Skoda Felicia
Service and Repair Manual

Mark Coombs and R M Jex

(3505 - 336 - 11AF3)

Models covered

Skoda Felicia Hatchback and Estate models, including special/limited editions
1.3 litre (1289 cc) and 1.6 litre (1598 cc) petrol engines
1.9 litre (1896 cc) diesel engine

Covers major mechanical features of Van, Pick-up and "Fun" models

© Haynes Group Limited 2003

A book in the **Haynes Service and Repair Manual Series**

All rights reserved. No part of this book may be reproduced or transmitted in any form or by any means, electronic or mechanical, including photocopying, recording or by any information storage or retrieval system, without permission in writing from the copyright holder.

ISBN 978 0 85733 749 8

British Library Cataloguing in Publication Data
A catalogue record for this book is available from the British Library.

Haynes Group Limited
Haynes North America, Inc

www.haynes.com

Authorised representative in the EU

HaynesPro BV
Stationsstraat 79 F, 3811MH Amersfoort, The Netherlands
gpsr@haynes.co.uk

Disclaimer

There are risks associated with automotive repairs. The ability to make repairs depends on the individual's skill, experience and proper tools. Individuals should act with due care and acknowledge and assume the risk of performing automotive repairs.

The purpose of this manual is to provide comprehensive, useful and accessible automotive repair information, to help you get the best value from your vehicle. However, this manual is not a substitute for a professional certified technician or mechanic.

This repair manual is produced by a third party and is not associated with an individual vehicle manufacturer. If there is any doubt or discrepancy between this manual and the owner's manual or the factory service manual, please refer to the factory service manual or seek assistance from a professional certified technician or mechanic.

Even though we have prepared this manual with extreme care and every attempt is made to ensure that the information in this manual is correct, neither the publisher nor the author can accept responsibility for loss, damage or injury caused by any errors in, or omissions from, the information given.

Contents

LIVING WITH YOUR SKODA FELICIA

MAINTENANCE

Routine maintenance and servicing

Contents

The Skoda Felicia was first launched onto the UK market in May 1995. The car is based on the outgoing Favorit range, but bears witness to the increasing influence of the parent Volkswagen Group in its improved build quality, and in its use of some proven VW engines.

The 1289 cc overhead valve engine is the only Skoda engine in the range, having first seen service in the Estelle, and latterly the Favorit, but it now offers the option of either Bosch single-point fuel injection, or an all-new multi-point injection system. A further advance on the multi-point injection engine is its distributorless ignition system.

February 1996 saw the introduction of the 1.6 litre engine, this being taken from the VW Polo. This modern overhead camshaft design features maintenance-free hydraulic tappets and multi-point fuel injection.

The engine range was completed in May 1997 with the introduction of the diesel models. Again, the 1.9 litre unit offered had first seen service in the VW Polo range, and features an overhead camshaft with hydraulic tappets. The engine also features a sophisticated 'walk-in' pre-heating system, first seen on the VW Golf.

In July 1997, all models received a minor facelift, the most obvious change being the adoption of the new 'family' chrome radiator grille.

The suspension at the front is of the MacPherson strut type, with coil springs and telescopic shock absorbers. Rear suspension incorporates trailing arms, a torsion beam, coil springs and telescopic shock absorbers.

Braking is by discs at the front and drums at the rear, utilising a dual-circuit hydraulic system. Anti-lock braking is offered as an option.

A wide range of standard and optional equipment is available within the range to suit most tastes, including central locking, electric windows and mirrors, driver and passenger air bags, and air conditioning.

Provided that regular servicing is carried out in accordance with the manufacturer's recommendations, the Felicia should prove a reliable and economical car. The engine compartment is well-designed, and most of the items needing frequent attention are easily accessible.

Skoda Felicia 1.6 GLXi Hatchback

Skoda Felicia 1.3 GLi Estate

Your Skoda Felicia manual

The aim of this manual is to help you get the best value from your vehicle. It can do so in several ways. It can help you decide what work must be done (even should you choose to get it done by a garage). It will also provide information on routine maintenance and servicing, and give a logical course of action and diagnosis when random faults occur. However, it is hoped that you will use the manual by tackling the work yourself. On simpler jobs it may even be quicker than booking the car into a garage and going there twice, to leave and collect it. Perhaps most important, a lot of money can be saved by avoiding the costs a garage must charge to cover its labour and overheads.

The manual has drawings and descriptions to show the function of the various components so that their layout can be understood. Tasks are described and photographed in a clear step-by-step sequence. The illustrations are numbered by the Section number and paragraph number to which they relate - if there is more than one illustration per paragraph, the sequence is denoted alphabetically.

References to the left or right of the vehicle are in the sense of a person in the driver's seat, facing forwards.

Acknowledgements

Thanks are due to Draper Tools Limited, who provided some of the workshop tools, and to all those people at Sparkford who helped in the production of this manual.

This manual is not a direct reproduction of the vehicle manufacturers data, and its publication should not be taken as implying any technical approval by the vehicle manufacturers or importers.

We take great pride in the accuracy of information given in this manual, but vehicle manufacturers make alterations and design changes during the production run of a particular vehicle of which they do not inform us. No liability can be accepted by the authors or publishers for loss, damage or injury caused by any errors in, or omissions from, the information given.

The Skoda Felicia Team

Haynes manuals are produced by dedicated and enthusiastic people working in close co-operation. The team responsible for the creation of this book included:

Authors	Mark Coombs R.M. Jex
Page Make-up	Steve Churchill
Workshop manager	Paul Buckland
Photo Scans	Paul Tanswell John Martin
Cover illustration & Line Art	Roger Healing
Wiring diagrams	Steve Tanswell

We hope the book will help you to get the maximum enjoyment from your car. By carrying out routine maintenance as described you will ensure your car's reliability and preserve its resale value.

Working on your car can be dangerous. This page shows just some of the potential risks and hazards, with the aim of creating a safety-conscious attitude.

General hazards

Scalding

• Don't remove the radiator or expansion tank cap while the engine is hot.
• Engine oil, automatic transmission fluid or power steering fluid may also be dangerously hot if the engine has recently been running.

Burning

• Beware of burns from the exhaust system and from any part of the engine. Brake discs and drums can also be extremely hot immediately after use.

Crushing

• When working under or near a raised vehicle, always supplement the jack with axle stands, or use drive-on ramps. *Never venture under a car which is only supported by a jack.*
• Take care if loosening or tightening high-torque nuts when the vehicle is on stands. Initial loosening and final tightening should be done with the wheels on the ground.

Fire

• Fuel is highly flammable; fuel vapour is explosive.
• Don't let fuel spill onto a hot engine.
• Do not smoke or allow naked lights (including pilot lights) anywhere near a vehicle being worked on. Also beware of creating sparks (electrically or by use of tools).
• Fuel vapour is heavier than air, so don't work on the fuel system with the vehicle over an inspection pit.
• Another cause of fire is an electrical overload or short-circuit. Take care when repairing or modifying the vehicle wiring.
• Keep a fire extinguisher handy, of a type suitable for use on fuel and electrical fires.

Electric shock

• Ignition HT voltage can be dangerous, especially to people with heart problems or a pacemaker. Don't work on or near the ignition system with the engine running or the ignition switched on.

• Mains voltage is also dangerous. Make sure that any mains-operated equipment is correctly earthed. Mains power points should be protected by a residual current device (RCD) circuit breaker.

Fume or gas intoxication

• Exhaust fumes are poisonous; they often contain carbon monoxide, which is rapidly fatal if inhaled. Never run the engine in a confined space such as a garage with the doors shut.
• Fuel vapour is also poisonous, as are the vapours from some cleaning solvents and paint thinners.

Poisonous or irritant substances

• Avoid skin contact with battery acid and with any fuel, fluid or lubricant, especially antifreeze, brake hydraulic fluid and Diesel fuel. Don't syphon them by mouth. If such a substance is swallowed or gets into the eyes, seek medical advice.
• Prolonged contact with used engine oil can cause skin cancer. Wear gloves or use a barrier cream if necessary. Change out of oil-soaked clothes and do not keep oily rags in your pocket.
• Air conditioning refrigerant forms a poisonous gas if exposed to a naked flame (including a cigarette). It can also cause skin burns on contact.

Asbestos

• Asbestos dust can cause cancer if inhaled or swallowed. Asbestos may be found in gaskets and in brake and clutch linings. When dealing with such components it is safest to assume that they contain asbestos.

Special hazards

Hydrofluoric acid

• This extremely corrosive acid is formed when certain types of synthetic rubber, found in some O-rings, oil seals, fuel hoses etc, are exposed to temperatures above 400°C. The rubber changes into a charred or sticky substance containing the acid. *Once formed, the acid remains dangerous for years. If it gets onto the skin, it may be necessary to amputate the limb concerned.*
• When dealing with a vehicle which has suffered a fire, or with components salvaged from such a vehicle, wear protective gloves and discard them after use.

The battery

• Batteries contain sulphuric acid, which attacks clothing, eyes and skin. Take care when topping-up or carrying the battery.
• The hydrogen gas given off by the battery is highly explosive. Never cause a spark or allow a naked light nearby. Be careful when connecting and disconnecting battery chargers or jump leads.

Air bags

• Air bags can cause injury if they go off accidentally. Take care when removing the steering wheel and/or facia. Special storage instructions may apply.

Diesel injection equipment

• Diesel injection pumps supply fuel at very high pressure. Take care when working on the fuel injectors and fuel pipes.

Warning: Never expose the hands, face or any other part of the body to injector spray; the fuel can penetrate the skin with potentially fatal results.

Remember...

DO

• Do use eye protection when using power tools, and when working under the vehicle.
• Do wear gloves or use barrier cream to protect your hands when necessary.
• Do get someone to check periodically that all is well when working alone on the vehicle.
• Do keep loose clothing and long hair well out of the way of moving mechanical parts.
• Do remove rings, wristwatch etc, before working on the vehicle – especially the electrical system.
• Do ensure that any lifting or jacking equipment has a safe working load rating adequate for the job.

DON'T

• Don't attempt to lift a heavy component which may be beyond your capability – get assistance.
• Don't rush to finish a job, or take unverified short cuts.
• Don't use ill-fitting tools which may slip and cause injury.
• Don't leave tools or parts lying around where someone can trip over them. Mop up oil and fuel spills at once.
• Don't allow children or pets to play in or near a vehicle being worked on.

The following pages are intended to help in dealing with common roadside emergencies and breakdowns. You will find more detailed fault finding information at the back of the manual, and repair information in the main chapters.

If your car won't start and the starter motor doesn't turn

☐ Open the bonnet and make sure that the battery terminals are clean and tight.

☐ Switch on the headlights and try to start the engine. If the headlights go very dim when you're trying to start, the battery is probably flat. Get out of trouble by jump starting (see next page) using a friend's car.

If your car won't start even though the starter motor turns as normal

☐ Is there fuel in the tank?
☐ Is there moisture on electrical components under the bonnet? Switch off the ignition, then wipe off any obvious dampness with a dry cloth. Spray a water-repellent aerosol product (WD-40 or equivalent) on ignition and fuel system electrical connectors like those shown in the photos. Pay special attention to the ignition coil wiring connector and HT leads. (Note that Diesel engines don't normally suffer from damp.)

A Check the security and condition of the battery connections.

B Check the connections to the ignition coil (1.3 litre MPi model shown).

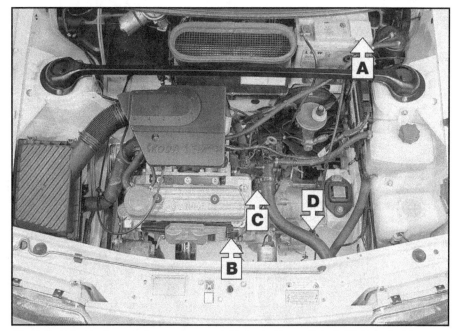

Check that electrical connections are secure (with the ignition switched off). Note that the large lead to the starter motor is permanently live. On petrol engine models, check the four spark plug leads and the ignition coil connections. Spray the connector plugs with a water-dispersant spray like WD-40 if you suspect a problem due to damp.

C Check that the wiring plug at the Hall sensor is securely connected (1.3 litre engine shown).

D Check that the starter motor connections are secure.

HAYNES HINT

Jump starting will get you out of trouble, but you must correct whatever made the battery go flat in the first place. There are three possibilities:

1 *The battery has been drained by repeated attempts to start, or by leaving the lights on.*

2 *The charging system is not working properly (alternator drivebelt slack or broken, alternator wiring fault or alternator itself faulty).*

3 *The battery itself is at fault (electrolyte low, or battery worn out).*

When jump-starting a car using a booster battery, observe the following precautions:

✔ Before connecting the booster battery, make sure that the ignition is switched off.

✔ Ensure that all electrical equipment (lights, heater, wipers, etc) is switched off.

✔ Take note of any special precautions printed on the battery case.

Jump starting

✔ Make sure that the booster battery is the same voltage as the discharged one in the vehicle.

✔ If the battery is being jump-started from the battery in another vehicle, the two vehicles MUST NOT TOUCH each other.

✔ Make sure that the transmission is in neutral

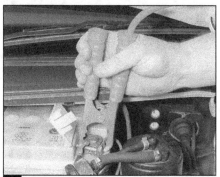

1 Connect one end of the red jump lead to the positive (+) terminal of the flat battery

2 Connect the other end of the red lead to the positive (+) terminal of the booster battery.

3 Connect one end of the black jump lead to the negative (-) terminal of the booster battery

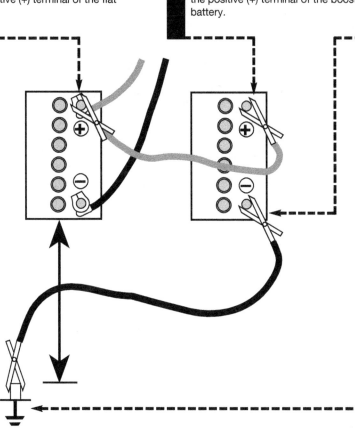

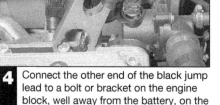

4 Connect the other end of the black jump lead to a bolt or bracket on the engine block, well away from the battery, on the vehicle to be started.

5 Make sure that the jump leads will not come into contact with the fan, drive-belts or other moving parts of the engine.

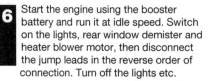

6 Start the engine using the booster battery and run it at idle speed. Switch on the lights, rear window demister and heater blower motor, then disconnect the jump leads in the reverse order of connection. Turn off the lights etc.

Wheel changing

 Warning: *Do not change a wheel in a situation where you risk being hit by another vehicle. On busy roads, try to stop in a lay-by or a gateway. Be wary of passing traffic while changing the wheel - it is easy to become distracted by the job in hand.*

Preparation

☐ When a puncture occurs, stop as soon as it is safe to do so.

☐ Park on firm level ground, if possible, and well out of the way of other traffic.

☐ Use hazard warning lights if necessary.

☐ If you have one, use a warning triangle to alert other drivers of your presence.

☐ Apply the handbrake and engage first or reverse gear (or Park on models with automatic transmission).

☐ Chock the wheel diagonally opposite the one being removed – a couple of large stones will do for this.

☐ If the ground is soft, use a flat piece of wood to spread the load under the jack.

Changing the wheel

1 The spare wheel and tools are stored in the luggage compartment. Fold back the floor covering and lift up the cover panel. Lift the jack and tool bag out of the spare wheel. Unscrew the retainer, and lift the spare wheel out of the vehicle.

2 Using the screwdriver tool, prise off the centre cover or wheel trim for access to the wheel bolts. Some models with alloy wheels have a centre cover which is removed with the special key provided in the tool bag.

3 Slacken each wheel bolt by a half turn, using the wheelbrace. If the bolts are too tight, DON'T stand on the wheelbrace to undo them - call for assistance from one of the motoring organisations.

4 Locate the jack head at the point in the lower sill flange indicated by the indentation in the sill (don't jack the vehicle at any other point of the sill). Two jacking points are provided on each side - use the one nearest the punctured wheel.

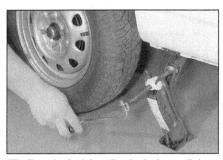

5 Turn the jack handle clockwise until the wheel is raised clear of the ground.

6 Unscrew the wheel bolts, recover the centre trim (where applicable) and remove the wheel.

7 Fit the spare wheel, and screw in the bolts. Lightly tighten the bolts with the wheelbrace, then lower the vehicle to the ground. Securely tighten the wheel bolts, then refit the wheel trim or centre cover, as applicable.

Finally...

☐ Remove the wheel chocks.

☐ Stow the punctured wheel and tools back in the luggage compartment, and secure them in position.

☐ Check the tyre pressure on the wheel just fitted. If it is low, or if you don't have a pressure gauge with you, drive slowly to the nearest garage and inflate the tyre to the right pressure.

☐ Have the damaged tyre or wheel repaired as soon as possible, or another puncture will leave you stranded.

☐ Note that the wheel bolts should be slackened and retightened to the specified torque at the earliest possible opportunity.

Identifying leaks

Puddles on the garage floor or drive, or obvious wetness under the bonnet or underneath the car, suggest a leak that needs investigating. It can sometimes be difficult to decide where the leak is coming from, especially if the engine bay is very dirty already. Leaking oil or fluid can also be blown rearwards by the passage of air under the car, giving a false impression of where the problem lies.

 Warning: Most automotive oils and fluids are poisonous. Wash them off skin, and change out of contaminated clothing, without delay.

 HAYNES HiNT *The smell of a fluid leaking from the car may provide a clue to what's leaking. Some fluids are distictively coloured. It may help to clean the car carefully and to park it over some clean paper overnight as an aid to locating the source of the leak. Remember that some leaks may only occur while the engine is running.*

Sump oil

Engine oil may leak from the drain plug...

Oil from filter

...or from the base of the oil filter.

Gearbox oil

Gearbox oil can leak from the seals at the inboard ends of the driveshafts.

Antifreeze

Leaking antifreeze often leaves a crystalline deposit like this.

Brake fluid

A leak occurring at a wheel is almost certainly brake fluid.

Power steering fluid

Power steering fluid may leak from the pipe connectors on the steering rack.

Towing

When all else fails, you may find yourself having to get a tow home – or of course you may be helping somebody else. Long-distance recovery should only be done by a garage or breakdown service. For shorter distances, DIY towing using another car is easy enough, but observe the following points:

☐ Use a proper tow-rope – they are not expensive. The vehicle being towed must display an 'ON TOW' sign in its rear window.

☐ Always turn the ignition key to the 'on' position when the vehicle is being towed, so that the steering lock is released, and that the direction indicator and brake lights will work.

☐ The rear towing eye is located behind a cover in the rear bumper moulding, which is prised out. The front towing eye is of the screw-in type, and is found in the toolkit in the spare wheel. The towing eye screws into the threaded hole next to the front number plate, and has a left-hand thread - ie it screws in anti-clockwise **(see illustration)**.

☐ Before being towed, release the handbrake and select neutral on the transmission.

☐ Note that greater-than-usual pedal pressure will be required to operate the brakes, since the vacuum servo unit is only operational with the engine running.

☐ The driver of the car being towed must keep the tow-rope taut at all times to avoid snatching.

☐ Make sure that both drivers know the route before setting off.

☐ Only drive at moderate speeds and keep the distance towed to a minimum. Drive smoothly and allow plenty of time for slowing down at junctions.

Front towing eye

Introduction

There are some very simple checks which need only take a few minutes to carry out, but which could save you a lot of inconvenience and expense.

These "Weekly checks" require no great skill or special tools, and the small amount of time they take to perform could prove to be very well spent, for example;

☐ Keeping an eye on tyre condition and pressures, will not only help to stop them wearing out prematurely, but could also save your life.

☐ Many breakdowns are caused by electrical problems. Battery-related faults are particularly common, and a quick check on a regular basis will often prevent the majority of these.

☐ If your car develops a brake fluid leak, the first time you might know about it is when your brakes don't work properly. Checking the level regularly will give advance warning of this kind of problem.

☐ If the oil or coolant levels run low, the cost of repairing any engine damage will be far greater than fixing the leak, for example.

Underbonnet check points

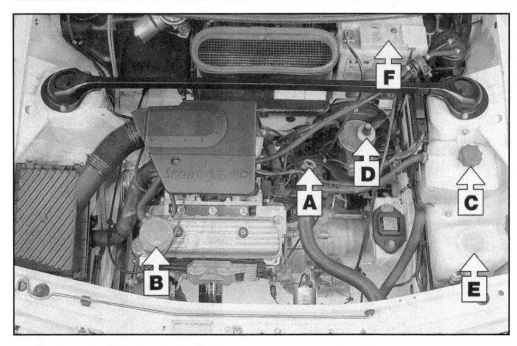

◀ **1.3 litre petrol**

A *Engine oil level dipstick*

B *Engine oil filler cap*

C *Coolant expansion tank*

D *Brake fluid reservoir*

E *Screen washer fluid reservoir*

F *Battery*

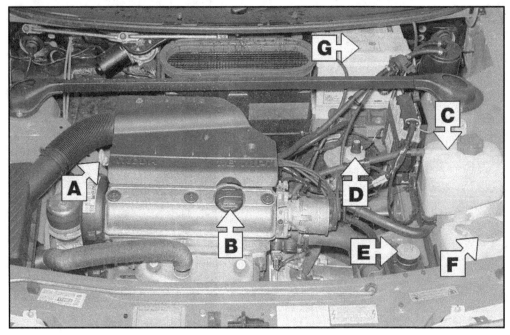

◀ **1.6 litre petrol**

A *Engine oil level dipstick*

B *Engine oil filler cap*

C *Coolant expansion tank*

D *Brake fluid reservoir*

E *Power steering fluid reservoir*

F *Screen washer fluid reservoir*

G *Battery*

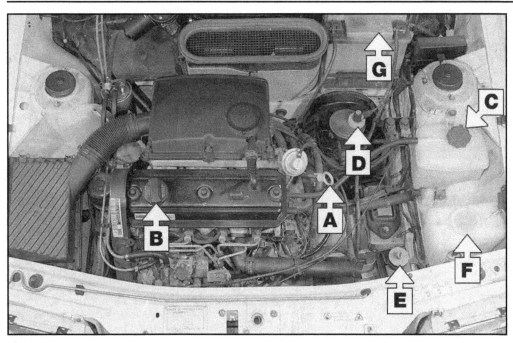

A *Engine oil level dipstick*
B *Engine oil filler cap*
C *Coolant expansion tank*
D *Brake fluid reservoir*
E *Power steering fluid reservoir*
F *Screen washer fluid reservoir*
G *Battery*

Engine oil level

Before you start

✔ Make sure that your car is on level ground.
✔ Check the oil level before the car is driven, or at least 5 minutes after the engine has been switched off.

> **HAYNES HiNT** *If the oil is checked immediately after driving the vehicle, some of the oil will remain in the upper engine components, resulting in an inaccurate reading on the dipstick!*

The correct oil

Modern engines place great demands on their oil. It is very important that the correct oil for your car is used (See "Lubricants, fluids and tyre pressures").

Car Care

● If you have to add oil frequently, you should check whether you have any oil leaks. Place some clean paper under the car overnight, and check for stains in the morning. If there are no leaks, the engine may be burning oil.

● Always maintain the level between the upper and lower dipstick marks (see photo 3). If the level is too low severe engine damage may occur. Oil seal failure may result if the engine is overfilled by adding too much oil.

1 The dipstick top is often brightly coloured for easy identification (see *Underbonnet check points* on pages 0•10 and 0•11 for exact location). Withdraw the dipstick.

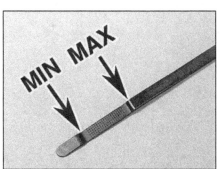
3 Note the oil level on the end of the dipstick, which should be between the MAX and MIN marks. If the oil level is only just above, or below, the MIN mark, topping-up is required.

2 Using a clean rag or paper towel, remove all oil from the dipstick. Insert the clean dipstick into the tube as far as it will go, then withdraw it again.

4 Oil is added through the filler cap. Lift off the cap and top-up the level. Add the oil slowly, checking the level on the dipstick often, and allowing time for the oil to fall to the sump. Add oil until the level is just up to the MAX mark on the dipstick - don't overfill (see *Car care left*).

Coolant level

Warning: *DO NOT attempt to remove the expansion tank pressure cap when the engine is hot, as there is a very great risk of scalding. Do not leave open containers of coolant about, as it is poisonous.*

Car Care

● With a sealed-type cooling system, adding coolant should not be necessary on a regular basis. If frequent topping-up is required, it is likely there is a leak. Check the radiator, all hoses and joint faces for signs of staining or wetness, and rectify as necessary.

● It is important that antifreeze is used in the cooling system all year round, not just during the winter months. Don't top-up with water alone, as the antifreeze will become too diluted.

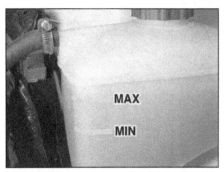

1 The coolant level varies with the temperature of the engine. When the engine is cold, the coolant level should be between the MAX and MIN marks. When the engine is hot, the level may rise slightly above the MAX mark.

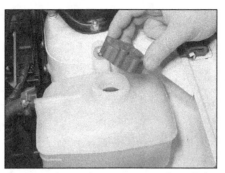

2 If topping up is necessary, **wait until the engine is cold**. Slowly unscrew the expansion tank cap, to release any pressure present in the cooling system, and remove it.

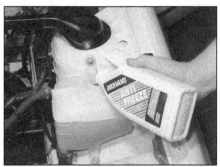

3 Add a mixture of water and antifreeze to the expansion tank until the coolant level is halfway between the level marks. Refit the cap and tighten it securely.

Brake fluid level

Warning:
● *Brake fluid can harm your eyes and damage painted surfaces, so use extreme caution when handling and pouring it.*
● *Do not use fluid that has been standing open for some time, as it absorbs moisture from the air, which can cause a dangerous loss of braking effectiveness.*

• *Make sure that your car is on level ground.*
• *The fluid level in the reservoir will drop slightly as the brake pads wear down, but the fluid level must never be allowed to drop below the "MIN" mark.*

Safety First!

● If the reservoir requires repeated topping-up this is an indication of a fluid leak somewhere in the system, which should be investigated immediately.

● If a leak is suspected, the car should not be driven until the braking system has been checked. Never take any risks where brakes are concerned.

1 The brake fluid reservoir is located on the left-hand side of the engine compartment. The MAX and MIN marks are indicated on the front of the reservoir.

2 The fluid level must be kept between the marks at all times. If topping-up is necessary, first wipe clean the area around the filler cap to prevent dirt entering the hydraulic system.

3 Unscrew the reservoir cap and carefully lift it out of position, taking care not to damage the level switch float. Place the cap and float on a piece of clean rag. Inspect the reservoir; if the fluid is dirty, the hydraulic system should be drained and refilled (see Chapter 1).

4 Carefully add fluid, taking care not to spill it onto the surrounding components. Use only the specified fluid; mixing different types can cause damage to the system. After topping-up to the correct level, securely refit the cap and wipe off any spilt fluid.

Tyre condition and pressure

It is very important that tyres are in good condition, and at the correct pressure - having a tyre failure at any speed is highly dangerous. Tyre wear is influenced by driving style - harsh braking and acceleration, or fast cornering, will all produce more rapid tyre wear. As a general rule, the front tyres wear out faster than the rears. Interchanging the tyres from front to rear ("rotating" the tyres) may result in more even wear. However, if this is completely effective, you may have the expense of replacing all four tyres at once! Remove any nails or stones embedded in the tread before they penetrate the tyre to cause deflation. If removal of a nail does reveal that the tyre has been punctured, refit the nail so that its point of penetration is marked. Then immediately change the wheel, and have the tyre repaired by a tyre dealer.

Regularly check the tyres for damage in the form of cuts or bulges, especially in the sidewalls. Periodically remove the wheels, and clean any dirt or mud from the inside and outside surfaces. Examine the wheel rims for signs of rusting, corrosion or other damage. Light alloy wheels are easily damaged by "kerbing" whilst parking; steel wheels may also become dented or buckled. A new wheel is very often the only way to overcome severe damage.

New tyres should be balanced when they are fitted, but it may become necessary to re-balance them as they wear, or if the balance weights fitted to the wheel rim should fall off. Unbalanced tyres will wear more quickly, as will the steering and suspension components. Wheel imbalance is normally signified by vibration, particularly at a certain speed (typically around 50 mph). If this vibration is felt only through the steering, then it is likely that just the front wheels need balancing. If, however, the vibration is felt through the whole car, the rear wheels could be out of balance. Wheel balancing should be carried out by a tyre dealer or garage.

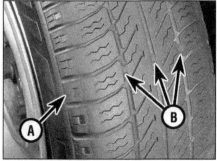

1 Tread Depth - visual check
The original tyres have tread wear safety bands (B), which will appear when the tread depth reaches approximately 1.6 mm. The band positions are indicated by a triangular mark on the tyre sidewall (A).

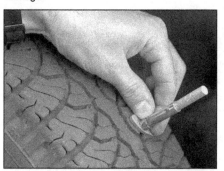

2 Tread Depth - manual check
Alternatively, tread wear can be monitored with a simple, inexpensive device known as a tread depth indicator gauge.

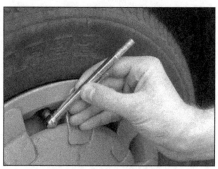

3 Tyre Pressure Check
Check the tyre pressures regularly with the tyres cold. Do not adjust the tyre pressures immediately after the vehicle has been used, or an inaccurate setting will result. Tyre pressures are shown on page 0•17.

Tyre tread wear patterns

Shoulder Wear

Underinflation (wear on both sides)
Under-inflation will cause overheating of the tyre, because the tyre will flex too much, and the tread will not sit correctly on the road surface. This will cause a loss of grip and excessive wear, not to mention the danger of sudden tyre failure due to heat build-up.
Check and adjust pressures
Incorrect wheel camber (wear on one side)
Repair or renew suspension parts
Hard cornering
Reduce speed!

Centre Wear

Overinflation
Over-inflation will cause rapid wear of the centre part of the tyre tread, coupled with reduced grip, harsher ride, and the danger of shock damage occurring in the tyre casing.
Check and adjust pressures

If you sometimes have to inflate your car's tyres to the higher pressures specified for maximum load or sustained high speed, don't forget to reduce the pressures to normal afterwards.

Uneven Wear

Front tyres may wear unevenly as a result of wheel misalignment. Most tyre dealers and garages can check and adjust the wheel alignment (or "tracking") for a modest charge.
Incorrect camber or castor
Repair or renew suspension parts
Malfunctioning suspension
Repair or renew suspension parts
Unbalanced wheel
Balance tyres
Incorrect toe setting
Adjust front wheel alignment
Note: *The feathered edge of the tread which typifies toe wear is best checked by feel.*

Screen washer fluid level*

* The underbonnet reservoir also serves the tailgate washer.

Screenwash additives not only keep the winscreen clean during foul weather, they also prevent the washer system freezing in cold weather - which is when you are likely to need it most. Don't top up using plain water as the screenwash will become too diluted, and will freeze during cold weather.

On no account use coolant antifreeze in the washer system - this could discolour or damage paintwork.

1 The screen washer fluid reservoir is located in the left-hand front corner of the engine compartment.

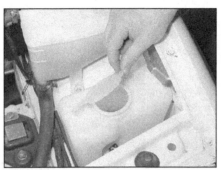

2 The screen washer level can be seen through the reservoir body. If topping-up is necessary, open the cap.

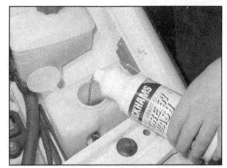

3 When topping-up the reservoir, add a screenwash additive in the quantities recommended on the bottle.

Power steering fluid level

Before you start:

✔ Park the vehicle on level ground.
✔ Set the steering wheel straight-ahead.
✔ The system must be at operating temperature.
✔ The engine should be turned off.

HAYNES HiNT *For the check to be accurate, the steering must not be turned once the engine has been stopped.*

Safety First!

● The need for frequent topping-up indicates a leak, which should be investigated immediately.

1 The reservoir is located at the front left-hand side of the engine compartment. Wipe clean the area around the reservoir filler neck and unscrew the filler cap/dipstick from the reservoir, using a suitable tool in the slot provided on the reservoir cap.

2 The filler cap has a dipstick attached, with MAX and MIN markings. Wipe the fluid dipstick attached to the cap clean with a clean non-fluffy rag, then screw the cap fully back into position, hand-tight.

3 Unscrew the cap once more, and note the reading on the dipstick. When the system is cold, the fluid level should be up to the MIN mark; when hot, it should be between the MAX and MIN marks.

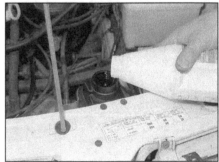

4 When topping-up, use the specified type of fluid and do not overfill the reservoir. Special hydraulic oil is used in the system, and ordinary automatic transmission fluid (ATF) **must not** be used. When the level is correct, securely refit the cap.

Wiper blades

Note: *Fitting details for wiper blades vary according to model, and according to whether genuine Skoda wiper blades have been fitted. Use the procedures and illustrations shown as a guide for your car.*

 If smearing is still a problem despite fitting new wiper blades, try cleaning the windscreen with neat screen-wash additive or methylated spirit.

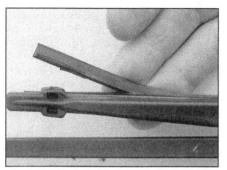

1 Check the condition of the wiper blades; if they are cracked or show any signs of deterioration, or if the glass swept area is smeared, renew them. Wiper blades should be renewed annually, regardless of their apparent condition.

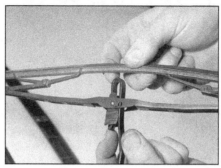

2 To remove a windscreen wiper blade, pull the arm fully away from the screen until it locks. Swivel the blade through 90°, press the locking tab with your fingers and slide the blade out of the arm's hooked end.

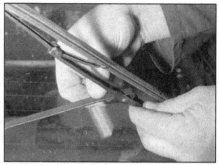

3 Don't forget to check the tailgate wiper blade as well (where applicable). Remove the blade using a similar technique to the windscreen wiper blades.

Battery

Caution: *Before carrying out any work on the vehicle battery, read the precautions given in "Safety first" at the start of this manual.*

✔ Make sure that the battery tray is in good condition, and that the clamp is tight. Corrosion on the tray, retaining clamp and the battery itself can be removed with a solution of water and baking soda. Thoroughly rinse all cleaned areas with water. Any metal parts damaged by corrosion should be covered with a zinc-based primer, then painted.

✔ Periodically (approximately every three months), check the charge condition of the battery as described in Chapter 5A.

✔ If the battery is flat, and you need to jump start your vehicle, see **Roadside Repairs**.

1 The battery is located at the rear of the engine compartment. The exterior of the battery should be inspected periodically for damage such as a cracked case or cover.

2 Check the tightness of battery clamps to ensure good electrical connections. You should not be able to move them. Also check each cable for cracks and frayed conductors.

Battery corrosion can be kept to a minimum by applying a layer of petroleum jelly to the clamps and terminals after they are reconnected.

3 If corrosion (white, fluffy deposits) is evident, remove the cables from the battery terminals, clean them with a small wire brush, then refit them. Automotive stores sell a tool for cleaning the battery post . . .

4 . . . as well as the battery cable clamps

Bulbs and fuses

✔ Check all external lights and the horn. Refer to the appropriate Sections of Chapter 12 for details if any of the circuits are found to be inoperative.

✔ Visually check all accessible wiring connectors, harnesses and retaining clips for security, and for signs of chafing or damage.

 HAYNES HiNT *If you need to check your brake lights and indicators unaided, back up to a wall or garage door and operate the lights. The reflected light should show if they are working properly.*

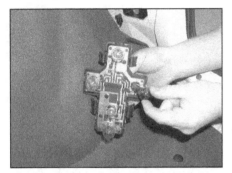

1 If a single indicator light, stop-light or headlight has failed, it is likely that a bulb has blown and will need to be replaced. Refer to Chapter 12 for details. If both stop-lights have failed, it is possible that the switch has failed (see Chapter 9).

2 If more than one indicator light or tail light has failed, it is likely that either a fuse has blown or that there is a fault in the circuit (see Chapter 12). The main fuses are located behind a cover below the passenger's side of the facia panel. Additional in-line fuses may be fitted on certain items.

3 To replace a blown fuse, simply pull it out and fit a new fuse of the correct rating (see Chapter 12). If the fuse blows again, it is important that you find out why - a checking procedure is given in Chapter 12.

Advanced driving

Many people see the words 'advanced driving' and believe that it won't interest them or that it is a style of driving beyond their own abilities. Nothing could be further from the truth. Advanced driving is straightforward safe, sensible driving - the sort of driving we should all do every time we get behind the wheel.

An average of 10 people are killed every day on UK roads and 870 more are injured, some seriously. Lives are ruined daily, usually because somebody did something stupid. Something like 95% of all accidents are due to human error, mostly driver failure. Sometimes we make genuine mistakes - everyone does. Sometimes we have lapses of concentration. Sometimes we deliberately take risks.

For many people, the process of 'learning to drive' doesn't go much further than learning how to pass the driving test because of a common belief that good drivers are made by 'experience'.

Learning to drive by 'experience' teaches three driving skills:

☐ Quick reactions. (Whoops, that was close!)
☐ Good handling skills. (Horn, swerve, brake, horn).
☐ Reliance on vehicle technology. (Great stuff this ABS, stop in no distance even in the wet...)

Drivers whose skills are 'experience based' generally have a lot of near misses and the odd accident. The results can be seen every day in our courts and our hospital casualty departments.

Advanced drivers have learnt to control the risks by controlling the position and speed of their vehicle. They avoid accidents and near misses, even if the drivers around them make mistakes.

The key skills of advanced driving are **concentration,** effective all-round **observation, anticipation** and **planning.** When **good vehicle handling** is added to

these skills, all driving situations can be approached and negotiated in a safe, methodical way, leaving nothing to chance.

Concentration means applying your mind to safe driving, completely excluding anything that's not relevant. Driving is usually the most dangerous activity that most of us undertake in our daily routines. It deserves our full attention.

Observation means not just looking, but seeing and seeking out the information found in the driving environment.

Anticipation means asking yourself what is happening, what you can reasonably expect to happen and what could happen unexpectedly. (One of the commonest words used in compiling accident reports is 'suddenly'.)

Planning is the link between seeing something and taking the appropriate action. For many drivers, planning is the missing link.

If you want to become a safer and more skilful driver and you want to enjoy your driving more, contact the Institute of Advanced Motorists at www.iam.org.uk, phone 0208 996 9600, or write to IAM House, 510 Chiswick High Road, London W4 5RG for an information pack.

Lubricants and fluids

Petrol engine	Multigrade engine oil, viscosity SAE 10W/40, 15W/40, or 15W/50, to API SG, VW 501 01, or VW 500 00
Diesel engine	Multigrade engine oil, viscosity SAE 10W/40, 15W/40, or 15W/50, to API CD, VW 500 00, or VW 505 00
Cooling system	Ethylene glycol-based antifreeze with corrosion inhibitor, specification TL-VW 774 C
Transmission and final drive	Gear oil, viscosity SAE 75W/90, to API GL4
Brake hydraulic system	Hydraulic fluid to FMVSS 116 DOT 4
Power steering	Hydraulic oil G 002 000
General greasing	Multi-purpose lithium-based grease

Choosing your engine oil

Engines need oil, not only to lubricate moving parts and minimise wear, but also to maximise power output and to improve fuel economy.

HOW ENGINE OIL WORKS

• Beating friction

Without oil, the moving surfaces inside your engine will rub together, heat up and melt, quickly causing the engine to seize. Engine oil creates a film which separates these moving parts, preventing wear and heat build-up.

• Cooling hot-spots

Temperatures inside the engine can exceed 1000° C. The engine oil circulates and acts as a coolant, transferring heat from the hot-spots to the sump.

• Cleaning the engine internally

Good quality engine oils clean the inside of your engine, collecting and dispersing combustion deposits and controlling them until they are trapped by the oil filter or flushed out at oil change.

OIL CARE - FOLLOW THE CODE

To handle and dispose of used engine oil safely, always:

OIL CARE

0800 66 33 66
www.oilbankline.org.uk

• **Avoid skin contact with used engine oil. Repeated or prolonged contact can be harmful.**
• **Dispose of used oil and empty packs in a responsible manner in an authorised disposal site. Call 0800 663366 to find the one nearest to you. Never tip oil down drains or onto the ground.**

Tyre pressures (cold)

	Front	Rear
Up to half-laden (normal usage)	2.0 bar (29 psi)	2.0 bar (29 psi)
Fully-laden:		
Petrol models	2.2 bar (32 psi)	2.6 bar (38 psi)
Diesel models	2.2 bar (32 psi)	2.8 bar (41 psi)

Note: *Pressures apply to original-equipment tyres, and may vary if any other make of tyre is fitted; check with the tyre manufacturer or supplier for the correct pressures if necessary.*

Notes

Chapter 1 Part A:
Routine maintenance & servicing - petrol models

Contents

Degrees of difficulty

| Easy, suitable for novice with little experience | | Fairly easy, suitable for beginner with some experience | | Fairly difficult, suitable for competent DIY mechanic | | Difficult, suitable for experienced DIY mechanic | | Very difficult, suitable for expert DIY or professional |

Lubricants and fluids

Refer to *Weekly checks*

Capacities

Engine oil (including oil filter):

1.3 litre engine	4.5 litres
1.6 litre engine	3.5 litres
Difference between MIN and MAX marks on dipstick	1.0 litre
Cooling system (approximate)	6.0 litres
Transmission (approximate)	2.4 litres
Fuel tank (all models)	42 litres

Engine

Valve clearances (1.3 litre engine):

Inlet	0.25 mm
Exhaust	0.20 mm

Cooling system

Antifreeze mixture:

50% antifreeze	Protection down to -37°C
55% antifreeze	Protection down to -45°C

Note: *Refer to antifreeze manufacturer for latest recommendations.*

Ignition system

Spark plugs:	Type	Electrode gap
1.3 litre:		
Engine code AMG	Bosch FR 7 LD+	0.9 mm
Multi-point fuel injection	Bosch FR 78 X	Not adjustable
All other engines	Bosch FR 7 D+	0.9 mm
1.6 litre	Bosch WR 7 LT+	1.0 mm

Brakes

Friction material minimum thickness:

Front brake pads	2.0 mm
Rear brake shoes	2.5 mm

Torque wrench settings

	Nm	lbf ft
Air cleaner top cover bolts - 1.3 litre, single-point injection	10	7
Coolant drain plugs - 1.3 litre engine:		
Coolant pipe drain plug	20	15
Cylinder block drain plug	25	18
Ignition coil unit mounting bolts	10	7
Roadwheel bolts	110	81
Rocker cover nuts	3	2
Spark plugs:		
Flat-seat (with washer)	30	22
Taper-seat (without washer)	15	11
Speedometer drive retaining plate bolt	10	7
Splash plate/rocker gear retaining bolt	30	22
Sump drain plug:		
1.3 litre engine	65	48
1.6 litre engine	30	22
Timing belt lower bolts (renew)	10	7
Transmission drain plug	35	25
Valve adjuster locknuts	18	13

The maintenance intervals in this manual are provided with the assumption that you, not the dealer, will be carrying out the work. These are the minimum maintenance intervals recommended by us for vehicles driven daily. If you wish to keep your vehicle in peak condition at all times, you may wish to perform some of these procedures more often. We encourage frequent maintenance, because it enhances the efficiency, performance and resale value of your vehicle.

If the vehicle is driven in dusty areas, used to tow a trailer, or driven frequently at slow speeds (idling in traffic) or on short journeys, more frequent maintenance intervals are recommended.

When the vehicle is new, it should be serviced by a factory-authorised dealer service department, in order to preserve the factory warranty.

Every 250 miles (400 km) or weekly
☐ Refer to *Weekly checks*

Every 5000 miles (7500 km)
Note: *Frequent oil and filter changes are good for the engine. We recommend changing the oil at the mileage specified here, or at least twice a year if the mileage covered is less.*
☐ Renew the engine oil and filter (Section 3)

Every 10 000 miles (15 000 km)
☐ Check the front brake pads and discs for wear (Section 4)
☐ Check the engine management system operation (Section 5)

Every 12 months, regardless of mileage
Note: *On models covering less than 10 000 miles (15 000 km) a year, also perform the tasks listed under the previous heading at this interval.*
☐ Check and adjust the valve clearances - 1.3 litre engine (Section 6)
☐ Check all components, pipes and hoses for fluid leaks (Section 7)
☐ Check the condition of the driveshaft gaiters (Section 8)
☐ Check the steering and suspension components for condition and security (Section 9)
☐ Check the condition of the exhaust system (Section 10)
☐ Check the condition of the coolant (Section 11)
☐ Check the operation of the clutch (Section 12)
☐ Lubricate all door locks and hinges, door stops, bonnet lock and release, and tailgate lock and hinges (Section 13)
☐ Check the exhaust emission level (Section 14)
☐ Check and if necessary adjust the headlight beam alignment (Section 15)
☐ Check the operation of the wiper/washer systems (Section 16)
☐ Carry out a road test (Section 17)

Every 20 000 miles (30 000 km)
☐ Renew the air filter element (Section 18)
☐ Renew the spark plugs - 1.3 litre engine (Section 19)
☐ Check the condition of the engine timing belt (Section 20)
☐ Lubricate the distributor - 1.3 litre engine (Section 21)
☐ Check the condition and tension of the auxiliary drivebelt(s) (Section 22)
☐ Carry out a visual check of the airbag(s) - where fitted (Section 23)
☐ Check the engine emission control systems (Section 24)
☐ Check the rear brake shoes and drums for wear (Section 25)
☐ Check the operation of the handbrake (Section 26)
☐ Check the underbody sealant for signs of damage (Section 27)
☐ Check the transmission oil level (Section 28)

Every 40 000 miles (60 000 km)
☐ Renew the spark plugs - 1.6 litre engine (Section 29)
☐ Renew the fuel filter (Section 30)
☐ Renew the transmission oil (Section 31)
☐ Renew the timing belt - 1.6 litre engine (Section 32)
Note: *The manufacturer does not give a recommended interval for timing belt renewal, and only specifies that a check should be carried out every 20 000 miles (30 000 km). However, we recommend that the belt is changed at this interval, regardless of its apparent condition.*

Every 2 years, regardless of mileage
☐ Renew the brake fluid (Section 33)

Every 3 years, regardless of mileage
☐ Renew the coolant (Section 34)

Underbonnet view of a 1.3 litre engine model

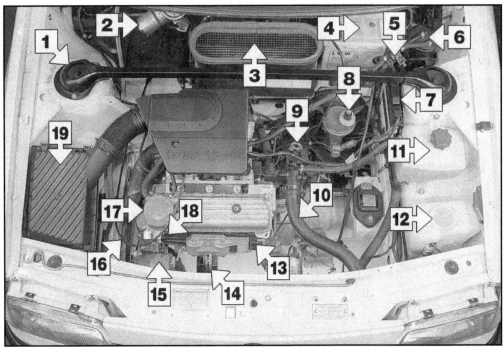

1 Suspension strut brace
2 Windscreen wiper motor
3 Heater/ventilation unit
4 Battery
5 Charcoal filter solenoid valve
6 Charcoal canister
7 Engine management ECU
8 Brake fluid reservoir
9 Engine oil dipstick
10 Radiator top hose
11 Coolant expansion tank
12 Washer fluid reservoir
13 Ignition coil unit
14 Engine oil filter
15 Alternator
16 Auxiliary drivebelt
17 Engine oil filler cap
18 No 1 spark plug (under coil unit)
19 Air cleaner housing

Underbonnet view of a 1.6 litre engine model

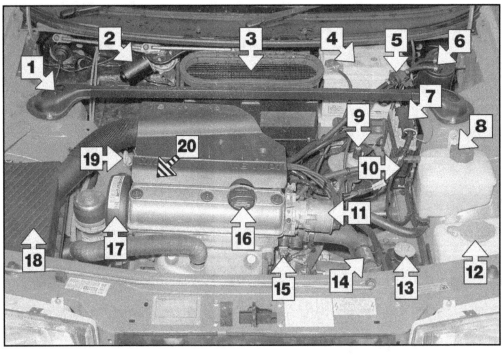

1 Suspension strut brace
2 Windscreen wiper motor
3 Heater/ventilation unit
4 Battery
5 Charcoal filter solenoid valve
6 Charcoal canister
7 Engine management ECU
8 Coolant expansion tank
9 Brake fluid reservoir
10 Ignition HT coil
11 Distributor
12 Washer fluid reservoir
13 Power steering fluid reservoir
14 Radiator top hose
15 Coolant temperature sensor
16 Engine oil filler cap
17 Timing belt upper cover
18 Air cleaner housing
19 Engine oil dipstick
20 No 1 spark plug (under throttle body cover)

Front underbody view (1.3 litre, undershields removed)

1 Alternator
2 Radiator bottom hose
3 Oil filter
4 Radiator cooling fan
5 Starter motor
6 Front brake caliper
7 Driveshaft
8 Wishbone/lower arm
9 Engine/transmission rear mounting
10 Gearchange linkage
11 Fuel/brake pipes
12 Catalytic converter
13 Track rod
14 Front brake hose
15 Engine oil drain plug
16 Lambda sensor
17 Transmission oil drain plug

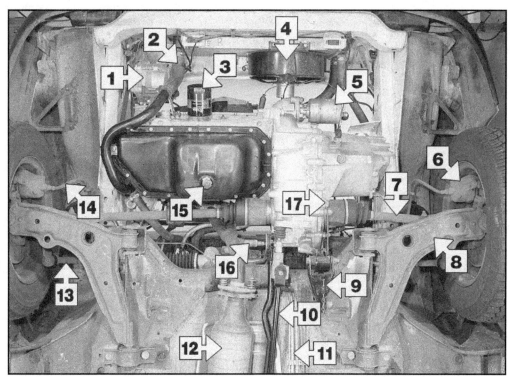

Rear underbody view

1 Rear brake hose
2 Fuel tank
3 Handbrake cable
4 Rear axle
5 Exhaust rear silencer
6 Rear strut lower mounting
7 Exhaust mounting
8 Rear towing eye
9 Fuel tank filler pipe
10 Fuel filter

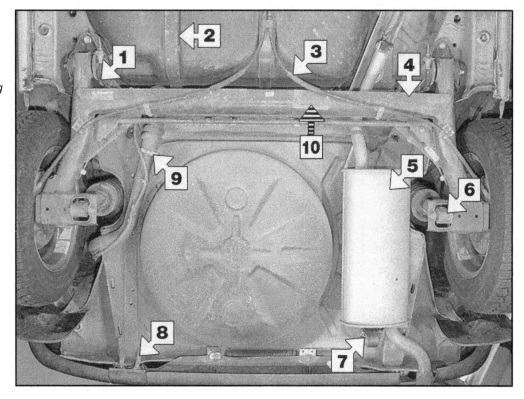

1 Introduction

General information

This Chapter is designed to help the home mechanic maintain his/her vehicle for safety, economy, long life and peak performance.

The Chapter contains a master maintenance schedule, followed by Sections dealing specifically with each task in the schedule. Visual checks, adjustments, component renewal and other helpful items are included. Refer to the accompanying illustrations of the engine compartment and the underside of the vehicle for the locations of the various components.

Servicing your vehicle in accordance with the mileage/time maintenance schedule and the following Sections will provide a planned maintenance programme, which should result in a long and reliable service life. This is a comprehensive plan, so maintaining some items but not others at the specified service intervals, will not produce the same results.

As you service your vehicle, you will discover that many of the procedures can - and should - be grouped together, because of the particular procedure being performed, or because of the proximity of two otherwise-unrelated components to one another. For example, if the vehicle is raised for any reason, the exhaust can be inspected at the same time as the suspension and steering components.

The first step in this maintenance programme is to prepare yourself before the actual work begins. Read through all the Sections relevant to the work to be carried out, then make a list and gather all the parts and tools required. If a problem is encountered, seek advice from a parts specialist, or a dealer service department.

2 Regular maintenance

1 If, from the time the vehicle is new, the routine maintenance schedule is followed closely, and frequent checks are made of fluid levels and high-wear items, as suggested throughout this manual, the engine will be kept in relatively good running condition, and the need for additional work will be minimised.
2 It is possible that there will be times when the engine is running poorly due to the lack of regular maintenance. This is even more likely if a used vehicle, which has not received regular and frequent maintenance checks, is purchased. In such cases, additional work may need to be carried out, outside of the regular maintenance intervals.
3 If engine wear is suspected, a compression test (refer to Chapter 2A or 2B, as applicable) will provide valuable information regarding the overall performance of the main internal components. Such a test can be used as a basis to decide on the extent of the work to be carried out. If, for example, a compression test indicates serious internal engine wear, conventional maintenance as described in this Chapter will not greatly improve the performance of the engine, and may prove a waste of time and money, unless extensive overhaul work is carried out first.
4 The following series of operations are those most often required to improve the performance of a generally poor-running engine:

Primary operations

a) Clean, inspect and test the battery (refer to Weekly checks).
b) Check all the engine-related fluids (refer to Weekly checks).
c) Check the condition and tension of the auxiliary drivebelt (Section 22).
d) Renew the spark plugs (Section 19 or 29).
e) Check the condition of the air filter, and renew if necessary (Section 18).
f) Renew the fuel filter (Section 30).
g) Check the condition of all hoses, and check for fluid leaks (Section 7).

5 If the above operations do not prove fully effective, carry out the following secondary operations:

Secondary operations

All items listed under *Primary operations*, plus the following:

a) Check the charging system (refer to Chapter 5A).
b) Check the ignition system (refer to Chapter 5B).
c) Check the fuel system (refer to Chapter 4A or 4B).

Every 5000 miles (7500 km)

3 Engine oil and filter renewal

1 Frequent oil and filter changes are the most important preventative maintenance procedures that can be undertaken by the DIY owner. As engine oil ages, it becomes diluted and contaminated, which leads to premature engine wear.
2 Before starting this procedure, gather

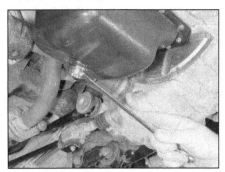

3.6 Unscrewing the engine oil drain plug

together all the necessary tools and materials. Also make sure that you have plenty of clean rags and newspapers handy to mop up any spills. Ideally, the engine oil should be warm as it will drain better and more built-up sludge will be removed with it. Take care, however, not to touch the exhaust or any other hot parts of the engine when working under the vehicle - this applies especially to the catalytic converter.
3 To avoid any possibility of injury through scalding, and to protect yourself from possible skin irritants and other harmful contaminants in used engine oils, it is advisable to wear non-permeable gloves when carrying out this work.
4 Access to the underside of the vehicle will be greatly improved if it can be raised on a lift, driven onto ramps or jacked up and supported on axle stands (see *Jacking and vehicle support*). Whichever method is chosen, make sure that the vehicle remains level, or if it is at an angle, that the drain plug (located on the underside of the sump) is at the lowest point.
5 Remove the full-width undershield by unscrewing the retaining screws. Side shields are also fitted - although their removal may not be essential for access, these metal shields

have sharp edges, and removal may be desirable for safety reasons.
6 Using a spanner or preferably a suitable socket and bar, slacken the drain plug about half a turn (see illustration). Position the draining container under the drain plug, then remove the plug completely (see Haynes Hint).

HAYNES HINT

Keep the drain plug pressed into the sump while unscrewing it by hand last couple of turns. As the plug releases, move it away sharply so the stream of oil issuing from the sump runs into the container, not up your sleeve

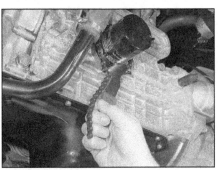

3.10 Loosening the oil filter using a chain-type removal tool

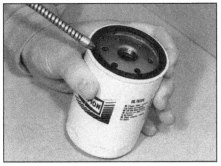

3.12 Apply a little engine oil to the new oil filter sealing ring

3.14 Fill the engine using the correct grade and quantity of oil

7 Allow some time for the old oil to drain, noting that it may be necessary to reposition the container as the oil flow slows to a trickle.
8 After all the oil has drained, wipe off the drain plug with a clean rag and, if necessary, renew the sealing washer. Clean the area around the drain plug opening and refit the plug. Tighten the plug securely, preferably to the specified torque using a torque wrench.
9 Move the container into position under the oil filter, which is located on the front of the cylinder block.
10 Using an oil filter removal tool if necessary, slacken the filter initially then unscrew it by hand the rest of the way **(see illustration)**. Empty the oil in the old filter into the container.
11 Use a clean rag to remove all oil, dirt and sludge from the filter sealing area on the engine. Check the old filter to make sure that the rubber sealing ring hasn't stuck to the engine. If it has, carefully remove it.
12 Apply a light coating of clean engine oil to the sealing ring on the new filter **(see**

illustration), then screw it into position on the engine. Tighten the filter firmly by hand only - do not use any tools.
13 Remove the old oil and all tools from under the vehicle and refit the undershield, then (if applicable) lower the vehicle to the ground.
14 Remove the oil filler cap and fill the engine, using the correct grade and type of oil **(see illustration)**. Pour in half the specified quantity of oil first, then wait a few minutes for the oil to fall to the sump. Continue adding oil a small quantity at a time until the level is up to the lower mark on the dipstick. Adding a further 1 litre will bring the level up to the upper mark on the dipstick.
15 Start the engine without revving, noting that the oil pressure warning light will take a second or two to go out. Run it for a few minutes, while checking for leaks around the oil filter seal and the sump drain plug.
16 Switch off the engine and wait a few minutes for the oil to settle in the sump once more. With the new oil circulated and the filter

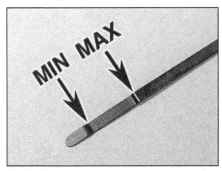

3.16 After running the engine, top-up the oil to the MAX mark on the dipstick

now completely full, recheck the level on the dipstick and add more oil as necessary **(see illustration)**.
17 Refit the undershield(s), tightening the screws securely, and lower the car to the ground.
18 Dispose of the used engine oil safely, with reference to *General repair procedures*.

Every 10 000 miles (15 000 km)

4 Front brake pad and disc check

1 Firmly apply the handbrake, then jack up the front of the car and support it securely on axle stands. Remove the front roadwheels.

2 For a comprehensive check, the brake pads should be removed and cleaned. The operation of the caliper can then also be checked, and the condition of the brake disc itself can be fully examined on both sides. Refer to Chapter 9 **(see Haynes Hint)**.

3 If any pad's friction material is worn to the specified thickness or less, *all four pads must be renewed as a set.*

5 Engine management system check

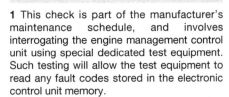

1 This check is part of the manufacturer's maintenance schedule, and involves interrogating the engine management control unit using special dedicated test equipment. Such testing will allow the test equipment to read any fault codes stored in the electronic control unit memory.
2 Unless a fault is suspected, this test is not essential, although it should be noted that it is recommended by the manufacturers.
3 It is possible for quite serious faults to occur in the engine management system without the owner being aware of it. Certain engine management system faults will cause the system to enter an emergency back-up mode, which is often so sophisticated that engine performance is not apparently much affected.

If a problem has caused the system to enter its back-up mode, this will usually be most apparent when starting and running from cold.

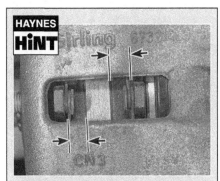

For a quick check, the thickness of the friction material on each brake pad can be measured through the aperture in the caliper body

6.4 Valve numbering and sequence - note splash plate retaining bolt (A)

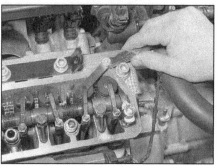

6.6a Checking an inlet valve clearance

6.6b Adjusting an exhaust valve clearance

Every 12 months, regardless of mileage

6 Valve clearance check and adjustment - 1.3 litre engine

Note: *On 1.6 litre engines, self-adjusting hydraulic tappets are fitted, making this task unnecessary.*

1 Obtaining the correct rocker arm/valve stem clearances is vitally important to the performance of the engine. If the clearances are too loose, the valves will open later and close earlier than was intended, and in turn reduce the efficiency of the engine. If, on the other hand, the clearances are too tight, there is a danger that, when the stems and pushrods expand with heat, they will not allow the valves to close fully, which will cause loss of compression and lead to burning of the valve head and valve seat.

2 The valve clearance adjustments should be made with the engine cold. Remove the rocker cover as described in Chapter 2A. It may be advantageous to remove the spark plugs at this stage, to enable the crankshaft to be rotated with the minimum of effort (refer to Section 19).

3 To improve access to the first two valves, unscrew the retaining bolt and remove the splash plate located under the oil filler cap **(refer to illustration 6.4)**

4 It is important that the clearance is set when the tappet of the valve being adjusted is on the heel of the cam (ie opposite the peak). This can be done by numbering the valves starting from the timing chain end of the engine **(see illustration)** and carrying out the adjustments in the following order, which also avoids the crankshaft being rotated more than necessary.

Valve fully open	Check and adjust
Valve No 8	*Valve No 1 (Ex)*
Valve No 6	*Valve No 3 (In)*
Valve No 4	*Valve No 5 (Ex)*
Valve No 7	*Valve No 2 (In)*
Valve No 1	*Valve No 8 (Ex)*
Valve No 3	*Valve No 6 (In)*
Valve No 5	*Valve No 4 (Ex)*
Valve No 2	*Valve No 7 (In)*

5 The correct valve clearance is given in the Specifications at the beginning of this Chapter. It is obtained by slackening the hexagonal locknut with a spanner while holding the ball-pin against rotation with a screwdriver.

6 Insert a feeler blade of thickness equal to the specified valve clearance between the valve stem head and the rocker arm and adjust the ball-pin until the feeler blade is a tight sliding fit **(see illustrations)**. Then, still holding the ball-pin in the correct position, tighten the locknut and recheck.

7 Turn the engine as necessary and repeat the procedure on the remaining valves.

8 Refit the splash plate, tightening the retaining bolt to the specified torque. Refit the rocker cover as described in Chapter 2A, and if applicable, the spark plugs as described in Section 19.

7 Hose and fluid leak check

1 Jack up the front of the vehicle and securely support it on axle stands. Visually inspect the engine joint faces, gaskets and seals for any signs of water or oil leaks. Pay particular attention to the areas around the camshaft cover, cylinder head, oil filter and

HAYNES HINT

A leak in the cooling system will usually show up as white- or rust-coloured deposits on the area adjoining the leak

sump joint faces. Bear in mind that, over a period of time, some very slight seepage from these areas is to be expected - what you are really looking for is any indication of a serious leak **(see Haynes Hint)**. Should a leak be found, renew the offending gasket or oil seal by referring to the appropriate Chapters in this manual.

2 Also check the security and condition of all the engine-related pipes and hoses. Ensure that all cable-ties or securing clips are in place and in good condition. Clips which are broken or missing can lead to chafing of the hoses, pipes or wiring, which could cause more serious problems in the future.

3 Carefully check the radiator hoses and heater hoses along their entire length. Renew any hose which is cracked, swollen or deteriorated. Cracks will show up better if the hose is squeezed. Pay close attention to the hose clips that secure the hoses to the cooling system components. Hose clips can pinch and puncture hoses, resulting in cooling system leaks.

4 Inspect all the cooling system components (hoses, joint faces etc.) for leaks. A leak in the cooling system will usually show up as white- or rust-coloured deposits on the area adjoining the leak. Where any problems of this nature are found on system components, renew the component or gasket with reference to Chapter 3.

5 With the vehicle raised at the rear, inspect the petrol tank and filler neck for punctures, cracks and other damage. The connection between the filler neck and tank is especially critical. Sometimes a rubber filler neck or connecting hose will leak due to loose retaining clamps or deteriorated rubber.

6 Carefully check all rubber hoses and metal fuel lines leading away from the petrol tank. Check for loose connections, deteriorated hoses, crimped lines, and other damage. Pay particular attention to the vent pipes and hoses, which often loop up around the filler neck and can become blocked or crimped. Follow the lines to the front of the vehicle, carefully inspecting them all the way **(see illustration)**. Renew damaged sections as necessary.

7 From within the engine compartment, check the security of all fuel hose attachments and pipe unions, and inspect the fuel hoses and vacuum hoses for kinks, chafing and deterioration.

8 Where applicable, check the condition of the power steering fluid hoses and pipes.

9 On completion, lower the vehicle to the ground.

8 Driveshaft gaiter check

1 With the vehicle raised and securely supported on axle stands, turn the steering to full left or right lock, then slowly rotate the roadwheel. Inspect the outer constant velocity (CV) joint rubber gaiters, squeezing the gaiters to open out the folds **(see illustration)**. Check for signs of cracking, splits or deterioration of the rubber, which may allow the grease to escape, or water and grit to enter. Also check the security and condition of the retaining clips. Repeat these checks on the inner CV joints. If any damage or deterioration is found, the gaiters should be renewed (see Chapter 8).

2 At the same time, check the general condition of the CV joints themselves by first holding the driveshaft and attempting to rotate the wheel. Repeat this check whilst holding the inner joint and attempting to rotate the driveshaft. Any appreciable movement indicates wear in the CV joints, wear in the driveshaft splines, or a loose hub nut.

9 Suspension and steering check

Front suspension and steering check

1 Raise the front of the vehicle, and securely support it on axle stands.

2 Visually inspect the balljoint dust covers and the steering rack gaiters for splits, chafing or deterioration **(see illustration)**. Any wear of these components will cause loss of lubricant, together with dirt and water entry, resulting in rapid deterioration of the balljoints or steering gear.

3 On vehicles with power steering, check the fluid hoses for chafing or deterioration, and the pipe and hose unions for fluid leaks. Also check for signs of fluid leakage under pressure from the steering gear rubber gaiters, which would indicate failed fluid seals within the steering gear.

4 Grasp the roadwheel at the 12 o'clock and 6 o'clock positions, and try to rock it **(see illustration)**. Very slight free play may be felt, but if the movement is appreciable, further investigation is necessary to determine the source. Continue rocking the wheel while an assistant depresses the footbrake. If the

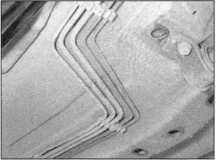

7.6 Check the metal fuel and brake lines along their entire length

movement is now eliminated or significantly reduced, it is likely that the hub bearings are at fault. If the free play is still evident with the footbrake depressed, then there is wear in the suspension joints or mountings.

5 Now grasp the wheel at the 9 o'clock and 3 o'clock positions, and try to rock it as before. Any movement felt now may again be caused by wear in the hub bearings or the steering track-rod balljoints. If the inner or outer balljoint is worn, the visual movement will be obvious.

6 Using a large screwdriver or flat bar, check for wear in the suspension mounting bushes by levering between the relevant suspension component and its attachment point. Some movement is to be expected as the mountings are made of rubber, but excessive wear should be obvious. Also check the condition of any visible rubber bushes, looking for splits, cracks or contamination of the rubber.

7 With the car standing on its wheels, have an assistant turn the steering wheel back and forth about an eighth of a turn each way. There should be very little, if any, lost movement between the steering wheel and roadwheels. If this is not the case, closely observe the joints and mountings previously described, but in addition, check the steering column universal joints for wear, and the rack-and-pinion steering gear itself.

Suspension strut/shock absorber check

8 Check for any signs of fluid leakage around the suspension strut/shock absorber body, or from the rubber gaiter around the piston rod. Should any fluid be noticed, the suspension

9.2 Checking a steering gear gaiter for signs of damage

8.1 Checking a driveshaft outer gaiter for signs of damage

strut/shock absorber is defective internally, and should be renewed. **Note:** *Suspension struts/shock absorbers should always be renewed in pairs on the same axle.*

9 The efficiency of the suspension strut/shock absorber may be checked by bouncing the vehicle at each corner. Generally speaking, the body will return to its normal position and stop after being depressed. If it rises and returns on a rebound, the suspension strut/shock absorber is probably suspect. Examine also the suspension strut/shock absorber upper and lower mountings for any signs of wear.

10 Exhaust system check

1 With the engine cold (at least an hour after the vehicle has been driven), check the complete exhaust system from the engine to the end of the tailpipe. The exhaust system is most easily checked with the vehicle raised on a hoist, or suitably supported on axle stands, so that the exhaust components are readily visible and accessible.

2 Check the exhaust pipes and connections for evidence of leaks, severe corrosion and damage. Make sure that all brackets and mountings are in good condition, and that all relevant nuts and bolts are tight **(see illustrations)**. Leakage at any of the joints or in other parts of the system will usually show up as a black sooty stain in the vicinity of the leak.

9.4 Check for wear in the hub bearings by grasping the wheel and trying to rock it

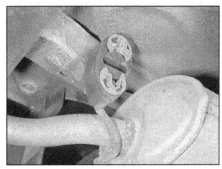

10.2a Check the condition of the exhaust mountings . . .

3 Rattles and other noises can often be traced to the exhaust system, especially the brackets and mountings. Try to move the pipes and silencers. If the components are able to come into contact with the body or suspension parts, secure the system with new mountings. Otherwise separate the joints (if possible) and twist the pipes as necessary to provide additional clearance.

11 Coolant condition check

⚠ **Warning: Wait until the engine is cold before starting this procedure. Do not allow antifreeze to come in contact with your skin, or with the painted surfaces of the vehicle. Rinse off spills immediately with plenty of water.**

1 Note that a tester will be required to check the coolant strength; these can be obtained relatively cheaply from most motor accessory shops.
2 With the engine completely cold, unscrew and remove the filler cap from the coolant expansion tank. Follow the instructions supplied with the tester and check the coolant mixture is sufficient to give protection down to temperatures well below freezing. If the coolant has been renewed at the specified intervals this shouldn't be a problem. However, if the coolant mixture is not strong enough to provide sufficient protection it will

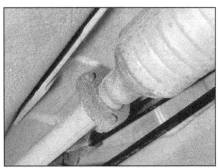

10.2b . . . and the tightness of all bolts and joints

be necessary to drain the cooling system and renew the coolant (see Section 34).
3 Once the test is complete, check the coolant level is correct (see *Weekly checks*) then securely refit the expansion tank cap.

12 Clutch check

1 Check and, if necessary adjust the clutch cable as described in Chapter 6.

13 Hinge and lock lubrication

1 Lubricate the hinges of the bonnet, doors and tailgate with a light general-purpose oil. Similarly, lubricate all latches, locks and lock strikers. At the same time, check the security and operation of all the locks, adjusting if necessary (see Chapter 11).
2 Lightly lubricate the bonnet release mechanism and cable with a suitable grease.

14 Exhaust emission check

This check is part of the manufacturer's maintenance schedule, and involves testing the exhaust emissions using an exhaust gas analyser. Unless a fault is suspected, this test is not essential, although it should be noted that it is recommended by the manufacturers. Adjusting the idle mixture is either not possible, or requires access to dedicated test equipment. Exhaust emissions testing is included as part of the MoT test.

15 Headlight beam alignment check

1 Refer to Chapter 12.

16 Wiper/washer system check

1 Check the condition of the wiper blades as described in *Weekly checks*.
2 Check that each of the washer jet nozzles are clear and that each nozzle provides a strong jet of washer fluid. The jets should be aimed to spray at a point slightly above the centre of the screen/headlight. Where there are two jets, aim one of the jets slightly above then centre of the screen/headlight and aim the other just below to ensure complete coverage of the screen. If necessary, adjust the jets using a pin.

17 Road test

Instruments and electrical equipment

1 Check the operation of all instruments and electrical equipment.
2 Make sure that all instruments read correctly, and switch on all electrical equipment in turn, to check that it functions properly.

Steering and suspension

3 Check for any abnormalities in the steering, suspension, handling or road feel.
4 Drive the vehicle, and check that there are no unusual vibrations or noises.
5 Check that the steering feels positive, with no excessive sloppiness, or roughness, and check for any suspension noises when cornering and driving over bumps.

Drivetrain

6 Check the performance of the engine, clutch, transmission and driveshafts.
7 Listen for any unusual noises from the engine, clutch and transmission.
8 Make sure that the engine runs smoothly when idling, and that there is no hesitation when accelerating.
9 Check that the clutch action is smooth and progressive, that the drive is taken up smoothly, and that the pedal travel is not excessive. Also listen for any noises when the clutch pedal is depressed.
10 Check that all gears can be engaged smoothly without noise, and that the gear lever action is not abnormally vague or notchy.

Check the operation and performance of the braking system

11 Make sure that the vehicle does not pull to one side when braking, and that the wheels do not lock prematurely when braking hard.
12 Check that there is no vibration through the steering when braking.
13 Check that the handbrake operates correctly without excessive movement of the lever, and that it holds the vehicle stationary on a slope.
14 Test the operation of the brake servo unit as follows. With the engine off, depress the footbrake four or five times to exhaust the vacuum. Hold the brake pedal depressed, then start the engine. As the engine starts, there should be a noticeable give in the brake pedal as vacuum builds up. Allow the engine to run for at least two minutes, and then switch it off. If the brake pedal is depressed now, it should be possible to detect a hiss from the servo as the pedal is depressed. After about four or five applications, no further hissing should be heard, and the pedal should feel considerably harder.

18.1 Release the wire clips around the top cover . . .

18.2a . . . then remove the three retaining bolts . . .

18.2b . . . and lift off the cover

Every 20 000 miles (30 000 km)

18 Air cleaner element renewal

1.3 litre models with single-point fuel injection

1 Release the over-centre wire clips around the air cleaner top cover **(see illustration)**.
2 Unscrew and remove the three bolts and carefully lift off the top cover, taking care not to disturb the air cleaner housing more than necessary **(see illustrations)**.
3 Lift out the air filter element **(see illustration)**.
4 Remove any debris inside the air cleaner housing, taking care not to let any fall into the throttle body.
5 Fit the new air filter element into position, noting any direction-of-fitting markings.
6 Refit the air cleaner top cover. Insert the three retaining bolts, and tighten to specified torque.
7 Secure the edges of the top cover by clipping on the over-centre wire clips.

1.3 litre models with multi-point fuel injection, and 1.6 litre models

8 Release the four over-centre wire clips around the air cleaner top cover **(see illustration)**.

9 The top cover can now be lifted sufficiently to withdraw the air filter element. Note the direction of fitting as the element is removed **(see illustration)**.
10 If greater access is required, using a suitable pair of pliers, compress the legs of the spring clip fitted to the top cover which secures the air inlet hose. Work the hose off the top cover stub, and remove the top cover. Alternatively, refer to Chapter 4B, and remove the air cleaner top cover together with the throttle body cover.
11 Remove any debris inside the air cleaner housing.
12 Fit the new air filter element into position, noting any direction-of-fitting markings. Fit the new element as noted on removal, and make sure the edges are securely seated.
13 Refit the air cleaner top cover, securing with the four wire clips. Where removed, refit the air inlet hose, securing with the spring clip, or refit the throttle body cover as described in Chapter 4B.

19 Spark plug renewal - 1.3 litre engine

1 The correct functioning of the spark plugs is vital for the correct running and efficiency of the engine. It is essential that the plugs fitted

are appropriate for the engine, and the suitable type is specified at the beginning of this Chapter. If this type is used and the engine is in good condition, the spark plugs should not need attention between scheduled replacement intervals. Spark plug cleaning is rarely necessary, and should not be attempted unless specialised equipment is available, as damage can easily be caused to the firing ends.
2 Before removing the spark plugs, allow the engine time to cool.

Models with a distributor

3 Mark the HT leads one to four to correspond to the cylinder the lead serves (No 1 cylinder is at the timing chain end of the engine). Either mark the leads with an indelible pen, or wrap an identifying label around each lead - do not cut or score the insulation. Pull the HT leads from the plugs by gripping the end fitting, not the lead, otherwise the lead connection may be fractured.

Models without a distributor

4 Disconnect the wiring plug from the end of the ignition coil unit **(see illustration)**.
5 Unscrew and remove the two socket-head bolts underneath the unit **(see illustrations)**.
6 Pull the coil unit off the spark plugs - do not pull sharply upwards, or the spark plugs may be damaged **(see illustration)**.

18.3 Lifting out the air filter element

18.8 Release the over-centre clips (two at the rear, two more at the front) . . .

18.9 . . . then lift the air cleaner top cover, and withdraw the filter element

19.4 Disconnect the wiring plug from the ignition coil unit

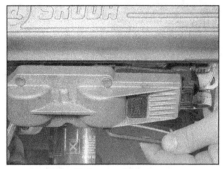

19.5a Using an Allen key . . .

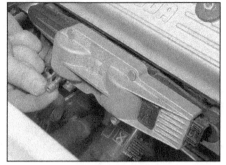

19.5b . . . unscrew and remove the two coil unit mounting bolts

All models

7 It is advisable to remove the dirt from the spark plug recesses using a clean brush, vacuum cleaner or compressed air before removing the plugs, to prevent the dirt dropping into the cylinders.

8 Unscrew the plugs using a spark plug spanner, suitable box spanner or a deep socket and extension bar **(see illustration)**. Keep the socket squarely on the spark plug - if it is forcibly moved to either side, the porcelain top of the spark plug may be broken off. As each plug is removed, note the angle of entry into the cylinder head - this will make screwing the plugs in easier.

9 Examination of the spark plugs will give a good indication of the condition of the engine. If the insulator nose of the spark plug is clean and white, with no deposits, this is indicative of a weak fuel mixture or too hot a plug (a hot

plug transfers heat away from the electrode slowly, a cold plug transfers heat away quickly).

10 If the tip and insulator nose are covered with hard black-looking deposits, then this is indicative that the fuel mixture is too rich. Should the plug be black and oily, then it is likely that the engine is fairly worn, as well as the mixture being too rich.

11 If the insulator nose is covered with light-tan to greyish-brown deposits, then the mixture is correct and it is likely that the engine is in good condition.

12 Finally, check that the spark plug body at the top of the threads is the same type on the plug just removed as the new ones. The plug should be of flat-seat design, with a washer, but some 135 engines may have taper-seat (or cone-seat) design plugs, without a washer - it is essential that the correct plugs are fitted,

as they are not interchangeable. At the time of writing, it appears that all UK-market Felicias are fitted with flat-seat plugs, as listed in the Specifications at the start of this Chapter - consult your Skoda dealer if in doubt.

13 The spark plug gap is of considerable importance as, if it is too large or too small, the size of the spark and its efficiency will be seriously impaired. For best results, the spark plug gap should be set in accordance with the Specifications at the beginning of this Chapter.

14 To set it, measure the gap with a feeler blade, and then bend the outer plug electrode until the correct gap is achieved **(see illustration)**. The centre electrode should never be bent, as this may crack the insulation and cause plug failure, if nothing worse.

15 Special spark plug electrode gap adjusting tools are available from most motor accessory shops **(see illustrations)**.

16 Before fitting the spark plugs, check that the threaded connector sleeves are tight, and that the plug exterior surfaces and threads are clean. Apply a light coating of copper-based brake grease to the spark plug threads, to aid removal next time.

17 Offer the plug into the hole at the angle noted on removal, and gently turn it until the thread catches **(see illustration)**. It's often difficult to screw in new spark plugs without cross-threading them - this can be avoided using a piece of rubber hose **(see Haynes Hint)**.

18 Remove the rubber hose (if used), and tighten the plug to the specified torque using

19.6 Pull the coil unit evenly off the spark plugs, and remove it

19.8 Remove the spark plugs using a deep socket

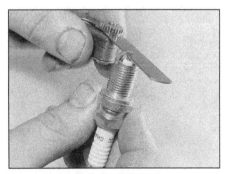

19.14 Measuring the spark plug electrode gap using a feeler blade

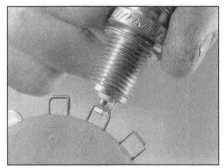

19.15a Measuring the spark plug electrode gap using a wire gauge

19.15b Adjusting the spark plug electrode gap using a special tool

the spark plug socket and a torque wrench. If a torque wrench is not available, tighten the plug by hand until it just seats, then tighten it by no more than a quarter of a turn further with the plug socket and handle. Refit the remaining spark plugs in the same manner.

19 On models with a distributor, reconnect the HT leads in their correct order, as marked on removal.

20 On models without a distributor, refit the ignition coil unit using a reversal of the removal procedure in paragraphs 4 to 6. Tighten the ignition coil unit mounting bolts to the specified torque.

20 Timing belt check - 1.6 litre engine

Note: *This check does not apply to the 1.3 litre engine, which has a chain-driven camshaft.*

1 Refer to Chapter 2B and remove the timing belt upper cover for access to the timing belt.

2 Examine the belt for signs of cracking or splitting, especially around the roots of the teeth, and for signs of fraying or separation of the belt plies. Also look for excess wear on the edges of the belt.

3 Using a spanner or socket on the crankshaft pulley bolt, turn the engine in its normal direction (clockwise, when viewed from the pulley end) and inspect the whole length of the belt.

4 If any damage is noted, the belt should be renewed as described in Chapter 2B. Remember - if the timing belt snaps while the

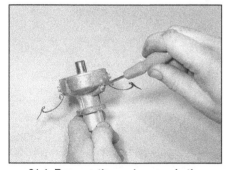

21.1 Remove the grub screw in the distributor body . . .

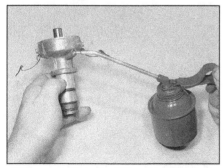

21.2 . . . and inject a little oil into the hole provided (distributor removed for clarity)

19.17 Insert the plug, and tighten it initially by hand

engine is running, severe damage will be caused to the cylinder head components, and possibly to the tops of the pistons.

5 If there is any sign that the belt is being contaminated with oil or other fluid, the belt should be changed and the source of the leak found and fixed, otherwise the new belt will quickly go the same way.

6 On completion, refit the timing belt upper cover as described in Chapter 2B.

21 Distributor lubrication - 1.3 litre engine

1 Remove the grub screw located in the distributor body **(see illustration)**.

2 Add a few drops of engine oil through the hole provided **(see illustration)**.

3 Take care not to allow oil to drip onto the auxiliary drivebelt, if done with the distributor in place.

4 Fit and tighten the grub screw on completion.

22 Auxiliary drivebelt check

1 The drivebelt should be visually inspected for signs of chafing, fraying, splitting and cracking. Twist the belt to examine the condition of the belt ribs **(see illustration)**.

2 To provide better access to the drivebelt, jack up the front right-hand corner of the vehicle, and remove the screws securing the

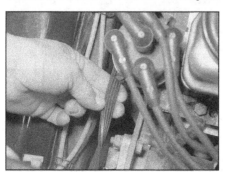

22.1 Twist the drivebelt to examine the belt ribs

HAYNES HINT

It is very often difficult to insert spark plugs into their holes without cross-threading them. To avoid this possibility, fit a short length of 5/16 inch internal diameter rubber hose over the end of the spark plug. The flexible hose acts as a universal joint to help align the plug with the plug hole. Should the plug begin to cross-thread, the hose will slip on the spark plug, preventing thread damage to the aluminium cylinder head

metal cover fitted over the drivebelt **(see illustration)**.

3 Use a spanner or socket on the crankshaft pulley bolt to turn the engine, so that the whole length of the belt can be checked.

4 If there are any signs that the drivebelt is in less-than-perfect condition, renew the drivebelt at the earliest opportunity - refer to Chapter 2A or 2B.

5 Models with the 1.6 litre engine (and 1.3 litre models with air conditioning) are equipped with an automatic tensioning device for the drivebelt, so unless this has failed, the belt tension should be correct.

6 On 1.3 litre models without air conditioning, test the drivebelt tension by pressing the top run of the belt between the alternator and coolant pump pulleys. If the belt deflects by less than 10 mm, or more than 15 mm, the belt tension should be reset as described in Chapter 2A.

7 On completion, where applicable, refit the drivebelt cover and lower the vehicle to the ground.

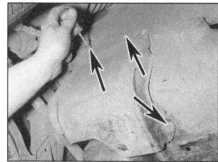

22.2 Remove the auxiliary drivebelt cover screws (arrowed)

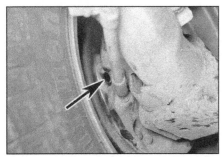

25.2 A quick check on the rear brake shoe friction material can be made using the inspection hole (arrowed) in the backplate

23 Airbag system check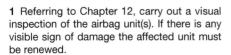

1 Referring to Chapter 12, carry out a visual inspection of the airbag unit(s). If there is any visible sign of damage the affected unit must be renewed.

24 Engine emission control system check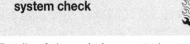

1 Details of the emissions control system components are given in Chapter 4D.
2 Checking consists simply of a visual check for obvious signs of damaged, perished, or leaking hoses and joints, or for loose, damaged or disconnected wiring.
3 Detailed checking and testing of the evaporative and/or exhaust emissions systems (as applicable) should be entrusted to a Skoda dealer.

25 Rear brake shoe and drum check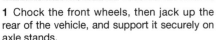

1 Chock the front wheels, then jack up the rear of the vehicle, and support it securely on axle stands.
2 For a quick check, the thickness of friction material remaining on one of the brake shoes

can be observed through the hole in the brake backplate which is exposed by prising out the sealing grommet (where fitted) **(see illustration)**. If a rod of the same diameter as the specified minimum friction material thickness is placed against the shoe friction material, the amount of wear can be assessed. A torch or inspection light will probably be required. If the friction material on any shoe is worn down to the specified minimum thickness or less, all four shoes must be renewed as a set.
3 For a comprehensive check, the brake drum should be removed and cleaned. This will allow the wheel cylinders to be checked, and the condition of the brake drum itself to be fully examined (see Chapter 9).

26 Handbrake check

1 Check and, if necessary, adjust the handbrake as described in Chapter 9.

27 Body corrosion check

1 With the vehicle raised and securely supported, carry out a thorough check of the vehicle underbody sealant for signs of damage. If any area of the underbody sealant shows visible damage, the affected area should be repaired to prevent possible problems with corrosion occurring at a later date.

28 Transmission oil level check

1 Park the car on a level surface. The oil level must be checked before the car is driven, or at least 5 minutes after the engine has been switched off. If the oil is checked immediately after driving the car, some of the oil will remain distributed around the transmission

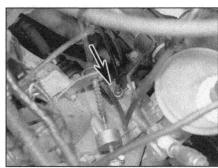

28.3a Undo the bolt (arrowed) then slide out the retaining plate . . .

components, resulting in an inaccurate level reading.
2 Wipe clean the area around the speedometer drive on the top of the transmission.
3 Slacken and remove the retaining bolt then slide out the retaining plate and withdraw the speedometer drive assembly from the transmission unit **(see illustrations)**.
4 The oil level is checked by using the speedometer drivegear as a dipstick. Wipe clean the drivegear then reinsert the speedometer drive fully into the transmission unit before removing it again. Measure the height the oil level extends up the drivegear; the oil level should be 4 mm above the base of the drivegear **(see illustration)**. It is permissible for level to be slightly higher then specified but it should never be allowed to fall below this.
5 If topping-up is necessary, add oil through the speedometer drivegear aperture until the level is correct; use only good-quality oil of the specified type (refer to *Lubricants and fluids*) **(see illustration)**.
6 If the transmission has been overfilled, siphon excess oil out through the speedometer drivegear aperture.
7 When the level is correct, inspect the speedometer drivegear sealing ring for signs of wear or deterioration and renew if necessary. Lubricate the sealing ring with a smear of transmission oil then ease the drive assembly into position. Engage the retaining plate with the drivegear slot then refit the retaining bolt, tightening it to the specified torque setting.

28.3b . . . and withdraw the speedometer drive assembly from the transmission unit

28.4 Use the speedometer drive as a dipstick to check the oil level. The level should be 4mm up from the base of the drivegear

28.5 If topping-up is necessary, add the specified type and grade of oil through the speedometer drive aperture

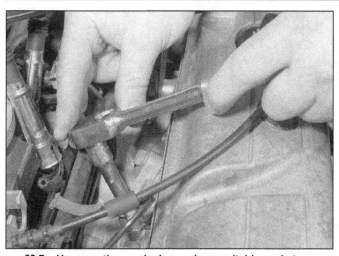

29.7a Unscrew the spark plugs using a suitable socket . . .

29.7b . . . and remove them from the cylinder head - note multi-earth-electrode spark plug

Every 40 000 miles (60 000 km)

29 Spark plug renewal - 1.6 litre engine

1 The correct functioning of the spark plugs is vital for the correct running and efficiency of the engine. It is essential that the plugs fitted are appropriate for the engine (a suitable type is specified at the beginning of this Chapter). If this type is used and the engine is in good condition, the spark plugs should not need attention between scheduled replacement intervals. Spark plug cleaning is rarely necessary, and should not be attempted unless specialised equipment is available, as damage can easily be caused to the firing ends.

2 Before removing the spark plugs, allow the engine time to cool.

3 To gain access to the spark plugs, unscrew and remove the three screws from the cover fitted over the throttle body, noting that the front screw is longer than the other two. Release any hoses or wiring clipped to the underside of the cover, and lift the cover away.

4 If the marks on the original-equipment spark plug (HT) leads cannot be seen, mark the leads 1 to 4, to correspond to the cylinder the lead serves (No 1 cylinder is at the timing belt end of the engine). Either mark the leads with an indelible pen, or wrap an identifying label around each lead - do not cut or score the insulation.

5 Metal heat shields are fitted to the lead end fittings. Pull the leads from the plugs by gripping the end fitting, not the lead, otherwise the lead connection may be fractured.

6 It is advisable to remove the dirt from the spark plug recesses using a clean brush, vacuum cleaner or compressed air before

removing the plugs, to prevent the dirt dropping into the cylinders.

7 Unscrew the plugs using a spark plug spanner, suitable box spanner or a deep socket and extension bar (see illustrations). Keep the socket squarely on the spark plug - if it is forcibly moved to either side, the porcelain top of the spark plug may be broken off. As each plug is removed, note the angle of entry into the cylinder head - this will make screwing the plugs in easier.

8 Examination of the spark plugs will give a good indication of the condition of the engine. If the insulator nose of the spark plug is clean and white, with no deposits, this is indicative of a weak fuel mixture or too hot a plug (a hot plug transfers heat away from the electrode slowly, a cold plug transfers heat away quickly).

9 If the tip and insulator nose are covered with hard black-looking deposits, then this is indicative that the fuel mixture is too rich. Should the plug be black and oily, then it is likely that the engine is fairly worn, as well as the mixture being too rich.

10 If the insulator nose is covered with light-tan to greyish-brown deposits, then the

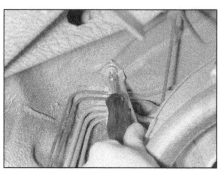

30.3a Remove the exhaust heat shield nuts . . .

mixture is correct and it is likely that the engine is in good condition.

11 The spark plugs fitted and recommended by the manufacturers have multiple earth electrodes, unlike conventional plugs, which have only one. No attempt should be made to adjust the plug gap on a spark plug with more than one earth electrode.

12 The rest of the procedure is as described for 1.3 litre engine models, in Section 19, paragraphs 16 to 19.

13 When the HT leads have been reconnected, refit the throttle body cover, tightening the screws securely.

30 Fuel filter renewal

⚠ *Warning: Refer to the notes in Safety first!, and follow them implicitly. Petrol is a highly-dangerous and volatile liquid, and the precautions necessary when handling it cannot be overstressed.*

1 Depressurise the fuel system with reference to Chapter 4A or 4B.

2 The fuel filter is situated underneath the rear of the vehicle, to the left and in front of the fuel tank. Access to the filter is poor. Chock the front wheels, then jack up the rear of the vehicle and support it securely on axle stands (see *Jacking and vehicle support*).

3 Remove the three nuts securing the exhaust heat shield, and manoeuvre the shield out around the exhaust pipe for access to the filter (see illustrations).

4 If you have them, fit hose clamps to the filter inlet and outlet hoses. These are not essential, but even with the system depressurised, there will still be an amount of petrol in the pipes (and the old filter), and this

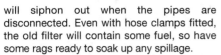

30.3b ... and manoeuvre the heat shield out past the exhaust pipe

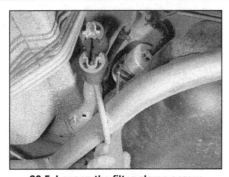

30.5 Loosen the filter clamp screw

30.6a The standard hose clips (arrowed) are of the spring type ...

will siphon out when the pipes are disconnected. Even with hose clamps fitted, the old filter will contain some fuel, so have some rags ready to soak up any spillage.

5 Loosen the retaining clamp screw, to allow some movement of the filter **(see illustration)**.

6 Release the hose clips and detach the hoses from the filter **(see illustrations)**. If spring-type clips are still fitted, discard them and fit proper (screw-type) petrol pipe clips when reassembling. Similarly, if the fuel hoses show any sign of perishing or cracking, particularly at the hose ends, renew the hoses.

7 Before removing the filter, note any direction-of-flow markings on the filter body, and check against the new filter - the arrow should point in the direction of fuel flow (towards the pipe leading to the front of the car).

8 Fit the new filter into position, with the flow marking arrow correctly orientated.

9 Reconnect the fuel hoses, using new clips if necessary. Ensure that no dirt is allowed to enter the hoses or filter connections. Tighten the filter retaining clamp screw, then release the hose clamps.

10 Start the engine (there may be a delay as the system re-pressurises and the new filter fills with fuel). Let the engine run for several minutes while you check the filter hose connections for leaks.

11 Refit the exhaust heat shield, then lower the vehicle to the ground.

 Warning: Dispose safely of the old filter; it will be highly flammable, and may explode if thrown on a fire.

31 Transmission oil renewal

1 This operation is much quicker and more efficient if the car is first taken on a journey of sufficient length to warm the engine/transmission up to normal operating temperature.

2 Park the car on level ground, switch off the ignition and apply the handbrake firmly. For improved access, jack up the front of the car and support it securely on axle stands (see *Jacking and vehicle support*). Note that the car must be lowered to the ground and level, to ensure accuracy, when refilling and checking the oil level.

3 Wipe clean the area around the speedometer drive on the top of the transmission.

4 Slacken and remove the retaining bolt then slide out the retaining plate and withdraw the speedometer drive assembly from the transmission unit (see Section 28). Inspect the drive sealing ring for signs of wear or deterioration and renew if necessary.

5 Wipe clean the area around the drain plug, which is situated on the base of the transmission unit, directly below the left-hand driveshaft inner CV joint. Position a suitable container under the drain plug and unscrew the plug **(see illustration)**.

6 Allow the oil to drain completely into the container. If the oil is hot, take precautions

against scalding. Clean the drain plug, being especially careful to wipe any metallic particles off the magnetic insert. Discard the sealing washer; it should be renewed whenever it is disturbed.

7 When the oil has finished draining, clean the drain plug threads and those of the transmission casing, fit a new sealing washer and refit the drain plug, tightening it to the specified torque wrench setting. If the car was raised for the draining operation, now lower it to the ground.

8 Refilling the transmission is an extremely awkward operation. Above all, allow plenty of time for the oil level to settle properly before checking it. Note that the car must be parked on flat level ground when checking the oil level.

9 Refill the transmission via the speedometer drive aperture with the exact amount of the specified type of oil then check the oil level as described in Section 28; if the correct amount was poured into the transmission and the level is not correct, refit the speedometer drive and take the car on a short journey so that the new oil is distributed fully around the transmission components, then check the level again on your return.

32 Timing belt renewal - 1.6 litre engine

Refer to Chapter 2B.

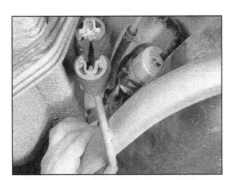

30.6b ... and must be released using suitable pliers

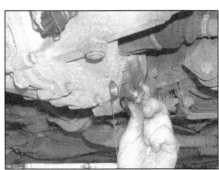

31.5 Unscrew the transmission drain plug and allow the oil to drain into a container

Every 2 years, regardless of mileage

33 Brake fluid renewal

> ⚠ **Warning: Brake hydraulic fluid can harm your eyes and damage painted surfaces, so use extreme caution when handling and pouring it. Do not use fluid that has been standing open for some time, as it absorbs moisture from the air. Excess moisture can cause a dangerous loss of braking effectiveness.**

1 The procedure is similar to that for the bleeding of the hydraulic system as described in Chapter 9, except that the brake fluid reservoir should be emptied by siphoning, using a clean poultry baster or similar before starting, and allowance should be made for the old fluid to be expelled when bleeding a section of the circuit.

2 Working as described in Chapter 9, open the first bleed screw in the sequence, and pump the brake pedal gently until nearly all the old fluid has been emptied from the master cylinder reservoir.

> **HAYNES HiNT** Old hydraulic fluid is invariably much darker in colour than the new, making it easy to distinguish the two.

3 Top-up to the MAX level with new fluid, and continue pumping until only the new fluid remains in the reservoir, and new fluid can be seen emerging from the bleed screw. Tighten the screw, and top the reservoir level up to the MAX level line.

4 Work through all the remaining bleed screws in the sequence until new fluid can be seen at all of them. Be careful to keep the master cylinder reservoir topped-up to above the MIN level at all times, or air may enter the system and greatly increase the length of the task.

5 When the operation is complete, check that all bleed screws are securely tightened, and that their dust caps are refitted. Wash off all traces of spilt fluid, and recheck the master cylinder reservoir fluid level.

6 Check the operation of the brakes before taking the car on the road.

Every 3 years, regardless of mileage

34 Coolant renewal

Cooling system draining

> ⚠ **Warning: Wait until the engine is cold before starting this procedure. Do not allow antifreeze to come in contact with your skin, or with the painted surfaces of the vehicle. Rinse off spills immediately with plenty of water. Never leave antifreeze lying around in an open container, or in a puddle in the driveway or on the garage floor. Children and pets are attracted by its sweet smell, but antifreeze can be fatal if ingested.**

1.3 litre engine

1 With the engine completely cold, firmly apply the handbrake then jack up the front of the vehicle and support it on axle stands.

2 Unscrew and remove the expansion tank filler cap then position a suitable container beneath the coolant drain plug which is located on the base of the metal pipe which runs underneath the crankshaft pulley **(see illustration)**.

3 Unscrew the drain plug and allow the coolant to drain into the container.

4 When the flow of coolant stops, reposition the container underneath the drain plug on the front, left-hand end of the cylinder block, directly above the oil pressure switch **(see illustration)**. Unscrew the drain plug and allow the remainder of the coolant to drain into the container.

5 If the coolant has been drained for a reason other than renewal, then provided it is clean and less than three years old, it can be re-used, though this is not recommended. Discard the drain plug sealing washers; they should be renewed whenever they are disturbed.

6 Clean the drain plug threads and fit the new sealing washers. Apply a smear of fresh sealant to each drain plug then refit them to the cylinder block and pipe and tighten to their specified torque settings.

1.6 litre engine

7 With the engine completely cold, unscrew and remove the expansion tank filler cap then position a suitable container beneath the radiator bottom hose connection.

8 Release the retaining clip then disconnect the bottom hose from the radiator and allow the coolant to drain into the container.

9 If the coolant has been drained for a reason other than renewal, then provided it is clean and less than three years old, it can be re-used, though this is not recommended.

10 Once the flow of the coolant stops, reconnect the coolant hose and secure it in position with the retaining clip.

Cooling system flushing

11 If coolant renewal has been neglected, or if the antifreeze mixture has become diluted, then in time, the cooling system may gradually lose efficiency, as the coolant passages become restricted due to rust, scale deposits, and other sediment. The cooling system efficiency can be restored by flushing the system clean.

12 The radiator should be flushed independently of the engine, to avoid unnecessary contamination.

Radiator flushing

13 To flush the radiator, disconnect the top and bottom hoses and any other relevant hoses from the radiator, with reference to Chapter 3.

14 Insert a garden hose into the radiator top inlet. Direct a flow of clean water through the radiator, and continue flushing until clean water emerges from the radiator bottom outlet.

15 If after a reasonable period, the water still does not run clear, the radiator can be flushed with a good proprietary cleaning agent. It is important that their manufacturer's instructions are followed carefully. If the contamination is particularly bad, insert the hose in the radiator bottom outlet, and reverse-flush the radiator.

Engine flushing

16 To flush the engine, remove the thermostat as described in Chapter 3, then temporarily refit the thermostat cover.

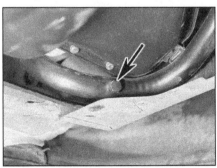

34.2 Coolant pipe drain plug - 1.3 litre engine

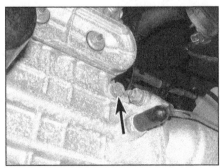

34.4 Cylinder block drain plug - 1.3 litre engine (viewed from below)

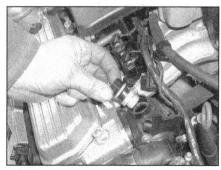

34.21 On 1.3 litre engines, remove the coolant temperature sensor from the thermostat housing to bleed the air from the engine as cooling system is refilled

17 With the top and bottom hoses disconnected from the radiator, insert a garden hose into the radiator top hose. Direct a clean flow of water through the engine, and continue flushing until clean water emerges from the radiator bottom hose.

18 On completion of flushing, refit the thermostat and reconnect the hoses with reference to Chapter 3.

Cooling system filling

19 Before attempting to fill the cooling system, make sure that all hoses and clips are in good condition, and that the clips are tight. Note that an antifreeze mixture must be used all year round, to prevent corrosion of the engine components (see following sub-Section).

1.3 litre engines

20 Ensure that both the drain plugs are securely tightened.

21 Lower the vehicle to the ground then remove the coolant temperature sensor from the top of the thermostat housing (see Chapter 3) **(see illustration)**.

22 Remove the expansion tank filler cap and slowly fill the system whilst keeping an eye on the thermostat housing. Once coolant free of air bubbles starts to flow from the housing aperture, refit the sensor as described in Chapter 3.

23 With the sensor in position, continue to slowly fill the system until the coolant level reaches the MAX mark on the side of the expansion tank.

24 Refit and tighten the expansion tank cap.

25 Start the engine, and allow it to run until it reaches normal operating temperature.

26 Stop the engine, and allow it to cool, then re-check the coolant level with reference to *Weekly checks*. Top-up the level if necessary and refit the expansion tank filler cap.

1.6 litre engine

27 Ensure that the bottom hose is reconnected to the radiator and secured in position with the retaining clip.

28 Remove the expansion tank filler cap and slowly fill the system until the coolant level reaches the MAX mark on the side of the expansion tank.

29 Refit and tighten the expansion tank filler cap.

30 Start the engine, and allow it to run until it reaches normal operating temperature.

31 Stop the engine, and allow it to cool, then re-check the coolant level with reference to *Weekly checks*. Top-up the level if necessary and refit the expansion tank filler cap.

Antifreeze mixture

32 The antifreeze should always be renewed at the specified intervals. This is necessary not only to maintain the antifreeze properties, but also to prevent corrosion which would otherwise occur as the corrosion inhibitors become progressively less effective.

33 Always use an ethylene-glycol based antifreeze which is suitable for use in mixed-metal cooling systems. The quantity of antifreeze and levels of protection are given in the Specifications.

34 Before adding antifreeze, the cooling system should be completely drained, preferably flushed, and all hoses checked for condition and security.

35 After filling with antifreeze, a label should be attached to the expansion tank, stating the type and concentration of antifreeze used, and the date installed. Any subsequent topping-up should be made with the same type and concentration of antifreeze.

36 Do not use engine antifreeze in the windscreen/tailgate washer system, as it will cause damage to the vehicle paintwork. A screenwash additive should be added to the washer system in the quantities stated on the bottle.

Chapter 1 Part B:
Routine maintenance & servicing - diesel models

Contents

Degrees of difficulty

Easy, suitable for novice with little experience | **Fairly easy,** suitable for beginner with some experience | **Fairly difficult,** suitable for competent DIY mechanic | **Difficult,** suitable for experienced DIY mechanic | **Very difficult,** suitable for expert DIY or professional

Lubricants and fluids

Refer to *Weekly checks*

Capacities

Engine oil

Including oil filter	5.0 litres
Difference between MIN and MAX marks on dipstick	1.0 litre

Cooling system

Approximate	6.0 litres

Transmission

Approximate	2.4 litres

Washer fluid reservoir

Without headlight washers	3.0 litres
With headlight washers	8.0 litres

Fuel tank

All models	42 litres

Cooling system

Antifreeze mixture:

50% antifreeze	Protection down to -37°C
55% antifreeze	Protection down to -45°C

Note: *Refer to antifreeze manufacturer for latest recommendations.*

Preheating system

Glow plugs	Bosch 0 250 201 032

Brakes

Friction material minimum thickness:

Front brake pads	2.0 mm
Rear brake shoes	2.5 mm

Torque wrench settings

	Nm	lbf ft
Coolant drain plug	20	15
Roadwheel bolts	110	81
Speedometer drive retaining plate bolt	10	7
Transmission drain plug	35	25

The maintenance intervals in this manual are provided with the assumption that you, not the dealer, will be carrying out the work. These are the minimum maintenance intervals recommended by us for vehicles driven daily. If you wish to keep your vehicle in peak condition at all times, you may wish to perform some of these procedures more often. We encourage frequent maintenance, because it enhances the efficiency, performance and resale value of your vehicle.

If the vehicle is driven in dusty areas, used to tow a trailer, or driven frequently at slow speeds (idling in traffic) or on short journeys, more frequent maintenance intervals are recommended.

When the vehicle is new, it should be serviced by a factory-authorised dealer service department, in order to preserve the factory warranty.

Every 250 miles (400 km) or weekly
- [ ] Refer to *Weekly checks*

Every 5000 miles (7500 km)
- [ ] Renew the engine oil and filter (Section 3)
- [ ] Drain water from fuel filter (Section 4)
- [ ] Check the front brake pads and discs for wear (Section 5)

Every 12 months, regardless of mileage
Note: *On models covering less than 5000 miles (7500 km) a year also perform the tasks listed under the previous heading at this interval.*
- [ ] Check and adjust the engine idle speed (Section 6)
- [ ] Check all components, pipes and hoses for fluid leaks (Section 7)
- [ ] Check the condition of the driveshaft gaiters (Section 8)
- [ ] Check the steering and suspension components for condition and security (Section 9)
- [ ] Check the condition of the exhaust system (Section 10)
- [ ] Check the condition of the coolant (Section 11)
- [ ] Check the operation of the clutch (Section 12)
- [ ] Lubricate all door locks and hinges, door stops, bonnet lock and release, and tailgate lock and hinges (Section 13)
- [ ] Check the exhaust emission level (Section 14)
- [ ] Check and if necessary adjust the headlight beam alignment (Section 15)
- [ ] Check the operation of the wiper/washer systems (Section 16)
- [ ] Carry out a road test (Section 17)

Every 20 000 miles (30 000 km)
- [ ] Renew the air filter element (Section 18)
- [ ] Renew the fuel filter (Section 19)
- [ ] Check the condition of the engine timing belt (Section 20)
- [ ] Check the condition and tension of the auxiliary drivebelt(s) (Section 21)
- [ ] Carry out a visual check of the airbag(s) - where fitted (Section 22)
- [ ] Check the engine emission control systems (Section 23)
- [ ] Check the rear brake shoes and drums for wear (Section 24)
- [ ] Check the operation of the handbrake (Section 25)
- [ ] Check the underbody sealant for signs of damage (Section 26)
- [ ] Check the transmission oil level (Section 27)

Every 40 000 miles (60 000 km)
- [ ] Renew the transmission oil (Section 28)
- [ ] Renew the timing belt (Section 29)
Note: *The manufacturer does not give a recommended interval for timing belt renewal and only specifies that a check should be carried out every 20 000 miles (30 000 km). However we recommend that the belt is changed at this interval, regardless of its apparent condition.*

Every 2 years, regardless of mileage
- [ ] Renew the brake fluid (Section 30)

Every 3 years, regardless of mileage
- [ ] Renew the coolant (Section 31)

Underbonnet view of a diesel engine

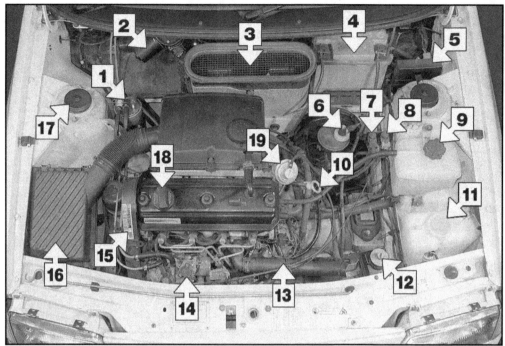

1 Fuel filter
2 Windscreen wiper motor
3 Heater/ventilation unit
4 Battery
5 Diesel/glow plug control unit
6 Brake fluid reservoir
7 EGR solenoid valve
8 Idle speed boost valve
9 Coolant expansion tank
10 Engine oil dipstick
11 Washer fluid reservoir
12 Power steering fluid reservoir
13 Radiator top hose
14 Fuel injection pump
15 Timing belt upper cover
16 Air cleaner housing
17 Suspension strut upper mounting
18 Engine oil filler cap
19 EGR valve

Front underbody view (undershields removed)

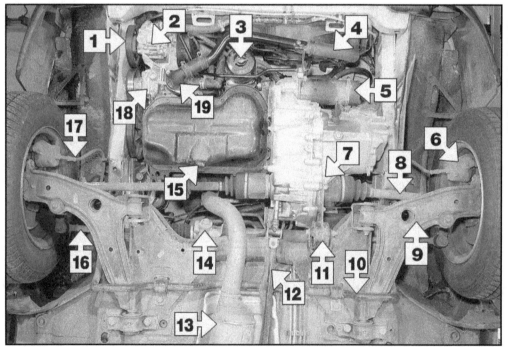

1 Auxiliary drivebelt
2 Power steering pump
3 Engine oil filter
4 Radiator bottom hose
5 Starter motor
6 Front brake caliper
7 Transmission oil drain plug
8 Driveshaft
9 Wishbone/lower arm
10 Anti-roll bar
11 Engine/transmission rear mounting
12 Gearchange linkage
13 Catalytic converter
14 Steering rack
15 Engine oil drain plug
16 Track rod
17 Front brake hose
18 Coolant pump
19 Thermostat housing

Rear underbody view

1   Rear brake hose
2   Fuel tank
3   Handbrake cable
4   Rear axle
5   Exhaust rear silencer
6   Rear strut lower mounting
7   Exhaust mounting
8   Rear towing eye
9   Fuel tank filler pipe

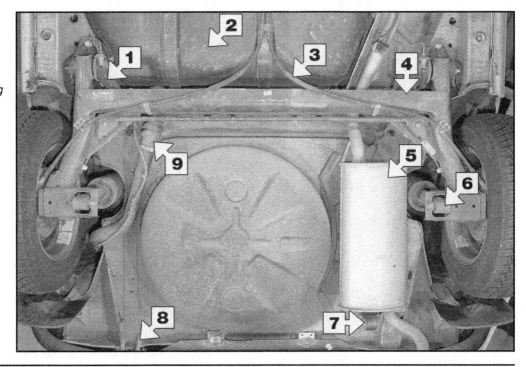

1 Introduction

General information

This Chapter is designed to help the home mechanic maintain his/her vehicle for safety, economy, long life and peak performance.

The Chapter contains a master maintenance schedule, followed by Sections dealing specifically with each task in the schedule. Visual checks, adjustments, component renewal and other helpful items are included. Refer to the accompanying illustrations of the engine compartment and the underside of the vehicle for the locations of the various components.

Servicing your vehicle in accordance with the mileage/time maintenance schedule and the following Sections will provide a planned maintenance programme, which should result in a long and reliable service life. This is a comprehensive plan, so maintaining some items but not others at the specified service intervals, will not produce the same results.

As you service your vehicle, you will discover that many of the procedures can - and should - be grouped together, because of the particular procedure being performed, or because of the proximity of two otherwise-unrelated components to one another. For example, if the vehicle is raised for any reason, the exhaust can be inspected at the same time as the suspension and steering components.

The first step in this maintenance programme is to prepare yourself before the actual work begins. Read through all the Sections relevant to the work to be carried out, then make a list and gather all the parts and tools required. If a problem is encountered, seek advice from a parts specialist, or a dealer service department.

2 Regular maintenance

1 If, from the time the vehicle is new, the routine maintenance schedule is followed closely, and frequent checks are made of fluid levels and high-wear items, as suggested throughout this manual, the engine will be kept in relatively good running condition, and the need for additional work will be minimised.
2 It is possible that there will be times when the engine is running poorly due to the lack of regular maintenance. This is even more likely if a used vehicle, which has not received regular and frequent maintenance checks, is purchased. In such cases, additional work may need to be carried out, outside of the regular maintenance intervals.
3 If engine wear is suspected, a compression test (refer to Chapter 2C) will provide valuable information regarding the overall performance of the main internal components. Such a test can be used as a basis to decide on the extent of the work to be carried out. If, for example, a compression test indicates serious

internal engine wear, conventional maintenance as described in this Chapter will not greatly improve the performance of the engine, and may prove a waste of time and money, unless extensive overhaul work is carried out first.
4 The following series of operations are those most often required to improve the performance of a generally poor-running engine:

Primary operations

a) Clean, inspect and test the battery (refer to Weekly checks).
b) Check all the engine-related fluids (refer to Weekly checks).
c) Check the condition and tension of the auxiliary drivebelt(s) (Section 21).
d) Check the condition of the air filter, and renew if necessary (Section 18).
e) Renew the fuel filter (Section 19).
f) Check the condition of all hoses, and check for fluid leaks (Section 7).

5 If the above operations do not prove fully effective, carry out the following secondary operations:

Secondary operations

All items listed under Primary operations, plus the following:
a) Check the charging system (refer to Chapter 5A).
b) Check the preheating system (refer to Chapter 5C).
c) Check the fuel system (refer to Chapter 4C).

3.6 Unscrewing the engine oil drain plug

3.10a Genuine Skoda filters have a slot in the base for a special tool . . .

3.10b . . . or for a home-made alternative

Every 5000 miles (7500 km)

3 Engine oil and filter renewal

1 Frequent oil and filter changes are the most important preventative maintenance procedures that can be undertaken by the DIY owner. As engine oil ages, it becomes diluted and contaminated, which leads to premature engine wear.

2 Before starting this procedure, gather together all the necessary tools and materials.

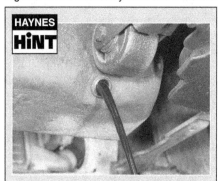

HAYNES HiNT

Keep the drain plug pressed into the sump while unscrewing it by hand last couple of turns. As the plug releases, move it away sharply so the stream of oil issuing from the sump runs into the container, not up your sleeve

Also make sure that you have plenty of clean rags and newspapers handy to mop up any spills. Ideally, the engine oil should be warm as it will drain better and more built-up sludge will be removed with it. Take care, however, not to touch the exhaust or any other hot parts of the engine when working under the vehicle - this applies especially to the catalytic converter.

3 To avoid any possibility of injury through scalding, and to protect yourself from possible skin irritants and other harmful contaminants in used engine oils, it is advisable to wear non-permeable gloves when carrying out this work.

4 Access to the underside of the vehicle will be greatly improved if it can be raised on a lift, driven onto ramps or jacked up and supported on axle stands (see *Jacking and vehicle support*). Whichever method is chosen, make sure that the vehicle remains level, or if it is at an angle, that the drain plug (located on the underside of the sump) is at the lowest point.

5 Remove the full-width undershield by unscrewing the retaining screws. Side shields are also fitted - although their removal may not be essential for access, these metal shields have sharp edges, and removal may be desirable for safety reasons.

6 Using a spanner or preferably a suitable socket and bar, slacken the drain plug about half a turn **(see illustration)**. Position the draining container under the drain plug, then remove the plug completely **(see Haynes Hint)**.

7 Allow some time for the old oil to drain,

noting that it may be necessary to reposition the container as the oil flow slows to a trickle.

8 After all the oil has drained, wipe off the drain plug with a clean rag and, if necessary, renew the sealing washer. Clean the area around the drain plug opening and refit the plug. Tighten the plug securely, preferably to the specified torque using a torque wrench.

9 Move the container into position under the oil filter, which is located on the front of the cylinder block.

10 Using an oil filter removal tool if necessary, slacken the filter initially then unscrew it by hand the rest of the way. A slot is provided in the base of a genuine Skoda filter, into which a suitable tool or lever can be inserted, to help unscrew it **(see illustrations)**. Empty the oil in the old filter into the container.

11 Use a clean rag to remove all oil, dirt and sludge from the filter sealing area on the engine. Check the old filter to make sure that the rubber sealing ring hasn't stuck to the engine. If it has, carefully remove it.

12 Apply a light coating of clean engine oil to the sealing ring on the new filter **(see illustration)**, then screw it into position on the engine. Tighten the filter firmly by hand only - do not use any tools.

13 Remove the old oil and all tools from under the vehicle and refit the undershield then (if applicable) lower the vehicle to the ground.

14 Remove the oil filler cap and fill the engine, using the correct grade and type of oil **(see illustrations)**. Pour in half the specified

3.12 Apply a little engine oil to the new oil filter sealing ring

3.14a Remove the oil filler cap . . .

3.14b . . . and fill the engine using the correct grade and quantity of oil

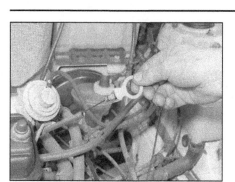

3.16a After running the engine, remove the dipstick . . .

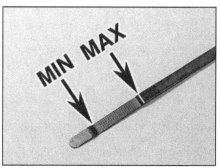

3.16b . . . and top-up the oil to the MAX mark on the dipstick

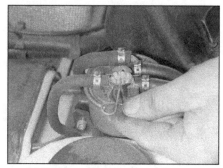

4.3 Slide out the R-clip securing the control valve

quantity of oil first, then wait a few minutes for the oil to fall to the sump. Continue adding oil a small quantity at a time until the level is up to the lower mark on the dipstick. Adding a further 1 litre will bring the level up to the upper mark on the dipstick.

15 Start the engine without revving, noting that the oil pressure warning light will take a second or two to go out. Run it for a few minutes, while checking for leaks around the oil filter seal and the sump drain plug.

16 Switch off the engine and wait a few minutes for the oil to settle in the sump once more. With the new oil circulated and the filter now completely full, recheck the level on the dipstick and add more oil as necessary **(see illustrations)**.

17 Refit the undershield(s), tightening the screws securely, and lower the car to the ground.

18 Dispose of the used engine oil safely, with reference to *General repair procedures*.

4 Fuel filter draining

1 From time to time, the water collected from the fuel by the filter unit must be drained out.
2 The fuel filter is mounted at the right-hand rear of the engine compartment.
3 At the top of the filter unit, pull out the R-clip and lift out the control valve, leaving the

fuel hoses attached **(see illustration)**.
4 Slacken the retaining bracket screw and lift the filter up slightly.
5 Position a container below the filter unit, and pad the surrounding area with rags to absorb any fuel that may be spilt.
6 Unscrew the drain valve at the base of the filter unit, until fuel starts to run out into the container **(refer to illustration 19.7)**. Keep the valve open until about 100 cc of fuel has been collected.
7 Refit the control valve to the top of the filter and insert the retaining clip. Close the drain valve and wipe off any surplus fuel from the nozzle.
8 Remove the collecting container and rags, then push the filter unit back into the retaining bracket and tighten the bracket screw.
9 Run the engine at idle, and check around the fuel filter for fuel leaks.
10 Raise the engine speed to about 2000 rpm several times, then allow the engine to idle again. Observe the fuel flow through the transparent hose leading to the fuel injection pump, and check that it is free of air bubbles.

5 Front brake pad and disc check

1 Firmly apply the handbrake, then jack up the front of the car and support it securely on axle stands. Remove the front roadwheels.

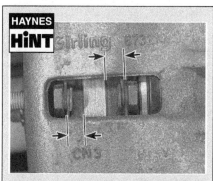

For a quick check, the thickness of the friction material on each brake pad can be measured through the aperture in the caliper body

2 For a comprehensive check, the brake pads should be removed and cleaned. The operation of the caliper can then also be checked, and the condition of the brake disc itself can be fully examined on both sides. Refer to Chapter 9 **(see Haynes Hint)**.
3 If any pad's friction material is worn to the specified thickness or less, *all four pads must be renewed as a set*.

Every 12 months, regardless of mileage

6 Idle speed check and adjustment

1 Start the engine and run it until it reaches its normal operating temperature. With the handbrake applied and the transmission in neutral, allow the engine to idle. Make sure that all electrical equipment (headlights, heated rear window, heater blower, etc) is switched off.
2 Using a diesel tachometer, check the idle speed against the Specifications at the start of this Chapter.

3 To adjust the idle speed, loosen the locknut on the idle speed stop screw, then adjust the screw as necessary **(see illustration)**. On completion, tighten the locknut.

7 Hose and fluid leak check

1 Jack up the front of the vehicle and securely support it on axle stands. Visually inspect the engine joint faces, gaskets and seals for any signs of water or oil leaks. Pay particular

6.3 Idle speed adjustment screw (arrowed)

A leak in the cooling system will usually show up as white- or rust-coloured deposits on the area adjoining the leak

attention to the areas around the camshaft cover, cylinder head, oil filter and sump joint faces. Bear in mind that, over a period of time, some very slight seepage from these areas is to be expected - what you are really looking for is any indication of a serious leak (see Haynes Hint). Should a leak be found, renew the offending gasket or oil seal by referring to the appropriate Chapters in this manual.

2 Also check the security and condition of all the engine-related pipes and hoses. Ensure that all cable-ties or securing clips are in place and in good condition. Clips which are broken or missing can lead to chafing of the hoses, pipes or wiring, which could cause more serious problems in the future.

3 Carefully check the radiator hoses and heater hoses along their entire length. Renew any hose which is cracked, swollen or deteriorated. Cracks will show up better if the hose is squeezed. Pay close attention to the hose clips that secure the hoses to the cooling system components. Hose clips can pinch and puncture hoses, resulting in cooling system leaks.

4 Inspect all the cooling system components (hoses, joint faces etc.) for leaks. A leak in the cooling system will usually show up as white- or rust-coloured deposits on the area adjoining the leak. Where any problems of this nature are found on system components, renew the component or gasket with reference to Chapter 3.

5 With the vehicle raised at the rear, inspect the petrol tank and filler neck for punctures, cracks and other damage. The connection between the filler neck and tank is especially critical. Sometimes a rubber filler neck or connecting hose will leak due to loose retaining clamps or deteriorated rubber.

6 Carefully check all rubber hoses and metal fuel lines leading away from the petrol tank. Check for loose connections, deteriorated hoses, crimped lines, and other damage. Pay particular attention to the vent pipes and hoses, which often loop up around the filler neck and can become blocked or crimped. Follow the lines to the front of the vehicle, carefully inspecting them all the way. Renew damaged sections as necessary.

7 From within the engine compartment, check the security of all fuel hose attachments and pipe unions, and inspect the fuel hoses and vacuum hoses for kinks, chafing and deterioration.

8 Where applicable, check the condition of the power steering fluid hoses and pipes.

9 On completion, lower the vehicle to the ground.

8 Driveshaft gaiter check

1 With the vehicle raised and securely supported on axle stands, turn the steering to full left or right lock, then slowly rotate the roadwheel. Inspect the outer constant velocity (CV) joint rubber gaiters, squeezing the gaiters to open out the folds (see illustration). Check for signs of cracking, splits or deterioration of the rubber, which may allow the grease to escape, or water and grit to enter. Also check the security and condition of the retaining clips. Repeat these checks on the inner CV joints. If any damage or deterioration is found, the gaiters should be renewed (see Chapter 8).

2 At the same time, check the general condition of the CV joints themselves by first holding the driveshaft and attempting to rotate the wheel. Repeat this check whilst holding the inner joint and attempting to rotate the driveshaft. Any appreciable movement indicates wear in the CV joints, wear in the driveshaft splines, or a loose hub nut.

9 Suspension and steering check

Front suspension and steering check

1 Raise the front of the vehicle, and securely support it on axle stands.

2 Visually inspect the balljoint dust covers and the steering rack gaiters for splits, chafing or deterioration (see illustration). Any wear of these components will cause loss of lubricant, together with dirt and water entry, resulting in rapid deterioration of the balljoints or steering gear.

3 On vehicles with power steering, check the fluid hoses for chafing or deterioration, and the pipe and hose unions for fluid leaks. Also check for signs of fluid leakage under pressure from the steering gear rubber gaiters, which would indicate failed fluid seals within the steering gear.

4 Grasp the roadwheel at the 12 o'clock and 6 o'clock positions, and try to rock it (see illustration). Very slight free play may be felt, but if the movement is appreciable, further investigation is necessary to determine the source. Continue rocking the wheel while an assistant depresses the footbrake. If the movement is now eliminated or significantly reduced, it is likely that the hub bearings are at fault. If the free play is still evident with the footbrake depressed, then there is wear in the suspension joints or mountings.

5 Now grasp the wheel at the 9 o'clock and 3 o'clock positions, and try to rock it as before. Any movement felt now may again be caused by wear in the hub bearings or the steering track-rod balljoints. If the inner or outer balljoint is worn, the visual movement will be obvious.

6 Using a large screwdriver or flat bar, check for wear in the suspension mounting bushes by levering between the relevant suspension component and its attachment point. Some movement is to be expected as the mountings are made of rubber, but excessive wear should be obvious. Also check the condition of any visible rubber bushes, looking for splits, cracks or contamination of the rubber.

8.1 Checking a driveshaft outer gaiter for signs of damage

9.2 Checking a steering gear gaiter for signs of damage

9.4 Check for wear in the hub bearings by grasping the wheel and trying to rock it

7 With the car standing on its wheels, have an assistant turn the steering wheel back and forth about an eighth of a turn each way. There should be very little, if any, lost movement between the steering wheel and roadwheels. If this is not the case, closely observe the joints and mountings previously described, but in addition, check the steering column universal joints for wear, and the rack-and-pinion steering gear itself.

Suspension strut/shock absorber check

8 Check for any signs of fluid leakage around the suspension strut/shock absorber body, or from the rubber gaiter around the piston rod. Should any fluid be noticed, the suspension strut/shock absorber is defective internally, and should be renewed. **Note:** *Suspension struts/shock absorbers should always be renewed in pairs on the same axle.*
9 The efficiency of the suspension strut/shock absorber may be checked by bouncing the vehicle at each corner. Generally speaking, the body will return to its normal position and stop after being depressed. If it rises and returns on a rebound, the suspension strut/shock absorber is probably suspect. Examine also the suspension strut/shock absorber upper and lower mountings for any signs of wear.

10 Exhaust system check

1 With the engine cold (at least an hour after the vehicle has been driven), check the complete exhaust system from the engine to the end of the tailpipe. The exhaust system is most easily checked with the vehicle raised on a hoist, or suitably supported on axle stands, so that the exhaust components are readily visible and accessible.
2 Check the exhaust pipes and connections for evidence of leaks, severe corrosion and damage. Make sure that all brackets and mountings are in good condition, and that all relevant nuts and bolts are tight **(see illustrations)**. Leakage at any of the joints or in other parts of the system will usually show

up as a black sooty stain in the vicinity of the leak.
3 Rattles and other noises can often be traced to the exhaust system, especially the brackets and mountings. Try to move the pipes and silencers. If the components are able to come into contact with the body or suspension parts, secure the system with new mountings. Otherwise separate the joints (if possible) and twist the pipes as necessary to provide additional clearance.

11 Coolant condition check

⚠️ **Warning: Wait until the engine is cold before starting this procedure. Do not allow antifreeze to come in contact with your skin, or with the painted surfaces of the vehicle. Rinse off spills immediately with plenty of water.**
1 Note that a tester will be required to check the coolant strength; these can be obtained relatively cheaply from most motor accessory shops.
2 With the engine completely cold, unscrew and remove the filler cap from the coolant expansion tank. Follow the instructions supplied with the tester and check the coolant mixture is sufficient to give protection down to temperatures well below freezing. If the coolant has been renewed at the specified intervals this shouldn't be a problem. However, if the coolant mixture is not strong enough to provide sufficient protection it will be necessary to drain the cooling system and renew the coolant (see Section 34).
3 Once the test is complete, check the coolant level is correct (see *Weekly checks*) then securely refit the expansion tank cap.

12 Clutch check

1 Check and, if necessary adjust the clutch cable as described in Chapter 6.

13 Hinge and lock lubrication

1 Lubricate the hinges of the bonnet, doors and tailgate with a light general-purpose oil. Similarly, lubricate all latches, locks and lock strikers. At the same time, check the security and operation of all the locks, adjusting if necessary (see Chapter 11).
2 Lightly lubricate the bonnet release mechanism and cable with a suitable grease.

14 Exhaust emission check

This check is part of the manufacturer's maintenance schedule, and involves testing the exhaust emissions using smoke testing equipment. Unless a fault is suspected, this test is not essential, although it should be noted that it is recommended by the manufacturers. Adjusting the idle mixture is either not possible, or requires access to dedicated test equipment. Exhaust emissions testing is included as part of the MoT test.

15 Headlight beam alignment check

1 Refer to Chapter 12.

16 Wiper/washer system check

1 Check the condition of the wiper blades as described in *Weekly checks*.
2 Check that each of the washer jet nozzles are clear and that each nozzle provides a strong jet of washer fluid. The jets should be aimed to spray at a point slightly above the centre of the screen/headlight. Where there are two jets, aim one of the jets slightly above then centre of the screen/headlight and aim the other just below to ensure complete coverage of the screen. If necessary, adjust the jets using a pin.

17 Road test

Instruments and electrical equipment

1 Check the operation of all instruments and electrical equipment.
2 Make sure that all instruments read correctly, and switch on all electrical equipment in turn, to check that it functions properly.

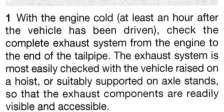
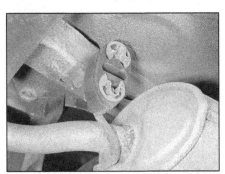

10.2a Check the condition of the exhaust mountings . . .

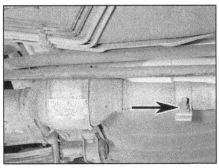

10.2b . . . and the tightness of all bolts and joints

Steering and suspension

3 Check for any abnormalities in the steering, suspension, handling or road feel.

4 Drive the vehicle, and check that there are no unusual vibrations or noises.

5 Check that the steering feels positive, with no excessive sloppiness, or roughness, and check for any suspension noises when cornering and driving over bumps.

Drivetrain

6 Check the performance of the engine, clutch, transmission and driveshafts.

7 Listen for any unusual noises from the engine, clutch and transmission.

8 Make sure that the engine runs smoothly when idling, and that there is no hesitation when accelerating.

9 Check that the clutch action is smooth and progressive, that the drive is taken up smoothly, and that the pedal travel is not excessive. Also listen for any noises when the clutch pedal is depressed.

10 Check that all gears can be engaged smoothly without noise, and that the gear lever action is not abnormally vague or notchy.

Check the operation and performance of the braking system

11 Make sure that the vehicle does not pull to one side when braking, and that the wheels do not lock prematurely when braking hard.

12 Check that there is no vibration through the steering when braking.

13 Check that the handbrake operates correctly without excessive movement of the lever, and that it holds the vehicle stationary on a slope.

14 Test the operation of the brake servo unit as follows. With the engine off, depress the footbrake four or five times to exhaust the vacuum. Hold the brake pedal depressed, then start the engine. As the engine starts, there should be a noticeable give in the brake pedal as vacuum builds up. Allow the engine to run for at least two minutes, and then switch it off. If the brake pedal is depressed now, it should be possible to detect a hiss from the servo as the pedal is depressed. After about four or five applications, no further hissing should be heard, and the pedal should feel considerably harder.

Every 20 000 miles (30 000 km)

18 Air cleaner element renewal

1 Release the four over-centre wire clips around the air cleaner top cover **(see illustration)**.

2 The top cover can now be lifted sufficiently to withdraw the air filter element. Note the direction of fitting as the element is removed **(see illustrations)**.

3 If greater access is required, using a suitable pair of pliers, compress the legs of the spring clip fitted to the top cover which secures the air inlet hose. Work the hose off the top cover stub, and remove the top cover.

4 Remove any debris inside the air cleaner housing.

5 Fit the new air filter element into position, noting any direction-of-fitting markings. Fit the new element as noted on removal, and make sure the edges are securely seated.

6 Refit the air cleaner top cover, securing with the four wire clips. Where removed, refit the air inlet hose, securing with the spring clip **(see illustration)**.

19 Fuel filter renewal

1 The fuel filter is mounted at the right-hand rear of the engine compartment.

2 Place a container below the filter, and pad the surrounding area with rags to absorb any fuel that may be spilt.

3 At the top of the filter unit, pull out the R-clip and lift out the control valve, leaving the fuel hoses attached **(refer to illustration 4.3)**.

4 Slacken the hose clips, and pull the fuel supply and delivery hoses from the ports on the of the filter unit. If crimp-type clips are fitted, cut them off using snips, and use proper fuel hose clips on refitting. Note the fitted position of each hose, in relation to the direction-of-flow arrows on top of the filter, to aid correct refitting.

Caution: Be prepared for an amount of fuel loss.

5 Using an Allen key, slacken the retaining bracket screw and lift the filter out **(see illustration)**.

6 Fill the new fuel filter with clean diesel fuel before fitting - this will make the engine easier to start. Fit the new fuel filter into the retaining bracket, and tighten the screw.

18.1 Release the over-centre clips (two at the rear, two more at the front) . . .

18.2a . . . then lift the air cleaner top cover . . .

18.2b . . . and withdraw the filter element

18.6 If removed, refit the air inlet hose securing clip

19.5 Slacken the retaining bracket screw using an Allen key

7 Fit a new O-ring seal to the control valve, then refit the control valve to the top of the filter, and insert the retaining clip **(see illustration)**.

8 Reconnect the fuel supply and delivery hoses, using the notes made during removal - note the fuel flow arrow markings next to each port. Where crimp-type hoses were originally fitted, use screw-type clips on refitting. Remove the collecting container and rags, and refit the inlet air hose to the air cleaner and inlet manifold (where removed).

9 Start and run the engine at idle, then check around the fuel filter for fuel leaks. **Note:** *It may take a few seconds of cranking before the engine starts, especially if the new filter was not primed with fuel before fitting.*

10 Raise the engine speed to about 2000 rpm several times, then allow the engine to idle again. Observe the fuel flow through the transparent hose leading to the fuel injection pump, and check that it is free of air bubbles.

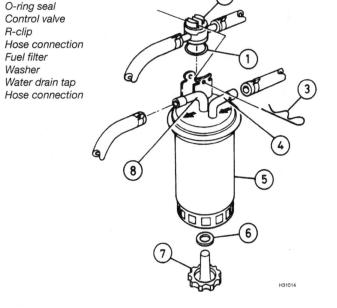

19.7 Fuel filter details

1   O-ring seal
2   Control valve
3   R-clip
4   Hose connection
5   Fuel filter
6   Washer
7   Water drain tap
8   Hose connection

H31014

20 Timing belt check

1 Refer to Chapter 2C and remove the timing belt upper cover for access to the timing belt.
2 Examine the belt for signs of cracking or splitting, especially around the roots of the teeth, and for signs of fraying or separation of the belt plies. Also look for excess wear on the edges of the belt.
3 Using a spanner or socket on the crankshaft pulley bolt, turn the engine in its normal direction (clockwise, when viewed from the pulley end) and inspect the whole length of the belt.
4 If any damage is noted, the belt should be renewed as described in Chapter 2C. Remember - if the timing belt snaps while the engine is running, severe damage will be caused to the cylinder head components, and possibly to the tops of the pistons.
5 If there is any sign that the belt is being contaminated with oil or other fluid, the belt should be changed and the source of the leak found and fixed, otherwise the new belt will quickly go the same way.

6 On completion, refit the timing belt upper cover as described in Chapter 2C.

21 Auxiliary drivebelt check

1 The drivebelt should be visually inspected for signs of chafing, fraying, splitting and cracking. Twist the belt to examine the condition of the belt ribs.
2 To provide better access to the drivebelt, jack up the front right-hand corner of the vehicle, and remove the screws securing the metal cover fitted over the drivebelt **(see illustration)**.
3 Use a suitable spanner or socket on the crankshaft pulley bolt to turn the engine, so that the whole length of the belt can be checked **(see illustration)**.

4 If there are any signs that the drivebelt is in less-than-perfect condition, renew the drivebelt at the earliest opportunity - refer to Chapter 2C.
5 All models are equipped with an automatic tensioning device for the drivebelt, so unless this has failed, the belt tension should be correct.
6 On completion, where applicable, refit the drivebelt cover and lower the vehicle to the ground.

22 Airbag system check

1 Referring to Chapter 12, carry out a visual inspection of the airbag unit(s). If there is any visible sign of damage the affected unit must be renewed.

23 Engine emission control system check

1 Details of the emissions control system components are given in Chapter 4D.
2 Checking consists simply of a visual check for obvious signs of damaged, perished, or leaking hoses and joints, or for loose, damaged or disconnected wiring.
3 Detailed checking and testing of the EGR system should be entrusted to a Skoda dealer.

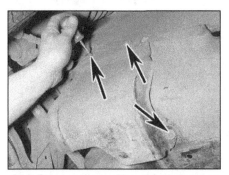

21.2 Remove the auxiliary drivebelt cover screws (arrowed)

21.3 Inspecting the whole length of the drivebelt is easier from below

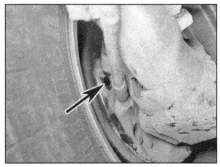

24.2 A quick check on the rear brake shoe friction material can be made using the inspection hole (arrowed) in the backplate

27.3a Undo the bolt (arrowed) then slide out the retaining plate . . .

27.3b . . . and withdraw the speedometer drive assembly from the transmission unit

24 Rear brake shoe and drum check

1 Chock the front wheels, then jack up the rear of the vehicle, and support it securely on axle stands.

2 For a quick check, the thickness of friction material remaining on one of the brake shoes can be observed through the hole in the brake backplate which is exposed by prising out the sealing grommet (where fitted) **(see illustration)**. If a rod of the same diameter as the specified minimum friction material thickness is placed against the shoe friction material, the amount of wear can be assessed. A torch or inspection light will probably be required. If the friction material on any shoe is worn down to the specified minimum thickness or less, all four shoes must be renewed as a set.

3 For a comprehensive check, the brake drum should be removed and cleaned. This will allow the wheel cylinders to be checked, and the condition of the brake drum itself to be fully examined (see Chapter 9).

25 Handbrake check

1 Check and, if necessary, adjust the handbrake as described in Chapter 9.

26 Body corrosion check

1 With the vehicle raised and securely supported, carry out a thorough check of the

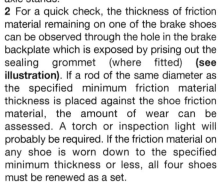

27.4 Use the speedometer drive as a dipstick to check the oil level. The level should be 4mm up from the base of the drivegear

vehicle underbody sealant for signs of damage. If any area of the underbody sealant shows visible damage, the affected area should be repaired to prevent possible problems with corrosion occurring at a later date.

27 Transmission oil level check

1 Park the car on a level surface. The oil level must be checked before the car is driven, or at least 5 minutes after the engine has been switched off. If the oil is checked immediately after driving the car, some of the oil will remain distributed around the transmission components, resulting in an inaccurate level reading.

2 Wipe clean the area around the speedometer drive on the top of the transmission.

3 Slacken and remove the retaining bolt then slide out the retaining plate and withdraw the speedometer drive assembly from the transmission unit **(see illustrations)**.

4 The oil level is checked by using the

27.5 If topping-up is necessary, add the specified type and grade of oil through the speedometer drive aperture

speedometer drivegear as a dipstick. Wipe clean the drivegear then reinsert the speedometer drive fully into the transmission unit before removing it again. Measure the height the oil level extends up the drivegear; the oil level should be 4 mm above the base of the drivegear **(see illustration)**. It is permissible for level to be slightly higher then specified but it should never be allowed to fall below this.

5 If topping-up is necessary, add oil through the speedometer drivegear aperture until the level is correct; use only good-quality oil of the specified type (refer to *Lubricants and fluids*) **(see illustration)**.

6 If the transmission has been overfilled, siphon excess oil out through the speedometer drivegear aperture.

7 When the level is correct, inspect the speedometer drivegear sealing ring for signs of wear or deterioration and renew if necessary. Lubricate the sealing ring with a smear of transmission oil then ease the drive assembly into position. Engage the retaining plate with the drivegear slot then refit the retaining bolt, tightening it to the specified torque setting.

Every 40 000 miles (60 000 km)

28 Transmission oil renewal

1 This operation is much quicker and more efficient if the car is first taken on a journey of sufficient length to warm the engine/transmission up to normal operating temperature.
2 Park the car on level ground, switch off the ignition and apply the handbrake firmly. For improved access, jack up the front of the car and support it securely on axle stands (see *Jacking and Vehicle Support*). Note that the car must be lowered to the ground and level, to ensure accuracy, when refilling and checking the oil level.
3 Wipe clean the area around the speedometer drive on the top of the transmission.
4 Slacken and remove the retaining bolt then slide out the retaining plate and withdraw the speedometer drive assembly from the transmission unit (see Section 27). Inspect the drive sealing ring for signs of wear or deterioration and renew if necessary.
5 Wipe clean the area around the drain plug, which is situated on the base of the

transmission unit, directly below the left-hand driveshaft inner CV joint **(see illustration)**. Position a suitable container under the drain plug and unscrew the plug.
6 Allow the oil to drain completely into the container. If the oil is hot, take precautions against scalding. Clean the drain plug, being especially careful to wipe any metallic particles off the magnetic insert. Discard the sealing washer; it should be renewed whenever it is disturbed.
7 When the oil has finished draining, clean the drain plug threads and those of the transmission casing, fit a new sealing washer and refit the drain plug, tightening it to the specified torque wrench setting. If the car was raised for the draining operation, now lower it to the ground.
8 Refilling the transmission is an extremely awkward operation. Above all, allow plenty of time for the oil level to settle properly before checking it. Note that the car must be parked on flat level ground when checking the oil level.
9 Refill the transmission via the speedometer drive aperture with the exact amount of the specified type of oil then check the oil level as described in Section 27; if the correct amount

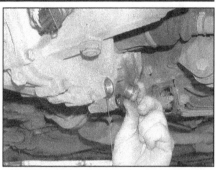

28.5 Unscrew the transmission drain plug and allow the oil to drain into a container

was poured into the transmission and the level is not correct, refit the speedometer drive and take the car on a short journey so that the new oil is distributed fully around the transmission components, then check the level again on your return.

29 Timing belt renewal

Refer to Chapter 2C.

Every 2 years, regardless of mileage

30 Brake fluid renewal

⚠ *Warning: Brake hydraulic fluid can harm your eyes and damage painted surfaces, so use extreme caution when handling and pouring it. Do not use fluid that has been standing open for some time, as it absorbs moisture from the air. Excess moisture can cause a dangerous loss of braking effectiveness.*

1 The procedure is similar to that for the bleeding of the hydraulic system as described in Chapter 9, except that the brake fluid reservoir should be emptied by siphoning,

using a clean poultry baster or similar before starting, and allowance should be made for the old fluid to be expelled when bleeding a section of the circuit.
2 Working as described in Chapter 9, open the first bleed screw in the sequence, and pump the brake pedal gently until nearly all the old fluid has been emptied from the master cylinder reservoir.

 Old hydraulic fluid is invariably much darker in colour than the new, making it easy to distinguish the two.

3 Top-up to the MAX level with new fluid, and continue pumping until only the new fluid

remains in the reservoir, and new fluid can be seen emerging from the bleed screw. Tighten the screw, and top the reservoir level up to the MAX level line.
4 Work through all the remaining bleed screws in the sequence until new fluid can be seen at all of them. Be careful to keep the master cylinder reservoir topped-up to above the MIN level at all times, or air may enter the system and greatly increase the length of the task.
5 When the operation is complete, check that all bleed screws are securely tightened, and that their dust caps are refitted. Wash off all traces of spilt fluid, and recheck the master cylinder reservoir fluid level.
6 Check the operation of the brakes before taking the car on the road.

Every 3 years, regardless of mileage

31 Coolant renewal

Cooling system draining

 Warning: Wait until the engine is cold before starting this procedure. Do not allow

antifreeze to come in contact with your skin, or with the painted surfaces of the vehicle. Rinse off spills immediately with plenty of water. Never leave antifreeze lying around in an open container, or in a puddle in the driveway or on the garage floor. Children and pets are attracted by its sweet smell, but antifreeze can be fatal if ingested.
1 With the engine completely cold, firmly

apply the handbrake then jack up the front of the vehicle and support it on axle stands.
2 Unscrew and remove the expansion tank filler cap.
3 Position a suitable container beneath the coolant drain plug which is located on the left-hand end of the metal pipe which runs along the front of the cylinder block **(see illustration)**. To improve access to the plug, undo the retaining screws and remove the

31.3 Coolant pipe drain plug location

undercover. Unscrew the drain plug and allow the coolant to drain into the container.

4 If the coolant has been drained for a reason other than renewal, then provided it is clean and less than three years old, it can be re-used, though this is not recommended. Discard the drain plug sealing washer; it should be renewed whenever it is disturbed.

5 When the flow of coolant stops, clean the drain plug threads and fit the new sealing washer. Apply a smear of fresh sealant to the drain plug threads then refit it to the pipe and tighten to the specified torque setting.

Cooling system flushing

6 If coolant renewal has been neglected, or if the antifreeze mixture has become diluted, then in time, the cooling system may gradually lose efficiency, as the coolant passages become restricted due to rust, scale deposits, and other sediment. The cooling system efficiency can be restored by flushing the system clean.

7 The radiator should be flushed independently of the engine, to avoid unnecessary contamination.

Radiator flushing

8 To flush the radiator, disconnect the top and bottom hoses and any other relevant hoses from the radiator, with reference to Chapter 3.

9 Insert a garden hose into the radiator top inlet. Direct a flow of clean water through the radiator, and continue flushing until clean water emerges from the radiator bottom outlet.

10 If after a reasonable period, the water still does not run clear, the radiator can be flushed with a good proprietary cleaning agent. It is important that their manufacturer's instructions are followed carefully. If the contamination is particularly bad, insert the hose in the radiator bottom outlet, and reverse-flush the radiator.

Engine flushing

11 To flush the engine, remove the thermostat as described in Chapter 3, then temporarily refit the thermostat cover.

12 With the top and bottom hoses disconnected from the radiator, insert a garden hose into the radiator top hose. Direct a clean flow of water through the engine, and continue flushing until clean water emerges from the radiator bottom hose.

13 On completion of flushing, refit the thermostat and reconnect the hoses with reference to Chapter 3.

Cooling system filling

14 Before attempting to fill the cooling system, make sure that all hoses and clips are in good condition, and that the clips are tight. Note that an antifreeze mixture must be used all year round, to prevent corrosion of the engine components (see following sub-Section).

15 Ensure that the drain plug is securely tightened then lower the vehicle to the ground.

16 Remove the expansion tank filler cap and slowly fill the system until the coolant level reaches the MAX mark on the side of the expansion tank.

17 Refit and tighten the expansion tank filler cap.

18 Start the engine, and allow it to run until it reaches normal operating temperature.

19 Stop the engine, and allow it to cool, then re-check the coolant level with reference to *Weekly checks*. Top-up the level if necessary and refit the expansion tank filler cap.

Antifreeze mixture

20 The antifreeze should always be renewed at the specified intervals. This is necessary not only to maintain the antifreeze properties, but also to prevent corrosion which would otherwise occur as the corrosion inhibitors become progressively less effective.

21 Always use an ethylene-glycol based antifreeze which is suitable for use in mixed-metal cooling systems. The quantity of antifreeze and levels of protection are given in the Specifications.

22 Before adding antifreeze, the cooling system should be completely drained, preferably flushed, and all hoses checked for condition and security.

23 After filling with antifreeze, a label should be attached to the expansion tank, stating the type and concentration of antifreeze used, and the date installed. Any subsequent topping-up should be made with the same type and concentration of antifreeze.

24 Do not use engine antifreeze in the windscreen/tailgate washer system, as it will cause damage to the vehicle paintwork. A screenwash additive should be added to the washer system in the quantities stated on the bottle.

Chapter 2 Part A:
1.3 litre petrol engine in-car repair procedures

Contents

Degrees of difficulty

Easy, suitable for novice with little experience 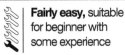	**Fairly easy,** suitable for beginner with some experience	**Fairly difficult,** suitable for competent DIY mechanic	**Difficult,** suitable for experienced DIY mechanic	**Very difficult,** suitable for expert DIY or professional 

Specifications

General

Type	Four-cylinder in-line, four stroke, liquid-cooled
Engine code:	
Low-compression, single-point injection	135B
Low-compression, multi-point injection	135M
High-compression, single-point injection	136B
High-compression, multi-point injection	136M
Bore	75.50 mm
Stroke	72.00 mm
Capacity	1289 cc
Firing order	1-3-4-2 (No 1 cylinder at crankshaft pulley end)
Direction of crankshaft rotation	Clockwise (when viewed from right-hand side of vehicle)
Compression ratio:	
135 engine	8.8 : 1
136 engine	9.7 : 1

Lubrication system

System pressure:	
Minimum @ 1500 rpm	3.5 bars
Maximum	5.8 bars
Oil pump type	Gear-driven, force-feed
Oil pump clearances:	
Drivegear shaft-to-cover:	
Standard	0.02 to 0.06 mm
Wear limit	0.15 mm
Pin-to-driven gear:	
Standard	0.014 to 0.050 mm
Wear limit	0.1 mm
Gear-to-pump cover (endfloat) - maximum	0.1 mm

Torque wrench settings

	Nm	lbf ft
Alternator adjustment link mounting bracket bolt (to cylinder head)* ..	26	19
Alternator lower mounting bracket nuts	24	18
Big-end (connecting rod) bearing cap nut	40	30
Camshaft sprocket bolt	35	26
Camshaft thrustplate bolts	8	6
Coolant pump mounting bolts	20	15
Crankshaft pulley bolt	120	89
Cylinder head bolts:		
Stage 1	17 to 20	13 to 15
Stage 2	Angle-tighten through a further 90°	
Stage 3	Angle-tighten through a further 90°	
Cylinder head nuts:		
With washer	26	19
Without washer (self-locking)	24	18
Distributor shaft extension tube bolts	8	6
Engine-to-transmission bolts	45	33
Engine/transmission left-hand mounting:		
Front bolt	60	44
Front nut	55	41
Rear bolt	55	41
Engine/transmission rear mounting	55	41
Engine/transmission right-hand mounting	50	37
Exhaust downpipe-to-manifold nuts	20	15
Exhaust manifold-to-cylinder head nuts	25	18
Flywheel bolts (new)*:		
Stage 1	30	22
Stage 2	Angle-tighten through a further 90°	
Flywheel cover plate bolts	10	7
Knock sensor	20	15
Main bearing cap bolt	75	55
Oil pressure switch	55	41
Oil pump pick-up/strainer	8	6
Pushrod cover nuts	4	3
Rear oil seal housing bolts	8	6
Roadwheel bolts	110	81
Rocker cover nuts	3	2
Rocker gear retaining bolts	30	22
Sump bolts	10	7
Sump drain plug	65	48
Timing chain cover bolts	8	6
Valve adjuster locknuts	18	13

Use thread-locking compound.

1 General information

How to use this Chapter

This Part of Chapter 2 describes those repair procedures that can reasonably be carried out on the engine while it remains in the vehicle. If the engine has been removed from the vehicle and is being dismantled as described in Part D, any preliminary dismantling procedures can be ignored.

Note that while it may be possible physically to overhaul items such as the piston/connecting rod assemblies while the engine is in the vehicle, such tasks are not usually carried out as separate operations, and usually require the execution of several additional procedures (not to mention the cleaning of components and of oilways); for this reason, all such tasks are classed as

major overhaul procedures, and are described in Part D of this Chapter.

Part D describes the removal of the engine/transmission from the vehicle and the full overhaul procedures that can then be carried out.

Engine description

The engine is an overhead valve (OHV), in-line four-cylinder unit, which is mounted transversely at the front of the vehicle; the clutch and transmission are situated on the left-hand end of the engine.

The engine is available in two different forms: a low-compression version (type 135) and a high-compression version (type 136). Apart from the different compression ratios, achieved by the use of different pistons (136 has flat-topped pistons whereas 135 has a recess in the piston crown), and different camshafts, both engines are of identical construction. The 136 engine can be identified by the presence of a yellow-painted Skoda

emblem at the front right-hand end of the cylinder head - on 135 engines, the emblem is not painted **(see illustration)**.

The cylinder block, cylinder head and rocker cover are all cast in aluminium alloy. The cylinder bores are formed by replaceable cast-iron cylinder liners that are located at

1.5 On models with the 136 engine, the Skoda emblem (arrowed) is painted yellow

their lower ends; sealing gaskets are fitted at the base of each liner to prevent the escape of coolant into the sump.

The crankshaft has three main bearings. The clutch and flywheel are located on a flange at the left-hand end. A double sprocket fitted onto the right-hand end serves to drive the camshaft via a double-row timing chain. The main bearings and the big-end bearings are of the shell type, whilst the connecting rod small-end bearings are of the bronze bush type, being pressed into the connecting rod and reamed to suit.

The camshaft has a helical gear on its right-hand end which drives the distributor, where applicable. The camshaft also drives the oil pump via the distributor shaft.

The force-feed lubrication system consists of a gear-driven pump, which draws oil from the sump through a strainer and circulates the lubricant to the various engine components, via a filter mounted externally on the front of the cylinder block.

Repair operations possible with the engine in the vehicle

The following work can be carried out with the engine in the vehicle:
a) Auxiliary drivebelt - removal and refitting.
b) Rocker cover - removal and refitting.
c) Rocker gear - removal and refitting.
d) Cylinder head - removal and refitting*.
e) Timing cover - removal and refitting.
f) Timing chain and sprockets - removal and refitting.
g) Oil cooler - removal and refitting.
h) Oil pump - removal, inspection and refitting.
i) Sump - removal and refitting.
j) Cylinder head and pistons - decarbonising.
k) Crankshaft oil seals - renewal.
l) Flywheel - removal, inspection and refitting.
m) Engine/transmission mountings - inspection and renewal.

*Cylinder head dismantling procedures are detailed in Chapter 2D.
Note: *It is possible to remove the pistons and connecting rods (after removing the cylinder head and sump) without removing the engine. However, this is not recommended. Work of this nature is more easily and thoroughly completed with the engine on the bench, as described in Chapter 2D.*

2 Compression test - description and interpretation

1 When engine performance is down, or if misfiring occurs which cannot be attributed to the ignition or fuel systems, a compression test can provide diagnostic clues as to the engine's condition. If the test is performed regularly, it can give warning of trouble before any other symptoms become apparent.

2 The engine must be fully warmed up to normal operating temperature, the battery must be fully charged, and the spark plugs must be removed (Chapter 1A). The aid of an assistant will also be required.

3 Disable the ignition system by disconnecting the ignition HT coil lead from the distributor cap, and earthing it on the cylinder block. Use a jumper lead or similar wire to make a good connection. On models without a distributor, disconnect the wiring plug from the ignition coil unit on the front of the cylinder head.

4 To prevent possible damage to the catalytic converter, depressurise and disable the fuel injection system by removing the fuel pump relay (see the relevant part of Chapter 4).

5 Fit a compression tester to the No 1 cylinder spark plug hole - the type of tester which screws into the plug thread is to be preferred.

6 Have the assistant hold the throttle wide open and crank the engine on the starter motor; after one or two revolutions, the compression pressure should build up to a maximum figure and then stabilise. Record the highest reading obtained.

7 Repeat the test on the remaining cylinders, recording the pressure in each.

8 All cylinders should produce very similar pressures, of the order of 11 to 15 bars. Any one cylinder reading below 10 bars, or a difference of more than 1.5 bars between cylinders, suggests a fault.

9 Note that the compression should build up quickly in a healthy engine; low compression on the first stroke, followed by gradually increasing pressure on successive strokes, indicates worn piston rings.

10 A low compression reading on the first stroke, which does not build up during successive strokes, indicates leaking valves or a blown head gasket (a cracked head could also be the cause). Deposits on the undersides of the valve heads can also cause low compression.

11 If the pressure in any cylinder is reduced to 10 bars or less, carry out the following test to isolate the cause. Introduce a teaspoonful of clean oil into that cylinder through its spark plug hole and repeat the test.

12 If the addition of oil temporarily improves the compression pressure, this indicates that bore or piston wear is responsible for the pressure loss. No improvement suggests that leaking or burnt valves, or a blown head gasket, may be to blame.

13 A low reading from two adjacent cylinders is almost certainly due to the head gasket having blown between them; the presence of coolant in the engine oil will confirm this.

14 If one cylinder is about 20 percent lower than the others and the engine has a slightly rough idle, a worn camshaft lobe could be the cause.

15 If the compression reading is unusually high, the combustion chambers are probably coated with carbon deposits. If this is the case, the cylinder head should be removed and decarbonised.

16 On completion of the test, refit the spark plugs and reconnect the ignition system. Refit the fuel pump relay (see the relevant part of Chapter 4).

3 Top Dead Centre (TDC) for No 1 piston - locating

1 Top dead centre (TDC) is the highest point in its travel up-and-down its cylinder bore that each piston reaches as the crankshaft rotates. While each piston reaches TDC both at the top of the compression stroke and again at the top of the exhaust stroke, for the purpose of timing the engine, TDC refers to the piston position (usually No 1) at the top of its compression stroke.

2 No 1 piston and cylinder are at the right-hand end of the engine. Note that the crankshaft rotates clockwise when viewed from the right-hand side of the vehicle.

3 Disconnect the battery negative terminal, and remove all the spark plugs as described in Chapter 1A.

4 On models with a distributor, unclip the distributor cap and remove the cap and HT leads.

5 Turn the steering onto full-right lock. Slacken and remove the three engine undershield right-hand side cover retaining screws, and remove the cover to gain access to the crankshaft pulley retaining bolt.

6 Using a socket and extension bar, applied to the crankshaft pulley bolt, rotate the crankshaft clockwise until the notch on the crankshaft pulley inner rim is aligned with the 0 on the timing chain cover **(see illustration)**. On models without a distributor, there may not be a notch in the pulley, although the timing scale is still present on the timing chain cover - in this case, establish TDC as described in paragraph 9, and make your own pulley mark opposite the 0 on the scale.

7 With the crankshaft in this position, Nos 1 and 4 cylinders are now at TDC, one of them on the compression stroke.

8 On models with a distributor, if the distributor rotor arm is pointing at the notch in

3.6 Crankshaft pulley timing mark at TDC

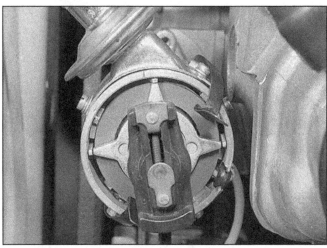

3.8 Distributor rotor arm aligned with notch showing No 1 cylinder firing position

4.2a Using a screwdriver, release the securing clips . . .

the distributor rim, then No 1 cylinder is correctly positioned (see illustration). If the rotor arm is pointing in the opposite direction, No 4 cylinder is on compression. Rotate the crankshaft one full turn (360°) clockwise until the rotor arm points at the notch. No 1 cylinder will then be at TDC on the compression stroke.

9 On models without a distributor, TDC on compression can only be established by turning the engine back a little from the position described in paragraph 6, and then forwards again to TDC with a finger placed over No 1 spark plug hole. If No 1 piston is rising on a compression stroke, pressure will be felt building up as the engine is turned forwards to TDC.

10 Once No 1 cylinder has been positioned at TDC on the compression stroke, TDC for any of the other cylinders can then be located by rotating the crankshaft clockwise 180° at a time and following the firing order (see Specifications).

4 Rocker cover - removal and refitting

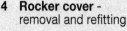
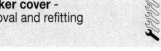

Removal

1 Disconnect the battery negative terminal.
2 Disconnect the breather hoses from the rocker cover oil filler neck (see illustrations).
3 Slacken and remove the two rocker cover retaining nuts, and lift off the rubber spacers (see illustrations).
4 Lift off the rocker cover and carefully remove the rubber seal from its groove (see illustration). Check the seal for signs of damage or distortion, and renew it if necessary.

Refitting

5 Carefully clean the cylinder head mating surfaces and the cover groove, removing all traces of oil. Fit the rubber seal to the rocker cover, ensuring it is correctly located in the groove (see illustration).
6 Refit the cover to the cylinder head, ensuring that the seal remains seated in its groove, then refit the spacers and nuts to the cover studs. Tighten both nuts to the specified torque setting.

4.2b . . . and disconnect the breather hoses from the rocker cover oil filler neck

4.3a Remove the retaining nuts (arrowed) . . .

4.3b . . . and lift off the rubber spacers

4.4 Lift the rocker cover away from the engine

4.5 Ensure that the rocker cover seal is correctly seated in its groove

4.7 Replace the original Skoda clips with screw-type clips when refitting

7 Connect the breather hose(s) to the cover oil filler neck. If the original Skoda clips are still fitted, use screw-type clips when refitting **(see illustration)**.

8 On completion, reconnect the battery. Check for oil leaks after the engine is next run.

5 Rocker gear - removal, inspection and refitting

Removal

1 Remove the rocker cover as described in Section 4.

2 Using a 10 mm Allen key, slacken and remove the two cylinder head bolts which secure the left- and right-hand rocker pedestals to the cylinder head.

5.4a To dismantle the rocker gear, remove the circlip . . .

5.7 On refitting, ensure all rocker arm adjusting screws are correctly located in the pushrod ends

3 Evenly and progressively slacken the four rocker gear retaining bolts by half a turn at a time, until all valve spring pressure has been relieved from the rocker arms. Remove the bolts, noting the correct fitted position of the oil splash plate which is fitted to the top of the right-hand pedestal, and lift the rocker gear assembly off the cylinder head **(see illustration)**.

4 If necessary, the rocker gear assembly can be dismantled by removing the circlip from one end of the rocker shaft and sliding the various components off the end of the shaft **(see illustrations)**. Keeping all components in their correct fitted order, make a note of each component's correct fitted position as it is removed, to ensure it is positioned correctly on reassembly.

Inspection

5 With the rocker gear dismantled, examine the rocker arm and shaft bearing surfaces for wear ridges and scoring. If there are obvious signs of wear the affected rocker arm(s) and/or shaft must be renewed.

Refitting

6 If the rocker gear was dismantled, reassemble it by reversing the dismantling sequence, and secure all components in position with the circlip. Ensure that the circlip is correctly located in its groove, and check that all rocker arms are free to rotate smoothly around the shaft.

7 Lower the rocker gear into position on the

5.4b . . . and slide off the various components keeping them in their correct fitted order

5.8a Don't forget to refit the oil splash plate to the right-hand pedestal

5.3 Slacken the retaining bolts and lift the rocker gear away from the cylinder head

cylinder head, ensuring that all the rocker arm adjusting screws correctly engage with their respective pushrod ends **(see illustration)**.

8 Refit the four rocker gear retaining bolts and, ensuring that the oil splash plate is correctly positioned on the right-hand pedestal, tighten them evenly and progressively to the specified torque setting **(see illustrations)**.

9 Refit the two cylinder head bolts securing the left- and right-hand pedestals in position and tighten them first to the specified Stage 1 torque setting, and then through the angles specified for their Stage 2 and 3 tightening. Refer to Section 6 for further information.

10 Adjust the valve clearances as described in Chapter 1A.

11 Refit the rocker cover as described in Section 4.

6 Cylinder head and manifolds - removal, separation and refitting

Removal

1 Disconnect the battery negative lead.

2 Set the engine to TDC as described in Section 3, then turn the crankshaft back by a few degrees, away from the TDC position. If preferred, for maximum safety, the pistons can be positioned halfway down their bores, with No 1 piston on its upstroke - ie 90° before TDC. It is important that the engine is **not** at TDC, to avoid the possibility of piston/valve contact when the head is refitted.

5.8b Tighten the rocker gear retaining bolts to the specified torque setting as described in text

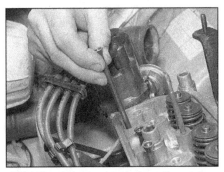

6.7 Lift out the pushrods from the engine and store them in a cardboard template

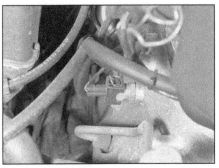

6.10a Disconnect the wiring plug from the injection system coolant temperature sensor

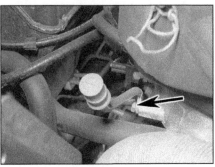

6.10b Remove the bolt (arrowed) and detach the CO sampling pipe

3 Drain the cooling system and remove the spark plugs as described in Chapter 1A.

4 On models with a distributor, remove the distributor cap and HT leads as described in Chapter 5B.

5 Remove the air cleaner and air inlet components as described in the relevant part of Chapter 4. Pull off the warm-air duct from the air cleaner inlet and the stub on the exhaust manifold collector plate.

6 Remove the rocker gear as described in Section 5.

7 Lift out each pushrod in turn and store it in its correct fitted order by pushing it through a clearly-marked cardboard template (see illustration). This will help ensure that the pushrods are refitted in their original positions on reassembly. Note that the inlet valve pushrods are made of aluminium, while the exhaust valve pushrods are steel.

8 Note that the following text assumes that the cylinder head will be removed with both inlet and exhaust manifolds attached; this is easier, but makes it a bulky and heavy assembly to handle. If it is wished first to remove the manifolds, proceed as described in the relevant part of Chapter 4.

9 Working as described in Chapter 4D, disconnect the exhaust system downpipe from the manifold.

10 On single-point injection models, disconnect the following from the inlet manifold/throttle body, as described in the relevant Sections of Chapter 4A:

a) Fuel supply and return hoses.
b) Throttle body wiring connectors. Free the wiring from any clips or ties, and lay it to one side.
c) Throttle cable.
d) Braking system vacuum servo unit hose.
e) Coolant hose(s).
f) Charcoal canister hose.
g) Coolant temperature sensor wiring connector (see illustration).
h) CO sampling pipe mounting bracket, where applicable (see illustration).

11 On multi-point injection models, disconnect the following as described in Chapter 4B:

a) Fuel supply and return hoses from the fuel rail (see illustration).
b) Vacuum hose from the fuel pressure regulator.
c) Fuel system wiring connectors, as necessary. Free the wiring from any clips or ties, and lay it to one side.
d) Inlet air temperature/pressure sensor wiring connector.
e) Charcoal canister hose.
f) Throttle cable.
g) Braking system vacuum servo unit hose from the inlet manifold.
h) Unbolt the support stay from the right-hand side of the inlet manifold.

12 Disconnect the coolant temperature gauge sensor wiring plug from the thermostat housing (see illustration). Disconnect the coolant hoses from the thermostat housing,

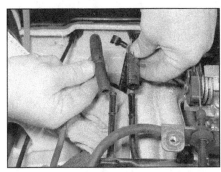

6.11 Disconnecting the fuel hoses from the fuel rail

referring to Chapter 3 for further information.

13 Disconnect the wiring connectors for the Hall sensor and for the lambda sensor. On models with single-point injection, both connectors are located on a bracket attached to the thermostat housing - the connector plugs should be removed from the bracket by sliding them out sideways. On multi-point injection models, the Hall sensor is disconnected at the top of the transmission - the lambda sensor plug is above and to the rear of it, and the plug slides out to the rear (see illustrations).

14 On models without air conditioning, slacken the alternator upper mounting bolt on the adjustment link. Remove the nut and bolt securing the adjustment link to the bracket on the cylinder head.

6.12 Disconnecting the wiring plug from the coolant temperature sensor (multi-point injection type shown)

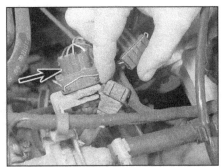

6.13a On single-point injection models, disconnect the Hall sensor plug, and slide it out of the mounting bracket - Lambda sensor plug arrowed

6.13b On multi-point injection models, disconnect and slide out the wiring plug for the Lambda sensor - Hall sensor wiring plug arrowed

15 Working in the **reverse** of the sequence shown later in this Section, progressively slacken the four cylinder head nuts, situated along the front edge of the head, and remove them. Remove the bolt securing the bracket for the alternator adjustment link (where applicable), and remove the bracket, noting its fitted location. Still following the sequence, slacken the eight remaining cylinder head bolts (two secure the rocker gear) by one turn at a time **(see illustration)**.

16 Remove each bolt along with its washer, and store it in its correct fitted order by pushing it through a clearly-marked cardboard template. This is particularly important as the bolts are three different lengths - bolts 8 and 9 in the tightening sequence are longer than the others, and bolt 10 is shorter. Note the correct fitted position of the engine lifting bracket fitted beneath the three rear bolts.

17 The joint between the cylinder head and gasket and the cylinder block/crankcase must now be broken without disturbing the wet liners; although these liners are better located and sealed than some wet-liner engines, there is still a risk of coolant and foreign matter leaking into the sump if the cylinder head is lifted carelessly. If care is not taken and the liners are moved, there is also a possibility of the bottom seals being disturbed, causing leakage after refitting the head.

Caution: If the liner bottom seals are disturbed, it will be necessary to remove the pistons and liners in order to fit new seals.

18 To break the joint, use the exhaust manifold as a leverage point, and gently rock the cylinder head free towards the front of the vehicle.

19 When the joint is broken, lift the cylinder head away; use assistance if possible, as it is a heavy assembly, especially if it is removed complete with the manifolds. Remove the gasket and discard it.

20 **Do not** attempt to rotate the crankshaft with the cylinder head removed, otherwise the cylinder liners may be displaced. Operations that would normally require the rotation of the crankshaft (eg cleaning the piston crowns), must be carried out with great care to ensure that no particles of dirt or foreign matter are left behind. If the crankshaft is to be turned, the liners must first be clamped in position using a couple of suitable bolts and large flat washers **(see illustration)**.

21 If the engine is to be left for any time with the head off, it might be worth attaching warning notices to ensure that no attempt is made to turn the engine if the liners are not clamped.

22 If the cylinder head is to be dismantled, then refer to the relevant Sections in Part D of this Chapter.

Manifold separation

23 Inlet manifold removal and refitting is described in Chapter 4A or B, as applicable.

24 Progressively slacken and remove the exhaust manifold retaining nuts; discard the old nuts if they are in poor condition. Lift the manifold away from the cylinder head, and recover the warm-air collector plate and gaskets. On models with single-point injection, the inlet and exhaust manifolds share one gasket, while separate gaskets are fitted on multi-point injection models.

25 Ensure that the mating surfaces are completely clean, then refit the exhaust manifold and warm-air collector plate, using new gasket(s). Fit new manifold retaining nuts, and tighten to the specified torque.

Preparation for refitting

26 Check the condition of the cylinder head bolts, paying particular attention to their threads, whenever they are removed. Keeping all the bolts in their correct fitted order, wash them and wipe dry, then check each for any sign of visible wear or damage, renewing any bolt if necessary. Considering the strain which the cylinder head bolts are under, it is recommended that they are renewed as a complete set whenever they are removed, regardless of their apparent condition.

27 The mating faces of the cylinder head, liners and cylinder block/crankcase must be perfectly clean before refitting the head. Refer to paragraph 20 before turning the engine to clean the piston crowns - the engine must not be turned if the cylinder liners have not been clamped.

28 Use a hard plastic or wood scraper to remove all traces of gasket and carbon; also clean the piston crowns. Take particular care, as the soft aluminium alloy is easily damaged. Also, make sure that the carbon is not allowed to enter the oil and water passages - this is particularly important for the lubrication system, as carbon could block the oil supply to any of the engine's components. Using adhesive tape and paper, seal the water, oil and bolt holes in the cylinder block/crankcase. To prevent carbon entering the gap between the pistons and bores, smear a little grease in the gap. After cleaning each piston, use a small brush to remove all traces of grease and carbon from the gap, then wipe away the remainder with a clean rag. Clean all the pistons in the same way.

29 Check the mating surfaces of the cylinder block/crankcase and the cylinder head for nicks, deep scratches and other damage. If slight, they may be removed carefully with a file, but if excessive, machining may be the only alternative to renewal.

30 If warpage is suspected of the cylinder head gasket surface, use a straight-edge to check it for distortion. Refer to Part D of this Chapter if necessary.

Refitting

31 Wipe clean the mating surfaces of the cylinder head and cylinder block/crankcase and position a new gasket on the cylinder block/crankcase surface. Ensure that the gasket is installed the correct way up, so that the holes in the gasket align with the oilways on the left- and right-hand ends of the cylinder block.

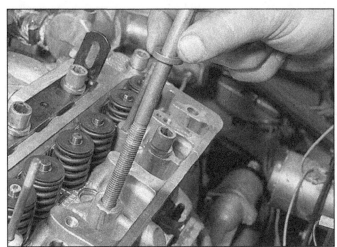

6.15 Slacken and remove the remaining cylinder head bolts

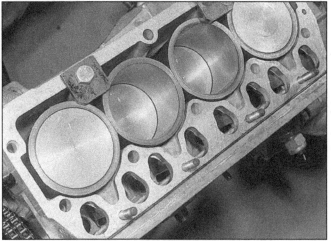

6.20 If the crankshaft is to be rotated with the head removed, the liners must be clamped in position as shown

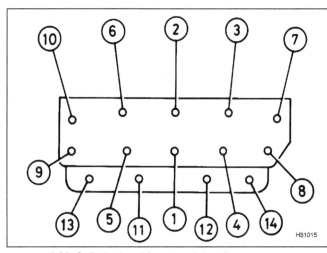

6.36 Cylinder head fastener tightening sequence

6.37 Tighten all bolts to the Stage 1 setting with a torque wrench

32 Locate the cylinder head on the studs, and carefully lower it into position.

33 Keeping all the cylinder head bolts and washers in their correct fitted order, wash them and wipe dry (if not already done), then lightly oil under the head and on the threads of each bolt. Carefully enter each bolt, (except the two which are also used to retain the rocker gear pedestals) into its original hole. Do not forget to refit the engine lifting bracket. Screw each bolt in by hand only until finger-tight.

34 Remove the pushrods from the cardboard template, and insert them into their original positions in the cylinder head, ensuring that each pushrod is correctly located in its cam follower.

35 Refit the rocker gear as described in Section 5. Tighten its four small inner retaining bolts to the specified torque, but tighten the two cylinder head bolts finger-tight only.

36 Working progressively and in the sequence shown (numbers 1 to 10), use first a torque wrench, then an ordinary socket extension bar, to tighten the cylinder head bolts in the stages given in the Specifications Section of this Chapter (see illustration).

37 First tighten all the bolts to the Stage 1 torque setting, using a torque wrench (see illustration).

38 Now angle-tighten the bolts, in the same sequence, through the specified Stage 2 angle, using a socket and extension bar. It is recommended that an angle-measuring gauge is used during this stage of the tightening, to ensure accuracy (see illustration). If a gauge is not available, use white paint to make alignment marks between the bolt head and cylinder head prior to tightening; the marks can then be used to check that the bolt has been rotated through the correct angle during tightening. Repeat the exercise for the Stage 3 setting.

39 Once the ten cylinder head bolts have been correctly tightened, apply a drop of engine oil to the threads and underside of the heads of the cylinder head nuts. Refit the nuts and washers onto the studs situated along the front edge of the cylinder head, not forgetting the bracket for the alternator adjustment link (where applicable). Tighten the four nuts to their specified torque setting in the order shown (numbers 11 to 14) (see illustration).

40 On models without air conditioning, fit and tighten the bolt which secures the bracket for the alternator adjustment link. Reconnect the adjustment link to the bracket, then tension the alternator drivebelt as described in Section 13.

41 Adjust the valve clearances as described

in Chapter 1A, then refit the rocker cover as described in Section 4 of this Chapter.

42 Connect all disturbed coolant hoses and reconnect the coolant temperature sensor wiring. It is recommended that the old Skoda hose clips (where fitted) are replaced with standard worm-drive type hose clips.

43 Working as described in the relevant Sections of Chapter 4, connect or refit all disturbed wiring and hoses to the inlet manifold and fuel system components, bearing in mind the point made above concerning the old hose clips. Reconnect and adjust the throttle cable.

44 Working as described in Chapter 4, reconnect the exhaust system downpipe to the manifold.

45 Refit and reconnect the wiring connectors for the Hall sensor and lambda sensor.

46 Where applicable, refit the distributor cap and HT leads as described in Chapter 5B.

47 Refit the air cleaner assembly as described in Chapter 4, and reconnect the battery negative lead.

48 Refill the cooling system and refit the spark plugs as described in Chapter 1A.

7 Timing cover, chain and sprockets - removal, inspection and refitting

Removal

1 Position No 1 cylinder at TDC as described in Section 3, then (where applicable) remove the distributor, complete with extension tube, as described in Chapter 5B.

2 Remove the alternator as described in Chapter 5A.

3 Remove the oil pick-up/strainer and withdraw the oil pump gears as described in Section 8.

4 To prevent crankshaft rotation while the pulley bolt is unscrewed, select top gear and have an assistant apply the brakes hard. If the

6.38 Use an angle gauge if available for the Stage 2 and 3 tightening

6.39 Tighten the cylinder head nuts to the specified torque

7.5 Remove the retaining bolt and washer, and slide off the crankshaft pulley

7.6 Undo the timing cover retaining bolts and remove the cover

TOOL TIP

The camshaft sprocket can be retained with a holding tool fabricated from two lengths of steel strip (one long, the other short) and three nuts and bolts. One nut and bolt form the pivot of the forked tool, with the remaining two nuts and bolts at the tips of the 'forks' to engage with the sprocket spokes

engine has been removed from the vehicle, lock the flywheel using the arrangement shown in Section 11.

5 Slacken and remove the pulley retaining bolt and washer, then slide the pulley off the crankshaft **(see illustration)**.

6 Slacken and remove all the timing chain cover retaining bolts and screws **(see illustration)**. Manoeuvre the cover downwards and away from the engine. Remove the gasket and discard it.

7 Using a flat-bladed screwdriver, bend back the tab of the camshaft bolt tab washer. To prevent camshaft rotation while the bolt is slackened, select top gear and have an assistant apply the brakes hard **(see Tool Tip)**.

8 Unscrew the camshaft bolt and remove it along with the tab washer and dished washer. Discard the tab washer; a new one must be used on refitting. Withdraw the distributor/oil

7.8a Remove the camshaft bolt, along with its tab washer and dished washer . . .

7.8b . . . and withdraw the drivegear

pump drivegear from the camshaft end, noting which way around it is fitted **(see illustrations)**.

9 Prior to removing the timing chain and sprockets, note the position of the sprocket timing marks and crankshaft and camshaft keyways **(refer to illustration 7.21)**.

10 Simultaneously withdraw the timing chain and sprockets from the crankshaft and camshaft, and manoeuvre the assembly away from the engine.

11 Remove the Woodruff key from the crankshaft keyway, noting which way around it is fitted. If the camshaft Woodruff key is a loose fit in the camshaft, remove it and store it with the sprocket for safe keeping.

12 With the Woodruff key removed, withdraw the shim, guide spacer and outer thrustwasher from the crankshaft end, noting which way around the guide spacer and thrustwasher are fitted.

Inspection

13 Examine the teeth on both the crankshaft and camshaft sprockets for signs of wear or damage such as chipped, hooked or missing teeth. If there is any sign of wear or damage on either sprocket, both sprockets and the chain should be renewed as a set.

14 Inspect the links of the timing chain for signs of wear on the rollers. The extent of wear on the chain can be judged by checking the amount by which the chain can be bent sideways: a new chain will have very little sideways movement.

15 If there is an excessive amount of side play in the timing chain, the chain must be

renewed. Note that it is a sensible precaution to renew the chain, regardless of its apparent condition, at about 30 000 miles or at a lesser mileage if the engine is undergoing a major overhaul.

16 Although not strictly necessary, it is always worth renewing the chain and sprockets as a matched set, since it is false economy to run a new chain on worn sprockets and *vice-versa*.

17 Inspect all other components for signs of wear or damage, and renew as necessary.

Refitting

18 Slide the outer thrustwasher over the end of the crankshaft, ensuring that its oil grooves are facing away from the bearing cap, then align the washer locating tab with its cut-out at the bottom of the cap, and press the thrustwasher into position in its recess **(see illustration)**.

19 With the thrustwasher in position, slide on the guide spacer, noting that its chamfered inner edge must face inwards, and refit the shim **(see illustrations)**.

20 Refit the Woodruff key to the crankshaft keyway so that its tapered end is innermost **(see illustration)**. Also refit the Woodruff key to the camshaft keyway if it was removed.

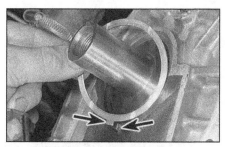

7.18 Refit the outer thrustwasher, ensuring its oil grooves are facing outwards, and locate its tab with the bearing cap cut-out (arrowed)

7.19a Slide on the guide spacer with its chamfered inner edge facing inwards . . .

7.19b ... and refit the shim

7.20 Refit the Woodruff key so that its tapered end is innermost

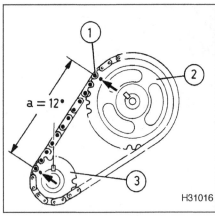

H31016

7.21 Crankshaft and camshaft Woodruff key and sprocket timing mark positions with No 1 cylinder at TDC

1 Timing chain
2 Camshaft sprocket
3 Crankshaft sprocket
a = 12 chain rollers

21 Engage the camshaft and crankshaft sprockets with the timing chain. The dot on the camshaft sprocket must be aligned with the twelfth timing chain roller along from the roller which aligns with the dot on the crankshaft sprocket, counting the roller above the crankshaft sprocket dot as number 1 **(see illustration)**.

22 Offer up the chain and sprocket assembly, and simultaneously slide on the sprockets, ensuring that the timing dot on each sprocket is facing outwards **(see illustration)**.

23 With the sprockets in position, recheck the position of the timing dots **(see illustration)**.

24 Locate the distributor/oil pump drivegear on the camshaft end, noting that its flange must face inwards, then refit the dished washer so that its concave face is outermost. Fit a new tab washer, engaging its locating peg with the slot in the drivegear, and refit the camshaft bolt. Tighten the bolt to the specified torque whilst using the method employed on removal to prevent rotation. Secure the bolt by bending up the tab washer against one of the flats of the bolt head **(see illustrations)**.

25 Remove all traces of oil and gasket from the mating surfaces of the timing chain cover and block. Inspect the crankshaft oil seal in the cover for signs of damage or deterioration, and renew it if necessary as described in Section 10.

26 Fit a new gasket over the locating pegs in the cylinder block, using a smear of grease to hold it in place **(see illustration)**.

27 Carefully manoeuvre the timing chain cover into position, and locate the cover on the pegs. Refit the cover retaining bolts and screws, and (where possible) tighten them to the specified torque.

28 Using a sharp knife, carefully trim of the ends of the gasket which protrude beyond the cylinder block sump mating face **(see illustration)**.

29 Align the crankshaft pulley slot with the Woodruff key and carefully slide the pulley onto the crankshaft, taking great care not to damage the oil seal lip. Refit the retaining bolt and washer, and tighten it by hand only.

30 Check that the inner and outer thrustwasher locating tabs are aligned with the cut-outs on the right-hand main bearing

7.22 Locate the timing chain and sprocket assembly on the crankshaft and camshaft ends

7.23 Recheck that the timing dots (arrowed) are still positioned as described in text

7.24a Tab washer locating peg correctly engaged with the drivegear

7.24b Bend tab washer up against one of camshaft bolt flats to secure it in position

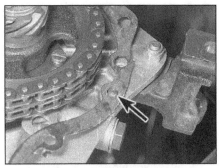

7.26 Locate a new gasket over pegs (arrowed) on block mating surface

7.28 Refit the timing cover and trim off the ends of the gasket which protrude beyond sump mating face

7.30 Ensure that the thrustwasher locating tabs are aligned with the bearing cap cut-outs

7.31 Tighten the crankshaft pulley retaining bolt to the specified torque

8.2a Undo the oil pump pick-up/strainer retaining bolts . . .

8.2b . . . then carefully lower it away from the engine . . .

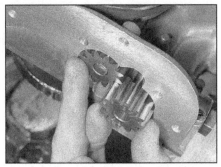

8.2c . . . and withdraw the oil pump gears

cap, and that the thrustwashers are correctly seated in their recesses (see illustration).
31 Tighten the crankshaft pulley bolt to the specified torque whilst preventing rotation using the method employed on removal (see illustration).
32 Note that if the thrustwashers are not properly seated, the crankshaft will lock up as the bolt is tightened, and the thrustwashers will be damaged. Check that the crankshaft rotates freely before proceeding further.
33 Refit the oil pump gears and the oil pick-up/strainer as described in Section 8, then refit the sump as described in Section 9.
34 Refit the alternator as described in Chapter 5A.
35 Where applicable, refit the distributor as described in Chapter 5B.

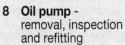

8 Oil pump -
removal, inspection and refitting

Removal

1 Remove the sump as described in Section 9.
2 Undo the four bolts securing the oil pump pick-up/strainer to the underside of the timing cover, and the single bolt securing it to the centre main bearing cap. Carefully lower the pick-up/strainer away from the timing cover, noting that the oil pump gears will drop out as soon as the cover is removed (see illustrations). Remove the gasket (where fitted) and discard it.

Inspection

3 Inspect the oil pump gears and the pump body for signs of wear ridges or obvious damage such as chipped teeth.
4 If the necessary measuring equipment is available, the extent of wear on the pump shafts and body can be determined by direct measurement.
5 If there is any obvious sign of wear, or if the tolerances given in the Specifications are exceeded, both the pump gears and the timing chain cover (which incorporates the oil pump body) must be renewed as a complete set (see illustration). Refer to Section 7 for information on timing chain cover removal and refitting.

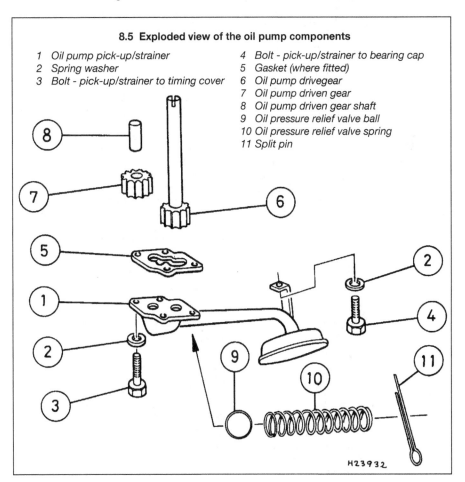

8.5 Exploded view of the oil pump components

1 Oil pump pick-up/strainer
2 Spring washer
3 Bolt - pick-up/strainer to timing cover
4 Bolt - pick-up/strainer to bearing cap
5 Gasket (where fitted)
6 Oil pump drivegear
7 Oil pump driven gear
8 Oil pump driven gear shaft
9 Oil pressure relief valve ball
10 Oil pressure relief valve spring
11 Split pin

H23932

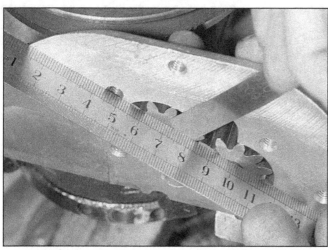

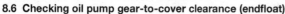

8.6 Checking oil pump gear-to-cover clearance (endfloat)

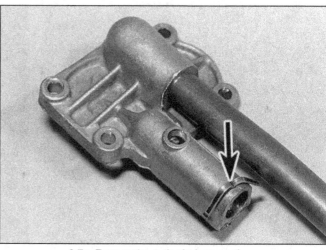

8.7a Extract the split pin (arrowed) . . .

6 Temporarily insert the gears into the pump body, and use a straight-edge and feeler blades to measure the gear-to-cover clearance (endfloat) **(see illustration)**. Skoda state that there must be a maximum of 0.1 mm clearance between the gears and cover. If there is approximately 0.1 mm clearance present, then the pick-up/strainer should be refitted without a gasket. If there is very little or no measurable clearance, then a gasket must be positioned behind the cover on refitting to provide the necessary clearance. If the clearance exceeds 0.1 mm, then the pump body and/or gears are worn, and the oil pump assembly must be renewed.

7 Extract the split pin from the pick-up/strainer assembly, and withdraw the oil pressure relief valve spring and ball **(see illustrations)**. Inspect the ball and spring for signs of wear or damage, and renew as necessary. If a new ball is to be fitted, insert the ball into position in the pick-up/strainer then, using a hammer and suitable soft-metal drift, tap the ball firmly into its seat; this will help the ball to seat properly and ensure correct operation of the valve. On refitting, secure the ball and spring in position with a new split pin.

Refitting

8 Where necessary, stick a new gasket onto the pick-up/strainer pipe mating surface, using a dab of grease to hold it in position.

9 Generously lubricate the oil pump gears and shafts, then insert the gears into the pump body. Holding them in position, offer up the pick-up/strainer and insert its five retaining bolts. Tighten the pick-up/strainer pipe retaining bolts to the specified torque.

10 Refit the sump as described in Section 9.

9 Sump - removal and refitting

Removal

1 Disconnect the battery negative lead.

2 Chock the rear wheels and apply the handbrake, then jack up the front of the vehicle and support it on axle stands (see *Jacking and vehicle support*).

3 Drain the engine oil, then clean and refit the engine oil drain plug, tightening it to the specified torque wrench setting. If the engine is nearing its service interval when the oil and filter are due for renewal, it is recommended that the filter is also removed and a new one fitted. After reassembly, the engine can then be replenished with fresh engine oil. Refer to Chapter 1A for further information.

4 From underneath the front of the vehicle, slacken and remove the bolt securing the coolant pipe to the bracket on the right-hand end of the sump **(see illustration)**.

5 Working in the **reverse** of the sequence shown, evenly and progressively slacken and remove the sump retaining bolts, noting the correct fitted position of the coolant pipe bracket which is fitted under the right-hand sump bolt.

6 Break the joint by striking the sump with the palm of the hand, then lower the sump away from the engine and withdraw it.

7 While the sump is removed, take the opportunity to clean the oil pump pick-up/strainer pipe mesh using a suitable solvent. Inspect the strainer mesh for signs of clogging or splitting and renew if necessary, referring to Section 8 for further information.

Refitting

8 Clean all traces of oil from the mating surfaces of the cylinder block/crankcase and sump, then use a clean rag to wipe out the sump and the engine's interior.

9 Fit a new sump gasket to the sump mating surface and offer up the sump to the cylinder block/crankcase. Refit the sump retaining bolts, not forgetting the coolant pipe bracket, and tighten them finger-tight only **(see illustrations)**.

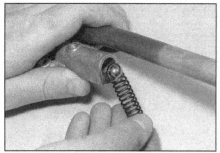

8.7b . . . and withdraw the pressure relief valve ball and spring from the pick-up/strainer

9.4 Undo the bolt securing the coolant pipe to the right-hand end of the sump

9.9a Fit a new gasket to the sump . . .

9.9b . . . and refit the sump to the engine

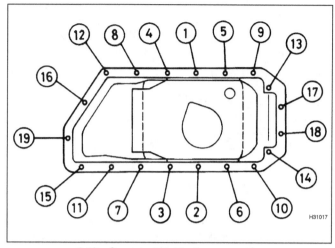

9.10a Sump bolt tightening sequence

10 Working in the sequence shown, tighten the sump bolts to the specified torque **(see illustrations)**.

11 Refit the coolant pipe retaining bolt and tighten it securely, then lower the vehicle to the ground and reconnect the battery negative lead.

12 Refill the engine with oil as described in Chapter 1A.

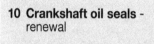

10 Crankshaft oil seals - renewal

Right-hand (pulley end) oil seal

1 Remove the crankshaft pulley as described in Section 7.

2 Carefully lever the old seal out of the timing chain cover using a suitable flat-bladed screwdriver, taking great care not to damage the cover or crankshaft **(see illustration)**.

3 Alternatively, punch or drill two small holes opposite each other in the seal, then screw a self-tapping screw into each and pull on the screws with pliers to extract the seal.

4 Clean the seal housing, and polish off any burrs or raised edges on the crankshaft which

may have caused the seal to fail in the first place.

5 Lubricate the lips of the new seal with clean engine oil, and press it into position until its outer edge is flush with the timing chain cover surface. If necessary, the seal can be tapped into position using a suitable tubular drift, such as a socket, which bears only on the hard outer edge of the seal **(see illustration)**. Note that the sealing lips must face inwards.

6 Clean off any traces of oil, then refit the crankshaft pulley as described in Section 7. Note that, should the crankshaft lock up as described, the sump will have to be removed to check the thrustwasher location.

Left-hand (flywheel end) oil seal

7 Remove the flywheel as described in Section 11.

8 Carefully punch or drill two small holes opposite each other in the seal. Screw a self-tapping screw into each hole, and pull on the screws with pliers to extract the seal **(see illustration)**.

9 Clean the seal housing, and polish off any burrs or raised edges on the crankshaft which may have caused the seal to fail in the first place.

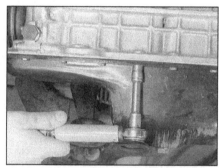

9.10b Tighten the sump retaining bolts to the specified torque setting as described in text

10 Lubricate the lips of the new seal and the crankshaft shoulder with clean engine oil, then offer the seal to the cylinder block/crankcase, ensuring its sealing lip is facing inwards.

11 Ease the sealing lip of the seal over the crankshaft shoulder by hand only, and press the seal evenly into its housing until its outer flange seats evenly on the housing shoulder. If necessary, a soft-faced mallet can be used to tap the seal gently into place.

12 Clean off any traces of oil, then refit the flywheel as described in Section 11.

10.2 Use a large flat-bladed screwdriver to prise out the crankshaft right-hand oil seal

10.5 Tap the new seal into position using a suitable tubular drift which bears only on the seal's hard outer edge

10.8 Using a self-tapping screw to remove the crankshaft left-hand oil seal

To prevent flywheel rotation as the retaining bolts are loosened or tightened, a locking tool can be made from a suitably thick piece of sheet metal, with a tooth shape to engage the flywheel teeth, and a bolt hole for attachment via one of the transmission housing bolts

11 Flywheel - removal, inspection and refitting

Removal

1 Remove the transmission as described in Chapter 7, then remove the clutch assembly as described in Chapter 6.
2 Prevent the flywheel from turning by locking the ring gear teeth as shown (see Tool Tip), or by bolting a strap between the flywheel and the cylinder block/crankcase.
3 Slacken and remove the flywheel retaining bolts; discard the bolts, as they must be renewed whenever they are disturbed.
4 Mark the relative positions of the flywheel centre and the crankshaft (see illustration). The marks are used when refitting to ensure that the flywheel is installed in its original fitted position; this is essential as the flywheel is balanced on the engine during manufacture.
5 Remove the flywheel. Do not drop it, as it is very heavy.

Inspection

6 If the clutch mating surface of the flywheel is deeply scored, cracked or otherwise

11.4 Prior to removing the flywheel, mark its correct fitted relationship with the crankshaft

damaged, the flywheel must be renewed, unless it is possible to have it surface-ground. Seek the advice of a Skoda dealer or engine reconditioning specialist.
7 If the ring gear is badly worn or has missing teeth, it must be renewed, but this job is best left to a Skoda dealer or engine reconditioning specialist. The temperature to which the new ring gear must be heated for installation (180° to 200°C) is critical and, if not done accurately, the hardness of the teeth will be destroyed.
8 If it is felt necessary, use the correct-size tap to clean the threads in the crankshaft of any old thread-locking fluid.

Refitting

9 Clean the mating surfaces of the flywheel and crankshaft, then fit the flywheel to the crankshaft. If the original flywheel is being refitted, aligning the marks made when dismantling. Note that if a new flywheel is being fitted, it can be installed in any position.
10 If the new flywheel retaining bolts are not supplied with their threads already pre-coated, apply a suitable thread-locking compound to the threads of each bolt. Fit the bolts, tightening them by hand only at this stage.
11 Lock the flywheel using the method employed on dismantling, and tighten the retaining bolts to the specified torque wrench setting.
12 Refit the clutch as described in Chapter 6, then remove the locking tool and refit the transmission as described in Chapter 7.

12 Engine/transmission mounting rubbers - inspection and renewal

Inspection

1 If improved access is required, raise the front of the vehicle and support it securely on axle stands (see *Jacking and Vehicle Support*).
2 Check each mounting rubber to see if it is cracked, hardened or separated from the metal at any point; renew the mounting if any such damage or deterioration is evident.
3 Check that all the mounting's fasteners are securely tightened; use a torque wrench to check if possible.
4 Using a large screwdriver or a pry bar, check for wear in the mounting by carefully levering against it to check for free play; where this is not possible, enlist the aid of an assistant to move the engine/transmission back and forth or from side to side while you watch the mounting. While some free play is to be expected even from new components, excessive wear should be obvious. If excessive free play is found, check first that the fasteners are correctly tightened before deciding that renewal of the mounting rubber is required.

Renewal - general information

Right-hand mounting

5 The right-hand engine mounting rubber is an integral part of the coolant pump casing. Removal and refitting of the mounting rubber from the pump requires the use of a hydraulic press and several special mandrels and spacers. Therefore, if the mounting requires renewal, remove the coolant pump as described in Chapter 3 and take it to your Skoda dealer. The dealer will have access to the equipment required to remove the old mounting rubber and install the new one.

Left-hand mounting

6 The left-hand engine mounting rubber is an integral part of the transmission end cover. Removal and refitting of the mounting rubber from the cover requires the use of a special Skoda service tool. Therefore, if the mounting requires renewal, remove the transmission as described in Chapter 7 and take it to your Skoda dealer. The dealer will have access to the necessary puller and will be able to remove the old mounting rubber and install the new one.

Rear mounting

7 There are two mounting rubbers in the rear mounting - the main one is pressed into the bracket attached to the rear of the transmission housing, and a smaller bush is fitted to the rear of the connecting link to the front subframe. If either mounting rubber requires renewal, it will be necessary to refer to a Skoda dealer. The dealer will have access to the equipment required to press out the old mounting rubber and install the new one.
8 To remove the main mounting, with the front of the car raised and supported, use another jack and block of wood to take the weight of the engine/transmission - for preference, do not jack under the sump. Remove the nut and through-bolt which secure the main mounting to the connecting link. Remove the two retaining bolts and the nut (or three nuts on later models) securing the mounting to the transmission housing, and remove the main mounting from under the car (see illustration).
9 To remove the connecting link, undo the nut securing the rear of the link to the

12.8 Engine/transmission rear mounting

mounting bracket on the front subframe, then slide out the through-bolt together with the washer. Undo the nut and remove the through-bolt securing the link to the main mounting bracket, and remove the link from underneath the vehicle.

10 Refitting is a reversal of the relevant removal procedure. Ensure that all mounting nuts and bolts are securely tightened.

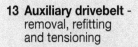

13 Auxiliary drivebelt - removal, refitting and tensioning

General information

1 Depending on the vehicle specification, the auxiliary drivebelt, which is driven from a pulley mounted on the crankshaft, will provide drive for the alternator, coolant pump and (on vehicles with air conditioning), the refrigerant compressor.

2 On models with air conditioning, the ribbed auxiliary belt is fitted with an automatic tensioning device; otherwise, the belt is tensioned by moving the alternator on its mountings.

3 On refitting, the auxiliary belt must be tensioned correctly, to ensure correct operation under all conditions, and for prolonged service life.

Removal

4 Park the vehicle on a level surface, apply the handbrake and chock the rear wheels. Loosen the right-hand front wheel bolts.

5 Raise the front of the car, rest it securely on axle stands and remove the right-hand front roadwheel.

6 Remove the screws, and lower the cover fitted over the drivebelt (see illustrations).

13.6a Remove the retaining screws (three in total) . . .

7 Examine the ribbed belt for manufacturer's markings, indicating the direction of rotation. If none are present, make some using typist's correction fluid or a dab of paint - do not cut or score the belt in any way.

Models without air conditioning

8 Slacken the alternator upper and lower mounting bolts by between one and two turns, and push the alternator to the rear to slacken the drivebelt (see illustration).

Models with air conditioning

9 Fit an open-end spanner to the tensioner centre nut, and rotate the assembly against its spring tension.

All models

10 Pull the belt off the alternator pulley (see illustration), then release it from the remaining pulleys, noting its routing.

Refitting and tensioning

Caution: Observe the manufacturer's direction of rotation markings on the belt, when refitting.

13.6b . . . and remove the drivebelt cover

Models without air conditioning

11 Fit the drivebelt around all the pulleys, ensuring that the belt ribs are engaged properly with the pulley grooves.

12 If not already done, loosen the alternator upper (adjustment link) and lower mountings. Tighten the adjustment link nut and bolt hand-tight, so that the alternator can still be moved.

13 Pull the alternator towards the front of the car to tension the drivebelt. Use a stout wooden lever between the alternator and the cylinder block if necessary, but take care not to lever against any part of the engine which may be damaged.

14 The drivebelt tension is correct when the belt can be deflected by 10 to 15 mm when depressed in the middle of its top run - between the alternator and coolant pump pulleys.

15 When the drivebelt tension is satisfactory, tighten the adjustment link nut and bolt (see illustration), followed by the alternator lower mountings.

Models with air conditioning

16 Pass the ribbed belt around the crankshaft

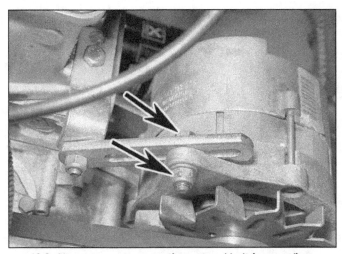

13.8 Alternator upper mounting nut and bolt (arrowed) on adjustment link

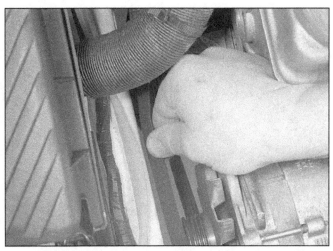

13.10 Removing the drivebelt from the alternator pulley

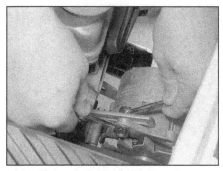

13.15 Tightening the alternator adjustment link nut and bolt

and refrigerant pump pulleys, ensuring that the ribs seat in the channels on the surface of the pulley **(see illustration)**.

17 Fit an open-end spanner to the tensioner centre nut, and rotate the assembly against its spring tension.

18 Pass the belt around the tensioner roller, then fit it over the remaining pulleys. Ensure that the belt ribs engage correctly with the pulley grooves, where applicable.

19 Release the spanner and allow the tensioner roller to tension the belt.

All models

20 Refit the drivebelt cover, tightening the screws securely.

21 Refit the right-hand front roadwheel and lower the car to the ground. Tighten the roadwheel bolts to the specified torque.

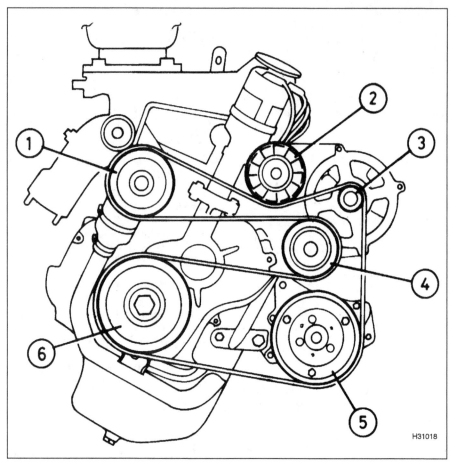

13.16 Auxiliary drivebelt run on models with air conditioning

1 Coolant pump	3 Alternator	5 Refrigerant pump
2 Roller	4 Tensioner	6 Crankshaft

Chapter 2 Part B:
1.6 litre petrol engine in-car repair procedures

Contents

Degrees of difficulty

Easy, suitable for novice with little experience		**Fairly easy,** suitable for beginner with some experience		**Fairly difficult,** suitable for competent DIY mechanic		**Difficult,** suitable for experienced DIY mechanic		**Very difficult,** suitable for expert DIY or professional	

Specifications

General

Type	Four-cylinder in-line, four stroke, liquid-cooled
Engine code	AEE
Bore	76.5 mm
Stroke	86.9 mm
Capacity	1598 cc
Firing order	1 - 3 - 4 - 2 (No 1 at timing belt end)
Direction of crankshaft rotation	Clockwise (when viewed from right-hand side of vehicle)
Compression ratio	9.8:1
Compression pressures:	
Wear limit	7.0 bar
Maximum difference between all cylinders	3.0 bar

Lubrication system

Oil pump type	Sump-mounted, chain-driven from crankshaft
Normal operating oil pressure	2.0 bar minimum (at 2000 rpm, oil temperature 80°C)
Oil pressure switch operating range	0.15 to 0.35 bar
Oil pump backlash	0.2 mm (wear limit)
Oil pump axial clearance	0.15 mm (wear limit)
Oil pump drive chain tension	4 mm (approx) deflection at mid-point between sprockets

Torque wrench settings

	Nm	lbf ft
Alternator mounting bolts	23	17
Alternator mounting bracket-to-engine bolts	45	33
Auxiliary drivebelt tensioner pulley bolt	45	33
Auxiliary drivebelt tensioner-to-bracket bolt	25	18
Big-end bearing cap bolts*:		
Stage 1	30	22
Stage 2	Angle-tighten a further 90°	
Camshaft bearing cap bolts	10	7
Camshaft bearing cap nuts:		
Stage 1	6	4
Stage 2	Angle-tighten a further 90°	
Camshaft cover bolts	10	7
Camshaft sprocket bolt*:		
Stage 1	20	15
Stage 2	Angle-tighten a further 90°	
Crankshaft main bearing cap bolts:		
Stage 1	65	48
Stage 2	Angle-tighten a further 90°	
Crankshaft oil seal housing bolts	10	7
Crankshaft pulley-to-crankshaft sprocket (socket-head bolts)	20	15
Crankshaft sprocket bolt - oil threads*:		
Stage 1	90	66
Stage 2	Angle-tighten a further 90°	
Cylinder head bolts:		
Stage 1	40	30
Stage 2	60	44
Stage 3	Angle-tighten a further 90°	
Stage 4	Angle-tighten a further 90°	
Dipstick tube bolts	10	7
Engine lifting eye bracket bolts	20	15
Engine right-hand mounting-to-block bolts*:		
Stage 1	40	30
Stage 2	Angle-tighten a further 90°	
Engine right-hand mounting-to-body bolts	50	37
Engine-to-transmission bolts	45	33
Engine/transmission left-hand mounting:		
Front bolt	60	44
Front nut	45	33
Rear bolt	45	33
Engine/transmission rear mounting:		
Front through-bolt/nut	45	33
Rear through-bolt/nut (to subframe)	77	57
Engine/transmission right-hand mounting bolts	50	37
Exhaust manifold	25	18
Exhaust manifold warm-air collector plate bolts	9	7
Exhaust pipe-to-manifold	25	18
Flywheel bolts*:		
Stage 1	60	44
Stage 2	Angle-tighten a further 90°	
Knock sensor	20	15
Oil pressure switch	20	15
Oil pump mounting bolts (timing belt end)	20	15
Oil pump pickup bracket bolts	10	7
Oil separator mounting bolts	10	7
Roadwheel bolts	110	81
Sump bolts	15	11
Sump drain plug	30	22
Timing belt cover bolts*	10	7
Timing belt guard/coolant pump mounting bolts	20	15
Timing belt inner cover-to-cylinder head bolts	10	7
Timing belt tensioner roller locknut	20	15

* Use new bolts/nuts

1 General information

Using this Chapter

This Part of Chapter 2 describes those repair procedures that can reasonably be carried out on the engine while it remains in the vehicle. If the engine has been removed from the vehicle and is being dismantled as described in Part D, any preliminary dismantling procedures can be ignored.

Note that while it may be possible physically to overhaul items such as the piston/connecting rod assemblies while the engine is in the vehicle, such tasks are not usually carried out as separate operations, and usually require the execution of several additional procedures (not to mention the cleaning of components and of oilways); for this reason, all such tasks are classed as major overhaul procedures, and are described in Part D of this Chapter.

Part D describes the removal of the engine/transmission from the vehicle and the full overhaul procedures that can then be carried out.

Engine description

The engine is a water-cooled, single overhead camshaft, in-line four-cylinder unit, with a cast-iron cylinder block and aluminium-alloy cylinder head. The engine is mounted transversely at the front of the vehicle, with the transmission bolted to the left-hand side of the engine.

The cylinder head carries the camshaft, which is driven by a toothed timing belt. It also houses the inlet and exhaust valves, which are closed by single coil springs, and which run in guides pressed into the cylinder head. The camshaft actuates the valves directly via hydraulic tappets, mounted in the cylinder head. The cylinder head contains integral oilways which supply and lubricate the tappets.

The crankshaft is supported by five main bearings, and crankshaft endfloat is controlled by a thrust bearing fitted between cylinder Nos 2 and 3.

Engine coolant is circulated by a pump, driven by the camshaft timing belt. For details of the cooling system, refer to Chapter 3.

Lubricant is circulated under pressure by a pump, driven by the crankshaft via a chain. Oil is drawn from the sump through a strainer, and then forced through an externally-mounted, replaceable screw-on filter. From there, it is distributed to the cylinder head, where it lubricates the camshaft journals and hydraulic tappets, and also to the crankcase, where it lubricates the main bearings, connecting rod big- and small-ends, gudgeon pins and cylinder bores.

Repairs possible with the engine installed in the vehicle

The following operations can be performed without removing the engine:

a) Auxiliary drivebelt - removal and refitting.
b) Camshaft - removal and refitting.*
c) Camshaft oil seal - renewal.
d) Camshaft sprocket - removal and refitting.
e) Coolant pump - removal and refitting (refer to Chapter 3).
f) Crankshaft oil seals - renewal.
g) Crankshaft sprocket - removal and refitting.
h) Cylinder head - removal and refitting.*
i) Engine mountings - inspection and renewal.
j) Oil pump and pickup assembly - removal and refitting.
k) Sump - removal and refitting.
l) Timing belt, sprockets and cover - removal, inspection and refitting.

*Cylinder head dismantling procedures are detailed in Chapter 2D, with details of camshaft and hydraulic tappet removal.
Note: *It is possible to remove the pistons and connecting rods (after removing the cylinder head and sump) without removing the engine . However, this is not recommended. Work of this nature is more easily and thoroughly completed with the engine on the bench, as described in Chapter 2D.*

2 Top Dead Centre (TDC) for No 1 piston - locating

General information

Note: *This sub-Section has been written with the assumption that the distributor, HT leads and timing belt are correctly fitted.*

1 The crankshaft and camshaft sprockets are driven by the timing belt, and rotate in phase with each other. When the timing belt is removed during servicing or repair, it is possible for the shafts to rotate independently of each other, and the correct phasing is then lost.

2 The design of the engines covered in this

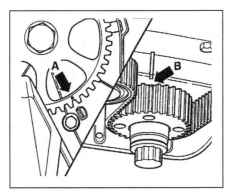

2.5 Camshaft sprocket (A) and crankshaft sprocket (B) TDC timing marks

Chapter is such that potentially damaging piston-to-valve contact may occur if the camshaft is rotated when any of the pistons are stationary at, or near, the top of its stroke.

3 For this reason, it is important that the correct phasing between the camshaft and crankshaft is preserved whilst the timing belt is off the engine. This is achieved by setting the engine in a reference condition (known as Top Dead Centre or TDC) before the timing belt is removed, and then preventing the shafts from rotating until the belt is refitted. Similarly, if the engine has been dismantled for overhaul, the engine can be set to TDC during reassembly to ensure that the correct shaft phasing is restored. **Note:** *The coolant pump is also driven by the timing belt, but the pump alignment with respect to the crankshaft and camshaft is not critical.*

4 TDC is the highest position a piston reaches within its respective cylinder - in a four-stroke engine, each piston reaches TDC twice per cycle; once on the compression stroke, and once on the exhaust stroke. In general, TDC normally refers to No 1 cylinder on the compression stroke (the cylinders are numbered 1 to 4, with No 1 being at the timing belt end of the engine).

5 The crankshaft sprocket has a notch ground away from one of its teeth which, when aligned with a reference marking on the crankshaft front oil seal flange, indicates that No 1 cylinder (and hence also No 4 cylinder) is at TDC. However, the crankshaft sprocket is only visible with the timing belt lower cover removed - there is also a notch in the crankshaft pulley, which, when aligned with a 0 mark moulded into the timing belt lower cover, indicates TDC. The camshaft sprocket is also equipped with a timing mark (a dot punched in its outer face) - when this is aligned with the raised pointer moulded into the timing belt inner cover, the engine is correctly synchronised, and the timing belt can then be refitted and tensioned **(see illustration)**.

6 The following sub-Sections describe setting the engine to TDC on No 1 cylinder.

Setting TDC on No 1 cylinder - timing belt fitted

7 Before starting work, disconnect the battery negative lead. **Note:** *If the vehicle has a security-coded radio, check that you have a copy of the code number before disconnecting the battery. Refer to your Skoda dealer if in doubt.*

8 Disable the ignition system by removing the distributor centre HT lead and grounding it on the cylinder block, using a jumper wire. Prevent any vehicle movement by applying the handbrake and chocking the rear wheels. Ensure that the transmission is in neutral.

9 On the distributor cap, note the position of the No 1 cylinder HT terminal with respect to the distributor body. On some models, the manufacturer provides a marking in the form of a small cut-out . If the terminal is not

2.25 Crankshaft sprocket chamfered tooth (1) and timing mark (2)

marked, follow the HT lead from the No 1 cylinder spark plug back to the distributor cap - No 1 cylinder is at the timing end of the engine - and using chalk or a pen (*not* a pencil), place a mark on the distributor body directly under the terminal.

10 Remove the distributor cap, as described in Chapter 5B.

11 Disconnect the HT leads from the spark plugs, noting their order of connection.

12 To bring any piston up to TDC, it will be necessary to rotate the crankshaft manually. This can be done by using a wrench and socket on the centre bolt that retains the crankshaft sprocket (refer to Section 5 for more detail).

13 Rotate the crankshaft in its normal direction of rotation until the distributor rotor arm electrode begins to approach the mark that was made on the distributor body.

HAYNES HINT *Remove all four spark plugs; this will make the engine easier to turn; refer to Chapter 1A for details.*

14 With reference to Section 4, remove the timing belt upper cover to expose the camshaft sprocket beneath.

15 Identify the timing marks on both the camshaft sprocket and the inner section of the timing belt cover. Continue turning the crankshaft clockwise until these marks are exactly aligned with each other.

16 At this point, identify the timing marks on the crankshaft pulley and the timing belt lower cover. The cover has a Z and a 0 mark moulded into it - when the notch in the rim of the crankshaft pulley aligns with the 0 mark, the engine is set to TDC.

17 Alternatively, check that the crankshaft sprocket and the crankshaft front oil seal flange timing marks are correctly aligned (**refer to illustration 2.5**). **Note**: *The crankshaft pulley and the lower timing belt cover must be removed to expose the crankshaft sprocket timing marks.*

18 Check that the centre of the distributor rotor arm electrode is now aligned with the No 1 terminal mark on the distributor body. If it proves impossible to align the rotor arm with the No 1 terminal whilst maintaining alignment of the camshaft timing marks, refer to

Chapter 5B and check that the distributor has been fitted correctly.

19 When all the above steps have been completed successfully, the engine will be set to TDC on No 1 cylinder.

Caution: If the timing belt is to be removed, ensure that the crankshaft, camshaft and intermediate shaft alignment is preserved by preventing the sprockets from rotating with respect to each other.

Setting TDC on No 1 cylinder - timing belt removed

20 This procedure has been written with the assumption that the timing belt has been removed and that the alignment between the camshaft and crankshaft has been lost, for example following engine removal and overhaul.

21 It is possible for damage to be caused by the piston crowns striking the valve heads, if the camshaft is rotated with the timing belt removed and the crankshaft set to TDC. For this reason, the TDC setting procedure must be carried out in a particular order, as described in the following paragraphs.

22 Before the cylinder head is refitted, use a wrench and socket on the crankshaft sprocket centre bolt to turn the crankshaft in its normal direction of rotation, until all four pistons are positioned **halfway down** their bores, with No 1 piston on its upstroke - i.e. around 90° before TDC.

23 With the cylinder head and camshaft sprocket fitted, identify the timing marks on both the camshaft sprocket and the inner section of the timing belt cover; refer to the illustration in *General Information.*

24 Turn the camshaft sprocket in its normal direction of rotation until the timing marks on the sprocket and timing belt inner cover are exactly aligned.

25 Identify the timing marks on the crankshaft sprocket and the crankshaft front oil seal flange. Using a socket and wrench on the crankshaft sprocket retaining bolt, turn the crankshaft through 90° (quarter of a turn) in its normal direction of rotation, to bring the timing marks into alignment **(see illustration)**.

26 Check that the centre of the distributor rotor arm electrode is now aligned with No 1 cylinder terminal marking on the distributor body. If it proves impossible to align the rotor arm with the No 1 terminal whilst maintaining the alignment of the camshaft timing marks, refer to Chapter 5B and check that the distributor has been fitted correctly.

27 When all the above steps have been completed successfully, the engine will be set at TDC on No 1 cylinder. The timing belt can now be fitted as described in Section 4.

Caution: Until the timing belt is fitted, ensure that the crankshaft, camshaft and intermediate shaft alignment is preserved by preventing the sprockets from rotating with respect to each other.

3 Cylinder compression test

1 When engine performance is down, or if misfiring occurs which cannot be attributed to the ignition or fuel systems, a compression test can provide diagnostic clues as to the engine's condition. If the test is performed regularly, it can give warning of trouble before any other symptoms become apparent.

2 The engine must be fully warmed-up to normal operating temperature, the battery must be fully charged, and all the spark plugs must be removed (refer to Chapter 1A). The aid of an assistant will also be required.

3 Disable the ignition system by disconnecting the ignition HT coil lead from the distributor cap and earthing it on the cylinder block. Use a jumper lead or similar wire to make a good connection.

4 To prevent possible damage to the catalytic converter, depressurise and disable the fuel injection system by removing the fuel pump fuse or relay (see the relevant part of Chapter 4).

5 Fit a compression tester to the No 1 cylinder spark plug hole - the type of tester which screws into the plug thread is preferable.

6 Have an assistant hold the accelerator pedal in the full-throttle position, then crank the engine on the starter motor; after one or two revolutions, the compression pressure should build up to a maximum figure, and then stabilise. Record the highest reading obtained.

7 Repeat the test on the remaining cylinders, recording the pressure in each. Keep the accelerator pedal fully depressed.

8 All cylinders should produce very similar pressures; a difference of more than 2 bars between any two cylinders indicates a fault (the manufacturer quotes a maximum difference between the highest and lowest of all four readings). Note that the compression should build up quickly in a healthy engine; low compression on the first stroke, followed by gradually-increasing pressure on successive strokes, indicates worn piston rings. A low compression reading on the first stroke, which does not build up during successive strokes, indicates leaking valves or a blown head gasket (a cracked head could also be the cause). Deposits on the undersides of the valve heads can also cause low compression.

9 Refer to the Specifications section of this Chapter, and compare the recorded compression figures with those stated by the manufacturer.

10 If the pressure in any cylinder is low, carry out the following test to isolate the cause. Introduce a teaspoonful of clean oil into that cylinder through its spark plug hole, and repeat the test.

11 If the addition of oil temporarily improves the compression pressure, this indicates that

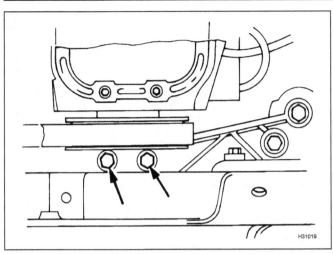

4.7 Remove the two mounting bolts (arrowed) - seen from below

4.10a Loosen the crankshaft pulley bolts, counterholding on the centre bolt . . .

bore or piston wear is responsible for the pressure loss. No improvement suggests that leaking or burnt valves, or a blown head gasket, may be to blame.

12 A low reading from two adjacent cylinders is almost certainly due to the head gasket having blown between them; the presence of coolant in the engine oil will confirm this.

13 If one cylinder is about 20 percent lower than the others and the engine has a slightly rough idle, a worn camshaft lobe could be the cause.

14 If the compression reading is unusually high, the combustion chambers are probably coated with carbon deposits. If this is the case, the cylinder head should be removed and decarbonised.

15 On completion of the test, refit the spark plugs and restore the ignition and fuel systems.

4 Timing belt and outer covers
- removal and refitting

General information

1 The primary function of the toothed timing belt is to drive the camshaft, but it is also used to drive the coolant pump. Should the belt slip or break in service, the valve timing will be disturbed and piston-to-valve contact may occur, resulting in serious engine damage. Similarly, the coolant pump may leak coolant onto the belt, or if the pump is severely worn, the pump may seize and break the belt.

2 For this reason, it is important that the timing belt is tensioned correctly, and inspected regularly for signs of wear or deterioration.

3 Note that the removal of the *inner* section of the timing belt cover is described as part of the camshaft oil seal renewal procedure; see Section 8.

Removal

4 Before starting work, immobilise the engine and vehicle as follows:

a) *Disconnect the battery negative lead, and position the lead away from the terminal.* **Note:** *If the vehicle has a security-coded radio, check that you have a copy of the code number before disconnecting the battery. Refer to your Skoda dealer if in doubt.*

b) *Prevent any vehicle movement by applying the handbrake and chocking the rear wheels. Ensure that the transmission is in neutral.*

c) *Loosen the right-hand front wheel bolts, then jack up the front of the car and support securely on axle stands (see Jacking and vehicle support).*

5 Access to the timing belt covers can be improved by removing the air cleaner housing, and the air ducting from the exhaust manifold and inner wing. Pull out the engine oil dipstick and place it to one side, out of the way.

6 To renew the belt, the engine right-hand mounting must be separated. Support the weight of the engine using an engine hoist from above, or using a securely-located hydraulic jack and suitable block of wood from below. Do not jack under the sump without using a block of wood to spread the

4.10b . . . and withdraw the crankshaft pulley

load, or the sump will be damaged. Skoda technicians use an engine support bar which locates in the inner wing channels.

7 With the engine securely supported, working from below, progressively loosen and remove the two engine mounting bolts directly above the crankshaft pulley, and recover the washers **(see illustration)**. If the engine is now lowered slightly, the mounting will separate, providing a gap for the timing belt to pass through.

8 The engine must now be lowered slightly, to allow the crankshaft pulley to be removed.

9 Remove the auxiliary drivebelt as described in Section 6.

10 Unscrew and remove the four crankshaft pulley retaining bolts - it should be possible to counterhold the pulley using a spanner or socket on the crankshaft sprocket bolt. Remove the crankshaft pulley **(see illustrations)**.

> **HAYNES HiNT** *To prevent the crankshaft drivebelt pulley from rotating whilst the bolts are being slackened, select top gear and get an assistant to apply the footbrake firmly. Failing this, grip the sprocket by wrapping a length of old rubber hose or inner tube around it. If top gear is selected to help in removing the pulley, make sure the transmission is returned to neutral before proceeding.*

11 Release the two retaining clips, unscrew the bolt, and remove the timing belt upper cover. Later models may have a further bolt at the front of the engine **(see illustrations)**.

12 Release the clip at the rear, then unscrew and remove the two retaining bolts, and remove the timing belt lower cover. To improve access to the front bolt, on models with power steering or air conditioning, rotate the auxiliary drivebelt tensioner clockwise and hold it out of the way using a spanner on the

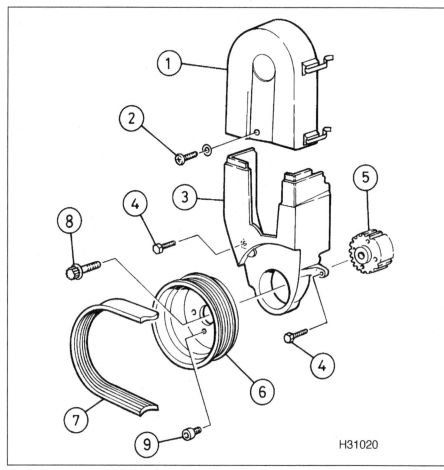

4.11a Timing belt covers and related components

1	Timing belt upper cover	4	Lower cover retaining	7	Auxiliary drivebelt
2	Upper cover retaining bolt		bolts	8	Crankshaft sprocket
	and washer	5	Crankshaft sprocket		bolt
3	Timing belt lower cover	6	Crankshaft pulley	9	Crankshaft pulley bolt

centre bolt. The tensioner can be removed completely, if preferred, by turning the centre bolt anti-clockwise; remove the bolt, washer and tensioner pulley.

13 Using the information in Section 2, set the engine to TDC on No 1 cylinder.

14 Examine the timing belt for manufacturer's markings that indicate the direction of rotation. If none are present, make your own using typist's correction fluid or a dab of paint - do

not cut or score the belt in any way

Caution: If the belt appears to be in good condition and can be re-used, it is essential that it is refitted the same way around, otherwise accelerated wear will result, leading to premature failure.

15 Loosen the tensioner roller locknut, and allow the tensioner to rotate anti-clockwise to relieve the tension on the belt **(see illustration)**.

16 Slide the belt off the sprockets, taking care to avoid twisting or kinking it excessively **(see illustration)**. Ensure that the sprockets remain aligned with their respective timing markings once the timing belt has been removed.

Caution: It is potentially damaging to allow the camshaft to turn with the timing belt removed and the engine set at TDC, as piston-to-valve contact may occur.

17 Examine the belt for evidence of contamination by coolant or lubricant. If this is the case, identify the source of the contamination before progressing any further. Check the belt for signs of wear or damage, particularly around the leading edges of the belt teeth. Renew the belt if its condition is in doubt; the cost of belt renewal is negligible compared with potential cost of the engine repairs, should the belt fail in service. Similarly, if the belt is known to have covered more than 30 000 miles, it is prudent to renew it regardless of condition, as a precautionary measure.

18 If the timing belt is not going to be refitted for some time, it is a wise precaution to hang a warning label on the steering wheel, to remind yourself (and others) not to attempt starting the engine. You may wish to further immobilise the engine against being started, perhaps by taping over the ignition switch.

Refitting

19 Ensure that the timing marks on the camshaft and crankshaft sprockets are correctly aligned with their corresponding TDC reference marks on the timing belt inner cover and crankshaft oil seal flange; refer to Section 2 for details.

20 Engage the timing belt teeth with the crankshaft sprocket, then manoeuvre it into position over the coolant pump and camshaft sprockets **(see illustration)**. Observe the direction of rotation markings on the belt.

21 Pass the flat side of the belt over the tensioner roller - avoid bending the belt back on itself or twisting it excessively as you do this. Ensure the front run of the belt is taut - ie all the slack should be in the section of the belt that passes over the tensioner roller.

22 Tension the belt as follows. Tighten the tensioner locknut lightly, then insert an Allen key into the adjustment hole, and turn the

4.11b Later models have a further upper belt cover retaining bolt (arrowed)

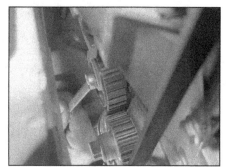

4.15 Loosening the belt tensioner locknut

4.16 Removing the timing belt

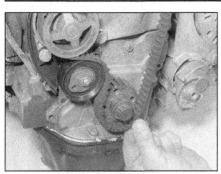

4.20 Engaging the timing belt with the crankshaft sprocket

4.22a Turn the tensioner clockwise using an Allen key until the pointer aligns with the slot in the tensioner baseplate

4.22b When the belt tension is correctly set, tighten the tensioner locknut

eccentrically-mounted tensioner clockwise until the slack in the belt is taken up. Continue turning the tensioner until the sliding pointer lines up with the notch in the tensioner baseplate. On completion, tighten the tensioner locknut to the specified torque **(see illustrations)**.

23 Using a spanner or wrench and socket on the crankshaft sprocket bolt, rotate the crankshaft through two complete revolutions, and reset the engine to TDC on No 1 cylinder, with reference to Section 2. Re-check the alignment of the tensioner, and adjust it if necessary.

24 Refer to Section 5 and test the operation of the tensioner.

25 Refit the lower and upper sections of the timing belt outer cover, refitting the clips and tightening the retaining bolts securely. Use new bolts on the timing belt lower cover.

26 Refit the pulley for the ribbed auxiliary drivebelt to the crankshaft sprocket, noting that the small hole in the pulley fits over a peg on the crankshaft sprocket **(see illustration)**. Insert and tighten the retaining bolts to the specified torque. Counterhold the sprocket using one of the methods described in paragraph 10.

27 Working from Section 6, refit and tension the auxiliary drivebelt.

28 Raise the engine back into a position

where the engine right-hand mounting can be reconnected.

29 Reconnect the engine right-hand mounting, and tighten the bolts to the specified torque. Remove the hoist or the jack on completion.

30 Refit the air cleaner warm air ducting to the exhaust manifold and air cleaner. Where applicable, restore the ignition and fuel systems by reconnecting the coil HT lead and refitting the fuel pump fuse or relay.

31 Reconnect the battery negative lead.

32 On completion, refer to Chapter 5B and check the ignition timing.

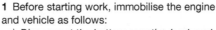

5 Timing belt sprockets and tensioner - removal, inspection and refitting

1 Before starting work, immobilise the engine and vehicle as follows:

a) *Disconnect the battery negative lead, and position the lead away from the terminal.* **Note:** *If the vehicle has a security-coded radio, check that you have a copy of the code number before disconnecting the battery. Refer to your Skoda dealer if in doubt.*

b) *Prevent any vehicle movement by applying the handbrake and chocking the*

rear wheels. Ensure that the transmission is in neutral.

Timing belt tensioner

Removal

2 With reference to Section 2, set the engine to TDC on No 1 cylinder.

3 Referring to Section 4, separate the engine right-hand mounting, then remove the auxiliary drivebelt, crankshaft pulley, and the timing belt upper and lower covers.

4 Slacken the locknut at the hub of the tensioner pulley, and allow the assembly to rotate anti-clockwise, relieving the tension on the timing belt.

5 Remove the locknut and slide the tensioner off its mounting stud.

Inspection

6 Wipe the tensioner clean, but do not use solvents that may contaminate the bearings. Spin the tensioner pulley on its hub by hand. Stiff movement or excessive freeplay is an indication of severe wear; the tensioner is not a serviceable component, and it should be renewed if its condition is less than perfect.

Refitting and testing

7 Slide the tensioner pulley over the mounting stud. The U-shape in the tensioner baseplate fits over the bolt shown **(see illustration)**.

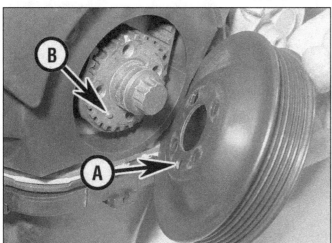

4.26 Refitting the crankshaft pulley - small hole (A) fits over peg (B) on crankshaft sprocket

5.7 Slide tensioner onto its mounting stud, fitting the U-shaped baseplate over the bolt (arrowed)

5.9a Apply pressure to the belt, and the tensioner pointer (arrowed) should move away from the central position . . .

5.9b . . . then return to correct alignment as pressure is released

To make a camshaft sprocket holding tool, obtain two lengths of steel strip about 6 mm thick by 30 mm wide or similar, one 600 mm long, the other 200 mm long (all dimensions approximate). Bolt the two strips together to form a forked end, leaving the bolt slack so that the shorter strip can pivot freely. At the end of each 'prong' of the fork, secure a bolt with a nut and a locknut, to act as the fulcrums; these will engage with the cut-outs in the sprocket, and should protrude by about 30mm

Refit the locknut and tighten it lightly - do not fully tighten the nut at this stage.

8 With reference to Section 4, tension the timing belt.

9 The operation of the belt tensioner can be tested as follows. Apply finger pressure to the timing belt at a point mid-way between the camshaft and crankshaft sprockets. The sliding pointer that protrudes from behind the tensioner roller should slide away from the alignment notch in the tensioner baseplate as pressure is applied, and then move back as the pressure is removed **(see illustrations)**. Any reluctance to return to the correct position indicates that the tensioner should be renewed - correct tension is critical to the operation of the belt, and the importance of the belt tensioner cannot be overstressed.

10 Referring to Section 4, refit the timing belt upper and lower covers, the crankshaft pulley, auxiliary drivebelt, and reconnect the engine right-hand mounting. Reconnect the battery negative lead.

11 With reference to Chapter 5B, check that the ignition timing is still within specifications.

Camshaft timing belt sprocket

Removal

12 With reference to Sections 2 and 4, remove the timing belt covers and set the engine to TDC on No 1 cylinder. Slacken the timing belt tensioner locknut and rotate it anti-clockwise to relieve the tension on the timing belt. Carefully slide the timing belt off the camshaft sprocket.

⚠️ *Warning: It is potentially damaging to allow the camshaft to turn with the timing belt removed and the engine set at TDC, as piston-to-valve contact may occur. Take care that the camshaft sprocket is not turned as it is removed. As a precaution against damage, Skoda recommend that the crankshaft be turned back a few degrees, away from TDC, while the camshaft sprocket is removed/refitted. The crankshaft may then be turned back to TDC when the timing belt is to be refitted.*

13 The camshaft sprocket must be held stationary whilst its retaining bolt is slackened; if access to the correct Skoda special tool is not possible, a simple home-made tool using basic materials may be fabricated **(see Tool Tip)**.

14 Using the home-made tool, brace the camshaft sprocket. Slacken and remove the retaining bolt.

15 Slide the camshaft sprocket from the end of the camshaft **(see illustration)**.

16 With the sprocket removed, look for signs of oil leaking from the camshaft oil seal. If necessary, refer to Section 8 and renew it.

17 Wipe the sprocket and camshaft mating surfaces clean.

Refitting

18 Offer up the sprocket to the camshaft, ensuring that the tooth in the rear of the sprocket hub engages with the keyway in the end of the camshaft.

19 Counterholding the camshaft sprocket as

for removal, fit and tighten the camshaft sprocket bolt to the specified torque, and then through the specified angle **(see illustration)**.

20 Working from Sections 2 and 4, check that the engine is still set to TDC on No 1 cylinder, then refit and tension the timing belt. Refit the timing belt covers and all other components removed for access, as described in Section 4. Reconnect the battery negative lead.

Crankshaft timing belt sprocket

Removal

21 With reference to Sections 2 and 4, remove the timing belt covers and set the engine to TDC on No 1 cylinder.

22 The crankshaft sprocket must be held stationary whilst its retaining bolt is slackened. If access to the correct Skoda flywheel locking tool is not available, lock the crankshaft in position by removing the starter motor, as described in Chapter 5A, to expose the flywheel ring gear. Then get an assistant insert a stout lever between the gear teeth and the transmission bellhousing whilst the sprocket retaining bolt is slackened.

23 Holding the engine against rotation as described in the previous paragraph, slacken the crankshaft sprocket bolt - do not remove it yet.

24 Ensure that the engine is still set to TDC, then slacken the timing belt tensioner centre nut and rotate it anti-clockwise to relieve the tension on the timing belt. Carefully slide the timing belt off the crankshaft sprocket.

25 Withdraw the bolt and slide off the crankshaft sprocket **(see illustrations)**.

26 With the sprocket removed, examine the crankshaft oil seal for signs of leaking. If necessary, refer to Section 9 and renew it.

5.15 Removing the camshaft sprocket - note the alignment tooth and keyway (arrowed)

5.19 Tighten the camshaft sprocket bolt to the specified torque, and then through the specified angle

5.25a Remove the crankshaft sprocket bolt . . .

5.25b . . . then slide the sprocket off the crankshaft

5.28 Crankshaft sprocket alignment tooth and keyway (arrowed)

27 Wipe the sprocket and crankshaft mating surfaces clean.

Refitting

28 Offer up the sprocket, engaging the tooth on the inside of the sprocket with the keyway in the end of the crankshaft **(see illustration)**. Insert a new bolt, and tighten it hand-tight at this stage. **Note:** *Due to the high torque to which the sprocket bolt must be tightened, there is a danger that the crankshaft sprocket may turn as it is tightened, particularly if the tool used to lock the flywheel ring gear slips. For this reason, it is recommended that the final tightening of the crankshaft sprocket bolt is delayed until after the timing belt has been fitted.*

29 Working from Sections 2 and 4, check that the engine is still set to TDC on No 1 cylinder, then refit and tension the timing belt.

30 Fit the new crankshaft sprocket bolt, and

5.30a Tighten the bolt to the specified torque . . .

5.30b . . . and then through the specified angle - use an angle gauge if available, to ensure accuracy

lightly oil the bolt threads. Tighten the bolt to the specified torque, then through the specified angle, using the method described in paragraph 22 to lock the flywheel **(see illustrations)**. If the engine is out of the car, have an assistant support the engine as the bolt is tightened - a great deal of effort will be required, and the engine may tip over.

31 Refit the timing belt covers and all other components removed for access, as described in Section 4. Reconnect the battery negative lead.

Coolant pump timing belt sprocket

32 The coolant pump sprocket is an integral part of the coolant pump assembly, and cannot be removed or renewed separately. To remove the coolant pump, refer to Chapter 3.

6 Auxiliary drivebelt - removal, refitting and tensioning

General information

1 Depending on the vehicle specification, the auxiliary drivebelt, which is driven from a pulley mounted on the crankshaft, will provide drive for the alternator, power steering pump and (on vehicles with air conditioning), the refrigerant compressor.

2 The ribbed auxiliary belt may be fitted with an automatic tensioning device, depending on its run (and hence the number of components it is driving). Otherwise, the belt is tensioned

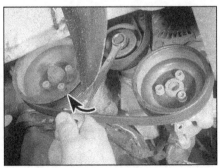

6.8 Rotate the auxiliary drivebelt tensioner clockwise to relieve the tension on the belt

by the alternator mountings, which have an in-built tensioning spring.

3 On refitting, the auxiliary belt must be tensioned correctly, to ensure correct operation under all conditions, and for prolonged service life.

Removal

4 Park the vehicle on a level surface, apply the handbrake and chock the rear wheels. Loosen the right-hand front wheel bolts.

5 Raise the front of the car, rest it securely on axle stands and remove the right-hand front roadwheel.

6 Remove the screws securing the cover fitted over the drivebelt.

7 Examine the ribbed belt for manufacturer's markings, indicating the direction of rotation. If none are present, make some using typist's correction fluid or a dab of paint - do not cut or score the belt in any way.

Models with automatic tensioner

8 Fit a ring spanner to the tensioner centre nut, and rotate the assembly clockwise, against its spring tension **(see illustration)**.

Models without automatic tensioner

9 Slacken the alternator upper and lower mounting bolts by between one and two turns.

10 Push the alternator down to its stop against the spring tension, so that it rotates around its uppermost mounting.

All models

11 Pull the belt off the alternator pulley, then release it from the remaining pulleys **(see illustration)**.

6.11 Removing the auxiliary drivebelt

7.1 Loosen and remove the socket-headed retaining bolts . . .

Refitting and tensioning

Caution: Observe the manufacturer's direction of rotation markings on the belt, when refitting.

12 Pass the ribbed belt underneath the crankshaft pulley, ensuring that the ribs seat in the channels on the surface of the pulley.

Models with automatic tensioner

13 Fit a ring spanner to the tensioner centre nut, and rotate the assembly clockwise, against its spring tension.

14 Pass the flat side of the belt underneath the tensioner roller, then fit it over the pulleys. Ensure that the belt ribs engage correctly with the pulley grooves.

15 Release the spanner and allow the tensioner roller to bear against the flat side of the belt.

Models without automatic tensioner

16 Repeatedly push the alternator down to its stop against the spring tension, so that it rotates around its uppermost mounting, and check that it moves back freely when released. If necessary, slacken the alternator mounting bolts by a further half a turn.

17 Keep the alternator pushed down against its stop, pass the belt over the alternator pulley, then release the alternator and allow it to tension the belt.

18 Start the engine and allow it to idle for about 10 seconds, leaving the alternator mounting bolts slackened.

19 Switch the engine off, then tighten first the lower, then the upper alternator mounting bolts to the specified torque.

7.2 . . . and lift off the camshaft cover

All models

20 Refit the drivebelt cover, and tighten the screws securely.

21 Refit the right-hand front roadwheel and lower the car to the ground. Tighten the roadwheel bolts to the specified torque.

7 Camshaft cover - removal and refitting

Removal

1 Slacken and withdraw the three socket-headed camshaft cover retaining bolts **(see illustration)**.

2 Lift the cover away from the cylinder head **(see illustration)**. If it sticks, do not attempt to lever it off with an implement - instead free it by working around the cover and tapping it lightly with a soft-faced mallet.

3 Recover the camshaft cover gasket; renew the gasket if damage or deterioration is evident.

4 Clean the mating surfaces of the cylinder head and camshaft cover thoroughly, removing all traces of oil and old gasket - take care to avoid damaging the surfaces as you do this.

Refitting

5 Refit the camshaft cover by following the removal procedure in reverse, noting the following points:

a) Before fitting the gasket, apply a smear of suitable sealant to the joint between the camshaft bearing caps at either end, and

the cylinder head.

b) Ensure that the gasket is correctly seated on the cylinder head, and take care to avoid displacing it as the camshaft cover is lowered into position.

c) Tighten the camshaft cover retaining bolts to the specified torque.

6 After the engine is next run, check for leaks.

8 Camshaft oil seal - renewal

1 Refer to Section 6 and remove the auxiliary drivebelt.

2 With reference to Sections 2, 4 and 5 of this Chapter, remove the crankshaft pulley and timing belt covers, then set the engine to TDC on No 1 cylinder and remove the timing belt, timing belt tensioner and camshaft sprocket.

3 After removing the retaining bolts, lift the timing belt inner cover away from the cylinder head - this will expose the oil seal **(see illustrations)**.

4 Remove the oil seal, using the same method as that described for the crankshaft oil seal removal, in Section 9.

5 Clean out the seal housing and sealing surface of the camshaft by wiping it with a lint-free cloth - avoid using solvents that may enter the cylinder head and affect component lubrication. Remove any swarf or burrs that may cause the seal to leak.

6 Lubricate the lip of the new oil seal with clean engine oil, and push it over the camshaft until it is positioned above its housing.

7 Using a hammer and a socket of suitable diameter, drive the seal squarely into its housing. **Note:** *Select a socket that bears only on the hard outer surface of the seal, not the inner lip which can easily be damaged.*

8 Refit the timing belt inner cover to the cylinder head, and tighten the retaining bolts to the specified torque.

9 With reference to Sections 2, 4 and 5 of this Chapter, refit the camshaft sprocket and the timing belt tensioner, then refit and tension the timing belt. On completion, refit the timing belt outer covers and other removed components.

10 With reference to Section 6, refit and tension the auxiliary drivebelt.

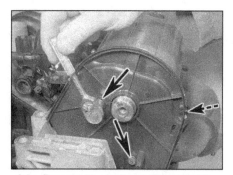

8.3a Remove two bolts on the end of the engine, and one at the front (arrowed) . . .

8.3b . . . and take off the timing belt inner cover

8.3c Camshaft oil seal (arrowed)

9.4 Drill a small hole into the old seal . . .

9.5a . . . then insert a self-tapping screw . . .

9.5b . . . and pull out the seal using pliers

9 Crankshaft oil seals - renewal

Crankshaft front oil seal

1 Drain the engine oil - see Chapter 1A.
2 Refer to Section 6 and remove the auxiliary drivebelt.
3 With reference to Sections 2, 4 and 5 of this Chapter, remove the crankshaft pulley, timing belt outer covers, timing belt and crankshaft sprocket.
4 Note the depth to which the old seal has been fitted, relative to its housing. Drill a small hole into the existing oil seal **(see illustration)**. Take great care to avoid drilling through into the seal housing or the crankshaft sealing surface. It may be necessary to drill another hole, if difficulty is experienced in pulling out the old seal, but we found that one hole was sufficient.
5 Thread a self-tapping screw into the hole, and using a pair of pliers, pull on the head of the screw to extract the oil seal **(see illustrations)**.
6 Clean out the seal housing and sealing surface of the crankshaft by wiping it with a lint-free cloth - avoid using solvents that may enter the crankcase and affect component lubrication. Remove any swarf or burrs that could cause the seal to leak.
7 Tape over the end of the crankshaft, to protect the new oil seal as it is fitted.
8 Lubricate the lip of the new oil seal with

clean engine oil, and position it over the housing **(see illustration)**.
9 The new seal must be fitted to the same depth as was noted for the old seal. Using a hammer and a socket of suitable diameter, drive the seal squarely into its housing. **Note:** *Select a socket that bears only on the hard outer surface of the seal, not the inner lip which can easily be damaged.* As an alternative, place the old oil seal over the new seal, then fit the sprocket and its bolt, and tighten the bolt a little at a time to press the new seal into position **(see illustrations)**. Be sure to remove the old oil seal before finally fitting and tightening the sprocket and its bolt.
10 With reference to Sections 2, 4 and 5 of this Chapter, refit the crankshaft sprocket, then refit and tension the timing belt. On completion, refit the timing belt outer covers, crankshaft pulley and other removed components.
11 The remainder of the refitting procedure is a reversal of removal, as follows:
a) With reference to Section 6, refit and tension the auxiliary drivebelt.
b) Refer to Chapter 1A and refill the engine with the correct grade and quantity of oil.

Crankshaft front oil seal housing - gasket renewal

12 Proceed as described in paragraphs 1 to 3 above, then refer to Section 14 and remove the sump.
13 Progressively slacken and then remove the oil seal housing retaining bolts from the cylinder block.

14 Lift the housing away from the cylinder block, together with the crankshaft oil seal, using a twisting motion to ease the seal along the crankshaft.
15 Recover the old gasket from the seal housing and the cylinder block. If it has disintegrated, scrape the remains off with a trimming knife blade. Take care to avoid damaging the mating surfaces.
16 Recover the sealing bush which fits between the seal housing and the cylinder block. If the bush shows signs of damage or deterioration, lightly oil and fit a new one to the oil seal housing.
17 Prise the old oil seal from the housing using a stout screwdriver.
18 Wipe the oil seal housing clean, and check it visually for signs of distortion or cracking. Lay the housing on a work surface, with the mating surface face down. Press in a new oil seal, using a block of wood as a press to ensure that the seal enters the housing squarely.
19 Smear the crankcase mating surface with multi-purpose sealant, and lay the new gasket in position.
20 Pad the end of the crankshaft with a layer of PVC tape; this will protect the oil seal as it is being fitted.
21 Lubricate the inner lip of the crankshaft oil seal with clean engine oil, then offer up the seal and its housing to the end of the crankshaft. Ease the seal along the shaft using a twisting motion, until the housing is flush with the crankcase. Ensure that the sealing bush fitted to the oil seal housing engages correctly with the crankcase.

9.8 Offering up the new oil seal - tape over the end of the crankshaft, to prevent the seal catching on the keyway

9.9a Fit the old seal over the new seal . . .

9.9b . . . then fit the crankshaft sprocket and bolt, and use the sprocket to press the new seal into place

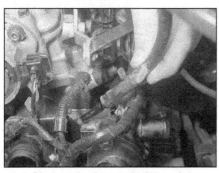

10.7 Disconnect the expansion tank hose, and all remaining hoses, from the thermostat housing

22 Insert new retaining bolts and tighten them progressively to the specified torque. *Caution: The housing is fabricated from a light alloy, and may be distorted if the bolts are not tightened progressively.*

23 Refer to Section 14 and refit the sump.

24 With reference to Sections 2, 4 and 5 of this Chapter, refit the crankshaft sprocket, then refit and tension the timing belt. On completion, refit the timing belt outer covers, crankshaft pulley and other removed components.

25 The remainder of the refitting procedure is a reversal of removal, as follows:
a) With reference to Section 6, refit and tension the auxiliary drivebelt.
b) Refer to Chapter 1A and refill the engine with the correct grade and quantity of oil.

Crankshaft rear oil seal (flywheel end)

26 Drain the engine oil - see Chapter 1A.

27 Refer to Chapter 7 and remove the transmission from the engine.

28 Refer to Section 12 of this Chapter and remove the flywheel, then refer to Chapter 6 and remove the clutch friction plate and pressure plate.

29 Progressively slacken and then remove the oil seal housing retaining bolts.

30 Lift the housing away from the cylinder block, together with the crankshaft oil seal, using a twisting motion to ease the seal along the shaft.

31 The rear oil seal is not available separately from the housing, and the seal and housing must therefore be renewed complete. The

original housing had an integral gasket - the replacement part does not, and a separate gasket must be obtained.

32 Thoroughly clean the mating surface of the cylinder block. Any sealant or old gasket can be scraped off with a trimming knife blade. Take care to avoid damaging the mating surface.

33 Smear the crankcase mating surface with multi-purpose sealant, and lay the new gasket in position.

34 A protective plastic sleeve is supplied with genuine Skoda crankshaft oil seals; when fitted over the end of the crankshaft, the sleeve prevents damage to the inner lip of the oil seal as it is being fitted. Use PVC tape to pad the end of the crankshaft if a sleeve is not available.

35 Lubricate the inner lip of the crankshaft oil seal with clean engine oil, then offer up the seal and its housing to the end of the crankshaft. Ease the seal along the shaft using a twisting motion, until the housing is flush with the crankcase.

36 Insert new retaining bolts and tighten them progressively to the specified torque. *Caution: The housing is fabricated from a light alloy, and may be distorted if the bolts are not tightened progressively.*

37 Refer to Section 14 and refit the sump.

38 Refer to Section 12 of this Chapter and refit the flywheel, then refer to Chapter 6 and refit the clutch friction plate and pressure plate.

39 Referring to Chapter 7, refit the transmission to the engine.

40 Refer to Chapter 1A and refill the engine with the correct grade and quantity of oil.

10 Cylinder head and manifolds - removal, separation and refitting

Removal

1 Select a solid, level surface to park the vehicle upon. Give yourself enough space to move around it easily.

2 Disconnect the battery negative lead, and position It away from the terminal. **Note:** *If the vehicle has a security-coded radio, check that you have a copy of the code number before*

disconnecting the battery cable. Refer to your Skoda dealer if in doubt.

3 Referring to Chapter 1A, drain the cooling system.

4 Remove the air cleaner and air inlet components as described in Chapter 4B. Pull off the warm-air duct from the air cleaner housing and the stub on the exhaust manifold collector plate.

5 Also in Chapter 4B, depressurise the fuel injection system.

6 Referring to Chapter 5B, remove the distributor cap, HT leads, rotor arm and flash shield. This is not essential to allow the cylinder head to be removed (if preferred, just the HT lead to the ignition coil can be disconnected), but it allows easier access, and should prevent damage to the distributor as the head is lifted away.

7 Referring to Chapter 3 if necessary, loosen the hose clips and disconnect the coolant hoses from the thermostat housing **(see illustration)**.

8 Disconnect the following electrical connections, labelling as necessary for refitting:
a) *The knock sensor and lambda sensor, both in a bracket above the flywheel. Slide the plugs out of the bracket.*
b) *The inlet air temperature/pressure sensor from the inlet manifold.*
c) *The throttle valve control unit.*
d) *The Hall sensor wiring plug from the distributor (see illustration).*
e) *The oil pressure switch from the rear of the cylinder head (see illustration).*
f) *The injector plug(s) and wiring harness from the inlet manifold, as necessary (refer to Chapter 4B). Unclip and disconnect the harness, and lay it to one side.*
g) *The coolant temperature sensor on the thermostat housing.*
h) *Once all the wiring plugs have been disconnected, release the wiring harness from any retaining ties, and move it to one side.*

9 Disconnect the following hoses:
a) *The inlet manifold hose leading to the charcoal canister solenoid valve on the left-hand inner wing (see illustration).*
b) *The brake servo vacuum hose from the inlet manifold.*

10.8a Disconnecting the distributor Hall sensor wiring plug . . .

10.8b . . . and the oil pressure switch wire

10.9 Disconnect the charcoal canister hose from the inlet manifold

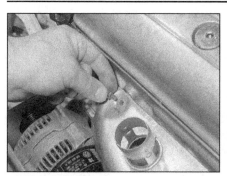

10.15a Remove the warm-air collector plate bolts . . .

10.15b . . . then lift off the plate . . .

10.15c . . . and remove the three exhaust manifold-to-downpipe nuts

c) *The fuel supply and return hoses from their connections at the fuel rail, noting the direction-of-flow and colour coding markings. Anticipate some loss of fuel. Plug or seal off the hose ends, to reduce further fuel loss and prevent the ingress of dirt.*

10 At the rear of the thermostat housing, slide out the wire clip which joins the thermostat housing to the coolant pump supply pipe running along the back of the engine block. Disconnect the remaining coolant hoses from the thermostat housing, noting their locations.

11 Refer to Section 6 and remove the auxiliary drivebelt.

12 With reference to Sections 2 and 4 of this Chapter, remove the crankshaft pulley and timing belt outer covers. Disengage the timing belt from the camshaft sprocket.

13 Once the timing belt has been disengaged, the engine can be raised back into its original position, and the right-hand engine mounting reconnected while the cylinder head is removed.

14 To avoid any possibility of piston-to-valve contact during cylinder head removal, it is recommended that the crankshaft be turned back a few degrees away from the TDC position, to take the pistons down the bores.

15 Remove the warm-air collector plate from the top of the exhaust manifold, then disconnect the exhaust downpipe from the manifold **(see illustrations)**. Recover the gasket.

16 Slacken and remove the bolt securing the engine oil dipstick tube to the rear of the cylinder head. Where applicable, unbolt and remove the inlet manifold support bracket.

17 Disconnect the accelerator cable as described in Chapter 4B.

18 Remove the camshaft cover as described in Section 7.

19 Working in the sequence shown, progressively loosen the cylinder head bolts by half a turn at a time, using a suitable socket, until all bolts can be unscrewed by hand **(see illustrations)**.

20 Check that nothing remains connected to the cylinder head, then lift the head away from the cylinder block; seek assistance if possible, as it is a heavy assembly, especially if it is being removed complete with the manifolds.

21 Remove the gasket from the top of the block. Do not discard the gasket yet.

22 If the cylinder head is to be dismantled for overhaul, refer to Chapter 2D.

Manifold separation

23 Inlet manifold removal and refitting is described in Chapter 4B.

24 Progressively slacken and remove the exhaust manifold retaining nuts; discard the old nuts if they are in poor condition. Lift the manifold away from the cylinder head, and recover the gaskets.

25 Ensure that the mating surfaces are completely clean, then refit the exhaust manifold, using new gaskets. Tighten the new retaining nuts to the specified torque.

Preparation for refitting

26 The mating faces of the cylinder head and cylinder block/crankcase must be perfectly clean before refitting the head. Use a hard plastic or wood scraper to remove all traces of gasket and carbon; also clean the piston crowns. Take particular care during the cleaning operations, as aluminium alloy is easily damaged. Also, make sure that the carbon is not allowed to enter the oil and water passages - this is particularly important for the lubrication system, as carbon could block the oil supply to the engine's components. Using adhesive tape and paper, seal the water, oil and bolt holes in the cylinder block/crankcase.

27 Check the mating surfaces of the cylinder block/crankcase and the cylinder head for nicks, deep scratches and other damage. If slight, they may be removed carefully with a file, but if excessive, machining may be the only alternative to renewal.

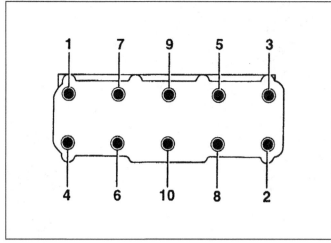

10.19a Cylinder head bolt LOOSENING sequence

10.19b Loosen the bolts by half a turn at a time, using a suitable splined socket

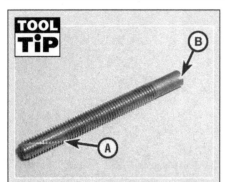

TOOL TIP

If a tap is not available, make a home-made substitute by cutting a slot (A) down the threads of one of the old cylinder head bolts. After use, the bolt head can be cut off, and the shank can then be used as an alignment dowel to assist cylinder head refitting. Cut a screwdriver slot (B) in the top of the bolt, to allow it to be unscrewed

28 If warpage of the cylinder head gasket surface is suspected, use a straight-edge to check it for distortion. Refer to Part D of this Chapter if necessary.
29 Check the condition of the cylinder head bolts, and particularly their threads, whenever they are removed. Wash the bolts in suitable solvent, and wipe them dry. Check each for any sign of visible wear or damage, renewing any bolt if necessary. Measure the length of each bolt, to check for stretching (although this is not a conclusive test, if all bolts have stretched by the same amount). Skoda do not actually specify that the bolts must be renewed, however, it is strongly recommended that the bolts should be renewed as a complete set whenever they are disturbed.
30 Clean out the cylinder head bolt drillings using a suitable tap. If a tap is not available, make a home-made substitute (see Tool Tip).
31 It is possible for the piston crowns to

10.32 Ensure that the gasket part number and TOP markings are face up

strike and damage the valve heads, if the camshaft is rotated with the timing belt removed and the crankshaft set to TDC. For this reason, the crankshaft must be set to a position other than TDC on No 1 cylinder, before the cylinder head is refitted. Set the crankshaft to TDC on No 1 cylinder, using the information in Section 2, then turn the crankshaft back by a few degrees, away from the TDC position. If preferred, for maximum safety, the pistons can be positioned halfway down their bores, with No 1 piston on its upstroke - ie 90° before TDC.

Refitting

32 Check that the new gasket is the same type as the one which was removed. Lay the new head gasket on the cylinder block, ensuring that the manufacturer's TOP and/or part number markings are face up (see illustration). Do not handle the gasket excessively before it is fitted, or it may become damaged.

HAYNES HiNT *Because no locating dowels are fitted, it may prove difficult to accurately align the head on the block when refitting. To overcome this, two of the old cylinder head bolts can be modified*

to act as locating dowels. Cut the heads off two of the bolts, and then cut a slot in the top of the bolt, so that a flat-bladed screwdriver may be used to unscrew the bolts from the block once the head is placed over them. Screw the two 'dowels' into place either end of the head, then lower the head into position over them. Fit two or more of the new head bolts to locate the head, then unscrew the dowels using a screwdriver.

33 Before fitting the cylinder head, check that the camshaft sprocket timing mark is aligned with the mark on the timing belt inner cover, as described in Section 2. Try to avoid turning the camshaft sprocket as the head is refitted.
34 With the help of an assistant, place the cylinder head and manifolds centrally on the cylinder block. Check that the head gasket is correctly seated before allowing the weight the full weight of the cylinder head to rest upon it.
35 Apply a smear of grease to the threads, and to the underside of the heads, of the cylinder head bolts; use a good-quality high-melting point grease.
36 Carefully enter each bolt into its relevant hole (do not drop them in) and screw in, by hand only, until finger-tight.
37 Working progressively and in the sequence shown, tighten the cylinder head bolts to their Stage 1 torque setting, using a torque wrench and suitable socket (see illustrations).
38 Working in the given sequence, tighten the bolts to their Stage 2 torque setting.
39 Now angle-tighten the bolts, in the same sequence, through the specified Stage 3 angle, using a socket and extension bar. It is recommended that an angle-measuring gauge is used during this stage of the tightening, to ensure accuracy (see illustration).

10.37a Cylinder head bolt TIGHTENING sequence

10.37b Tighten all bolts in sequence to the specified torque

10.39 Use an angle gauge to ensure accuracy when angle-tightening the cylinder head bolts

40 If a gauge is not available, use white paint to make alignment marks between the bolt head and cylinder head prior to tightening; the marks can then be used to check that the bolt has been rotated through the correct angle during tightening. Repeat the exercise for the Stage 4 setting.

41 Refit the camshaft cover, as described in Section 7.

42 If removed, refit the distributor components as described in Chapter 5B.

43 Refit the hose securing clip for the coolant pump supply pipe-to-thermostat housing connection.

44 Reconnect the accelerator cable, and adjust if necessary, as described in Chapter 4B.

45 Fit the dipstick tube back onto the head, and tighten the securing bolt.

46 Reconnect the exhaust front pipe to the manifold, using a new gasket - refer to Chapter 4D. Refit the warm air collector plate.

47 Refer to Section 2 and follow the procedure for setting the engine to TDC on No 1 cylinder with the timing belt removed.

48 Support the engine, then disconnect the right-hand engine mounting and lower the engine down slightly. Referring to Section 4, refit the timing belt and outer covers, and the crankshaft pulley.

49 The engine can now be raised back into position, and the right-hand engine mounting reconnected as described in Section 4.

50 Refit and tension the auxiliary drivebelt as described in Section 6.

51 The remainder of the refitting sequence is a reversal of the removal procedure, as follows:

a) *Reconnect the fuel hoses, coolant hoses, brake servo vacuum hose and charcoal canister hose.*
b) *Reconnect the wiring plugs disconnected in paragraph 8.*
c) *Refit the air cleaner housing as described in Chapter 4B.*
d) *Refill the cooling system as described in Chapter 1A, and check the oil level as described in Weekly checks.*
e) *Restore the battery connection.*

11 Hydraulic tappets - operation check

> ⚠ *Warning: After fitting hydraulic tappets, wait a minimum of 30 minutes (or preferably, leave overnight) before starting the engine, to allow the tappets time to settle, otherwise the pistons may strike the valve heads.*

1 The hydraulic tappets are self-adjusting, and require no attention whilst in service.

2 If the hydraulic tappets become excessively noisy, their operation can be checked as described below.

3 Run the engine until it reaches its normal operating temperature. Increase the engine speed to around 2500 rpm (fast idle) for about 2 minutes, then switch off the engine. Refer to Section 7 and remove the camshaft cover.

4 Rotate the camshaft by turning the crankshaft with a socket and wrench, until the first cam lobe over No 1 cylinder is pointing upwards.

5 Using a feeler blade, measure the clearance between the base of the cam lobe and the top of the tappet. If the clearance is greater than 0.2mm, then the tappet is defective and must be renewed.

6 If the clearance is less than 0.2 mm, press down on the top of the tappet, until it is felt to contact the top of the valve stem **(see illustration)**. Use a wooden or plastic implement that will not damage the surface of the tappet.

7 If the tappet travels more than 0.2 mm before making contact, then it is defective and must be renewed.

8 Hydraulic tappet removal and refitting is described as part of the cylinder head overhaul sequence - see Chapter 2D for details.

12 Flywheel - removal, inspection and refitting

Removal

1 Remove the transmission and clutch as described in Chapters 7 and 6 respectively.

2 Lock the flywheel in position using a home-made locking tool, fabricated from a piece of scrap metal. Bolt it to one of the transmission bellhousing mounting holes **(see illustration)**. Mark the position of the flywheel with respect to the crankshaft using a dab of paint.

3 Slacken and withdraw the flywheel mounting bolts, then lift off the flywheel.

Caution: Get an assistant to help, as the flywheel is extremely heavy.

Inspection

4 If the flywheel's clutch mating surface is deeply scored, cracked or otherwise damaged, the flywheel must be renewed. However, it may be possible to have it surface-ground; seek the advice of a Skoda dealer or engine reconditioning specialist.

5 If the ring gear is badly worn or has missing teeth, the flywheel must be renewed.

Refitting

6 Clean the mating surfaces of the flywheel and crankshaft. Remove any remaining locking compound from the threads of the crankshaft holes, using the correct-size tap, if available.

> **HAYNES HiNT** *If a suitable tap is not available, cut two slots down the threads of one of the old flywheel bolts with a hacksaw, and use the bolt to remove the locking compound from the threads.*

7 If the new flywheel retaining bolts are not supplied with their threads already pre-coated, apply a suitable thread-locking compound to the threads of each bolt **(see illustration)**.

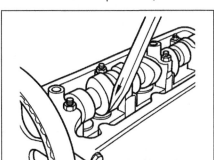

11.6 Press down on the tappet, until it contacts the top of the valve stem

12.2 Flywheel locked in position with a home-made tool

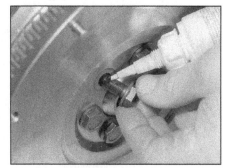

12.7 Apply locking fluid to the new flywheel bolts, if necessary

12.9 Tighten the flywheel bolts to the specified torque

8 Offer up the flywheel to the crankshaft, using the alignment marks made during removal, and fit the new retaining bolts.
9 Lock the flywheel using the method employed on dismantling, and tighten the retaining bolts to the specified torque **(see illustration)**.
10 Refit the clutch as described in Chapter 6. Remove the locking tool, and refit the transmission as described in Chapter 7.

13 Engine/transmission mountings - inspection and renewal

Inspection

1 If improved access is required, raise the front of the car and support it securely on axle stands.

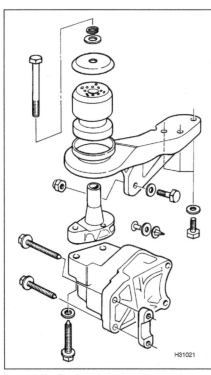

13.7b Engine right-hand mounting components

2 Check the mounting rubbers to see if they are cracked, hardened or separated from the metal at any point; renew the mounting if any such damage or deterioration is evident.
3 Check that all the mounting's fasteners are securely tightened; use a torque wrench to check if possible.
4 Using a large screwdriver or a crowbar, check for wear in the mounting by carefully levering against it to check for free play. Where this is not possible, enlist the aid of an assistant to move the engine/transmission back and forth, or from side to side, while you watch the mounting. While some free play is to be expected even from new components, excessive wear should be obvious. If excessive free play is found, check first that the fasteners are correctly secured, then renew any worn components as described below.

Renewal

Right-hand mounting

5 Disconnect the battery negative lead, and position it away from the terminal.
6 Support the weight of the engine from above using a hoist or lifting beam, or support it from below using a securely-located trolley jack and suitable block of wood underneath the sump. Do not jack directly under the sump without using a block of wood, or the sump may be damaged.
7 With the engine supported from above or below, slacken and withdraw the upper through-bolt, and separate the engine mounting. The rubber mounting can now be dismantled - take note of the fitted order and orientation of all components **(see illustrations)**.
8 The remaining bolts can now be removed, and the upper part of the mounting removed from the inner wing.
9 If required, the lower part of the mounting can be removed from the engine block after the timing belt covers have been removed (see Section 4).
10 Refitting is a reversal of removal, noting the following points:
a) Use new bolts, and apply a little oil to their threads before fitting.
b) Tighten all bolts to the specified torque, where given.

14.6 Removing the sump bolts (seen with engine removed and inverted, for clarity)

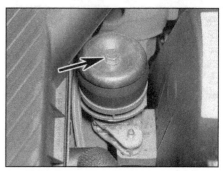

13.7a Engine right-hand mounting - through-bolt arrowed

Left-hand mounting

11 Refer to Chapter 2A, Section 12.

Rear mounting

12 Refer to Chapter 2A, Section 12.

14 Sump - removal and refitting

Removal

1 Park the vehicle on a level surface, apply the handbrake and chock the rear wheels.
2 Raise the front of the vehicle, and rest it securely on axle stands or wheel ramps; refer to *Jacking and vehicle support*.
3 Disconnect the battery negative lead, and position it away from the terminal.
4 Refer to Chapter 1A and drain the engine oil.
5 Disconnect the exhaust system downpipe from the exhaust manifold, as described in Chapter 4D. By releasing the exhaust system from its mountings, it should be possible to lower the system sufficiently to gain clearance to lower the sump. Take care that the wiring for the lambda sensor is not strained as the exhaust is lowered - disconnect the wiring plug if necessary.
6 Working around the outside of the sump, progressively slacken and withdraw the sump retaining bolts **(see illustration)**.
7 Break the joint by striking the sump with the palm of your hand, then lower the sump and withdraw it from underneath the vehicle.
8 While the sump is removed, take the opportunity to check the oil pump pick-up/strainer for signs of clogging or disintegration. If necessary, remove the pump as described in Section 15, and clean or renew the strainer.

Refitting

9 Clean all traces of sealant or old gasket, as applicable, from the mating surfaces of the cylinder block/crankcase and sump, then use a clean rag to wipe out the sump.
10 Ensure that the sump and cylinder block/crankcase mating surfaces are clean and dry, then apply a 2 to 3 mm bead of

suitable silicone sealant to the sump mating surface. Run the bead of sealant around the inside of the bolt holes.

 Warning: Take care not to apply excessive amounts of sealant, in the hope of obtaining a better seal - if too much is applied, the excess may enter the sump and then block the oil pump strainer, causing oil starvation.

11 The sump should be offered into position immediately, and the retaining bolts tightened hand-tight initially.

> **HAYNES HiNT** To make aligning the sump easier, obtain two or three M6 studs, and screw them by a few threads into opposite sides of the cylinder block/crankcase mating surface. The sump can be offered into position and fitted over the studs, then the remaining sump bolts can be fitted and hand-tightened. Remove the studs, and fit the rest of the sump bolts.

12 Progressively tighten the sump bolts to the specified torque. Refer to the sealant manufacturer's advice on the length of time required for the sealant to set. Typically, it is advisable to wait for several hours before filling the engine with oil. If the car is to be left for some time with no oil in the sump, ensure that the battery remains disconnected, so that no attempt is made to start the engine.

13 Refit the exhaust downpipe as described in Chapter 4D.

14 Lower the car to the ground, then refer to Chapter 1A and refill the engine with the specified grade and quantity of oil.

15 Restore the battery connection, then run the engine and check for leaks.

15.3 Oil pump components

1 Crankshaft sprocket
2 Oil pump
3 Mounting bolts
4 Guide rail (not fitted to all models)
5 Guide rail bolts
6 Drive chain

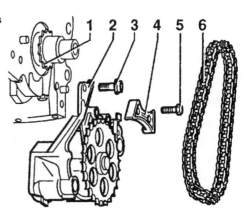

15 Oil pump and pickup - removal, inspection and refitting

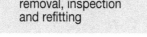

Removal

1 Refer to Section 14 and remove the sump from the crankcase.

2 With reference to Section 9, remove the front (timing belt end) crankshaft oil seal and housing.

3 Slacken and remove the bolts securing the oil pump to the timing belt end of the crankcase **(see illustration)**.

4 Remove the bolts securing the oil pump pickup to the crankcase bracket.

5 Disengage the pump sprocket from the drive chain, and remove the oil pump and pickup from the engine.

Inspection

6 Remove the screws from the mating flange, and lift off the pickup tube and oil pump cover. Recover the O-ring seal, where fitted.

7 Clean the pump thoroughly, and inspect the gear teeth for signs of damage or wear.

8 Check the condition of the oil pump drive chain; if the links appear excessively worn or are particularly loose, renew the chain.

9 Check the pump backlash by inserting a feeler blade between the meshed gear teeth; rotate the gears against each other slightly, to give the maximum clearance **(see illustration)**. Compare the measurement with the limit quoted in Specifications.

10 Check the pump axial clearance as follows. Lay an engineer's straight edge across the oil pump casing, then using a feeler blade, measure the clearance between the straight edge and the pump gears **(see illustration)**. Compare the measurement with the limit quoted in Specifications.

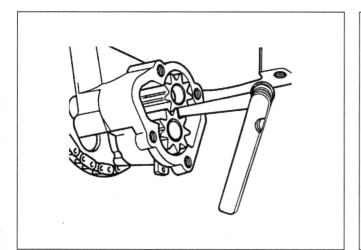

15.9 Checking oil pump backlash

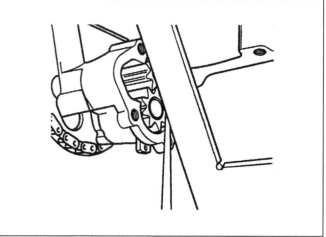

15.10 Checking oil pump axial clearance

11 If either measurement is outside of the specified limit, this indicates that the pump is worn and must be renewed.

Refitting

12 Reassemble the oil pickup to the oil pump, using a new O-ring seal, where applicable. Tighten the retaining bolts securely.

13 Offer up the oil pump to the end of the crankcase. Fit the drive chain over the oil pump sprocket, then engage it with the crankshaft sprocket.

14 Fit the pump mounting bolts to the timing belt end of the engine, and hand-tighten them.

15 Tension the drive chain by applying finger pressure to it at a point midway between the two sprockets **(see illustration)**. Adjust the position of the pump on its mountings until the tension is as given in the Specifications. On completion, tighten the mounting bolts to the specified torque.

16 Fit and tighten the fixings for the pickup tube to crankcase bracket.

17 With reference to Section 9, refit the crankshaft oil seal housing, using a new gasket and oil seal.

18 Refer to Section 14 and refit the sump.

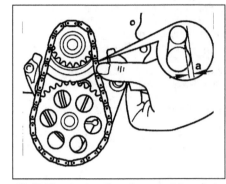

15.15 Tensioning the oil pump drive chain

For deflection (a), see Specifications

Chapter 2 Part C:
Diesel engine in-car repair procedures

Contents

Auxiliary drivebelt - removal, refitting and tensioning 6
Camshaft - removal and overhaul . . . . .See Chapter 2D
Camshaft cover - removal and refitting 7
Camshaft oil seal - renewal 8
Crankshaft oil seals - renewal 10
Cylinder compression test 3
Cylinder head - dismantling and overhaul . . . . .See Chapter 2D
Cylinder head and manifolds - removal, separation and refitting . . . 11
Engine mountings - inspection and renewal 14
Engine oil and filter - renewal .See Chapter 1B
Engine oil level - check . . . . .See *Weekly checks*
Flywheel - removal, inspection and refitting 13
General information 1
Hydraulic tappets - operation check 12
Intermediate shaft oil seal - renewal 9
Oil pump and pickup - removal and refitting 16
Sump - removal, inspection and refitting 15
Timing belt and outer covers - removal and refitting 4
Timing belt tensioner and sprockets - removal and refitting 5
Top Dead Centre (TDC) for No 1 piston - locating 2

Degrees of difficulty

Easy, suitable for novice with little experience	**Fairly easy,** suitable for beginner with some experience	**Fairly difficult,** suitable for competent DIY mechanic	**Difficult,** suitable for experienced DIY mechanic	**Very difficult,** suitable for expert DIY or professional

Specifications

General

Engine code	AEF
Bore	79.5 mm
Stroke	95.5 mm
Capacity	1896 cc
Firing order	1 - 3 - 4 - 2 (No 1 at timing belt end)
Direction of crankshaft rotation	Clockwise (when viewed from right-hand side of vehicle)
Compression ratio	22.5:1
Compression pressures:	
Wear limit	26 bar
Maximum difference between all cylinders	5 bar

Lubrication system

Oil pump type	Sump-mounted, driven indirectly from intermediate shaft
Normal operating oil pressure	2.0 bar minimum (at 2000 rpm, oil temperature 80°C)
Oil pump backlash	0.20 mm (wear limit)
Oil pump axial clearance	0.15 mm (wear limit)

Torque wrench settings

	Nm	lbf ft
Alternator mounting bracket-to-engine bolts	25	18
Auxiliary belt tensioner adjustment bolt	10	7
Auxiliary belt tensioner pulley bolt (left-hand thread)	20	15
Auxiliary belt tensioner-to-bracket bolts	20	15
Big-end bearing cap bolts*:		
Stage 1	30	22
Stage 2	Angle-tighten a further 90°	
Camshaft bearing cap nuts	20	15
Camshaft cover nuts	10	7
Camshaft sprocket bolt	45	33
Coolant pump pulley bolts	25	18
Crankshaft front oil seal housing bolts:		
Upper bolt	10	7
Lower bolts	25	18
Crankshaft main bearing cap bolts*:		
Stage 1	65	48
Stage 2	Angle-tighten a further 90°	
Crankshaft pulley bolts	25	18
Crankshaft rear oil seal housing bolts	10	7
Crankshaft sprocket bolt (oiled)*:		
Stage 1	90	66
Stage 2	Angle-tighten a further 90°	
Cylinder head bolts*:		
Stage 1	40	30
Stage 2	60	44
Stage 3	Angle-tighten a further 90°	
Stage 4	Angle-tighten a further 90°	
Dipstick tube		
Lower bolt	45	33
Upper bolt	10	7
Engine lifting eye bolt	20	15
Engine right-hand mounting-to-block bolts	45	33
Engine right-hand mounting-to-body bolts	50	37
Engine-to-transmission bolts	45	33
Engine/transmission left-hand mounting:		
Front bolt	60	44
Front nut	45	33
Rear bolt	45	33
Engine/transmission rear mounting:		
Front through-bolt/nut	45	33
Rear through-bolt/nut (to subframe)	77	57
Exhaust downpipe-to-manifold nuts	40	30
Exhaust gas recirculation valve bolts	25	18
Exhaust manifold-to-cylinder head nuts	25	18
Flywheel mounting bolts*:		
Stage 1	60	44
Stage 2	Angle-tighten a further 90°	
Glow plugs	25	18
Injection pump mounting nuts/bolts	25	18
Injection pump sprocket bolts	25	18
Injector pipe unions	25	18
Inlet pipe cover bolts	10	7
Inlet pipe/manifold securing bolts	25	18
Intermediate shaft oil seal housing bolts	25	18
Intermediate shaft sprocket bolt	45	33
Oil cooler retaining nut	25	18
Oil filter mounting bracket bolts	25	18
Oil pressure switch	25	18
Oil pump cover screws	10	7
Oil pump mounting bolts	25	18
Oil pump pickup tube screws	10	7
Piston oil jet (use suitable locking fluid)	10	7
Roadwheel bolts	110	81
Sump drain plug	30	22
Sump retaining bolts	20	15
Timing belt inner cover-to-cylinder head bolts	10	7
Timing belt lower cover bolts	10	7
Timing belt tensioner roller locknut	20	15
Vacuum pump clamp bolt	20	15

Use new nuts/bolt(s)

1 General information

Using this Chapter

This Part of Chapter 2 describes those repair procedures that can reasonably be carried out on the engine while it remains in the vehicle. If the engine has been removed from the vehicle and is being dismantled as described in Part D, any preliminary dismantling procedures can be ignored.

Note that while it may be possible physically to overhaul items such as the piston/connecting rod assemblies while the engine is in the vehicle, such tasks are not usually carried out as separate operations, and usually require the execution of several additional procedures (not to mention the cleaning of components and of oilways); for this reason, all such tasks are classed as major overhaul procedures, and are described in Part D of this Chapter.

Part D describes the removal of the engine/transmission from the vehicle and the full overhaul procedures that can then be carried out.

Engine description

The engine is a water-cooled, single overhead camshaft, in-line four cylinder unit with a cast-iron cylinder block and aluminium-alloy cylinder head. The engine is mounted transversely at the front of the vehicle, with the transmission bolted to the left-hand side.

The cylinder head carries the camshaft, which is driven by a toothed timing belt. It also houses the inlet and exhaust valves, which are closed by single springs, and which run in guides pressed into the cylinder head. The camshaft actuates the valves directly via hydraulic tappets, mounted in the cylinder head. The cylinder head contains integral oilways which supply and lubricate the tappets.

The diesel engine fitted to the Felicia is an indirect injection engine, and the cylinder head incorporates renewable swirl chambers.

The crankshaft is supported by five main bearings, and endfloat is controlled by a thrust bearing fitted between cylinders No 2 and 3.

A timing belt-driven intermediate shaft is fitted, which provides drive for the brake servo vacuum pump and the oil pump.

Engine coolant is circulated by a pump, driven by the auxiliary drivebelt. For details of the cooling system, refer to Chapter 3.

Lubricant is circulated under pressure by a pump, driven by the intermediate shaft. Oil is drawn from the sump through a strainer, and then forced through an externally-mounted, replaceable screw-on filter. From there, it is distributed to the cylinder head, where it lubricates the camshaft journals and hydraulic tappets, and also to the crankcase, where it lubricates the main bearings, connecting rod big- and small-ends, gudgeon pins and cylinder bores. Oil jets are fitted to the base of each cylinder - these spray oil onto the underside of the pistons, to improve cooling. An oil cooler, supplied with engine coolant, reduces the temperature of the oil before it re-enters the engine.

Repairs possible with the engine installed in the vehicle

The following operations can be performed without removing the engine:

a) Auxiliary drivebelt - removal and refitting.
b) Camshaft - removal and refitting. *
c) Camshaft oil seal - renewal.
d) Camshaft sprocket - removal and refitting.
e) Coolant pump - removal and refitting (refer to Chapter 3)
f) Crankshaft oil seals - renewal.
g) Crankshaft sprocket - removal and refitting.
h) Cylinder head - removal and refitting. *
i) Engine mountings - inspection and renewal.
j) Intermediate shaft oil seal - renewal.
k) Oil pump and pickup assembly - removal and refitting.
l) Sump - removal and refitting.
m) Timing belt, sprockets and cover - removal, inspection and refitting.

*Cylinder head dismantling procedures are in Chapter 2D, and also contain details of camshaft and hydraulic tappet removal.

Note: It is possible to remove the pistons and connecting rods (after removing the cylinder head and sump) without removing the engine from the vehicle. However, this procedure is not recommended. Work of this nature is more easily and thoroughly completed with the engine on the bench - refer to Chapter 2D.

2 Top Dead Centre (TDC) for No 1 piston - locating

1 Remove the camshaft cover, auxiliary drivebelt and timing belt outer covers as described in Sections 7, 6 and 4 respectively.
2 Remove the inspection bung from the transmission bellhousing. Rotate the crankshaft clockwise with a wrench and socket, or a spanner, until the mark machined onto the edge of the flywheel is in the centre of the inspection hole in the bellhousing **(see illustration)**.
3 To lock the engine in the TDC position, the camshaft (not the sprocket) and fuel injection pump sprocket must be secured in a reference position, using special locking tools. Improvised tools may be fabricated, but due to the exact measurements and machining involved, it is strongly recommended that a kit of locking tools is either borrowed or hired from a Skoda dealer, or purchased from a reputable tool manufacturer - for example, Sykes Pickavant produce a kit of camshaft and fuel injection pump sprocket locking tools specifically for the engine covered in this Chapter.
4 Engage the edge of the locking bar with the slot in the end of the camshaft **(see illustration)**.
5 With the locking bar still inserted, turn the camshaft slightly (by turning the crankshaft clockwise, as before), so that the locking bar rocks to one side, allowing one end of the bar to contact the cylinder head surface. At the other side of the locking bar, measure the gap between the end of the bar and the cylinder head using a feeler blade.
6 Turn the camshaft back slightly, then pull out the feeler blade. The idea now is to level the locking bar by inserting two feeler blades,

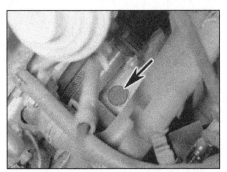

2.2a Remove the rubber plug (arrowed) . . .

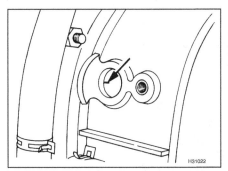

2.2b . . . to access the TDC '0' marking (arrowed) on the flywheel

2.4 Engage the locking bar with the slot in the camshaft

each with a thickness equal to *half* the originally measured gap, on either side of the camshaft between each end of the locking bar and the cylinder head **(see illustration)**. This centres the camshaft, and sets the valve timing in reference condition.

7 Insert the locking pin through the fuel injection pump sprocket alignment hole, and into the slot in the hub **(see illustration)**. This locks the fuel injection pump in a reference condition.

8 The engine is now set to TDC on No 1 cylinder.

3 Cylinder compression test

Compression test

Note: *A compression tester specifically designed for diesel engines must be used for this test.*

1 When engine performance is down, or if misfiring occurs, a compression test can provide diagnostic clues as to the engine's condition. If the test is performed regularly, it can give warning of trouble before any other symptoms become apparent.

2 A compression tester specifically intended for diesel engines must be used, because of the higher pressures involved. The tester is connected to an adapter which screws into the glow plug or injector hole. It is unlikely to be worthwhile buying such a tester for occasional use, but it may be possible to borrow or hire one - if not, have the test

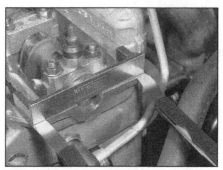

2.6 Camshaft centred and locked using locking bar and feeler gauges

performed by a garage.

3 Unless specific instructions to the contrary are supplied with the tester, observe the following points:

a) *The battery must be in a good state of charge, the air filter must be clean, and the engine should be at normal operating temperature.*

b) *All four injectors (or all four glow plugs) should be removed before starting the test. If removing the injectors, also remove the flame shield washers, otherwise they may be blown out.*

c) *The stop solenoid must be disconnected, to prevent the engine from running or fuel from being discharged.*

d) *Disconnect the main engine wiring harness connector multi-plug (behind the left-hand suspension strut turret) before starting the test.*

4 There is no need to hold the accelerator pedal down during the test, because the

diesel engine air inlet is not throttled.

5 Skoda specify wear limits for compression pressures - refer to the Specifications. Seek the advice of a Skoda dealer or other diesel specialist if in doubt as to whether a particular pressure reading is acceptable.

6 The cause of poor compression is less easy to establish on a diesel engine than on a petrol one. The effect of introducing oil into the cylinders (wet testing) is not conclusive, because there is a risk that the oil will sit in the swirl chamber, instead of passing to the rings. However, the following can be used as a rough guide to diagnosis.

7 All cylinders should produce very similar pressures; a difference of more than 5 bar between any two cylinders indicates the existence of a fault. Note that the compression should build up quickly in a healthy engine; low compression on the first stroke, followed by gradually-increasing pressure on successive strokes, indicates worn piston rings. A low compression reading on the first stroke, which does not build up during successive strokes, indicates leaking valves or a blown head gasket (a cracked head could also be the cause).

8 A low reading from two adjacent cylinders is almost certainly due to the head gasket having blown between them; the presence of coolant in the engine oil will confirm this.

9 If the compression reading is unusually high, the cylinder head surfaces, valves and pistons are probably coated with carbon deposits. If this is the case, the cylinder head should be removed and decarbonised (refer to Part D of this Chapter).

Leakdown test

10 A leakdown test measures the rate at which compressed air fed into the cylinder is lost. It is an alternative to a compression test, and in many ways it is better, since the escaping air provides easy identification of where pressure loss is occurring (piston rings, valves or head gasket).

11 The equipment needed for leakdown testing is unlikely to be available to the home mechanic. If poor compression is suspected, have the test performed by a suitably-equipped garage.

4 Timing belt and outer covers - removal and refitting

General information

1 The primary function of the toothed timing belt is to drive the camshaft, but it is also used to drive the fuel injection pump and intermediate shaft. Should the belt slip or break in service, the valve timing will be disturbed, and piston-to-valve contact may occur, resulting in serious engine damage.

2 For this reason, it is important that the timing belt is tensioned correctly, and inspected regularly for signs of wear or deterioration.

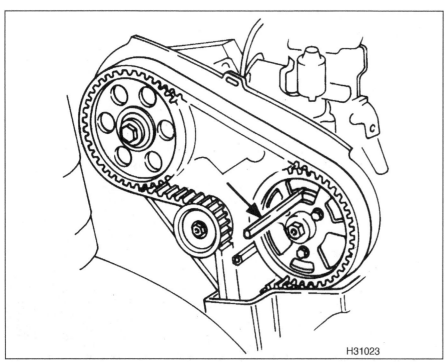

H31023

2.7 Injection pump sprocket locked using locking pin (arrowed)

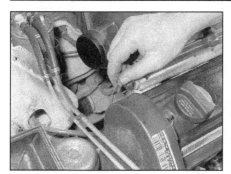

4.13a Prise open the spring clip at the top . . .

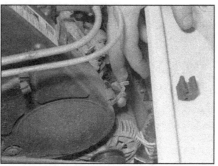

4.13b . . . and at the front . . .

4.13c . . . then remove the retaining screw . . .

3 Note that the removal of the *inner* section of the timing belt cover is described as part of the camshaft oil seal renewal procedure; see Section 8.

Removal

4 Before starting work, immobilise the engine and vehicle as follows:
a) *Disconnect the battery negative lead, and position the lead away from the terminal.*
b) *Prevent any vehicle movement by applying the handbrake and chocking the rear wheels. Ensure that the transmission is in neutral.*

5 Access to the timing belt covers can be improved by removing the air cleaner from the inner wing, and the inlet hose from the inlet manifold cover - refer to Chapter 4C.

6 To renew the belt, the engine right-hand mounting and the engine/transmission rear mounting must first be removed. Support the weight of the engine using an engine hoist from above, or using a securely-located hydraulic jack and suitable block of wood from below. Do not jack directly under the sump, or the sump will be damaged. Skoda technicians use an engine support bar which locates in the inner wing channels.

7 With the engine securely supported, progressively loosen the mounting bolts and remove the engine right-hand mounting and the engine/transmission rear mounting from the vehicle (see Section 14). Also unbolt the lower part of the right-hand mounting from the cylinder head.

8 Refer to Section 2, and using the engine alignment markings, set the engine to TDC on No 1 cylinder.

9 With reference to Section 6, remove the auxiliary drivebelt.

10 The engine must now be lowered slightly, to permit removal of the auxiliary drivebelt pulleys.

11 Slacken and withdraw the bolts, and lift off the coolant pump pulley and the crankshaft pulley.

 HAYNES HINT *To prevent the crankshaft drivebelt pulley from rotating whilst the bolts are being slackened, select top gear and get an assistant to apply the footbrake firmly. Failing this, grip the*

sprocket by wrapping a length of old rubber hose or inner tube around it. If top gear is selected to help in removing the pulley, make sure the transmission is returned to neutral before proceeding.

12 Unscrew and remove the auxiliary drivebelt tensioner pulley bolt, noting that it has a **left-hand thread** (ie it unscrews **clockwise**), and remove the drivebelt tensioner pulley.

13 Release the uppermost part of the timing belt outer cover by prising open the metal spring clips and removing the retaining screw. Detach the fuel pipes from the locating clip, and move them clear of the work area **(see illustrations)**. Lift the cover away from the engine.

14 Remove the retaining bolts and clips, and lift off the timing belt lower cover.

15 Ensure that the sprocket locking pin is firmly in position (see Section 2), then loosen the three outer sprocket securing bolts by half a turn.

Caution: Do not loosen the sprocket centre nut, as this will alter the fuel injection pump's basic timing setting.

16 With reference to Section 5, relieve the tension on the timing belt by slackening the tensioner mounting nut slightly, allowing the tensioner to pivot away from the belt.

17 Examine the timing belt for manufacturer's markings that indicate the direction of rotation. If none are present, make your own using typist's correction fluid or a dab of paint - do not cut or score the belt in any way.

Caution: If the belt appears to be in good condition and can be re-used, it is essential that it is refitted the same way around, otherwise accelerated wear will result, leading to premature failure.

18 Slide the belt off the sprockets, taking care to avoid twisting or kinking it excessively.

19 Examine the belt for evidence of contamination by coolant or lubricant. If this is the case, find the source of the contamination before progressing any further. Check the belt for signs of wear or damage, particularly around the leading edges of the belt teeth. Renew the belt if its condition is in doubt; the cost of belt renewal is negligible compared with potential cost of the engine repairs, should the belt fail in

4.13d . . . and detach the fuel pipes from the timing belt upper cover

service. Similarly, if the belt is known to have covered more than 30 000 miles, it is prudent to renew it regardless of condition, as a precautionary measure.

20 If the timing belt is not going to be refitted for some time, it is a wise precaution to hang a warning label on the steering wheel, to remind yourself (and others) not to try and start the engine. You may wish to further immobilise the engine against being started, perhaps by taping over the ignition switch.

Refitting

21 Ensure that the crankshaft is still set to TDC on No 1 cylinder, as described in Section 2.

22 Refer to Section 5 and slacken the camshaft sprocket bolt by half a turn. Release the sprocket from the camshaft taper mounting by carefully tapping it with a pin punch, inserted through the hole provided in the timing belt inner cover **(see illustration)**.

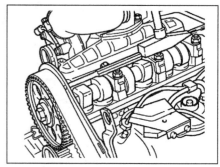

4.22 Releasing the camshaft sprocket from the taper using a pin punch

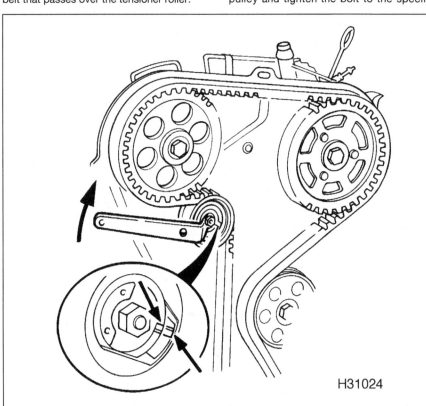

4.27a Tensioning the timing belt using a pair of circlip pliers in the belt tensioner

23 Loop the timing belt loosely under the crankshaft sprocket.

Caution: Observe the direction of rotation markings on the belt.

24 Engage the timing belt teeth with the crankshaft sprocket, then manoeuvre it into position over the camshaft and injection pump sprockets. Ensure the belt teeth seat correctly on the sprockets. **Note:** *Slight adjustments to the position of the camshaft sprocket (and injection pump sprocket) may be necessary to achieve this.*

25 Pass the flat side of the belt over the intermediate shaft pulley and tensioner roller - avoid bending the belt back on itself or twisting it excessively as you do this.

26 Ensure that the front run of the belt is taut - ie all the slack should be in the section of the belt that passes over the tensioner roller.

27 Tension the belt by turning the eccentrically-mounted tensioner clockwise; two holes are provided in the side of the tensioner hub for this purpose - a pair of sturdy right-angled circlip pliers is a suitable substitute for the correct Skoda tool. Turn the tensioner until the notch and the raised portion are aligned, then tighten the tensioner locknut to the specified torque **(see illustrations).**

28 At this point, check that the crankshaft is still set to TDC on No 1 cylinder (see Section 2).

29 Refer to Section 5 and tighten the camshaft sprocket bolt to the specified torque.

30 Tighten the three injection pump sprocket outer bolts, then remove the sprocket locking pin.

31 With reference to Section 2, remove the camshaft locking bar.

32 Using a spanner or wrench and socket on the crankshaft sprocket bolt, rotate crankshaft through two complete revolutions. Reset the engine to TDC on No 1 cylinder, with reference to Section 2 and check that the fuel injection pump sprocket locking pin can be inserted. Re-check the timing belt tension and adjust it, if necessary.

33 Refer to Section 5 and test the operation of the tensioner.

34 Refit the upper and lower sections of the timing belt outer cover, securing with the clips and tightening the retaining bolts securely.

35 Refit the auxiliary drivebelt tensioner pulley and tighten the bolt to the specified

torque, noting that it has a **left-hand thread** (ie it tightens **anti-clockwise**).

36 Refit the coolant pump pulley, and tighten the retaining bolts to the specified torque.

37 Refit the crankshaft auxiliary belt pulley and tighten the retaining bolts to the specified torque, using the method employed during removal. Note that the offset of the pulley mounting holes allows only one fitting position.

38 Working from Section 6, refit and tension the auxiliary drivebelt.

39 Raise the engine back into a position where the engine right-hand mounting can be refitted.

40 Refit the engine right-hand mounting and the engine/transmission rear mounting, and tighten the bolts to the specified torque. Lower the hoist or the jack on completion.

41 Reconnect the inlet air hose to the inlet manifold cover and the connection on the inner wing.

42 Restore the battery connection.

43 On completion, refer to Chapter 4C and check the fuel injection pump timing.

5 Timing belt tensioner and sprockets - removal and refitting

1 Before starting work, immobilise the engine and vehicle as follows:
 a) *Disconnect the battery negative lead, and position the lead away from the terminal.*
 b) *Prevent any vehicle movement by applying the handbrake and chocking the rear wheels. Ensure that the transmission is in neutral.*

Timing belt tensioner

Removal

2 With reference to the relevant paragraphs of Sections 2 and 4, set the engine to TDC on No 1 cylinder, then remove the upper and lower sections of the timing belt outer cover.

3 Slacken the retaining nut at the hub of the tensioner roller and allow the assembly to rotate anti-clockwise, relieving the tension on the timing belt. Remove the nut and slide the tensioner off its mounting stud **(see illustrations).**

5.3a Remove the tensioner nut and recover the washer

4.27b Alignment marks on belt tensioner pulley and hub

H31024

5.3b Slide the tensioner off its mounting stud

Inspection

4 Wipe the tensioner clean, but do not use solvents that may contaminate the bearings. Spin the tensioner pulley on its hub by hand. Stiff movement or excessive freeplay is an indication of severe wear; the tensioner is not a serviceable component, and should be renewed.

Refitting and testing

5 Slide the tensioner pulley over the mounting stud, and refit the tensioner retaining nut - do not fully tighten the nut at this stage.
6 With reference to Section 4, refit and tension the timing belt.
7 The operation of the tensioner can be tested as follows. Apply finger pressure to the timing belt at a point mid-way between the camshaft and injection pump sprockets. The tensioner pulley alignment marks should move apart as pressure is applied, and then move back and line up again as the pressure is removed **(see illustration)**.
8 Any reluctance to return to the correct position indicates that the tensioner should be renewed - correct tension is critical to the operation of the belt, and the importance of the belt tensioner cannot be overstressed.
9 Referring to Section 4, refit the timing belt upper and lower covers, the auxiliary drivebelt pulleys, auxiliary drivebelt, the engine mountings, and all other components removed for access. Reconnect the battery negative lead.

Camshaft timing belt sprocket

Removal

10 Referring to Sections 2 and 4, set the engine to TDC on No 1 cylinder, then remove the timing belt outer covers. Slacken the tensioner centre nut and allow it to rotate anti-clockwise, to relieve the tension on the timing belt. Carefully slide the timing belt off the camshaft sprocket.
11 The camshaft sprocket must be held stationary whilst its retaining bolt is slackened; if access to the correct Skoda special tool is not possible, a simple home-made tool may be fabricated using basic materials **(see Tool Tip)**.
12 Using the home-made tool, brace the camshaft sprocket and slacken and remove the retaining bolt.

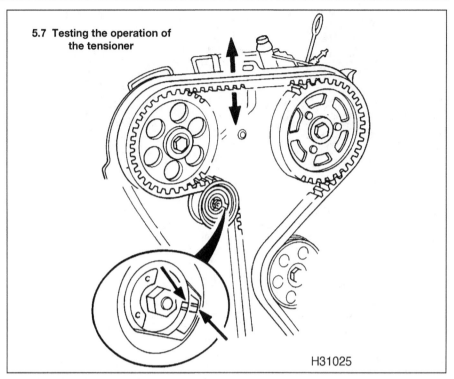

5.7 Testing the operation of the tensioner

H31025

⚠ *Warning: It is potentially damaging to allow the camshaft to turn with the timing belt removed and the engine set at TDC, as piston-to-valve contact may occur. Take care that the camshaft sprocket is not turned as it is removed. As a precaution against damage, Skoda recommend that the crankshaft be turned back a few degrees, away from TDC, while the camshaft sprocket is removed/refitted. The crankshaft may then be turned back to TDC when the timing belt is to be refitted.*
13 Slide the camshaft sprocket from the end of the camshaft.
14 With the sprocket removed, examine the camshaft oil seal for signs of leaking. If necessary, refer to Section 8 and renew it.
15 Wipe the sprocket and camshaft mating surfaces clean.

Refitting

16 Ensure the lug in the rear of the sprocket hub engages with recess in the end of the camshaft.
17 Working from Sections 2 and 4, check that the engine is still set to TDC on No 1 cylinder, then refit and tension the timing belt.
18 Referring to Section 4, refit the timing belt upper and lower covers, the auxiliary drivebelt pulleys, auxiliary drivebelt, the engine mountings, and all other components removed for access. Reconnect the battery negative lead.

Crankshaft timing belt sprocket

Removal

19 Referring to Sections 2 and 4, set the engine to TDC on No 1 cylinder, then remove

the timing belt outer covers. Slacken the tensioner centre nut and allow it to rotate anti-clockwise, to relieve the tension on the timing belt. Carefully slide the timing belt off the camshaft sprocket.
20 The crankshaft sprocket must be held stationary whilst its retaining bolt is slackened. If access to the correct Skoda flywheel locking tool is not available, lock the crankshaft in position by removing the starter motor, as described in Chapter 5A, to expose

TOOL TiP

To make a camshaft sprocket holding tool, obtain two lengths of steel strip about 6mm thick by 30 mm wide or similar, one 600 mm long, the other 200 mm long (all dimensions approximate). Bolt the two strips together to form a forked end, leaving the bolt slack so that the shorter strip can pivot freely. At the end of each 'prong' of the fork, secure a bolt with a nut and a locknut, to act as the fulcrums; these will engage with the cut-outs in the sprocket, and should protrude by about 30mm

5.24a Insert the crankshaft sprocket bolt . . .

5.24b . . . tighten it to the Stage 1 torque . . .

5.24c . . . then through the Stage 2 angle

the flywheel ring gear. Get an assistant insert a stout lever between the ring gear teeth and the transmission bellhousing whilst the sprocket retaining bolt is slackened.

21 Withdraw the bolt and lift off the sprocket.

22 With the sprocket removed, examine the crankshaft oil seal for signs of leaking. If necessary, refer to Section 10 and renew it.

23 Wipe the sprocket and crankshaft mating surfaces clean.

Refitting

24 Offer up the sprocket to the crankshaft, engaging the lug on the inside of the sprocket with the recess in the end of the crankshaft. Oil the threads of a new retaining bolt, then insert and tighten it to the specified torque **(see illustrations)**. **Note:** *If preferred, final tightening of the sprocket bolt may be delayed until after the timing belt has been refitted - this will prevent possible engine damage if the sprocket should turn as the bolt is tightened.*

25 Working from Sections 2 and 4, check that the engine is still set to TDC on No 1 cylinder, then refit and tension the timing belt.

26 Referring to Section 4, refit the timing belt upper and lower covers, the auxiliary drivebelt pulleys, auxiliary drivebelt, the engine mountings, and all other components removed for access. Reconnect the battery negative lead.

Intermediate shaft sprocket

Removal

27 With reference to Sections 2 and 4, remove the timing belt covers and set the engine to TDC on No 1 cylinder. Slacken the

tensioner centre nut and rotate it anti-clockwise to relieve the tension on the timing belt. Carefully slide the timing belt off the camshaft sprocket.

28 The intermediate shaft sprocket must be held stationary whilst its retaining bolt is slackened; if access to the correct Skoda special tool is not possible, a simple home-made tool may be fabricated using basic materials as described in the camshaft sprocket removal sub-Section.

29 Using a socket and extension bar, brace the intermediate shaft sprocket. Slacken and remove the retaining bolt, and slide the sprocket from the end of the intermediate shaft **(see illustration)**. Where applicable, recover the Woodruff key from the keyway.

30 With the sprocket removed, examine the intermediate shaft oil seal for signs of leaking. If necessary, refer to Section 9 and renew it.

31 Wipe the sprocket and shaft mating surfaces clean.

Refitting

32 Where applicable, fit the Woodruff key into the keyway, with the plain surface facing upwards. Offer up the sprocket to the intermediate shaft, engaging the slot in the sprocket with the Woodruff key.

33 Tighten the sprocket retaining bolt to the specified torque; hold the sprocket using the method employed during removal.

34 With reference to Section 2, check that the engine is still set to TDC on No 1 cylinder. Working from Section 4, refit and tension the timing belt.

35 Referring to Section 4, refit the timing belt

upper and lower covers, the auxiliary drivebelt pulleys, auxiliary drivebelt, the engine mountings, and all other components removed for access. Reconnect the battery negative lead.

Fuel injection pump sprocket

36 Refer to Chapter 4C.

6 Auxiliary drivebelt - removal, refitting and tensioning

General information

1 The auxiliary drivebelt, which is driven from a pulley mounted on the crankshaft, provides drive for the alternator, power steering pump, and coolant pump.

2 The ribbed auxiliary belt is fitted with an automatic tensioning device.

Removal

3 Park the vehicle on a level surface, apply the handbrake and chock the rear wheels. Loosen the right-hand front wheel bolts.

4 Raise the front of the car, rest it securely on axle stands and remove the right-hand front roadwheel.

5 Remove the screws, and lower the metal cover fitted over the drivebelt **(see illustrations)**.

6 Examine the ribbed belt for manufacturer's markings, indicating the direction of rotation. If none are present, make some using typist's correction fluid or a dab of paint - do not cut or score the belt in any way.

5.29 Brace the intermediate shaft sprocket, then remove the retaining bolt

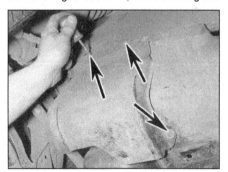

6.5a Remove the cover screws (arrowed) . . .

6.5b . . . and lower the cover for access to the drivebelt

7 Fit an open-ended 15 mm spanner (or an adjustable spanner) to the tensioner lever, and rotate the tensioner pulley anti-clockwise, against its spring tension.

8 Pull the belt off the alternator pulley, then release it from the remaining pulleys **(see illustration)**.

Refitting and tensioning

Caution: Observe the manufacturer's direction of rotation markings on the belt, when refitting.

9 Pass the ribbed belt underneath the crankshaft pulley, ensuring that the ribs seat in the channels on the surface of the pulley.

10 Fit an open-ended 15 mm spanner (or an adjustable spanner) to the tensioner lever, and rotate the tensioner pulley anti-clockwise, against its spring tension.

11 Pass the flat side of the belt underneath the tensioner roller, then fit it over the pulleys. Ensure that the belt ribs engage correctly with the pulley grooves.

12 Release the spanner and allow the tensioner roller to bear against the flat side of the belt.

13 Refit the drivebelt cover, and tighten the screws securely.

14 Refit the right-hand front roadwheel and lower the car to the ground. Tighten the roadwheel bolts to the specified torque.

7 Camshaft cover - removal and refitting

Removal

1 Disconnect the crankcase breather pipe from the camshaft cover. If the sealing grommet is damaged, obtain a new one for reassembly.

2 Prise off the cover caps, then slacken and remove the three camshaft cover retaining nuts - recover the washers and seals, noting their fitted positions. If any of the washers are damaged, new ones should be obtained for reassembly.

3 Lift the cover away from the cylinder head; if it sticks, do not attempt to lever it off - instead free it by working around the cover and tapping it lightly with a soft-faced mallet.

4 Recover the camshaft cover gasket. Inspect the gasket carefully, and renew it if damage or deterioration is evident.

5 Clean the mating surfaces of the cylinder head and camshaft cover thoroughly, removing all traces of oil and old gasket - take care to avoid damaging the surfaces as you do this.

Refitting

6 Refit the camshaft cover by following the removal procedure in reverse, noting the following points:

a) Ensure that the gasket is correctly seated on the cylinder head - the projections on

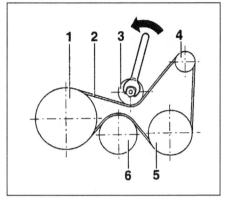

6.8 Rotate the auxiliary drivebelt tensioner pulley anti-clockwise to relieve the tension on the belt

1	Crankshaft pulley	5	Power steering
2	Auxiliary drivebelt		pump pulley
3	Tensioner pulley	6	Coolant pump
4	Alternator pulley		pulley

the gasket should locate into the holes provided in the cylinder head mating surface.

b) Ensure that the sealing cones are still in place on the three camshaft cover studs.

c) Take care to avoid displacing the gasket as the camshaft cover is lowered into position.

d) Fit the washers and seals in the order noted on removal, then fit and tighten the camshaft cover retaining nuts to the specified torque. Fit the cover caps over the nuts.

e) Refit the crankcase breather pipe to the camshaft cover, using a new sealing grommet if necessary.

8 Camshaft oil seal - renewal

1 Refer to Section 6 and remove the auxiliary drivebelt.

2 With reference to Sections 2, 4 and 5 of this Chapter, remove the auxiliary belt pulleys and timing belt upper cover. Set the engine to TDC on No 1 cylinder and remove the timing belt, timing belt tensioner, and the camshaft and fuel injection pump sprockets.

3 After removing the retaining bolts, lift the timing belt inner cover away from the engine.

4 Working from the relevant Section of Chapter 2D, carry out the following:

a) Unbolt the camshaft No 1 bearing cap, and slide off the old camshaft oil seal **(see illustration)**.

b) Lubricate the surface of a new camshaft oil seal with clean engine oil, and fit it over the end of the camshaft.

c) Apply a suitable sealant to the mating surface of the bearing cap, then refit it and tighten its mounting nuts progressively to the specified torque.

5 With reference to Sections 2, 4 and 5 of this Chapter, refit the timing belt inner cover, belt tensioner and timing sprockets, then refit and tension the timing belt. On completion, refit the timing belt outer covers and all other components removed for access.

6 With reference to Section 6, refit and tension the auxiliary drivebelt.

9 Intermediate shaft oil seal - renewal

1 Refer to Section 6 and remove the auxiliary drivebelt.

2 With reference to Sections 2, 4 and 5 of this Chapter, remove the auxiliary belt pulleys and timing belt upper cover. Set the engine to TDC on No 1 cylinder and remove the timing belt, timing belt tensioner and the intermediate shaft sprocket.

3 With reference to Chapter 2D, remove the intermediate shaft flange, and renew the shaft and flange oil seals.

4 With reference to Sections 2, 4 and 5 of this Chapter, refit the timing belt tensioner and intermediate shaft sprocket, then refit and tension the timing belt. On completion, refit the timing belt outer covers and all other components removed for access.

5 With reference to Section 6, refit and tension the auxiliary drivebelt.

10 Crankshaft oil seals - renewal

Crankshaft front oil seal

1 Refer to Chapter 1B and drain the engine oil.

2 Refer to Section 6 and remove the auxiliary drivebelt.

3 With reference to Sections 2, 4 and 5 of this Chapter, remove the auxiliary belt pulleys, timing belt outer covers, timing belt and crankshaft sprocket.

4 Drill two small holes into the existing oil seal, diagonally opposite each other. Take great care to avoid drilling through into the seal housing or crankshaft sealing surface.

8.4 Remove the camshaft bearing cap and slide off the oil seal

10.4 Removing the crankshaft front oil seal using self-tapping screws

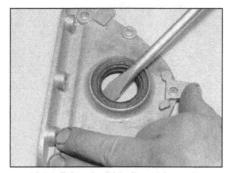

10.14 Prise the old oil seal from the housing

10.16 Locate the new crankshaft front oil seal housing gasket in position

Thread two self-tapping screws into the holes, and using two pairs of pliers, pull on the heads of the screws to extract the oil seal **(see illustration)**.

5 Clean out the seal housing and sealing surface of the crankshaft by wiping it with a lint-free cloth - avoid using solvents that may enter the crankcase and affect component lubrication. Remove any swarf or burrs that could cause the seal to leak.

6 Smear the lip of the new oil seal with clean engine oil, and position it over the housing.

7 Using a hammer and a socket of suitable diameter, drive the seal squarely into its housing. **Note:** *Select a socket that bears only on the hard outer surface of the seal, not the inner lip, which can easily be damaged.*

8 With reference to Sections 2, 4 and 5 of this Chapter, refit the crankshaft sprocket, then refit and tension the timing belt. On completion, refit the timing belt outer covers, auxiliary drivebelt pulleys, and all other components removed for access.

9 The remainder of the refitting procedure is a reversal of removal, as follows:
  a) *With reference to Section 6, refit and tension the auxiliary drivebelt.*
  b) *Refer to Chapter 1B and refill the engine with the correct grade and quantity of oil.*

Crankshaft front oil seal housing - gasket renewal

10 Proceed as described in paragraphs 1 to 3 above, then refer to Section 15 and remove the sump.

11 Progressively slacken and then remove the oil seal housing retaining bolts.

12 Lift the housing away from the cylinder block, together with the crankshaft oil seal, using a twisting motion to ease the seal along the shaft.

13 Recover the old gasket from the seal housing on the cylinder block. If it has disintegrated, scrape the remains off with a trimming knife blade. Take care to avoid damaging the mating surfaces.

14 If necessary, prise the old oil seal from the housing using a stout screwdriver **(see illustration)**.

15 Wipe the oil seal housing clean, and check it visually for signs of distortion or cracking. Lay the housing on a work surface, with the mating surface face down. If removed, press in a new oil seal, using a block of wood as a press to ensure that the seal enters the housing squarely.

16 Smear the crankcase mating surface with suitable multi-purpose sealant, and lay the new gasket in position **(see illustration)**.

17 Pad the end of the crankshaft with a layer of PVC tape; this will protect the oil seal as it is being fitted.

18 Lubricate the inner lip of the crankshaft oil seal with clean engine oil, then offer up the seal and its housing to the end of the crankshaft **(see illustration)**. Ease the seal along the shaft using a twisting motion, until the housing is flush with the crankcase.

19 Insert the bolts and tighten them to the specified torque.

Caution: The housing is light alloy, and may be distorted if the bolts are not tightened progressively.

20 Refer to Section 15 and refit the sump.

21 With reference to Sections 2, 4 and 5 of this Chapter, refit the crankshaft timing belt sprocket, then refit and tension the timing belt. On completion, refit the timing belt outer covers, auxiliary drivebelt pulleys, and all other components removed for access.

22 The remainder of the refitting procedure is a reversal of removal, as follows:
  a) *With reference to Section 6, refit and tension the auxiliary drivebelt.*
  b) *Refer to Chapter 1B and refill the engine with the correct grade and quantity of oil.*

Crankshaft rear oil seal (flywheel end)

23 Proceed as described in paragraphs 1 to 3 above, then refer to Section 15 and remove the sump.

24 Refer to Chapter 7 and remove the transmission from the engine.

25 Refer to Section 13 of this Chapter and remove the flywheel; refer to Chapter 6 and remove the clutch friction plate and pressure plate.

26 Where applicable, remove the retaining bolts and lift the intermediate plate away from the cylinder block.

27 Progressively slacken and then remove the oil seal housing retaining bolts.

28 Lift the housing away from the cylinder block, together with the crankshaft oil seal, using a twisting motion to ease the seal along the shaft.

29 Recover the old gasket from the seal housing cylinder block. If it has disintegrated, scrape the remains off with a trimming knife blade. Take care to avoid damaging the mating surfaces.

30 The rear oil seal is not available separately from the housing, and the seal and housing must therefore be renewed complete.

31 Smear the crankcase mating surface with suitable multi-purpose sealant, and lay the new gasket in position **(see illustration)**.

32 A protective plastic sleeve is usually supplied with genuine Skoda crankshaft oil seal housings; when fitted over the end of the crankshaft, the sleeve prevents damage to the inner lip of the oil seal as it is being fitted **(see illustration)**. Use PVC tape to pad the end of the crankshaft if a sleeve is not provided.

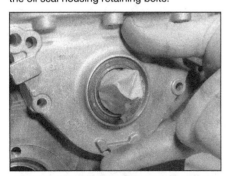

10.18 Offer up the seal and its housing to the end of the crankshaft

10.31 Locate the new crankshaft rear oil seal housing gasket in position

10.32 A protective plastic cap is supplied with genuine crankshaft oil seal housings

10.33 Fitting the crankshaft rear oil seal housing

10.34 Tightening the crankshaft rear oil seal housing retaining bolts

33 Lubricate the inner lip of the crankshaft oil seal with clean engine oil, then offer up the seal housing to the end of the crankshaft **(see illustration)**. Ease the seal along the shaft using a twisting motion, until the housing is flush with the crankcase.

34 Insert the retaining bolts and tighten them progressively to the specified torque **(see illustration)**.

Caution: The housing is light alloy, and may be distorted if the bolts are not tightened progressively.

35 Refer to Section 15 and refit the sump.

36 Refer to Chapter 6 and refit the flywheel, pressure plate and clutch friction plate.

37 With reference to Chapter 7, refit the transmission to the engine.

38 On completion, refer to Chapter 1B and refill the engine with the correct grade and quantity of oil.

11 Cylinder head and manifolds
- removal, separation and refitting

Removal

1 Select a level surface to park the vehicle upon. Give yourself enough space to move around it easily.

2 Disconnect the battery negative lead, and position it away from the terminal.

3 With reference to Chapter 1B, drain the cooling system.

4 Refer to Section 6 and remove the auxiliary drivebelt.

5 Compress the legs of the spring clip, and release the inlet air trunking from the inlet manifold cover.

6 Refer to Chapter 3 and perform the following:
  a) Slacken the clips and disconnect the radiator hoses from the ports on the cylinder head.
  b) Slacken the clips and disconnect the expansion tank hose, and the heater inlet and outlet coolant hoses, from the ports on the cylinder head.

7 Refer to Chapter 4C and carry out the following:
  a) Disconnect and remove the injector fuel supply pipes from the injectors and the injection pump head **(see illustration)**.
  b) Disconnect the injector return hose from the injection pump fuel return port.
  c) Unplug all fuel system electrical cabling at the relevant connectors, labelling each cable to aid refitting later.

8 With reference to Sections 2, 4 and 7, carry out the following:
  a) Remove the camshaft cover.

  b) Remove the timing belt outer covers, and disengage the timing belt from the camshaft sprocket.
  c) Remove the timing belt tensioner, camshaft sprocket and fuel injection pump sprocket.

9 Once the timing belt has been disengaged, the engine can be raised back into its original position, and the engine right-hand mounting refitted while the cylinder head is removed.

10 To avoid any possibility of piston-to-valve contact during cylinder head removal, it is recommended that the crankshaft be turned back a few degrees away from the TDC position, to take the pistons down the bores.

11 Slacken and withdraw the retaining screws, and lift off the timing belt inner cover.

12 Refer to Chapter 4D and 5C as necessary, and carry out the following:
  a) Working from underneath the car, remove the bolts and separate the exhaust downpipe from the exhaust manifold flange. Alternatively, removing the inlet manifold cover and pipes as described in paragraphs 20 and 21 will provide better access from above.
  b) Remove the EGR valve and its connecting pipework from the inlet and exhaust manifolds.
  c) Unbolt the supply cable from the glow plug in cylinder No 4 **(see illustration)**.

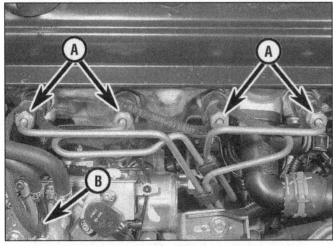

11.7 General view of the fuel injector pipes (A) and the return hose connection (B)

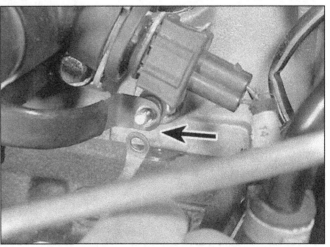

11.12 Unbolt the electrical supply cable from No 4 cylinder glow plug

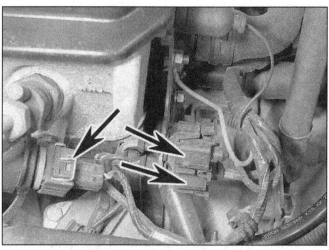

11.13 Disconnect the coolant temperature sensor wiring plug (left) and the two plugs adjacent (arrowed)

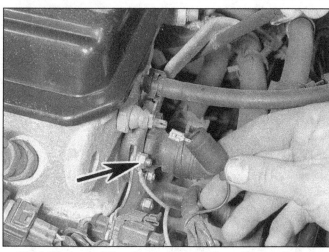

11.14 Disconnect the oil pressure switch, and the earth lead below (arrowed)

13 Disconnect the wiring plug from the coolant temperature sensor, and the two wiring plugs in the adjacent bracket **(see illustration)**.

14 Disconnect the oil pressure switch wiring plug, and the earth lead below it **(see illustration)**.

15 Progressively slacken the cylinder head bolts, by half a turn at a time, until all bolts can be unscrewed by hand **(see illustration)**. Discard the bolts - new ones must be fitted on reassembly.

16 Check that nothing remains connected to the cylinder head, then lift the head away from the cylinder block; seek assistance if possible, as it is a heavy assembly, especially if it is being removed complete with the manifolds.

17 If the head will not release, bear in mind that it is located on two dowels - do not strike the head from the side. Rock the head off using the manifolds for leverage - prising between the head and block will damage the mating faces, and is not recommended.

18 Remove the gasket from the top of the block, noting the locating dowels. If the dowels are a loose fit, remove them and store them with the head for safe-keeping. Do not discard the gasket yet - it will be needed for identification purposes.

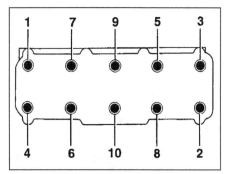

11.15 Cylinder head bolt LOOSENING sequence

19 If the cylinder head is to be dismantled for overhaul, refer to Chapter 2D.

Manifold separation

20 With the cylinder head on a work surface, slacken and withdraw the five inlet manifold cover bolts. Lift the cover away, and recover the gasket.

21 Loosen and remove the inlet manifold/inlet pipe retaining bolts, and remove the four pipes and manifold from the cylinder head. Recover the manifold-to-cylinder head gasket.

22 Progressively slacken and remove the exhaust manifold retaining nuts; discard the old nuts if they are in poor condition. Lift the manifold away from the cylinder head, and recover the gasket.

23 Ensure that the inlet and exhaust manifold mating surfaces are completely clean. Refit the exhaust manifold, using a new gasket. Tighten the new exhaust manifold retaining nuts to the specified torque.

24 Fit a new inlet manifold gasket to the cylinder head, then lift the inlet manifold into position. Fitting each inlet pipe in turn, insert the retaining bolts and tighten them to the specified torque.

Preparation for refitting

25 The mating faces of the cylinder head and cylinder block/crankcase must be perfectly clean before refitting the head. Use a hard plastic or wood scraper to remove all traces of gasket and carbon; also clean the piston crowns. Take particular care during the cleaning operations, as aluminium alloy is easily damaged. Also, make sure that the carbon is not allowed to enter the oil and water passages - this is particularly important for the lubrication system, as carbon could block the oil supply to the engine's components. Using adhesive tape and paper, seal the water, oil and bolt holes in the cylinder block/crankcase.

26 Check the mating surfaces of the cylinder block/crankcase and the cylinder head for nicks, deep scratches and other damage. If slight, they may be removed carefully with abrasive paper, but note that head machining will not be possible - refer to Chapter 2D. If warpage of the cylinder head gasket surface is suspected, use a straight-edge to check it for distortion. Refer to Part D of this Chapter if necessary.

27 Clean out the cylinder head bolt drillings using a suitable tap. If a tap is not available, make a home-made substitute **(see Tool Tip)**.

28 It is possible for the piston crowns to strike and damage the valve heads, if the camshaft is rotated with the timing belt removed and the crankshaft set to TDC. For this reason, the crankshaft must be set to a position other than TDC on No 1 cylinder, before the cylinder head is refitted. Set the crankshaft to TDC on No 1 cylinder, using the

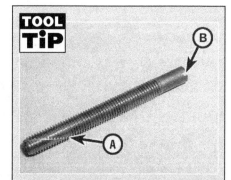

If a tap is not available, make a home-made substitute by cutting a slot (A) down the threads of one of the old cylinder head bolts. After use, the bolt head can be cut off, and the shank can then be used as an alignment dowel to assist cylinder head refitting. Cut a screwdriver slot (B) in the top of the bolt, to allow it to be unscrewed

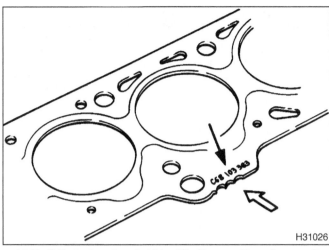

11.29 Cylinder head gasket identification markings (arrowed)

11.33 Oil the cylinder head bolt threads, then place each bolt into its relevant hole

information in Section 2, then turn the crankshaft back by a few degrees, away from the TDC position. If preferred, for maximum safety, the pistons can be positioned halfway down their bores, with No 1 piston on its upstroke - ie 90° before TDC.

Refitting

29 Examine the old cylinder head gasket for manufacturer's identification markings. These will either be in the form of punched holes/ notches or a part number, on the edge of the gasket **(see illustration)**. Unless new pistons have been fitted, the new cylinder head gasket must be the same type as the old one.

Where no locating dowels are fitted, it may prove difficult to accurately align the head on the block when refitting. To overcome this, two of the old cylinder head bolts can be modified to act as locating dowels. Cut the heads off two of the bolts, and then cut a slot in the top of the bolt, so that a flat-bladed screwdriver may be used to unscrew the bolts from the block once the head is placed over them. Screw the two 'dowels' into place either end of the head, then lower the head into position over them. Fit two or more of the new head bolts to locate the head, then unscrew the dowels using a screwdriver

30 If new piston assemblies have been fitted as part of an engine overhaul, before purchasing the new cylinder head gasket, refer to Chapter 2D and measure the piston projection. Purchase a new gasket according to the results of the measurement (see Chapter 2D Specifications).

31 Lay the new head gasket on the cylinder block, engaging it with the locating dowels. If no dowels are fitted, or if the originals are lost or damaged, make up some substitutes **(see Tool Tip)**. Ensure that the manufacturer's TOP and/or part number markings are face up. Do not handle the gasket excessively before it is fitted, or it may become damaged.

32 With the help of an assistant, place the cylinder head and manifolds centrally on the cylinder block, ensuring that the locating dowels engage with the recesses in the cylinder head. Check that the head gasket is correctly seated before allowing the full weight of the cylinder head to rest upon it.

33 Apply a little oil to the threads, and to the underside of the heads, of the new cylinder head bolts **(see illustration)**.

34 Carefully enter each bolt into its relevant hole (*do not drop them in*) and screw in, by hand only, until finger-tight.

35 Working progressively and in the sequence shown **(see illustration)**, tighten the cylinder head bolts to their Stage 1 torque setting, using a torque wrench and suitable socket. Repeat the exercise in the same sequence for the Stage 2 torque setting.

36 Once all the bolts have been tightened to their Stage 2 settings, working again in the given sequence, angle-tighten the bolts through the specified Stage 3 angle, using a socket and extension bar. It is recommended that an angle-measuring gauge is used during this stage of the tightening, to ensure accuracy. If a gauge is not available, use white paint to make alignment marks between the bolt head and cylinder head prior to tightening; the marks can then be used to check the bolt has been rotated through the

correct angle during tightening. Repeat for the Stage 4 setting.

37 Refit the timing belt inner cover, tightening the retaining bolts securely.

38 Refer to Section 2 and set the engine to TDC on No 1 cylinder.

39 Support the engine, then disconnect the engine mountings as described in Section 4 and lower the engine down slightly. Referring to Section 5, refit the timing belt sprockets. Using the information in Section 4, refit and tension the timing belt and outer covers, and the crankshaft pulley.

40 The engine can now be raised back into position, and the engine mountings refitted as described in Section 4.

41 Refit and tension the auxiliary drivebelt as described in Section 6.

42 The remainder of refitting is a reversal of the removal procedure, as follows:

a) *Refer to Chapter 4D and refit the exhaust downpipe, EGR valve and glow plug cabling.*

b) *Refer to Chapter 4C and refit the injector fuel supply hoses to the injectors and the injection pump head. Reconnect all fuel system electrical cabling. Refit the injector bleed hose to the injection pump fuel return port.*

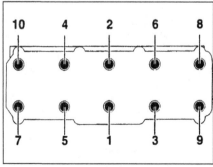

11.35 Cylinder head bolt TIGHTENING sequence

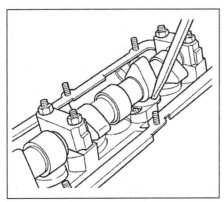

12.6 Press down on the tappet, until it contacts the top of the valve stem

c) *Reconnect the engine harness multi-plug connector.*
d) *Refit the camshaft cover (see Section 7).*
e) *Reconnect the radiator, expansion tank and heater coolant hoses, referring to Chapter 3 for guidance. Reconnect the coolant temperature sensor wiring.*
f) *Restore the battery connection.*

43 On completion, refer to Chapter 1B and refill the engine cooling system with the correct quantity of new coolant.

12 Hydraulic tappets - operation check

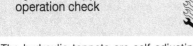

1 The hydraulic tappets are self-adjusting, and require no attention whilst in service.
2 If the hydraulic tappets become excessively noisy, their operation can be checked as described below.
3 Run the engine until it reaches its normal operating temperature. Increase the engine speed to around 2500 rpm (fast idle) for about 2 minutes, then switch off the engine. Refer to Section 7 and remove the camshaft cover.
4 Rotate the camshaft by turning the crankshaft with a socket and wrench, until the first cam lobe over No 1 cylinder is pointing upwards.
5 Using a feeler blade, measure the clearance between the base of the cam lobe and the top of the tappet. If the clearance is greater than 0.1mm, then the tappet is defective and must be renewed.
6 If the clearance is less than 0.1 mm, press down on the top of the tappet, until it is felt to contact the top of the valve stem **(see illustration)**. Use a wooden or plastic implement that will not damage the surface of the tappet.
7 If the tappet travels more than 1.0 mm before making contact, then it is defective and must be renewed.
8 Hydraulic tappet removal and refitting is described as part of the cylinder head overhaul sequence - see Chapter 2D for details.

> **Warning: After fitting hydraulic tappets, wait a minimum of 30 minutes (or leave overnight) before starting the engine, to allow the tappets time to settle, otherwise the pistons may strike the valve heads.**

13 Flywheel - removal, inspection and refitting

Removal of the flywheel is as described in Section 12 of Chapter 2B.

14 Engine mountings - inspection and renewal

Refer to Section 13 of Chapter 2B.

15 Sum - removal, inspection and refitting

Removal

1 Disconnect the battery negative cable, and position it away from the terminal.
2 Refer to Chapter 1B and drain the engine oil.
3 Park the vehicle on a level surface, apply the handbrake and chock the rear wheels.
4 Raise the front of the vehicle, rest it securely on axle stands or wheel ramps; refer to *Jacking and vehicle support*.
5 Working around the outside of the sump, progressively slacken and withdraw the sump retaining bolts. A knuckle joint or other flexible fitting may be required to reach the two sump bolts at the transmission end.
6 Break the joint by striking the sump with the palm of your hand, then lower the sump and withdraw it from underneath the vehicle. Recover and discard the sump gasket. Where a baffle plate is fitted, note that it can only be removed once the oil pump has been unbolted (see Section 16).
7 While the sump is removed, take the opportunity to check the oil pump pick-up/strainer for signs of clogging or disintegration. If necessary, remove the pump as described in Section 16, and clean or renew the strainer.

Refitting

8 Clean all traces of sealant from the mating surfaces of the cylinder block/crankcase and sump, then use a piece of clean rag to wipe out the sump.
9 Ensure that the sump and cylinder block/crankcase mating surfaces are clean and dry, then apply a coating of suitable sealant to the sump and crankcase mating surfaces.

10 Lay a new sump gasket in position on the sump mating surface, then offer up the sump and refit the retaining bolts. Tighten the nuts and bolts evenly and progressively to the specified torque.
11 Refer to Chapter 1B and refill the engine with the specified grade and quantity of oil.
12 Restore the battery connection.

16 Oil pump and pickup - removal and refitting

General information

1 The oil pump and pickup are both mounted in the sump. Drive is taken from the intermediate shaft, which rotates at half crankshaft speed.

Removal

2 Refer to Section 15 and remove the sump from the crankcase.
3 Slacken and remove the bolts securing the oil pump to the base of the crankcase **(see illustration)**.
4 Lower the oil pump and pickup away from the crankcase. Where applicable, recover the baffle plate.

Inspection

5 Remove the screws from the mating flange, and lift off the pickup tube. Recover the O-ring seal. Slacken and withdraw the screws, then remove the oil pump cover.
6 Clean the pump thoroughly, and inspect the gear teeth for signs of damage or wear.
7 Check the pump backlash by inserting a feeler blade between the meshed gear teeth; rotate the gears against each other slightly, to give the maximum clearance **(see illustration)**. Compare the measurement with the limit quoted in Specifications.
8 Check the pump axial clearance as follows. Lay an engineer's straight edge across the oil pump casing, then using a feeler blade, measure the clearance between the straight edge and the pump gears **(see illustration)**. Compare the measurement with the limit quoted in Specifications.
9 If either measurement is outside of the specified limit, this indicates that the pump is worn and must be renewed.

Refitting

10 Refit the oil pump cover, then fit and tighten the screws to the specified torque.
11 Reassemble the oil pickup to the oil pump, using a new O-ring seal. Tighten the retaining screws to the specified torque.
12 Where applicable, fit the crankcase baffle plate in place.
13 Offer up the oil pump to the crankcase, then fit the mounting bolts and tighten them to the specified torque.
14 Refer to Section 15 and refit the sump.

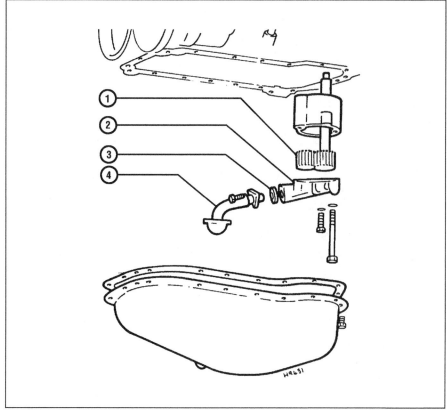

16.3 Oil pump components

1 Oil pump gears   2 Oil pump cover   3 O-ring seal   4 Pickup tube

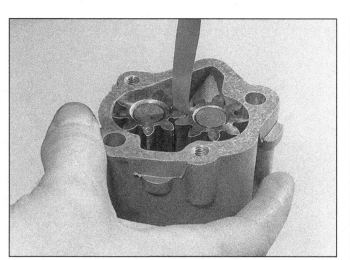

16.7 Checking the oil pump backlash

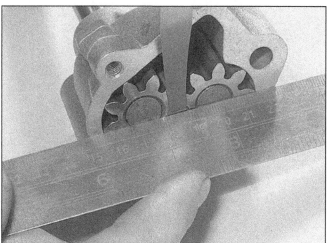

16.8 Checking the oil pump axial clearance

Notes

Chapter 2 Part D:
Engine removal and overhaul procedures

Contents

Degrees of difficulty

Easy, suitable for novice with little experience	Fairly easy, suitable for beginner with some experience	Fairly difficult, suitable for competent DIY mechanic ⚙	Difficult, suitable for experienced DIY mechanic ⚙	Very difficult, suitable for expert DIY or professional ⚙

Specifications

Cylinder head

Cylinder head gasket surface, maximum distortion:
Petrol engines	0.05 mm
Diesel engines	0.1 mm
Minimum cylinder head height (1.6 litre engine only)	135.6 mm
Maximum swirl chamber projection (diesel engine only)	0.05 mm

Valves

1.3 litre engine

Seat angle	45°

Head diameter:
Inlet	34 mm
Exhaust	30 mm

Stem diameter:
Standard	8 mm
Oversize	8.25 mm

Valve spring free length:
Inner spring	43.60 mm

Outer spring:
135 engines	45.85 mm
136 engines	46.5 mm

1.6 litre engine

Seat angle	45°

Head diameter:
Inlet	35.6 mm
Exhaust	29.0 mm

Valve stem diameter:
Inlet	6.963 mm
Exhaust	6.943 mm

Diesel engine

Seat angle	45°

Head diameter:
Inlet	36.0 mm
Exhaust	31.0 mm

Valve stem diameter:
Inlet	7.97 mm
Exhaust	7.95 mm

Camshaft

1.3 litre engine

Drive	Chain, from crankshaft at pulley end
Number of bearings	3
Camshaft journal diameter:	
Pulley end	38.950 to 38.975 mm
Middle	38.450 to 38.475 mm
Flywheel end	29.959 to 29.980 mm
Camshaft bearing internal diameter:	
Pulley end	39.000 to 39.025 mm
Middle	38.500 to 38.525 mm
Flywheel end	30.000 to 30.021 mm
Camshaft bearing running clearance	0.025 to 0.075 mm
Camshaft endfloat	0.020 to 0.066 mm
Cam follower outer diameter:	
Standard	20.980 to 21.000 mm
Oversize	21.193 to 21.200 mm
Cam follower bore internal diameter:	
Standard	21.000 to 21.021 mm
Oversize	21.200 to 21.221 mm

1.6 litre and diesel engines

Endfloat	0.15 mm
Maximum runout	0.01 mm
Maximum running clearance:	
Diesel engines	0.11 mm
Petrol engines	0.10 mm

Cylinder block

1.3 litre engine

Material	Aluminium alloy
Cylinder liner diameter:	
Standard - class A	75.500 mm nominal
Standard - class B	75.510 mm nominal
Standard - class C	75.520 mm nominal
Tolerance on nominal diameter	+ 0.009 mm / - 0 mm
Cylinder liner protrusion above cylinder block surface:	
Standard	0.07 to 0.12 mm
Maximum difference between any two liners	0.04 mm

1.6 litre engine

Material	Cast iron
Bore diameter:	
Standard	76.51 mm
1st oversize	76.76 mm
2nd oversize	77.01 mm
3rd oversize	77.26 mm

Diesel engine

Material	Cast iron
Bore diameter:	
Standard	79.51 mm
1st oversize	79.76 mm
2nd oversize	80.01 mm

Pistons and piston rings

1.3 litre engine

	New	Wear limit
Piston diameter:		
Standard - class A	75.475 mm	
Standard - class B	75.485 mm	
Standard - class C	75.495 mm	
Diametrical tolerance (all pistons)	± 0.009 mm	
Piston-to-bore clearance	0.025 mm	
Piston ring-to-groove clearance:		
Top compression ring	0.040 to 0.072 mm	
Second compression ring	0.030 to 0.062 mm	
Piston ring end gap:		
Compression rings	0.25 to 0.40 mm	1.00 mm
Oil scraper ring	0.20 to 0.35 mm	1.00 mm

Pistons and piston rings (continued)

1.6 litre engine

Piston diameter:
Standard	76.470 mm
1st oversize	76.720 mm
2nd oversize	76.970 mm
3rd oversize	77.220 mm

Piston ring-to-groove wall clearance:
Compression rings	0.04 to 0.08 mm (wear limit: 0.15 mm)

Oil scraper ring:
One-part	0.04 to 0.08 mm (wear limit: 0.15 mm)
Three-part	Not measurable

Piston ring end gap:	New	Wear limit
1st compression ring	0.20 to 0.50 mm	1.0 mm
2nd compression ring	0.40 to 0.70 mm	1.0 mm

Oil scraper ring:
	New	Wear limit
One-part	0.25 to 0.50 mm	1.0 mm
Three-part	0.40 to 1.40 mm	N/A

Diesel engine

Piston diameter:
Standard	79.48 mm
1st oversize	79.73 mm
2nd oversize	79.98 mm

Piston ring-to-groove wall clearance:
1st compression ring	0.09 to 0.12 mm (wear limit: 0.25 mm)
2nd compression ring	0.05 to 0.08 mm (wear limit: 0.25 mm)
Oil scraper ring	0.03 to 0.06 mm (wear limit: 0.15 mm)

Piston ring end gap:	New	Wear limit
1st compression ring	0.20 to 0.40 mm	1.2 mm
2nd compression ring	0.20 to 0.40 mm	0.6 mm
Oil scraper ring	0.25 to 0.50 mm	1.2 mm

Piston projection at TDC:
0.66 to 0.86 mm	Gasket with 1 hole/notch
0.87 to 0.90 mm	Gasket with 2 holes/notches
0.91 to 1.02 mm	Gasket with 3 holes/notches

Connecting rods

1.6 litre engine

Bearing shell pre-tension - minimum	1.5 mm

Diesel engine

Big-end thrust clearance	0.37 mm

Crankshaft

1.3 litre engine

Number of main bearings	3

Main bearing journal diameter:
Standard	60.00 mm
1st regrind	59.75 mm
2nd regrind	59.50 mm
3rd regrind	59.25 mm
Diametrical tolerance (all journals)	-0.010 to -0.029 mm

Main bearing shell thickness:
Standard	2.495 mm
1st regrind	2.620 mm
2nd regrind	2.745 mm
3rd regrind	2.870 mm
Thickness tolerance (all bearings)	+0.000 to -0.010 mm
Main bearing running clearance	0.016 to 0.065 mm

Crankpin journal diameter:
Standard	45.00 mm
1st regrind	44.75 mm
2nd regrind	44.50 mm
3rd regrind	44.25 mm
Diametrical tolerance (all journals)	-0.009 to -0.025 mm

Crankshaft (continued)

1.3 litre engine (continued)

Crankpin bearing shell thickness:
Standard	1.490 mm
1st regrind	1.615 mm
2nd regrind	1.740 mm
3rd regrind	1.865 mm
Thickness tolerance (all bearings)	+0.000 to -0.010 mm

Big-end bearing running clearance .... 0.019 to 0.060 mm

Main bearing No 1 journal width:
Standard	31.500 mm
1st regrind	31.625 mm
2nd regrind	31.750 mm
3rd regrind	31.875 mm
Width tolerance	-0.000 to +0.025 mm

Thrustwasher thickness:
Standard	1.490 mm
1st regrind	1.615 mm
2nd regrind	1.740 mm
3rd regrind	1.865 mm
Thickness tolerance (all washers)	+0.000 to -0.010 mm

Crankshaft endfloat .... 0.04 to 0.1 mm

1.6 litre engine

Maximum endfloat:
New	0.07 to 0.18 mm
Wear limit	0.20 mm

Main bearing journal diameters:
Standard	54.00 mm
1st undersize	53.75 mm
2nd undersize	53.50 mm
3rd undersize	53.25 mm
Tolerance	-0.022 to -0.037 mm

Main bearing running clearances:
Standard	0.03 to 0.08 mm
Service limit	0.17 mm

Crankpin journal diameters:
Standard	47.80 mm
1st undersize	47.55 mm
2nd undersize	47.30 mm
3rd undersize	47.05 mm
Tolerance	-0.022 to -0.037 mm

Big-end running clearance:
New	0.006 to 0.047 mm

Wear limit .... 0.091 mm

Diesel engine

Maximum endfloat:
New	0.07 to 0.17 mm
Service limit	0.37 mm

Main bearing journal diameters:
Standard	54.00 mm
1st undersize	53.75 mm
2nd undersize	53.50 mm
3rd undersize	53.25 mm
Tolerance	-0.022 to -0.042 mm

Main bearing running clearances:
Standard	0.03 to 0.08 mm
Service limit	0.17 mm

Crankpin journal diameters:
Standard	47.80 mm
1st undersize	47.55 mm
2nd undersize	47.30 mm
3rd undersize	47.05 mm
Tolerance	-0.022 to -0.042 mm

Big-end running clearance (wear limit) .... 0.08 mm

Torque wrench settings

Refer to Chapter 2A, 2B or 2C Specifications, as appropriate

1 Engine and transmission removal - preparation and precautions

If you have decided that the engine must be removed for overhaul or major repair work, several preliminary steps should be taken.

Locating a suitable place to work is extremely important. Adequate work space, along with storage space for the vehicle, will be needed. If a workshop or garage is not available, at the very least a solid, level, clean work surface is required.

If possible, clear some shelving close to the work area, and use it to store the engine components and ancillaries as they are removed and dismantled. In this manner, the components stand a better chance of staying clean and undamaged during the overhaul. Laying out components in groups together with their fixings bolts, screws etc will save time and avoid confusion when the engine is refitted.

Clean the engine compartment and engine/transmission before beginning the removal procedure; this will help visibility and help to keep tools clean.

The help of an assistant should be available; there are certain instances when one person cannot safely perform all of the operations required to remove the engine from the vehicle. Safety is of primary importance, considering the potential hazards involved in this kind of operation. A second person should always be in attendance to offer help in an emergency. If this is the first time you have removed an engine, advice and aid from someone more experienced would also be beneficial.

Plan the operation ahead of time. Before starting work, obtain (or arrange for the hire of) all of the tools and equipment you will need. Access to the following items will allow the task of removing and refitting the engine/transmission to be completed safely and with relative ease: a heavy-duty trolley jack - rated in excess of the combined weight of the engine and transmission, complete sets of spanners and sockets as described in the front of this manual, wooden blocks, and plenty of rags and cleaning solvent for mopping up spilled oil, coolant and fuel. A selection of different-sized plastic storage bins will also prove useful for keeping dismantled components grouped together. If any of the equipment must be hired, make sure that you arrange for it in advance, and perform all of the operations possible without it beforehand; this may save you time and money.

Plan on the vehicle being out of use for quite a while, especially if you intend to carry out an engine overhaul. Read through the whole of this Section and work out a strategy based on your own experience and the tools, time and workspace available to you. Some of the overhaul processes may have to carried

out by a Skoda dealer or an engineering works - these establishments often have busy schedules, so it would be prudent to consult them before removing or dismantling the engine, to get an idea of the amount of time required to carry out the work.

When removing the engine from the vehicle, be methodical about the disconnection of external components. Labelling cables and hoses as they are removed will greatly assist the refitting process.

Always be extremely careful when removing the engine/transmission assembly from the engine bay. Serious injury can result from careless actions. If help is required, it is better to wait until it is available rather than risk personal injury and/or damage to components by continuing alone. By planning ahead and taking your time, a job of this nature, although major, can be accomplished successfully and without incident.

On all models described in this manual, the engine and transmission are removed as a complete assembly, and are lowered out of the vehicle. The vehicle must therefore be securely supported at a height which leaves sufficient clearance for the combined engine/transmission unit to be withdrawn from underneath.

2 Engine and transmission - removal, separation and refitting

Removal

Note: *The engine can be removed from the vehicle only as a complete unit with the transmission; the two are then separated for overhaul. The engine/transmission unit is lowered out of the vehicle. The vehicle must therefore be securely supported at a height which leaves sufficient clearance for the combined engine/transmission unit to be withdrawn from underneath.*

1 Park the vehicle on firm, level ground, then remove the bonnet as described in Chapter 11.
2 If the engine is to be dismantled, drain the oil and remove the oil filter (see the relevant part of Chapter 1). Clean and refit the drain plug, tightening it securely.

2.7 Disconnect the gearchange linkage roll pin and steady rod

2.6 Disconnect the wiring plug for the lambda sensor

3 Firmly apply the handbrake and slacken the front wheel bolts. Jack up the front of the vehicle and support it securely on axle stands, bearing in mind the note made at the start of the this Section (see *Jacking and vehicle support*). Remove both front roadwheels.
4 Drain the transmission oil as described in the relevant part of Chapter 1, then clean and refit the drain plug and tighten it securely.
5 Drain the cooling system as described in the relevant part of Chapter 1.
6 Unbolt the front exhaust pipe from the manifold as described in Chapter 4D. On petrol engine models, trace the wiring for the lambda sensor back from the sensor to the wiring plug, and disconnect it; slide the plug out of its mounting bracket **(see illustration)**. Detach the exhaust mountings as required, and lower the pipe out of the way, bearing in mind that the engine/transmission unit will be being lowered out of the engine bay.
7 Working as described in Chapter 7, disconnect the gearchange linkage selector rod and steady rod from the transmission **(see illustration)**.
8 Remove the air cleaner (or just the air cleaner trunking) as described in the relevant part of Chapter 4. On 1.3 litre and 1.6 litre models with multi-point fuel injection, remove the throttle body cover.
9 Disconnect the battery and remove the alternator as described in Chapter 5A.
10 Rotate the clutch adjusting nut in an anti-clockwise direction to obtain maximum clutch cable free play **(see illustration)**. Release the inner cable from the clutch release lever and free the outer cable from its mounting bracket.

2.10 Clutch adjuster nut (arrowed)

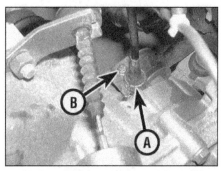

2.11 Speedometer cable retaining collar (A) and drivegear retaining plate bolt (B)

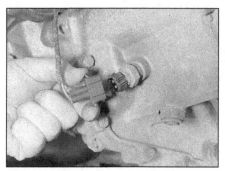

2.12 Disconnect the reversing light switch

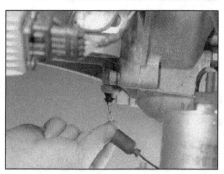

2.14 Disconnecting the oil pressure switch - 1.3 litre engine shown

Unbolt and remove the clutch cable support bracket, together with the earth wiring, where applicable.

11 Unscrew the knurled retaining collar, and pull the speedometer cable upwards to disconnect its drive from the rear of the transmission. Alternatively, unscrew the retaining plate bolt, and remove the speedometer drivegear from the transmission **(see illustration)**.

12 Disconnect the wiring from the reversing light switch, located on the front underside of the transmission **(see illustration)**. Unclip the switch wiring from the starter motor, where applicable.

13 Slide back the rubber insulating boot from the starter motor solenoid main terminal, then remove the nut and disconnect the battery lead. Carefully disconnect the spade connector from the solenoid.

14 Disconnect the wiring connector from the

2.15a Coolant temperature sender on coolant elbow - diesel models

oil pressure switch, situated on the lower front of the cylinder block on 1.3 litre models, on the rear of the head on 1.6 litre models, or on the left-hand end of the cylinder head on diesel models **(see illustration)**.

15 Disconnect the wiring connector from the coolant temperature gauge sender unit on the thermostat housing or coolant elbow, and from the radiator cooling fan switch and motor **(see illustrations)**. Disconnect the hoses from the radiator and thermostat housing/coolant elbow as necessary. Given the risk of damage as the engine is removed, it is advisable to remove the radiator and fan completely - on diesel engine models, this is essential to provide clearance.

16 On models with power steering or air conditioning, remove the auxiliary drivebelt as described in Chapter 2A, 2B or 2C.

17 On vehicles with air conditioning, refer to Chapter 3 and carry out the following additional operations:

a) Disconnect the vacuum hose from the vacuum reservoir.

b) Disconnect the wiring plug from the compressor.

c) Unbolt the air conditioning compressor from the engine, and tie it up out of the way. Make sure the refrigerant hoses are not under strain.

18 On models with power steering, refer to Chapter 10 and remove the pump. There's no need to disconnect the fluid lines, as long as the pump is positioned so that the pipes are not under strain (or likely to be damaged during engine removal).

Petrol models

19 On 1.3 litre single-point injection models, disconnect the following from the inlet manifold/throttle body, as described in the relevant Sections of Chapter 4A:

a) Fuel supply and return hoses.

b) Throttle body wiring connectors. Free the wiring from any clips or ties, and lay it to one side.

c) Throttle cable.

d) Braking system vacuum servo unit hose.

e) Coolant hose(s).

f) Charcoal canister hose.

g) Coolant temperature sensor wiring connector **(see illustration)**.

h) CO sampling pipe mounting bracket.

20 On 1.3 litre and 1.6 litre multi-point injection models, disconnect the following as described in Chapter 4B:

a) Fuel supply and return hoses from the fuel pressure regulator.

b) Vacuum hose from the fuel pressure regulator.

c) Fuel system wiring connectors, as necessary. Free the wiring from any clips or ties, and lay it to one side.

d) Inlet air temperature/pressure sensor wiring connector.

e) Ignition coil unit wiring connector (1.3 litre models) **(see illustration)**.

f) Charcoal canister hose.

g) Throttle cable.

h) Braking system vacuum servo unit hose from the inlet manifold.

i) Knock sensor wiring connector on the rear of the engine block **(see illustration)**.

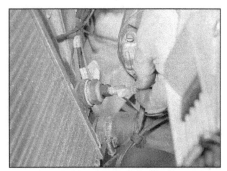

2.15b Disconnecting the radiator fan switch . . .

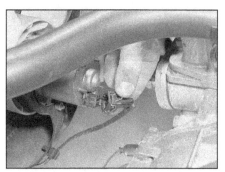

2.15c . . . and the radiator fan motor

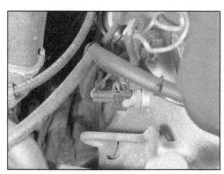

2.19 Coolant temperature sensor at the rear of the inlet manifold

2.20a Unplug the wiring connector from the ignition coil unit

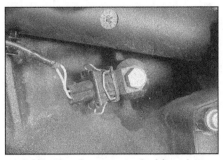

2.20b Knock sensor and wiring plug (1.6 litre) - seen with engine removed, for clarity

2.21 Hall sensor wiring plug is on the distributor on 1.6 litre models

21 Disconnect the wiring plug for the Hall sensor. On 1.3 litre models, the three-pin wiring plug is either on a bracket attached to the thermostat housing, or on top of the transmission housing. On 1.6 litre models, the Hall sensor wiring plug is on the distributor **(see illustration)**.
22 If not already done, disconnect the wiring from the ignition coil.
23 Referring to Chapter 5B, remove the distributor cap, rotor arm and flash shield, as applicable.

Diesel models

24 Refer to Chapter 9 and disconnect the brake servo vacuum hose from the vacuum pump.
25 Refer to Chapter 4D if necessary, and disconnect the vacuum hose from the EGR valve.

26 Carry out the following operations, referring to Chapter 4C where necessary:
a) Slacken and withdraw the banjo bolts, then disconnect the fuel supply and return hoses from the fuel injection pump.
b) Release the clip, then disconnect the injector bleed hose from the port on the fuel return union.
c) Slacken the clips and remove the inlet air hose from the inlet manifold cover.
d) Disconnect the accelerator cable and cold start accelerator cable from the fuel injection pump.
e) Disconnect the EGR valve and idle speed boost valve wiring connectors at the rear of the engine compartment, noting their locations **(see illustration)**.
f) Unplug the wiring harness at the multiway connector situated behind the left-hand suspension strut turret **(see illustration)**.

The connector is a screw fit; twist the housing to unlock the two halves, then pull them apart and recover the internal seal; note the red alignment marking for use when reconnecting. Cover the connector housings with a plastic bag to prevent the ingress of dirt or water.
g) *Disconnect the two wiring plugs mounted in a bracket at the left-hand end of the engine **(see illustrations)**, and the earth wire from the bracket above. Cover the connector housings with a plastic bag to prevent the ingress of dirt or water. Release the harness from all the retaining clips.*
h) *Where applicable, disconnect the wiring plug for the alternator harness **(see illustration)**.*

All models

27 With reference to Chapter 5B and Chapter 4A, B or C as applicable, identify those sections of the engine, ignition and fuelling system electrical harness that remain connected to sensors and actuators on the engine. Establish which connectors must be separated to permit engine removal, labelling each connector carefully as it is disconnected, to ensure correct refitting.
28 Depending on model, one or more earth straps will be fitted, either at the transmission, close to the engine right-hand mounting, or near the base of the dipstick tube - disconnect the straps to allow the engine/transmission to be removed.

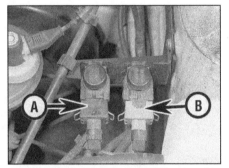

2.26a Wiring plugs for the EGR solenoid valve (A) and idle speed boost valve (B)

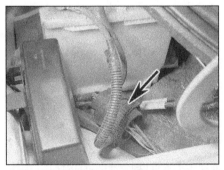

2.26b Wiring harness multiway connector - unscrew to disconnect

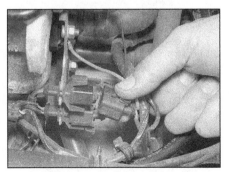

2.26c Disconnect the upper . . .

2.26d . . . and lower wiring plugs, and the earth wire above

2.26e Where applicable, disconnect the alternator harness wiring plug (arrowed)

2.32 Engine/transmission rear mounting

2.33 Transmission left-hand mounting

29 Refer to Chapter 8 and pull the driveshafts out from the transmission. Once the driveshafts have been separated, tie them up using wire or string, to prevent damage to the CV joints.

30 Connect a hoist or engine support bar, and raise it so that the weight of the engine and transmission are just supported. Arrange the hoist and sling so that the engine and transmission are kept level when they are being withdrawn from the vehicle. It is not advisable to support the engine/transmission entirely from below, because this is less safe, and because the engine/transmission must be lowered to the floor to be withdrawn under the front bumper - anything under the engine will prevent it from being lowered fully.

31 To avoid damage to the sump, arrange a piece of board or some old carpet below the engine, onto which the assembly can be lowered. Bear in mind that the assembly must be slid out forwards under the front bumper - a wheeled trolley of some kind would be ideal.

32 Unscrew and remove the through-bolt from the engine/transmission rear mounting, referring to Chapter 2A or 2B as necessary **(see illustration)**.

33 Before removing the transmission left-hand mounting, mark its fitted location from below. Remove the self-locking nut and the two bolts, and take off the mounting plate from the top of the mounting **(see illustration)**.

34 On 1.3 litre engine models, lever out the plug from the right-hand inner wing which allows the engine right-hand mounting through-bolt to be withdrawn. Unscrew the

through-bolt nut, then withdraw the through-bolt **(see illustrations)**.

35 On 1.6 litre and diesel engine models, working from below, remove the two engine right-hand mounting bolts directly above the crankshaft pulley, and recover the washers.

36 Check around the engine and transmission assembly to ensure that all associated attachments are disconnected and positioned out of the way. Engage the services of an assistant to help in guiding the assembly clear of surrounding components, especially the exhaust downpipe and the power steering fluid pipework, where applicable. Carefully lower the engine/transmission assembly to the floor, then remove the assembly from under the front of the vehicle.

37 Once the engine/transmission assembly is clear of the vehicle, move it to an area where it can be cleaned and worked on.

Separation

38 Rest the engine and transmission assembly on a firm, flat surface, and use wooden blocks as wedges to keep the unit steady.

39 Remove the starter motor, referring to Chapter 5A if necessary.

40 Where applicable, undo the flywheel cover plate retaining bolts, and remove the plate from the transmission.

41 Slacken and remove the nuts/bolts securing the transmission housing to the engine, noting that one of the bolts is used to secure the clutch cable support bracket removed earlier. Move the gearbox squarely

away from the engine to release it from its locating dowels, and separate the two. Collect the locating dowels if they are loose enough to be extracted.

42 If required, remove the clutch release mechanism, pressure plate and friction plate as described in Chapter 6.

Refitting

43 If the engine and transmission have not been separated, go to paragraph 46.

43 Smear a little high-melting-point grease on the splines of the transmission input shaft. Do not use an excessive amount, as there is the risk of contaminating the clutch friction plate. Carefully offer up the transmission to the cylinder block, guiding the dowels into the mounting holes in cylinder block.

44 Refit the bellhousing nuts/bolts, hand-tightening them to secure the transmission in position. **Note:** *Do not tighten them to force the engine and transmission together.* Ensure that the bellhousing and cylinder block mating faces will butt together evenly without obstruction, before tightening the bolts and nuts to their specified torque. Note that one of the bolts secures the clutch cable support bracket removed earlier.

45 Where applicable, refit the flywheel cover plate and secure with the retaining bolts.

46 Slide the engine/transmission assembly into position under the front of the car.

47 Attach the jib of the engine hoist or support bar to the lifting eyelets on the cylinder head, and raise the engine and transmission from the ground.

48 With the help of an assistant, raise and guide the engine/transmission into position until the engine right-hand mounting can be reconnected. Tighten the bolts (or the through-bolt and nut) to the specified torque. On 1.3 litre engine models, refit the access plug to the right-hand inner wing.

49 Reconnect the transmission left-hand mounting, not forgetting the plate fitted to the top of the mounting. Leave the nuts and bolts loose until the marks on the underside of the mounting made on removal are completely aligned. Tighten the bolts and self-locking nut to the specified torque.

50 Reconnect the engine/transmission rear mounting, tightening the nuts/bolts to the specified torque.

51 Detach the engine hoist or engine support bar from the lifting eyelets.

52 The remainder of the refitting sequence is a direct reversal of the removal procedure, noting the following points:

a) Ensure that all sections of the wiring harness follow their original routing; use new cable-ties to secure the harness in position, keeping it away from sources of heat and abrasion.

b) Ensure that all hoses are correctly routed and are secured with the correct hose clips, where applicable. If the hose clips originally fitted were of the crimp variety, they cannot be used again; proprietary

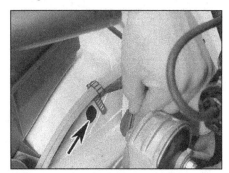

2.34a Remove the rubber plug from the hole (arrowed) in the inner wing

2.34b Unbolting the engine right-hand mounting

worm-drive clips must be fitted in their place, unless otherwise specified.

c) When reconnecting the gearchange linkage, use a new roll pin and secure with a worm-drive clip (see Chapter 7).

d) Refill the cooling system as described in Chapter 1A or B.

e) Refill the engine with appropriate grades and quantities of oil (Chapter 1A or B).

f) On diesel models, with reference to Chapter 4D, after reconnecting the cold start accelerator cable to the fuel injection pump, check and if necessary adjust the operation of the cold start acceleration system.

53 When the engine is started for the first time, check for air, coolant, lubricant and fuel leaks from manifolds, hoses etc. If the engine has been overhauled, read the notes in Section 15 before attempting to start it.

3 Engine overhaul - preliminary information

It is much easier to dismantle and work on the engine if it is mounted on a portable engine stand. These stands can often be hired from a tool hire shop. Before the engine is mounted on a stand, the flywheel should be removed, so that the stand bolts can be tightened into the end of the cylinder block/crankcase.

If a stand is not available, it is possible to dismantle the engine with it blocked up on a sturdy workbench, or on the floor. Be very careful not to tip or drop the engine when working without a stand.

If you intend to obtain a reconditioned engine, all ancillaries must be removed first, to be transferred to the replacement engine (just as they will if you are doing a complete engine overhaul yourself). These components include the following:

Petrol engines

a) Power steering pump (Chapter 10) - where applicable.

b) Air conditioning compressor (Chapter 3) - where applicable.

c) Alternator (including mounting brackets)and starter motor (Chapter 5A).

d) The ignition system and HT components, including all sensors, distributor, HT leads and spark plugs, as applicable (Chapters 1A and 5B).

e) The fuel injection system components (Chapter 4A or B).

f) All electrical switches, actuators and sensors, and the engine wiring harness (Chapter 4A or B, Chapter 5B, Chapter 12).

g) Inlet and exhaust manifolds (Chapter 4).

h) Engine oil dipstick and tube (Chapter 2A or B).

i) Engine mountings (Chapter 2A or B).

j) Flywheel/driveplate (Chapter 2A or B).

k) Clutch components (Chapter 6).

Diesel engines

a) Power steering pump (Chapter 10) - where applicable.

b) Air conditioning compressor (Chapter 3) - where applicable.

c) Alternator (including mounting brackets)and starter motor (Chapter 5A).

d) The glow plug/pre-heating system components (Chapter 5C)

e) All fuel system components, including the fuel injection pump, all sensors and actuators (Chapter 4C)

f) The brake vacuum pump (Chapter 9)

g) All electrical switches, actuators and sensors, and the engine wiring harness (Chapter 4C, Chapter 12).

h) Inlet and exhaust manifolds (the relevant part of Chapter 4).

i) The engine oil level dipstick and its tube (Chapter 2C)

j) Engine mountings (Chapter 2C).

k) Flywheel (Chapter 2C).

l) Clutch components (Chapter 6).

Note: When removing the external components from the engine, pay close attention to details that may be helpful or important during refitting. Note the fitted position of gaskets, seals, spacers, pins, washers, bolts, and other small components.

If you are obtaining a short engine (the engine cylinder block/crankcase, crankshaft, pistons and connecting rods, all fully assembled), then the cylinder head, sump and baffle plate, oil pump, timing chain/belt (together with its covers), auxiliary drivebelt, coolant pump, thermostat housing, coolant outlet elbows, oil filter housing (and where applicable, oil cooler) will also have to be removed.

If you are planning a full overhaul, the engine can be dismantled in the order given below:

a) Inlet and exhaust manifolds.

b) Timing chain/belt, sprockets and belt tensioner.

c) Cylinder head.

d) Flywheel.

e) Sump.

f) Oil pump.

g) Piston/connecting rod assemblies.

h) Crankshaft.

4.9 Keep groups of components together in labelled bags or boxes

4 Cylinder head - dismantling, cleaning, inspection and assembly

Note: New and reconditioned cylinder heads are available from Skoda, and from engine specialists. Specialist tools are required for the dismantling and inspection procedures, and new components may not be readily available. It may, therefore, be more practical for the home mechanic to buy a reconditioned head, rather than to dismantle, inspect and recondition the original head.

Dismantling

1.3 litre engine

1 Using a valve spring compressor, compress each valve spring in turn until the split collets can be removed. Release the compressor, and lift off the spring retainer and both the outer and inner springs.

2 If, when the valve spring compressor is screwed down, the spring retainer refuses to free and expose the split collets, gently tap the top of the tool, directly over the retainer with a light hammer. This will free the retainer.

3 Lift both the inner and outer spring seats off the valve guide, then use a pair of pliers to carefully extract the valve stem seal from the guide.

4 Withdraw the valve through the combustion chamber.

5 It is essential that each valve is stored together with its collets, retainer, springs and spring seats, and that all valves are kept in their correct sequence, unless they are so badly worn that they are to be renewed. If they are going to be kept and used again, place each valve assembly in a labelled polythene bag or similar small container.

1.6 litre and diesel engines

6 On diesel engines, remove the injectors and glow plugs (see Chapter 4C and Chapter 5C). Remove the coolant outlet elbow, together with its gasket/O-ring.

7 On 1.6 litre engines, unscrew the thermostat housing and oil pressure switch from the cylinder head.

8 Remove the camshaft timing belt sprocket (Part B or C of this Chapter).

9 It is important that groups of components are kept together when they are removed and, if still serviceable, refitted in the same groups. If they are refitted randomly, accelerated wear leading to early failure will occur. Stowing groups of components in plastic bags or storage bins will help to keep everything in the right order. Label parts according to their fitted location, eg No 1 exhaust, No 2 inlet, etc - note that No 1 cylinder is nearest the timing belt end of the engine **(see illustration)**.

10 Check that the manufacturer's identification markings are visible on camshaft bearing caps **(see illustration)**; if none can be

4.10 Camshaft bearing cap identification marks

4.15a Valve spring compressor jaws located on the upper spring seat . . .

4.15b . . . and on the valve head

found, make your own using a scriber or centre-punch. The camshaft bearing cap nuts must be removed progressively and in sequence to avoid stressing the camshaft, as follows.

11 Slacken the nuts from bearing caps Nos 5, 1 and 3 first, then at bearing caps 2 and 4. Slacken the nuts alternately and diagonally half a turn at a time until they can be removed by hand. **Note:** *Camshaft bearing caps are numbered 1 to 5 from the timing belt end.*

12 Slide the oil seal from the sprocket end of the camshaft and discard it; a new one must be used on reassembly.

13 Carefully lift the camshaft from the cylinder head - do not tilt it. Support both ends as it is removed so that the journals and lobes are not damaged.

14 Lift the hydraulic tappets from their bores and store them with the valve contact surface facing downwards, to prevent the oil from draining out. Alternatively, place the tappets in a tray full of oil, sufficiently deep to prevent the tappets draining. Make a note of the position of each tappet, as they must be fitted to the same valves on reassembly - accelerated wear leading to early failure will result if they are interchanged.

15 Turn the cylinder head over, and rest it on one side. Using a valve spring compressor, compress each valve spring in turn, extracting the split collets when the upper valve spring seat has been pushed far enough down the valve stem to free them **(see illustrations)**. If the spring seat sticks, tap the upper jaw of the compressor with a hammer to free it.

16 Release the valve spring compressor and

remove the upper spring seat and valve spring.

17 Use a pair of pliers to extract the valve stem oil seal. Withdraw the valve itself from the head gasket side of the cylinder head. If the valve sticks in the guide, carefully deburr the end face with fine abrasive paper. Repeat this process for the remaining valves.

18 On diesel engines, if the swirl chambers are badly coked or burned and are in need of renewal, insert a pin punch through each injector hole, and carefully drive out the swirl chambers using a mallet **(see illustration)**.

Cleaning

19 Using a suitable degreasing agent, remove all traces of oil deposits from the cylinder head, paying particular attention (as applicable) to the camshaft journal bearings, hydraulic tappet bores, valve guides and oilways. Scrape off any traces of old gasket from the mating surfaces, taking care not to score or gouge them. If using emery paper, do not use a grade of less than 100. Turn the head over and using a blunt blade, scrape any carbon deposits from the combustion chambers and ports.

Caution: Do not erode the sealing surface of the valve seat. Finally, wash the entire head casting with a suitable solvent to remove the remaining debris.

20 Clean the valve heads and stems using a fine wire brush. If the valve is heavily coked, scrape off the majority of the deposits with a blunt blade first, then use the wire brush.

Caution: Do not erode the sealing surface of the valve face.

21 Thoroughly clean the remainder of the components using solvent and allow them to dry completely. Discard the oil seals, as new items must be fitted when the cylinder head is reassembled.

Inspection

Cylinder head casting

Note: *On diesel engines, the cylinder heads and valves cannot be reworked (although valves may be lapped in); new or exchange units must be obtained.*

22 Examine the head casting closely to identify any damage sustained or cracks that may have developed. Pay particular attention to the areas around the mounting holes, valve seats and spark plug holes. If cracking is discovered between the valve seats, consult a Skoda dealer **(see illustration)**.

23 Moderately pitted and scorched valve seats can be repaired by lapping the valves in during reassembly, as described later in this Chapter. Badly worn or damaged valve seats may be restored by recutting; this is a highly specialised operation involving precision machining and accurate angle measurement and as such should be entrusted to a professional cylinder head re-builder.

24 Measure any distortion of the gasketed surfaces using a straight edge and a set of feeler blades **(see illustration)**. Take one measurement longitudinally on both the inlet and exhaust manifold mating surfaces. Take several measurements across the head gasket surface, to assess the level of distortion in all planes. Compare the measurements with the

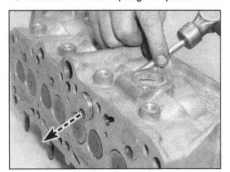

4.18 Swirl chamber removal (diesel engine)

4.22 Look for cracking between the valve seats

4.24 Measuring the distortion of the cylinder head gasketed surface

figures in the Specifications. On petrol engines, if the head is distorted out of specification, it may be possible to repair it by smoothing down any high-spots on the surface with fine abrasive paper.

25 Minimum cylinder head heights (measured between the cylinder head gasket surface and the cylinder head cover gasket surface), where quoted by the manufacturer, are listed in Specifications. If the cylinder head is to be professionally machined, bear in mind the following:

a) *The minimum cylinder head height dimension (where specified) must be adhered to.*

b) *The valve seats will need to be recut to suit the new height of the cylinder head, otherwise valve-to-piston crown contact may occur.*

c) *Before the valve seats can be recut, check that there is enough material left on the cylinder head to allow repair; if too much material is removed, the valve stem may protrude too far above the top of the valve guide, and this would prevent the hydraulic tappets from operating correctly. Refer to a professional head rebuilder or machine shop for advice.*

Note: *Depending on engine type, it may be possible to obtain new valves with shorter valve stems - refer to your Skoda dealer for advice.*

Camshaft - 1.6 litre and diesel engines

Note: *for information on camshaft removal and refitting on 1.3 litre engines, refer to Section 5.*

26 The camshaft is identified by means of markings stamped onto the side of the shaft, between the inlet and exhaust lobes **(see illustration)**. Refer to your Skoda dealer or engine overhaul specialist for an explanation of the markings.

27 Visually inspect the camshaft for evidence of wear on the surfaces of the lobes and journals. Normally their surfaces should be smooth and have a dull shine; look for scoring, erosion or pitting and areas that appear highly polished - these are signs that wear has begun to occur. Accelerated wear will occur once the hardened exterior of the camshaft has been damaged, so always renew worn items. **Note:** *If these symptoms are visible on the tips of the camshaft lobes, check the corresponding tappet, as it will probably be worn as well.*

28 On diesel engines, examine the vacuum pump drivegear for signs of wear or damage.

29 If the machined surfaces of the camshaft appear discoloured or blued, it is likely that it has been overheated at some point, probably due to inadequate lubrication. This may have distorted the shaft, so check the runout as follows: place the camshaft between two V-blocks and using a DTI gauge, measure the runout at the centre journal. If it exceeds the figure quoted in the Specifications at the start of this Chapter, camshaft renewal should be considered.

30 To measure the camshaft endfloat, temporarily refit the camshaft to the cylinder head, then fit the first and last bearing caps and tighten the retaining nuts to the specified first stage torque setting - refer to *Reassembly* for details. Anchor a DTI gauge to the timing belt end of the cylinder head, and align the gauge probe with the camshaft axis. Push the camshaft to one end of the cylinder head as far as it will travel, then rest the DTI gauge probe on the end of the camshaft, and zero the gauge display. Push the camshaft as far as it will go to the other end of the cylinder head, and record the gauge reading **(see illustration)**. Verify the reading by pushing the camshaft back to its original position and checking that the gauge indicates zero again. **Note:** *The hydraulic tappets must **not** be fitted to the cylinder whilst this measurement is being taken.*

31 Check that the camshaft endfloat measurement is within the limit listed in the Specifications. Wear outside of this limit is unlikely to be confined to any one component, so renewal of the camshaft, cylinder head and bearing caps must be considered; seek the advice of a cylinder head rebuilding specialist.

32 The difference between the outside diameters of the camshaft bearing surfaces and the internal diameters formed by the bearing caps and the cylinder head must now be measured, this dimension is known as the camshaft running clearance.

33 The dimensions of the camshaft bearing journals are not quoted by the manufacturer, so running clearance measurement by means of a micrometer and a bore gauge or internal vernier calipers cannot be recommended in this case.

34 Another (more accurate) method of measuring the running clearance involves the use of Plastigauge. This is a soft, plastic material supplied in thin sticks of about the same diameter as a sewing needle. Lengths of Plastigauge are cut to length as required, laid on the camshaft bearing journals and crushed as the bearing caps are temporarily fitted and tightened. The Plastigauge spreads widthways as it is crushed; the running clearance can then be determined by measuring the increase in width using the card gauge supplied with the Plastigauge kit.

35 The following paragraphs describe this measurement procedure step by step, but note that a similar method is used to measure the crankshaft running clearances; refer to Section 12 for further guidance.

36 Ensure that the cylinder head, bearing cap and camshaft bearing surfaces are completely clean and dry. Lay the camshaft in position in the cylinder head.

37 Lay a length of Plastigauge on top of each of the camshaft bearing journals.

38 Lubricate each bearing cap with a little silicone release agent, then place them in position over the camshaft and tighten the retaining nuts down to the specified torque -

4.26 Camshaft identification markings

refer to *Reassembly* later in this Section for guidance. **Note:** *Where the torque setting is expressed in several stages, tighten the cap fixings to the first stage only. Do not rotate the camshaft whilst the bearing caps are in place, as the measurements will be affected.*

39 Carefully remove the bearing caps again, lifting them vertically away from the camshaft to avoid disturbing the Plastigauge. The Plastigauge should remain on the camshaft bearing surface, squashed into a uniform sausage shape. If it disintegrates as the bearing caps are removed, re-clean the components and repeat the exercise, using a little more release agent on the bearing cap.

40 Hold the scale card supplied with the kit against each bearing journal, and match the width of the crushed Plastigauge with the graduated markings on the card; use this to determine the running clearances.

41 Compare the camshaft running clearance measurements with those listed in the Specifications; if any are outside the specified tolerance, the camshaft and cylinder head should be renewed. Note that undersize camshafts with bearing shells may be obtained from Skoda dealers, but only as part of an exchange cylinder head package.

42 On completion, remove the bearing caps and camshaft, and clean of all remaining traces of Plastigauge and silicone release agent.

Valves and associated components

Note: *On all engines, the valve heads cannot be re-cut (although they may be lapped in); new or exchange valves must be obtained.*

4.30 Checking camshaft endfloat using a DTI gauge

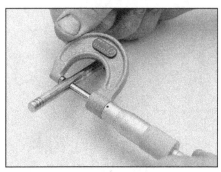

4.43 Measure the diameter of a valve stem with a micrometer

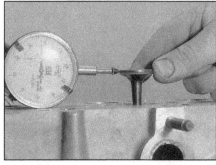

4.47 Measure the maximum deflection of the valve in its guide, using a DTI gauge

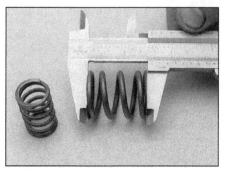

4.49 Measure the free length of each of the valve springs

43 Examine each valve closely for signs of wear. Inspect the valve stems for wear ridges, scoring or variations in diameter; measure their diameters at several points along their lengths with a micrometer **(see illustration)**.

44 The valve heads should not be cracked, badly pitted or charred. Note that light pitting of the valve head can be rectified by grinding-in the valves during reassembly, as described later in this Section.

45 Check that the valve stem end face is free from excessive pitting or indentation; this would be caused (on 1.6 litre and diesel engines) by defective hydraulic tappets.

46 Place the valves in a V-block and using a DTI gauge, measure the runout at the valve head. A maximum figure is not quoted by the manufacturer, but the valve should be renewed if the runout appears excessive.

47 Insert each valve into its respective guide in the cylinder head, and set up a DTI gauge against the edge of the valve head. With the valve end face flush with the top of the valve guide, measure the maximum side-to-side deflection of the valve in its guide **(see illustration)**.

48 If the deflection appears excessive, the valve and valve guide should be renewed as a pair. **Note:** *Valve guides are an interference fit in the cylinder head, and their removal requires access to a hydraulic press. For this reason, it would be wise to entrust the job to an engineering workshop or head rebuilding specialist.*

49 Using vernier calipers, measure the free length of each of the valve springs **(see illustration)**. As a manufacturer's figure is not

quoted, the only way to check the length of the springs is by comparison with a new component. Note that valve springs are usually renewed during a major engine overhaul.

50 Stand each spring on its end on a flat surface, against an engineer's square **(see illustration)**. Check the squareness of the spring visually; if it appears distorted, renew the spring. No squareness limits are specified by the manufacturers.

51 Measuring valve spring pre-load involves compressing the valve by applying a specified weight and measuring the reduction in length. This may be a difficult operation to conduct in the home workshop, so it would be wise to approach your local garage or engineering workshop for assistance. Weakened valve springs will at best increase engine running noise and at worst cause poor compression, so defective items should be renewed.

Valve grinding

52 To achieve a gas-tight seal between the valves and their seats, it will be necessary to grind, or lap, the valves in. To complete this process, you will need a quantity of fine/coarse grinding paste and a grinding tool - this can either be of the dowel and rubber sucker type, or the automatic type which are driven by a rotary power tool.

53 Smear a small quantity of *fine* grinding paste on the sealing face of the valve head. Turn the cylinder head over so that the combustion chambers are facing upwards, and insert the valve into the correct guide. Attach the grinding tool to the valve head and

using a backward/forward rotary action, grind the valve head into its seat **(see illustration)**. Periodically lift the valve and rotate it to redistribute the grinding paste.

54 Continue this process until the contact between valve and seat produces an unbroken, matt grey ring of uniform width, on both faces. Repeat the operation for the remaining valves.

55 If the valves and seats are so badly pitted that coarse grinding paste must be used, check first that there is enough material left on both components to make this operation worthwhile. On 1.6 litre and diesel engines, if too little material is left remaining, the valve stems may protrude too far above their guides, impeding the correct operation of the hydraulic tappets. Refer to a machine shop or cylinder head rebuilding specialist for advice.

56 Assuming the repair is feasible, work as described in the previous paragraph but use the coarse grinding paste initially, to achieve a dull finish on the valve face and seat. Then, wash off coarse paste with solvent and repeat the process using fine grinding paste to obtain the correct finish.

57 When all the valves have been ground in, remove all traces of grinding paste from the cylinder head and valves with solvent, and allow them to dry completely.

Reassembly - 1.3 litre engine

Caution: Unless all new components are to be used, maintain groups when refitting valve train components - do not mix components between cylinders, and ensure that components are refitted in their original positions.

58 Lubricate the stems of the valves, and insert them into their original locations **(see illustration)**. If new valves are being fitted, insert them into the locations to which they have been ground.

59 Working on the first valve, first refit the inner and outer spring seats over the valve guide **(see illustrations)**.

60 If genuine Skoda valve guide seals are being fitted, fit one of the plastic seal protectors supplied with the seal kit to the end of the valve stem; these protect the seal lip from being damaged as it passes over the valve end.

4.50 Checking the squareness of a valve spring

4.53 Grinding-in a valve

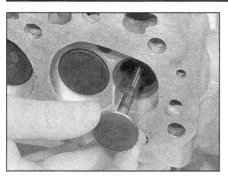

4.58 Lubricate the valve stem, then insert into its guide

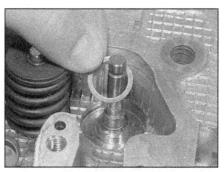

4.59a Refit the inner . . .

4.59b . . . and outer spring seats

61 Dip the new valve guide seal in fresh engine oil, then carefully locate it over the valve and onto the guide. Take care not to damage the seal as it is passed over the valve stem **(see illustration)**.

62 Use a suitable socket or metal tube to press the seal firmly onto the guide **(see illustration)**. Where fitted, remove the seal protector.

63 Locate the inner and outer springs on their seats, and refit the spring retainer **(see illustrations)**.

64 Using a valve spring compressor, compress the valve spring, then locate the split collets in the recess in the valve stem **(see illustration)**. Release the compressor, then repeat the procedure on the remaining valves.

> **HAYNES HiNT** *Use a little grease to hold the collets in place.*

65 With all the valves installed, place the cylinder head flat on the bench and, using a hammer and interposed block of wood, tap the end of each valve stem to settle the components.

66 Refer to Chapter 2A and refit the cylinder head to the cylinder block.

Reassembly - 1.6 litre and diesel engines

Caution: Unless all new components are to be used, maintain groups when refitting valve train components - do not mix

components between cylinders, and ensure that components are refitted in their original positions.

67 Where necessary on diesel engines, fit new swirl chambers by driving them squarely into their housings with a mallet - use a block of wood to protect the face of the swirl chamber. Note the locating recess on the side of the chamber and the corresponding groove in the housing **(see illustrations)**.

68 On completion, the projection of the swirl chamber from the face of the cylinder head must be measured using a DTI gauge and compared with the limit quoted in the Specifications **(see illustration)**. If this limit is exceeded, there is a risk that the chamber may be struck by the piston, and in this case the advice of a professional cylinder head rebuilder or machine shop should be sought.

4.61 Fitting the valve guide oil seal. Note the seal protector (arrowed) supplied with genuine parts

4.62 Use a socket to press the seal onto the valve guide

4.63a Refit the inner and outer valve springs . . .

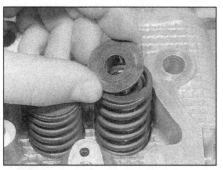

4.63b . . . and install the spring retainer

4.64 Compress the valve spring and install the collets, using a dab of grease to hold them in position

4.67a Swirl chamber locating recess (diesel engine)

4.67b Fitting a swirl chamber

4.68 Measuring swirl chamber projection using a DTI gauge

4.69 Fit the lower spring seat in place, with the convex face facing the cylinder head

69 Turn the head over and place it on a stand, or wooden blocks. Where applicable, fit the first lower spring seat into place, with the convex side facing the cylinder head **(see illustration)**.

4.70a Lubricate the valve stem with clean engine oil and insert it into the guide

70 Working on one valve at a time, lubricate the valve stem with clean engine oil, and insert it into the guide. Fit one of the protective plastic sleeves supplied with the new valve stem oil seals over the valve end face - this will protect the oil seal whilst it is being fitted **(see illustrations)**.

71 Dip a new valve stem seal in clean engine oil, and carefully push it over the valve and onto the top of the valve guide - take care not to damage the stem seal as it passes over the valve end face. Use a suitable long-reach socket to press it firmly into position **(see illustrations)**.

72 Locate the valve spring over the valve stem **(see illustration)**.

73 Fit the upper seat over the top of the springs, then using a valve spring compressor, compress the springs until the upper seat is pushed beyond the collet grooves in the valve stem. Refit the split collet, using a dab of grease to hold the two

halves in the grooves **(see illustrations)**. Gradually release the spring compressor, checking that the collet remains correctly seated as the spring extends. When correctly seated, the upper seat should force the two halves of the collet together, and hold them securely in the grooves in the end of the valve.

74 Repeat this process for the remaining sets of valve components. To settle the components after installation, strike the end of each valve stem with a mallet, using a block of wood to protect the stem from damage. Check before progressing any further that the spilt collets remain firmly held in the end of the valve stem by the upper spring seat.

75 Smear some clean engine oil onto the sides of the hydraulic tappets, and fit them into position in their bores in the cylinder head **(see illustration)**. Push them down until they contact the valves, then lubricate the camshaft lobe contact surfaces.

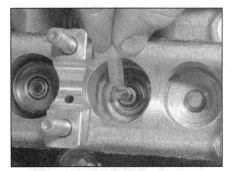

4.70b Fit one of the protective plastic sleeves over the valve end face

4.71a Fit a new valve stem seal over the valve

4.71b Use a long-reach socket to press on the oil seal

4.72 Fitting a valve spring

4.73a Fit the upper seat over the top of the valve spring

4.73b Use grease to hold the two halves of the split collet in the groove

4.75 Fit the tappets into their bores in the cylinder head

4.76a Lubricate the camshaft bearings with clean engine oil . . .

4.76b . . . then lower the camshaft into position on the cylinder head

76 Lubricate the camshaft and cylinder head bearing journals with clean engine oil, then carefully lower the camshaft into position on the cylinder head **(see illustrations)**. Support the ends of the shaft as it is inserted, to avoid damaging the lobes and journals.
77 On diesel engines, with reference to Chapter 2C, lubricate the lip of a new camshaft oil seal with clean engine oil, and locate it over the end of the camshaft **(see illustration)**. Slide the seal along the camshaft until it locates in the lower half of its housing in the cylinder head.
78 Oil the upper surfaces of the camshaft bearing journals, then fit the bearing caps in place as described below.

1.6 litre engine

79 Note the fitted orientation of the camshaft

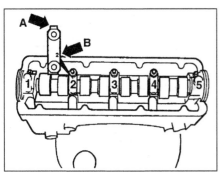

4.79 Petrol engine camshaft bearing cap orientation

A Cast lug
B Identification number

4.81 Smear the mating surfaces of cap No 1 with sealant

bearing caps. The wider cast lugs must be positioned on the inlet side of the head, and the bearing cap identification numbers must be readable from the exhaust side **(see illustration)**.
80 Fit caps Nos 2 and 4 over the camshaft, and tighten the retaining nuts alternately and diagonally to the specified Stage 1 torque.
81 Smear the mating surfaces of caps Nos 1 and 5 with sealant **(see illustration)**. Locate caps Nos 1, 3 and 5 over the camshaft, then fit and tighten the nuts to the specified Stage 1 torque.
82 Working in a diagonal sequence, tighten all the bearing cap bolts to the specified Stage 2 angle - use an angle gauge, if available, to ensure accuracy.
83 Fit the bolts to bearing cap No 5, and tighten to the specified torque.
84 With reference to Chapter 2B, lubricate the lip of a new camshaft oil seal with clean engine oil, and locate it over the end of the camshaft **(see illustration)**. Using a mallet and a long-reach socket of an appropriate diameter, drive the seal squarely into its housing until it bears against the inner stop - do not attempt to force it in any further.
85 Refit the thermostat housing and oil pressure switch.

Diesel engine

86 The bearing cap mounting holes are drilled off-centre; ensure that they are fitted the correct way around **(see illustration)**.
87 When fitting the bearing caps, the camshaft lobes for No 1 cylinder must be facing upwards.

4.84 Fitting a new camshaft oil seal

4.77 Fitting the camshaft oil seal (diesel engine)

88 Fit caps Nos 2 and 4 over the camshaft, and tighten the retaining nuts alternately and diagonally to the specified torque.
89 Now fit caps Nos 1, 3 and 5 over the camshaft and tighten the nuts to the specified torque. Ensure that cap No 5 is correctly located by lightly tapping the end of the camshaft.
90 Refit the coolant outlet elbow, using a new gasket/O-ring as necessary.
91 Refit the fuel injectors and glow plugs, with reference to Chapters 4C and 5C.

All engines

92 With reference to Chapter 2B or C as applicable, carry out the following:
a) Refit the timing belt sprocket to the camshaft.
b) Refit the inlet and exhaust manifolds, complete with new gaskets.
93 Refer to Chapter 2B or C as applicable, and refit the cylinder head to the cylinder block.

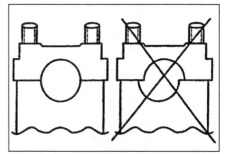

4.86 The camshaft bearing caps on diesel engines are drilled off-centre, to ensure they are refitted the correct way round

5.4a Withdraw the cam followers from the block . . .

5.4b . . . and store them in a partitioned container

5.6 Checking camshaft endfloat

5 Camshaft and followers (1.3 litre engine) - removal, inspection and refitting

Removal

1 Remove the rocker gear as described in Chapter 2A.

2 Lift out each pushrod in turn, and store it in its correct fitted order by pushing it through a clearly-marked cardboard template. This will help ensure that the pushrods are refitted in their original positions on reassembly. Note that the inlet valve pushrods are made of aluminium - those for the exhaust valves are made of cast iron.

3 Undo the four retaining nuts securing the cam follower cover to the front of the cylinder block, then remove the washers and seals from the cover studs. Carefully prise the cover

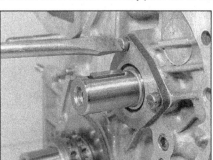

5.8a Undo the thrustplate retaining screws . . .

away from the cylinder block, and remove it along with its rubber seal.

4 Withdraw each cam follower in turn, and either label the individual followers or place them in a small partitioned container **(see illustrations)**. This will help ensure that, if the followers are to be re-used, they are refitted in their original positions; this is essential to minimise the amount of wear between the followers and cam lobes.

5 Remove the timing chain and sprockets as described in Chapter 2A.

6 Prior to removing the camshaft, check the endfloat as follows. Temporarily refit the distributor/oil pump drivegear, dished washer, tab washer and sprocket bolt to the end of the camshaft, and tighten the bolt to the specified torque. Set up a dial gauge on the end of the camshaft, and measure the endfloat whilst moving the camshaft to and fro **(see illustration)**.

7 If the endfloat exceeds the specified limit, renew the camshaft thrustplate on refitting.

8 Remove the temporarily-installed components, then slacken and remove the three screws securing the camshaft thrustplate to the cylinder block. Remove the plate and withdraw the camshaft from the block **(see illustrations)**.

Inspection

9 Inspect the cam followers for wear ridges and pitting of their camshaft lobe contact surfaces.

10 Insert each follower into its respective bore in the cylinder block, and check that it is free to move smoothly up and down, but that

there is no excessive side-to-side movement of the follower.

11 If the necessary measuring equipment is available, the amount of wear on the followers and their bores in the cylinder block can be checked by direct measurement **(see illustration)**.

12 If any of the cam followers are badly marked or excessively-worn (compare with the figures quoted in the Specifications), it will be necessary to renew the affected follower(s).

13 If the amount of side-to-side movement of any follower in its bore seems excessive, or if any of the bores in the cylinder block have worn beyond their specified limits, it will be necessary to have the bores in the cylinder block reamed and to install oversize cam followers. This task should be entrusted to a Skoda dealer, who will be able to obtain a set of oversize followers, and will have the necessary tools to ream out the bores.

14 Examine the camshaft lobes and bearing journals for signs of wear such as pitting or scoring, along with the camshaft bearings which are in the cylinder block.

15 If the necessary measuring equipment is available, measure the diameter of the camshaft journals **(see illustration)** and the internal diameter of each bearing in the cylinder block, and compare the results to the figures given in the Specifications. The bearing running clearance can be calculated by subtracting the camshaft journal outer diameter from the bearing internal diameter.

16 If the camshaft lobes or the bearing journals are badly worn, the camshaft must be

5.8b . . . remove the thrustplate . . .

5.8c . . . and withdraw the camshaft

5.11 Measuring a cam follower diameter

5.15 Measuring a camshaft bearing journal

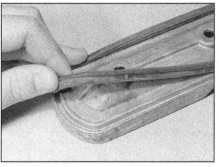

5.23 Ensure seal is correctly located in cam follower cover groove

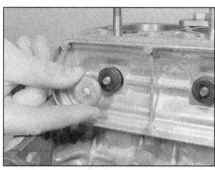

5.25a Fit the seals and washers onto the cover studs . . .

5.25b . . . then tighten the retaining nuts

renewed. If the camshaft bearings are excessively-worn (compare with the figures quoted in the Specifications), then the advice of a Skoda dealer or engine repair specialist must be sought. It may be possible to have the cylinder block bored out and camshaft bearing shells installed. If this is not possible, the block will have to be renewed.

17 Inspect the camshaft thrustplate for signs of scuffing, and renew if worn.

Refitting

18 Liberally oil the camshaft lobes and bearing journals, then slide the camshaft into position in the cylinder block.

19 Fit the camshaft thrustplate over the camshaft end, and securely tighten its three retaining screws. Check the camshaft endfloat as described in paragraph 6.

20 Refit the timing chain and sprockets as described in Chapter 2A.

21 Liberally oil the outer surfaces of the cam followers, and insert them into their respective bores in the cylinder block. If the original followers are being re-used, ensure they are refitted in their original locations to minimise wear.

22 Examine the cam follower cover seal for signs of damage or deterioration, and renew if necessary; if the seal is undamaged, it can be re-used.

23 Ensure the cover and block mating surfaces are clean, and the seal is correctly located in its groove in the cover **(see illustration)**.

24 Refit the cover to the cylinder block, ensuring that the seal does not distort as the cover is fitted.

25 Slide the seals and flat washers onto the cover studs, then refit the cover retaining nuts and tighten them to the specified torque setting **(see illustrations)**.

26 Remove the pushrods from the cardboard template, and insert them into their original positions in the cylinder head, ensuring that each pushrod is correctly located in its cam follower.

27 Refit the rocker gear as described in Chapter 2A, adjusting the valve clearances as described in Chapter 1A before installing the rocker cover.

6 Intermediate shaft (diesel engine) - removal and refitting

Removal

1 Refer to Chapter 2C and carry out the following:

a) *Remove the timing belt.*

b) *Remove the intermediate shaft sprocket.*

2 Before the shaft is removed, the endfloat must be checked. Anchor a DTI gauge to the cylinder block, with its probe in line with the intermediate shaft centre axis. Push the shaft into the cylinder block to the end of its travel, zero the DTI gauge and then draw the shaft out to the opposite end of its travel **(see illustration)**. The manufacturers do not quote a figure for intermediate shaft endfloat - as a guide, the figure for camshaft endfloat may be used. Renew the shaft if the endfloat appears excessive.

3 Slacken the retaining bolts and withdraw the intermediate shaft flange. Recover the O-ring seal, then press out the oil seal **(see illustrations)**.

4 Withdraw the intermediate shaft from the cylinder block, and inspect the drive gear at the end of the shaft; if the teeth show signs of excessive wear, or are damaged in any way, the shaft should be renewed.

5 If the oil seal has been leaking, check the shaft mating surface for signs of scoring or damage.

Refitting

6 Liberally oil the intermediate shaft bearing surfaces and drive gear, then carefully guide the shaft into the cylinder block and engage the journal at the leading end with its support bearing.

7 Press a new shaft oil seal into its housing in

6.2 Check the intermediate shaft endfloat using a DTI gauge

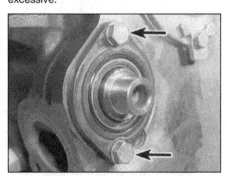

6.3a Slacken the retaining bolts (arrowed) . . .

6.3b . . . and withdraw the intermediate shaft flange

6.3c Press out the oil seal . . .

6.3d . . . then recover the O-ring seal

7.2 Connecting rod assemblies are numbered with their cylinder number

the intermediate shaft flange, and fit a new O-ring seal to the inner sealing surface of the flange.

8 Lubricate the inner lip of the seal with clean engine oil, and slide the flange and seal over the end of the intermediate shaft. Ensure that the O-ring is correctly seated, then fit the flange retaining bolts and tighten them to the specified torque. Check that the intermediate shaft can rotate freely.

9 With reference to Chapter 2C, refit the timing belt sprocket to the intermediate shaft and tighten the centre bolt to the specified torque.

7 Pistons and connecting rods - removal and inspection

Removal

1.3 litre engine

1 Remove the cylinder head, sump and oil pump gears as described in Chapter 2A. Ensure that the cylinder liners are securely clamped in position.

2 Prior to removing the connecting rods, note the two numbers which are stamped on one side of each assembly, next to the connecting rod/big-end cap mating surface; one on the big-end cap and one on the connecting rod (see illustration). These numbers indicate the cylinder number of each respective connecting rod assembly, No 1 cylinder being at the right-hand end (nearest the timing chain).

3 If any of the numbers are no longer visible, or the number stamped on the assembly does not correspond to the cylinder to which it is fitted, use a hammer and centre-punch or paint to mark each connecting rod and big-end bearing cap with its respective cylinder number on the flat, machined surface provided.

4 With the connecting rods still installed on the crankshaft, use a feeler blade to check the amount of endfloat between the caps and crankshaft webs. If the measured endfloat greatly exceeds the specified tolerance, then the affected connecting rods will require renewal.

5 Rotate the crankshaft until Nos 2 and 3 cylinder pistons are at the bottom of their stroke.

6 Unscrew and remove the big-end bearing cap nuts, and withdraw the cap, complete with bearing shell, from the connecting rod.

7 If only the bearing shells are being attended to, push the connecting rod up and off the crankpin, ensuring that the connecting rod big-ends do not mark the cylinder bore walls, then remove the upper bearing shell.

8 Keep the cap, nuts and (if they are to be refitted) the bearing shells together in their correct sequence.

9 With Nos 2 and 3 cylinder big-ends disconnected, repeat the procedure (exercising great care to prevent damage to any of the components) to remove Nos 1 and 4 cylinder bearing caps.

10 Remove the ridge of carbon from the top of each bore. Push each piston/connecting rod assembly up, and remove it from the top

of the bore, taking great care to ensure the connecting rod big-ends do not mark the cylinder bore walls. Immediately refit the bearing cap, shells and nuts to each piston/connecting rod assembly, so that they are all kept together as a matched set.

1.6 litre and diesel engines

11 Refer to Part B or C of this Chapter and remove the cylinder head, sump and baffle plate, oil pump and pickup, as applicable.

12 With the pistons sitting halfway down their bores, carefully feel around the tops of the cylinder bores. Any wear ridges found at the point where the pistons reach top dead centre must be removed, otherwise the pistons may be damaged when they are pushed out of their bores. This can be accomplished with a scraper or ridge reamer.

13 Scribe the number of each piston on its crown, to allow identification later; note that No 1 is at the timing belt end of the engine.

14 Using a set of feeler blades, measure the big-end to crankpin web thrust clearance at each connecting rod, and record the measurements for later reference.

15 On diesel engines, remove the retaining screw and withdraw the piston cooling jets from their mounting holes (see illustrations).

16 Rotate the crankshaft until pistons Nos 1 and 4 are at bottom dead centre. Unless they are already identified, mark the big-end bearing caps and connecting rods with their respective piston numbers, using a centre-punch or a scribe (see illustration). Note the orientation of the bearing caps in relation to the connecting rod; it may be difficult to see

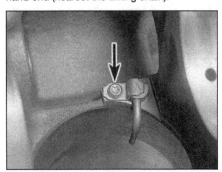

7.15a Remove the piston cooling jet retaining screw (arrowed) . . .

7.15b . . . and withdraw the jet from its mounting hole

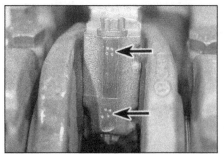

7.16 Mark the big-end caps and connecting rods with their piston numbers (arrowed)

7.21a Insert a small screwdriver into the slot, and prise off the gudgeon pin circlips

7.21b Push out the gudgeon pin, and separate the piston and connecting rod

7.22 Piston rings can be removed using an old feeler blade

the manufacturer's markings at this stage, so scribe alignment arrows on them both to ensure correct reassembly.

17 Note the fitted orientation of the connecting rods and caps in relation to the timing belt end of the engine. Depending on engine code, there will be some form of marking on the side of rod and cap which faces the timing belt end - this may be a punch mark, cut-out, raised dot or a different profile in the casting. Make your own marks on the timing belt side of the rod and cap if the manufacturer's marks are unclear.

18 Unbolt the bearing cap bolts, half a turn at a time, until they can be removed by hand. Recover the bottom shell bearing, and tape it to the cap for safe keeping. Note that if the shell bearings are to be re-used, they must be refitted to the same connecting rod.

19 Drive the pistons out of the top of their bores by pushing on the underside of the piston crown with a piece of dowel or a hammer handle. As the piston and connecting rod emerge, recover the top shell bearing and tape it to the connecting rod for safekeeping.

20 Turn the crankshaft through half a turn and working as described above, remove Nos 2 and 3 pistons and connecting rods. Remember to maintain the components in their cylinder groups, whilst they are in a dismantled state.

Inspection

21 Insert a small flat-bladed screwdriver into the removal slot, and prise the gudgeon pin circlips from each piston. Push out the gudgeon pin, and separate the piston and connecting rod **(see illustrations)**. Discard the circlips, as new items must be fitted on reassembly. If the pin proves difficult to remove, heat the piston to 60°C with hot water - the resulting expansion will then allow the two components to be separated.

22 Before an inspection of the pistons can be carried out, the existing piston rings must be removed, using a removal/installation tool, or an old feeler blade if such a tool is not available **(see illustration)**. Always remove the upper piston rings first, expanding them to clear the piston crown. The rings are very brittle and will snap if they are stretched too much - sharp edges are produced when this

happens, so protect your eyes and hands. Discard the rings on removal, as new items must be fitted when the engine is reassembled.

23 Use a section of old piston ring to scrape the carbon deposits out of the ring grooves, taking care not to score or gouge the edges of the groove.

24 Carefully scrape away all traces of carbon from the top of the piston. A hand-held wire brush (or a piece of fine emery cloth) can be used, once the majority of the deposits have been scraped away. Be careful not to remove any metal from the piston, as it is relatively soft. **Note:** *Take care to preserve the piston number markings that were made during removal.*

25 Once the deposits have been removed, clean the pistons and connecting rods with paraffin or a suitable solvent, and dry thoroughly. Make sure that the oil return holes in the ring grooves are clear.

26 Examine the piston for signs of terminal wear or damage. Some normal wear will be apparent, in the form of a vertical grain on the piston thrust surfaces and a slight looseness of the top compression ring in its groove. Abnormal wear should be carefully examined, to assess whether the component is still serviceable and what the cause of the wear might be.

27 Scuffing or scoring of the piston skirt may indicate that the engine has been overheating, through inadequate cooling, lubrication or abnormal combustion temperatures. Scorch marks on the skirt indicate that blow-by has occurred, perhaps caused by worn bores or

piston rings. Burnt areas on the piston crown are usually an indication of pre-ignition, pinking or detonation. In extreme cases, the piston crown may be melted by operating under these conditions. Corrosion pit marks in the piston crown indicate that coolant has seeped into the combustion chamber and/or the crankcase. The faults causing these symptoms must be corrected before the engine is brought back into service, or the same damage will recur.

28 Check the pistons, connecting rods, gudgeon pins and bearing caps for cracks. Lay the connecting rods on a flat surface, and look along the length to see if it appears bent or twisted. If you have doubts about their condition, get them measured at an engineering workshop. Inspect the small-end bush bearing for signs of wear or cracking.

29 Using a micrometer, measure the diameter of all four pistons at a point 10 mm from the bottom of the skirt, at right-angles to the gudgeon pin axis **(see illustration)**. Compare the measurements with those listed in the Specifications. If the piston diameter is out of the tolerance band listed for its particular size, then it must be renewed. **Note:** *If the cylinder block was re-bored during a previous overhaul (or if new liners have been fitted, on 1.3 litre engines), oversize pistons may have been fitted.* Record the measurements and use them to check the piston clearances when the cylinder bores are measured, later in this Chapter.

30 Hold a new piston ring in the appropriate groove, and measure the ring-to-groove clearance using a feeler blade **(see illustration)**.

7.29 Using a micrometer, measure the diameter of all four pistons

7.30 Measuring the piston ring-to-groove clearance using a feeler blade

7.31 Measuring gudgeon pin diameter

Note that the rings are of different widths, so use the correct ring for the groove. Compare the measurements with those listed; if the clearances are outside of the tolerance band, then the piston must be renewed. Confirm this by checking the width of the piston ring with a micrometer.

31 Using internal/external vernier calipers, measure the connecting rod small-end internal diameter and the gudgeon pin external diameter **(see illustration)**. Subtract the gudgeon pin diameter from the small-end diameter to obtain the clearance. If this measurement is outside its specification (where given), then the piston and connecting rod bush will have to be resized and a new gudgeon pin installed. An engineering workshop will have the equipment needed to undertake a job of this nature.

32 On 1.3 litre engines, the connecting rods are grouped into two weight groups, to allow for manufacturing tolerances. The weight group of each assembly is indicated by a dot of paint on the big-end bearing cap; lighter rods are marked with a dot of yellow paint, and the heavier rods are marked with a dot of blue paint. Skoda state that all four connecting rods must be of the same weight group, therefore it will be necessary to state the required weight group when ordering new connecting rods. If the weight group markings are no longer visible, take the original connecting rod along to your Skoda dealer, who will be able to identify its weight group by weighing it.

33 The orientation of the piston with respect to the connecting rod must be correct when the two are reassembled. The piston crown is

marked with an arrow (which may be obscured by carbon deposits).

34 On 1.3 litre engines, the arrow points towards the front (oil filter side) of the engine, and the oilway in the connecting rod faces the rear.

35 On 1.6 litre and diesel engines, the piston crown arrow points towards the timing belt end of the engine when the piston is installed. The connecting rod and its bearing cap both have recesses machined into them, close to their mating surfaces - these recesses must both face the same way as the arrow on the piston crown (ie towards the timing belt end of the engine) when correctly installed. Reassemble the two components to satisfy this requirement.

36 Lubricate the gudgeon pin and small-end bush with clean engine oil. Slide the pin into the piston, engaging the connecting rod small-end **(see illustration)**. Fit two new circlips to the piston at either end of the gudgeon pin, such that their open ends are facing 180° away from the removal slot in the piston. Repeat this operation for the remaining pistons.

8 Crankshaft - removal and inspection

Removal

1.3 litre engine

1 Remove the cylinder head and the timing chain and sprockets as described in Chapter 2A. Ensure the cylinder liners are securely clamped in position.

2 Free the connecting rod big-end caps from the crankshaft and, if necessary, remove the connecting rods as described in Section 7.

3 Prior to removing the crankshaft, temporarily refit the following components to the right-hand end of the crankshaft:

a) Slide the outer thrustwasher onto the crankshaft, ensuring that its oil grooves are facing away from the bearing cap, then locate the thrustwasher tab with its cut-out in the bearing cap, and press the thrustwasher into its recess; check that the inner thrustwasher tab is also correctly located in its cap cut-out.

7.36 Align the gudgeon pin with the connecting rod small-end bore, then press the pin in

b) With the thrustwasher in position, slide on the large spacer (chamfered inner edge facing towards block), the shim, the Woodruff key (tapered end innermost) and the timing chain sprocket.

c) Fit the crankshaft pulley, pulley bolt and washer; tighten the bolt to the specified torque, preventing flywheel rotation using the arrangement shown in Part A, Section 11. Note that if the thrustwashers are not properly located, the crankshaft will lock up as the bolt is tightened, and both thrustwashers will be damaged.

4 Position a dial gauge with its probe in contact with the end of the crankshaft. Push the crankshaft fully one way, and zero the gauge. Push the crankshaft fully the other way and check the endfloat **(see illustration)**. The result can be compared with the value given in the Specifications, and will give an indication as to whether new thrustwashers are required.

5 If a dial gauge is not available, feeler gauges can be used. First push the crankshaft fully towards the flywheel end of the engine, then use feeler gauges to measure the gap between the web of No 1 crankpin and the thrustwasher **(see illustration)**.

6 Once the crankshaft endfloat has been checked, remove all the components which were temporarily installed on the crankshaft right-hand end. Remove the flywheel as described in Part A.

7 Slacken and remove its retaining screws **(see illustration)**, and slide the flywheel-end oil seal housing off the end of the crankshaft, noting whether a gasket is fitted behind the

8.4 Using a dial gauge to measure crankshaft endfloat

8.5 Checking crankshaft endfloat using feeler blades

8.7 Undo the retaining screws and remove the flywheel-end oil seal housing

8.8 Main bearing caps are numbered for identification purposes

8.15 Measuring crankshaft endfloat using a DTI gauge

8.16 Measuring crankshaft endfloat using feeler blades

housing or not. If there is a gasket, remove and discard it; a new one must be fitted on reassembly.

8 Identification numbers should be visible on each main bearing cap **(see illustration)**. The caps are numbered 1 to 3, with No 1 being the right-hand (pulley-end) cap. If no marks are visible, stamp the bearing caps with a centre-punch as was done for the connecting rods, and mark them in such a way as to indicate their fitted direction.

9 Slacken and remove the main bearing cap bolts, and withdraw the caps complete with bearing shells.

10 Remove the crankshaft, and slide the thrustwasher off its right-hand end, noting which way around it is fitted.

11 Remove the upper main bearing shells from the cylinder block, and store them with their respective partners from the main bearing caps so that all shells can be identified and (if necessary) refitted in their original locations.

1.6 litre and diesel engines

12 Note: *If no work is to be done on the pistons and connecting rods, then removal of the cylinder head and pistons will not be necessary. Instead, the pistons need only be pushed far enough up the bores so that they are positioned clear of the crankpins. The use of an engine stand is strongly recommended.*

13 With reference to Chapter 2B or C as applicable, carry out the following:

a) *Remove the crankshaft timing belt sprocket.*
b) *Remove the clutch components and the flywheel.*
c) *Remove the sump, baffle plate (where applicable), oil pump and pickup.*
d) *Remove the front and rear crankshaft oil seals and their housings.*

14 Remove the pistons and connecting rods, as described in Section 7 (refer to the Note above).

15 Carry out a check of the crankshaft endfloat, as follows. **Note:** *This can only be accomplished when the crankshaft is still installed in the cylinder block/crankcase, but is free to move.* Set up a DTI gauge so that the probe is in line with the crankshaft axis and is in contact with a fixed point on end of the crankshaft. Push the crankshaft along its axis

to the end of its travel, and then zero the gauge. Push the crankshaft fully the other way, and record the endfloat indicated on the dial **(see illustration)**. Compare the result with the figure given in the Specifications and establish whether new thrustwashers are required.

16 If a dial gauge is not available, feeler blades can be used. First push the crankshaft fully towards the flywheel end of the engine, then use a feeler blade to measure the gap between cylinder No 2 crankpin web and the main bearing thrustwasher **(see illustration)**. Compare the results with the Specifications.

17 Observe the manufacturer's identification marks on the main bearing caps **(see illustration)**. The number relates to the position in the crankcase, as counted from the timing belt end of the engine.

18 Loosen the main bearing cap bolts one quarter of a turn at a time, until they can be removed by hand. Using a soft-faced mallet, strike the caps lightly to free them from the crankcase. Recover the lower main bearing shells, taping them to the cap for safekeeping. Mark them with indelible ink to aid identification, but do not score or scratch them in any way.

19 Carefully lift the crankshaft out, taking care not to dislodge the upper main bearing shells **(see illustration)**. It would be wise to get an assistant's help, as the crankshaft is heavy. Set it down on a clean, level surface and chock it with blocks to prevent it from rolling.

20 Extract the upper main bearing shells from the crankcase, and tape them to their

respective bearing caps. Remove the two thrustwasher bearings from either side of No 3 crank web.

21 With the shell bearings removed, observe the recesses machined into the bearing caps and crankcase - these provide location for the lugs which protrude from the shell bearings and so prevent them from being fitted incorrectly.

Inspection

22 Wash the crankshaft in a suitable solvent and allow it to dry. Flush the oil holes thoroughly, to ensure that are not blocked - use a pipe cleaner or a needle brush if necessary. Remove any sharp edges from the edge of the hole which may damage the new bearings when they are installed.

23 Inspect the main bearing and crankpin journals carefully; if uneven wear, cracking, scoring or pitting are evident, the crankshaft should be reground by an engineering workshop, and refitted to the engine with undersize bearings.

24 Use a micrometer to measure the diameter of each main bearing journal **(see illustration)**. Taking a number of measurements on the surface of each journal will reveal if it is worn unevenly. Differences in diameter measured at 90° intervals indicate that the journal is out of round. Differences in diameter measured along the length of the journal, indicate that the journal is tapered. Again, if wear is detected, the crankshaft must be reground by an engineering workshop, and undersize bearings will be needed (refer to *Reassembly*)

8.17 Manufacturer's identification markings on the main bearing caps (arrowed)

8.19 Lifting the crankshaft from the crankcase

8.24 Use a micrometer to measure the diameter of each main bearing journal

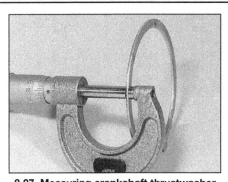

8.27 Measuring crankshaft thrustwasher thickness

25 Check the oil seal journals at either end of the crankshaft. If they appear excessively scored or damaged, they may cause the new seals to leak when the engine is reassembled. It may be possible to repair the journal; seek the advice of an engineering workshop or your Skoda dealer.

26 Measure the crankshaft runout by setting up a DTI gauge on the centre main bearing and rotating the shaft in V-blocks. The maximum deflection of the gauge will indicate the runout. Take precautions to protect the bearing journals and oil seal mating surfaces from damage during this procedure. A maximum runout figure is not quoted by the manufacturer, but use the figure of 0.05 mm as a rough guide. If the runout exceeds this figure, crankshaft renewal should be considered - consult your Skoda dealer or an engine rebuilding specialist for advice.

27 On 1.3 litre engines, using a micrometer, measure the crankshaft thrustwasher thickness **(see illustration)**. Compare the readings obtained with the measurements given in the Specifications. If either of the thrustwashers are worn beyond the specified tolerances for their relevant size group, renew both washers as a pair. Note that if the crankshaft has been reground, one of the thrustwashers will be thicker than the other. Ensure that the thicker of the thrustwashers is always installed as the inner thrustwasher (ie next to the crankshaft web).

28 Refer to Section 10 for details of main and big-end bearing inspection.

9 Cylinder block/ crankcase casting - cleaning and inspection

Cleaning

1 Remove all external components and electrical switches/sensors from the block. For complete cleaning, the core plugs should ideally be removed. Drill a small hole in the plugs, then insert a self-tapping screw into the hole. Extract the plugs by pulling on the screw with a pair of grips, or by using a slide hammer.

2 Scrape all traces of gasket and sealant from the cylinder block/crankcase, taking care not to damage the sealing surfaces.

3 Remove all oil gallery plugs (where fitted). The plugs are usually very tight - they may have to be drilled out, and the holes re-tapped. Use new plugs when the engine is reassembled.

4 If the casting is extremely dirty, it should be steam-cleaned. After this, clean all oil holes and galleries one more time. Flush all internal passages with warm water until the water runs clear. Dry thoroughly, and apply a light film of oil to all mating surfaces and cylinder bores, to prevent rusting. If you have access to compressed air, use it to speed up the drying process, and to blow out all the oil holes and galleries **(see illustration)**.

 Warning: Wear eye protection when using compressed air!

5 If the castings are not very dirty, you can do an adequate cleaning job with hot, soapy water and a stiff brush. Take plenty of time, and do a thorough job. Regardless of the cleaning method used, be sure to clean all oil holes and galleries very thoroughly, and to dry all components well. Protect the cylinder bores as described above, to prevent rusting.

6 All threaded holes must be clean, to ensure accurate torque readings during reassembly. To clean the threads, run the correct-size tap into each of the holes to remove rust, corrosion, thread sealant or sludge, and to restore damaged threads **(see illustration)**. If possible, use compressed air to clear the holes of debris produced by this operation.
Note: *Take extra care to exclude all cleaning liquid from blind tapped holes, as the casting may be cracked by hydraulic action if a bolt is threaded into a hole containing liquid.*

7 Apply suitable sealant to the new oil gallery plugs, and insert them into the holes in the block. Tighten them securely.

8 If the engine is not going to be reassembled immediately, cover it with a large plastic bag to keep it clean; protect all mating surfaces and the cylinder bores as described above, to prevent rusting.

Inspection

1.3 litre engine

9 Visually check the castings for cracks and corrosion. Look for stripped threads in the threaded holes. If there has been any history of internal water leakage, it may be worthwhile having an engine overhaul specialist check the cylinder block/crankcase with special equipment. If defects are found have them repaired, if possible, or renew the assembly.

10 Remove the liners as described in paragraph 26, and check the bore of each liner for scuffing and scoring. The liners are grouped into three size classes to allow for manufacturing tolerances; the size group is stamped on the side of the each liner.

11 Measure the diameter of each cylinder liner just below the wear ridge at the top of the bore, halfway down the bore, and just up from the base of the bore. Take measurements both parallel to the crankshaft axis and at right-angles to it.

12 Compare the results with the Specifications for the relevant class of liner given at the beginning of this Chapter; if any measurement exceeds the tolerances specified, the liner must be renewed.

13 To measure the piston-to-bore clearance, measure the bore and piston skirt as described in Section 7, and subtract the skirt diameter from the bore measurement.

14 Alternatively, insert each piston into the original bore, select a feeler blade, and slip it into the bore along with the piston. The piston must be aligned exactly in its normal attitude, and the feeler blade must be between the piston and bore on one of the thrust faces, just up from the bottom of the bore.

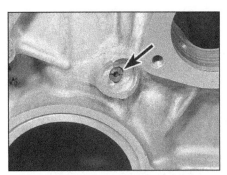

9.4 Clean all cylinder block oilways (1.3 litre engine timing chain oil jet arrowed)

9.6 To clean the cylinder block threads, run a correct-size tap into the holes

15 If the clearance is excessive, a new piston will be required. If the piston binds at the lower end of the bore and is loose towards the top, the bore is tapered. If tight spots are encountered as the piston/feeler gauge blade is rotated in the bore, the bore is out-of-round.

16 Repeat this procedure for the remaining pistons and cylinder liners.

17 If the cylinder liner walls are badly scuffed or scored, or if they are excessively-worn, out-of-round or tapered, obtain new cylinder liners; new pistons will also be required.

18 Skoda state that all the pistons and liners installed in the engine must be of the same size class. The liner size class is stamped on the outer surface of the liner, and the piston size class is stamped on the piston crown.

19 If the bores are in reasonably good condition and not worn to the specified limits, and if the piston-to-bore clearances can be maintained properly, then it may only be necessary to renew the piston rings.

20 If this is the case, the bores should be honed to allow the new rings to bed in correctly and provide the best possible seal.

21 Honing involves using an abrasive tool to produce a fine, cross-hatch pattern on the inner surface of the bore. This has the effect of seating the piston rings, resulting in a good seal between the piston and cylinder. There are two types of honing tool available to the home mechanic, both are driven by a rotary power tool, such as a drill. The bottle brush hone is a stiff, cylindrical brush with abrasive stones bonded to its bristles. The more conventional surfacing hone has abrasive stones mounted on spring-loaded legs. For the inexperienced home mechanic, satisfactory results will be achieved more easily using the bottle brush hone. **Note:** *If you are unwilling to tackle cylinder bore honing, an engineering workshop will be able to carry out the job for you at a reasonable cost.*

22 Carry out the honing as follows; you will need one of the honing tools described above, a power drill/air wrench, a supply of clean rags, some honing oil and a pair of safety glasses.

23 Fit the honing tool in the drill chuck. Lubricate the cylinder bores with honing oil and insert the honing tool into the first bore, compressing the stones to allow it to fit. Turn on the drill and as the tool rotates, move it up and down in the bore at a rate that produces a fine cross-hatch pattern on the surface. The lines of the pattern should ideally cross at about 50 to 60°, although some piston ring manufacturer's may quote a different angle; check the literature supplied with the new rings **(see illustration)**.

 Warning: Wear safety glasses to protect your eyes from debris flying off the honing tool.

24 Use plenty of oil during the honing process. Do not remove any more material than is necessary to produce the required

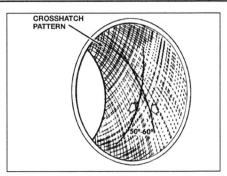

9.23 Cylinder bore honing pattern

finish. When removing the hone tool from the bore, do not pull it out whilst it is still rotating; maintain the up/down movement until the chuck has stopped, then withdraw the tool whilst rotating the chuck by hand, in the normal direction of rotation.

25 Wipe out the oil and swarf with a rag and proceed to the next bore. When all four bores have been honed, thoroughly clean the whole cylinder block in hot soapy water to remove all traces of honing oil and debris. The block is clean when a clean rag, moistened with new engine oil does not pick up any grey residue when wiped along the bore.

26 To remove the liners, invert the cylinder block/crankcase and support it on blocks of wood, then use a hard wood drift to tap out each liner from the crankshaft side.

27 When all the liners are released, tip the cylinder block/crankcase on its side, and remove each liner from the cylinder head side.

28 Remove the sealing washer from the base of the liner, and measure its thickness. The washer is available in various sizes, and is used to adjust the cylinder liner protrusion (see paragraph 33); obtain a new washer of the relevant thickness for each liner to use on refitting.

29 If the liners are to be re-used, mark each one by sticking masking tape on its right-hand (timing chain) face and writing the cylinder number on the tape.

30 To install the liners, thoroughly clean the liner mating surfaces in the cylinder block/crankcase, and use fine abrasive paper to polish away any burrs or sharp edges which might damage the liner sealing washer.

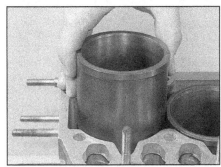

9.32 . . . and install the liner in the block

9.31 Fit a sealing washer of the required thickness to the base of the liner . . .

31 Clean the liners and wipe dry, then fit a new sealing washer of the required thickness to the base of each liner **(see illustration)**. Apply a thin coat of engine oil to the bore.

32 If the original liners are being refitted, use the marks made on removal to ensure that each is refitted the same way round into its original bore. Insert each liner into the cylinder block/crankcase, taking great care not to displace the washer, and press it home as far as possible by hand **(see illustration)**. Using a hammer and a block of wood, tap each liner lightly but fully onto its locating shoulder.

33 With all four liners installed, using a dial gauge or a straight-edge and feeler blade, check that the protrusion of each liner above the upper surface of the cylinder block is within the limits given in the Specifications, and that the maximum difference between any two liners is not exceeded **(see illustration)**.

34 If this is not the case, it will be necessary to remove the appropriate liner and to obtain another sealing washer of the required thickness. Washers are available in three thicknesses; 0.10 mm, 0.12 mm and 0.14 mm.

35 Fit the necessary washer to the liner, then install the liner and recheck the protrusion.

36 Repeat as necessary until all liner protrusions are within the specified limits and the maximum difference between any two is not exceeded, then securely clamp the liners in position **(see illustration)**.

1.6 litre and diesel engines

37 Visually check the casting for cracks and corrosion. Look for stripped threads in the

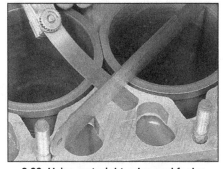

9.33 Using a straight-edge and feeler blade to check liner protrusion

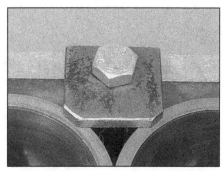

9.36 Once liner protrusions are within specified limits, clamp all the liners in position

threaded holes. If there has been any history of internal water leakage, it may be worthwhile having an engine overhaul specialist check the cylinder block/crankcase with professional equipment. If defects are found, have them repaired if possible; if not, a new block will be required.

38 Check the cylinder bores for scuffing or scoring. Any evidence of this kind of damage should be cross-checked with an inspection of the pistons: see Section 7 of this Chapter. If the damage is in its early stages, it may be possible to repair the block by reboring it. Seek the advice of an engineering workshop before you progress.

39 To allow an accurate assessment of the wear in the cylinder bores to be made, their diameter must be measured at a number of points, as follows. Insert a bore gauge into bore No 1, and take three measurements in line with the crankshaft axis; one at the top of the bore, roughly 10 mm below the bottom of the wear ridge, one halfway down the bore and one at a point roughly 10 mm the bottom of the bore. **Note:** *Stand the cylinder block*

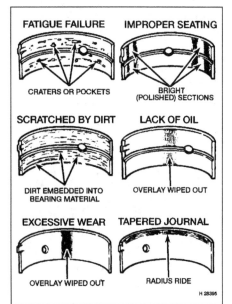

10.1 Typical bearing failures

squarely on a workbench during this procedure, inaccurate results may be obtained if the measurements are taken when the engine mounted on a stand.

40 Rotate the bore gauge through 90°, so that it is at right-angles to the crankshaft axis and repeat the measurements detailed in paragraph 39. Record all six measurements, and compare them with the data listed in the Specifications. If the difference in diameter between any two cylinders exceeds the wear limit, or if any one cylinder exceeds its maximum bore diameter, then *all four* cylinders will have to be rebored and oversize pistons will have to be fitted. Note that the imbalances produced by not reboring all the cylinders together would render the engine unusable.

41 Use the piston diameter measurements recorded earlier (see Section 7) to calculate the piston-to-bore clearances. Figures are not available from the manufacturer, so seek the advice of your Skoda dealer or engine reconditioning specialist.

42 Place the cylinder block on a level work surface, crankcase downwards. Use a straight edge and a set of feeler blades to measure the distortion of the cylinder head mating surface in both planes. If the measurement exceeds the specified figures, repair may be possible by machining (on petrol engines) - consult your dealer for advice. On diesel engines, machining the head is not permissible.

43 Before the engine can be reassembled, the cylinder bores must be honed as described in paragraphs 21 to 25.

44 Apply a light coating of engine oil to the mating surfaces and cylinder bores to prevent rust forming. Wrap the block in a plastic bag until reassembly.

10 Main and big-end bearings - inspection and selection

Inspection

1 Even though the main and big-end bearings should be renewed during the engine overhaul, the old bearings should be retained for close examination, as they may reveal valuable information about the condition of the engine **(see illustration)**.

2 Bearing failure can occur due to lack of lubrication, the presence of dirt or other foreign particles, overloading the engine, or corrosion. Regardless of the cause of bearing failure, the cause must be corrected before the engine is reassembled, to prevent it from happening again.

3 When examining the bearing shells, remove them from the cylinder block/crankcase, the main bearing caps, the connecting rods and the connecting rod big-end bearing caps. Lay them out on a clean surface in the same general position as their location in the engine. This will enable you to match any

bearing problems with the corresponding crankshaft journal. *Do not* touch any shell's internal bearing surface with your fingers while checking it, or the delicate surface may be scratched.

4 Dirt and other foreign matter gets into the engine in a variety of ways. It may be left in the engine during assembly, or it may pass through filters or the crankcase ventilation system. It may get into the oil, and from there into the bearings. Metal chips from machining operations and normal engine wear are often present. Abrasives are sometimes left in engine components after reconditioning, especially when parts are not thoroughly cleaned using the proper cleaning methods. Whatever the source, these foreign objects often end up embedded in the soft bearing material, and are easily recognised. Large particles will not embed in the bearing, but will score or gouge the bearing and journal. The best prevention for this cause of bearing failure is to clean all parts thoroughly, and keep everything spotlessly-clean during engine assembly. Frequent and regular engine oil and filter changes are also recommended.

5 Lack of lubrication (or lubrication breakdown) has a number of interrelated causes. Excessive heat (which thins the oil), overloading (which squeezes the oil from the bearing face) and oil leakage (from excessive bearing clearances, worn oil pump or high engine speeds) all contribute to lubrication breakdown. Blocked oil passages, which usually are the result of misaligned oil holes in a bearing shell, will also oil-starve a bearing, and destroy it. When lack of lubrication is the cause of bearing failure, the bearing material is wiped or extruded from the steel backing of the bearing. Temperatures may increase to the point where the steel backing turns blue from overheating.

6 Driving habits can have a definite effect on bearing life. Full-throttle, low-speed operation (labouring the engine) puts very high loads on bearings, tending to squeeze out the oil film. These loads cause the bearings to flex, which produces fine cracks in the bearing face (fatigue failure). Eventually, the bearing material will loosen in pieces, and tear away from the steel backing.

7 Short-distance driving leads to corrosion of bearings, because insufficient engine heat is produced to drive off the condensed water and corrosive gases. These products collect in the engine oil, forming acid and sludge. As the oil is carried to the engine bearings, the acid attacks and corrodes the bearing material.

8 Incorrect bearing installation during engine assembly will lead to bearing failure as well. Tight-fitting bearings leave insufficient bearing running clearance, and will result in oil starvation. Dirt or foreign particles trapped behind a bearing shell result in high spots on the bearing, which lead to failure.

9 *Do not* touch any shell's internal bearing surface with your fingers during reassembly;

there is a risk of scratching the delicate surface, or of depositing particles of dirt on it.

10 As mentioned at the beginning of this Section, the bearing shells should be renewed as a matter of course during engine overhaul; to do otherwise is false economy.

Selection - main and big-end bearings

11 To select the required bearing shells, it will first be necessary to determine the size group of the crankshaft bearing journals; ie, are they standard or have they been reground? To do this, measure the bearing journal diameter and compare the measurements obtained with the figures given in the Specifications at the start of this Chapter to find which size group the bearing journals belong (see Section 8 for further information).

12 Alternatively (on 1.3 litre engines only), the size group of the crankshaft journals can be determined by measuring the thickness of the original bearing shells, using a suitable micrometer, then comparing then readings obtained with those given in the Specifications **(see illustration)**. Note that great care must be taken not to mark the surface of the bearing shells. It is preferable to use the crankshaft journal measurements, since the bearing shells are far more difficult to measure accurately and more likely to wear, therefore giving a false reading.

13 Once the bearing journal size group is known, the correct thickness bearing shells can be selected.

14 Main and big-end bearings for the engines described in this Chapter are available in standard sizes and a range of undersizes to suit reground crankshafts - refer to Specifications for details.

15 The running clearances will need to be checked when the crankshaft is refitted with its new bearings (see Sections 12 and 14).

---

11 Engine overhaul -
reassembly sequence

1 Before reassembly begins, ensure that all new parts have been obtained, and that all necessary tools are available. Read through the entire procedure to familiarise yourself with the work involved, and to ensure that all items necessary for reassembly of the engine are at hand. In addition to all normal tools and materials, thread-locking compound will be needed. A suitable tube of liquid sealant will also be required for the joint faces that are without gaskets. It is recommended that the manufacturer's own products are used, which are specially formulated for this purpose; the relevant product names are quoted in the text of each Section where they are required.

2 In order to save time and avoid problems, engine reassembly should ideally be carried out in the following order:

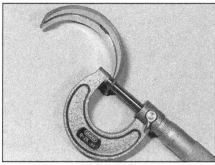

10.12 Measuring bearing shell thickness

1.3 litre engine

a) Crankshaft.
b) Piston/connecting rod assemblies.
c) Cylinder head (see Chapter 2A).
d) Camshaft and followers.
e) Timing chain and sprockets (see Chapter 2A).
f) Flywheel (see Chapter 2A).
g) Sump (see Chapter 2A).
h) Engine external components.

1.6 litre and diesel engines

a) Crankshaft.
b) Piston/connecting rod assemblies.
c) Oil pump (see Chapter 2B or 2C).
d) Sump (see Chapter 2B or 2C).
e) Flywheel/driveplate (see Chapter 2B or 2C).
f) Cylinder head and gasket (see Chapter 2B or 2C).
g) Timing belt tensioner, sprockets and timing belt (see Chapter 2B or2 C).
h) Engine external components and ancillaries.
i) Auxiliary drivebelts, pulleys and tensioners (see Chapter 2B or2 C).

3 At this stage, all engine components should be absolutely clean and dry, with all faults repaired. The components should be laid out (or in individual containers) on a completely clean work surface.

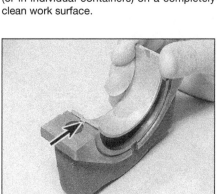

12.2a Lower main bearing shells are plain and have a central locating tab (arrowed) . . .

12 Crankshaft -
refitting and running clearance check

1.3 litre engine

Main bearing running clearance check

1 Clean the backs of the bearing shells and the bearing locations in both the cylinder block/crankcase and the main bearing caps.

2 Press the bearing shells into their locations, ensuring that the tab on each shell engages in the notch in the cylinder block/crankcase or main bearing cap location, and taking care not to touch any shell's bearing surface with your fingers. Note that it is not possible to interchange upper and lower main bearing shells, since their locating tabs are offset **(see illustrations)**.

3 If the original main bearing shells are being re-used, these must be refitted to their original locations in the cylinder block/crankcase and main bearing caps.

4 If the original or a newly-reground crankshaft and genuine Skoda bearings are to be installed, a further check will not be necessary.

5 The main bearing running clearance should be checked if there is any doubt about the amount of crankshaft wear that has taken place, if the crankshaft has been reground and is to be refitted with non-genuine undersized bearing shells, or if non-genuine bearing shells are to be fitted. If the clearance is to be checked, it can be done in either of two ways.

6 One method (which will be difficult to achieve without a range of internal micrometers or internal/external expanding calipers) is to refit the main bearing caps to the cylinder block/crankcase, with bearing shells in place. With the bearing cap retaining bolts tightened to the specified torque, measure the internal diameter of each assembled pair of bearing shells. If the diameter of each corresponding crankshaft journal is measured and then subtracted from the bearing internal diameter, the result will be the main bearing running clearance.

12.2b . . . whilst upper main bearing shells are grooved and have an offset locating tab (arrowed)

12.10 Place the length of Plastigauge on the journal to be measured, parallel to the crankshaft axis

12.13 Using the scale on the envelope provided to check (at its widest point) the width of the crushed Plastigauge and measure the bearing running clearance

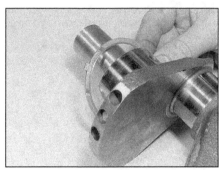

12.19 Fit the inner thrustwasher to the crankshaft, so that its oil grooves face the crankshaft web . . .

7 The second (and more accurate) method is to use a product known as Plastigauge. This consists of a fine thread of perfectly-round plastic which is compressed between the bearing shell and the journal. When the shell is removed, the plastic is deformed and can be measured with a special card gauge supplied with the kit. The running clearance is determined from this gauge.

8 Plastigauge is sometimes difficult to obtain, but enquiries at one of the larger specialist quality motor factors should produce the name of a stockist in your area. The procedure for using Plastigauge is as follows.

9 With the main bearing upper shells in place, carefully lay the crankshaft in position. Do not use any lubricant; the crankshaft journals and bearing shells must be perfectly clean and dry.

10 Cut off a length of the appropriate size Plastigauge for each main bearing (they should be slightly shorter than the width of the main bearings) and place one length on each crankshaft journal axis **(see illustration)**.

11 With the main bearing lower shells in position, refit the main bearing caps and tighten their retaining bolts to the specified torque setting. Take great care not to disturb the Plastigauge or rotate the crankshaft at any time during this operation.

12 Once all bearing cap bolts have been tightened to the specified torque, carefully undo the bolts and remove the bearing caps, again taking great care not to disturb the Plastigauge or rotate the crankshaft.

13 Compare the width of the crushed

Plastigauge on each journal with the scale printed on the Plastigauge envelope to obtain the main bearing running clearance **(see illustration)**.

14 If the clearance is not as specified, the bearing shells may be the wrong size (or excessively-worn if the original shells are being re-used). Before deciding that different size shells are needed, make sure that no dirt or oil was trapped between the bearing shells and the caps or cylinder block/crankcase when the clearance was measured. If the Plastigauge was wider at one end than at the other, the journal may be tapered, and would need regrinding.

15 If the main bearing running clearance is excessive even with new bearing shells of the correct size fitted, it will be necessary to have the crankshaft ground down to the next specified size and to fit oversize main bearing shells (see Section 8).

16 If all is well, carefully scrape away all traces of the Plastigauge material from the crankshaft and bearing shells, using a fingernail or other object which is unlikely to score the shells.

Final refitting

17 Carefully lift the crankshaft out of the cylinder block once more.

18 Place the bearing shells in their locations as described in paragraphs 1 to 3. If new shells are being fitted, ensure that all traces of the protective grease are cleaned off using paraffin. Wipe dry the shells and bearing journals with a lint-free cloth. Liberally lubricate each bearing shell in the cylinder block/crankcase.

19 Slide the inner thrustwasher onto the right-hand end of the crankshaft, ensuring its lubrication grooves are facing towards the crankshaft web **(see illustration)**.

20 Carefully lower the crankshaft into position in the block **(see illustration)**, then lubricate the bearing shells and crankshaft journals with clean engine oil.

21 Position the thrustwasher locating tab so that it is pointing directly upwards; this will ensure that it aligns with the cut-out in the bearing cap when the cap is installed **(see illustration)**.

22 Refit the main bearing caps, using the marks made or noted on removal to ensure that they are refitted in their original positions. Align the thrustwasher tab with the cut-out in the right-hand bearing cap, and press the thrustwasher into its recess.

23 Install the main bearing cap bolts, and tighten them evenly and progressively to the specified torque setting **(see illustration)**.

24 Check that the crankshaft is free to turn, then check the endfloat as described in Section 8. Note that great care must be taken to ensure that the inner and outer thrustwasher locating tabs are properly seated in their grooves on the main bearing cap before the crankshaft pulley bolt is tightened. If the thrustwashers are not properly seated, the crankshaft will lock up as the bolt is tightened, and the thrustwashers will be damaged.

25 Remove all traces of gasket or sealant from the flywheel end oil seal housing and cylinder block mating surfaces.

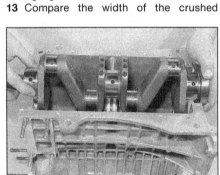

12.20 . . . then carefully lower the crankshaft into the cylinder block

12.21 Align the thrustwasher tab with the cut-out in the bearing cap when installing No 1 cap (arrowed)

12.23 Tighten the main bearing cap bolts evenly and progressively to the specified torque setting

12.26 Fit a new seal to the flywheel end oil seal housing . . .

12.28 . . . then slide the housing over the crankshaft and onto its locating dowels (arrowed)

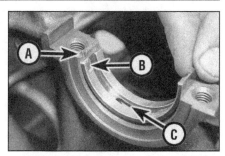

12.32 Bearing shells correctly refitted

A *Recess in bearing*   B *Lug on bearing shell*
   saddle   C *Oil hole*

26 Carefully lever the old seal out of the housing, and press a new seal into position so that it seats evenly on the housing shoulder. If necessary, a soft-faced mallet can be used to tap the seal gently into place **(see illustration)**. Note that the oil seal sealing lip should face inwards.

27 If an oil seal housing gasket was noted on removal, fit a new gasket over the locating dowels on the cylinder block. If no gasket was noted on removal, apply a thin film of gasket sealant to the oil seal housing mating surface.

28 Ease the oil seal onto the crankshaft end, taking care not to damage its sealing lip. Slide the housing into position on the cylinder block, so that it engages with its locating dowels **(see illustration)**.

29 Refit the housing retaining screws, and tighten them securely. If a gasket has been fitted, use a sharp knife to trim off the ends of the gasket which protrude beyond the cylinder block sump mating face.

30 Install the connecting rod assemblies as described in Section 14.

1.6 litre and diesel engines

31 Place the cylinder block on a clean, level work surface, with the crankcase facing upwards. Unbolt the bearing caps and carefully release them from the crankcase; lay them out in order to ensure correct reassembly. If they are still in place, remove the bearing shells from the caps and the crankcase, and wipe out the inner surfaces with a clean rag - they must be kept spotlessly clean.

32 Clean the rear surface of the new bearing shells with a rag, and lay them on the bearing

saddles. Ensure that the orientation lugs on the shells engage with the recesses in the saddles, and that the oil holes are correctly aligned **(see illustration)**. Do not hammer or otherwise force the bearing shells into place. It is critically important that the surfaces of the bearings are kept free from damage and contamination.

33 Give the newly-fitted bearing shells and the crankshaft journals a final clean with a rag. Check that the oil holes in the crankshaft are free from dirt, as any left here will become embedded in the new bearings when the engine is first started.

34 Carefully lay the crankshaft in the crankcase, taking care not to dislodge the bearing shells.

Main bearing running clearance check

35 Refer to paragraphs 5 to 16, noting that the bearing caps should be tightened just to the Stage 1 torque setting for this check, not further to the Stage 2 angle.

Final refitting

36 Lift the crankshaft out of the crankcase. Wipe off the surfaces of the bearings in the crankcase and the bearing caps. Fit the thrust bearings either side of the No 3 bearing saddle, between cylinders No 2 and 3. Use a small quantity of grease to hold them in place; ensure that they are seated correctly in the machined recesses, with the oil grooves facing outwards

37 Liberally coat the bearing shells in the crankcase with clean engine oil of the appropriate grade.

38 Lower the crankshaft into position so that No 2 and 3 cylinder crankpins are at TDC; No 1

and 4 cylinder crankpins will then be at BDC, ready for fitting No 1 piston.

39 Lubricate the lower bearing shells in the main bearing caps with clean engine oil, then fit the thrustwashers to either side of bearing cap No 3, noting that the lugs protruding from the washers engage the recesses in the side of the bearing cap **(see illustration)**. Make sure that the locating lugs on the shells are still engaged with the corresponding recesses in the caps.

40 Fit the main bearing caps in the correct order and orientation - No 1 bearing cap must be at the timing belt end of the engine, and the bearing shell locating recesses in the bearing saddles and caps must be adjacent to each other **(see illustration)**. Insert the bearing cap bolts (new bolts on diesel engines) and hand-tighten them only.

41 Working from the centre bearing cap outwards, tighten the retaining bolts to the specified Stage 1 torque **(see illustration)**.

42 Working in the same sequence, tighten the bolts further to the specified Stage 2 angle. Use an angle-measuring gauge, if available, to ensure accuracy.

43 Refit the crankshaft rear oil seal housing, together with a new oil seal; refer to Part B or C (as applicable) of this Chapter for details.

44 Check that the crankshaft rotates freely by turning it by manually. If resistance is felt, re-check the running clearances, as described above.

45 Carry out a check of the crankshaft endfloat as described at the beginning of Section 8. If the thrust surfaces of the crankshaft have been checked and new thrust bearings have been fitted, then the endfloat should be within specification.

12.39 Fitting the thrustwashers to No 3 bearing cap

12.40 Fitting a main bearing cap in place

12.41 Tighten the bearing cap bolts to the specified torque

13 Pistons and piston rings - assembly

1 At this point, it is assumed that the pistons have been correctly assembled to their respective connecting rods, and that the piston ring-to-groove clearances have been checked. If not, refer to Section 7.

2 Before the rings can be fitted to the pistons, the end gaps must be checked with the rings fitted into the cylinder bores.

3 Lay out the piston assemblies and the new ring sets on a clean work surface so that the components are kept together in their groups during and after end gap checking. Place the crankcase on the work surface on its side, allowing access to the top and bottom of the bores.

4 Take the No 1 piston top ring and insert it into the top of the bore. Using the No 1 piston as a ram, push the ring close to the bottom of the bore, at the lowest point of the piston travel. Ensure that it is perfectly square in the bore by pushing firmly against the piston crown.

5 Use a set of feeler blades to measure the gap between the ends of the piston ring; the correct blade will just pass through the gap with a minimal amount of resistance **(see illustration)**. Compare this measurement with the wear limit listed in the Specifications. Check that you have the correct ring before deciding that a gap is incorrect. Repeat the operation for all rings.

6 If new rings are being fitted, it is unlikely that the end gaps will be too small. If a measurement is found to be undersize, it must be corrected or there is the risk that the ends of the ring may contact each other during operation, possibly resulting in engine damage. Ensure that the ring has been fitted in its correct location, and consult your parts supplier if the ring end gap is still too small.

7 When all the piston ring end gaps have been verified, they can be fitted to the pistons. Work from the lowest ring groove (oil control ring) upwards. Note that the oil control ring comprises two side rails separated by a expander ring. Note also that the two compression rings are different in cross-section, and so must be fitted in the correct

groove and the right way up, using a piston ring fitting tool. Both of the compression rings have marks stamped on one side to indicate the top facing surface **(see illustration)**. Ensure that these marks face up when the rings are fitted.

8 Distribute the end gaps around the piston, spaced at 120° intervals to the each other. **Note:** *If the piston ring manufacturer supplies specific fitting instructions with the rings, follow these exclusively.*

14 Piston and connecting rod assemblies - refitting and big-end bearing clearance check

1.3 litre engine

Big-end bearing running clearance check

1 If the original or a newly-reground crankshaft and genuine Skoda bearings are to be installed, a further check will not be necessary.

2 The main bearing running clearance should be checked if there is any doubt about the amount of crankshaft wear that has taken place, if the crankshaft has been reground and is to be refitted with non-genuine undersized bearing shells, or if non-genuine bearing shells are to be fitted. If the clearance is to be checked, it can be done in either of two ways.

3 One method is to refit the big-end bearing cap to the connecting rod, with bearing shells in place. With the cap retaining nuts tightened to the specified torque, use an internal micrometer or vernier caliper to measure the internal diameter of each assembled pair of bearing shells. If the diameter of each corresponding crankpin journal is measured and then subtracted from the bearing internal diameter, the result will be the big-end bearing running clearance.

4 The second method is to use Plastigauge as described in Section 12.

5 Place a strand of Plastigauge on each (cleaned) crankpin journal and refit the (clean) piston/connecting rod assemblies, shells and big-end bearing caps, tightening the nuts to the specified torque wrench settings. Take care not to disturb the Plastigauge or rotate the connecting rod at any time during this operation.

6 Dismantle the assemblies without rotating the crankshaft, and use the scale printed on the Plastigauge envelope to obtain the big-end bearing running clearance. On completion of the measurement, carefully scrape off all traces of Plastigauge from the journal and shells, using a fingernail or other object which will not score the components.

Final refitting

7 Note that the following procedure assumes that the cylinder liners have been refitted to the cylinder block/crankcase and clamped in position as described in Section 9, and that the crankshaft and main bearing caps are in place. It is of course possible to refit the piston/connecting rod assemblies before installing the crankshaft.

8 Clean the backs of the bearing shells and the bearing recesses in both the connecting rod and the big-end bearing cap. If new shells are being fitted, ensure that all traces of the protective grease are cleaned off using paraffin. Wipe dry the shells and connecting rods with a lint-free cloth.

9 Press the bearing shells into their locations, ensuring that the tab on each shell engages in the notch in the connecting rod or big-end bearing cap, and taking care not to touch any shell's bearing surface with your fingers. Note that if the original bearing shells are to be re-used, they must be installed in their original fitted positions.

10 Lubricate the cylinder bores, the pistons and piston rings, then lay out each piston/connecting rod assembly in its respective position.

11 Starting with assembly No 1, make sure that the piston rings are still spaced as described in Section 13, then clamp them in position with a piston ring compressor.

12 Insert the piston/connecting rod assembly into the top of liner No 1, ensuring that the arrow on the piston crown or near the gudgeon pin bore (as applicable) points towards the front of the engine; note that the oilway on the connecting rod should face towards the rear of the engine.

13 Using a block of wood or a hammer handle against the piston crown, tap the assembly into the liner until the piston crown is flush with the top of the liner **(see illustration)**.

14 Check that the bearing shell is still correctly installed, then liberally lubricate the crankpin and both bearing shells.

15 Taking great care not to mark the liner bores, pull the piston/connecting rod assembly down the bore and onto the crankpin.

16 Refit the big-end bearing cap and shell, noting that the cap and connecting rod faces with the stamped marks must match **(see illustration)**.

17 Refit the bearing cap nuts, noting that the collar of the nut must face the bearing cap, and tighten them evenly and progressively to the specified torque setting **(see illustrations)**.

13.5 Checking a piston ring end gap using a feeler blade - 1.3 litre engine shown

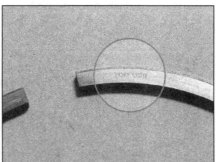

13.7 Piston ring TOP marking

After the nuts are tightened, check that the crankshaft is free to rotate before moving onto the next assembly.

18 Repeat the procedure for the remaining three piston/connecting rod assemblies.

19 With all piston/connecting rod assemblies installed, check that the crankshaft is free to rotate before proceeding further. Some stiffness is to be expected with new components, but there must be no tight spots or binding.

1.6 litre and diesel engines

Big-end bearing running clearance check

Note: *At this point, it is assumed that the crankshaft is fitted to the engine, as described in Section 12.*

20 As with the main bearings (Section 12), a running clearance must exist between the big-end crankpin and its bearing shells to allow oil to circulate. There are two methods of checking the size of the running clearance, as described in the following paragraphs.

21 Place the cylinder block on a clean, level work surface, with the crankcase facing upwards. Position the crankshaft such that crankpins No 1 and 4 are at BDC.

22 The first method is the least accurate and involves bolting bearing caps to the big-ends, away from the crankshaft, with the bearing shells in place. **Note:** *Correct orientation of the bearing caps is critical; refer to the notes in Section 7. The internal diameter formed by the assembled big-end is then measured using internal vernier calipers. The diameter of the respective crankpin is then subtracted from this measurement and the result is the running clearance.*

23 The second method of carrying out this check involves the use of Plastigauge, in the same manner as the main bearing running clearance check (see Section 12) and is much more accurate than the previous method. Clean all four crankpins with a clean rag. With crankpins No 1 and 4 at BDC initially, place a strand of Plastigauge on each crankpin journal.

24 Fit the upper big-end bearing shells to the connecting rods, ensuring that the locating lugs and recesses engage correctly.

14.13 Using a piston ring compressor to clamp piston rings while piston/connecting rod assembly is fitted to cylinder liner

Temporarily refit the piston/connecting rod assemblies to the crankshaft; refit the big-end bearing caps, using the manufacturer's markings to ensure that they are fitted the correct way around - refer to *Final refitting* for details.

25 Tighten the bearing cap nuts/bolts to the specified Stage 1 torque only - no further. Take care not to disturb the Plastigauge or rotate the connecting rod during the tightening process.

26 Dismantle the assemblies without rotating the connecting rods. Use the scale printed on the Plastigauge envelope to determine the big-end bearing running clearance and compare it with the figures listed in Specifications.

27 If the clearance is significantly different from that expected, the bearing shells may be the wrong size (or excessively worn, if the original shells are being re-used). Make sure that no dirt or oil was trapped between the bearing shells and the caps or connecting rods when the clearance was measured. Re-check the diameters of the crankpins. Note that if the Plastigauge was wider at one end than at the other, the crankpins may be tapered. When the problem is identified, fit new bearing shells or have the crankpins reground to a listed undersize, as appropriate.

28 Upon completion, carefully scrape away all traces of the Plastigauge material from the crankshaft and bearing shells. Use a plastic or wooden scraper, which will be soft enough to prevent scoring of the bearing surfaces.

14.17a ... then refit the bearing cap nuts, noting that the collar of the nut must abut the cap

14.17b Tighten the bearing cap nuts evenly and progressively to the specified torque setting

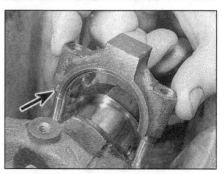

14.16 Refit the bearing cap, aligning the stamped marks (arrowed) . . .

Bearing shell pre-tension check - 1.6 litre engine

29 Using internal and external vernier calipers, measure the internal diameter of the assembled connecting rod and big-end bearing cap, and the diameter of its bearing shells, as shown **(see illustration)**. Subtract the connecting rod internal diameter from the shell diameter to obtain the shell pre-tension. If the figure obtained is less than the specified minimum, new shells should be fitted.

Final refitting

30 Note that the following procedure assumes that the crankshaft main bearing caps are in place (see Section 12).

31 Ensure that the bearing shells are correctly fitted, as described earlier in this Section. If new shells are being fitted, ensure that all traces of the protective grease are cleaned off using paraffin. Wipe dry the shells and connecting rods with a lint-free cloth.

32 Lubricate the cylinder bores, the pistons, and piston rings with clean engine oil. Lay out each piston/connecting rod assembly in order on a work surface.

33 Start with piston/connecting rod assembly No 1. Make sure that the piston rings are still spaced as described in Section 13, then clamp them in position with a piston ring compressor.

34 Insert the piston/connecting rod assembly into the top of cylinder No 1. Lower the big-end in first, guiding it to protect the cylinder bores.

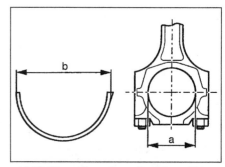

14.29 Dimensions for calculation of big-end bearing shell pre-tension

a Connecting rod internal diameter
b Bearing shell diameter

14.39 Tightening the big-end bearing cap bolts to the Stage 1 . . .

35 Ensure that the orientation of the piston in its cylinder is correct - the piston crown, connecting rods and big-end bearing caps have markings, which must point towards the timing belt end of the engine when the piston is installed in the bore - refer to Section 7 for details.

36 Using a block of wood or hammer handle against the piston crown, tap the assembly into the cylinder until the piston crown is flush with the top of the cylinder.

37 Ensure that the bearing shell is still correctly installed. Liberally lubricate the crankpin and both bearing shells with clean engine oil. Taking care not to mark the cylinder bores, tap the piston/connecting rod assembly down the bore and onto the crankpin.

38 Oil the threads and contact faces of the new retaining bolts with clean engine oil. Refit the big-end bearing cap, tightening its new retaining bolts finger-tight at first. Note that the orientation of the bearing cap with respect to the connecting rod must be correct when the two components are reassembled. The connecting rod and its corresponding bearing cap both have markings machined into them, close to their mating surfaces - these must both face in the same direction as the arrow on the piston crown (ie towards the timing belt end of the engine) when correctly installed - refer to Section 7 for details.

39 Tighten the bolts half a turn at a time to the specified Stage 1 torque **(see illustration)**.

40 Now tighten the bolts further to the specified Stage 2 angle. Use an angle-measuring gauge, if available, to ensure accuracy **(see illustration)**.

14.40 . . . and Stage 2 torque settings

41 Refit the remaining three piston/connecting rod assemblies in the same way.

42 Rotate the crankshaft by hand. Check that it turns freely; some stiffness is to be expected if new parts have been fitted, but there should be no binding or tight spots.

Diesel engines

43 If new pistons are to be fitted, or if a new short engine is to be installed, the projection of the piston crowns above the cylinder head at TDC must be measured, to determine the type of head gasket that should be fitted.

44 Turn the cylinder block over (so that the crankcase is facing downwards) and rest it on a stand or wooden blocks. Anchor a DTI gauge to the cylinder block, and zero it on the head gasket mating surface. Rest the gauge probe on No 1 piston crown and turn the crankshaft slowly by hand so that the piston reaches and then passes through TDC. Measure and record the maximum deflection at TDC.

45 Repeat the measurement at piston No 4, then turn the crankshaft through 180° and take measurements at pistons Nos 2 and 3.

46 If the measurements differ from piston to piston, take the highest figure and use this to determine the head gasket type that must be used - refer to the Specifications for details.

47 Note that if the original pistons have been refitted, then a new head gasket of the same type as the original item must be fitted; refer to Chapter 2C for details of how to identify different head gasket types.

---

15 Engine -
initial start-up after
overhaul and reassembly

1 Refit the remainder of the engine components in the order listed in Section 11, referring to Part A, B or C where necessary. Refit the engine (and transmission) to the vehicle as described in Section 2. Double-check the engine oil and coolant levels and make a final check that everything has been reconnected. Make sure that there are no tools or rags left in the engine compartment.

Petrol models

2 Remove the spark plugs, referring to Chapter 1A for details.

3 The engine must be immobilised such that it can be turned over using the starter motor, without starting - disable the fuel pump by unplugging the fuel pump relay from the relay board; refer to the relevant part of Chapter 4 for details. Alternatively, identify and remove the fuel pump fuse.

Caution: On vehicles with a catalytic converter, it is potentially damaging to immobilise the engine by disabling the ignition system without first disabling the fuel system, as unburnt fuel could be supplied to the catalyst. When the engine is later started, the unburnt fuel in the

converter may ignite and irreparably damage the converter.

4 Turn the engine using the starter motor until the oil pressure warning light goes out. If the light fails to extinguish after several seconds of cranking, check the engine oil level and that the oil filter is secure. Assuming these are correct, check the security of the oil pressure switch wiring - do not progress any further until you are satisfied that oil is being pumped around the engine at sufficient pressure.

5 Refit the spark plugs, and reconnect the fuel pump relay (or refit the fuel pump fuse).

Diesel models

6 Disconnect the electrical wiring from the fuel cut-off valve (stop solenoid) at the fuel injection pump - refer to Chapter 4C for details.

7 Turn the engine using the starter motor until the oil pressure warning light goes out.

8 If the light fails to extinguish after several seconds of cranking, check the engine oil level and that the oil filter is secure. Assuming these are correct, check the security of the oil pressure switch wiring - do not progress any further until you are satisfied that oil is being pumped around the engine at sufficient pressure.

9 Reconnect the fuel cut-off valve wiring.

All models

10 Start the engine, but be aware that as fuel system components have been disturbed, the cranking time may be a little longer than usual.

11 While the engine is idling, check for fuel, water and oil leaks. Don't be alarmed if there are some odd smells and the occasional plume of smoke as components heat up and burn off oil deposits.

12 On petrol models, the idle speed may be rather erratic until the ECU has re-learned its adaptive values for all idle conditions.

13 On 1.6 litre and diesel engines, the hydraulic tappets may initially run noisily, but the engine should quieten down after a few seconds running.

14 Assuming all is well, keep the engine idling until hot water is felt circulating through the top hose.

15 On diesel models, check the fuel injection pump timing and engine idle speed, referring to Chapter 4C and Chapter 1B.

16 After a few minutes, recheck the oil and coolant levels, and top-up as necessary.

17 On all the engines described in this Chapter, there is no need to re-tighten the cylinder head bolts/nuts once the engine has been run following reassembly.

18 If new pistons, rings or crankshaft bearings have been fitted, the engine must be treated as new, and run-in for the first 600 miles (1000 km). *Do not* operate the engine at full-throttle, or allow it to labour at low engine speeds in any gear. It is recommended that the engine oil and filter are changed at the end of this period.

Chapter 3
Cooling, heating and ventilation systems

Contents

Degrees of difficulty

Easy, suitable for novice with little experience	Fairly easy, suitable for beginner with some experience	Fairly difficult, suitable for competent DIY mechanic 	Difficult, suitable for experienced DIY mechanic	Very difficult, suitable for expert DIY or professional

Specifications

General

Maximum system pressure	1.2 to 1.5 bar

Thermostat

Opening temperature (approximate):	
Starts opening	85 to 89°C
Fully open	103°C
Minimum valve lift	7 mm

Torque wrench settings

	Nm	lbf ft
Cooling fan switch	40	30
Coolant pump:		
1.3 litre petrol engine:		
Pump housing nuts	20	15
1.6 litre petrol engine:		
Pump retaining bolts	20	15
Diesel engine:		
Pump-to-housing bolts	10	7
Pump pulley bolts	25	18
Pump housing-to-cylinder block bolts	25	18
Injection pump lower mounting bolt	25	18
Thermostat cover bolts	10	7

1 General information and precautions

General information

1 The cooling system is of pressurised type, comprising a coolant pump (driven by the timing belt on 1.6 litre engines and the auxiliary drivebelt on the other engines), an aluminium crossflow radiator, an electric cooling fan, a thermostat, heater matrix, and all associated hoses and switches.

2 The system functions as follows. Cold coolant in the bottom of the radiator passes through the bottom hose to the coolant pump, where it is pumped around the cylinder block and head passages, and through the oil cooler (where fitted). After cooling the cylinder bores, combustion surfaces and valve seats, the coolant reaches the underside of the thermostat, which is initially closed. The coolant passes through the heater, and is returned via the cylinder block to the coolant pump.

3 When the engine is cold, the coolant circulates only through the cylinder block, cylinder head, and heater. When the coolant reaches a predetermined temperature, the thermostat opens, and the coolant passes through the top hose to the radiator. As the coolant circulates through the radiator, it is cooled by the inrush of air when the car is in forward motion. The airflow is supplemented by the action of the electric cooling fan when necessary. Upon reaching the bottom of the radiator, the coolant has now cooled, and the cycle is repeated.

4 The electric cooling fan mounted on the back of the radiator are controlled by a thermostatic switch. At a predetermined coolant temperature, the switch actuates the fan.

3.2a Release the retaining clips . . .

Precautions

⚠ **Warning: Do not attempt to remove the expansion tank filler cap, or to disturb any part of the cooling system, while the engine is hot, as there is a high risk of scalding. If the expansion tank filler cap must be removed before the engine and radiator have fully cooled (even though this is not recommended), the pressure in the cooling system must first be relieved. Cover the cap with a thick layer of cloth to avoid scalding, and slowly unscrew the filler cap until a hissing sound is heard. When the hissing has stopped, indicating that the pressure has reduced, slowly unscrew the filler cap until it can be removed; if more hissing sounds are heard, wait until they have stopped before unscrewing the cap completely. At all times, keep well away from the filler cap opening, and protect your hands.**

⚠ **Warning: Do not allow antifreeze to come into contact with your skin, or with the painted surfaces of the vehicle. Rinse off spills immediately, with plenty of water. Never leave antifreeze lying around in an open container, or in a puddle in the driveway or on the garage floor. Children and pets are attracted by its sweet smell, but antifreeze can be fatal if ingested.**

⚠ **Warning: If the engine is hot, the electric cooling fan may start rotating even if the engine is not running. Be careful to keep your hands,**

hair, and any loose clothing well clear when working in the engine compartment.

⚠ **Warning: Refer to Section 10 for precautions to be observed when working on models equipped with air conditioning.**

2 Cooling system hoses - disconnection and renewal

Note: *Refer to the warnings given in Section 1 of this Chapter before proceeding. Hoses should only be disconnected once the engine has cooled sufficiently to avoid scalding.*

1 If the checks described in the relevant part of Chapter 1 reveal a faulty hose, it must be renewed as follows.

2 First drain the cooling system (see the relevant part of Chapter 1). If the coolant is not due for renewal, it may be re-used, providing it is collected in a clean container.

3 To disconnect a hose, release the retaining clips and move them along the hose, clear of the relevant inlet/outlet. There are two different types of clip, the standard jubilee-type clip and spring clips which are released by squeezing their ends together with a pair of pliers. Carefully work the hose free; hoses can be removed with relative ease when new - on an older car, they may have stuck.

4 If a hose proves to be difficult to remove, try to release it by rotating its ends before attempting to free it. Gently prise the end of the hose with a blunt instrument (such as a flat-bladed screwdriver), but do not apply too much force, and take care not to damage the pipe stubs or hoses. Note in particular that the radiator inlet stub is fragile; do not use excessive force when attempting to remove the hose. If all else fails, cut the hose with a sharp knife, then slit it so that it can be peeled off in two pieces. Although this may prove expensive if the hose is otherwise undamaged, it is preferable to buying a new radiator. Check first, however, that a new hose is readily available.

5 When fitting a hose, first slide the clips onto the hose, then work the hose into position. On some hose connections alignment marks are provided on the hose and union; if marks are present, ensure they are correctly aligned.

 If the hose is stiff, use a little soapy water as a lubricant, or soften the hose by soaking it in hot water. Do not use oil or grease, which may attack the rubber.

6 Ensure the hose is correctly routed then secure it in position with the retaining clips.

7 Refill the cooling system with reference to the relevant part of Chapter 1.

8 Check thoroughly for leaks as soon as possible after disturbing any part of the cooling system.

3 Radiator - removal, inspection and refitting

Note: *If leakage is the reason for removing the radiator, bear in mind that minor leaks can often be cured using a radiator sealant with the radiator in situ.*

Removal

1 Disconnect the battery negative lead then drain the cooling system as described in the relevant part of Chapter 1. Proceed as described under the relevant sub-heading.

Petrol engine models

2 Release the retaining clips and disconnect the top and bottom hoses from the radiator. On 1.3 litre models also disconnect the expansion tank hose **(see illustrations)**.

3 Disconnect the wiring connectors from the cooling fan motor and the fan switch and unclip the wiring from the radiator and shroud **(see illustration)**.

4 Slacken and remove the retaining bolts securing the radiator to the bonnet lock crossmember.

5 Free the radiator from its lower mountings and manoeuvre it out from the engine compartment, taking care not to lose the mounting rubbers **(see illustrations)**. **Note:** *On some models it maybe necessary to unbolt and remove the strengthening bar linking the bonnet crossmember to the front valance to gain the necessary clearance for removal.*

3.2b . . . and disconnect the upper (expansion tank hose arrowed) . . .

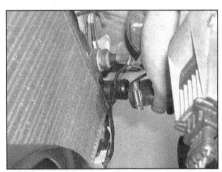

3.2c . . . lower coolant hose from the radiator

3.3 Disconnect the wiring connector from the cooling fan and free the wiring from the shroud

3.5a Manoeuvre the radiator assembly out of position . . .

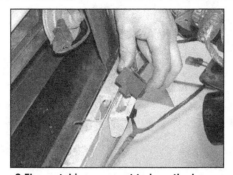

3.5b . . . taking care not to lose the lower mounting rubbers

4.3 Release the retaining clips and disconnect the coolant hoses from the thermostat housing (later 1.3 litre engine shown)

Diesel engine models

6 Release the retaining clip and disconnect the top hose from the radiator.

7 Slacken and remove the bolt securing the bottom hose coolant pipe to its mounting bracket. Release the retaining clip then free the pipe from thermostat housing hose and remove it from the engine compartment.

8 Remove the cooling fan assembly as described in Section 5.

9 Disconnect the wiring connector from the fan switch which is screwed into the radiator.

10 On models with power steering, unbolt from the fluid reservoir from the crossmember and position it clear of the radiator. Keep the reservoir upright to avoid fluid spillage.

11 Slacken and remove the retaining bolts securing the radiator to the bonnet lock crossmember.

12 Free the radiator from its lower mountings and manoeuvre it out from the engine compartment, taking care not to lose the mounting rubbers.

Inspection

13 If the radiator has been removed due to suspected blockage, reverse-flush it as described in the relevant part of Chapter 1. Clean dirt and debris from the radiator fins, using an air line (in which case, wear eye

protection) or a soft brush. Be careful, as the fins are sharp, and easily damaged.

14 If necessary, a radiator specialist can perform a flow test on the radiator, to establish whether an internal blockage exists.

15 A leaking radiator must be referred to a specialist for permanent repair. Do not attempt to weld or solder a leaking radiator, as damage to the plastic components may result.

16 In an emergency, minor leaks from the radiator can be cured by using a suitable radiator sealant, in accordance with its manufacturer's instructions, with the radiator *in situ*.

17 If the radiator is to be sent for repair or renewed, remove the cooling fan switch.

18 Inspect the condition of the radiator lower mounting rubbers, and renew them if necessary.

Refitting

19 Refitting is a reversal of removal, bearing in mind the following points.

a) *Ensure that the radiator is correctly engaged with its lower mounting rubbers and securely tighten the retaining bolts.*

b) *Make sure all coolant hoses are correctly reconnected and securely retained by their clips.*

c) *On completion, refill the cooling system as described in the relevant part of Chapter 1.*

---

4 Thermostat -
removal, testing and refitting

Removal

1 Disconnect the battery negative lead then drain the cooling system as described in the relevant part of Chapter 1. Proceed as described under the relevant sub-heading.

Petrol engine models

2 The thermostat housing is mounted on the left-hand end of the cylinder head.

3 Release the retaining clip(s) and disconnect the coolant hose(s) from the thermostat cover **(see illustration)**.

4 Unscrew the retaining bolts and remove the thermostat housing cover and sealing ring/ gasket from the engine **(see illustrations)**. Discard the sealing ring/gasket; a new one must be used on refitting.

5 On early (pre February 1996) 1.3 litre models and all 1.6 litre models, remove the thermostat from its housing, noting which way around it is fitted.

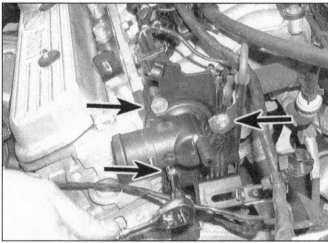

4.4a Slacken and remove the retaining bolts (arrowed) . . .

4.4b . . . and remove the thermostat housing cover

4.6a On later 1.3 litre models, free the retaining clip from the housing cover . . .

4.6b . . . then remove the spring . . .

4.6c . . . and thermostat plunger

6 On later (February 1996 on) 1.3 litre models, the thermostat assembly is clipped into the thermostat housing cover. Noting each components correct fitted location, unclip the retaining clip from the cover then remove the spring and thermostat plunger **(see illustrations)**.

Diesel engine models

7 The thermostat is fitted to the base of the coolant pump housing. To improve access, firmly apply the handbrake then jack up the front of the vehicle and support it on axle stands. Undo the retaining screws and remove the undercover panel from the front of the vehicle.

8 Release the retaining clip and disconnect the coolant hose from the thermostat cover **(see illustration)**.

9 Unscrew the retaining bolts and remove the thermostat housing cover and sealing ring. Discard the sealing ring; a new one must be used on refitting.

10 Remove the thermostat, noting which way around it is fitted **(see illustration)**.

Testing

Note: *On later (February 1996 on) 1.3 litre models, testing must be carried out with the thermostat components assembled in the housing cover.*

11 A rough test of the thermostat may be made by suspending it with a piece of string in a container full of water. Heat the water to bring it to the boil - the thermostat must open by the time the water boils. If not, renew it.

12 If a thermometer is available, the precise opening temperature of the thermostat may be determined; compare with the figures given in the Specifications. The opening temperature should also be marked on the thermostat.

13 A thermostat which fails to close as the water cools must also be renewed.

Refitting

Petrol engine models

14 On later (February 1996 on) 1.3 litre models, fit the thermostat plunger and spring to the housing cover and secure them in position with the retaining clip.

15 On early (pre February 1996) 1.3 litre models and all 1.6 litre models, fit the thermostat to the housing making sure it is correctly located.

16 On all models, fit the new sealing ring/gasket (as applicable) then refit the thermostat cover to the housing. Ensure the cover is correctly seated then refit the retaining bolts, tightening them to the specified torque setting.

17 Reconnect the coolant hose(s) to the cover and secure it in position with the retaining clip(s).

18 Refill the cooling system as described in the relevant part of Chapter 1 and reconnect the battery.

Diesel engine models

19 Fit the new sealing ring to the thermostat cover.

20 Fit the thermostat to the housing, making sure it is correctly located, then refit the cover. Refit the retaining bolts and tighten them to the specified torque.

21 Reconnect the coolant hose and secure it in position with the retaining clip.

22 Refit the undercover (where removed), tightening its retaining screws securely, then lower the vehicle to the ground.

23 Refill the cooling system as described in the relevant part of Chapter 1, and reconnect the battery.

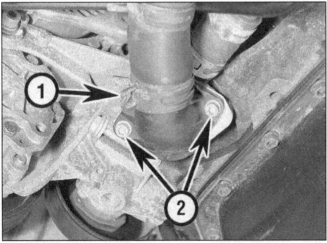

4.8 On diesel engines, release the retaining clip (1) and disconnect the coolant hose then unscrew the bolts (2) and remove the thermostat housing cover . . .

4.10 . . . and thermostat

5.6a Disconnect the wiring connector from the fan motor . . .

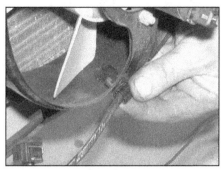

5.6b . . . then unclip the motor wiring from the shroud

5.6c Slacken and remove the retaining bolts (upper bolts arrowed) . . .

5 Cooling fan - testing, removal and refitting

Testing

1 Current supply to the cooling fan(s) is via the ignition switch and a fuse (see Chapter 12). The circuit is completed by the cooling fan thermostatic switch, which is mounted in the side of the radiator.

2 If a fan does not appear to work, run the engine until normal operating temperature is reached, then allow it to idle. The fan should cut in within a few minutes (before the temperature gauge needle enters the red section). If not, switch off the ignition and disconnect the wiring plug from the cooling fan switch. Bridge the relevant contacts in the wiring plug (see Wiring diagrams at the end of this manual - some models have two-stage switches) using a length of spare wire, and switch on the ignition. If the fan now operates, the switch is probably faulty, and should be renewed.

3 If the fan still fails to operate, check that battery voltage is available at the feed wire to the switch; if not, then there is a fault in the feed wire (possibly due to a fault in the fan motor, or a blown fuse). If there is no problem with the feed, check that there is continuity between the switch earth terminal and a good earth point on the body; if not, then the earth connection is faulty, and must be re-made.

4 If the switch and the wiring are in good condition, the fault must lie in the motor itself. The motor can be checked by disconnecting it from the wiring loom and connecting a 12-volt supply directly to it.

Removal

5 Disconnect the battery negative terminal.

6 Disconnect the wiring connector from the fan motor then slacken and remove the retaining bolts and remove the fan shroud assembly from the rear of the radiator **(see illustrations)**.

7 If necessary, slacken and remove the retaining nuts and washers and separate the motor and shroud **(see illustration)**. The fan blade can be pulled off from the motor once its retaining clip has been removed.

Refitting

8 Fit the motor assembly to the shroud and refit the washers and retaining nuts, tightening them securely. Where necessary, seat the fan blade on the motor spindle and secure it in position with the retaining clip.

9 Refit the shroud assembly to the radiator and securely tighten its retaining bolts.

10 Reconnect the wiring connector to the motor then reconnect the battery.

6 Cooling system electrical switches and sensors - testing, removal and refitting

Cooling fan thermostatic switch

Testing

1 Testing of the switch is described in Section 5, as part of the cooling fan test procedure.

Removal

Note: *The engine and radiator should be cold before removing the switch.*

2 The switch is screwed into the side of the radiator.

3 Disconnect the battery negative lead then drain the cooling system to just below the level of the switch (as described in the relevant part of Chapter 1). Alternatively, have ready a suitable bung to plug the switch aperture in the radiator when the switch is removed. If this method is used, take great care not to damage the radiator, and do not

5.6d . . . then free the motor assembly and remove it from the rear of the radiator (1.3 litre engine shown)

use anything which will allow foreign matter to enter the radiator.

4 Disconnect the wiring plug from the switch **(see illustration)**.

5 Carefully unscrew the switch from the radiator, and recover the sealing washer. If the system has not been drained, plug the switch aperture to prevent further coolant loss.

Refitting

6 Refitting is a reversal of removal, using a new sealing washer. Tighten the switch to the specified torque and refill (or top-up) the cooling system as described in the relevant part of Chapter 1.

7 On completion, start the engine and run it until it reaches normal operating temperature. Continue to run the engine, and check that the cooling fan cuts in and out correctly.

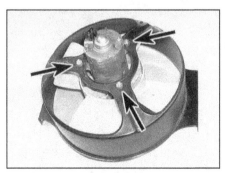

5.7 Fan motor is secured to the shroud by nuts (arrowed)

6.4 Disconnect the wiring connector from the fan switch

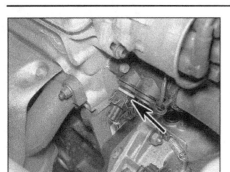

6.8a Coolant temperature sensor location
- 1.6 litre petrol engine

6.8b Coolant temperature sensor location
- diesel engine

6.14 Disconnecting the wiring connector
from the coolant temperature sensor -
later 1.3 litre petrol engine

Coolant temperature gauge sensor

Testing

8 On petrol engines the coolant temperature gauge sensor is fitted to the thermostat housing on the left-hand end of the cylinder head and on diesel engines it is fitted to the coolant outlet union on the front of the cylinder head **(see illustrations)**. *Note: On 1.3 litre petrol engines with a single-point fuel injection system, the sensor controls only the temperature gauge. On all other engines the sensor also performs the fuel injection (petrol engine) or preheating (diesel engine) system temperature sensor function.*

9 The temperature gauge is fed with a stabilised voltage from the instrument panel feed (via the ignition switch and a fuse). The gauge earth is controlled by the sensor. The sensor contains a thermistor - an electronic component whose electrical resistance decreases at a predetermined rate as its temperature rises. When the coolant is cold, the sensor resistance is high, current flow through the gauge is reduced, and the gauge needle points towards the blue (cold) end of the scale. As the coolant temperature rises and the sensor resistance falls, current flow increases, and the gauge needle moves towards the upper end of the scale. If the sensor is faulty, it must be renewed.

10 If the gauge develops a fault, first check the other instruments; if they do not work at all, check the instrument panel electrical feed. If the readings are erratic, there may be a fault

in the voltage stabiliser, which will necessitate renewal of the stabiliser (the stabiliser is integral with the instrument panel printed circuit board - see Chapter 12). If the fault lies in the temperature gauge alone, check it as follows.

11 If the gauge needle remains at the cold end of the scale when the engine is hot, disconnect the sensor wiring plug, and earth the relevant wire to the cylinder head. If the needle then deflects when the ignition is switched on, the sensor unit is proved faulty, and should be renewed. If the needle still does not move, remove the instrument panel (Chapter 12) and check the continuity of the wire between the sensor unit and the gauge, and the feed to the gauge unit. If continuity is shown, and the fault still exists, then the gauge is faulty, and the gauge unit should be renewed.

12 If the gauge needle remains at the hot end of the scale when the engine is cold, disconnect the sensor wire. If the needle then returns to the cold end of the scale when the ignition is switched on, the sensor unit is proved faulty, and should be renewed. If the needle still does not move, check the remainder of the circuit as described previously.

Removal

Note: *The engine should be cold before removing the switch.*

13 Either partially drain the cooling system to just below the level of the sensor (as described in the relevant part of Chapter 1), or

have ready a suitable plug which can be used to plug the sensor aperture whilst it is removed. If a plug is used, take great care not to damage the sensor unit aperture, and do not use anything which will allow foreign matter to enter the cooling system.

14 Disconnect the wiring connector from the sensor and identify wether the sensor is a push-fit or a screw-fit **(see illustration)**.

15 On screw-fit sensors, unscrew the sensor from the engine and recover its sealing washer.

16 On push-fit sensors, depress the sensor unit and slide out its retaining clip. Withdraw the sensor from the engine and recover its sealing ring **(see illustrations)**.

Refitting

17 On screw-fit sensors, fit a new sealing washer then fit the sensor, tightening it securely.

18 On push-fit sensor units, fit a new sealing ring then push the sensor fully into its aperture and secure it in position with the retaining clip.

19 Reconnect the wiring connector then refill the cooling system as described in the relevant part of Chapter 1 or top-up as described in *Weekly checks*.

Fuel injection system temperature sensor - petrol engines

20 On 1.3 litre single-point injection engines a separate fuel injection system temperature sensor is screwed into the rear of the inlet manifold **(see illustration)**. On all other engines, the fuel injection temperature sensor

6.16a On push-fit sensors, slide out the
retaining clip ...

6.16b ... then lift out the sensor ...

6.16c ... and recover the sealing ring

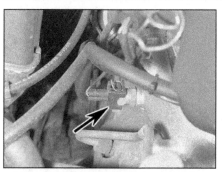

6.20 Fuel injection system temperature sensor location - 1.4 litre single-point injection petrol engine

is combined with the temperature gauge sensor and is fitted to the thermostat housing on the left-hand end of the cylinder head.

21 The sensor is a thermistor (see paragraph 9). The fuel injection/engine management electronic control unit (ECU) supplies the sensor with a set voltage and then, by measuring the current flowing in the sensor circuit, it determines the engine's temperature. This information is then used, in conjunction with other inputs, to control the injector timing, the idle speed etc.

22 If the sensor circuit should fail to provide adequate information, the ECU's back-up facility will override the sensor signal. In this event, the ECU assumes a predetermined setting which will allow the fuel injection/engine management system to run, albeit at reduced efficiency. When this occurs, the warning light on the instrument panel will come on, and the advice of a Skoda dealer should be sought. The sensor itself can only be tested using special Skoda diagnostic equipment (see the relevant part of Chapter 4). *Do not* attempt to test the circuit using any other equipment, as there is a high risk of damaging the ECU.

Removal and refitting

23 Refer to paragraphs 13 to 19.

Preheating system temperature sensor - diesel engine

Testing

24 Refer to Chapter 5C for details on the operation of the preheating system.

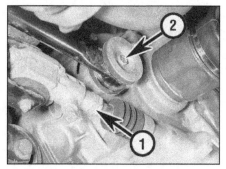

7.5 Remove the clip (1) then tap out the roll pin and detach the selector rod from the transmission then unbolt the steady rod (2)

Removal and refitting

25 The sensor is combined with the temperature gauge sensor and is fitted to the coolant outlet union on the front of the cylinder head. Removal and refitting is as described in paragraphs 13 to 19.

---

7 Coolant pump - removal and refitting

1.3 litre petrol engine

Note: *If the coolant pump is faulty there are two options. One is to renew the complete pump and housing assembly the other is to remove the remove the assembly and take it to a Skoda dealer for overhaul (all the pump components are available individually but overhaul requires the use of several special tools and a hydraulic press). Consult your Skoda dealer for the cost/availability of parts and decide which option to take before removal.*

Removal

1 Drain the cooling system as described in the relevant part of Chapter 1. The coolant pump is an integral part of the engine/transmission right-hand mounting assembly and removal is as follows.

2 Remove the air cleaner assembly as described in the relevant part of Chapter 4.

3 Remove the auxiliary drivebelt as described in the relevant part of Chapter 2.

4 Slacken and remove the bolt securing the coolant pipe to the right-hand end of the engine then slacken the retaining clip and detach the pipe from the coolant pump hose **(see illustration)**.

5 Working at the transmission end of the gearchange selector rod, remove the retaining clip to gain access to the roll pin **(see illustration)**. If the original clip is still fitted, discard it and replace it with a jubilee-type hose clip on refitting. Tap the roll pin out of position and discard it; a new one must be used on refitting.

6 Slacken and remove the bolt securing the gearchange steady rod to the transmission unit and recover the washers and mounting rubber.

7.11 Unscrew the retaining nuts and remove the pump/mounting bracket assembly from the engine

7.4 On 1.3 litre engines, slacken and remove the bolt securing the coolant pipe to the right-hand end of the engine

7 Position a jack with interposed block of wood under the engine and raise it until its is supporting the engine/transmission unit. Alternatively, attach a hoist or support bar to the engine lifting eye on the cylinder head and take the weight of the engine from above.

8 Slacken and remove the nut and through bolt from the engine/transmission unit rear mounting.

9 Unscrew the retaining nut and remove the right-hand mounting through-bolt. To gain the required clearance for through-bolt removal, remove the plug from the right-hand valance (see the relevant part of Chapter 2); the through-bolt can then be withdrawn through the hole and out from under the wing.

10 Make alignment marks between the right-hand mounting bracket and body then undo the retaining bolts and manoeuvre the bracket out of position.

11 Slacken and remove the retaining nuts securing the pump/mounting bracket assembly to the cylinder block. Slide the assembly off of its mounting studs and remove it from the vehicle, raising/lower the engine/transmission unit as necessary taking care to place any excess strain on the exhaust system and engine wiring/hoses **(see illustration)**.

12 Remove the housing gasket and discard; a new one must be used on refitting.

Refitting

13 Ensure the pump housing and block mating surfaces are clean and dry then fit the new gasket to the housing studs **(see illustration)**.

7.13 On refitting ensure the mating surfaces are clean and dry then fit a new pump gasket

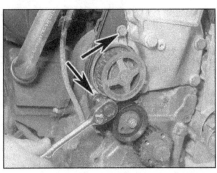

7.28a On 1.6 litre petrol engines, undo the two bolts (arrowed) . . .

14 Fit the pump housing assembly to the cylinder block and tighten its retaining nuts to the specified torque.
15 Refit the right-hand mounting bracket to the body and refit the retaining bolts. Align the marks made prior to removal then tighten the bolts to the specified torque (see the relevant part of Chapter 2).
16 Align the right-hand mounting with the bracket then refit the through bolt and nut, tightening it by hand only at this stage. Refit the access plug to the wing valance.
17 Refit the though bolt to the rear engine/transmission mounting and lightly tighten its nut.
18 Remove the jack/hoist/support bar (as applicable) from the engine. Rock the engine/transmission unit to settle it in position then tighten both the right-hand and rear mounting through bolts to their specified torque settings (see the relevant part of Chapter 2).

7.29 . . . then withdraw the pump from the cylinder block

7.30 Prior to refitting, fit a new sealing ring to the rear of the pump

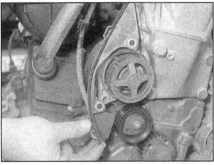

7.28b . . . and remove the timing belt rear cover

19 Remove all traces of locking compound from the gearchange steady rod bolt threads. Ensure the mounting rubbers and washer are correctly positioned then reconnect the rod to the transmission housing. Apply a few drops of locking compound (Skoda recommend the use of Loctite 270 or Three Bond 1305) to the retaining bolt threads then refit the bolt and tighten it to the specified torque setting (see Chapter 7).
20 Reconnect the selector rod to the transmission and secure it in position with a new roll pin. Secure the roll pin in position using a jubilee-type hose clip.
21 Reconnect the coolant pipe to the pump hose. Refit the pipe retaining bolt, tightening it securely, then securely tighten the pump hose retaining clip.
22 Refit the auxiliary drivebelt as described in the relevant part of Chapter 2.
23 Refit the air cleaner assembly as described in the relevant part of Chapter 4.
24 Refit the undercover, tightening its retaining screws securely, then lower the vehicle to the ground.
25 Refill the cooling system as described in the relevant part of Chapter 1.

1.6 litre petrol engine

Removal

26 Remove the timing belt as described in the relevant part of Chapter 2.
27 Drain the cooling system as described in the relevant part of Chapter 1.
28 Slacken and remove the pump retaining bolts then remove the timing belt rear cover from the pump **(see illustrations)**.
29 Remove the pump from the cylinder block **(see illustration)**. Recover the sealing ring and discard it; a new one must be used on refitting.

Refitting

30 Fit a new sealing ring to the pump and locate the pump in the cylinder block **(see illustration)**. Fit the timing belt rear cover and refit the pump retaining bolts, tightening them to the specified torque.
31 Refit the timing belt as described in the relevant part of Chapter 2.
32 On completion refill the cooling system as described in the relevant part of Chapter 1.

Diesel engine

Removal

33 Drain the cooling system as described in the relevant part of Chapter 1.
34 Remove the alternator as described in Chapter 5A.
35 Remove the power steering pump as described in Chapter 10 noting that there is no need to disconnect the hydraulic pipe/hose from the pump. Unbolt the pump from its mountings and position it clear of the coolant pump housing.
36 Slacken and remove the bolt securing the injection pump rear bracket to the top of the pump housing/mounting bracket assembly **(see illustration)**.

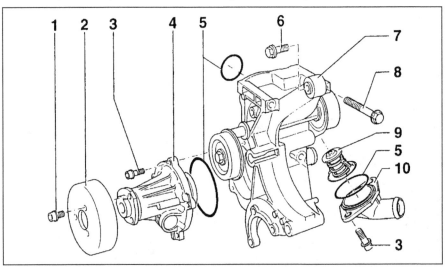

7.36 Coolant pump housing/mounting bracket assembly - diesel engine

1 Pulley bolt	4 Coolant pump	7 Pump housing/mounting bracket	8 Mounting bolt
2 Pulley	5 Sealing ring		9 Thermostat
3 Retaining bolt	6 Injection pump bolt		10 Thermostat cover

37 Release the retaining clips and disconnect the coolant hoses from the rear of the pump housing/mounting bracket assembly.
38 Slacken and remove the retaining bolts and remove the pump housing/mounting bracket assembly from the front of the cylinder block. Recover the sealing ring which is fitted between the housing and block and discard it; a new one should be used on refitting.
39 With the assembly on a bench, unscrew the retaining bolts and remove the pulley from the pump. Undo the pump retaining bolts and remove the pump from the housing. Discard the sealing ring, a new one must be used on refitting.

Refitting

40 Ensure that the pump and housing mating surfaces are clean and dry then fit the new sealing ring.
41 Fit the coolant pump to the housing and evenly tighten its retaining bolts to the specified torque setting. Refit the pulley to the pump and tighten its retaining bolts to the specified torque
42 Fit the new sealing ring to the housing assembly recess and refit the housing to the cylinder block. Refit the retaining bolts and tighten them to the specified torque setting in the order shown in **illustration 7.42 (see illustration).**
43 Connect the coolant hoses to the housing and secure them in position with the retaining clips.
44 Refit the alternator and power steering pump and install the auxiliary drivebelt (see the relevant part of Chapters 2, 5 and 10).

45 On completion refill the cooling system as described in the relevant part of Chapter 1.

8 Heating and ventilation system - general information

1 The heating/ventilation system consists of a fully adjustable blower motor (housed behind the facia), face level vents in the centre and at each end of the facia, and air ducts to the front footwells.
2 The control unit is located in the facia, and the controls operate flap valves to deflect and mix the air flowing through the various parts of the heating/ventilation system. The flap valves are contained in the air distribution housing, which acts as a central distribution unit, passing air to the various ducts and vents.
3 Cold air enters the system through the grille at the rear of the engine compartment. If required, the airflow is boosted by the blower, and then flows through the various ducts, according to the settings of the controls. Stale air is expelled through ducts at the rear of the vehicle. If warm air is required, the cold air is passed over the heater matrix, which is heated by the engine coolant.
4 The outside air supply to the vehicle can be closed off which is useful to prevent unpleasant odours entering from outside the vehicle. This is achieved either by setting the blower motor switch to position 0 or using the intake flap valve switch (where fitted). This feature should only be used briefly, as the recirculated air inside the vehicle will soon become stale.

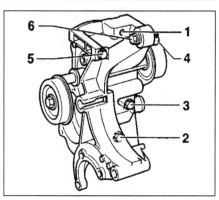

7.42 Tighten the coolant pump housing/mounting bracket bolts to the specified torque in the sequence shown

9 Heater/ventilation components - removal and refitting

Models not fitted with air conditioning

Heater/ventilation housing assembly

1 Where necessary, unscrew the suspension strut upper mounting nuts and remove the strut brace from the vehicle (see illustrations).
2 Working as described in the relevant part of Chapter 4 carry out the following.
a) On 1.3 litre petrol engines fitted with a single-point fuel injection system, remove the air cleaner assembly.
b) On 1.3 litre petrol engines fitted with a multi-point fuel injection system, unbolt the throttle body assembly from the inlet manifold and position it clear of the housing (see illustration). Note that there is no need to any hoses/wiring or the accelerator cable; they can all be left attached.
c) On 1.6 litre petrol engines, remove the air inlet pipe.
d) On diesel engine models remove the inlet manifold upper section.
3 Prise off the retaining clips securing the intake to the top of the heater/ventilation housing and remove the intake duct assembly from the engine compartment (see illustrations).

9.1a Unscrew the strut upper mounting nuts . . .

9.1b . . . and lift off the strut brace (where fitted)

9.2 On 1.3 litre multi-point injection models unbolt the throttle body assembly from the manifold

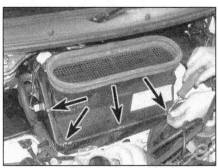

9.3a Prise off the retaining clips (arrowed) . . .

9.3b . . . and remove the intake duct assembly from the housing

9.8 Slacken the retaining clips and detach the coolant hoses (arrowed) from the housing

9.9 Slacken and remove the retaining nuts and washers . . .

4 Remove the battery as described in Chapter 5A.

5 Remove the instrument panel and the cigarette lighter as described in Chapter 12.

6 Locate the heater control panel wiring connector on the left-hand side of the housing and disconnect it. If the connector is awkward to reach, disconnect it as the housing is removed.

7 Reach in through the cigarette lighter aperture and unclip the rear footwell duct from the base of the heater/ventilation housing.

8 Working in the engine compartment, clamp the heater matrix coolant hoses to minimise coolant loss. Position a wad of rag beneath the matrix unions, to catch any spilt coolant, then release the retaining clips and disconnect both hoses. Mop up any spilt coolant and rinse off with water. Position absorbent rags around the housing to catch any further coolant spilt as the housing is removed **(see illustration)**.

9 Slacken and remove the nuts securing the heater/ventilation housing assembly to the bulkhead **(see illustration)**.

10 With the aid of an assistant, ensure the control panel is freed from the facia then lift the housing and control panel assembly out of position and remove it from the vehicle. As the unit is removed make sure all the necessary clips and ties have been released and try and keep the heater matrix unions uppermost to prevent coolant spillage **(see illustrations)**.

11 Refitting is the reverse of removal, noting the following points.

a) Prior to refitting, check the housing bulkhead gasket for signs of wear or damage and renew if necessary.

b) Ensure the housing assembly is correctly seated and that the ventilation ducts and elbows are all securely joined before securing the housing in position with the retaining nuts.

c) Ensure the coolant hoses are securely reconnected to the matrix.

d) On completion, top-up the cooling system as described in Weekly checks or the relevant part of Chapter 1.

Heater/ventilation control panel

12 Remove the heater/ventilation housing and control panel assembly as described in paragraphs 1 to 10.

13 Note the correct fitted location of each cable (the cable end fittings are colour-coded) then, using pliers, release the retaining clips and detach the cables from the panel **(see illustration)**.

14 Disconnect the wiring connector from the blower motor switch and separate the control panel from the housing **(see illustration)**.

15 Refitting is a reversal of removal, ensuring that the control cables are securely reconnected to their original locations and are correctly routed. Check the operation of the controls prior to refitting the housing assembly to the vehicle.

Blower motor - petrol engine models

16 Remove the retaining clips securing the intake to the heater/ventilation housing then remove the intake duct from the housing **(see illustrations)**.

9.10a . . . then remove the heating/ventilation housing assembly from the engine compartment . . .

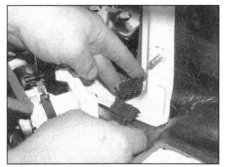

9.10b . . . where necessary, disconnecting its wiring connector as it becomes accessible

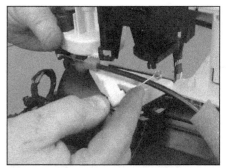

9.13 Unclip the control cables from the base of the panel . . .

9.14 . . . then disconnect the wiring connector and separate the panel and housing

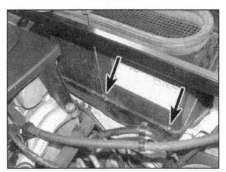

9.16a Remove the retaining clips . . .

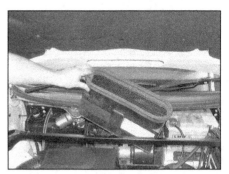

9.16b . . . then lift off the intake duct from the housing

9.18a Disconnect the wiring connector . . .

9.18b . . . then free the wiring grommet and the wiring from the housing

9.19a Undo the retaining screws (arrowed) . . .

9.19b . . . then lift the blower motor mounting plate assembly away from the housing

9.20a Unclip the covers . . .

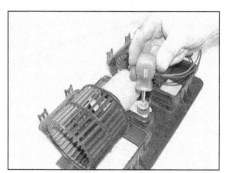

9.20b . . . then undo the mounting screw . . .

17 To improve access, remove the battery as described in Chapter 5A.
18 Trace the wiring back from the blower motor to its connector. Disconnect the connector and free the wiring grommet from housing **(see illustrations)**.
19 Undo the retaining screws then unclip and remove the blower motor mounting plate assembly from the housing **(see illustrations)**.
20 Unclip the covers from the mounting plate then slacken the mounting screw and separate the blower motor and plate **(see illustrations)**.
21 Refitting is the reverse of removal. On completion, refit the battery and check the motor spins freely.

Blower motor - diesel engine models

22 To improve access, remove the battery as described in Chapter 5A.

9.20c . . . and separate the blower motor and mounting plate

23 Unclip and remove the intake from the heater/ventilation housing.
24 Disconnect the blower motor wiring connector and detach the wiring.
25 Slacken and remove the nuts securing the blower motor mounting plate then manoeuvre the assembly out from the heater/ventilation housing **(see illustration)**.
26 Remove the retaining clips then lift off the covers to expose the blower motor. Slacken the clamp screw and separate the blower motor from its mounting plate.

27 Refitting is the reverse of removal. On completion, refit the battery and check the motor spins freely.

Blower motor resistor - petrol engine models

28 The blower motor resistor is situated in the engine compartment where it is fitted to the right-hand side of the heater/ventilation housing assembly. On left-hand drive models access to the resistor can be improved by removing the battery (see Chapter 5A).

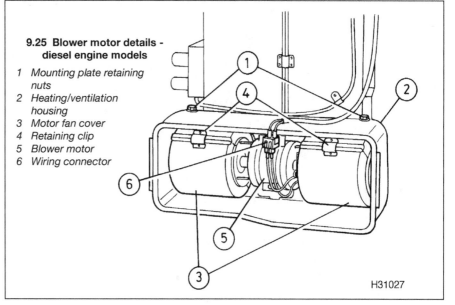

9.25 Blower motor details - diesel engine models

1 *Mounting plate retaining nuts*
2 *Heating/ventilation housing*
3 *Motor fan cover*
4 *Retaining clip*
5 *Blower motor*
6 *Wiring connector*

H31027

9.29a On petrol engine models disconnect the wiring connector . . .

9.29b . . . then unclip the blower motor resistor from the housing

9.36 Undo the retaining screw and carefully slide the heater matrix out of position

29 Disconnect the wiring connector then unclip the resistor and remove it from the housing (see illustrations).
30 Refitting is the reverse of removal, ensuring the resistor is clipped securely into the housing.

Blower motor resistor - diesel engine models

31 The blower motor resistor is situated in the engine compartment where it is fitted to the left-hand side of the heater/ventilation housing assembly. Access to the resistor can be improved by removing the battery (see Chapter 5A).
32 Disconnect the wiring connectors from the resistor, noting each ones correct fitted location.
33 Slacken and remove the retaining screws and remove the resistor from the housing.
34 Refitting is the reverse of removal.

Heater matrix - petrol engine models

35 Remove the heater/ventilation housing assembly as described in paragraphs 1 to 10.

36 Undo the retaining screw and slide the matrix out from the housing (see illustration). *Caution: Take care not to cut your hands as the matrix fins are extremely sharp.*
37 Prior to refitting, check that the matrix sealing foam is in good condition. Slide the matrix carefully into position then securely tighten its retaining screw before refitting the housing assembly (see paragraph 11).

Heater matrix - diesel engine models

38 On left-hand drive models, remove the battery as described in Chapter 5A.
39 On all models, clamp the heater matrix coolant hoses to minimise coolant loss and position a wad of rag beneath the matrix unions, to catch any spilt coolant. Release the retaining clips and disconnect both hoses. Mop up any spilt coolant and rinse off with water. Position absorbent rags around the housing to catch any further coolant spilt as the matrix is removed.
40 Slacken the clamp bolts and free the control cables from the heater matrix thermostat linkage (see illustration). Release

the retaining clip and detach the upper outer cable then unscrew the upper and lower retaining nut and remove the heater/ventilation flap lever from the housing.
41 Carefully unclip the top of the matrix cover from the housing and remove the cover.
42 Slide the matrix carefully out of position, take care not to damage the matrix cooling fins.
Caution: Take care not to cut your hands as the matrix fins are extremely sharp.
43 Refitting is the reverse of removal ensuring the matrix sealing foam is in good condition.

Models equipped with air conditioning

⚠️ *Warning: Do not attempt to open the refrigerant circuit. Refer to the precautions given in Section 10.*

Heater/ventilation housing assembly and control panel

44 Removal and refitting must be entrusted to a Skoda dealer. This is necessary since removal requires the refrigerant pipes to be disconnect from the evaporator expansion valve (see Section 10).

Blower motor

45 Working in the engine compartment, remove the retaining fasteners then unclip and remove the heatshield from the heating/ventilation housing.
46 Locate the blower motor wiring connector at the front of the housing then disconnect the connector and push the wiring grommet into the housing.
47 Disconnect the vacuum hose from the intake flap diaphragm unit and detach the rod from the diaphragm linkage.
48 Remove the retaining screws and clips then lift the intake duct off from the top of the heater/ventilation housing, freeing it from the blower motor wiring.
49 Slacken and remove the retaining screws then lift the blower motor assembly out of position.
50 Refitting is the reverse of removal, ensuring the wiring grommet is correctly located in the intake duct. On completion check the operation of the intake duct flap.

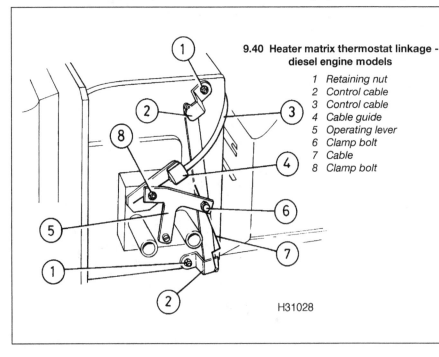

9.40 Heater matrix thermostat linkage - diesel engine models

1 Retaining nut
2 Control cable
3 Control cable
4 Cable guide
5 Operating lever
6 Clamp bolt
7 Cable
8 Clamp bolt

H31028

Blower motor resistor

51 The blower motor resistor is situated in the engine compartment where it is fitted to the left-hand side of the heater/ventilation housing assembly. Access to the resistor can be improved by removing the battery (see Chapter 5A).

52 Disconnect the wiring connector then unclip the resistor and remove it from the housing.

53 Refitting is the reverse of removal, ensuring the resistor is clipped securely into the housing.

Heater matrix

54 Removal and refitting must be entrusted to a Skoda dealer. This is necessary since removal requires the heater/ventilation housing to be removed from the vehicle which requires the refrigerant pipes to be disconnect from the evaporator expansion valve (see Section 10).

10 Air conditioning system - general information and precautions

General information

1 An air conditioning system is available on certain models. It enables the temperature of incoming air to be lowered, and also dehumidifies the air, which makes for rapid demisting and increased comfort.

2 The cooling side of the system works in the same way as a domestic refrigerator. Refrigerant gas is drawn into a belt-driven compressor, and passes into a condenser mounted on the front of the radiator, where it loses heat and becomes liquid. The liquid passes through an expansion valve to an evaporator, where it changes from liquid under high pressure to gas under low pressure. This change is accompanied by a drop in temperature, which cools the evaporator. The refrigerant returns to the compressor, and the cycle begins again.

3 Air blown through the evaporator passes to the heater/ventilation housing, where it is mixed with hot air blown through the heater matrix to achieve the desired temperature in the passenger compartment.

4 The heating side of the system works in the same way as on models without air conditioning (see Section 8).

5 Any problems with the air conditioning system should be referred to an Skoda dealer.

Precautions

6 When an air conditioning system is fitted, it is necessary to observe special precautions when dealing with any part of the system, or its associated components.

7 Never attempt to open any air conditioning system pipe/hose union. If for any reason the system must be disconnected, the vehicle should be taken to a Skoda dealer or air conditioning system specialist with the necessary equipment to safely discharge the refrigerant before opening the circuit. Once the work is complete they can then safely recharge the circuit with the correct type and amount fresh refrigerant.

8 The refrigerant is potentially dangerous, and should only be handled by qualified persons. Uncontrolled discharging of the refrigerant is dangerous for the following reasons.

a) If it is splashed onto the skin, it can cause frostbite.

b) The refrigerant is heavier than air and so displaces oxygen. In a confined space which is not adequately ventilated this could lead to a risk of suffocation. The gas is odourless and colourless so there is no warning of its presence in the atmosphere.

c) Although not poisonous, in the presence of a naked flame (including a cigarette) it forms a noxious gas which causes nausea, headaches, etc.

9 Do not operate the air conditioning system if it is known to be short of refrigerant, as this may damage the compressor.

11 Air conditioning system components - removal and refitting

 Warning: Do not attempt to open the refrigerant circuit. Refer to the precautions given in Section 10.

1 The only operation which can be carried out easily without discharging the refrigerant is the renewal of the compressor drivebelt. This is described in the relevant part of Chapter 1. All other operations must be referred to a Skoda dealer or an air conditioning specialist.

2 If necessary, the compressor can be unbolted and moved aside, without disconnecting the refrigerant pipes, after removing the drivebelt.

Chapter 4 Part A:
Fuel system - single-point petrol injection

Contents

Degrees of difficulty

Easy, suitable for novice with little experience		Fairly easy, suitable for beginner with some experience		Fairly difficult, suitable for competent DIY mechanic		Difficult, suitable for experienced DIY mechanic		Very difficult, suitable for expert DIY or professional

Specifications

Fuel system data

System type	Bosch Mono-Motronic
Fuel pump type	Electric, immersed in fuel tank
Fuel pump delivery rate	1000 cm^3 / min (battery voltage of 12.5 V)
Regulated fuel pressure	0.8 to 1.2 bar
Engine idle speed	750 to 850 rpm (non-adjustable, electronically controlled)
Maximum engine speed	5800 rpm (governed electronically)
Injector electrical resistance	Less than 3.0 ohms at 15 to 30°C

Recommended fuel

Minimum octane rating (all models)	95 RON unleaded

Torque wrench settings

	Nm	lbf ft
Air cleaner housing nuts/bolts	10	7
Fuel tank mounting bolts	25	18
Injector cap/inlet air temperature sensor housing screw	5	4
Inlet manifold retaining nuts	25	18
Throttle body mounting flange-to-inlet manifold bolts	10	7
Throttle body through-bolts	15	11
Throttle valve positioning module screws	6	4

1 General information and precautions

General information

The Bosch Mono-Motronic system is a self-contained engine management system, which controls both the fuel injection and ignition. This Chapter deals with the fuel injection system components only - refer to Chapter 5B for details of the ignition system components.

The fuel injection system comprises a fuel tank, an electric fuel pump, a fuel filter, fuel supply and return lines, a throttle body with an integral electronic fuel injector, and an Electronic Control Unit (ECU) together with its associated sensors, actuators and wiring.

The fuel pump delivers a constant supply of fuel through a cartridge filter to the throttle body, at a slightly higher pressure than required - the fuel pressure regulator (integral with the throttle body) maintains a constant fuel pressure at the fuel injector, and returns excess fuel to the tank via the return line. This constant flow system also helps to reduce fuel temperature and prevents vaporisation.

The fuel injector is opened and closed by an Electronic Control Unit (ECU), which calculates the injection timing and duration according to engine speed, throttle position and rate of opening, inlet air temperature, coolant temperature, road speed and exhaust gas oxygen content information, received from sensors mounted on the engine.

Inlet air is drawn into the engine through the air cleaner, which contains a renewable paper filter element. The inlet air temperature is regulated by a vacuum-operated valve mounted in the air cleaner inlet trunking, which blends air at ambient temperature with warm air, drawn from over the exhaust manifold. Vacuum supply to the valve is regulated by a temperature switch mounted in the air cleaner.

Engine speed information is derived from the Hall sensor mounted on top of the transmission housing, from the rotational speed of the flywheel.

The temperature of the air entering the throttle body is measured by a sensor mounted directly above the injector. This information is used by the ECU to fine-tune the fuelling requirements for different operating temperatures.

Idle speed control is achieved partly by an electronic throttle positioning module, mounted on the front of the throttle body, and partly by the ignition system, which gives fine control of the idle speed by altering the ignition timing. As a result, manual adjustment of the engine idle speed is not necessary, or possible. Information on throttle position and the rate of throttle opening is provided by the throttle position sensor (or throttle valve potentiometer), located on the left-hand side of the throttle body.

The exhaust gas oxygen content is constantly monitored by the ECU via the Lambda sensor, which is mounted in the front part of the exhaust pipe. The ECU then uses this information to modify the injection timing and duration to maintain the optimum air/fuel ratio - a result of this is that manual adjustment of the idle exhaust CO content is not necessary. All models covered by this Manual are fitted with a catalytic converter - see Chapter 4D for details.

In addition, the ECU controls the operation of the activated charcoal filter evaporative loss system - refer to Chapter 4D for further details.

It should be noted that fault diagnosis of the Bosch Mono-Motronic system is only possible with dedicated electronic test equipment. A diagnostic socket is provided, under the right-hand end of the facia panel. Problems with the system's operation should be referred to a Skoda dealer, who should be able to read any fault codes stored in the system ECU with diagnostic test equipment.

Once the fault has been identified, the removal/refitting sequences detailed in the following Sections will then allow the appropriate component(s) to be renewed as required.

Precautions

 Warning: Petrol is extremely flammable - great care must be taken when working on any part of the fuel system.

Do not smoke, or allow any naked flames or uncovered light bulbs near the work area. Note that gas powered domestic appliances with pilot flames, such as heaters boilers and tumble-dryers, also present a fire hazard - bear this in mind if you are working in an area where such appliances are present. Always keep a suitable fire extinguisher close to the work area, and familiarise yourself with its operation before starting work. Wear eye protection when working on fuel systems, and wash off any fuel spilt on bare skin immediately with soap and water. Note that fuel vapour is just as dangerous as liquid fuel - possibly more so; a vessel that has been emptied of liquid fuel will still contain vapour, and can be potentially explosive.

Many of the operations described in this Chapter involve the disconnection of fuel lines, which may cause an amount of fuel spillage. Before commencing work, refer to the above Warning and the information in Safety first! at the beginning of this manual.

Residual fuel pressure always remain in the fuel system, long after the engine has been switched off. This pressure must be relieved in a controlled manner before work can commence on any component in the fuel system - refer to Section 8 for details.

When working with fuel system components, pay particular attention to cleanliness - dirt entering the fuel system may cause blockages, which will lead to poor running.

In the interests of personal safety and equipment protection, many of the procedures in this Chapter suggest that the negative lead be removed from the battery terminal. *This firstly eliminates the possibility of accidental short-circuits being caused as the vehicle is being worked upon, and secondly prevents damage to electronic components (eg sensors, actuators, ECUs) which are particularly sensitive to the power surges caused by disconnection or reconnection of the wiring harness whilst they are still live.*

It should be noted, however, that the engine management system has a learning capability, that allows the system to adapt to the engine's running characteristics as it wears with use. This learnt information is lost when the battery is disconnected, and the system will then take a short period of time to re-learn the engine's characteristics - this may be manifested (temporarily) as rough idling, reduced throttle response and possibly a slight increase in fuel consumption, until the system re-adapts. The re-adaptation time will depend on how often the vehicle is used and the driving conditions encountered.

2 Air cleaner - removal and refitting

Removal

1 Release the over-centre wire clips around the air cleaner top cover, then unscrew and remove the three bolts and lift off the top cover (refer to Chapter 1A if necessary). Lift out the air filter element.

2 Unclip the accelerator cable from the front underside of the housing, and disconnect the warm-air supply tube from the temperature control valve housing. On models with the 136B engine, loosen the clip and disconnect the air inlet hose either from the air cleaner housing or from the resonator box **(see illustrations)**.

3 Lift the housing away from the throttle body slightly, then disconnect the temperature switch vacuum pipe underneath which leads to the throttle body - the other vacuum hose to the capsule can be left attached **(see illustration)**.

2.2a Unclip the accelerator cable from the housing . . .

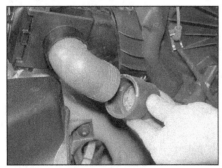

2.2b . . . and pull off the warm-air supply tube

2.2c On models with the 136B engine, disconnect the air inlet hose

2.3 Lift up the housing, and disconnect the vacuum pipe from the base of the air temperature vacuum switch

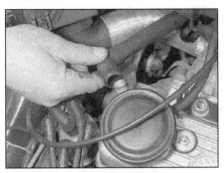

2.4 Pull off the crankcase breather hose from the rocker cover

2.6 Air cleaner spout securing screw

4 Pull off the larger crankcase breather pipe from the engine top cover **(see illustration)**. Unclip the smaller hose leading from the engine top cover, and the charcoal canister hose, from underneath the air cleaner housing.
5 The air cleaner housing can now be removed from the engine compartment.
6 If required, the air cleaner inlet spout on 135B engines can be removed by taking out the retaining screw **(see illustration)**.
7 To remove the air inlet temperature control valve housing, disconnect the vacuum pipe from the capsule, then release the two spring clips and slide the housing out of its location **(see illustrations)**.
8 On models with the 136B engine, a resonator box is fitted in the air inlet to reduce induction noise. The box is secured by two plastic nuts - one at the front, and one onto the suspension strut turret at the rear **(see illustration)**.

Refitting

9 Refit the air cleaner and air inlet system components by following the removal procedure in reverse. Make sure that the vacuum connection to the underside of the housing is securely made. The air cleaner housing must be correctly mounted on the throttle body, to ensure there is no air leakage - check the condition of the rubber seal which fits over the top of the throttle body, and renew it if necessary.

2.7a Disconnect the vacuum pipe . . .

2.7b . . . release the two spring clips . . .

2.7c . . . and slide out the temperature valve housing

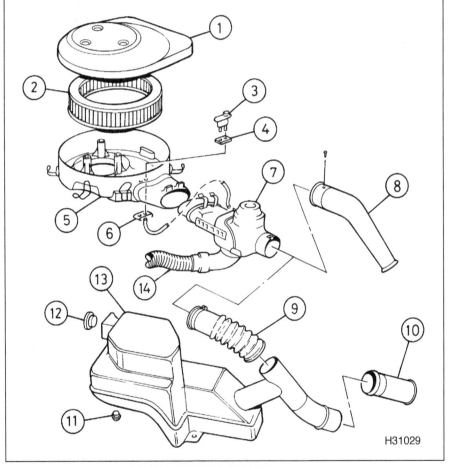

H31029

2.8 Air cleaner and related components

1 Air cleaner top cover	6 Retaining plate	11 Rubber mounting
2 Air filter element	7 Vacuum capsule	12 Mounting
3 Air temperature vacuum switch	8 Inlet spout (135B engine)	13 Resonator box (136B engine)
4 Seal	9 Inlet hose	14 Warm-air supply tube
5 Air cleaner housing	10 Inlet spout (136B engine)	

4.2 Unhook the inner cable from the throttle valve

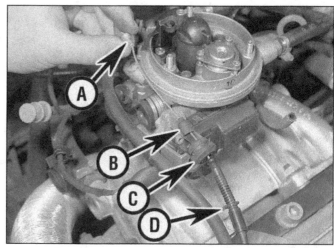

4.3 Throttle cable disconnected from the throttle body

A *Inner cable end fitting*   C *Cable outer grommet*
B *Cable outer end cover*   D *Cable adjuster circlip*

3 Inlet air temperature vacuum switch - removal and refitting

Removal

1 Remove the air cleaner housing as described in Section 2.
2 Pull off the remaining vacuum pipe (leading to the vacuum capsule on the temperature control valve housing) from the vacuum switch, noting its location.
3 Using a small flat-bladed screwdriver, prise off the retaining plate from below the vacuum switch. The plate will probably be quite stiff, but work carefully, to avoid damaging the pipe stubs.
4 Remove the vacuum switch from the air cleaner housing, and recover the seal.

Refitting

5 Refit the vacuum switch by following the removal procedure in reverse. If the seal is damaged or deteriorated, fit a new one when reassembling. Press the retaining plate firmly into position over the pipe stubs.

4 Accelerator cable - removal, refitting and adjustment

Removal

1 Remove the air cleaner housing as described in Section 2.
2 At the throttle body, disconnect the accelerator cable inner from the throttle valve spindle plate by pulling on the cable inner and detaching the cable end fitting **(see illustration)**.
3 Remove the cover from the end of the cable outer, and extract the cable outer grommet from the mounting bracket. The grommet can now be slid off the end of the cable **(see illustration)**.
4 Working inside the vehicle, release the cable nipple from the clevis at the top of the pedal.
5 Release the cable from its clips and guide it out through the bulkhead grommet.

Refitting

6 Refit the accelerator cable by following the removal procedure in reverse.

Adjustment

7 At the throttle body, fix the position of the cable outer in its mounting bracket by inserting the metal clip in one of the locating slots, such that there is no slack in the cable when the throttle valve lever is touching the idle position stop **(see illustrations)**.

5 Bosch Mono-Motronic system components - removal and refitting

Note: *Observe the precautions in Section 1 before working on any component in the fuel system.*

Throttle body

Removal

1 Refer to Section 2 and remove the air cleaner housing.
2 Refer to Section 8 and depressurise the fuel system, then disconnect the battery negative lead and position it away from the terminal.
3 Disconnect the fuel supply and return hoses from the ports on the side of the throttle body. Note the arrows that denote the direction of fuel flow, and mark the hoses accordingly **(see illustrations)**.

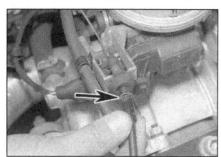

4.7a Pull the cable outer to assess the slack in the cable - adjuster circlip arrowed

4.7b Adjust the cable by inserting the circlip into one of the slots in the cable outer

5.3a Throttle body fuel supply connection . . .

5.3b . . . and fuel return connection

5.4a Disconnecting the fuel injector
wiring plug . . .

5.4b . . . throttle valve positioning
module plug . . .

5.4c . . . and throttle position sensor plug

5.6 Throttle body through-bolts (A), upper-
to-lower body through-bolts (B), injector
securing screw (C), and fuel pressure
regulator screws (D)

5.11 Removing the injector securing
screw

4 Unplug the wiring harness from the throttle body at the connectors, labelling them to aid correct refitting later **(see illustrations)**.
5 Refer to Section 4 and disconnect the accelerator cable from the throttle body.
6 Loosen and remove the through-bolts which secure the throttle body to the inlet manifold **(see illustration)**. Lift the throttle body away from the inlet manifold, recovering the gasket (where applicable). Unless specifically required, it is not recommended that the upper and lower halves of the throttle body are separated - these are held together by two inner through-bolts. If the two halves are split, a new gasket must be used on reassembly.

Refitting

7 Refitting is a reversal of removal; renew all gaskets where appropriate. Tighten the

through-bolts securely. On completion, check and if necessary adjust the accelerator cable.

Fuel injector

Removal

8 Refer to Section 2 and remove the air cleaner housing.
9 Refer to Section 8 and depressurise the fuel system, then disconnect the battery negative lead and position it away from the terminal.
10 Unplug the wiring connector from the injector **(refer to illustration 5.4a)**.
11 Remove the screw and lift off the injector retaining cap/inlet air temperature sensor housing **(see illustration)**. Recover the gasket.
12 Release the securing washer (where fitted), then lift the injector out of the throttle body, recovering the O-ring seals **(see illustration)**.

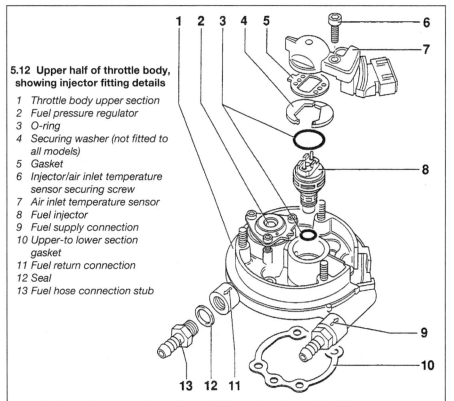
5.12 Upper half of throttle body, showing injector fitting details

1 Throttle body upper section
2 Fuel pressure regulator
3 O-ring
4 Securing washer (not fitted to all models)
5 Gasket
6 Injector/air inlet temperature sensor securing screw
7 Air inlet temperature sensor
8 Fuel injector
9 Fuel supply connection
10 Upper-to lower section gasket
11 Fuel return connection
12 Seal
13 Fuel hose connection stub

5.27 Throttle valve positioning module retaining screws (arrowed)

13 Check the injector electrical resistance using a multimeter, and compare the result with the Specifications.

Refitting

14 Refit the injector by following the removal procedure in reverse, renewing all O-ring seals and gaskets. Apply a suitable sealant to the screw threads, then insert and tighten the retaining screw to the specified torque.

Inlet air temperature sensor

15 The inlet air temperature sensor is an integral part of the injector retaining cap. Removal is as described in the previous sub-Section.

Fuel pressure regulator

Removal

16 If the operation of the fuel pressure regulator is in question, dismantle the unit as described below, then check the cleanliness and integrity of the internal components. **Note:** *The fuel pressure regulator components are matched to the upper part of the throttle body during manufacture. If the pressure regulator is defective, Skoda state that the upper part of the throttle body must be renewed complete. Consult your parts supplier for the latest advice.*

17 Remove the air cleaner housing, with reference to Section 2.

18 Refer to Section 8 and depressurise the fuel system, then disconnect the battery negative lead and position it away from the terminal.

19 With reference to the relevant sub-

Section, remove the screw and lift off the inlet air temperature sensor/injector cap.

20 Slacken and withdraw the three Torx retaining screws and lift off the fuel pressure regulator retaining frame.

21 Lift out the upper cover, spring and membrane.

22 Clean all the components thoroughly, then inspect the membrane for cracks or splits.

Refitting

23 Reassemble the pressure regulator by following the removal procedure in reverse.

Throttle valve positioning module

Removal

24 Disconnect the battery negative lead and position it away from the terminal. Remove the air cleaner housing, with reference to Section 2.

25 Refer to Section 4 and disconnect the accelerator cable from the throttle body.

26 Unplug the connector from the side of the throttle valve positioning module.

27 Remove the retaining screws **(see illustration)** and lift the module, together with the accelerator cable outer mounting bracket, away from the throttle body.

Refitting

28 Refitting is a reversal of removal. Note that if a new module has been fitted, the adjustment of the idle switch will need to be checked - refer to a Skoda dealer for advice as this operation requires access to dedicated test equipment.

Throttle position sensor

29 Refer to the relevant sub-Section and remove the throttle body. The throttle position sensor is an integral part of the lower section of the throttle body, and cannot be renewed separately.

Idle switch

30 Refer to the relevant sub-Section and remove the throttle valve positioning module. The idle switch is an integral part of the module, and cannot be renewed separately.

31 Where a new throttle valve positioning module has been fitted, the adjustment of the

idle switch will need to be checked - refer to a Skoda dealer for advice as this operation requires access to dedicated test equipment.

Lambda sensor

Removal

32 Refer to Chapter 4D.

Coolant temperature sensor

33 The temperature sensor for the fuel injection system is fitted into the rear of the inlet manifold - a separate sensor is fitted for the temperature gauge (see Chapter 3). If the injection system sensor develops a fault, the engine will run particularly poorly when warming up.

34 The sensor may be tested by measuring its resistance, which will be higher when the engine is cold (typically 2000 ohms), lower when hot (typically 300 ohms).

35 If an open-circuit reading is obtained, renew the sensor. If the measured resistance varies with temperature, have the unit checked by a Skoda dealer or electrical specialist before condemning it. A fault in the sensor will sometimes generate a fault code in the injection system ECU - a Skoda dealer can check the ECU for fault codes.

36 To remove the sensor, the cooling system must be drained. Either drain the whole system as described in Chapter 1A, or disconnect one of the coolant hoses from the manifold, and allow the manifold to drain. Alternatively, have ready a plug which will fit into the hole in the rear of the manifold, to prevent too much coolant being lost when the sensor is unscrewed.

37 Disconnect the wiring plug, and unscrew the sensor from the rear of the manifold **(see illustration)**. Recover the seal, and discard it - a new one should be used on refitting.

38 Fit a new seal to the new sensor, and screw the sensor into position.

39 Reconnect the sensor wiring plug, and refill or top-up the cooling system, as necessary.

Hall sensor

40 Refer to Chapter 5B.

Electronic control unit (ECU)

41 The ECU is located at the rear left-hand side of the engine compartment **(see illustration)**. The unit is coded, and should not be removed without consulting a Skoda dealer, otherwise it may not function correctly when the multi-plug is reconnected.

Fuel pump relay and fuses

42 The fuel pump relay and fuel injection system fuses are located in the fuse/relay panel in the passenger compartment - refer to Chapter 12.

43 The fuel pump relay is in position 5 on the relay panel, and the fuel pump is fed by fuse number 4.

44 The relay can be simply pulled from its socket - it is best to note which way round it

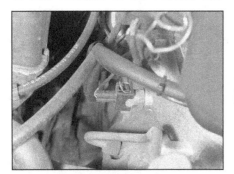

5.37 Coolant temperature sensor - fuel injection system

5.41 Mono-Motronic electronic control unit (ECU)

6.5 Slacken the access hatch screws, and lift the hatch away from the floorpan

6.6 Unplug the wiring harness connector from the sender unit

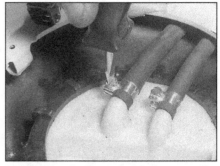

6.7 Slacken the hose clips and remove the fuel pipes from the ports at the sender unit

fits, to make refitting easier, although it will only fit one way round.

45 The fuse is removed in the same way as all other fuses (refer to Chapter 12 if necessary).

46 Note that removing the main injection system fuse (number 1) will erase the learned adaptive values from the ECU memory (as will disconnecting the battery). These values will be re-learned when the engine is next started. The best way to achieve this is to start the engine and allow it to idle for a few minutes, before continuing driving as normal - the idle speed in particular may be a little erratic for a time until the system finds the optimum settings.

Use a pair of water pump pliers to grip and rotate the fuel tank sender unit plastic securing ring

6 Fuel pump and gauge sender unit - removal and refitting

Note: *Observe the precautions in Section 1 before working on any component in the fuel system.*

⚠️ **Warning: Avoid direct skin contact with fuel - wear protective clothing and gloves when handling fuel system components. Ensure that the work area is well-ventilated to prevent the build-up of fuel vapour.**

General information

1 The fuel pump and gauge sender unit are combined in one assembly, which is mounted on the top of the fuel tank. Access is via a hatch provided in the load space floor. The unit protrudes into the fuel tank, and its removal involves exposing the contents of the tank to the atmosphere.

Removal

2 Depressurise the fuel system as described in Section 8.
3 Ensure that the vehicle is parked on a level surface, then disconnect the battery negative lead and position it away from the terminal.
4 Fold the rear seat forwards, and remove the trim from the load space floor.
5 Slacken and withdraw the access hatch screws, and lift the hatch away from the floorpan **(see illustration)**.

6 Unplug the wiring harness connector from the pump/sender unit **(see illustration)**.
7 Pad the area around the supply and return fuel hoses with rags to absorb any spilt fuel, then slacken the hose clips and remove them from the ports at the sender unit **(see illustration)**. Observe the supply and return arrows markings on the ports - label the fuel hoses accordingly to ensure correct refitting later.
8 Unscrew the plastic securing ring and lift it out **(see Tool Tip)**. Turn the pump/sender unit to the left to release it from its bayonet fitting and lift it out, holding it above the level of the fuel in the tank until the excess fuel has drained out. Recover the rubber seal **(see illustrations)**.
9 Remove the pump/sender unit from the vehicle and lay it on an absorbent card or rag. Inspect the float at the end of the sender unit swinging arm for punctures and fuel ingress - renew the unit if it appears damaged.
10 The fuel pick-up incorporated in the assembly is spring-loaded, to ensure that it always draws fuel from the lowest part of the tank. Check that the pick-up is free to move under spring tension with respect to the sender unit body.
11 Inspect the rubber seal from the fuel tank aperture for signs of fatigue - renew it if necessary.
12 Inspect the sender unit wiper and track; clean off any dirt and debris that may have accumulated, and look for breaks in the track **(see illustration)**.

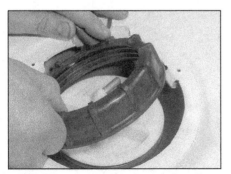

6.8a Unscrew the plastic securing ring and lift it out

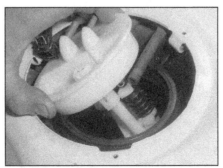

6.8b Lift out the sender unit . . .

6.8c . . . and recover the rubber seal

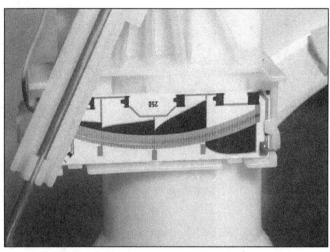

6.12 Look for breaks in the sender unit wiper track

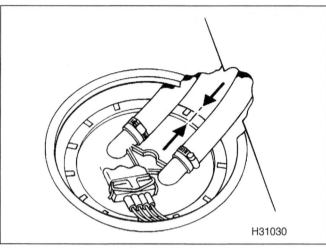

6.13 The arrow marks on the sender unit body and the fuel tank must be aligned

Refitting

13 Refit the sender unit by following the removal procedure in reverse, noting the following points:

a) Take care not to bend the float arm as the unit is refitted.

b) When correctly installed, the pump/sender unit float arm must be at 90° to the centre-line of the vehicle.

c) Smear the tank aperture rubber seal with clean fuel before fitting it in position.

d) The arrow markings on the sender unit body and the fuel tank must be aligned **(see illustration)**.

e) Reconnect the fuel hoses to the correct ports - observe the direction-of-flow arrow markings.

7 Fuel tank -
removal and refitting

Note: *Refer to the warning note in Section 1 before proceeding.*

Removal

1 A fuel tank drain plug is not provided; it is therefore preferable to carry out the removal operation when the tank is nearly empty. Before proceeding, disconnect the battery negative lead, and syphon or hand-pump the remaining fuel from the tank.

2 Chock the front wheels, jack up the rear of the vehicle and support it on axle stands, allowing sufficient room under the vehicle to lower and withdraw the tank. Remove the right-hand rear wheel to improve access on that side.

3 Remove the access cover and disconnect the wiring, fuel supply and return hoses from the top of the sender unit as described in the previous Section.

4 Working underneath the vehicle, unscrew the worm-drive clips and detach the fuel filler pipe from the tank **(see illustration)**.

5 Prise open the retaining clips, and release the handbrake cables from their locating clips on the underside of the tank retaining strap **(see illustration)** and the rear axle beam each side. Move each cable out of the way, and tie them back so that they are clear of the fuel tank.

6 Support the weight of the fuel tank, then undo the retaining strap bolts **(see illustration)**, pivot the straps downwards and lower the fuel tank. Note that one of the fuel tank strap bolts also secures one of the exhaust system mountings - support the exhaust if necessary. As the tank is lowered, guide it clear of the surrounding components and withdraw it from under the vehicle. Allow for the spillage of any remaining fuel in the tank. Plug all hoses and cover their unions to prevent the entry of dirt and the escape of fuel.

7 If the tank is contaminated with sediment or water, wash it out with clean fuel. If the tank is damaged or leaks, it should be inspected by a fuel tank repair specialist for possible repair, or else renewed.

Refitting

8 Refitting is the reverse of the removal procedure, noting the following points:

a) When lifting the tank back into position, take care to ensure none of the hoses get trapped between the tank and vehicle body.

b) Ensure that all pipes and hoses are correctly routed, are not kinked, and are securely held in position with their retaining clips.

c) Tighten the tank mounting bolts to the specified torque.

d) On completion, refill the tank with fuel, and exhaustively check for signs of leakage prior to taking the vehicle out on the road.

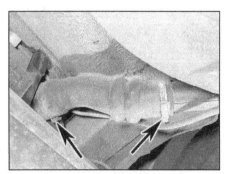

7.4 Fuel filler pipe-to-tank connections (arrowed)

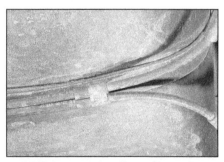

7.5 Prise open the clip to release the handbrake cables from the tank retaining strap

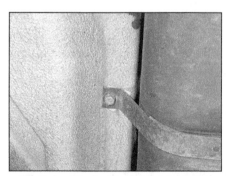

7.6 One of the fuel tank retaining strap bolts

8 Fuel injection system - depressurisation

Note: *Observe the precautions in Section 1 before working on any component in the fuel system.*

⚠️ **Warning: The following procedure will merely relieve the pressure in the fuel system - remember that fuel will still be present in the system components and take precautions accordingly before disconnecting any of them.**

1 The fuel system referred to in this Section is defined as the tank-mounted fuel pump, the fuel filter, the fuel injector, the throttle body-mounted fuel pressure regulator, and the metal pipes and flexible hoses of the fuel lines between these components. All these contain fuel, which will be under pressure while the engine is running and/or while the ignition is switched on. The pressure will remain for some time after the ignition has been switched off, and must be relieved before any of these components are disturbed for servicing work. Ideally, the engine should be allowed to cool completely before work commences.

2 Disconnect the battery negative terminal.

3 Referring to Section 5, remove the fuel pump relay and/or the fuel pump fuse.

4 With the fuel pump disabled, temporarily reconnect the battery negative terminal and crank the engine for about ten seconds. The engine may fire and run for a while, but let it continue running until it stops. The fuel injector should have opened enough times during cranking to considerably reduce the line fuel pressure, and reduce the risk of fuel spraying out when a fuel line is disturbed.

5 Take out the ignition key and disconnect the battery negative terminal. The fuel pump relay or fuse may now be refitted, provided that the battery is not reconnected, nor the ignition switched on, until all work on the fuel system is complete.

⚠️ **Warning: If the fuel pump is not disabled and the ignition is switched on with the fuel system open, fuel will be ejected from the open connection at full pressure!**

6 Place a suitable container beneath the relevant connection/union to be disconnected, and have a large rag ready to soak up any escaping fuel not being caught by the container.

7 Slowly loosen the connection or union nut (as applicable) to avoid a sudden release of pressure, and position the rag around the connection to catch any fuel spray which may be expelled. Once the pressure has been released, disconnect the fuel line. Insert plugs to minimise fuel loss and prevent the entry of dirt into the fuel system.

9 Inlet manifold - removal and refitting

Note: *Observe the precautions in Section 1 before working on any component in the fuel system.*

Removal

1 Disconnect the battery negative lead and position it away from the terminal.

2 Refer to Chapter 1A and drain the coolant from the engine. Alternatively, disconnect one of the coolant hoses from the rear of the manifold, and drain the manifold.

3 With reference to Section 5, disconnect all wiring connectors and hoses from the throttle body. Alternatively, the throttle body can be removed completely.

4 Slacken the clips and remove the coolant hoses from the inlet manifold.

9.6 Disconnect the wiring plug from the coolant temperature sensor (arrowed)

5 Refer to Chapter 9 and disconnect the brake servo vacuum hose from the port on the inlet manifold.

6 Disconnect the wiring for the coolant temperature sensor at the connector on the rear of the manifold **(see illustration)**.

7 Just above the temperature sensor, disconnect the vacuum pipe which runs to the rocker cover.

8 Remove the retaining bolt and detach the CO sampling pipe (where fitted) from the rear of the inlet manifold **(see illustration)**.

9 To allow the manifold to be withdrawn, all cables and hoses must be released from their manifold securing clips. Note the location and routing of all hoses and cables as they are detached, as an aid to reassembly.

10 Progressively slacken and remove the six inlet manifold retaining nuts **(see illustration)**, then loosen the manifold from the cylinder head. Take care not to damage the gasket, unless it is to be renewed in any case.

11 Make a final check to ensure that nothing remains connected to the manifold, then manoeuvre it out of the engine bay. If required, the throttle body mounting flange can be removed by unscrewing the retaining nuts and lifting it from the inlet manifold **(see illustration)**.

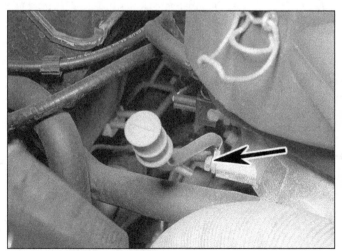

9.8 CO sampling pipe bracket retaining bolt (arrowed)

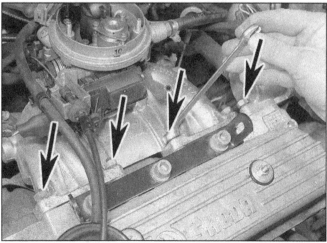

9.10 Four of the inlet manifold retaining nuts (arrowed) - two more below manifold

12 If the gasket is damaged or in poor condition, it must be renewed. As a combined inlet/exhaust manifold is used, the exhaust manifold will need to be removed also (Chapter 4D).

Refitting

13 Refitting is the reverse of the removal procedure, noting the following points:

a) *Ensure that the manifold and cylinder head mating surfaces are clean and dry.*

b) *Tighten the manifold retaining nuts to the specified torque setting.*

c) *Ensure that all relevant cables and hoses are reconnected to their original positions and are securely held (where necessary) by their retaining clips.*

d) *Where removed, refit the throttle body (or reconnect the plugs and hoses) as described in Section 5.*

e) *On completion, refill or top-up the cooling system (see Chapter 1A or Weekly checks).*

10 Fuel injection system - testing and adjustment

1 If a fault appears in the fuel injection system, first ensure that all the system wiring connectors are securely connected and free of corrosion. Then ensure that the fault is not due to poor maintenance; ie, check that the air cleaner filter element is clean, the spark plugs are in good condition and correctly gapped, the cylinder compression pressures are correct, the ignition timing is correct and the engine breather hoses are clear and undamaged, referring to Chapter 1A, Chapter 2A and Chapter 5B for further information.

2 If these checks fail to reveal the cause of the problem, the vehicle should be taken to a suitably-equipped Skoda dealer for testing. A diagnostic socket is provided (under the right-hand end of the facia panel) into which a dedicated electronic test equipment can be plugged. The test equipment is capable of interrogating the engine management system ECU electronically and accessing its internal fault log. In this manner, faults can be pinpointed quickly and simply, even if their occurrence is intermittent. Testing all the system components individually in an attempt to locate the fault by elimination is a time-consuming operation that is unlikely to be fruitful (particularly if the fault occurs dynamically) and carries high risk of damage to the ECU's internal components.

3 Experienced home mechanics equipped with an accurate tachometer and a carefully-calibrated exhaust gas analyser may be able to check the exhaust gas CO content and the engine idle speed; if these are found to be out of specification, then the vehicle must be taken to a suitably-equipped Skoda dealer for assessment. Neither the air/fuel mixture (exhaust gas CO content) nor the engine idle speed are manually adjustable; incorrect test results indicate a fault within the fuel injection system.

11 Unleaded petrol - general information and usage

Note: *The information given in this Chapter is correct at the time of writing, and applies only to petrols currently available in the UK. Check with a Skoda dealer, as more up-to-date information may be available. If travelling abroad, consult one of the motoring organisations (or a similar authority) for advice on the petrols available and their suitability for your vehicle.*

1 The fuel recommended by Skoda is given in the Specifications of this Chapter.

2 RON and MON are different testing standards; RON stands for Research Octane Number (also written as RM), while MON stands for Motor Octane Number (also written as MM).

3 Vehicles equipped with a catalytic converter (as all fuel-injected models covered by this Manual are) must not be run on leaded fuel (eg UK 4-star) or the catalyst will be damaged (see Chapter 4D).

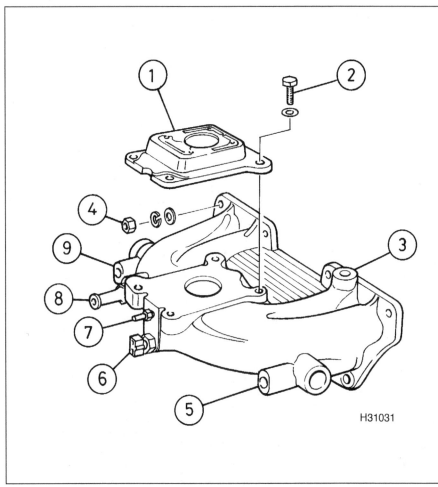

H31031

9.11 Inlet manifold details

1 *Throttle body mounting flange*
2 *Flange bolt*
3 *Inlet manifold*
4 *Manifold nut*
5 *Coolant hose to heater*
6 *Coolant temperature sensor (injection system)*
7 *Vacuum connection to rocker cover*
8 *Brake servo vacuum hose connection*
9 *Coolant hose to thermostat housing*

Chapter 4 Part B:
Fuel system - multi-point petrol injection

Contents

Degrees of difficulty

Easy, suitable for novice with little experience	Fairly easy, suitable for beginner with some experience	Fairly difficult, suitable for competent DIY mechanic	Difficult, suitable for experienced DIY mechanic	Very difficult, suitable for expert DIY or professional

Specifications

System type

1.3 litre engine, codes 135M and 136M	Simos 2P
1.6 litre engine, code AEE	Magneti-Marelli 1AV

Fuel system data

Fuel pump type	Electric, immersed in fuel tank
Fuel pump delivery rate	1100 cm^3 / min (battery voltage of 12.5 V)
Regulated fuel pressure	2.5 bar
Engine idle speed (non-adjustable, electronically controlled):	
1.3 litre engine	790 ± 25 rpm
1.6 litre engine	640 to 790 rpm
Idle CO content (non-adjustable, electronically controlled)	0.5 % max
Injector electrical resistance	15 to 20 ohms

Recommended fuel

Minimum octane rating (all models)	95 RON unleaded

Torque wrench settings

	Nm	lbf ft
1.3 litre engine		
Fuel pressure regulator mounting bracket bolt	8	6
Fuel rail mounting bolts	20	15
Inlet manifold to cylinder head	25	18
Throttle body mounting bolts	10	7
1.6 litre engine		
Fuel rail mounting bolts	10	7
Inlet manifold to cylinder head	20	15
Throttle body mounting bolts	10	7

1 General information and precautions

General information

The Simos 2P and Magneti-Marelli 1AV systems are self-contained engine management systems, which control both the fuel injection and ignition. This Chapter deals with the fuel system components only - see Chapter 5B for details of the ignition system.

The fuel injection system comprises a fuel tank, an electric fuel pump, a fuel filter, fuel supply and return lines, a throttle body, a fuel rail, a fuel pressure regulator, four electronic fuel injectors, and an Electronic Control Unit (ECU) together with its associated sensors, actuators and wiring. The two systems used are broadly similar - the only significant differences lie in the inlet manifold details and the ECUs.

The fuel pump delivers a constant supply of fuel through a cartridge filter to the fuel rail, at a slightly higher pressure than required - the fuel pressure regulator maintains a constant fuel pressure to the fuel injectors, and returns excess fuel to the tank via the return line. This constant flow system also helps to reduce fuel temperature, and prevents vaporisation.

The fuel injectors are opened and closed by an Electronic Control Unit (ECU), which calculates the injection timing and duration according to engine speed, crankshaft position, throttle position and rate of opening, inlet manifold depression, inlet air temperature, coolant temperature, and exhaust gas oxygen content information, received from sensors mounted on and around the engine.

2.1 Release the air cleaner top cover clips (four in total)

Inlet air is drawn into the engine through the air cleaner, which contains a renewable paper filter element. The inlet air temperature is regulated by a valve mounted in the air cleaner housing, which blends air at ambient temperature with hot air, drawn from over the exhaust manifold.

The temperature of the air entering the throttle body is measured by a sensor mounted on the inlet manifold. This sensor also monitors the pressure in the inlet manifold. This information is used by the ECU to fine-tune the fuelling requirements for different operating conditions.

Idle speed control is achieved partly by an electronic throttle valve positioning module on the throttle body, and partly by the ignition system, which gives fine control of the idle speed by altering the ignition timing. As a result, manual adjustment of the engine idle speed is not necessary or possible. Information on throttle position and the rate of throttle opening is provided by the throttle position sensor (or throttle valve potentiometer) and idle/full-throttle switches, incorporated into the throttle valve positioning module.

The exhaust gas oxygen content is constantly monitored by the ECU via the lambda sensor, which is mounted in the front section of the exhaust pipe, ahead of the catalytic converter. The ECU then uses this information to modify the injection timing and duration to maintain the optimum air/fuel ratio - a result of this is that manual adjustment of the idle exhaust CO content is not necessary or possible. All models are fitted with a catalytic converter - see Chapter 4D.

Where fitted, the ECU controls the operation of the activated charcoal filter evaporative loss system - refer to Chapter 4D for further details.

It should be noted that fault diagnosis of all the engine management systems described in this Chapter is only possible with dedicated electronic test equipment. Problems with the systems operation should therefore be referred to a Skoda dealer for assessment. Once the fault has been identified, the removal/refitting sequences detailed in the following Sections will then allow the appropriate component(s) to be renewed as required.

Precautions

 Warning: Petrol is extremely flammable - great care must be taken when working on any part of the fuel system.
Do not smoke, or allow any naked flames or uncovered light bulbs near the work area. Note that gas powered domestic appliances with pilot flames, such as heaters boilers and tumble-dryers, also present a fire hazard - bear this in mind if you are working in an area where such appliances are present. Always keep a suitable fire extinguisher close to the work area, and familiarise yourself with its operation before starting work. Wear eye protection when working on fuel systems, and wash off any fuel spilt on bare skin immediately with soap and water. Note that fuel vapour is just as dangerous as liquid fuel - possibly more so; a vessel that has been emptied of liquid fuel will still contain vapour, and can be potentially explosive.
Many of the operations described in this Chapter involve the disconnection of fuel lines, which may cause an amount of fuel spillage. Before commencing work, refer to the above Warning and the information in Safety first! at the beginning of this manual.
Residual fuel pressure always remain in the fuel system, long after the engine has been switched off. This pressure must be relieved in a controlled manner before work can commence on any component in the fuel system - refer to Section 9 for details.

When working with fuel system components, pay particular attention to cleanliness - dirt entering the fuel system may cause blockages, which will lead to poor running.

In the interests of personal safety and equipment protection, many of the procedures in this Chapter suggest that the negative lead be removed from the battery terminal. This firstly eliminates the possibility of accidental short-circuits being caused as the vehicle is being worked upon, and secondly prevents damage to electronic components (eg sensors, actuators, ECUs) which are particularly sensitive to the power surges caused by disconnection or reconnection of the wiring harness whilst they are still live.

It should be noted, however, that the engine management systems described in this Chapter (and Chapter 5B) have a learning capability, that allows the system to adapt to the engine's running characteristics as it wears with use. This learnt information is lost when the battery is disconnected, and the system will then take a short period of time to re-learn the engine's characteristics - this may be manifested (temporarily) as rough idling, reduced throttle response and possibly a slight increase in fuel consumption, until the system re-adapts. The re-adaptation time will depend on how often the vehicle is used and the driving conditions encountered.

2 Air cleaner and inlet system - removal and refitting

Removal

1.3 litre models

1 Release the over-centre wire clips around the air cleaner top cover (see illustration).
2 Unscrew and remove the three bolts from the cover fitted over the throttle body (see illustrations), and unclip the charcoal canister hose and any wiring from the underside of the cover.

2.2a Remove the bolts securing the throttle body cover from the top . . .

2.2b . . . left-hand rear of the manifold . . .

2.2c . . . and right-hand rear of the manifold

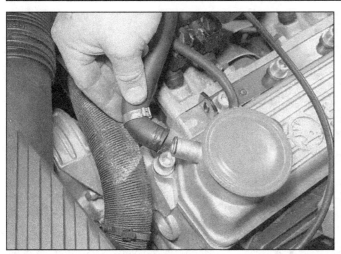

2.3a Remove the large-diameter breather hose from the rocker cover . . .

2.3b . . . and unclip the pressure regulator vacuum hose

3 Pull off the large-diameter breather hose from the engine top cover, and unclip the fuel pressure regulator vacuum hose from under the air inlet hose **(see illustrations)**.
4 Remove the throttle body cover, together with the air cleaner top cover and inlet hose **(see illustration)**.

1.6 litre models

5 Unscrew and remove the three screws from the cover fitted over the throttle body, noting that the front screw is longer than the other two **(see illustrations)**.

2.4 Removing the throttle body cover, air cleaner cover and inlet hose

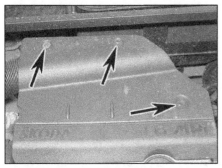

2.5a Throttle body cover screws (arrowed)

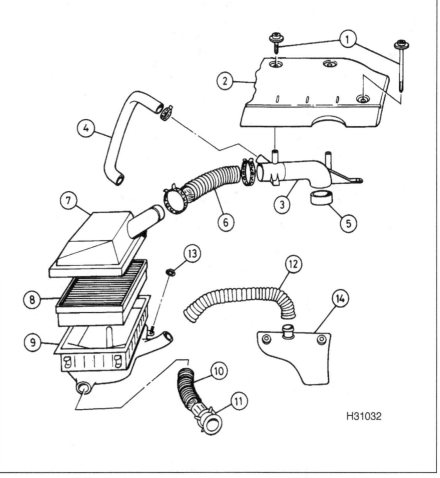

2.5b Air cleaner and related components - 1.6 litre models

1 Throttle body cover retaining screws
2 Throttle body cover
3 Air inlet pipe
4 Crankcase breather hose
5 Seal
6 Air inlet hose
7 Air cleaner top cover
8 Air filter element
9 Air cleaner housing
10 Inlet hose
11 Inlet spout
12 Warm-air hose
13 Plastic nut
14 Warm-air collector plate

H31032

2.11 Disconnecting the warm-air hose from the air cleaner housing

2.12a Unscrew the plastic nut . . .

2.12b . . . then release the housing from the inner wing rubber mountings, and remove

6 Release any hoses or wiring clipped to the underside of the cover, and lift the cover away.

7 Release the over-centre wire clips around the air cleaner top cover.

8 Disconnect the crankcase breather hose from the top of the air inlet pipe. If removal of the inlet pipe will be hindered by any hoses or wiring, unclip it and move it aside.

9 Unscrew and remove the three screws securing the air inlet pipe, and remove it together with the air cleaner top cover and inlet hose.

All models

10 Check the condition of the rubber seal which fits over the top of the throttle body (where applicable), and renew it if damaged.

11 If the air cleaner housing is to be removed from the inner wing, lift out the air filter element and disconnect the warm-air hose from the base of the housing (see illustration).

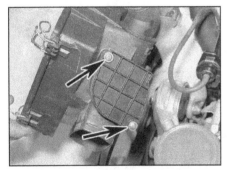

2.13 Warm-air control valve retaining screws (arrowed)

12 The housing is secured by a plastic nut at the front, and by two rubber mountings at the side pressed into holes in the inner wing. Unscrew the nut, release the housing from the rubber mountings and remove it from the engine compartment (see illustrations).

13 The control valve for the flap which admits manifold-heated warm air can be removed after unscrewing the two retaining screws at the front of the housing (see illustration).

Refitting

14 Refit the air cleaner components by following the removal procedure in reverse. The connection to the throttle body must be airtight, as any air leakage would seriously affect running (see illustration).

3 Inlet air temperature control system - general information

General information

1 The inlet air temperature control system consists of a temperature-controlled flap valve, mounted inside the air cleaner housing, and a duct to the warm-air collector plate over the exhaust manifold.

2 The temperature sensor in the flap valve housing senses the temperature of the inlet air, and opens the valve when a preset lower limit is reached. As the flap valve opens, warm air drawn from around the exhaust manifold blends with the inlet air (see illustration).

3 As the temperature of the inlet air rises, the sensor closes the flap progressively, until the warm-air supply from the exhaust manifold is completely closed off, and only air at ambient temperature is admitted to the air cleaner.

4 If a hairdryer and suitable freeze spray is available, the action of the sensor can be tested.

5 To remove the sensor and flap valve assembly, refer to Section 2.

4 Accelerator cable - removal, refitting and adjustment

Note: *Observe the precautions in Section 1 before working on any component in the fuel system.*

Removal

1 Remove the cover fitted over the throttle body as described in Section 2.

2 At the throttle body, disconnect the accelerator cable inner from the throttle valve spindle plate by pulling on the cable inner and detaching the cable end fitting (see illustration).

3 Remove the cover from the end of the cable outer, and pull the cable back through the grommet. Extract the cable outer grommet from the mounting bracket (see illustrations). The grommet can now be slid off the end of the cable.

2.14 When refitting the throttle body cover, check the condition of the rubber seal

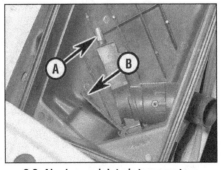

3.2 Air cleaner inlet air temperature sensor (A) and flap valve (B)

4.2 Disconnect the cable inner from the throttle spindle

4.3a Pull off the cover from the cable outer, and pull the cable back through the grommet . . .

4.3b . . . then extract the grommet from the cable mounting bracket

4.4 Unhook the cable end fitting (arrowed) from the bush at the top of the pedal

4 Working inside the vehicle, unhook the cable end fitting from the bush at the top of the pedal **(see illustration)**.
5 Release the cable from its clips **(see illustration)** and guide it out through the bulkhead grommet.

Refitting

6 Refit the accelerator cable by following the removal procedure in reverse.

Adjustment

7 At the throttle body, fix the position of the cable outer in its mounting bracket by inserting the metal clip in one of the locating slots **(see illustration)**, such that when the accelerator is depressed fully, the throttle valve is just touching its end stop.

4.5 Unclipping the cable from the warm-air duct

5 Simos 2P system components - removal and refitting

Note: *Observe the precautions in Section 1 before working on any component in the fuel system.*

Throttle body

Removal

1 Remove the throttle body top cover and air cleaner top cover as described in Section 2.
2 Refer to Section 4 and detach the accelerator cable from the throttle valve lever.
3 Disconnect the battery negative lead, and position it away from the terminal.
4 Unplug the wiring connector from the throttle positioner module **(see illustration)**.

4.7 Adjust the accelerator cable, then fix the cable using the metal clip in one of the slots

5 Disconnect the vacuum hose (from the engine top cover) and the hose for the charcoal canister, from the front of the throttle body **(see illustrations)**.
6 Slacken and withdraw the four through-bolts **(see illustration)**, then lift the throttle body away from the inlet manifold. Recover and discard the gasket.

Refitting

7 Refitting is a reversal of removal, noting the following:
a) Use a new throttle body-to-inlet manifold gasket.
b) Tighten the throttle body through-bolts to the specified torque.
c) Ensure that all hoses and electrical connectors are refitted securely.
d) With reference to Section 4, check and if necessary adjust the accelerator cable.

5.4 Disconnecting the throttle positioner wiring plug

5.5a Unscrew the retaining clip, and disconnect the vacuum hose . . .

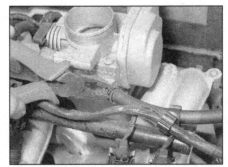

5.5b . . . then release the clip and detach the charcoal canister hose

5.6 Unscrew the four throttle body through-bolts (arrowed)

5.11a Disconnect the injector wiring plugs, noting their locations for refitting

5.11b Release the wiring harness clips . . .

5.11c . . . and move the harness to one side

5.12a Release the hose clips . . .

5.12b . . . and detach the fuel hoses - use a rag to catch any spilled fuel

5.13a Disconnect the vacuum hose from the fuel pressure regulator . . .

Fuel injectors and fuel rail

Note: *Observe the precautions in Section 1 before working on any component in the fuel system. If a faulty injector is suspected, before* removing the injectors, it is worth trying the effect of one of the proprietary injector-cleaning treatments. These can be added to the petrol in the tank, and are intended to clean the injectors as you drive.

Removal

8 Refer to Section 9 and depressurise the fuel system.
9 Disconnect the battery negative lead, and position it away from the terminal.
10 Remove the throttle body top cover and air cleaner top cover as described in Section 2.
11 Unplug the injector harness connectors, labelling them to aid correct refitting later. Unclip the wiring harness clips from the top of the fuel rail, and lay the harness to one side **(see illustrations)**.
12 Slacken the clips and disconnect the fuel supply and return hoses from the end of the fuel rail **(see illustrations)**. *Carefully* note the

fitted positions of the hoses - the supply hose is nearest the throttle body.
13 Disconnect the vacuum hose from the front of the fuel pressure regulator, and the smaller hose from the engine top cover. Unclip the charcoal canister hose from the rear of the fuel rail **(see illustrations)**.
14 Slacken and withdraw the two fuel rail mounting bolts, then carefully lift the rail away from the inlet manifold, together with the injectors. Anticipate some fuel spillage - keep the fuel rail as level as possible as it is removed. Make sure the injector O-ring seals remain in place as they emerge from the manifold.
15 The injectors can be removed individually from the fuel rail by extracting the relevant metal clip and easing the injector out of the rail. Recover the injector upper O-ring seals **(see illustrations)**.

5.13b . . . and from the engine top cover

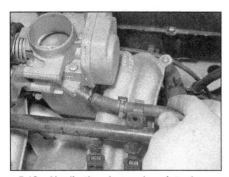

5.13c Unclip the charcoal canister hose from the fuel rail

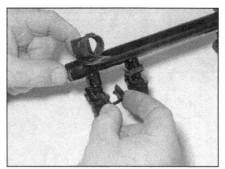

5.15a Withdraw the injector retaining clip . . .

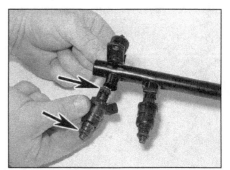

5.15b . . . and ease the injector out of the fuel rail - check the O-ring seals (arrowed)

5.22 Disconnect the pressure regulator
vacuum hose

5.24a Unscrew the retaining bolt . . .

5.24b . . . and unhook the retaining plate
from the top of the regulator

16 If required, remove the fuel pressure regulator, referring to the relevant sub-Section for guidance.
17 Check the electrical resistance of the injector using a multimeter and compare it with the Specifications.

Refitting

18 Refit the injectors and fuel rail by following the removal procedure in reverse, noting the following points:
a) *Renew the injector O-ring seals if they appear worn or damaged.*
b) *Ensure that the injector retaining clips are securely seated.*
c) *Check that the fuel supply and return hoses are reconnected correctly.*
d) *Check that all vacuum and electrical connections are remade correctly and securely.*
e) *On completion, check exhaustively for fuel leaks before bringing the vehicle back into service.*

Fuel pressure regulator

Note: *Observe the precautions in Section 1 before working on any component in the fuel system.*

Removal

19 Refer to Section 9 and depressurise the fuel system.
20 Disconnect the battery negative lead, and position it away from the terminal.
21 Remove the throttle body top cover and air cleaner top cover as described in Section 2.
22 Disconnect the vacuum hose from the

front of the fuel pressure regulator **(see illustration)**.
23 Be prepared for some fuel spillage as the regulator is removed - place a wad of rag below the unit.
24 Remove the bolt below the pressure regulator vacuum port, recover the washer, and unhook the retaining plate from the front of the unit **(see illustrations)**.
25 Pull the regulator out of its location in the fuel rail, ensuring that the O-ring seals are withdrawn with the unit **(see illustration)**.

Refitting

26 Refit the fuel pressure regulator by following the removal procedure in reverse, noting the following points:
a) *Renew the O-ring seals if they appear worn or damaged **(see illustration)**.*
b) *Ensure that the regulator retaining plate is correctly engaged at the top, and tighten the bolt to the specified torque..*
c) *Refit the regulator vacuum hose securely.*

Throttle valve positioning module

27 The throttle valve positioner is integral with the throttle body, and is not available separately. If a fault is suspected, have the vehicle checked by a Skoda dealer before fitting a new throttle body assembly.

Inlet manifold air temperature/pressure sensor

Removal

28 The sensor is fitted to the rear of the inlet manifold.

5.25 Removing the pressure regulator

29 Disconnect the battery negative lead, and position it away from the terminal.
30 Remove the throttle body top cover and air cleaner top cover as described in Section 2.
31 Disconnect the wiring plug from the sensor **(see illustration)**.
32 Remove the two retaining screws, and pull the sensor from the manifold. Recover the seal **(see illustration)**.

Refitting

33 Refitting is a reversal of removal. Renew the seal if it appears damaged, and tighten the retaining screws securely.

Coolant temperature sensor

34 The fuel injection system temperature sensor is combined with the temperature gauge sensor - refer to Chapter 3.

5.26 Check the condition of the O-ring
seals

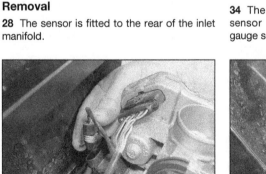

5.31 Disconnect the air temperature/
pressure sensor wiring plug . . .

5.32 . . . then remove the screws and
withdraw the sensor - note the seal

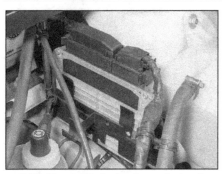

5.38 Simos 2P electronic control unit (ECU)

Lambda sensor

35 Refer to Chapter 4D.

Hall sensor

36 Refer to Chapter 5B.

Knock sensor

37 Refer to Chapter 5B.

Electronic control unit (ECU)

38 The ECU is located at the rear left-hand side of the engine compartment **(see illustration)**. The unit is coded, and should not be removed without consulting a Skoda dealer, otherwise it may not function correctly when the multi-plug is reconnected.

Fuel pump relay and fuses

39 The fuel pump relay and fuel injection system fuses are located in the fuse/relay panel in the passenger compartment - refer to Chapter 12.
40 The fuel pump relay is in position 5 on the relay panel, and the fuel pump is fed by fuse number 4.
41 The relay can be simply pulled from its socket - it is best to note which way round it fits, to make refitting easier, although it will only fit one way round.
42 The fuse is removed in the same way as all other fuses (refer to Chapter 12 if necessary).
43 Note that removing the main injection system fuse (number 1) will erase the learned adaptive values from the ECU memory (as will disconnecting the battery). These values will be re-learned when the engine is next started.

6.6a Remove the through-bolts . . .

6.4 Disconnect the throttle potentiometer wiring plug

The best way to achieve this is to start the engine and allow it to idle for a few minutes, before continuing driving as normal - the idle speed in particular may be a little erratic for a time until the system finds the optimum settings.

---

6 Magneti-Marelli 1AV system components - removal and refitting

Note: Observe the precautions in Section 1 before working on any component in the fuel system.

Throttle body

Removal

1 Remove the throttle body top cover and air inlet pipe as described in Section 2.
2 Refer to Section 4 and detach the accelerator cable from the throttle valve lever.
3 Disconnect the battery negative lead, and position it away from the terminal.
4 Unplug the wiring connector from the throttle positioner module **(see illustration)**.
5 Disconnect the hose for the charcoal canister from the front of the throttle body **(see illustration)**.
6 Slacken and withdraw the four mounting bolts, then lift the throttle body away from the inlet manifold. Recover and discard the sealing washer **(see illustrations)**.

Refitting

7 Refitting is a reversal of removal, noting the following:

6.6b . . . lift away the throttle body . . .

6.5 Disconnect the charcoal canister hose from the stub on the throttle body

a) Use a new throttle body-to-inlet manifold sealing washer.
b) Tighten the throttle body mounting bolts to the specified torque.
c) Ensure that all hoses and electrical connectors are refitted securely.
d) With reference to Section 4, check and if necessary adjust the accelerator cable.

Fuel injectors and fuel rail

Note: Observe the precautions in Section 1 before working on any component in the fuel system. If a faulty injector is suspected, before removing the injectors, it is worth trying the effect of one of the proprietary injector-cleaning treatments. These can be added to the petrol in the tank, and are intended to clean the injectors as you drive.

Removal

8 Refer to Section 9 and depressurise the fuel system.
9 Disconnect the battery negative lead, and position it away from the terminal.
10 Remove the throttle body top cover as described in Section 2.
11 Unplug the injector harness connectors, labelling them to aid correct refitting later. Unclip the wiring harness clips from the top of the fuel rail, and lay the harness to one side **(see illustrations)**.
12 Disconnect the vacuum hose from the port on the bottom of the fuel pressure regulator.
13 Anticipate some fuel spillage as the fuel hoses are removed by placing a wad of rag below the connections. Slacken the clips and

6.6c . . . and recover the sealing washer

6.11a Disconnect the injector wiring plugs . . .

6.11b . . . then unclip the harness retaining clips, and move the wiring harness to one side

6.13 Fuel supply and return connections at the fuel rail - note direction-of-flow arrows

disconnect the fuel supply and return hoses from the end of the fuel rail. *Carefully* note the fitted positions of the hoses, if no markings are found **(see illustration)**.

14 Slacken and withdraw the two fuel rail mounting bolts, then carefully lift the rail away from the inlet manifold, together with the injectors. Make sure the injector lower O-ring seals remain in place as they emerge from the manifold **(see illustration)**.

15 The injectors can be removed individually from the fuel rail by extracting the relevant metal clip and easing the injector out of the rail. Recover the injector upper O-ring seals **(see illustrations)**.

16 If required, remove the fuel pressure regulator, referring to the relevant sub-Section for guidance.

17 Check the electrical resistance of the injector using a multimeter and compare it with the Specifications.

Refitting

18 Refit the injectors and fuel rail by following the removal procedure in reverse, noting the following points:
a) Renew the injector O-ring seals if they appear worn or damaged.
b) Ensure that the injector retaining clips are securely seated.
c) Check that the fuel supply and return hoses are reconnected correctly.
d) Check that all vacuum and electrical connections are remade correctly and securely.
e) On completion, check exhaustively for fuel leaks before bringing the vehicle back into service.

Fuel pressure regulator

Note: *Observe the precautions in Section 1 before working on any component in the fuel system.*

Removal

19 Refer to Section 9 and depressurise the fuel system.

20 Disconnect the battery negative lead, and position it away from the terminal.

21 Remove the throttle body top cover as described in Section 2.

22 Disconnect the vacuum hose from the port on the bottom of the fuel pressure regulator **(see illustration)**.

23 Slacken the clip and disconnect the fuel supply hose from the fuel rail. This will allow the majority of fuel in the regulator to drain out. Be prepared for an amount of fuel loss - position a small container and some old rags underneath the fuel regulator housing.

24 Extract the retaining clip from the top of the regulator housing and lift out the regulator body, recovering the O-ring seals **(see illustrations)**.

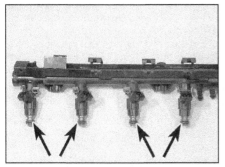

6.14 As the fuel rail is removed, recover the injector lower O-ring seals (arrowed)

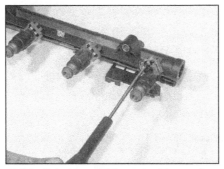

6.15a Using a suitable screwdriver, prise out the injector securing clip . . .

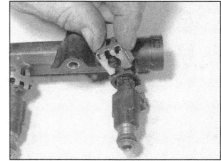

6.15b . . . and remove it from the fuel rail

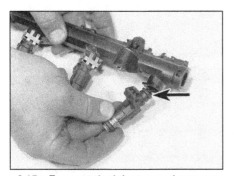

6.15c Ease out the injector, and recover the upper O-ring seal (arrowed)

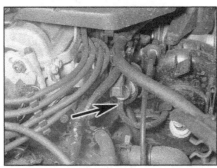

6.22 Fuel pressure regulator vacuum hose (arrowed)

6.24a The fuel pressure regulator is mounted in the end of the fuel rail (arrowed)

Refitting

25 Refit the fuel pressure regulator by following the removal procedure in reverse, noting the following points:
  a) Renew the O-ring seals if they appear worn or damaged.
  b) Ensure that the regulator retaining clip is securely seated.
  c) Refit the regulator vacuum hose securely.

Throttle valve positioning module

26 The throttle valve positioner is integral with the throttle body, and is not available separately. If a fault is suspected, have the vehicle checked by a Skoda dealer before fitting a new throttle body assembly.

Inlet manifold air temperature/pressure sensor

Removal

27 The sensor is fitted to the right-hand end of the inlet manifold **(see illustration)**.
28 Disconnect the battery negative lead, and position it away from the terminal.
29 Remove the throttle body top cover as described in Section 2.
30 Disconnect the wiring plug from the sensor.
31 Remove the two retaining screws, and pull the sensor from the manifold.

Refitting

32 Refitting is a reversal of removal, tightening the retaining screws securely.

Coolant temperature sensor

33 The fuel injection system temperature sensor is combined with the temperature gauge sensor - refer to Chapter 3.

Lambda sensor

34 Refer to Chapter 4D.

Hall sensor

35 Refer to Chapter 5B.

Knock sensor

36 Refer to Chapter 5B.

Electronic control unit (ECU)

37 The ECU is located at the rear left-hand side of the engine compartment. The unit is coded, and should not be removed without consulting a Skoda dealer, otherwise it may not function correctly when the multi-plug is reconnected.

Fuel pump relay and fuses

38 The fuel pump relay and fuel injection system fuses are located in the fuse/relay panel in the passenger compartment - refer to Chapter 12.
39 The fuel pump relay is in position 5 on the relay panel, and the fuel pump is fed by fuse number 4.
40 The relay can be simply pulled from its socket - it is best to note which way round it fits, to make refitting easier, although it will only fit one way round.

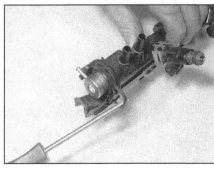
6.24b To remove the pressure regulator, prise out the retaining clip and withdraw it from the fuel rail

41 The fuse is removed in the same way as all other fuses (refer to Chapter 12 if necessary).
42 Note that removing the main injection system fuse (number 1) will erase the learned adaptive values from the ECU memory (as will disconnecting the battery). These values will be re-learned when the engine is next started. The best way to achieve this is to start the engine and allow it to idle for a few minutes, before continuing driving as normal - the idle speed in particular may be a little erratic for a time until the system finds the optimum settings.

7 Fuel pump and gauge sender unit - removal and refitting

Note: *Observe the precautions in Section 1 before working on any component in the fuel system.*
  Refer to the information in Chapter 4A, Section 6.

8 Fuel tank - removal and refitting

Note: *Observe the precautions in Section 1 before working on any component in the fuel system.*
  Refer to the information in Chapter 4A, Section 7.

6.27 Inlet manifold air temperature/pressure sensor location

9 Fuel injection system - depressurisation

Note: *Observe the precautions in Section 1 before working on any component in the fuel system.*
  Refer to the information in Chapter 4A, Section 8.

10 Inlet manifold - removal and refitting

Note: *Observe the precautions in Section 1 before working on any component in the fuel system.*

Removal

1 Refer to Section 9 and depressurise the fuel system, then disconnect the battery negative lead and position it away from the terminal.

1.3 litre models

2 Remove the throttle body top cover and air cleaner top cover as described in Section 2.
3 Refer to Section 4 and detach the accelerator cable from the throttle valve lever. Remove the cable outer from the support clip, and lay it to one side.
4 Unplug the wiring connector from the throttle positioner module, and from the inlet air temperature/pressure sensor.
5 Disconnect the hose for the charcoal canister, and the smaller vacuum hose from the engine top cover, from the front of the throttle body.
6 Unplug the injector harness connectors, labelling them to aid correct refitting later. Unclip the wiring harness clips from the top of the fuel rail, and lay the harness to one side.
7 Disconnect the vacuum hose from the front of the fuel pressure regulator.
8 Anticipate some fuel spillage as the fuel hoses are removed by placing a wad of rag below the connections. Slacken the clips and disconnect the fuel supply and return hoses from the end of the fuel rail. *Carefully* note the fitted positions of the hoses - the supply hose is nearest the throttle body.
9 Trace the brake servo vacuum hose from the servo on the bulkhead to the port on the left-hand side of the inlet manifold, and disconnect it at the port.
10 At the right-hand side of the inlet manifold, unbolt the support stay from the manifold **(see illustration)**.
11 Check around the inlet manifold to ensure that nothing else remains connected to it that will impede its removal.
12 Progressively slacken the six inlet manifold retaining nuts and bolts (four visible from above, two from below) **(see illustration)**. Do not confuse the inlet manifold fasteners with those for the exhaust manifold.

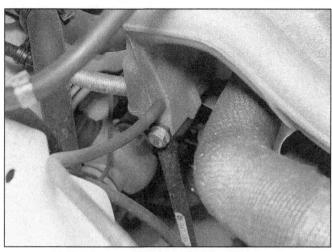

10.10 Inlet manifold support stay retaining bolt

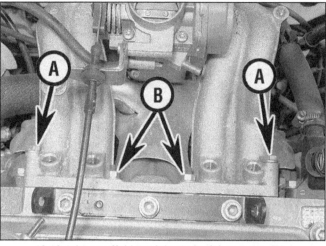

10.12 Inlet manifold retaining bolts (A) and nuts (B) - two more on underside

Ease the manifold away from the cylinder head, and out of the engine compartment, taking care not to spill any fuel remaining in the fuel rail. Recover and discard the two gaskets.

1.6 litre models

13 Remove the throttle body top cover and the air inlet pipe as described in Section 2.

14 Refer to Section 4 and detach the accelerator cable from the throttle valve lever. Remove the cable outer from the support clip on the manifold, and lay it to one side.

15 Unplug the wiring connector from the throttle positioner module, and from the inlet air temperature/pressure sensor.

16 Disconnect the hose for the charcoal canister from the front of the throttle body.

17 Unplug the injector harness connectors, labelling them to aid correct refitting later. Unclip the wiring harness clips from the top of the fuel rail, and lay the harness to one side.

18 Disconnect the vacuum hose from the port on the bottom of the fuel pressure regulator.

19 Anticipate some fuel spillage as the fuel hoses are removed by placing a wad of rag below the connections. Slacken the clips and disconnect the fuel supply and return hoses from the end of the fuel rail. *Carefully* note the fitted positions of the hoses.

20 Disconnect the brake servo vacuum hose from the port on the left-hand side of the inlet manifold **(see illustration)**.

21 Progressively slacken and remove the inlet manifold-to-cylinder head bolts. Move the manifold away from the head, and recover the O-ring seals **(see illustrations)**.

Refitting

22 Refit the inlet manifold by following the removal procedure in reverse, noting the following points:

a) Use new manifold gaskets or O-ring seals, as applicable.

b) Tighten the manifold-to-cylinder head fasteners to the specified torque.

c) Check that all vacuum, electrical and fuel system connections are remade correctly and securely.

d) Adjust the accelerator cable as described in Section 4.

e) On completion, check exhaustively for fuel leaks before bringing the vehicle back into service.

11 Fuel injection system - testing and adjustment

1 If a fault appears in the fuel injection system, first ensure that all the system wiring connectors are securely connected and free of corrosion. Then ensure that the fault is not due to poor maintenance; ie, check that the air cleaner filter element is clean, the spark plugs are in good condition and correctly gapped, the cylinder compression pressures are correct, the ignition timing is correct and the engine breather hoses are clear and undamaged, referring to Chapter 1A, Chapter 2A or B and Chapter 5B.

2 If these checks fail to reveal the cause of the problem, the vehicle should be taken to a suitably-equipped Skoda dealer for testing. A diagnostic connector is incorporated in the engine management system wiring harness (under the right-hand end of the facia panel), into which a dedicated electronic test equipment can be plugged. The test equipment is capable of interrogating the engine management system ECU electronically and accessing its internal fault log. In this manner, faults can be pinpointed quickly and simply, even if their occurrence is intermittent. Testing

10.20 Brake servo vacuum connection (arrowed) to the inlet manifold

10.21a Unscrew the inlet manifold bolts . . .

10.21b . . . and recover the O-ring seals

all the system components individually in an attempt to locate the fault by elimination is a time-consuming operation that is unlikely to be fruitful (particularly if the fault occurs dynamically), and carries high risk of damage to the ECU's internal components.

3 Experienced home mechanics equipped with an accurate tachometer and a carefully-calibrated exhaust gas analyser may be able to check the exhaust gas CO content and the engine idle speed; if these are found to be out of specification, then the vehicle must be taken to a suitably-equipped Skoda dealer for assessment. Neither the air/fuel mixture (exhaust gas CO content) nor the engine idle speed are manually adjustable; incorrect test results indicate a fault within the fuel injection system.

12 Unleaded petrol -
general information and usage

Note: *The information given in this Chapter is correct at the time of writing, and applies only to petrols currently available in the UK. Check with a Skoda dealer as more up to date information may be available. If travelling abroad, consult one of the motoring organisations (or a similar authority) for advice on the petrols available and their suitability for your vehicle.*

1 The fuel recommended by Skoda is given in the Specifications of this Chapter.

2 RON and MON are different testing standards; RON stands for Research Octane Number (also written as RM), while MON stands for Motor Octane Number (also written as MM).

Chapter 4 Part C:
Fuel system - diesel

Contents

Degrees of difficulty

Easy, suitable for novice with little experience		Fairly easy, suitable for beginner with some experience		Fairly difficult, suitable for competent DIY mechanic		Difficult, suitable for experienced DIY mechanic		Very difficult, suitable for expert DIY or professional	

Specifications

General

Firing order	1-3-4-2
Maximum engine speed	5050 ± 100 rpm
Engine idle speed	940 ± 20 rpm
Engine idle speed boost (not adjustable)	1050 ± 50 rpm

Torque wrench settings

	Nm	lbf ft
Fuel tank retaining bolts	25	18
Idle speed boost locknut	6	4
Immobiliser control unit retaining bolt	25	18
Injection pump fuel supply and return banjo bolts	25	18
Injection pump front mounting bracket-to-block	10	7
Injection pump mounting bolts:		
Front mounting bolts	25	18
Rear support bolt	10	7
Injection pump sprocket bolts	25	18
Injector fuel pipe unions	25	18
Injectors	70	52

1 General information and precautions

General information

The fuel system comprises a fuel tank, a fuel injection pump, an engine-bay mounted fuel filter with an integral water separator, fuel supply and return lines, and four fuel injectors.

The injection pump is driven at half crankshaft speed by the camshaft timing belt. Fuel is drawn from the fuel tank, through the filter by the injection pump, which then distributes the fuel under very high pressure to the injectors via separate delivery pipes.

The injectors are spring-loaded mechanical valves, which open when the pressure of the fuel supplied to them exceeds a specific limit. Fuel is then sprayed from the injector nozzle into the cylinder via a swirl chamber (indirect injection). Two-stage injectors are fitted, which open in steps as the supplied fuel pressure rises; this improves the engines combustion characteristics.

The basic injection timing is set by the position of the injection pump on its mounting bracket. When the engine is running, the injection timing is advanced and retarded mechanically by the injection pump itself, and is influenced primarily by the accelerator position and engine speed.

The engine is stopped by means of a solenoid-operated fuel cut-off valve, which interrupts the flow of fuel to the injection pump when de-activated. The fuel cut-off valve (known generally as the stop solenoid) is linked on most models to an anti-theft immobiliser - until the immobiliser is disabled, no fuel will be available to the system, and the engine will not start.

When starting from cold, the engine idle speed is raised by means of a vacuum-operated automatic idle boost actuator, mounted on the side of the injection pump. For information on the glow plug system fitted to aid cold starting, refer to Chapter 5C.

A diesel control unit is fitted, which controls the operation of the glow plugs and the EGR system. The unit is fitted next to the glow plug relay in the left rear corner of the engine compartment.

1.8 Throttle potentiometer (arrowed)

Information on engine load is supplied to the diesel control unit by a potentiometer attached to the throttle lever **(see illustration)**. A start-of-injection valve fitted to the injection pump relays information on pump timing to the diesel control unit.

The fuel injection pump is equipped with an electronic self-diagnosis and fault logging system, incorporated into the diesel control unit. The diagnostic connector is located under the right-hand end of the facia panel; interrogation of this system is only possible with dedicated electronic test equipment. Problems with the system's operation should therefore be referred to a Skoda dealer for assessment. Once the fault has been identified, the removal/refitting sequences detailed in the following Sections will then allow the appropriate component(s) to be renewed as required.

Precautions

Many of the operations described in this Chapter involve the disconnection of fuel lines, which may cause an amount of fuel spillage. Before commencing work, refer to the warnings below and the information in *Safety first!* at the beginning of this manual.

⚠️ *Warning: When working on any part of the fuel system, avoid direct contact skin contact with diesel fuel - wear protective clothing and gloves when handling fuel system components. Ensure that the work area is well-ventilated, to prevent the build-up of diesel fuel vapour.*

Fuel injectors operate at extremely high pressures, and the jet of fuel produced at the nozzle is capable of piercing skin, with potentially fatal results. When working with pressurised injectors, take great care to avoid exposing any part of the body to the fuel spray. It is recommended that any pressure testing of the fuel system components should be carried out by a diesel fuel systems specialist.

Under no circumstances should diesel fuel be allowed to come into contact with coolant hoses - wipe off accidental spillage immediately. Hoses that have been contaminated with fuel for an extended period should be renewed. Diesel fuel systems are particularly sensitive to contamination from dirt, air and water. Pay particular attention to cleanliness when working on any part of the fuel system, to

prevent the ingress of dirt. Thoroughly clean the area around fuel unions before disconnecting them. Store dismantled components in sealed containers, to prevent contamination and the formation of condensation. Only use lint-free cloths and clean fuel for component cleansing. Avoid using compressed air when cleaning components in situ.

2 Air cleaner assembly and air inlet components - removal and refitting

Removal

Air cleaner

1 Remove the air cleaner element, as described in Chapter 1B.

2 Working in the engine compartment, compress the legs of the large spring clips using pliers, and disconnect the air inlet trunking from the inlet manifold cover **(see illustration)**. The air cleaner top cover and inlet trunking can now be removed.

3 The air cleaner housing is mounted on the right-hand side inner wing. The housing is secured by a plastic nut at the front, and by two rubber mountings at the side pressed into holes in the inner wing. Unscrew the nut, release the housing from the rubber mountings and remove it from the engine compartment.

Inlet manifold and cover

4 Loosen and remove the five inlet manifold cover retaining bolts **(see illustration)**.

5 Pull the breather hose out of the camshaft cover **(see illustration)**, or release the retaining clip and pull the breather hose from the inlet manifold cover.

6 If not already done, release the retaining clip and disconnect the air inlet trunking **(see illustration)**.

7 Lift away the inlet manifold cover, tipping it towards the rear of the engine compartment **(see illustration)**. The cover cannot be removed until the air inlet pipes and inlet manifold have been removed. Check the condition of the rubber seal, and fit a new one if necessary.

2.2 Release the spring clip securing the air inlet trunking

2.4 Inlet manifold cover retaining bolts (arrowed)

2.5 Pulling the breather hose out of the camshaft cover

2.6 Releasing the air inlet trunking from the air cleaner top cover

2.7 Inlet manifold cover removed for access to air inlet pipes and inlet manifold

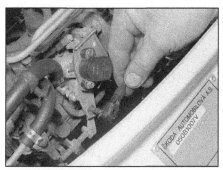

3.4 Pull off the accelerator cable end fitting from the injection pump lever

8 Loosen and remove the bolts securing the air inlet pipes - these bolts also secure the manifold - and lift the pipes and manifold from the rear of the cylinder head, along with the manifold cover. Recover the manifold gasket.

Refitting

9 Refitting is a reversal of removal. If the inlet manifold was removed, use a new manifold gasket; check the breather hose for blockages or signs of splitting, and clean or renew it if necessary.

3 Accelerator cable - removal, refitting and adjustment

Removal

1 Refer to Chapter 11 and remove the facia trim panels from underneath the steering column.
2 Depress the accelerator pedal slightly, then unhook the accelerator cable end from the bush at the top of the pedal.
3 Pass the cable through the bulkhead, releasing it from the bulkhead grommet.
4 Working in the engine bay, pull off the accelerator cable end fitting from the fuel injection pump lever. Recover the rubber bush which fits inside the cable end fitting **(see illustration)**.
5 Remove the cover from the end of the cable outer, and pull the cable back through the grommet. Extract the cable outer grommet from the mounting bracket **(see illustration)**.

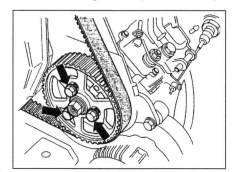

6.6 Loosen and remove ONLY the three pulley-to-hub bolts (arrowed)

6 Release the cable from its securing clips and guide it out through the bulkhead grommet.

Refitting

7 Refit the accelerator cable by following the removal procedure in reverse.

Adjustment

8 At the fuel injection pump, fix the position of the cable outer in its mounting bracket by inserting the metal clip in one of the locating grooves, such that when the accelerator is depressed fully, the throttle lever just touches its end stop.

4 Fuel tank sender unit - removal and refitting

Note: *Observe the precautions in Section 1 before working on any component in the fuel system.*
Refer to Chapter 4A, Section 6.

5 Fuel tank - removal and refitting

Note: *Observe the precautions in Section 1 before working on any component in the fuel system.*
Refer to the information in Chapter 4A, Section 7.

6 Fuel injection pump - removal and refitting

Note: *The injection pump timing is checked statically, as is normally the case with diesel engines. The timing would normally be checked using a dial test indicator (DTI) to measure fuel pump lift. However, the injection pump timing setting is expressed as a dimension from the flywheel TDC mark to a fixed point on the engine, and accurate setting must therefore be carried out using dedicated Skoda equipment.*

Removal

1 Disconnect the battery negative lead and

6.8a Slacken the rigid fuel pipe unions at the rear of the injection pump

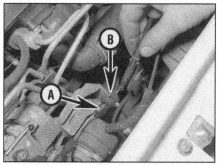

3.5 Pull back the cover (A) from the cable outer, then pull out the grommet (B)

position it away from the terminal.
2 Remove the air cleaner inlet trunking as described in Section 2.
3 Owing to the extremely limited working room around the pump, it may be helpful to remove the radiator, with reference to Chapter 3.
4 With reference to Chapter 2C, carry out the following:
a) *Remove the camshaft cover and timing belt outer cover.*
b) *Set the engine to TDC on cylinder No 1.*
c) *Remove the timing belt from the camshaft and fuel injection pump sprockets.*
5 The timing belt sprocket must now be removed from the injection pump shaft. The sprocket must be braced whilst its fixings are loosened - a home-made tool can easily be fabricated for this purpose; refer to Section 5 of Chapter 2C for further details.
6 Loosen the three bolts and remove the sprocket from the pump hub **(see illustration)**.
Caution: On no account should the nut seen at the centre of the sprocket be slackened, as this will alter the basic injection timing.
7 Disconnect the fuel supply and return hoses from the pump, taking care to minimise fuel loss, and labelling them if necessary for accurate refitting. Also disconnect the fuel leak-off hose from the fuel return connection.
8 Using a pair of spanners (a slotted ring spanner may be required), slacken the rigid fuel pipe unions on the injection pump and at each end of the injectors, then lift the fuel pipe assembly away from the engine **(see illustrations)**.

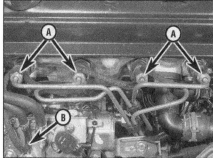

6.8b Fuel injector unions (A) and injector leak-off hose connection (B)

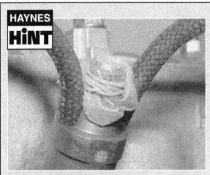

Hint 1: Cut the fingertips from an old pair of rubber gloves and secure them over the fuel ports with elastic bands

Hint 2: Fit a short length of hose over the banjo bolt (arrowed) so that the drillings are covered, then thread the bolt back into its injection pump port

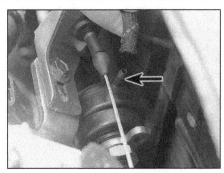

6.10 Disconnecting the idle speed boost actuator vacuum pipe - connection arrowed

Caution: Be prepared for some fuel leakage during this operation, position a small container under the union to be slackened and pad the area with old rags, to catch any spilt diesel. Take great care to avoid stressing the rigid fuel pipes as they are removed.

9 Cover the open pipes and ports to prevent the ingress of dirt and excess fuel leakage **(see Haynes Hints 1 and 2)**.

10 Disconnect the vacuum pipe from the idle speed boost actuator on the injection pump **(see illustration)**.

11 Referring to Section 3, disconnect the accelerator cable from the injection pump bracket.

12 Disconnect the wiring plugs from the following components/locations, labelling the plugs to aid refitting:

a) *Oil pressure switch on the left-hand end of the cylinder head.*
b) *Oil temperature/pressure switch on the oil filter mounting bracket.*
c) *Glow plugs.*
d) *Two injection pump harness connectors mounted in a bracket on the left-hand end of the cylinder block. Separate both plug halves, noting the location of each, then slide them out of the bracket (see illustrations).*
e) *Coolant temperature sender on the coolant elbow at the front of the cylinder head (see illustration).*

13 Before removing the pump, mark the

position of the mounting bolts in their elongated holes. The pump can then be refitted in this reference position, to allow an approximate injection timing setting to be achieved when the pump is refitted (refer to the Note at the start of this Section).

14 Loosen and remove the rear support bolt and the three mounting bolts at the sprocket end, supporting the pump as the last is removed **(see illustrations)**. Check that nothing remains connected, then lift the injection pump from the engine bay.

Refitting

15 Offer up the injection pump to the engine, then insert the mounting nuts/bolts and tighten to the specified torque. **Note:** *The mounting holes are elongated to allow adjustment - if a new pump is being fitted, then mount it such that the bolts are initially at the centre of the holes, to allow the maximum range of pump timing adjustment. Alternatively, if the existing pump is being refitted, use the markings made during removal for alignment.*

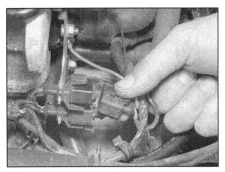

6.12a Disconnect the upper . . .

6.12b . . . and lower wiring plugs on the left-hand end of the engine . . .

6.12c . . . and the coolant temperature sensor wiring plug

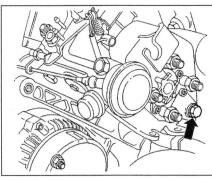

6.14a Injection pump rear support bolt . . .

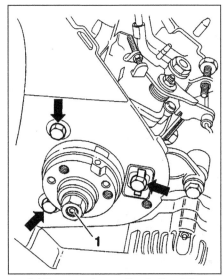

6.14b . . . and mounting bolts at the sprocket end (arrowed)

On no account loosen the centre nut (1)

16 Prime the injection pump by fitting a small funnel to the fuel supply and return pipe unions, and filling the cavity with clean diesel. Pad the area around the unions with clean dry rags to absorb any spillage.

17 Reconnect the fuel pipes to the injectors and injection pump, then tighten the unions to the correct torque using a pair of spanners.

18 Reconnect the fuel supply and return pipes to the pump, using new sealing washers. Tighten the banjo bolts to the specified torque.

19 Reconnect all wiring plugs to the engine and injection pump, as applicable, using the labels fitted on disconnection to aid refitting.

20 Reconnect the vacuum pipe to the idle speed boost valve.

21 Referring to Section 3, reconnect and adjust the accelerator cable.

22 Offer up the injection pump sprocket, and fit the three retaining bolts in the centre of the slotted holes. Hand-tighten the bolts at this stage.

23 Lock the injection pump sprocket in position by inserting a bar or bolt through its alignment hole and into the drilling in the pump hub. Ensure that there is minimal play in the sprocket, once it has been locked in position.

24 Refit and tension the timing belt as described in Chapter 2C.

25 The injection pump timing must now be checked and if necessary adjusted by a Skoda dealer; refer to Note 1 at the start of this Section. If a new pump has been fitted, your Skoda dealer will need to match the new pump to the electronic immobiliser (where fitted).

26 Check and if necessary adjust the idle speed as described in Chapter 1B, the maximum engine speed (Section 7), and the idle speed boost (Section 8).

27 The rest of the refitting procedure is a direct reversal of removal.

7 Maximum engine speed - checking and adjustment

Warning: This operation should not be carried out if the condition of the camshaft timing belt is at all questionable. This check requires that the engine be run at maximum speed, which places considerable strain on the timing belt. Provided the belt is known to be in good condition, there should be no problem, but if the belt breaks, considerable engine damage would result.

Note: *Observe the precautions in Section 1 before working on any component in the fuel system.*

1 Start the engine and let it warm up to normal operating temperature.

2 Ensure that the handbrake is firmly applied and the transmission is in neutral, then have an assistant depress the accelerator fully.

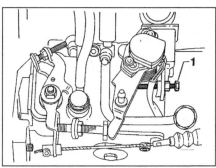

7.4 Maximum engine speed adjusting screw (1)

3 Using a diesel tachometer, check that the maximum engine speed is as quoted in the Specifications.

Caution: Do not maintain maximum engine speed for more than two or three seconds.

4 If adjustment is necessary, remove the locking wire and protective cap from the adjusting screw. Adjust the maximum engine speed by slackening the locknut and rotating the adjusting screw **(see illustration)**.

5 Re-check the setting, then tighten the locknut. Refit the locking wire and protective cap.

8 Idle speed boost - checking

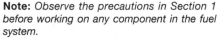

Note: *Observe the precautions in Section 1 before working on any component in the fuel system.*

1 The idle speed boost valve is mounted at the rear of the engine compartment, next to the EGR solenoid valve (the idle speed boost valve has a grey connector) **(see illustration)**. It operates when the engine is cold, or when a load is placed on the engine which would normally cause the idle speed to drop (eg switching on the headlights, heated rear window, etc). The system will not necessarily provide a fast idle, such as a choke control might on a petrol engine, but is intended rather to maintain the idle speed, regardless of engine temperature or load. If the system does not appear to be operating properly, check as follows.

2 With reference to Chapter 1B, check and if necessary adjust the idle speed.

3 Start the engine, then switch on as many electrical loads as possible. Provided the battery and charging system are in good condition, the idle speed should not drop significantly.

4 With the engine warm, pull off the vacuum hose from the boost valve vacuum capsule. The idle speed should rise to the value specified at the start of this Chapter.

5 The idle speed boost is not adjustable. If the boost valve is not operating correctly, check the vacuum hose for splits, and that the linkage is not binding **(see illustration)**. The

8.1 The idle speed boost valve (arrowed) has a grey connector plug

operating cable should be set so that there is slight play between the clamp and the operating lever. If the valve is faulty, it should be renewed complete.

9 Fuel injection pump timing - testing and adjustment

Checking and setting the injection pump timing using a dial test indicator (DTI) is not possible, since Skoda do not quote timing figures for use with a DTI - a special Skoda setting rig is required to set the timing with the necessary degree of accuracy.

10 Injectors - general information, removal and refitting

Warning: Exercise extreme caution when working on the fuel injectors. Never expose the hands or any part of the body to injector spray, as the high working pressure can cause the fuel to penetrate the skin, with possibly fatal results. You are strongly advised to have any work which involves testing the injectors under pressure carried out by a dealer or fuel injection specialist. Refer to the precautions given in Section 1 of this Chapter before proceeding.

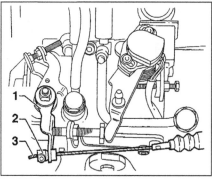

8.5 Idle speed boost operating linkage

1 Operating lever *3 Operating*
2 Cable clamp *cable*

10.7a Removing an injector from the cylinder head

10.7b Recover the heat shield washer

General information

1 Injectors do deteriorate with prolonged use, and it is reasonable to expect them to need reconditioning or renewal after 60 000 miles (100 000 km) or so. Accurate testing, overhaul and calibration of the injectors must be left to a specialist. A defective injector which is causing knocking or smoking can be located without dismantling as follows.

2 Run the engine at a fast idle. Gradually slacken each injector union in turn, placing rag around the union to catch spilt fuel and being careful not to expose the skin to any spray. When the union on the defective injector is slackened, the knocking or smoking will stop.

Removal

Note: *Take great care not to allow dirt into the injectors or fuel pipes during this procedure. Do not drop the injectors, nor allow the needles at their tips to become damaged. The injectors are precision-made to fine limits, and must not be handled roughly.*

3 Disconnect the battery negative lead.

4 Cover the alternator with a clean cloth or plastic bag, to protect it if fuel is spilt onto it.

5 Carefully clean around the injectors and pipe union nuts, and disconnect the return pipes from the injectors.

6 Wipe clean the pipe unions, then slacken the union nut securing the relevant injector pipes to each injector, and the relevant union nuts securing the pipes to the rear of the injection pump (pipes are removed as one assembly). As each pump union nut is slackened, retain the adapter with a suitable open-ended spanner to prevent it being unscrewed from the pump. With the union nuts undone, remove the injector pipes from the engine. Cover the injector and pipe unions to prevent the entry of dirt into the system.

HAYNES HiNT *Cut the fingertips from an old rubber glove, and secure them over the open unions with elastic bands to prevent dirt ingress (see Section 6).*

7 Unscrew each injector using a 27 mm deep socket or box spanner, and remove from the cylinder head. Recover the heat shield washer, and discard it - new washers must be used when refitting **(see illustrations)**. If the injectors are not being overhauled, label them so they can be refitted in their original positions.

Refitting

8 Fit a new heat shield washer to the cylinder head, noting that it must be fitted with its concave side facing downwards (towards the cylinder head) **(see illustration)**.

9 Screw the injector into position and tighten it to the specified torque **(see illustration)**.

10 Refit the injector pipes, and tighten the union nuts to the specified torque setting. Position any clips attached to the pipes as noted before removal.

11 Reconnect the return pipe to the injector.

12 Restore the battery connection and check the running of the engine.

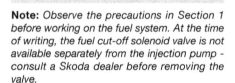

11 Fuel cut-off solenoid valve - removal and refitting

Note: *Observe the precautions in Section 1 before working on the fuel system. At the time of writing, the fuel cut-off solenoid valve is not available separately from the injection pump - consult a Skoda dealer before removing the valve.*

Removal

1 The fuel cut-off solenoid valve, commonly known as the stop solenoid, is located at the rear of the injection pump.

2 Disconnect the battery negative lead and position it away from the terminal.

3 Pull off the cover over the top of the valve.

4 Trace the wiring from the valve body to the immobiliser control unit. Unscrew the bolt, recover the spacer, and remove the control unit from the base of the injection pump.

5 Unscrew and withdraw the valve body from the injection pump, using the hex cast into the base of the valve, and taking care not to place the wiring to the immobiliser unit under strain. Recover the O-ring seal, spring and plunger.

Refitting

6 Refitting is a reversal of removal, using a new O-ring seal. Tighten the valve body securely into the pump.

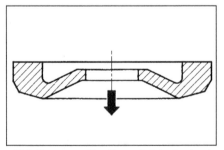

10.8 Cross-section through injector heat shield, to show fitting orientation

Arrow points towards cylinder head

10.9 Screw the injector into position and tighten it to the specified torque

Chapter 4 Part D:
Emission control and exhaust systems

Contents

Degrees of difficulty

Easy, suitable for novice with little experience		Fairly easy, suitable for beginner with some experience		Fairly difficult, suitable for competent DIY mechanic	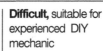	Difficult, suitable for experienced DIY mechanic		Very difficult, suitable for expert DIY or professional	

Specifications

Torque wrench settings	Nm	lbf ft
Catalytic converter flange (1.3 litre models):		
Bolts	13	10
Nuts	15	11
EGR valve clamp screw	10	7
EGR valve-to-exhaust manifold nuts (renew)	25	18
EGR valve-to-inlet manifold bolts	25	18
Exhaust downpipe-to-manifold nuts:		
1.3 litre models	20	15
1.6 litre models	25	18
Diesel models	40	30
Exhaust manifold-to-cylinder head nuts	25	18
Exhaust system clamp nuts/bolts:		
Diesel models	70	52
Petrol models	20	15
Lambda sensor:		
1.3 litre models	50	37
1.6 litre models	55	41

1 General information

Emission control systems

All petrol-engined models use unleaded fuel, and are controlled by engine management systems that are tuned to give the best compromise between driveability, fuel consumption and exhaust emission production. In addition, a number of systems are fitted that help to minimise other harmful emissions. All petrol models are fitted with a crankcase emission-control system that reduces the release of pollutants from the engine's lubrication system, and a catalytic converter that reduces exhaust gas pollutants. Petrol engine models have an evaporative loss emission control system that reduces the release of gaseous hydrocarbons from the fuel tank.

All diesel-engined models also have a crankcase emission control system. In addition, all diesel models are fitted with an oxidation catalytic converter and an Exhaust Gas Recirculation (EGR) system to reduce exhaust emissions.

Crankcase emission control

To reduce the emission of unburned hydrocarbons from the crankcase into the atmosphere, the engine is sealed, and the blow-by gases and oil vapour are drawn from inside the crankcase, into the air cleaner, to be burned by the engine during normal combustion.

Under conditions of high manifold depression (idling, deceleration) the gases will be sucked positively out of the crankcase. Under conditions of low manifold depression (acceleration, full-throttle running) the gases are forced out of the crankcase by the (relatively) higher crankcase pressure; if the engine is worn, the raised crankcase pressure (due to increased blow-by) will cause some of the flow to return under all manifold conditions.

2.3 Disconnect the charcoal canister purge valve wiring connector

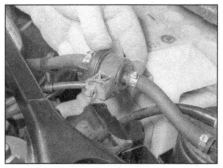

2.4 Slide the purge valve upwards off the mounting bracket

Exhaust emission control - petrol models

To minimise the amount of pollutants which escape into the atmosphere, all models are fitted with a catalytic converter in the exhaust system. The fuelling system is of the closed-loop type, in which a lambda sensor in the exhaust system provides the engine management system ECU with constant feedback, enabling the ECU to adjust the air/fuel mixture to optimise combustion.

The lambda sensor has a heating element built-in that is controlled by the ECU through the lambda sensor relay, to quickly bring the sensor's tip to its optimum operating temperature. The sensor's tip is sensitive to oxygen, and relays a voltage signal to the ECU that varies according on the amount of oxygen in the exhaust gas. If the inlet air/fuel mixture is too rich, the exhaust gases are low in oxygen, so the sensor sends a low-voltage signal, the voltage rising as the mixture weakens and the amount of oxygen rises in the exhaust gases. Peak conversion efficiency of all major pollutants occurs if the inlet air/fuel mixture is maintained at the chemically-correct ratio for the complete combustion of petrol of 14.7 parts (by weight) of air to 1 part of fuel (the stoichiometric ratio). The sensor output voltage alters in a large step at this point, the ECU using the signal change as a reference point, and correcting the inlet air/fuel mixture accordingly by altering the fuel injector pulse width. Details of lambda sensor removal and refitting are given in Section 4.

Exhaust emission control - diesel models

An oxidation catalyst is fitted in the exhaust system of all diesel-engined models. This has the effect of removing a large proportion of the gaseous hydrocarbons, carbon monoxide and particulates present in the exhaust gas.

An Exhaust Gas Recirculation (EGR) system is fitted to all diesel models. This reduces the level of nitrogen oxides produced during combustion, by introducing a proportion of the exhaust gas back into the inlet manifold, under certain engine operating conditions, via a plunger valve. The system is controlled electronically by the diesel control unit (see Chapter 4C, Section 1).

Evaporative emission control - petrol models

To minimise the escape of unburned hydrocarbons into the atmosphere, an evaporative loss emission control system is fitted to all petrol models. The fuel tank filler cap is sealed, and a charcoal canister is mounted on the left-hand inner wing to collect the petrol vapours released from the fuel contained in the fuel tank. It stores them until they can be drawn from the canister (under the control of the fuel-injection/ignition system ECU) via the purge valve into the inlet tract, where they are then burned by the engine during normal combustion.

To ensure that the engine runs correctly when it is cold and/or idling, and to protect the catalytic converter from the effects of an over-rich mixture, the purge control valve is

not opened by the ECU until the engine has warmed up, and the engine is under load; the valve solenoid is then modulated on and off to allow the stored vapour to pass into the inlet tract.

Exhaust systems

The exhaust system comprises the exhaust manifold, front downpipe, a catalytic converter, two silencer boxes, a number of mounting brackets, and a series of connecting pipes. On 1.6 litre and diesel engine models, the downpipe and catalytic converter are one unit, while a separate downpipe and converter are fitted on 1.3 litre models.

2 Evaporative loss emission control system - information and component renewal

Information

1 The evaporative loss emission control system consists of the purge valve, the activated charcoal filter canister, and a series of connecting hoses.

2 The purge valve is mounted on a bracket at the rear of the left-hand inner wing, and the charcoal canister is mounted behind it in a clamp bracket.

Component renewal

Purge valve

3 Ensure that the ignition is switched off, then unplug the wiring harness from the purge valve at the connector **(see illustration)**.

4 Slide the purge valve upwards to release its rubber mounting from the bracket **(see illustration)**.

5 Slacken the clips and pull the hoses off the purge valve ports. Make a note of their orientation to aid refitting later.

6 Refitting is a reversal of removal.

Charcoal canister

7 Disconnect the hoses from the top of the canister, noting which ports they connect to. Remove the clamp bolt and lift the canister out of the bracket **(see illustrations)**.

8 Refitting is a reversal of removal.

3 Crankcase emission system - general information

1 The crankcase emission control system consists of a series of hoses that connect the crankcase vent to the engine top cover vent (where applicable) and the air cleaner.

2 An oil separator unit is fitted on 1.6 litre models. This is a large plastic housing, bolted to the rear of the engine block, and sealed to the block openings by two O-ring seals **(see illustrations)**. If the unit has become blocked,

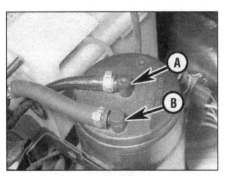

2.7a Charcoal canister pipe from fuel tank (A) and pipe to purge valve (B)

2.7b Remove the clamp bolt (arrowed) and lift out the canister

3.2a Oil separator unit retaining bolts (seen with engine removed, for clarity)

3.2b Oil separator unit removed, showing O-ring seals (arrowed)

Refitting

5 Apply a little anti-seize grease to the sensor threads only - keep the probe tip clean.
6 Refit the sensor to its housing, tightening it to the correct torque. Restore the harness connection. Note that the type of lambda sensor fitted depends on vehicle specification - the sensor may not be interchangeable with one obtained from another model.

it may be worth trying to clean it out using a suitable solvent before renewing the complete unit. The unit cannot be dismantled for servicing.
3 The system requires no attention other than to check at regular intervals that the hose(s) are free of blockages and undamaged.

4   Lambda sensor (petrol models) - removal and refitting

Removal

1 The lambda sensor is threaded into the exhaust downpipe, ahead of the catalytic converter (see illustration).
2 Disconnect the battery negative lead and position it away from the terminal.
3 Unplug the wiring harness from the lambda

sensor at the connector, which is located in a bracket attached to the thermostat housing. If two connectors are present in this bracket, the one for the lambda sensor is the lower of the two (see illustration). Separate the connector plug halves, and slide the plug out of the bracket.
4 Note: *As a flying lead remains connected to the sensor after it has been disconnected, if the correct-size spanner is not available, a slotted socket will be required to remove the sensor.* Working under the vehicle, slacken and withdraw the sensor, taking care to avoid damaging the sensor probe as it is removed.

5   EGR system (diesel models) - general information and component removal

General information

1 The EGR system consists of the EGR valve, the EGR solenoid valve, the diesel control unit and a connecting vacuum hose.
2 The EGR valve is mounted on a flange joint at the inlet manifold, and is connected to a second flange joint at the exhaust manifold by a semi-flexible pipe (see illustration).
3 The EGR solenoid valve/modulator valve is mounted on a bracket at the rear of the engine compartment.
4 The EGR system is under the control of the diesel control unit mounted at the rear of the

4.1 Lambda sensor (arrowed) on 1.3 litre engine model

4.3 Disconnecting the lambda sensor wiring plug

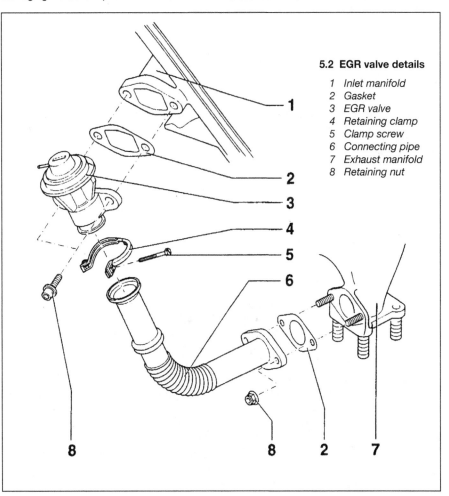

5.2 EGR valve details

1   Inlet manifold
2   Gasket
3   EGR valve
4   Retaining clamp
5   Clamp screw
6   Connecting pipe
7   Exhaust manifold
8   Retaining nut

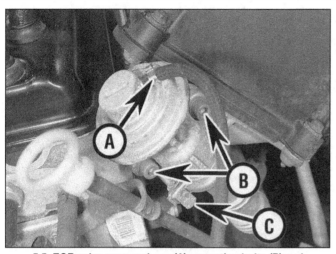

5.5 EGR valve vacuum hose (A), mounting bolts (B) and clamp screw (C)

5.9 Disconnecting the wiring plug from the EGR solenoid valve

engine compartment, next to the glow plug relay. The control unit enables the EGR system only between 825 rpm and 3200 rpm - outside this engine speed range, the system is switched off. The system is also disabled during the first two seconds of acceleration, and if the vehicle is operating at more than 1000 metres above sea level.

Component renewal

EGR valve

5 Disconnect the vacuum hose from the port at the top of the EGR valve **(see illustration)**.
6 Slacken and withdraw the bolts that secure the EGR valve to the inlet manifold flange. Recover and discard the gasket from the joint.
7 Remove the clamp screw from the EGR valve retaining ring, and lift the EGR valve out of the semi-flexible pipe. If required, unscrew the retaining nuts and disconnect the semi-flexible pipe from the exhaust manifold; recover the gasket.
8 Refitting is a reversal of removal, noting the following points:
  a) Use a new flange joint gasket.
  b) If the semi-flexible pipe has been removed, use a new gasket on refitting. Fit the retaining bolts loosely, and ensure that the pipe is unstressed before

tightening the bolts to the specified torque.

EGR solenoid valve

9 Ensure that the ignition is switched off, then disconnect the wiring plug from the valve **(see illustration)**. The idle speed boost valve's grey connector distinguishes it from that for the EGR solenoid valve next to it.
10 Slacken the clips and pull the hoses off the valve ports. Make a *careful* note of their orientation to aid refitting later.
11 Remove the retaining screws and lift off the valve.
12 Refitting is a reversal of removal.
Caution: Ensure that the vacuum hoses are refitted correctly; combustion and exhaust smoke production can be drastically affected by an incorrectly operating EGR system.

6 Exhaust manifold - removal and refitting

Exhaust manifold removal is described as part of the cylinder head dismantling sequence; refer to Chapter 2A, B or C as applicable.

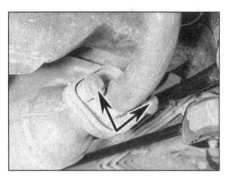

7.6 Downpipe-to-catalytic converter bolts (arrowed)

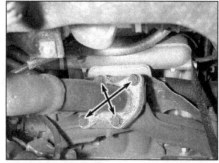

7.7 Downpipe-to-manifold nuts (arrowed)

7 Exhaust system - general information and component renewal

General information

1 On all models, the exhaust system is made up of the front downpipe, a catalytic converter, the centre section incorporating the front silencer, and the tail section which contains the rear silencer. **Note:** *On 1.6 litre and diesel engine models, the catalytic converter is one unit with the downpipe, while on 1.3 litre models, the downpipe and converter are separate.*
2 On all models, the system is suspended throughout its entire length by rubber mountings, which are secured to the underside of the vehicle by metal brackets.

Removal

⚠ *Warning: Allow ample time for the exhaust system to cool before starting work. In particular, the catalytic converter (where applicable) runs at very high temperatures, and severe burns will result if it is carelessly handled. If there is any chance that the system may still be hot, wear suitable gloves.*

3 Each exhaust section can be removed individually, bearing in mind the Note in paragraph 1.
4 To remove the system or part of the system, first jack up the front or rear of the car and support it on axle stands (see *Jacking and vehicle support*). Alternatively, position the car over an inspection pit or on car ramps.

Downpipe (1.3 litre models)

5 Refer to Section 4 and remove the lambda sensor.
6 Support the weight of the catalytic converter. Loosen and remove the two bolts from the converter front flange, and recover the washers and springs **(see illustration)**.

7.8 Catalytic converter (petrol model), showing front and rear flange joints

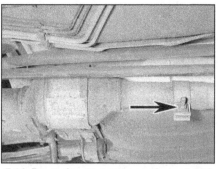

7.11 Downpipe-to-centre section nut and clamp bolt (arrowed) - diesel model shown

7.15 Tailpipe/rear silencer clamping ring and bolt

As the joint separates, recover the sealing ring, noting its direction of fitting (flat side to the front).

7 Supporting the weight of the downpipe, progressively loosen and remove the four downpipe-to-manifold nuts **(see illustration)**, and lower the downpipe out from under the vehicle.

Catalytic converter (1.3 litre models)

8 Support the weight of the catalytic converter. Loosen and remove the three nuts, bolts and washers from the converter rear flange **(see illustration)**.

9 Loosen and remove the two bolts from the converter front flange, and recover the washers and springs. As the joint separates, recover the sealing ring, noting its direction of fitting (flat side to the front). Lower the converter carefully to the ground (refer to Section 8), and remove it from under the vehicle.

Downpipe and catalytic converter (1.6 litre and diesel models)

10 Place blocks of wood under the front silencer or downpipe to act as a support. On 1.6 litre models, refer to Section 4 and remove the lambda sensor from the exhaust downpipe.

11 Slacken and remove the nut and clamp bolt securing the downpipe to the centre section **(see illustration)**. On 1.6 litre models, recover the washer and spacer.

12 Undo the nuts and separate the downpipe from the exhaust manifold. Recover the gasket. Disconnect the pipe from the centre section, and withdraw the downpipe carefully (see Section 8) from underneath the vehicle.

Centre section/front silencer

13 Support the catalytic converter, then slacken the clamp or flange bolts and disengage the front of the centre section from the converter. On 1.3 litre models, recover the gasket.

14 Slacken the clamp bolt at the rear of the centre section. Unhook the centre section from its mountings, then separate the front and rear joints from the clamps and remove it from the vehicle. The rubber mountings are secured by two large circlips, which must be slid out before the mounting can be detached.

Tailpipe/rear silencer

15 Slacken the clamping ring bolt and disengage the tailpipe at the joint **(see illustration)**.

16 Unhook the tailpipe from its mounting rubbers and remove it from the vehicle. The tailpipe rubber mounting is secured by two large circlips, which must be slid out before the rubber mounting can be detached **(see illustration)**.

Heatshield(s)

17 The heatshields are secured to the underside of the body by a mixture of nuts, bolts and clips. Each shield can be removed once the relevant exhaust section has been removed. Note that if the shield is being removed to gain access to a component located behind it, in some cases it may prove sufficient to remove the retaining nuts and/or bolts and simply lower the shield, removing the need to disturb the exhaust system **(see illustration)**.

Refitting

18 Each section is refitted by a reverse of the removal sequence, noting the following points:
a) *Ensure that all traces of corrosion have been removed from the flanges, and renew all necessary gaskets. If the clamp nuts and bolts are in less than perfect condition, fit new ones.*
b) *Inspect the rubber mountings for signs of damage or deterioration, and renew as*

7.16 Removing one of the circlips securing the tailpipe rubber mounting

necessary. Liquid soap can be useful in helping to slide the rubber mountings onto the metal pegs under the car.
c) *On joints which are secured by clamping rings, apply a smear of exhaust system jointing paste to the joint mating surfaces to ensure an gas-tight seal.*
d) *Prior to finally tightening the exhaust system fasteners, ensure that all rubber mountings are correctly located, and that there is adequate clearance between the exhaust system and vehicle underbody.*
e) *Tighten the clamping ring nuts evenly and progressively to the specified torque.*

8 Catalytic converter - general information and precautions

The catalytic converter is a reliable and simple device which needs no maintenance in itself, but there are some facts of which an owner should be aware if the converter is to function properly for its full service life.

Petrol models

a) *DO NOT use leaded (UK 4-star) petrol in a car with a catalytic converter - the lead will coat the precious metals' reagents, reducing their converting efficiency, and will eventually destroy the converter.*
b) *Always keep the ignition and fuel systems well-maintained in accordance with the manufacturer's schedule (see Chapter 1A or 1B).*

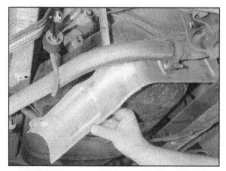

7.17 With care, the heatshields can be removed without disturbing the exhaust system

c) If the engine develops a misfire, do not drive the car at all (or at least as little as possible) until the fault is cured.

d) DO NOT push- or tow-start the car - this will soak the catalytic converter in unburned fuel, causing it to overheat when the engine does start.

e) DO NOT switch off the ignition at high engine speeds, ie do not blip the throttle immediately before switching off.

f) In some cases a sulphurous smell (like that of rotten eggs) may be noticed from the exhaust. This is common to many catalytic converter-equipped cars and once the car has covered a few thousand miles the problem should disappear. Low-quality fuel with a high sulphur content will exacerbate this effect.

g) The catalytic converter, used on a well-maintained and well-driven car, should last between 50 000 and 100 000 miles - if the converter is no longer effective it must be renewed.

Petrol and diesel models

h) DO NOT use fuel or engine oil additives - these may contain substances harmful to the catalytic converter.

i) DO NOT continue to use the car if the engine burns oil to the extent of leaving a visible trail of blue smoke.

j) Remember that the catalytic converter operates at very high temperatures. DO NOT, therefore, park the car in dry undergrowth, over long grass or piles of dead leaves after a long run.

k) Remember that the catalytic converter is FRAGILE - do not strike it with tools during servicing work, and take care if handling it once it has been removed.

Chapter 5 Part A:
Starting and charging systems

Contents

Degrees of difficulty

Easy, suitable for novice with little experience	Fairly easy, suitable for beginner with some experience	Fairly difficult, suitable for competent DIY mechanic 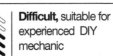	Difficult, suitable for experienced DIY mechanic	Very difficult, suitable for expert DIY or professional

Specifications

General
System type . . . . 12-volt, negative earth

Starter motor
Rating:
    1.3 litre engines up to June 1995 . . . . 12V, 0.8 kW
    1.3 litre and 1.6 litre engines, June 1995-on . . . . 12V, 1.0 kW
    Diesel engines . . . . 12V, 1.8 kW

Alternator
Minimum brush length . . . . 5 mm (tolerance +1mm, -0 mm)
Ratings . . . . 55 to 90 A (depending on model and equipment)

Torque wrench settings

	Nm	lbf ft
1.3 litre models		
Alternator adjustment link mounting bracket bolt (to cylinder head)* . .	26	19
Alternator lower mounting bracket nuts	24	18
1.6 litre models		
Alternator mounting bolts	23	17
Alternator mounting bracket-to-engine bolts	45	33
Diesel models		
Alternator mounting bracket-to-engine bolts	25	18
All models		
Battery clamping plate bolts	16	12
Starter motor cable nuts	14	10
Starter motor mounting:		
Nuts	50	37
Bolts/studs	60	44
Strut brace nuts (renew)	20	15

* Use thread locking compound.

1 General information and precautions

General information

The engine electrical system consists mainly of the charging and starting systems. Because of their engine-related functions, these are covered separately from the body electrical devices such as the lights, instruments, etc (which are covered in Chapter 12). On petrol engine models refer to Part B of this Chapter for information on the ignition system, and on diesel models refer to Part C for the pre-heating system.

The electrical system is of the 12-volt negative earth type.

The battery may of the low maintenance or maintenance-free (sealed for life) type and is charged by the alternator, which is belt-driven from the crankshaft pulley.

The starter motor is of the pre-engaged type, with an integral solenoid. On starting, the solenoid moves the drive pinion into engagement with the flywheel ring gear before the starter motor is energised. Once the engine has started, a one-way clutch prevents the motor armature being driven by the engine until the pinion disengages from the flywheel.

Further details of the various systems are given in the relevant Sections of this Chapter. While some repair procedures are given, the usual course of action is to renew the component concerned. The owner whose interest extends beyond mere component renewal should obtain a copy of the *Automobile Electrical & Electronic Systems Manual*, available from the publishers of this manual.

Precautions

⚠ *Warning: It is necessary to take extra care when working on the electrical system to avoid damage to semi-conductor devices (diodes and transistors), and to avoid the risk of personal injury. In addition to the precautions given in Safety first!, observe the following when working on the system:*

Always remove rings, watches, etc before working on the electrical system. Even with the battery disconnected, capacitive discharge could occur if a component's live terminal is earthed through a metal object. This could cause a shock or nasty burn.

Do not reverse the battery connections. Components such as the alternator, electronic control units, or any other components having semi-conductor circuitry could be irreparably damaged.

Never disconnect the battery terminals, the alternator, any electrical wiring or any test instruments when the engine is running.

Do not allow the engine to turn the alternator when the alternator is not connected.

Never test for alternator output by 'flashing' the output lead to earth.

Always ensure that the battery negative lead is disconnected when working on the electrical system.

If the engine is being started using jump leads and a slave battery, connect the batteries *positive-to-positive* and *negative-to-negative* (see *Booster battery (jump) starting*). This also applies when connecting a battery charger.

Never use an ohmmeter of the type incorporating a hand-cranked generator for circuit or continuity testing.

Before using electric-arc welding equipment on the car, *disconnect the battery, alternator and components such as the electronic control units* (where applicable) to protect them from the risk of damage.

Most radio/cassettes fitted as standard equipment by Skoda have a built-in security code to deter thieves. If the power source to the unit is cut, the anti-theft system will activate. Even if the power source is immediately reconnected, the radio/cassette unit will not function until the correct security code has been entered. Therefore, *if you do not know the correct security code for the radio/cassette unit, do not disconnect the battery negative terminal* or remove the radio/cassette unit from the vehicle. On models with a pull-out stereo, the anti-theft system may activate if the unit is removed from the vehicle for more than 24 hours. Refer to your Skoda dealer for further information on whether the unit fitted to your car has a security code.

On vehicles equipped with a Skoda anti-theft alarm, before disconnecting the battery, *ensure that the alarm is disabled using the special key in the rear of the alarm module*. If this is not done, the alarm will sound when the battery is reconnected.

2 Battery - testing, charging and electrolyte level check

Standard and low-maintenance battery - testing

1 If the vehicle covers a small annual mileage, it is worthwhile checking the specific gravity of the electrolyte every three months to determine the state of charge of the battery. Use a hydrometer to make the check, and compare the results with the following table. Note that the specific gravity readings assume an electrolyte temperature of 15°C (60°F); for every 10°C (18°F) below 15°C (60°F) subtract 0.007. For every 10°C (18°F) above 15°C (60°F) add 0.007.

	Above 25°C	Below 25°C
Fully charged	1.210 to 1.230	1.270 to 1.290
70% charged	1.170 to 1.190	1.230 to 1.250
Discharged	1.050 to 1.070	1.110 to 1.130

2 If the battery condition is suspect, first check the specific gravity of electrolyte in each cell. A variation of 0.040 or more between any cells indicates loss of electrolyte or deterioration of the internal plates.

3 If the specific gravity variation is 0.040 or more, the battery should be renewed. If the cell variation is satisfactory but the battery is discharged, it should be charged as described later in this Section.

Maintenance-free battery - testing

4 In cases where a sealed for life maintenance-free battery is fitted, topping-up and testing of the electrolyte in each cell is not possible. The condition of the battery can therefore only be tested using a battery condition indicator or a voltmeter.

5 Certain models my be fitted with a maintenance-free battery, with a built-in charge condition indicator. The indicator is located in the top of the battery casing, and indicates the condition of the battery from its colour. If the indicator shows green, then the battery is in a good state of charge. If the indicator turns darker, eventually to black, then the battery requires charging, as described later in this Section. If the indicator shows clear/yellow, then the electrolyte level in the battery is too low to allow further use, and the battery should be renewed. **Do not** attempt to charge, load or jump start a battery when the indicator shows clear/yellow.

6 If testing the battery using a voltmeter, connect the voltmeter across the battery and note the voltage. The test is only accurate if the battery has not been subjected to any kind of charge for the previous six hours. If this is not the case, switch on the headlights for 30 seconds, then wait four to five minutes before testing the battery after switching off the headlights. All other electrical circuits must be switched off, so check that the doors and tailgate are fully shut when making the test.

7 If the voltage reading is less than 12.2 volts, then the battery is discharged, whilst a reading of 12.2 to 12.4 volts indicates a partially discharged condition.

8 If the battery is to be charged, remove it from the vehicle and charge it as described later in this Section.

Standard and low maintenance battery - charging

Note: *The following is intended as a guide only. Always refer to the manufacturer's recommendations (often printed on a label attached to the battery) before charging a battery.*

9 Charge the battery at a rate equivalent to 10% of the battery capacity (eg for a 55 Ah battery charge at 5.5 A) and continue to charge the battery at this rate until no further rise in specific gravity is noted over a four-hour period.

10 Alternatively, a trickle charger charging at the rate of 1.5 amps can safely be used overnight.

11 Specially rapid boost charges which are claimed to restore the power of the battery in 1 to 2 hours are not recommended, as they can cause serious damage to the battery plates through overheating. If the battery is completely flat, Skoda recommend that recharging should take at least 24 hours.

12 While charging the battery, note that the temperature of the electrolyte should never exceed 37.8°C (100°F).

Maintenance-free battery - charging

Note: *The following is intended as a guide only. Always refer to the manufacturer's recommendations (often printed on a label attached to the battery) before charging a battery.*

13 This battery type takes considerably longer to fully recharge than the standard type, the time taken being dependent on the extent of discharge, but it can take anything up to three days.

14 A constant voltage type charger is required, to be set, when connected, to 13.9 to 14.9 volts with a charger current below 25 amps. Using this method, the battery should be useable within three hours, giving a voltage reading of 12.5 volts, but this is for a partially-discharged battery and, as mentioned, full charging can take far longer.

15 If the battery is to be charged from a fully-discharged state (condition reading less than 12.2 volts), have it recharged by your Skoda dealer or local automotive electrician, as the charge rate is higher and constant supervision during charging is necessary.

Battery electrolyte level check

⚠️ **Warning:** *The electrolyte inside a battery is diluted acid - it is a good idea to wear suitable rubber gloves. When topping-up, don't overfill the cells so that the electrolyte overflows. In the event of any spillage, rinse the electrolyte off without delay. Refit the cell covers and rinse the battery with copious quantities of clean water. Don't attempt to siphon out any excess electrolyte.*

16 Some models covered by this Manual may be fitted with a maintenance-free battery as standard equipment, or may have had one fitted as a replacement. If the battery in your vehicle is marked Freedom, Maintenance-Free or similar, no electrolyte level checking is required (the battery is often completely sealed, preventing any topping-up).

17 Batteries which do require their electrolyte level to be checked can be recognised by the presence of removable covers over the six battery cells - the battery casing is also sometimes translucent, so that the electrolyte level can be more easily checked **(see illustration)**. Make sure you do not have a maintenance-free battery before attempting to top up the electrolyte level.

18 Remove the cell covers and either look down inside the battery to see the level web, or check the level using any markings provided on the battery casing. The electrolyte should at least cover the battery plates. If necessary, top up a little at a time with distilled (deionised) water until the level in all six cells is correct - don't fill the cells up to the brim. Wipe up any spillage, then refit the cell covers.

3 Battery - removal and refitting

Removal

1 Note: *If the vehicle has a security-coded radio, check that you have a copy of the code number before disconnecting the battery cable; refer to the caution in Section 1. On models with a Skoda alarm, disable the alarm unit using the special key in the rear of the alarm module.*

2 Slacken the clamp nut and disconnect the battery negative lead from the terminal **(see illustrations)**. Take care to identify the battery leads, as both main leads are black in colour.

3 Unclip the plastic cover and disconnect the battery positive lead in the same manner as the negative lead.

4 At the base of the battery, slacken and withdraw the clamp bolts **(see illustration)**, then lift off the clamping plate.

5 To make removing the battery easier,

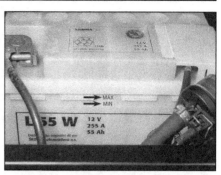

2.17 Battery electrolyte MAX and MIN marks

unbolt and remove the strut brace (where applicable). To provide extra clearance, it may be necessary to remove the top cover from the heater/ventilation unit (see Chapter 3). On petrol models, lift the canister purge solenoid valve off its mounting peg, and move it aside - there should be no need to detach the hoses.

6 Where applicable, disconnect the vent pipe from the top of the battery, and remove the battery from the engine bay

Refitting

7 Refitting the battery is a reversal of the removal procedure, noting the following points:

a) *Make sure the clamping plate locates in the base of the battery.*

b) *Tighten the clamping plate bolts to the correct torque.*

c) *Fit the positive lead first, then the negative lead - make sure the connections are clean, and tighten the clamp bolts securely.*

d) *Where applicable, refit the strut brace using new self-locking nuts tightened to the specified torque.*

e) *On models with a Skoda alarm, remember to switch the alarm unit back on using the special key.*

f) *On petrol models, disconnecting the battery will have erased the adaptive values for the engine management system. The system will re-learn these values when the vehicle is next used, but the idle speed in particular may be a little erratic for a time.*

3.2a Loosen the clamp nut . . .

3.2b . . . and disconnect the battery negative lead - position it away from the battery terminal

3.4 Unscrew and remove the battery clamp bolts

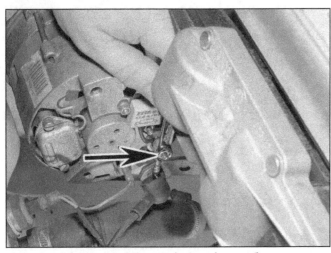

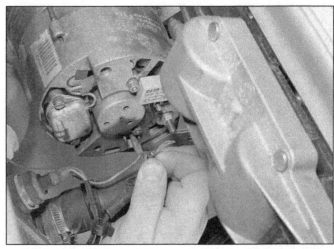

5.3a Unscrew the terminal nut (arrowed) . . .   5.3b . . . and disconnect the power cable from the alternator

4 Alternator/charging system - testing in vehicle

Note: *Refer to Safety first! and Section 1 of this Chapter before starting work.*

1 If the charge warning light fails to illuminate when the ignition is switched on, first check the alternator wiring connections for security. If satisfactory, check that the warning light bulb has not blown, and that the bulbholder is secure in its location in the instrument panel. If the light still fails to illuminate, check the continuity of the warning light feed wire from the alternator to the bulbholder. If all is satisfactory, the alternator is at fault and should be renewed or taken to an auto-electrician for testing and repair.

2 Similarly, if the charge warning light comes on with the ignition, but is then slow to go out when the engine is started, this may indicate an impending alternator problem. Check all the items listed in the preceding paragraph, and refer to an auto-electrical specialist if no obvious faults are found.

3 If the charge warning light illuminates when the engine is running, stop the engine and check that the drivebelt is correctly tensioned (see Chapter 2A, B or C, as applicable) and

that the alternator connections are secure. If all is so far satisfactory, check the alternator brushes and slip rings as described in Section 6. If the fault persists, the alternator should be renewed, or taken to an auto-electrician for testing and repair.

4 If the alternator output is suspect even though the warning light functions correctly, the regulated voltage may be checked as follows.

5 Connect a voltmeter across the battery terminals, and start the engine.

6 Increase the engine speed until the voltmeter reading remains steady; the reading should be approximately 12 to 13 volts, and no more than 14 volts.

7 Switch on as many electrical accessories (eg, the headlights, heated rear window and heater blower) as possible, and check that the alternator maintains the regulated voltage at around 13 to 14 volts.

8 If the regulated voltage is not as stated, this may be due to worn brushes, weak brush springs, a faulty voltage regulator, a faulty diode, a severed phase winding or worn or damaged slip rings. The brushes and slip rings may be checked (see Section 6), but if the fault persists, the alternator should be renewed or taken to an auto-electrician.

5 Alternator - removal and refitting

Removal

1 Disconnect the battery negative lead and position it away from the terminal - refer to the precautions in Section 1.

2 Remove the auxiliary drivebelt from the alternator pulley (see Chapter 2A, B or C, as applicable).

1.3 litre models

3 Remove the protective cap, slacken and withdraw the nut and washers, then disconnect the power cable from the alternator at the screw terminal post **(see illustrations)**.

4 Unplug the sense cable from the alternator at the connector **(see illustration)**.

5 Slacken and remove the upper mounting bolt(s) **(see illustrations)**.

6 Loosen the lower mounting nut and bolt, then pivot the alternator towards the radiator for improved access **(see illustrations)**.

7 Remove the lower through-bolt, and lift the alternator away from its mounting bracket.

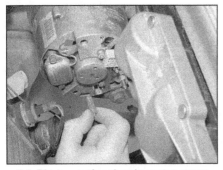

5.4 Disconnecting the alternator sense cable

5.5a Either unbolt the adjustment link from the cylinder head bracket . . .

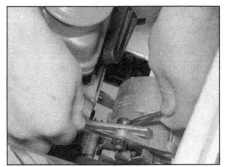

5.5b . . . or remove the adjustment link nut and bolt

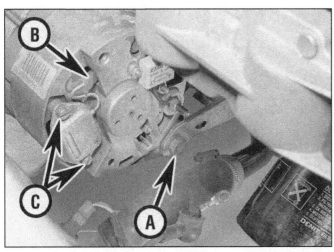

5.6a Alternator lower mounting bolt (A) - note regulator module wiring (B) and retaining screws (C)

5.6b Pivot the alternator towards the radiator to improve access to the through-bolt and nut (arrowed)

1.6 litre and diesel models

8 Unplug the sense cable from the alternator at the connector (see illustration).

9 Remove the protective cap, or slide back the rubber boot, for access to the power cable retaining nut. Slacken and withdraw the nut and washers, then disconnect the power cable from the alternator at the screw terminal post (see illustrations).

10 Slacken and remove the lower, then the upper bolts (see illustrations), then lift the alternator away from its bracket. Where applicable, pivot the drivebelt tensioner roller out of the way to gain access to the lower mounting bolt.

All models

11 Refer to Section 6 if the removal of the brush holder/voltage regulator module is required.

Refitting

12 Refitting is a reversal of removal. Refer to the relevant Part of Chapter 2 for details of refitting and tensioning the auxiliary drivebelt.

13 On completion, tighten the alternator mounting bolts to the specified torque.

6 Alternator - brush holder/regulator module renewal

1 Remove the alternator as described in Section 5.

2 Place the alternator on a clean work surface, with the pulley facing down.

3 On 1.6 litre and diesel models, remove the retaining screws, then prise open the clips and lift the plastic cover from the rear of the alternator (see illustrations).

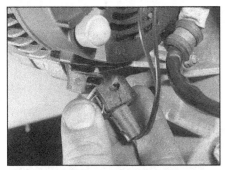

5.8 Unplug the sense cable from the alternator at the connector

5.9a Remove the protective cap . . .

5.9b . . . remove the nut and washers, then disconnect the power cable

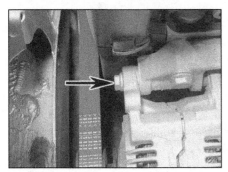

5.10a Alternator upper mounting bolt . . .

5.10b . . . and lower mounting bolt

6.3a Remove the retaining screws (arrowed) . . .

6.3b ... then prise open the clips ...

6.3c ... and lift the plastic cover from the rear of the alternator (1.6 litre model shown)

6.4a Remove the brush holder/voltage regulator module screws ...

6.4b ... then lift the module away from the alternator (1.6 litre model shown)

4 Slacken and withdraw the brush holder/voltage regulator module screws, unplug the wiring connector, then lift the module away from the alternator (see illustrations).
5 Measure the free length of the brush contacts - where applicable, take the measurement from the manufacturer's emblem etched on the side of the brush contact, to the shallowest part of the curved end face of the brush (see illustration). Check the measurement with the Specifications; renew the

module if the brushes are worn below the minimum limit.
6 Inspect the surfaces of the slip rings, at the end of the alternator shaft (see illustration). If they appear excessively worn, burnt or pitted, then renewal must be considered; refer to an automobile electrical system specialist for further guidance.
7 Reassemble the alternator by following the dismantling procedure in reverse. On completion, refer to Section 5 and refit the alternator.

7 Starting system - testing

Note: *Refer to the precautions given in Safety first! and in Section 1 of this Chapter before starting work.*
1 If the starter motor fails to operate when the ignition key is turned to the appropriate position, the following possible causes may be to blame:
a) *The battery is faulty.*
b) *The electrical connections between the switch, solenoid, battery and starter motor are somewhere failing to pass the necessary current from the battery through the starter to earth.*
c) *The solenoid is faulty.*
d) *The starter motor is mechanically or electrically defective.*
2 To check the battery, switch on the headlights. If they dim after a few seconds, this indicates that the battery is discharged - recharge (see Section 2) or renew the battery. If the headlights glow brightly, operate the ignition switch and observe the lights. If they dim, then this indicates that current is reaching the starter motor, therefore the fault must lie in the starter motor. If the lights continue to glow brightly (and no clicking sound can be heard from the starter motor solenoid), this indicates that there is a fault in the circuit or solenoid - see following paragraphs. If the starter motor turns slowly when operated, but the battery is in good condition, then this indicates that either the starter motor is faulty, or there is considerable resistance somewhere in the circuit.
3 If a fault in the circuit is suspected, disconnect the battery leads (including the earth connection to the body), the starter/ solenoid wiring and the engine/transmission earth strap. Thoroughly clean the connections,

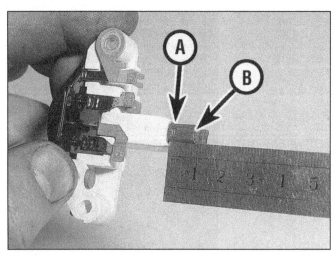

6.5 Measure the alternator brush length from the emblem (A) to the lowest point on the end face (B) - see text

6.6 Inspect the surfaces of the slip rings (arrowed), at the end of the alternator shaft

8.2a Unscrew the retaining nut . . .

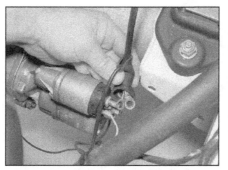

8.2b . . . and detach the wiring from the threaded connection

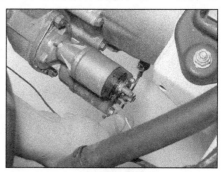

8.2c Unplug the remaining connection to the solenoid

and reconnect the leads and wiring, then use a voltmeter or test light to check that full battery voltage is available at the battery positive lead connection to the solenoid, and that the earth is sound. Smear petroleum jelly around the battery terminals to prevent corrosion - corroded connections are amongst the most frequent causes of electrical system faults.

4 If the battery and all connections are in good condition, check the circuit by disconnecting the wire from the solenoid blade terminal. Connect a voltmeter or test light between the wire end and a good earth (such as the battery negative terminal), and check that the wire is live when the ignition switch is turned to the start position. If it is, then the circuit is sound - if not the circuit wiring can be checked as described in Chapter 12.

5 The solenoid contacts can be checked by connecting a voltmeter or test light between the battery positive feed connection on the starter side of the solenoid, and earth. When the ignition switch is turned to the start position, there should be a reading or lighted bulb, as applicable. If there is no reading or lighted bulb, the solenoid is faulty and should be renewed.

6 If the circuit and solenoid are proved sound, the fault must lie in the starter motor. Remove the starter as described in Section 8. It may be possible to have the starter motor overhauled by a specialist, but check on the availability and cost of spares before proceeding, as it may prove more economical to obtain a new or exchange motor.

8 Starter motor - removal and refitting

Removal

1 Disconnect the battery negative lead, and position the lead away from the battery terminal. This is especially important when working on the starter motor, as the supply cable to the motor is permanently live.

2 Pull off the protective rubber boot and disconnect the wires from the rear of the starter solenoid, noting their relative terminal positions **(see illustrations)**.

3 Unclip the wiring for the reversing light switch, and move it to one side **(see illustration)**. It may be wise to also disconnect

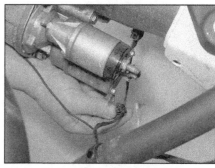

8.3 Unclip the reversing light switch wiring from the starter body

the wiring plug from the reversing light switch itself, to prevent possible damage to the wiring as the starter is removed.

4 While supporting the weight of the starter motor, unscrew the starter motor-to-transmission nuts and withdraw the motor **(see illustrations)**.

Refitting

5 Refitting is the reverse of the removal procedure; tighten the mountings to the specified torque.

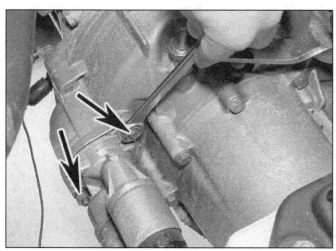

8.4a Unscrew the mounting nuts (arrowed) . . .

8.4b . . . and withdraw the starter motor from the transmission housing

9 Starter motor - overhaul

If the starter motor is thought to be defective, it should be removed from the vehicle and taken to an auto-electrician for assessment. In the majority of cases, new starter motor brushes can be fitted at a reasonable cost; unlike alternator brushes, those for the starter motor usually have to be soldered in place, rather than renewed as a unit. However, check the cost of repairs first, as it may prove more economical to purchase a new or exchange motor.

Chapter 5 Part B:
Ignition system - petrol engines

Contents

Degrees of difficulty

Easy, suitable for novice with little experience	Fairly easy, suitable for beginner with some experience	Fairly difficult, suitable for competent DIY mechanic	Difficult, suitable for experienced DIY mechanic 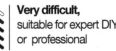	Very difficult, suitable for expert DIY or professional 

Specifications

General

Type*:
1.3 litre engine, codes 135B and 136B	Bosch Mono-Motronic
1.3 litre engine, codes 135M and 136M	Simos 2P (distributorless)
1.6 litre engine, code AEE	Magneti-Marelli 1AV
Ignition timing	Controlled by engine management system

*Refer to Chapter 2A or 2B for engine code listings.

Ignition coil

Bosch Mono-Motronic
Primary winding resistance	0.5 to 0.7 ohms
Secondary resistance	3000 to 4000 ohms

Magneti-Marelli 1AV
Primary winding resistance	0.5 to 1.5 ohms
Secondary resistance	3000 to 4000 ohms

Spark plugs

See Chapter 1A Specifications

HT leads

Resistance value (nominal)	30 000 ohms per metre length

Torque wrench settings

	Nm	lbf ft
Distributor clamp bolts:		
Bosch Mono-Motronic	10	7
Magneti-Marelli 1AV	25	18
Hall sensor retaining bolt	10	7
Ignition coil mounting nuts/bolts	10	7
Knock sensor mounting bolt	20	15

1 General information

The Bosch Mono-Motronic, Simos 2P, and Magneti-Marelli 1AV systems are self-contained engine management systems, which control both the fuel injection and ignition. This Chapter deals with the ignition system components only - refer to Chapter 4A or 4B for details of the fuel system components.

Bosch Mono-Motronic and Magneti-Marelli 1AV

The ignition system comprises four spark plugs, five HT leads, the distributor, an electronic ignition coil, and an Electronic Control Unit (ECU) together with its associated sensors, actuators and wiring. The component layout varies, but the basic operation is the same for all models.

The basic operation is as follows: the ECU supplies a voltage to the input stage of the ignition coil, which causes the primary windings in the coil to be energised. The supply voltage is periodically interrupted by the ECU, and this results in the collapse of primary magnetic field, which then induces a much larger voltage in the secondary coil, called the HT voltage. This voltage is directed, by the distributor via the HT leads, to the spark plug in the cylinder currently on its ignition stroke. The spark plug electrodes form a gap small enough for the HT voltage to arc across, and the resulting spark ignites the fuel/air mixture in the cylinder. The timing of this sequence of events is critical, and is regulated solely by the ECU.

The ECU calculates and controls the ignition timing and dwell angle primarily according to engine speed, crankshaft position and inlet manifold depression information, received from sensors mounted on and around the engine. Other parameters that affect ignition timing are throttle position and rate of opening, inlet air temperature, coolant temperature and on Magneti-Marelli systems, engine knock. Again, these are monitored via sensors mounted on the engine.

Knock control is employed on 1.6 litre engines with the Magneti-Marelli system. The knock sensor is mounted on the cylinder block, and has the ability to detect engine pre-ignition (or pinking) before it actually becomes audible. If pre-ignition occurs, the ECU retards the ignition timing of the cylinder that is pre-igniting in steps until the pre-ignition ceases. The ECU then advances the ignition timing of that cylinder in steps until it is restored to normal, or until pre-ignition occurs again.

Idle speed control is achieved partly by an electronic throttle valve positioning module, mounted on the side of the throttle body, and partly by the ignition system, which gives fine control of the idle speed by altering the ignition timing. As a result, manual adjustment of the engine idle speed is not necessary or possible.

On certain systems, the ECU has the ability to perform multiple ignition cycles during cold starting. During cranking, each spark plug fires several times per ignition stroke, until the engine starts. This greatly improves the engine's cold starting performance.

It should be noted that comprehensive fault diagnosis of all the engine management systems described in this Chapter is only possible with dedicated electronic test equipment. Problems with the system's operation that cannot be pinpointed by following the basic guidelines in Section 2 should therefore be referred to a Skoda dealer for assessment. Once the fault has been identified, the removal/refitting sequences detailed in the following Sections will then allow the appropriate component(s) to renewed as required.

Simos 2P

On the Simos 2P system, the ignition system is of the static (distributorless) type, consisting of two twin-output ignition coils. The ignition coils are housed in a single unit, which is mounted directly above the spark plugs - no HT leads are fitted.

Each ignition coil serves two cylinders (one coil supplies cylinders 1 and 4, and the other cylinders 2 and 3).

Under the control of the ECU, the ignition coils operate on the wasted spark principle, ie. each spark plug sparks twice for every cycle of the engine, once during the compression stroke and once during the exhaust stroke. The spark voltage is greatest

in the cylinder which is under compression; in the cylinder on its exhaust stroke, the compression is low and this produces a very weak spark which has no effect on the exhaust gases. This arrangement means that direct ignition can be employed without the need for a separate ignition coil for each cylinder.

The ECU uses its inputs from the various sensors to calculate the required ignition advance setting and coil charging time, depending on engine temperature, load and speed. At idle speeds, the ECU varies the ignition timing to alter the torque characteristic of the engine, enabling the idle speed to be controlled. This system operates in conjunction with the throttle valve positioner - see Chapter 4B for details.

A knock sensor is incorporated into the ignition system. Mounted on the rear of the cylinder block, the sensor detects the high frequency vibrations caused when the engine starts to pre-ignite, or pink. Under these conditions, the knock sensor sends an electrical signal to the ECU, which in turn retards the ignition advance setting in small steps until the pinking ceases.

2 Ignition system - testing and component checking

⚠ *Warning: Extreme care must be taken when working on the system with the ignition switched on; it is possible to get a substantial electric shock from a vehicle's ignition system. Persons with cardiac pacemaker devices should keep well clear of the ignition circuits, components and test equipment. Always switch off the ignition before disconnecting or connecting any component and when using a multi-meter to check resistances.*

Simos distributorless system

1 On models with the Simos distributorless system, very little testing is possible by the DIY mechanic.
2 In the event of any problem, check the wiring connectors to the ignition coil unit and Hall sensor, and the wiring harness back from the connectors for any obvious defects.
3 Ensure that the coil unit is securely fitted onto all four spark plugs, and that the spark plugs themselves are satisfactory. Be aware that a wasted-spark system will put more work into the spark plugs than a conventional system - if the spark plugs have not been checked for some time, they should not be overlooked.
4 Remove and inspect the Hall sensor as described in Section 6.
5 If these checks do not reveal the cause of the problem, take the vehicle to a Skoda dealer for a more thorough check with diagnostic equipment.

All other systems

General

6 Most ignition system faults are likely to be due to loose or dirty connections or to tracking (unintentional earthing) of HT voltage due to dirt, dampness or damaged insulation, rather than by the failure of any of the system's components. **Always** check all wiring thoroughly before condemning an electrical component, and work methodically to eliminate all other possibilities before deciding that a particular component is faulty. In damp conditions, try the effect of spraying the HT components with a little water-dispersant spray such as WD40.
7 The old practice of checking for a spark by holding the live end of an HT lead a short distance away from the engine is not recommended; not only is there a high risk of an electric shock, but the HT coil could be damaged. Similarly, **never** try to diagnose misfires by pulling off one HT lead at a time.

Engine will not start

8 If the engine either will not turn over at all, or only turns very slowly, check the battery and starter motor. Connect a voltmeter across the battery terminals (meter positive probe to battery positive terminal), disconnect the ignition coil HT lead from the distributor cap and earth it, then note the voltage reading obtained while turning over the engine on the starter for (no more than) ten seconds. If the reading obtained is less than approximately 9.5 volts, first check the battery, starter motor and charging systems (see Chapter 5A).
9 If the engine turns over at normal speed but will not start, check the HT circuit by connecting a timing light (following the manufacturer's instructions) and turning the engine over on the starter motor; if the light flashes, voltage is reaching the spark plugs, so these should be checked first. If the light does not flash, check the HT leads themselves, followed by the distributor cap, carbon brush and rotor arm.
10 If there is a spark, check the fuel system for faults, referring to the relevant part of Chapter 4 for further information.
11 If there is no spark, there may be a problem with the LT side of the system. Check for a 12-volt supply to the ignition coil, and for poor connections or damaged wiring. Check the coil itself as described later in this Section. If the coil is not receiving a 12-volt supply, this suggests a problem with the ignition switch, or possibly a blown fuse (see Chapter 12).
12 Remember that a fault with the anti-theft alarm or immobiliser (where fitted) could be responsible for a non-starting engine. Make sure first that the system has been correctly disabled by referring to the vehicle handbook or instructions.
13 If there is still no spark, then the problem must lie within the engine management system. In these cases, the vehicle should be referred to a Skoda dealer for assessment.

2.28a Release the two spring clips . . .

2.28b . . . and lift off the distributor cap

Engine misfires

14 An irregular misfire suggests either a loose connection or intermittent fault on the LT circuit, or an HT fault on the coil side of the rotor arm. A fault with the Hall sensor could also be responsible for erratic running - refer to Section 6.

15 With the ignition switched off, check carefully through the system, ensuring that all connections are clean and securely fastened. If the equipment is available, check the LT circuit for poor connections or damaged wiring.

16 Check that the HT coil, the distributor cap and the HT leads are clean and dry. Check the leads themselves and the spark plugs (by substitution, if necessary), then check the distributor cap, carbon brush and rotor arm.

17 Regular misfiring is almost certainly due to a fault in the distributor cap, HT leads or spark plugs. Use a timing light (paragraph 9) to check whether HT voltage is present at all leads.

18 If HT voltage is not present on one particular lead, the fault will be in that lead or in the distributor cap. If HT is present on all leads, the fault will be in the spark plugs; check and renew them if there is any doubt about their condition.

19 If no HT voltage is present, check the HT coil; its secondary windings may be breaking down under load.

Other problems

20 Problems with the system's operation that cannot be pinpointed by following the guidelines in the preceding paragraphs should be referred to a Skoda dealer for assessment.

Ignition component checking

Note: *This Section does not apply to the Simos distributorless system.*

HT leads

21 The spark plug (HT) leads should be checked whenever new spark plugs are fitted (see Chapter 1A).

22 Pull the leads from the plugs by gripping the end fitting, not the lead, otherwise the lead connection may be fractured.

> **HAYNES HiNT** *Ensure that the leads are numbered before removing them, to avoid confusion when refitting*

23 Check inside the end fitting for signs of corrosion, which will look like a white crusty powder. Push the end fitting back onto the spark plug, ensuring that it is a tight fit on the plug. If not, remove the lead again and use pliers to carefully crimp the metal connector inside the end fitting until it fits securely on the end of the spark plug.

24 Using a clean rag, wipe the entire length of the lead to remove any built-up dirt and grease. Once the lead is clean, check for burns, cracks and other damage. Do not bend the lead too much, nor pull the lead lengthways - the conductor inside might break.

25 Disconnect the other end of the lead from the distributor cap. Again, pull only on the end fitting. Check for corrosion and a tight fit in the same manner as the spark plug end. If an ohmmeter is available, check the resistance of the lead by connecting the meter between the spark plug end of the lead and the segment inside the distributor cap. Refit the lead securely on completion.

26 Check the remaining leads one at a time, in the same way. Do not forget to check the king lead, which runs from the centre terminal of the distributor cap to the coil.

27 If new spark plug (HT) leads are required, buy a set for your specific car and engine.

Distributor cap

28 Release the spring clips and remove the distributor cap **(see illustrations)**. Wipe it clean, and carefully inspect it inside and out for signs of cracks, black carbon tracks (tracking) and worn, burned or loose contacts; check that the cap's carbon brush is unworn,

free to move against spring pressure, and making good contact with the rotor arm.

> **HAYNES HiNT** *When fitting a new cap, remove the leads from the old cap one at a time, and fit them to the new cap in the same location*

29 Do not simultaneously remove all the leads from the old cap, or firing order confusion may occur. When refitting, tighten the cap retaining screws securely, or ensure that the cap clips engage correctly.

30 Even with the ignition system in first-class condition, some engines may still occasionally experience poor starting attributable to damp ignition components. To disperse moisture, a water-dispersant aerosol should be applied.

Rotor arm

31 With reference to the previous sub-Section, remove the distributor cap.

32 Inspect the rotor arm; it is common practice to renew the cap and rotor arm whenever new spark plug (HT) leads are fitted. However, on 1.3 litre models, the rotor arm is bonded to the distributor shaft, and will probably be damaged if an attempt is made to remove it - refer to a Skoda dealer for advice. On 1.6 litre models, the rotor arm can be pulled off the shaft **(see illustration)**.

2.32 Removing the rotor arm from the end of the distributor shaft

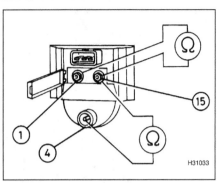

2.36 Ignition coil resistance test points

1   LT '–' terminal   15 LT '+' terminal
4   HT terminal

33 Check the condition of the rotor arm contacts - one in the centre of the arm, for the distributor cap carbon contact, and one in the end of the arm, which contacts the distributor cap segments for each HT lead. Clean off any carbon deposits using fine emery paper, and wipe the rotor arm clean.

34 Refitting is a reversal of removal - ensure that the rotor arm alignment lug engages with the recess in the distributor shaft, before refitting the distributor cap.

Ignition coil

35 Disconnect the LT wiring plug and the HT (king) lead from the ignition coil.

36 Connect a multimeter between terminals 1(–) and 15(+), and check that the resistance of the primary windings is as given in the Specifications **(see illustration)**.

37 Connect the multimeter between terminals 4 (HT) and 15(+), and check that the resistance of the secondary windings is as given in the Specifications.

38 Reconnect the wiring.

39 If the coil body is hot to the touch after the engine has been running, this may indicate an internal insulation fault.

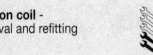

3 Ignition coil - removal and refitting

Removal

1 Ensure that the ignition is switched off, then disconnect the battery negative lead and position it away from the terminal.

Bosch Mono-Motronic

2 The ignition coil is mounted at the front of

the right-hand inner wing, adjacent to the distributor.

3 Disconnect the LT wiring plug and the HT lead from the coil **(see illustration)**.

4 Unscrew and remove the mounting bolts, and remove the coil.

Simos 2P

5 The ignition coil unit is fitted over the four spark plugs, at the front of the engine.

6 Disconnect the wiring plug from the end of the coil unit **(see illustration)**.

7 Unscrew and remove the two socket-head bolts underneath the unit **(see illustrations)**.

8 Pull the unit off the spark plugs - do not pull sharply upwards, or the spark plugs may be damaged **(see illustration)**.

Magneti-Marelli 1AV

9 The ignition coil is fitted to the left-hand inner wing, adjacent to the ECU.

10 Disconnect the LT wiring plug and the HT lead from the coil.

11 Unscrew and remove the mounting nuts/bolts, and remove the coil and mounting plate.

Refitting

12 Refitting is a reversal of removal. Ensure that all wiring connections are correctly and securely remade.

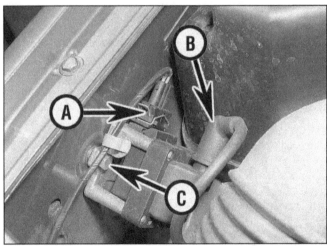

3.3 Ignition coil LT wiring plug (A), HT lead (B) and one of the mounting bolts (C)

3.6 Disconnect the wiring plug from the coil unit

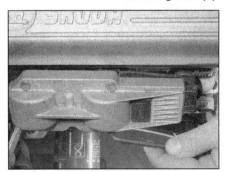

3.7a Using an Allen key . . .

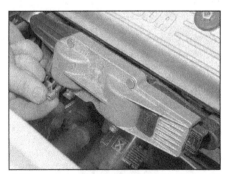

3.7b . . . unscrew and remove the two coil unit mounting bolts

3.8 Pull the coil unit evenly off the spark plugs, and remove it

4.9 Distributor/extension tube clamp nut and alignment index marks

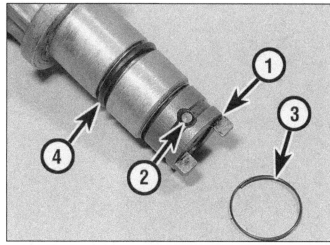

4.11 Distributor drive coupling (1), retaining pin (2), spring (3) and O-ring seal (4)

4 Distributor - removal and refitting

Note: *This Section does not apply to the Simos distributorless system.*

Removal

1 Disconnect the battery negative lead and position it away from the terminal.
2 Set the engine to TDC on cylinder No 1, referring to Chapter 2A or B as applicable.

4.12 Disconnecting the distributor cap earth braid

3 If required, unplug all five HT leads from the distributor cap, labelling them to aid refitting later. It is preferable, however, to remove the distributor cap with all leads attached - the leads can then be transferred one at a time to a new cap, if one is being fitted.

Bosch Mono-Motronic

4 Release the retaining clips, detach the distributor cap and position it out of the way.
5 Mark the base of the distributor in relation to the engine block, as a reference for refitting.
6 The distributor can be removed and refitted in one of two ways, according to preference. It can either be removed complete with the extension tube, or separately. The latter method is preferable.
7 To remove the distributor complete with the extension tube, undo the two extension tube flange-to-timing cover retaining bolts, then withdraw the distributor and tube from the timing cover.
8 As the distributor and tube are withdrawn, it will be noted that the rotor will turn as the shaft pinion disengages from the helical drive gear on the camshaft. Note the final position of the rotor once the distributor is withdrawn, to provide a guide to the required preset position when refitting.

9 To detach the distributor from the extension tube, first mark their relative positions to ensure correct timing when refitting, then slacken the clamp nut and bolt, and withdraw the distributor **(see illustration)**.
10 Do not disturb the crankshaft setting while the distributor is removed, nor rotate the distributor shaft.
11 Remove the O-ring seal from the groove in the distributor; this must be renewed whenever it is disturbed **(see illustration)**.

Magneti-Marelli 1AV

12 Unplug the earth braid from the metal screening cap **(see illustration)**.
13 Unplug the Hall sensor wiring connector from the distributor body **(see illustration)**.
14 Release the retaining clips, detach the distributor cap and position it out of the way **(see illustrations)**.
15 Check at this point that the centre of the rotor arm electrode is aligned with the cylinder No 1 marking on the distributor body.
16 Mark the relationship between the distributor body and the mounting flange by scribing arrows on each, or painting an alignment mark between them **(see illustration)**.

4.13 Unplug the Hall sensor cable from the distributor body at the connector

4.14a Using a suitable screwdriver, release the spring clips . . .

4.14b . . . and lift away the distributor cap

4.16 Alignment marks (arrowed) painted between distributor body and mounting flange

4.17a Loosen the clamp bolts (arrowed) using an Allen key . . .

17 Slacken and remove the clamp bolts, then withdraw the distributor body from the cylinder head. It may be necessary to work the distributor from side to side, to release the large O-ring seal **(see illustrations)**.

18 Recover the O-ring seal from the bottom of the distributor and inspect it. Renew the seal if it appears at all worn or damaged.

Refitting

Bosch Mono-Motronic

19 First check that No 1 cylinder is still at TDC. Turn the distributor shaft to align the rotor arm tip with the notch in the top rim of the distributor body. If the extension tube is still on the engine, check that the distributor drive dog aligns with the engagement slot of the extension shaft **(see illustration)**. If refitting the distributor and extension tube as an assembly, align the rotor arm to the pre-setting position noted during removal (paragraph 8).

20 With the index marks in alignment, refit the distributor. If necessary, turn the rotor arm very slightly to allow the drive dog or the gear teeth to mesh. Refit the mounting bolts and tighten them to the specified torque.

21 Refit the distributor cap, ensuring that it is correctly located, then reconnect the HT leads between the spark plugs and the distributor cap. The firing order is 1-3-4-2.

22 Fit the HT king lead between the coil and the centre terminal on the distributor cap.

23 If a new distributor is accurately fitted, the ignition timing should be very close to the optimum setting. However, the setting should be checked by a Skoda dealer at the earliest opportunity.

Magneti-Marelli 1AV

24 First check that No 1 cylinder is still at TDC. Install the distributor, engaging its drive dog with the hole in the camshaft drive flange, and loosely fit the clamp bolts. Rotate the distributor body such that the alignment marks made during removal line up. The centre of the rotor arm electrode should point directly at the No 1 cylinder mark on the distributor body **(see illustration)**.

25 Refit the distributor cap, pressing the retaining clips firmly into place.

26 Reconnect the Hall sensor wiring to the distributor.

27 Refit the screening cap earth braid.

28 Working from the No 1 terminal, connect the HT leads between the spark plugs and the distributor cap. The firing order is 1-3-4-2.

29 Fit the HT king lead between the coil and the centre terminal on the distributor cap.

30 If a new distributor is accurately fitted, the ignition timing should be very close to the optimum setting. However, the setting should be checked by a Skoda dealer at the earliest opportunity.

5 Ignition timing - checking and adjusting

The ignition timing is under the control of the engine management system ECU, and cannot be set manually (at least not to the required accuracy) without access to dedicated electronic test equipment. A basic setting cannot be quoted because the ignition timing is constantly being altered to control engine idle speed (see Section 1 for details).

The vehicle must be taken to a Skoda dealer if the timing requires checking or adjustment.

6 Ignition system sensors - removal and refitting

1 Many of the engine management system sensors provide signals for both the fuel injection and ignition systems. Those specific to the ignition system are detailed in this Section.

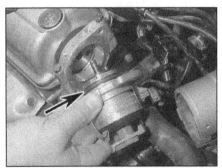

4.17b . . . and remove the distributor - note the large O-ring seal (arrowed)

4.19 Extension shaft position - No 1 cylinder at TDC

4.24 Rotor arm contact aligned with raised notch in distributor body (arrowed)

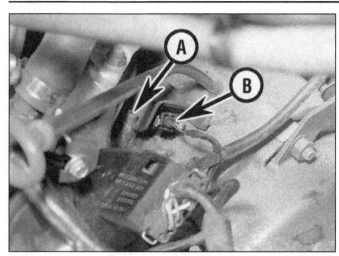

6.4a Knock sensor heat shield bolt (A) and wiring plug (B) -
1.3 litre engine

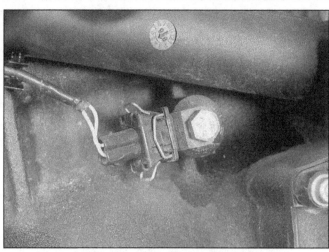

6.4b Knock sensor and wiring plug (1.6 litre engine) -
seen with engine removed, for clarity

2 Those sensors that are common to both systems are detailed in Chapter 4A or 4B. These include the coolant temperature sensor, the inlet air temperature/pressure sensor, and the throttle potentiometer and idle switch (incorporated in the throttle valve positioner module).

Knock sensor

Removal

3 Disconnect the battery negative lead and position it away from the terminal.
4 The knock sensor is mounted on the rear of the cylinder block; access to the sensor is poor from above (especially on 1.6 litre models). Where a heat shield is fitted,

unscrew the socket-head bolt and remove the shield **(see illustrations)**.
5 Unplug the harness wiring from the sensor at the connector.
6 Slacken and withdraw the mounting bolt and lift off the sensor.

Refitting

7 Refitting is a reversal of removal, but note that the sensor's operation will be affected if its mounting bolt is not tightened to exactly the specified torque.

Hall sensor

Bosch Mono-Motronic

8 The Hall sensor is mounted on top of the transmission housing.
9 Separate the three-pin wiring connector which is located in a bracket attached to the thermostat housing. Slide the wiring plug out of the bracket **(see illustrations)**.
10 Unscrew the retaining bolt from the transmission housing, and withdraw the sensor **(see illustrations)**. Check the sensor tip for signs of damage or dirt build-up.

6.9a Disconnect the sensor multi-plug . . .

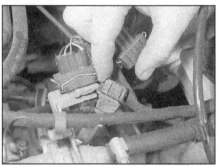

6.9b . . . then slide the lower half of the plug out of the mounting bracket

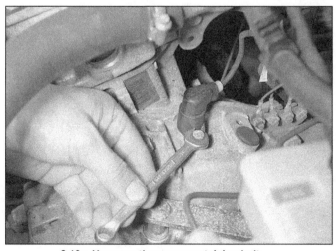

6.10a Unscrew the sensor retaining bolt . . .

6.10b . . . then withdraw the sensor from the transmission

6.12a On the Simos system, the Hall sensor plug is on top of the sensor . . .

6.12b . . . disconnect the plug . . .

6.12c . . . then unbolt and withdraw the sensor from the transmission

11 Refitting is a reversal of removal. Clean the sensor tip before fitting the sensor into the transmission housing, and tighten the bolt to the specified torque.

Simos 2P

12 Removal and refitting of the Hall sensor is as described for the Mono-Motronic system in paragraphs 8 to 11, except that the wiring connector is situated directly on top of the sensor itself, rather than in a bracket **(see illustrations)**.

Magneti-Marelli 1AV

13 The sensor is an integral part of the distributor assembly. It can be removed and renewed separately, but dismantling of the distributor will be necessary. It is therefore recommended that this operation is entrusted to an automotive electrical specialist.

Chapter 5 Part C:
Pre-heating system - diesel models

Contents

Degrees of difficulty

Easy, suitable for novice with little experience		Fairly easy, suitable for beginner with some experience		Fairly difficult, suitable for competent DIY mechanic		Difficult, suitable for experienced DIY mechanic		Very difficult, suitable for expert DIY or professional	

Specifications

Glow plugs
Electrical resistance .... 1.5 ohms (approx)
Current consumption .... 8 amps (per glow plug)

Torque wrench setting	Nm	lbf ft
Glow plugs	25	18

1 General information

To assist cold starting, diesel-engined models are fitted with a pre-heating system, which comprises four glow plugs, a control unit, a facia-mounted warning light and the associated electrical wiring.

The glow plugs are miniature electric heating elements, encapsulated in a metal case, with a probe at one end and electrical connection at the other. Each swirl chamber/inlet tract has a glow plug threaded into it, the glow plug probe being positioned directly in line with incoming spray of fuel. When the glow plug is energised, the fuel passing over it is heated, allowing its optimum combustion temperature to be achieved more readily when it reaches the cylinder.

The duration of the pre-heating period is governed by a control unit (see Chapter 4C, Section 1), which monitors the temperature of the engine via the coolant temperature sensor, and alters the pre-heating time to suit the conditions.

A facia-mounted warning light informs the driver that pre-heating is taking place. The light extinguishes when sufficient pre-heating has taken place to allow the engine to be started, but power will still be supplied to the glow plugs for a further period until the engine is started. If no attempt is made to start the engine, the power supply to the glow plugs is switched off to prevent battery drain and glow plug burn-out. Note that on certain models, the warning light will also illuminate during normal driving if a pre-heating system malfunction occurs.

Generally, pre-heating is triggered by the ignition key being turned to the second position. However, Felicia models are additionally equipped with a pre-heating system that activates when the driver's door is opened, and then shut. Note that the system only functions once each time the engine is started - if the driver's door is opened, shut, and then no attempt is made to start the vehicle within a certain period, subsequent opening and shutting of the door will not reset the system. Refer to the vehicle

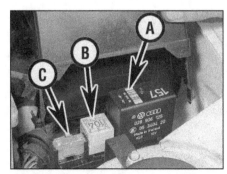

2.3 Diesel/glow plug control unit (A), glow plug relay (B) and glow plug supply fuse (C)

handbook for further information.

After the engine has been started, the glow plugs continue to operate for up to 3 minutes (afterglow or post-heating). This helps to improve fuel combustion whilst the engine is warming up, resulting in quieter, smoother running and reduced exhaust emissions.

2 Glow plug control system components - removal and refitting

Removal

Control unit

1 The control unit is located on a bracket at the rear of the left-hand inner wing, next to the glow plug relay.
2 Disconnect the battery negative lead and position it away from the terminal.
3 Where applicable, release the securing clips and lift off the plastic cover (see illustration).
4 Unplug the control unit and remove it from the mounting bracket.

Relay

5 Removal of the glow plug relay is as described in paragraphs 2 to 4 above.

Refitting

6 Refitting is a reversal of removal. Ensure that all wiring connections are securely made.

3.6 Glow plug and supply cable retaining nut (arrowed) - coolant temperature sensor disconnected

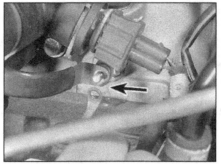

3.13a Supply cable (arrowed) removed from No 4 cylinder glow plug

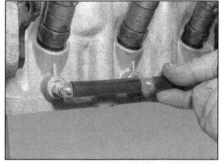

3.13b Remove the nuts and washers from the glow plug terminal. Lift off the bus bar/supply cable

3 Glow plugs -
testing, removal and refitting

Testing

1 If the system malfunctions, testing is ultimately by substitution of known good units, or by taking the vehicle to a Skoda dealer to have the control unit fault code memory interrogated using diagnostic equipment. Some preliminary checks may be made as described in the following paragraphs.

2 Check the two system fuses located in the bracket containing the glow plug relay at the left rear of the engine compartment. One is a 5-amp fuse, and the larger one is rated 50 amps. If the 50-amp fuse has blown, this would indicate a serious wiring fault - on no account replace this fuse (in particular) more than once without establishing the reason for it failing, and don't substitute anything else, or you could have an electrical fire.

3 Disconnect the wiring plug from the coolant temperature sensor. This simulates a cold engine, and will ensure that the pre-heating system operates. **Note:** *Switching on the ignition with the coolant temperature sensor disconnected will cause the control unit to register a fault code, which would then have to be erased by a Skoda dealer, using diagnostic equipment. If preferred, leave the temperature sensor connected and perform*

this test when the engine is cold.
4 Connect a voltmeter or 12-volt test light between the glow plug supply cable and a good earth point on the engine.
*Caution: **Make sure that the live connection is kept well clear of the engine and bodywork.***
5 Have an assistant activate the pre-heating system (either using the ignition key, or opening the driver's door, as applicable) and check that a battery voltage is applied to the glow plug electrical connection. (Note that the voltage will drop to zero when the pre-heating period ends).
6 If no supply voltage can be detected at the glow plug, then either the glow plug relay or the supply cabling must be faulty **(see illustration)**.
7 To locate a faulty glow plug, first disconnect the battery negative lead and position it away from the terminal.
8 Refer to the next sub-Section and remove the supply cabling from the glow plug terminal. Measure the electrical resistance between the glow plug terminal and the engine earth. A reading of anything more than a few ohms indicates that the plug is defective.
9 If a suitable ammeter is available, connect it between the glow plug and its supply cable. Temporarily reconnect the battery negative lead.
10 If possible, start the engine as normal, and with the engine idling (in the post-heating period) measure the steady-state current

consumption (ignore the initial current surge, which will be about 50% higher). Compare the result with the Specifications. Each plug will draw 8 amps, so a reading of 32 amps indicates all four plugs are satisfactory; 24 amps would show that one plug is suspect, 16 amps would mean two plugs suspect, and so on.
11 As a final check, remove the glow plugs and inspect them visually, as described in the next sub-Section.

Removal

12 If not already done, disconnect the battery negative lead and position it away from the terminal.
13 Remove the nuts and washers from the glow plug terminal. Lift off the bus bar/supply cable **(see illustrations)**.
14 Slacken and withdraw the glow plug **(see illustration)**.
15 Inspect the glow plug probe for signs of damage. A badly burned or charred probe is usually an indication of a faulty fuel injector - refer to Chapter 4C.

> ⚠ *Warning: Under no circumstances should the glow plugs be tested outside the engine. A correctly-functioning glow plug will become red-hot in a very short time!*

Refitting

16 Refitting is a reversal of removal. Tighten the glow plugs to the specified torque **(see illustration)**, and reconnect the coolant temperature sensor wiring plug (where applicable) on completion.

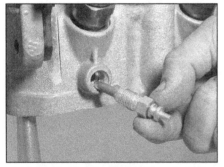

3.14 Slacken and withdraw the glow plug (seen with cylinder head removed)

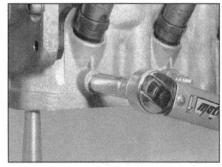

3.16 Tighten the glow plug to the specified torque

Chapter 6
Clutch

Contents

Degrees of difficulty

Easy, suitable for novice with little experience	Fairly easy, suitable for beginner with some experience	Fairly difficult, suitable for competent DIY mechanic	Difficult, suitable for experienced DIY mechanic	Very difficult, suitable for expert DIY or professional

Specifications

Type . . . . Single dry plate with diaphragm spring, cable-operated

Torque wrench settings	Nm	lbf ft
Pressure plate retaining bolts	25	18
Release fork retaining bolt	25	18

1 General information

1 The clutch consists of a friction plate, a pressure plate assembly, a release bearing and the release mechanism; all of these components are contained in the large cast-aluminium alloy bellhousing, sandwiched between the engine and the transmission. The clutch release mechanism is cable-operated.
2 The friction plate is fitted between the engine flywheel and the clutch pressure plate, and is allowed to slide on the transmission input shaft splines.
3 The pressure plate assembly is bolted to the engine flywheel. When the engine is running, drive is transmitted from the crankshaft, via the flywheel, to the friction plate (these components being clamped securely together by the pressure plate assembly) and from the friction plate to the transmission input shaft.
4 To interrupt the drive, the spring pressure must be relaxed. Depressing the clutch pedal pulls the control cable inner wire, and this rotates the release fork by acting on the lever at the fork's upper end. The release fork then presses the release bearing against the pressure plate spring fingers. This causes the springs to deform and releases the clamping force on the pressure plate. To ensure correct operation, the clutch must be regularly adjusted.

2 Clutch pedal - removal and refitting

Right-hand drive models

Note: *It is possible to change the clutch pedal pivot bushes without removing the pedal assembly (access is poor though). Extract the split pin from either side of the pedal pivot and slide back the thrustwashers to enable the pivot bushes to be freed from the pedal bore and removed from the brake pedal shaft. Lubricate the new bushes with multi-purpose grease (Skoda recommend the use of Litol 24 or G000062 grease - available from your dealer) and fit them to brake pedal shaft.*

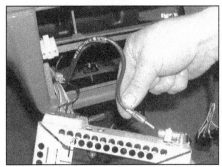

2.3a Disconnect the aerial lead . . .

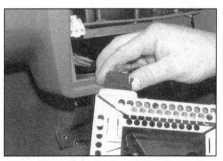

2.3b . . . then unclip the wiring connector and remove the radio/cassette unit frame from the facia

2.5 Unhook the assist spring (arrowed) from the clutch pedal

Locate both bushes correctly in the pedal bore and secure the pedal in position with two new split pins, ensuring the thrustwashers are correctly positioned between the pedal and pins. On completion check the cable adjustment as described in Section 3.

2.6 Unhook the cable (arrowed) from the upper end of the accelerator pedal

Removal

1 Working in the engine compartment, disconnect the battery negative terminal then locate the transmission end of the clutch cable and fully slacken the adjuster nut to obtain maximum freeplay in the cable.

2 Remove the centre console as described in Chapter 11.

3 Remove the radio/cassette unit (see Chapter 12) then bend back the retaining tangs and slide the unit mounting frame out from the facia. Disconnect the aerial lead and unclip the wiring connector then remove the mounting frame from the vehicle **(see illustrations)**.

4 Unclip the duct linking the base of the heater/ventilation housing to the rear footwell duct and remove it from the vehicle.

5 Unhook the assist spring from the clutch pedal **(see illustration)**. Reach up behind the facia and remove the clutch cable retaining

clip from the pedal then free the cable end fitting from its pivot.

6 Unhook the accelerator cable from the upper end of the pedal **(see illustration)**.

7 Disconnect the wiring connectors from the stop-light switch which is screwed into the top of the pedal assembly right-hand mounting bracket **(see illustration)**.

8 Working in the passenger footwell, remove the retaining clip then remove the trim cover from the pedal assembly left-hand mounting bracket. The fastener is released by pressing out its centre pin then prising it out of position **(see illustrations)**.

9 Remove the retaining clip and slide out the clevis pin securing the braking system servo unit pushrod to the pedal linkage **(see illustration)**.

10 Undo the retaining nuts and remove the accelerator pedal stop and the footrest from the left-hand side of the clutch pedal **(see illustrations)**.

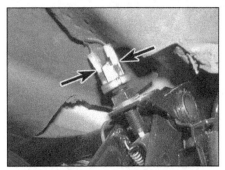

2.7 Disconnect the wiring connectors (arrowed) from the stop-light switch

2.8a Press out the centre pin then remove the fastener . . .

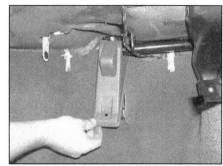

2.8b . . . and lift off the trim cover from the pedal assembly left-hand bracket

2.9 Remove the retaining clip and slide out the clevis pin securing the servo unit pushrod to the pedal linkage

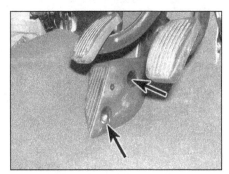

2.10a Undo the retaining nuts (arrowed) and remove the footrest . . .

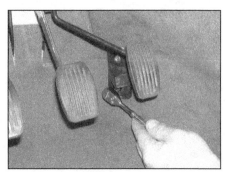

2.10b . . . and accelerator pedal stop from the driver's side footwell

11 Release the retaining clips and peel back the carpet from the bulkhead to gain access to the pedal bracket lower mounting nuts (see illustration).
12 Slacken and remove the nuts securing the pedal assembly left- and right-hand mounting brackets in position (see illustration). Recover the lower mounting plates from the engine compartment.
13 Manoeuvre the pedal assembly out of position and remove it from the vehicle.
14 With the assembly on a bench, carefully unhook the brake pedal return spring from behind the servo unit lever. Remove the circlips from the brake pedal shaft and separate the mounting brackets, pivot bushes and return spring from the pedal assembly. No further dismantling is possible; the clutch pedal and brake pedal are supplied as an assembly (the pivot bushes and split pins are available separately to enable renewal - see note at the start of this Section).

Refitting

15 Refitting is the reverse of removal, noting the following points.
  a) Lubricate the pivot bushes and clevis pin with multi-purpose grease (Skoda recommend the use of Litol 24 or G000062 grease - available from your dealer).
  b) Reconnect the accelerator cable to the pedal and check the cable adjustment as described in the relevant part of Chapter 4.
  c) Reconnect the clutch cable and adjust as described in Section 3.
  d) On completion reconnect the battery and check the operation of the stop-light switch (see Chapter 9 for details).

Left-hand drive models

Removal

16 Working in the engine compartment, disconnect the battery negative terminal then locate the transmission end of the clutch cable and fully slacken the adjuster nut to obtain maximum freeplay in the cable.
17 Unhook the assist spring from the clutch pedal. Reach up behind the facia and remove the clutch cable retaining clip from the pedal then free the cable end fitting from its pivot.
18 Slide off the retaining clip from the end of the pedal pivot shaft then slide the pedal out of position and remove it from the mounting bracket, complete with the assist spring.
19 Inspect the pedal for signs of wear or damage and renew if necessary. The pedal pivot bush also doubles as the brake pedal pivot. If the bush is to be renewed it will be necessary to firmly support the brake pedal whilst the original is slid out of position and the new one installed.

Refitting

20 Fit the assist spring to the clutch pedal then lubricate the pivot shaft and bush with multi-purpose grease (Skoda recommend the use of Litol 24 or G000062 grease - available from your dealer).

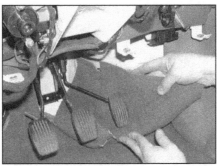

2.11 Fold back the carpet to gain access to the pedal mounting bracket lower nuts

21 Slide the pedal into position, making sure the assist spring remains correctly positioned, and secure it in position with the retaining clip.
22 Lubricate the clutch cable end fitting with multi-purpose grease then reconnect the cable to the pedal, securing it in position with the retaining clip.
23 Hook the assist spring over the pedal then adjust the clutch cable as described in Section 3. On completion reconnect the battery.

3   **Clutch cable -**
     removal, refitting
     and adjustment

Removal

1 Disconnect the battery negative terminal.
2 From inside the vehicle, reach up behind the facia and unhook the assist spring from the clutch cable. Remove the retaining clip from the top of the pedal and free the cable end fitting from its pivot.
3 Return to the engine compartment and locate the transmission end of the clutch cable.
4 On right-hand drive models, remove the locking clip from the inner cable then unscrew the adjuster nut and remove the end fittings and rubber spacer from the cable end (see illustration). Free the outer cable from the mounting bracket and slide off the rubber gaiter, locating collar, rubber spacer and washer.
5 On left-hand drive models, remove the locking clip from the inner cable then unscrew the adjuster nut and remove the washer, rubber spacer and locating collar from the cable end. Free the outer cable from the release lever and remove the end fitting, rubber spacer and locating collar.
6 On all models, work back along the cable, releasing it from all the necessary retaining clips whilst noting its correct routing. Free the clutch from the bulkhead and remove it from the vehicle, recovering the locating collar and sealing grommet from its bulkhead end.
7 Examine the cable, looking for worn end fittings or a damaged outer casing, and for signs of fraying of the inner wire. Check the cable's operation; the inner wire should move smoothly and easily through the outer casing.

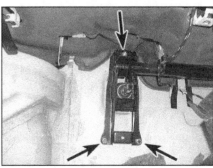

2.12 Slacken and remove the upper and lower mounting nuts then manoeuvre the pedal linkage assembly out of position

Remember that a cable that appears serviceable when tested off the car may well be much heavier in operation when in its working position. Renew the cable if it shows signs of excessive wear or any damage.

Refitting

8 Apply a thin smear of multi-purpose grease to the cable end fittings then slide the locating collar and sealing grommet onto the bulkhead end of the cable.
9 Manoeuvre the cable into position and pass the cable through the engine compartment bulkhead, making sure the grommet and locating sleeve are correctly located.
10 From inside the vehicle, hook the cable end fitting onto the clutch pedal and secure it in position with the retaining clip.
11 Return to the engine compartment and ensure that the cable is correctly routed and retained by all the relevant retaining clips and guides.
12 On right-hand drive models, slide the washer, rubber spacer, locating collar and rubber gaiter onto the transmission end of the cable. Locate the collar correctly in the mounting bracket then fit the inner end fitting, rubber spacer and outer end fitting onto the cable. Ensure all components are correctly positioned then screw the adjuster nut onto the cable end.
13 On left-hand drive models, slide the locating collar, rubber spacer and end fitting onto the cable and seat the cable assembly in the release lever. Fit the locating collar, rubber spacer and washer onto the cable then ensure

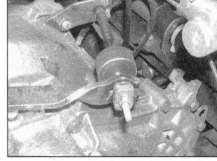

3.4 The clutch cable adjuster nut is located on the top of the transmission unit

all components are correctly located and screw the adjuster nut onto the cable end.

14 Reconnect the battery then hook the assist spring back onto/over the clutch pedal before adjusting the cable as follows.

Adjustment

15 The clutch cable adjustment is set by checking the clutch pedal height in relation to the brake pedal. If the cable is correctly adjusted the clutch pedal should be level with the brake pedal (±3 mm) and there should be no freeplay in the cable. If adjustment is necessary, proceed as follows.

16 Working in the engine compartment, locate the end of the clutch cable which is situated on the top of the transmission unit.

17 Remove the locating clip from the inner cable and adjust the clutch pedal height by rotating the adjuster nut on the threaded end of the cable. Once the cable is correctly adjusted, refit the locating clip to the end of the inner cable ensuring that it is tight against the release lever/mounting bracket (as applicable).

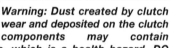

4 Clutch assembly - removal, inspection and refitting

⚠️ *Warning: Dust created by clutch wear and deposited on the clutch components may contain asbestos, which is a health hazard. DO NOT blow it out with compressed air, or inhale any of it. DO NOT use petrol or petroleum-based solvents to clean off the dust. Brake system cleaner or methylated spirit should be used to flush the dust into a suitable receptacle. After the clutch components are wiped clean with rags, dispose of the contaminated rags and cleaner in a sealed, marked container.*
Note: *Although some friction materials may no longer contain asbestos, it is safest to assume that they do, and to take precautions accordingly.*

4.2 Prior to removal, make alignment marks between the pressure plate and flywheel

Removal

1 Unless the complete engine/transmission unit is to be removed from the car and separated for major overhaul (see Chapter 2D), the clutch can be reached by removing the transmission as described in Chapter 7.

2 Before disturbing the clutch, use a dab of paint or a marker pen to mark the relationship of the pressure plate assembly to the flywheel **(see illustration)**.

3 Working in a diagonal sequence, slacken the pressure plate bolts by half a turn at a time, until spring pressure is released and the bolts can be unscrewed by hand.

4 Prise the pressure plate assembly off its locating dowels (where fitted), and collect the friction plate, noting which way round the friction plate is fitted **(see illustrations)**.

Inspection

Note: *Due to the amount of work necessary to remove and refit clutch components, it is usually considered good practice to renew the clutch friction plate, pressure plate assembly and release bearing as a matched set, even if only one of these is actually worn enough to require renewal. It is also worth considering the renewal of the clutch components on a preventive basis if the engine and/or transmission have been removed for some other reason.*

5 Remove the clutch assembly.

6 When cleaning clutch components, read first the warning at the beginning of this Section; remove dust using a clean, dry cloth, and working in a well-ventilated atmosphere.

7 Check the friction plate facings for signs of wear, damage or oil contamination. If the friction material is cracked, burnt, scored or damaged, or if it is contaminated with oil or grease (shown by shiny black patches), the friction plate must be renewed. No measurements are given by Skoda to judge the amount of friction plate wear which has taken place. As a guide, if the rivet heads are less than 0.3 mm below the friction material surface the plate can be considered worn and should be renewed. Seek the advice of your Skoda dealer if there is any doubt about the plate condition.

8 If the friction material is still serviceable, check that the centre boss splines are unworn, that the torsion springs are in good condition and securely fastened, and that all the rivets are tight. If any wear or damage is found, the friction plate must be renewed.

9 If the friction material is fouled with oil, this must be due to an oil leak from the crankshaft left-hand oil seal, from the sump-to-cylinder block joint, or from the transmission input shaft. Renew the seal or repair the joint, as appropriate, as described in the relevant part of Chapter 2 or Chapter 7, before installing the new friction plate.

10 Check the pressure plate assembly for obvious signs of wear or damage; shake it to check for loose rivets or worn or damaged fulcrum rings, and check that the drive straps securing the pressure plate to the cover do not show signs (such as a deep yellow or blue discoloration) of overheating. Check the diaphragm spring fingers for signs of wear or damage and check that the height of each finger above the pressure plate machined face. If the finger height exceeds the specified service limit or the diaphragm spring is worn or damaged, or if its pressure is in any way suspect, the pressure plate assembly should be renewed.

4.4a Remove the pressure plate from the flywheel . . .

4.4b . . . and withdraw the friction plate, noting which way around it is fitted

4.19 Centralise the friction plate with a clutch aligning tool then tighten the pressure plate retaining bolts to the specified torque in a diagonal sequence

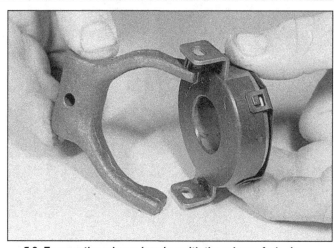

5.9 Engage the release bearing with the release fork pin . . .

11 Examine the machined bearing surfaces of the pressure plate and of the flywheel; they should be clean, completely flat, and free from scratches or scoring. If either is discoloured from excessive heat, or shows signs of cracks, it should be renewed - although minor damage of this nature can sometimes be polished away using emery paper. Using a straight edge and feeler blades check the pressure plate surface for warpage at several points around its diameter, if the warpage exceeds the specified limit the plate must be renewed.

12 Check that the release bearing contact surface rotates smoothly and easily, with no sign of noise or roughness. Also check that the surface itself is smooth and unworn, with no signs of cracks, pitting or scoring. If there is any doubt about its condition, the bearing must be renewed.

Refitting

13 On reassembly, ensure that the bearing surfaces of the flywheel and pressure plate are completely clean, smooth, and free from oil or grease. Use solvent to remove any protective grease from new components.

14 Apply a very thin film of high-temperature grease (Skoda recommend the use of Kluber Microlube GL202, GL261 or GL262 or alternatively Mobil lithium 932 or 933 - available from your Skoda dealer) to the splines of the clutch friction plate taking care not to contaminate the friction material. Ensure all excess grease is removed to avoid the possibility of the friction material becoming contaminated in use.

15 Fit the friction plate so that its spring hub assembly faces away from the flywheel; there may also be a marking showing which way round the plate is to be refitted.

16 Refit the pressure plate assembly, aligning the marks made on dismantling (if the original pressure plate is re-used). Where necessary, ensure the plate is correctly located on its dowels. Fit the pressure plate

bolts, but tighten them only finger-tight, so that the friction plate can still be moved.

17 The friction plate must now be centralised, so that when the transmission is refitted, its input shaft will pass through the splines at the centre of the friction plate.

18 Centralisation can be achieved by passing a screwdriver or other long bar through the friction plate and into the hole in the crankshaft; the friction plate can then be moved around until it is centred on the crankshaft hole. Alternatively, a clutch-aligning -tool can be used to eliminate the guesswork; these can be obtained from most accessory shops. A home-made aligning tool can be fabricated from a length of metal rod or wooden dowel which fits closely inside the crankshaft hole, and has insulating tape wound around it to match the diameter of the friction plate splined hole.

19 When the friction plate is centralised, tighten the pressure plate bolts evenly and in a diagonal sequence to the specified torque setting **(see illustration)**. Ensure the pressure plate is drawn squarely onto the flywheel, to prevent the pressure plate being distorted.

20 Refit the transmission as described in Chapter 7.

5 Clutch release mechanism - removal, inspection and refitting

Note: *Refer to the warning concerning the dangers of asbestos dust at the beginning of Section 4.*

Removal

1 Unless the complete engine/transmission unit is to be removed from the car and separated for major overhaul (see Chapter 2D), the clutch release mechanism can be reached by removing the transmission only, as described in Chapter 7.

2 Slacken and remove the retaining bolt and

washer securing the release fork to the lever shaft.

3 Unhook the spring from the top of the shaft then withdraw the lever from the transmission housing. Remove the release fork and bearing assembly, noting which way around the fork is fitted, then separate the two components.

Inspection

4 Check the release mechanism, renewing any component which is worn or damaged. Carefully check all bearing surfaces and points of contact.

5 When checking the release bearing itself, note that it is often considered worthwhile to renew it as a matter of course. Check that the contact surface rotates smoothly and easily, with no sign of noise or roughness, and that the surface itself is smooth and unworn, with no signs of cracks, pitting or scoring. If there is any doubt about its condition, the bearing must be renewed.

6 If the release lever shaft bush is worn it can be renewed. Tap the old bush out of position with a hammer and punch and tap the new one into position using a socket, which bears only on the bush outer edge, as a drift.

Refitting

7 Ensure all components are clean and dry and remove all traces of locking compound from the release fork and retaining bolt threads. Ensure the release lever shaft bush is correctly seated in the transmission housing.

8 Apply a thin smear of high-temperature grease (Skoda recommend the use of Kluber Microlube GL202, GL261 or GL262 or alternatively Mobil lithium 932 or 933 - available from your Skoda dealer) to the contact areas of the release lever shaft, release fork and release bearing. Do not apply excess grease as there is a risk that the clutch friction material may be contaminated.

9 Assembly the release bearing and fork, ensuring the fork is the right way around, and locate the fork upper pin in the release bearing slot **(see illustration)**.

5.10a ... then slide the bearing and fork assembly onto the guide sleeve and insert the release lever, aligning its hole with that of the fork

5.10b Apply a drop of locking compound to the threads of the release fork bolt before refitting it and tightening to the specified torque

10 Slide the release fork and bearing assembly onto the transmission guide sleeve then insert the release lever. Apply a drop of locking compound (Skoda recommend the use of Three bond or Aldurit - available from your Skoda dealer) to the retaining bolt threads then align the lever shaft hole with the fork and screw in the retaining bolt and washer **(see illustrations)**. Ensure the bolt is correctly aligned with the shaft hole then tighten it to the specified torque.

11 Hook the spring onto the top of the release lever and check the operation of the mechanism before refitting the transmission as described in Chapter 7.

Chapter 7
Manual transmission

Contents

Degrees of difficulty

Easy, suitable for novice with little experience	Fairly easy, suitable for beginner with some experience	Fairly difficult, suitable for competent DIY mechanic	Difficult, suitable for experienced DIY mechanic	Very difficult, suitable for expert DIY or professional

Specifications

General

Type	Manual, five forward speeds and reverse. Synchromesh on all forward speeds

Torque wrench settings

	Nm	lbf ft
Clutch release bearing guide sleeve screws	8	6
Drain plug	60	44
Gearchange mechanism:		
Steady rod-to-transmission bolt	10	7
Steady rod-to-body bolts	20	15
Selector rod-to-lever bolt nut	18	13
Left-hand mounting plate:		
Front bolt	60	44
Front bolt nut	55	41
Rear bolt	55	41
Rear mounting link:		
Link-to-body bolt	100	74
Link-to-transmission mounting bolt	55	41
Reversing light switch	20	15
Speedometer drive retaining plate bolt	10	7
Transmission-to-engine nuts/bolts	45	33

1 General information

1 The transmission is contained in a cast-aluminium alloy casing bolted to the engine's left-hand end, and consists of the gearbox and final drive differential.

2 Drive is transmitted from the crankshaft via the clutch to the input shaft, which has a splined extension to accept the clutch friction plate, and rotates in sealed ball-bearings. From the input shaft, drive is transmitted to the output shaft, which rotates in a roller bearing at its right-hand end, and a sealed ball-bearing at its left-hand end. From the output shaft, the drive is transmitted to the differential crownwheel, which rotates with the differential case and planetary gears, thus driving the sun gears and driveshafts. The rotation of the planetary gears on their shaft allows the inner roadwheel to rotate at a slower speed than the outer roadwheel when the car is cornering.

3 The input and output shafts are arranged side by side, parallel to the crankshaft and driveshafts, so that their gear pinion teeth are in constant mesh. In the neutral position, the output shaft gear pinions rotate freely, so that drive cannot be transmitted to the crownwheel.

4 Gear selection is via a floor-mounted lever and selector rod mechanism. The selector rod causes the appropriate selector fork to move its respective synchro-sleeve along the shaft, to lock the gear pinion to the synchro-hub. Since the synchro-hubs are splined to the output shaft, this locks the pinion to the shaft, so that drive can be transmitted. To ensure that gear-changing can be made quickly and quietly, a synchro-mesh system is fitted to all forward gears, consisting of baulk rings and spring-loaded fingers, as well as the gear pinions and synchro-hubs. The synchro-mesh cones are formed on the mating faces of the baulk rings and gear pinions.

2.2a Remove the retaining clip (arrowed) . . .

2.2b . . . and tap out the roll pin securing the selector rod to the transmission unit

2 Gearchange linkage -
removal and refitting

Removal

Note: *A new selector shaft roll pin will be required on refitting.*

1 Park the vehicle on level ground, switch off the ignition, and apply the handbrake firmly. Jack up the front of the vehicle and support it securely on axle stands.

2 Working at the transmission end of the selector rod, remove the retaining clip to gain access to the roll pin. If the original clip is still fitted, discard it and replace it with a jubilee-type hose clip on refitting. Tap the roll pin out of position and discard it; a new one must be used on refitting **(see illustrations)**.

3 Slacken and remove the nut and pivot bolt

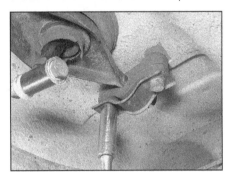

2.5 Gearchange linkage steady rod is secured to the body by two bolts . . .

securing the selector rod to the base of the gearchange lever/mounting plate then free the front end of the rod from the transmission shaft and remove the rod from the vehicle **(see illustration)**. Recover the pivot bush(es) from the gearchange lever.

4 Unscrew the knob from the gearchange lever and free the lever gaiter from the centre console and slide it off the lever.

5 From underneath the vehicle, slacken and remove the bolts and retaining plate securing the steady rod rear mounting to the body **(see illustration)**. Remove the mounting rubber from the steady rod, taking care not to lose its spacers.

6 Slacken and remove the bolt securing the gearchange steady rod to the transmission unit and recover the washers and mounting rubber **(see illustration)**. Manoeuvre the steady rod and gearchange lever assembly out from underneath the vehicle.

7 If necessary, the rod and lever assembly can be dismantled once the sealing boots and circlip have been removed. Note the correct fitted location of each component as it is removed to avoid problems on reassembly.

8 Thoroughly clean all components and check them for wear or damage, renewing all worn or faulty items (most components are available separately).

Refitting

9 Refitting is the reverse of the removal procedure, noting the following points.

a) *Apply a smear of multi-purpose grease to all linkage pivot points.*

b) *Remove all traces of locking compound*

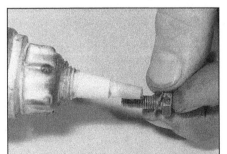

2.9a On refitting apply thread locking compound to the steady rod and selector rod bolts . . .

2.3 Slacken and remove the nut and pivot bolt securing the selector rod to the lever

from the steady rod retaining bolt threads. On refitting, apply a few drops of locking compound (Skoda recommend the use of Loctite 270 or Three Bond 1305) to all three bolts prior to installation and tighten them to their specified torque settings **(see illustration)**.

c) *Clean the selector rod to lever bolt threads and apply a few drops of locking to them prior to refitting (see b). Refit the nut and tighten to the specified torque.*

d) *Secure the selector rod to the transmission with a new roll pin then secure the roll pin in position using a jubilee-type hose clip* **(see illustration)**.

3 Oil seals -
renewal

Driveshaft oil seals

Note: *A new driveshaft inner joint circlip will be required.*

1 Chock the rear wheels, apply the handbrake, then jack up the front of the car and support it on axle stands. Remove the appropriate front roadwheel.

2 Drain the transmission oil as described in the relevant part of Chapter 1 or be prepared for some fluid loss as the driveshaft is removed.

3 Working as described in Chapter 8, free the inner end of the driveshaft from the transmission, and place it clear of the seal, noting that there is no need to unscrew the

2.9b . . . and secure the selector rod in position with a new roll pin

2.6 . . . and the transmission by a single bolt

3.3 If both driveshafts are to be removed it will be necessary to support one of the differential side gears (see text)

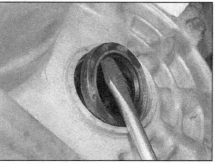

3.4 Lever out the oil seal using a large flat-bladed screwdriver . . .

3.5 . . . and tap the new seal into position with a tubular drift

driveshaft retaining nut; the driveshaft can be left secured to the hub. Support the driveshaft, to avoid placing any strain on the driveshaft joints or gaiters.

Caution: If both driveshafts are to be disconnected from the transmission unit at the same time, it will be necessary to retain one of the differential side gears to prevent the possibility of both side gears falling into the transmission unit. Once the first driveshaft has been disconnected, insert a length of clean metal rod/tubing approximately 26 mm in diameter into the inner bore of the differential side gear and leave it protruding out from the transmission housing; if necessary tape the rod/tubing to the transmission unit to prevent it falling out (see illustration). If the differential side gears drop into the transmission unit, the only way to realign them is to remove the transmission unit from the vehicle and have the unit rebuilt by a transmission specialist.

4 Carefully prise the oil seal out of the transmission using a large flat-bladed screwdriver (see illustration).
5 Remove all traces of dirt from the area around the oil seal aperture, then apply a smear of grease to the outer lip of the new oil seal. Ensure the seal is correctly positioned, with its sealing lip facing inwards, and drive it squarely into position, using a suitable tubular drift (such as a socket) which bears only on the hard outer edge of the seal (see illustration).
6 Ensure the seal is correctly located in the

transmission housing then fit a new circlip to the driveshaft inner joint and refit the driveshaft (see Chapter 8).
7 Refill/top-up the transmission with the specified type of oil and check the oil level as described in the relevant part of Chapter 1.

Selector shaft oil seal

Note: *A new selector shaft roll pin will be required.*
8 Park the vehicle on level ground then firmly apply the handbrake. Jack up the front of the vehicle and support it securely on axle stands.
9 Working at the transmission end of the selector rod, remove the retaining clip to gain access to the roll pin. If the original clip is still fitted, discard it and replace it with a jubilee-type hose clip on refitting.
10 Using a hammer and punch, tap the roll pin out of position and disconnect the selector rod from the transmission. Discard the roll pin, which must be renewed whenever it is disturbed.
11 Remove the selector shaft gaiter then, using a screwdriver or long-nosed pliers, carefully lever the seal out of the housing and slide it off the end of the shaft (see illustrations). Be prepared for oil spillage by positioning a container beneath the transmission unit.
12 Before fitting a new seal, check the selector shaft seal rubbing surface for signs of burrs, scratches or other damage which may have caused the seal to fail in the first place. It may be possible to polish away minor faults of this sort using fine abrasive paper; more

serious defects will require the renewal of the selector shaft.
13 Apply a smear of grease to the outer edge and sealing lip of the new seal, then carefully slide the seal along the selector rod. Press the seal fully into position in the gearbox housing and refit the gaiter, ensuring that it is correctly seated on the seal shoulder.
14 Reconnect the selector rod to the shaft, and align the roll pin holes. Tap a new roll pin into position using a hammer and punch, and secure it in position by tightening a jubilee-type hose clip around it.
15 On completion, check the transmission oil level as described in the relevant part of Chapter 1.

Input shaft oil seal

16 Remove the transmission unit from the vehicle and dismantle the clutch release mechanism as described in Chapter 6.
17 Undo the retaining screws securing the clutch release bearing guide sleeve in position and slide the guide off the input shaft (see illustration). Note that the sleeve may be a tight-fit in the transmission housing and prove difficult to remove.
18 Carefully lever the oil seal out of the guide by using a suitable flat-bladed screwdriver.
19 Before fitting a new seal, check the input shaft's seal rubbing surface for signs of burrs, scratches or other damage which may have caused the seal to fail in the first place. It may be possible to polish away minor faults of this sort using fine abrasive paper, however, more serious defects will require the renewal of the input shaft.

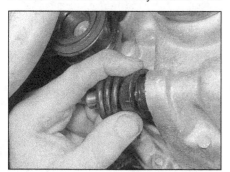

3.11a Remove the rubber gaiter . . .

3.11b . . . and extract the selector shaft seal from the transmission housing

3.17 Clutch release bearing guide sleeve is retained by two screws

4.4 The reversing light switch is screwed into the base of the transmission housing

20 Dip the new seal in clean oil and fit it to the rear of the guide sleeve, making sure its sealing lip is facing outwards (inwards when the sleeve assembly is in position on the transmission).

21 Ensure that the input shaft is clean and greased to protect the seal lips on refitting then carefully slide the guide sleeve into position, taking care not to damage the oil seal lips. Press/tap the sleeve fully into the transmission housing then refit the retaining screws, tightening them to the specified torque setting.

4 Reversing light switch - testing, removal and refitting

Testing

1 The reversing light circuit is controlled by a plunger-type switch that is screwed into the base of the transmission casing. If a fault develops in the circuit, first ensure that the circuit fuse has not blown.

2 To test the switch, disconnect the wiring connector(s). Use a multimeter (set to the resistance function) or a battery-and-bulb test circuit to check that there is continuity between the switch terminals only when reverse gear is selected. If this is not the case, and there are no obvious breaks or other damage to the wires, the switch is faulty, and must be renewed.

5.1 The speedometer drive (arrowed) is situated at the rear of the transmission unit

Removal

Note: *A new sealing washer will be required on refitting.*

3 Firmly apply the handbrake then jack up the front of the vehicle and support it on axle stands.

4 Disconnect the wiring connector(s) from the reversing light switch (see illustration).

5 Be prepared for oil loss when the switch is removed and have ready a suitable plug to plug the transmission aperture whilst the switch is removed.

6 Wipe clean the area around the switch then unscrew it and remove it from the transmission unit along with its sealing washer. Plug the switch aperture to minimise oil loss.

Refitting

7 Fit a new sealing washer to the switch then remove the plug from the transmission and quickly screw in the switch. Tighten the switch to the specified torque.

8 Work back along the switch wiring, securing it in position with all the relevant clips and ties, and reconnect the wiring connector(s).

9 Lower the vehicle to the ground and check the transmission oil level as described in the relevant part of Chapter 1.

5 Speedometer drive - removal and refitting

Removal

1 Working in the engine compartment, locate the speedometer drive which is situated at the rear of the transmission unit (see illustration). Slacken the knurled retaining ring securing the speedometer cable to its drive but do not disconnect it yet.

2 Slacken and remove the retaining bolt and slide out the speedometer drive retaining plate.

3 Use the speedometer cable to pull the drive assembly out of position then unscrew the drive assembly from the cable retaining ring and remove it from the vehicle.

4 Examine the speedometer drivegear for signs of chipped or missing teeth; renew if damaged. Inspect the speedometer drive sealing ring for signs of damage or deterioration, and renew if necessary.

Refitting

5 Ensure the sealing ring is correctly seated on the speedometer drive and apply a smear of oil to it to ease installation.

6 Fit the drive to the end of the speedometer cable and lightly tighten the retaining ring.

7 Ease the speedometer drive assembly back into the transmission unit, ensuring the gear teeth engage correctly.

8 Once the drive is correctly positioned refit

the retaining plate, ensuring it is correctly located in the drive slots, and tighten the retaining bolt to the specified torque.

9 Slacken the cable retaining ring to relieve and tension in the cable then retighten it securely.

6 Transmission - removal and refitting

Removal

Note: *New mounting bolt nuts will be required on refitting as will new driveshaft inner joint circlips.*

1 Chock the rear wheels, then firmly apply the handbrake. Jack up the front of the vehicle, and securely support it on axle stands. Remove both front roadwheels.

2 Undo the retaining screws and fasteners and remove the undercover (where fitted) from the front of the vehicle.

3 Drain the transmission oil as described in the relevant part of Chapter 1. Refit the drain plug, using a new sealing washer, and tighten it to the specified torque setting.

4 On 1.3 litre engines remove the hall (crankshaft) sensor from the transmission housing and on models with single-point injection referring to Chapter 4A, remove the air cleaner housing from the throttle body.

5 On all models remove the starter motor as described in Chapter 5A.

6 Unscrew the knurled retaining ring and disconnect the speedometer cable from its drive on the rear of the transmission unit.

7 Slacken the clutch cable adjusting nut, to obtain maximum freeplay in the clutch cable, then unhook the cable from the clutch release lever and mounting bracket and position it clear of the transmission unit (see Chapter 6). Unhook the spring and remove it from the upper end of the release fork pivot shaft.

8 Remove the retaining clip from the transmission end of the selector rod to gain access to the roll pin. If the original clip is still fitted, discard it and replace it with a jubilee-type hose clip on refitting. Using a hammer and punch, tap the roll pin out of position and disconnect the rod from the transmission. Discard the roll pin, which must be renewed whenever it is disturbed.

9 Slacken and remove the bolt securing the gearchange steady rod to the transmission unit then free the rod and recover the washers.

10 Disconnect the wiring connector(s) from the reversing light switch.

11 Unscrew the retaining bolts and remove the flywheel lower cover plate from the base of the transmission housing (see illustrations).

12 Working as described in Chapter 8, free the inner end of the left-hand driveshaft from the transmission, noting that there is no need to

unscrew the driveshaft retaining nut; the driveshaft can be left secured to the hub. Support the driveshaft, to avoid placing any strain on the driveshaft joints or gaiters.

13 Insert a length of clean metal rod/tubing approximately 26 mm in diameter into the inner bore of the left differential side gear and leave it protruding out from the transmission housing. If necessary tape the rod/tubing to the transmission unit to prevent it falling out.

Caution: If both driveshafts are disconnected from the transmission unit at the same time without supporting the differential side gear, there is a possibility that the side gears could move and fall into the transmission unit. If the differential side gears are allowed to drop into the transmission unit, the only way to realign them is to remove the transmission unit from the vehicle and have the unit rebuilt by a transmission specialist.

14 Once the left-hand differential side gear is securely supported, working as described in Chapter 8, disconnect the right-hand driveshaft from the transmission unit. Support the driveshaft to avoid placing any strain on the driveshaft joints or gaiters.

15 Place a jack with a block of wood beneath the engine, to take the weight of the engine. Alternatively, attach a couple of lifting eyes to the engine, and fit a hoist or support bar to take the engine weight. Also place a jack and block of wood beneath the transmission, and raise the jack to take the weight of the transmission.

16 Slacken and remove the nuts and bolts securing the engine/transmission rear mounting link to the transmission and body and remove the link **(see illustration)**. Discard the nuts, new ones should be used on refitting.

17 Slacken and remove the nut from the engine/transmission mounting left-hand mounting plate front bolt then slacken and remove both bolts and lift off the mounting plate. Discard the mounting bolt nut, a new one should be used on refitting.

18 With the jack positioned beneath the transmission taking the weight, slacken and remove the remaining nuts and bolts securing the transmission housing to the engine. Note the correct fitted positions of each nut/bolt, and the necessary brackets, as they are removed, to use as a reference on refitting **(see illustration)**. Make a final check that all components have been disconnected, and are positioned clear of the transmission so that they will not hinder the removal procedure.

19 With the nuts/bolts removed, lower the transmission unit slightly until there is sufficient clearance to be able to slide the unit to the left to free it from its mounting studs. Once the transmission is free, lower the jack and manoeuvre the unit out from under the car. Remove the locating dowels from the transmission or engine if they are loose, and keep them in a safe place.

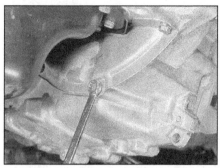

6.11a Undo the retaining bolts . . .

Refitting

20 Apply a thin smear of high-temperature grease (Skoda recommend the use of Kluber Microlube GL202, GL261 or GL262 or alternatively Mobil lithium 932 or 933 - available from your Skoda dealer) to the clutch release bearing, fork and guide sleeve contact surfaces and check the operation of the clutch release mechanism (see Chapter 6). Also apply a thin smear of grease to the transmission input shaft splines; do not apply too much grease otherwise the clutch friction plate may be contaminated.

21 Ensure the locating dowels are correctly positioned then lift the transmission unit into position. Ease the transmission unit onto the engine then refit the retaining nuts and bolts, ensuring all necessary brackets are correctly positioned. Tighten the nuts and bolts lightly only at this stage.

22 Raise the transmission unit up into position ensuring the transmission housing is correctly aligned with the left-hand mounting aperture.

23 Refit the left-hand mounting plate then refit the retaining bolts, tightening them to their specified torque settings. Fit the new mounting nut to the front bolt and tighten it to the specified torque.

24 Refit the rear mounting link then refit the mounting bolts and screw on the new nuts. Remove the jack from the beneath the transmission unit and the engine support

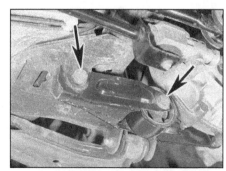

6.16 Slacken and remove the bolts (arrowed) and remove the rear mounting link from the transmission

6.11b . . . and remove the flywheel lower cover plate from the transmission housing

bar/hoist. Rock the engine/transmission unit to settle it in position then tighten the rear mounting link bolt nuts to their specified torque settings.

25 The remainder of refitting is the reverse of removal, noting the following points.

a) Tighten all nuts and bolts to their specified torque settings (where given).
b) Renew the right-hand driveshaft oil seal (see Section 3) then refit the driveshafts as described in Chapter 8, renewing the inner joint circlip prior to refitting. Once the right-hand shaft is correctly fitted, remove the support bar/tube and repeat the operation on the left-hand driveshaft.
c) Secure the gearchange selector rod in position with a new roll pin and position a jubilee-type hose clip over the pin (see Section 2).
d) Remove all traces of locking compound from the steady rod-to-transmission bolt threads prior to refitting. Apply a few drops of locking compound (Skoda recommend the use of Loctite 270 or Three Bond 1305) to all the bolt prior to installation and tighten it to the specified torque.
e) Reconnect the clutch cable and adjust it as described in Chapter 6.
f) On completion, refill the transmission with the specified type and quantity of lubricant then check the oil level as described in the relevant part of Chapter 1.

6.18 Note the correct fitted position of all brackets when removing the transmission nuts/bolts

7 Transmission overhaul - general information

1 Overhauling a manual transmission unit is a difficult and involved job for the DIY home mechanic. In addition to dismantling and reassembling many small parts, clearances must be precisely measured and, if necessary, changed by selecting shims and spacers. Internal transmission components are also often difficult to obtain, and in many instances, extremely expensive. Because of this, if the transmission develops a fault or becomes noisy, the best course of action is to have the unit overhauled by a specialist repairer, or to obtain an exchange reconditioned unit.

2 Nevertheless, it is not impossible for the more experienced mechanic to overhaul the transmission, provided the special tools are available, and the job is done in a deliberate step-by-step manner, so that nothing is overlooked.

3 The tools necessary for an overhaul include internal and external circlip pliers, bearing pullers, a slide hammer, a set of pin punches, a dial test indicator, and possibly a hydraulic press. In addition, a large, sturdy workbench and a vice will be required.

4 During dismantling of the transmission, make careful notes of how each component is fitted, to make reassembly easier and more accurate.

5 Before dismantling the transmission, it will help if you have some idea what area is malfunctioning. Certain problems can be closely related to specific areas in the transmission, which can make component examination and replacement easier. Refer to the *Fault finding* Section of this manual for more information.

Chapter 8
Driveshafts

Contents

Degrees of difficulty

Easy, suitable for novice with little experience	Fairly easy, suitable for beginner with some experience	Fairly difficult, suitable for competent DIY mechanic	Difficult, suitable for experienced DIY mechanic	Very difficult, suitable for expert DIY or professional

Specifications

Lubrication (overhaul only - see text)

Type:
   Outer joint . . . . Shell GL245MO or SWC 423MB*
   Inner joint . . . . Shell GL240 or SWC 423B*
Amount per joint:
   Outer joint . . . . 80 gm
   Inner joint . . . . 100 gm
*See your Skoda dealer for details

Torque wrench settings

	Nm	lbf ft
Anti-roll bar connecting link nut	33	24
Hub nut	300	221
Lower arm balljoint clamp bolt nut	65	48
Roadwheel bolts	110	81
Vibration damper retaining screws	15	11

1 General information

1 Drive is transmitted from the differential to the front wheels by means of two solid-steel driveshafts. Both driveshafts are splined at their outer ends, to accept the wheel hubs, and are secured to the hub by a large nut. The inner end of each driveshaft is splined to the differential side gears. A damper is fitted to the (longer) right-hand driveshaft to dampen out vibrations.

2 Constant velocity (CV) joints are fitted to each end of the driveshafts, to ensure the smooth and efficient transmission of drive at all the angles possible as the roadwheels move up and down with the suspension, and as they turn from side to side under steering. The outer joint is of the ball-and-cage type and the inner joint is of the tripod-type.

2 Driveshafts - removal and refitting

Removal

Note: *A new hub nut, lower arm balljoint clamp bolt nut and driveshaft inner joint circlip will be required on refitting.*

1 Remove the wheel trim/hub cap (as applicable) then slacken the hub nut with the vehicle resting on its wheels. Also slacken the wheel bolts.

2 Chock the rear wheels of the car, firmly apply the handbrake, then jack up the front of the car and support it on axle stands. Remove the appropriate front roadwheel.

3 Working as described in the relevant part of Chapter 1, drain the transmission oil then fit a new sealing washer to the drain plug. Refit the drain plug and tighten to the specified torque.

4 On models equipped with ABS, remove the wheel sensor from the hub as described in Chapter 9.

5 Extract the split pin then unscrew the retaining nut from the track rod balljoint and free the balljoint from the hub (see Chapter 10).

6 Slacken and remove the hub nut and washer. If the nut was not slackened with the wheels on the ground (see paragraph 1), refit at least two roadwheel bolts to the front hub, tightening them securely, then have an assistant firmly depress the brake pedal to prevent the front hub from rotating, whilst you slacken and remove the hub bolt. Alternatively, a tool can be fabricated from two lengths of steel strip (one long, one short) and a nut and bolt; the nut and bolt forming the pivot of a forked tool. Discard the hub nut, a new one should be used on refitting.

7 On models with an anti-roll bar, slacken and remove the nut securing the anti-roll bar connecting link to the lower arm and remove the washer and lower mounting rubber.

2.9 Free the lower arm balljoint from the swivel hub then move the hub assembly outwards and free it from the driveshaft outer joint

2.10 Carefully lever the inner joint out of the transmission using a suitable bar and remove the driveshaft from the vehicle

8 On all models, slacken and remove the lower arm balljoint clamp bolt and nut from the base of the swivel hub. Carefully lever down on the lower arm to free the balljoint from the swivel hub clamp; on models with an anti-roll bar take care not to lose the upper mounting rubber and washer from the connecting link. Discard the clamp bolt nut, a new one should be used on refitting.

9 Carefully pull the swivel hub assembly outwards and free it from the driveshaft outer joint splines **(see illustration)**. If necessary, the shaft can be tapped out of hub using a soft-faced mallet. Once the outer joint is freed from the hub ensure the driveshaft is supported; do not allow it to hang down as this could damage the constant velocity joints/gaiters.

10 Taking care not to damage the housing, insert a flat bar or large screwdriver inbetween the inner joint and the transmission and carefully lever the joint out of position **(see illustration)**.

11 Remove the driveshaft from the vehicle taking care not to damage the differential oil seal. **Note:** *Do not allow the vehicle to rest on its wheels with one or both driveshafts removed, as damage to the wheel bearing(s) may result. If moving the vehicle is unavoidable, temporarily insert the outer end of the driveshaft(s) in the hub(s) and tighten the driveshaft nut(s). Support the inner end(s) of the driveshaft(s) to avoid damage.*
Caution: If both driveshafts are to be

removed at the same time, it will be necessary to retain one of the differential side gears to prevent the possibility of both side gears falling into the transmission unit. Once the first driveshaft has been removed, insert a length of clean metal rod/tubing approximately 26 mm in diameter into the inner bore of the differential side gear and leave it protruding out from the transmission housing; if necessary tape the rod/tubing to the transmission unit to prevent it falling out (see illustration). If the differential side gears drop into the transmission unit, the only way to realign them is to remove the transmission unit from the vehicle and have the unit rebuilt by a transmission specialist.

Refitting

12 Before installing the driveshaft, examine the driveshaft oil seal in the transmission for signs of damage or deterioration and, if necessary, renew it, as described in Chapter 7. It is highly recommended that the seal is renewed, regardless of its apparent condition.
13 Using a small screwdriver, remove the original circlip from the end of the inner constant velocity joint splines and discard it. Fit a new circlip making sure it is correctly located in the inner joint recess.
14 Thoroughly clean the driveshaft splines, and the apertures in the transmission and hub assembly. Apply a thin film of grease to the oil

2.11 If both driveshafts are to be removed it will be necessary to support one of the differential side gears (see text)

2.15 On refitting take care not to damage the differential oil seal when engaging the inner joint splines with those of the side gear

seal lips, and to the driveshaft splines and shoulders. Check that all gaiter clips are securely fastened.
15 Offer up the driveshaft, and locate the joint splines with those of the differential side gear, taking great care not to damage the oil seal **(see illustration)**. Push the joint fully into position and check that it is securely retained by the circlip.
16 Locate the outer constant velocity joint splines with those of the swivel hub, and slide the joint back into position in the hub. Refit the washer to the outer joint and screw on the new hub nut, tightening it lightly only at this stage.
17 Align the lower arm balljoint shank with the swivel hub clamp then insert the clamp bolt and fit the new nut, tightening it to the specified torque. On models with an anti-roll bar, align the connecting link with the lower arm as the balljoint is located, making sure the upper mounting rubber and washer are correctly fitted.
18 Where necessary, refit the lower mounting rubber and washer to the anti-roll bar connecting link then refit the retaining nut and tighten to the specified torque.
19 Locate the track rod balljoint shank correctly in the swivel hub bore and securely tighten its retaining nut. Secure the nut in position with a new split pin.
20 On models with ABS, refit the wheel sensor to the hub as described in Chapter 9.
21 Refit the roadwheel then lower the vehicle to the ground and tighten the wheel bolts to the specified torque.
22 With the vehicle resting on its wheels, tighten the hub nut to the specified torque then refit the wheel trim/hub cap (as applicable).
23 Refill the transmission unit with the specified type and amount of oil as described in the relevant part of Chapter 1.

3 Driveshaft rubber gaiters - renewal

1 Remove the driveshaft from the vehicle as described in Section 2 and proceed as described under the relevant sub-heading.

Outer joint

2 Secure the driveshaft in a vice equipped with soft jaws, and release the gaiter retaining clips. If necessary, the retaining clips can be cut to release them.
3 Fold back the rubber gaiter to expose the outer constant velocity joint. Scoop out the excess grease.
4 Using a hammer and suitable soft metal drift, sharply strike the inner member of the outer joint to drive it off the end of the shaft **(see illustration)**. The joint is retained on the driveshaft by a circlip, and striking the joint in this manner forces the circlip into its groove, so allowing the joint to slide off.

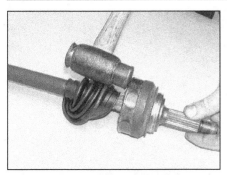

3.4 Free the outer joint from the driveshaft end by striking it with a soft-faced mallet or hammer and soft-metal drift

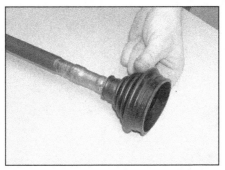

3.11 Tape over the splines then slide the new outer gaiter onto the shaft, taking care to displace its plastic bush

3.12 Remove the tape then fit the new circlip to the driveshaft groove

5 Once the joint assembly has been removed, remove the circlip from the groove in the driveshaft splines, and discard it. A new circlip must be fitted on reassembly.

6 Remove the rubber gaiter from the driveshaft and discard it.

7 With the constant velocity joint removed from the driveshaft, thoroughly clean the joint using paraffin, or a suitable solvent, and dry it thoroughly. Carry out a visual inspection of the joint.

8 Move the inner splined driving member from side to side, to expose each ball in turn at the top of its track. Examine the balls for cracks, flat spots, or signs of surface pitting.

9 Inspect the ball tracks on the inner and outer members. If the tracks have widened, the balls will no longer be a tight fit. At the same time, check the ball cage windows for wear or cracking between the windows.

10 If the constant velocity joint is found to be worn or damaged, it will be necessary to renew it. If the joint is in satisfactory condition, obtain a new gaiter, retaining clips, circlip and the correct type and quantity of grease (see Specifications).

11 Tape over the splines on the end of the driveshaft, then slide the new gaiter onto the

shaft taking care not to displace the plastic bush from inside the gaiter inner lip **(see illustration)**.

12 Remove the tape then fit the new circlip, making sure it is correctly located in the driveshaft groove **(see illustration)**.

13 Work the grease well into the ball tracks of the outer joint then fill the gaiter with any excess **(see illustration)**.

14 Locate the outer joint on the driveshaft splines and slide it on until the inner member abuts the circlip. Tap the joint outer member sharply with hammer and soft-metal drift to force the inner member over the circlip and fully onto the driveshaft **(see illustration)**. Pull on the joint assembly to make sure the joint is securely retained by the circlip.

15 Locate the outer lip of the gaiter in the groove on the joint outer member then slide the inner lip upto to the ridge on the driveshaft. Lift the inner lip of the gaiter to equalise the air pressure inside.

16 Ensure the gaiter is correctly located then secure it in position with the retaining clips. Note that there are two possible types of retaining clip which are secured as follows.

17 The most frequently used type of clip simply clips around the gaiter and is secured

in position by compressing its raised section. In the absence of the special tool, carefully compress the clip raised section using a pair of side cutters taking great care not to cut through the clip.

18 The other less-commonly type of clip is in the form of a metal strap with a buckle at one end. Pass the end of the strap through the buckle slot then seat the clip on the gaiter. Using a hook fabricated out of welding rod and a pair of pliers, pull the clip tightly to remove all slack then bend the strap back over the buckle. Cut off the excess then bend the strap end behind the buckle before folding the buckle firmly down onto the strap to secure the clip in position **(see illustrations)**.

19 Ensure both the inner and outer clips are correctly fitted then check that the constant velocity joint moves freely in all directions before refitting the driveshaft as described in Section 2.

Inner joint

20 Secure the driveshaft upright in a vice equipped with soft jaws, and release the gaiter retaining clips. If necessary, the retaining clips can be cut to release them.

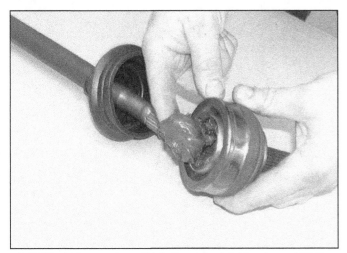

3.13 Work the grease well into the outer joint tracks and fill the gaiter with any excess

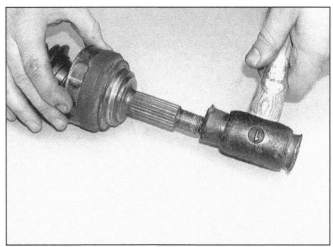

3.14 Locate the outer joint on the driveshaft splines and tap it into position over the circlip. Ensure that the joint is securely retained by the circlip before proceeding

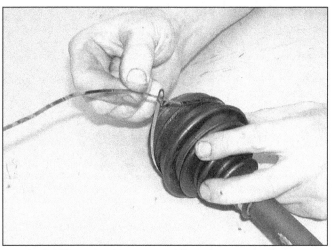

3.18a Where buckle-type retaining clips are supplied . . .

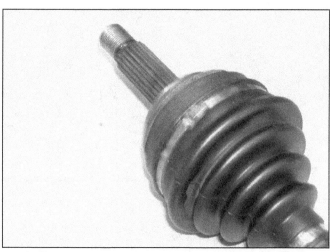

3.18b . . . secure them in position as described in the text

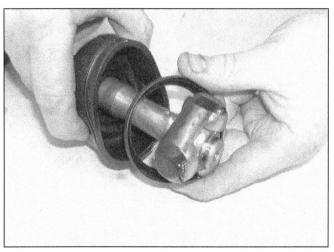

3.23 Manoeuvre the outer member off over the tripod joint noting which way around it is fitted

3.24 Remove the circlip then slide the tripod joint assembly off from the driveshaft end

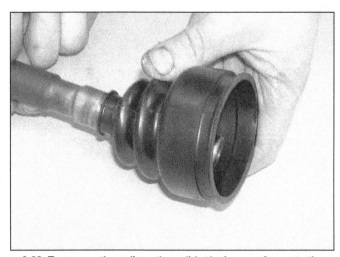

3.28 Tape over the splines then slide the inner gaiter onto the driveshaft

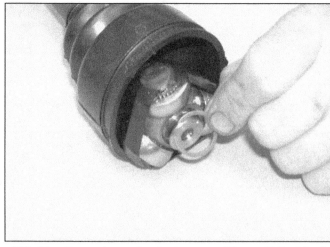

3.31 Align the marks made prior to removal then refit the tripod joint and secure it in position with the new circlip

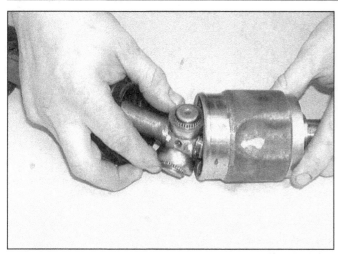

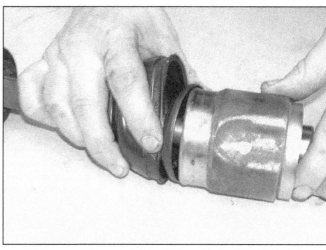

3.32a Remove the tape from the tripod joint then refit the outer member, ensuring the marks made prior to removal are correctly aligned . . .

3.32b . . . and secure it in position with the retaining plate

21 Fold the gaiter back and scoop out excess grease from the joint then, using paint or a suitable marker pen, make alignment marks between the joint outer member and the driveshaft.

22 Unclip the retaining plate from the end of the outer member then lift the joint outer member off from the driveshaft, taking care not to displace the rollers from the tripod joint. Wipe away the grease from the tripod joint then wrap adhesive tape around the joint to secure the rollers in position. **Note:** *It is essential that all the inner joint components are refitted in their original locations on refitting so it is important that the rollers and tripod remain correctly mated whilst the outer member is removed. Failure to do this will lead to increased wear in the joint assembly.*

23 Manoeuvre the outer member retaining plate off over the tripod joint noting which way around it is fitted **(see illustration)**.

24 Mark the relative position of the tripod joint in relation to the driveshaft then remove circlip from the driveshaft end and pull off the tripod joint **(see illustration)**. If it is tight, draw the joint off the driveshaft end using a two or three-legged bearing puller. Ensure that the legs of the puller are located behind the joint

inner member, and do not contact the joint rollers. Alternatively, support the inner member of the tripod joint, and press the shaft out of the joint using a hydraulic press, ensuring that no load is applied to the joint rollers.

25 With the tripod joint removed, the gaiter can be slid off from the driveshaft.

26 Thoroughly clean all the constant velocity joint components using paraffin, or a suitable solvent, and dry them thoroughly - take great care not to remove the alignment marks made on dismantling. Carry out a visual inspection of the joint.

27 Examine the tripod joint, rollers and outer member for any signs of scoring or wear, and for smoothness of movement of the rollers on the tripod stems. If any component is worn, the complete joint assembly must be renewed. If the joint is in satisfactory condition, obtain a new gaiter, retaining clips, circlip and the correct type and quantity of grease (see Specifications).

28 Tape over the splines on the end of the driveshaft then carefully slide the new gaiter onto the shaft and locate it in the driveshaft groove **(see illustration)**.

29 Remove the tape from the driveshaft end then fit the outer member retaining plate,

ensuring it is the correct way around .

30 Align the marks made on dismantling and engage the tripod joint with the driveshaft splines. Tap the joint fully onto the shaft using a hammer and soft metal drift, taking great care not to damage the driveshaft splines or joint rollers.

31 Secure the tripod joint in position with the new circlip, making sure it is correctly located in the driveshaft groove **(see illustration)**.

32 Remove the tape from around the joint then align the marks made on removal and fit the outer member. Ensure the joint components are correctly assembled then secure the outer member in position with the retaining plate **(see illustrations)**.

33 Evenly distribute the special grease around the tripod joint and outer member, working the grease well into the joint rollers, and pack the gaiter with the remainder **(see illustration)**.

34 Locate the outer lip of the gaiter in the groove on the joint outer member then lift the outer lip of the gaiter to equalise the air pressure inside **(see illustration)**.

35 Fit both the inner and outer retaining clips to the gaiter as described in paragraph 17 or 18 (as applicable) **(see illustrations)**.

3.33 Work the grease it the joint rollers and fill the gaiter with any excess

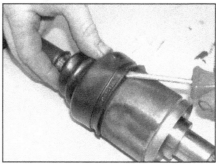

3.34 Seat the gaiter correctly on the joint and driveshaft then lift the outer lip to equalise pressure within the gaiter

3.35a where buckle-type retaining clips are supplied, pass the end of the strap through the buckle slot . . .

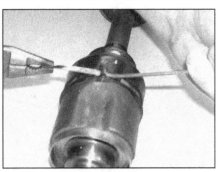

3.35b . . . then, using a hooked piece of wire and a pair of pliers, pull the clip tightly before bending the strap back over the buckle

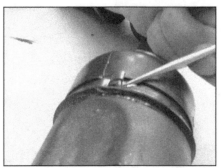

3.35c Cut off the excess then bend the strap end behind the buckle . . .

3.35d . . . before folding the buckle firmly down onto the strap

36 Check that the constant velocity joint moves freely in all directions, then refit the driveshaft to the vehicle as described in Section 2.

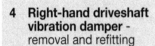

4 Right-hand driveshaft vibration damper -
removal and refitting

Removal

1 Firmly apply the handbrake then jack up the front of the vehicle and support it on axle stands.
2 Slacken and remove the retaining screws then separate the two halves of the damper and remove them from the right-hand driveshaft **(see illustration)**.
3 Check the damper rubbers for signs of damage or deterioration and renew if necessary. Each rubber is bonded to the damper (Skoda recommend the use of Chemopren 25 adhesive).

Refitting

4 Ensure the damper and driveshaft mating surfaces are clean and dry.

5 Locate the damper halves on the driveshaft, making sure both are correctly engaged with the shaft lugs. Refit the retaining screws, tightening them to the specified torque, then lower the vehicle to the ground.

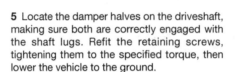

5 Driveshaft overhaul -
general information

1 If any of the checks described in the relevant part of Chapter 1 reveal wear in any driveshaft joint, first remove the roadwheel trim or centre cap (as appropriate) and check that the hub nut is tightened to the specified torque. If the nut is loose, obtain a new one and tighten it to the specified torque. If the nut is tight, refit the centre cap/trim and repeat the check on the other hub nut.
2 Road test the vehicle, and listen for a metallic clicking from the front as the vehicle is driven slowly in a circle on full-lock. If a clicking noise is heard, this indicates wear in the outer constant velocity joint. This means that the joint must be renewed; reconditioning is not possible.

4.2 Undo the retaining screws (arrowed) and remove the two halves of the vibration damper from the right-hand driveshaft

3 If vibration, consistent with road speed, is felt through the car when accelerating first check that the vibration damper is securely fitted to the right-hand driveshaft and is in good condition (Section 4). If the damper is alright, there is a possibility of wear in the inner constant velocity joints.
4 To check the joints for wear, remove the driveshafts, then dismantle them as described in Section 3; if any wear or free play is found, the affected joint must be renewed.

Chapter 9
Braking system

Contents

Degrees of difficulty

Easy, suitable for novice with little experience	**Fairly easy,** suitable for beginner with some experience	**Fairly difficult,** suitable for competent DIY mechanic	**Difficult,** suitable for experienced DIY mechanic	**Very difficult,** suitable for expert DIY or professional

Specifications

Front brakes
Disc thickness:
New . . . . 12.9 mm
Minimum . . . . 11.4 mm
Maximum disc run-out . . . . 0.1 mm
Brake pad friction material minimum thickness . . . . 2.0 mm

Rear drum brakes
Drum internal diameter:
New . . . . 200 mm
Maximum diameter after machining . . . . 201 mm
Brake shoe friction material minimum thickness . . . . 2.5 mm

Torque wrench settings	Nm	lbf ft
ABS wheel sensor bolt	10	7
Disc retaining screw	8	6
Front brake caliper:		
Guide pin bolts	35	26
Mounting bolts	60	44
Load-sensitive regulating valve axle bolt nut	20	15
Master cylinder retaining nuts	20	15
Roadwheel bolts	110	81
Vacuum pump clamp bolt - diesel engine	20	15
Vacuum servo unit mounting nuts	20	15
Wheel cylinder retaining bolts	6	4

1 General information

1 The braking system is of the servo-assisted, dual-circuit hydraulic type. Under normal circumstances, both circuits operate in unison. However, in the event of hydraulic failure in one circuit, full braking force will still be available at two wheels. An anti-lock braking system (ABS) was fitted as standard on some higher specification models and offered as an optional extra on others. Refer to Section 19 for details.

2 All models are fitted with front disc brakes and rear drum brakes. The front disc brakes are actuated by single-piston sliding type calipers, which ensure that equal pressure is applied to each disc pad. The rear drum brakes, the rear brakes incorporate leading and trailing shoes, which are actuated by twin-piston wheel cylinders. A self-adjust mechanism is incorporated, to automatically compensate for brake shoe wear. As the brake shoe linings wear, the footbrake operation automatically operates the adjuster mechanism, which effectively lengthens the shoe strut and repositions the brake shoes, to remove the lining-to-drum clearance.

3 On models not fitted with ABS a pressure regulating valve is incorporated into the hydraulic circuit to each rear brake; the valve(s) can either be of the pressure-sensitive or load-sensitive type. On models with pressure-sensitive valves, there are two separate valves (one for each rear brake) which are screwed directly into the master cylinder ports. On models with a load-sensitive valve, the valve is mounted onto the vehicle body and is linked to the rear axle by a spring. The valve(s) regulate the hydraulic pressure applied to the rear brakes and so helps prevent rear wheel lock-up during emergency braking.

4 The handbrake provides an independent mechanical means of rear brake application.

⚠ **Warning: When servicing any part of the system, work carefully and methodically; also observe scrupulous cleanliness when overhauling any part of the hydraulic system. Always renew components (in axle sets, where applicable) if in doubt about their condition, and use only genuine Skoda replacement parts, or at least those of known good quality. Note the warnings given in Safety first and at relevant points in this Chapter concerning the dangers of asbestos dust and hydraulic fluid.**

2 Hydraulic system - bleeding

⚠ **Warning: Hydraulic fluid is poisonous; wash off immediately and thoroughly in the case of skin contact, and seek immediate medical advice if any fluid is swallowed or gets into the eyes. Certain types of hydraulic fluid are inflammable, and may ignite when allowed into contact with hot components; when servicing any hydraulic system, it is safest to assume that the fluid is inflammable, and to take precautions against the risk of fire as though it is petrol that is being handled. Hydraulic fluid is also an effective paint stripper, and will attack plastics; if any is spilt, it should be washed off immediately, using copious quantities of fresh water. Finally, it is hygroscopic (it absorbs moisture from the air) - old fluid may be contaminated and unfit for further use. When topping-up or renewing the fluid, always use the recommended type, and ensure that it comes from a freshly-opened sealed container.**
Caution: On models equipped with ABS, disconnect the battery before disconnecting any braking system hydraulic union and do not reconnect the battery until after the hydraulic system has been bled. Failure to do this could lead to air entering the hydraulic unit. If air becomes trapped in the hydraulic unit, it may become impossible to remove using the conventional method described below. If this is the case, the only way to bleed the unit is to take the vehicle to a Skoda dealer who has access to the electronic tester (VAG 1552) required to bleed the hydraulic unit.

General

1 The correct operation of any hydraulic system is only possible after removing all air from the components and circuit; this is achieved by bleeding the system.

2 During the bleeding procedure, add only clean, unused hydraulic fluid of the recommended type; never re-use fluid that has already been bled from the system. Ensure that sufficient fluid is available before starting work.

3 If there is any possibility of incorrect fluid being already in the system, the brake components and circuit must be flushed completely with uncontaminated, correct fluid, and new seals should be fitted to the various components.

4 If hydraulic fluid has been lost from the system, or air has entered because of a leak, ensure that the fault is cured before proceeding further.

5 Park the vehicle on level ground, switch off the engine and select first or reverse gear then chock the wheels and release the handbrake.

6 Check that all pipes and hoses are secure, unions tight and bleed screws closed. Clean any dirt from around the bleed screws.

7 Unscrew the master cylinder reservoir cap, and top the master cylinder reservoir up to the MAX level line; refit the cap loosely, and remember to maintain the fluid level at least above the MIN level line throughout the procedure, or there is a risk of further air entering the system.

8 There are a number of one-man, do-it-yourself brake bleeding kits currently available from motor accessory shops. It is recommended that one of these kits is used whenever possible, as they greatly simplify the bleeding operation, and also reduce the risk of expelled air and fluid being drawn back into the system. If such a kit is not available, the basic (two-man) method must be used, which is described in detail below.

9 If a kit is to be used, prepare the vehicle as described previously, and follow the kit manufacturer's instructions, as the procedure may vary slightly according to the type being used; generally, they are as outlined below in the relevant sub-section.

10 Whichever method is used, the same sequence must be followed (paragraphs 11 and 12) to ensure that the removal of all air from the system.

Bleeding sequence

11 If the system has been only partially disconnected, and suitable precautions were taken to minimise fluid loss, it should be necessary only to bleed that part of the system (ie the primary or secondary circuit).

12 If the complete system is to be bled, then it should be done working in the following sequence:

    a) Right-hand rear brake.
    b) Left-hand rear brake.
    c) Right-hand front brake.
    d) Left-hand front brake.

Bleeding - basic (two-man) method

13 Collect a clean glass jar, a suitable length of plastic or rubber tubing which is a tight fit over the bleed screw, and a ring spanner to fit the screw. The help of an assistant will also be required.

14 Remove the dust cap from the first screw in the sequence. Fit the spanner and tube to the screw, place the other end of the tube in the jar, and pour in sufficient fluid to cover the end of the tube.

15 Ensure that the master cylinder reservoir fluid level is maintained at least above the MIN level line throughout the procedure.

16 Have the assistant fully depress the brake pedal several times to build up pressure, then maintain it on the final downstroke.

17 While pedal pressure is maintained, unscrew the bleed screw (approximately one turn) and allow the compressed fluid and air to flow into the jar. The assistant should maintain pedal pressure, following it down to the floor if necessary, and should not release it until instructed to do so. When the flow stops, tighten the bleed screw again, have the assistant release the pedal slowly, and recheck the reservoir fluid level.

18 Repeat the steps given in paragraphs 16 and 17 until the fluid emerging from the bleed screw is free from air bubbles. If the master

cylinder has been drained and refilled, and air is being bled from the first screw in the sequence, allow approximately five seconds between cycles for the master cylinder passages to refill.

19 When no more air bubbles appear, securely tighten the bleed screw then remove the tube and spanner, and refit the dust cap. Do not overtighten the bleed screw.

20 Repeat the procedure on the remaining screws in the sequence, until all air is removed from the system and the brake pedal feels firm again.

Bleeding - using a one-way valve kit

21 As their name implies, these kits consist of a length of tubing with a one-way valve fitted, to prevent expelled air and fluid being drawn back into the system; some kits include a translucent container, which can be positioned so that the air bubbles can be more easily seen flowing from the end of the tube.

22 The kit is connected to the bleed screw, which is then opened **(see illustration)**. The user returns to the driver's seat, depresses the brake pedal with a smooth, steady stroke, and slowly releases it; this is repeated until the expelled fluid is clear of air bubbles.

23 Note that these kits simplify work so much that it is easy to forget the master cylinder reservoir fluid level; ensure that this is maintained at least above the MIN level line at all times.

Bleeding - using a pressure-bleeding kit

24 These kits are usually operated by the reservoir of pressurised air contained in the spare tyre. However, note that it will probably be necessary to reduce the pressure to a lower level than normal; refer to the instructions supplied with the kit.

25 By connecting a pressurised, fluid-filled container to the master cylinder reservoir, bleeding can be carried out simply by opening each screw in turn (in the specified sequence), and allowing the fluid to flow out until no more air bubbles can be seen in the expelled fluid.

26 This method has the advantage that the large reservoir of fluid provides an additional safeguard against air being drawn into the system during bleeding.

27 Pressure-bleeding is particularly effective when bleeding difficult systems, or when bleeding the complete system at the time of routine fluid renewal.

All methods

28 When bleeding is complete, and firm pedal feel is restored, wash off any spilt fluid, securely tighten the bleed screws and refit their dust caps.

29 Check the hydraulic fluid level in the master cylinder reservoir, and top-up if necessary (see *Weekly checks*).

30 Discard any hydraulic fluid that has been

2.22 Bleeding the brakes with a one-way valve kit

bled from the system; it will not be fit for re-use.

31 Check the feel of the brake pedal. If it feels at all spongy, air must still be present in the system, and further bleeding is required. Failure to bleed satisfactorily after a reasonable repetition of the bleeding procedure may be due to worn master cylinder seals. **Note:** *On models equipped with ABS if there is any doubt about the operation of the braking system, take the vehicle to a Skoda dealer to have the system checked and bled using the special electronic tester (VAG 1552).*

3 Hydraulic pipes and hoses - renewal

Note: *Before starting work, refer to the note at the beginning of Section 2 concerning the dangers of hydraulic fluid.*

Models not equipped with an anti-lock braking system (ABS)

1 If any pipe or hose is to be renewed, minimise fluid loss by first removing the master cylinder reservoir cap, then tightening it down onto a piece of polythene to obtain an airtight seal. Alternatively, flexible hoses can be sealed, if required, using a proprietary brake hose clamp; metal brake pipe unions can be plugged (if care is taken not to allow dirt into the system) or capped immediately they are disconnected **(see illustration)**. Place a wad of rag under any union that is to

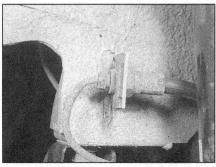

3.2 Typical flexible hose to brake pipe union clipped to the vehicle underbody

3.1 Flexible brake hoses can be sealed using a clamp

be disconnected, to catch any spilt fluid.

2 If a flexible hose is to be disconnected, unscrew the brake pipe union nut before removing the spring clip which secures the hose to its mounting bracket **(see illustration)**.

3 To unscrew the union nuts, it is preferable to obtain a brake pipe spanner of the correct size; these are available from most large motor accessory shops **(see illustration)**. Failing this, a close-fitting open-ended spanner will be required, though if the nuts are tight or corroded, their flats may be rounded-off if the spanner slips. In such a case, a self-locking wrench is often the only way to unscrew a stubborn union, but it follows that the pipe and the damaged nuts must be renewed on reassembly. Always clean a union and surrounding area before disconnecting it. If disconnecting a component with more than one union, make a careful note of the connections before disturbing any of them.

4 If a brake pipe is to be renewed, it can be obtained, cut to length and with the union nuts and end flares in place, from Skoda dealers. All that is then necessary is to bend it to shape, following the line of the original, before fitting it to the car. Alternatively, most motor accessory shops can make up brake pipes from kits, but this requires very careful measurement of the original, to ensure that the replacement is of the correct length. The safest answer is usually to take the original to the shop as a pattern.

5 On refitting, do not overtighten the union nuts. It is not necessary to exercise brute force to obtain a sound joint.

3.3 Using a brake pipe spanner to unscrew a pipe union nut

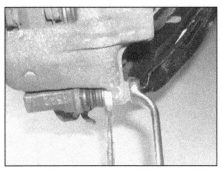

4.3 Slacken and remove the lower guide pin bolt . . .

4.4 . . . then pivot the caliper upwards and away from the pads

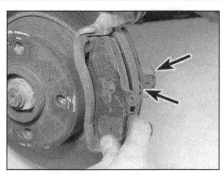

4.5 Lift the pads out from the mounting bracket (anti-rattle springs arrowed)

6 Ensure that the pipes and hoses are correctly routed, with no kinks, and that they are secured in the clips or brackets provided. After fitting, remove the polythene from the reservoir, and bleed the hydraulic system as described in Section 2. Wash off any spilt fluid, and check carefully for fluid leaks.

Models equipped with an anti-lock braking system (ABS)

Caution: On models equipped with ABS, disconnect the battery before disconnecting any braking system hydraulic union and do not reconnect the battery until after the hydraulic system has been bled. Failure to do this could lead to air entering the hydraulic unit. If air becomes trapped in the hydraulic unit, it may become impossible to remove using the conventional method (see Section 2). If this is the case, the only way to bleed the unit is to take the vehicle to a Skoda dealer who has access to the electronic tester (VAG 1552) required to bleed the hydraulic unit.

7 Refer to the information given in paragraphs 1 to 6. If a brake pipe is to be disconnected from the hydraulic unit or master cylinder, it is essential that the unit port and pipe are sealed up immediately to prevent fluid loss and allow the entry of air. This will minimise the risk of air getting trapped into the hydraulic unit (see Caution). Prior to reconnecting the pipe, ensure both the port and pipe are full of fluid.

4 Front brake pads - renewal

⚠️ *Warning: Renew both sets of front brake pads at the same time - never renew the pads on only one wheel, as uneven braking may result. Note that the dust created by wear of the pads may contain asbestos, which is a health hazard. Never blow it out with compressed air, and don't inhale any of it. An approved filtering mask should be worn when working on the brakes. DO NOT use petrol or petroleum-based solvents to clean brake parts; use brake cleaner or methylated spirit only.*

1 Chock the rear wheels, apply the handbrake, then jack up the front of the vehicle and support it on axle stands. Remove the front roadwheels.
2 Push the piston into its bore by pulling the caliper outwards.
3 Slacken and remove the caliper lower guide pin bolt, using a slim open-ended spanner to prevent the guide pin from rotating **(see illustration)**.
4 Pivot the caliper away from the brake pads and mounting bracket, and tie it to the suspension strut using a suitable piece of wire **(see illustration)**. Do not allow the caliper to hang down by the hose.
5 Withdraw the two brake pads from the caliper mounting bracket **(see illustration)**.

6 First measure the thickness of each brake pads friction material **(see illustration)**. If the friction material of either pad is worn at any point to the specified minimum thickness or less, all four pads must be renewed. Also, the pads should be renewed if any are fouled with oil or grease; there is no satisfactory way of degreasing friction material, once contaminated. If any of the brake pads are worn unevenly, or are fouled with oil or grease, trace and rectify the cause before reassembly.
7 If the brake pads are still serviceable, carefully clean them using a clean, fine wire brush or similar, paying particular attention to the sides and back of the metal backing. Clean out the grooves in the friction material, and pick out any particles of embedded debris. Carefully clean the pad locations in the caliper mounting bracket.
8 Prior to fitting the pads, check that the guide pins are free to slide easily in the caliper mounting bracket, and check that the rubber guide pin gaiters are undamaged **(see illustration)**. Brush the dust and dirt from the caliper and piston, but **do not** inhale it, as it is injurious to health. Inspect the dust seal around the piston for damage, and the piston for evidence of fluid leaks, corrosion or damage. If attention to any of these components is necessary, refer to Section 8.
9 If new brake pads are to be fitted, the caliper piston must be pushed back into the cylinder to make room for them. Either use a G-clamp or similar tool, or use suitable pieces of wood as levers. Provided that the master cylinder reservoir has not been overfilled with hydraulic fluid, there should be no spillage, but keep a careful watch on the fluid level while retracting the piston. If the fluid level rises above the MAX level line at any time, the surplus should be siphoned off or ejected via a plastic tube connected to the bleed screw (see Section 2). *Caution: Do not syphon the fluid by mouth, as it is poisonous; use a syringe or an old poultry baster.*
10 Remove all traces of locking compound from the guide pin and bolt threads. If the threads are damaged, the bolt should be renewed.
11 Fit the brake pads to the caliper mounting bracket, ensuring that the friction material of each pad is against the brake disc.

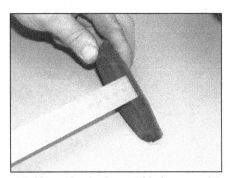

4.6 Measuring brake pad friction material thickness

4.8 Check the guide pins are free to slide in the caliper bracket and the gaiters are undamaged

12 Pivot the caliper down into position over the pads making sure the pad anti-rattle springs are correctly positioned against the caliper body.

13 Apply a few drops of locking compound (Skoda recommend the use of Loctite 243) to the guide pin bolt threads then press down on the caliper and screw in the bolt. Tighten the guide pin bolt to the specified torque setting, while retaining the guide pin with an open-ended spanner **(see illustrations)**.

14 Depress the brake pedal repeatedly, until the pads are pressed into firm contact with the brake disc, and normal (non-assisted) pedal pressure is restored.

15 Repeat the above procedure on the remaining front brake caliper.

16 Refit the roadwheels, then lower the vehicle to the ground and tighten the roadwheel bolts to the specified torque setting.

17 Check the hydraulic fluid level as described in *Weekly checks*.

 HAYNES HINT *New pads will not give full braking efficiency until they have bedded in. Be prepared for this, and avoid hard braking as far as possible for the first hundred miles or so after pad renewal.*

5 Rear brake shoes - renewal

 Warning: Brake shoes must be renewed on both rear wheels at the same time - never renew the

4.13a Apply locking compound to the guide pin bolt threads . . .

shoes on only one wheel, as uneven braking may result. Also, the dust created by wear of the shoes may contain asbestos, which is a health hazard. Never blow it out with compressed air, and don't inhale any of it. An approved filtering mask should be worn when working on the brakes. DO NOT use petrol or petroleum-based solvents to clean brake parts; use brake cleaner or methylated spirit only.

1 Remove the brake drum (see Section 7).

2 Working carefully, and taking the necessary precautions, remove all traces of brake dust from the brake drum, backplate and shoes.

3 Measure the thickness of each brake shoes friction material at several points; if either shoes friction material is worn at any point to the specified minimum thickness or less, all four shoes must be renewed as a set. The shoes should also be renewed if any are fouled with oil or grease; there is no satisfactory way of degreasing friction material, once contaminated.

4.13b . . . then refit the bolt and tighten it to the specified torque

4 If any of the brake shoes are worn unevenly, or fouled with oil or grease, trace and rectify the cause before reassembly.

5 To renew the brake shoes, proceed as follows. If the all components are in good condition, refit the brake drum (Section 7).

6 Note the position of each shoe, the wedge key, strut and the location of each of the springs, to aid refitting later **(see illustration)**.

7 Using a pair of pliers, remove the shoe retainer spring cups by depressing and turning them through 90°. With the cups removed, lift off the springs and withdraw the retainer pins **(see illustrations)**.

8 Ease the shoes out one at a time from the lower pivot point, to release the tension of the return spring, then disconnect the lower return spring from both shoes **(see illustrations)**.

9 Ease the upper end of both shoes out from their wheel cylinder locations, taking care not to damage the wheel cylinder seals, and disconnect the handbrake cable from the trailing shoe **(see illustration)**. The brake

5.6 Note the correct fitted locations of all springs before disturbing the brake shoes

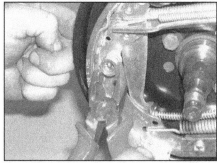
5.7a Release the shoe retainer spring cup by depressing it and rotate through 90° . . .

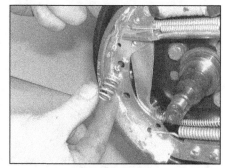
5.7b . . . then lift off the spring and remove the retainer pin

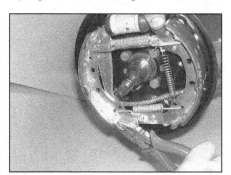
5.8a Ease the shoes out from the lower pivot point . . .

5.8b . . . and detach the lower return spring

5.9 Disconnect the handbrake cable and remove the shoe assembly from the vehicle

5.10 Unhook the adjuster wedge key spring and remove it

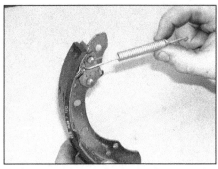

5.16a Hook the tensioning spring onto the leading shoe . . .

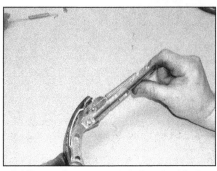

5.16b . . . then engage the strut with the opposite end of the spring and pivot it down into the leading shoe slot

shoe and adjuster strut assembly can then be manoeuvred out of position and away from the backplate. Do not depress the brake pedal until the brakes are reassembled; wrap a strong elastic band around the wheel cylinder pistons to retain them.

10 Make a note of the correct fitted positions of all components, then unhook and remove the spring from the adjuster wedge key **(see illustration)**.

11 Unhook the upper return spring and remove the trailing shoe from the leading shoe and strut.

12 Withdraw the wedge key, noting which way around it is fitted, then ease the strut out from the leading shoe and detach the tensioning spring.

13 Examine all components for signs of wear or damage, and renew as necessary. All return springs should be renewed, regardless of their

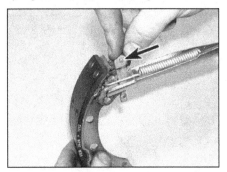

5.17 Insert the wedge key into position ensuring its peg (arrowed) is facing away from the shoe

apparent condition. Although linings are available separately (without shoes) from Skoda dealers, renewal of the shoes complete with linings is to be preferred, unless the necessary skills and equipment are available to fit new linings to the old shoes.

14 Peel back the rubber protective caps, and check the wheel cylinder for fluid leaks or other damage; check that both cylinder pistons are free to move easily. Refer to Section 9, if necessary, for information on wheel cylinder overhaul.

15 Apply a little brake grease to the contact areas of the strut and handbrake lever.

16 Hook the tensioning spring into the leading shoe. Engage the strut with the opposite end of the spring, and pivot the strut into position in the leading shoe slot **(see illustrations)**.

17 Insert the wedge key between the leading shoe and pushrod, making sure it is fitted the correct way around **(see illustration)**.

18 Fit the upper return spring to the leading shoe and engage the spring in its hole in the trailing shoe. Ensure the spring is correctly fitted then pivot the trailing shoe into position making sure both the shoe and handbrake lever are correctly engaged with the strut **(see illustrations)**.

19 Fit the spring to the wedge key, and hook it onto the leading shoe.

20 Prior to installation, clean the backplate, and apply a thin smear of high-temperature brake grease or anti-seize compound to all those surfaces of the backplate which bear on the shoes, particularly the wheel cylinder

pistons and lower pivot point. Do not allow the lubricant to foul the friction material.

21 Remove the elastic band fitted to the wheel cylinder, and offer up the shoe assembly.

22 Connect the handbrake cable to the handbrake lever, and locate the top of the shoes in the wheel cylinder piston slots.

23 Fit the lower return spring to the shoes, then lever the bottom of the shoes onto the bottom anchor.

24 Tap the shoes to centralise them with the backplate, then refit the shoe retainer pins and springs, and secure them in position with the spring cups.

25 Refit the brake drum as described in Section 7.

26 Repeat the above procedure on the remaining rear brake.

27 Once both sets of rear shoes have been renewed, adjust the lining-to-drum clearance by firmly depressing the brake pedal until normally (non-assisted) pedal pressure returns.

28 Check and, if necessary, adjust the handbrake as described in Section 14.

29 On completion, check the hydraulic fluid level as described in *Weekly checks*.

> **HAYNES HINT** *New shoes will not give full braking efficiency until they have bedded in. Be prepared for this, and avoid hard braking as far as possible for the first hundred miles or so after shoe renewal.*

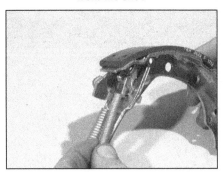

5.18a Fit the upper return spring to the leading shoe . . .

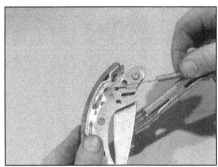

5.18b . . . then hook it onto the trailing shoe . . .

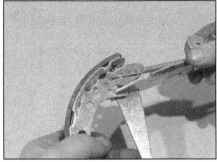

5.18c . . . before pivoting the shoe into position in the strut

6.6 Slacken and remove the mounting bolts and slide the complete brake caliper assembly off from the disc

6.7 Slacken and remove the retaining screw and remove the brake disc from the hub

6 Front brake disc - inspection, removal and refitting

Note: Before starting work, refer to the note at the beginning of Section 4 concerning the dangers of asbestos dust.

Inspection

Note: If either disc requires renewal, BOTH should be renewed at the same time, to ensure even and consistent braking. New brake pads should also be fitted.

1 Apply the handbrake, then jack up the front of the car and support it on axle stands. Remove the appropriate front roadwheel.
2 Slowly rotate the brake disc so that the full area of both sides can be checked; remove the brake pads if better access is required to the inboard surface. Light scoring is normal in the area swept by the brake pads, but if heavy scoring or cracks are found, the disc must be renewed.
3 It is normal to find a lip of rust and brake dust around the disc's perimeter; this can be scraped off if required. If, however, a lip has formed due to excessive wear of the brake pad swept area, then the disc's thickness must be measured using a micrometer. Take measurements at several places around the disc, at the inside and outside of the pad swept area; if the disc has worn at any point to the specified minimum thickness or less, the disc must be renewed.
4 If the disc is thought to be warped, it can be checked for run-out. Either use a dial gauge mounted on any convenient fixed point, while the disc is slowly rotated, or use feeler blades to measure (at several points all around the disc) the clearance between the disc and a fixed point, such as the caliper mounting bracket. If the measurements obtained are at the specified maximum or beyond, the disc is excessively warped, and must be renewed; however, it is worth checking first that the hub

bearing is in good condition (Chapters 1A, 1B and/or 10).
5 Check the disc for cracks, especially around the wheel bolt holes, and any other wear or damage, and renew if necessary.

Removal

6 Slacken and remove the two bolts securing the brake caliper mounting bracket to the swivel hub. Slide the caliper assembly off of the disc and tie the assembly to the front coil spring, using a piece of wire or string, to avoid placing any strain on the hydraulic brake hose **(see illustration)**.
7 Slacken and remove the retaining screw and remove the brake disc from the hub. If it is tight, lightly tap its rear face with a hide or plastic mallet **(see illustration)**.

Refitting

8 Ensure that the mating surfaces of the disc and hub are clean and flat. If a new disc is been fitted, use a suitable solvent to wipe any preservative coating from the disc.
9 Fit the disc to the hub and tighten its retaining screw to the specified torque.
10 Slide the brake caliper assembly into position, making sure the brake pads pass either side of the disc, and tighten its mounting bolts to the specified torque.

11 Refit the roadwheel then lower the vehicle to the ground and tighten the wheel bolts to the specified torque. Apply the footbrake several times to force the pads back into contact with the disc before driving the vehicle.

7 Rear brake drum - removal, inspection and refitting

Note: Before starting work, refer to the note at the beginning of Section 5 concerning the dangers of asbestos dust.

Removal

1 Chock the front wheels, then jack up the rear of the vehicle and support it on axle stands. Remove the appropriate rear wheel.
2 Using a hammer and a large flat-bladed screwdriver, carefully tap and prise the cap out of the centre of the brake drum **(see illustration)**. Discard the cap if it is disfigured during removal.
3 Extract the split pin from the hub nut and remove the locking cap **(see illustration)**. Discard the split pin; a new one must be used on refitting.

7.2 Carefully tap the cap out from the centre of the brake drum to gain access to the hub nut

7.3 Extract the split pin and remove the locking cap from the hub nut

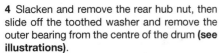

7.4a Slacken and remove the hub nut . . .

7.4b . . . then slide off the toothed washer . . .

7.4c . . . and withdraw the outer bearing . . .

4 Slacken and remove the rear hub nut, then slide off the toothed washer and remove the outer bearing from the centre of the drum **(see illustrations)**.

5 It should now be possible to withdraw the brake drum assembly from the stub axle by hand **(see illustration)**. It may be difficult to remove the drum, due to the tightness of the hub bearing on the stub axle, or due to the brake shoes binding on the inner circumference of the drum. If the bearing is tight, tap the periphery of the drum using a hide or plastic mallet, or use a universal puller, secured to the drum with the wheel bolts, to pull it off. If the brake shoes are binding, first check that the handbrake is fully released, then continue as follows.

6 Referring to Section 14, fully slacken the handbrake adjustment, to obtain maximum freeplay in the cable.

7 Insert a screwdriver through one of the wheel bolt holes in the brake drum, and lever

7.5 . . . before removing the brake drum

up the wedge key in order to allow the brake shoes to retract fully **(see illustrations)**. The brake drum can now be withdrawn.

Inspection

Note: *If either drum requires renewal, BOTH should be renewed at the same time, to ensure even and consistent braking. New brake shoes should also be fitted.*

8 Working carefully, remove all traces of brake dust from the drum, but avoid inhaling the dust, as it is injurious to health.

9 Clean the outside of the drum, and check it for obvious signs of wear or damage, such as cracks around the roadwheel bolt holes; renew the drum if necessary.

10 Examine carefully the inside of the drum. Light scoring of the friction surface is normal, but if heavy scoring is found, the drum must be renewed. It is usual to find a lip on the drum's inboard edge which consists of a mixture of rust and brake dust; this should be scraped away, to leave a smooth surface which can be polished with fine (120- to 150-grade) emery paper. If, however, the lip is due to the friction surface being recessed by wear, then the drum must be renewed.

11 If the drum is thought to be excessively worn, or oval, its internal diameter must be measured at several points using an internal micrometer. Take measurements in pairs, the second at right-angles to the first, and compare the two, to check for signs of ovality. Provided that it does not enlarge the drum to beyond the specified maximum diameter, it may be possible to have the drum refinished

by skimming or grinding; if this is not possible, the drums on both sides must be renewed. Note that if the drum is to be skimmed, BOTH drums must be refinished, to maintain a consistent internal diameter on both sides.

Refitting

12 If a new brake drum is to be installed, use a suitable solvent to remove any preservative coating that may have been applied to its interior. If necessary, install the bearing races, inner bearing and oil seal as described in Chapter 10, and thoroughly grease the outer bearing.

13 Prior to refitting, fully retract the brakes shoes by lifting up the wedge key.

14 Apply a smear of grease to the drum oil seal, and carefully slide the assembly onto the stub axle.

15 Fit the outer bearing and toothed thrustwasher, ensuring its tooth is correctly engaged in the axle slot.

16 Refit the hub nut, tightening it to the point where it just contacts the washer whilst rotating the brake drum to settle the hub bearings in position. Gradually slacken the hub nut until the position is found where it is just possible to move the toothed washer from side-to-side using a screwdriver **(see illustration)**. **Note:** *Only a small amount of force should be needed to move the washer.* When the hub nut is correctly positioned, refit the locking cap and secure the nut in position with a new split pin.

17 Fit the cap to the centre of the brake drum, driving it fully into position.

7.7a If the drum is tight, insert a screwdriver in through one of the wheel bolt holes . . .

7.7b . . . and lever up on the wedge key to fully retract the brake shoes (shown with drum removed for clarity)

7.16 Adjust the hub bearing as described in text

18 With both drums in position, adjust the lining-to-drum clearance by firmly depressing the brake pedal until normally (non-assisted) pedal pressure returns.

19 Repeat the above procedure on the remaining rear brake assembly (where necessary), then check and, if necessary, adjust the handbrake cable (see Section 14).

20 On completion, refit the roadwheel(s), then lower the vehicle to the ground and tighten the wheel bolts to the specified torque.

8 Front brake caliper -
removal, overhaul and refitting

Caution: On models equipped with ABS, disconnect the battery before disconnecting any braking system hydraulic union and do not reconnect the battery until after the hydraulic system has been bled. Failure to do this could lead to air entering the hydraulic unit. If air becomes trapped in the hydraulic unit, it may become impossible to remove using the conventional method (see Section 2). If this is the case, the only way to bleed the unit is to take the vehicle to a Skoda dealer who has access to the electronic tester (VAG 1552) required to bleed the hydraulic unit.

Note: *Before starting work, refer to the note at the beginning of Section 2 concerning the dangers of hydraulic fluid, and to the warning at the beginning of Section 4 concerning the dangers of asbestos dust.*

Removal

1 Apply the handbrake, then jack up the front of the vehicle and support it on axle stands. Remove the appropriate roadwheel.

2 Minimise fluid loss by first removing the master cylinder reservoir cap, and then tightening it down onto a piece of polythene, to obtain an airtight seal. Alternatively, use a brake hose clamp, a G-clamp or a similar tool to clamp the flexible hose.

3 Clean the area around the caliper hose union, then loosen the union.

4 Slacken and remove the upper and lower caliper guide pin bolts, using a slim open-ended spanner to prevent the guide pin itself from rotating. Lift the caliper away from the brake disc, then unscrew the caliper from the end of the brake hose; plug the hose end to minimise fluid loss and prevent dirt entry. Note that the brake pads need not be disturbed, and can be left in position in the caliper mounting bracket.

Overhaul

5 With the caliper on the bench, wipe away all traces of dust and dirt, but *avoid inhaling the dust, as it is injurious to health.*

6 Withdraw the partially ejected piston from the caliper body, and remove the dust seal **(see illustration)**.

<table><tr><td>HAYNES HiNT</td><td>*If the piston cannot be withdrawn by hand, it can be pushed out by applying compressed air to the brake hose union hole. Only low pressure should be required, such as is generated by a foot pump. As the piston is expelled take great care not to trap your fingers between the piston and caliper.*</td></tr></table>

7 Using a small screwdriver, extract the piston hydraulic seal, taking great care not to damage the caliper bore.

8 Thoroughly clean all components, using only methylated spirit, isopropyl alcohol or clean hydraulic fluid as a cleaning medium. Never use mineral-based solvents such as petrol or paraffin, as they will attack the hydraulic system's rubber components. Dry the components immediately, using compressed air or a clean, lint-free cloth. Use compressed air to blow clear the fluid passages.

9 Check all components, and renew any that are worn or damaged. Check particularly the cylinder bore and piston; these should be renewed (note that this means the renewal of the complete body assembly) if they are scratched, worn or corroded in any way. Similarly check the condition of the guide pins and their gaiters; both pins should be undamaged and (when cleaned) a reasonably tight sliding fit in the caliper bracket. If there is any doubt about the condition of any component, renew it.

10 If the assembly is fit for further use, obtain the appropriate repair kit; the components are available from Skoda dealers in various combinations. All rubber seals should be renewed as a matter of course; these should never be re-used.

11 On reassembly, ensure that all components are clean and dry.

12 Soak the piston and the new piston (fluid) seal in clean hydraulic fluid. Smear clean fluid on the cylinder bore surface.

13 Fit the new piston (fluid) seal, using only your fingers (no tools) to manipulate it into the cylinder bore groove.

14 Fit the new dust seal to the rear of the piston and offer up the piston to the caliper body. Seat the inner lip of the dust seal correctly in the caliper bore groove then carefully ease the piston squarely into the cylinder bore using a twisting motion. Press the piston fully into position then seat the outer lip of the dust seal in the piston groove.

15 If the guide pins are being renewed, lubricate the pin shafts with the special grease supplied (Skoda recommend the use of Lukosan M11 or M14) in the repair kit and fit the gaiters to the pin grooves. Insert the pins into the caliper bracket and seat the gaiters correctly in the bracket grooves.

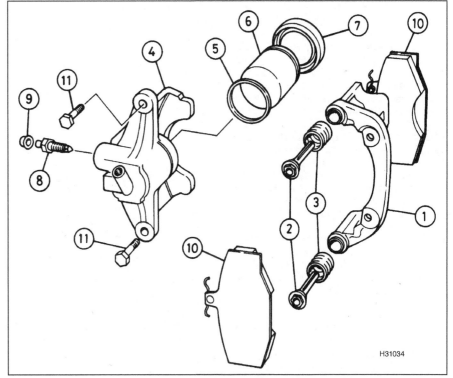

8.6 Exploded view of a front brake caliper

1 Mounting bracket	3 Gaiter	6 Piston	9 Dust cap
2 Guide pin	4 Caliper body	7 Dust seal	10 Brake pads
	5 Fluid seal	8 Bleed screw	11 Guide pin bolts

Refitting

16 Remove all traces of locking compound from the guide pin and bolt threads. If the threads are damaged, the bolts should be renewed.

17 Screw the caliper body fully onto the flexible hose union.

18 Ensure that the brake pads are still correctly fitted in the caliper mounting bracket then refit the caliper, making sure the pad anti-rattle springs are correctly positioned against the caliper body

19 Apply a few drops of locking compound (Skoda recommend the use of Loctite 243) to the threads of each guide pin bolt. Press the caliper into position then fit both guide pin bolts and tighten them to the specified torque whilst retaining the guide pins with an open-ended spanner.

20 Securely tighten the brake hose union nut then remove the brake hose clamp or polythene (where fitted).

21 Bleed the hydraulic system as described in Section 2. Note that, providing the precautions described were taken to minimise brake fluid loss, it should only be necessary to bleed the relevant front brake.

22 Refit the roadwheel, then lower the vehicle to the ground and tighten the roadwheel bolts to the specified torque.

---

9   Rear wheel cylinder -
removal, overhaul and refitting

Caution: On models equipped with ABS, disconnect the battery before disconnecting any braking system hydraulic union and do not reconnect the battery until after the hydraulic system has been bled. Failure to do this could lead to air entering the hydraulic unit. If air becomes trapped in the hydraulic unit, it may become impossible to remove using the conventional method (see Section 2). If this is the case, the only way to bleed the unit is to take the vehicle to a Skoda dealer who has access to the electronic tester (VAG 1552) required to bleed the hydraulic unit.

Note: *Before starting work, refer to the note at the beginning of Section 2 concerning the dangers of hydraulic fluid, and to the warning at the beginning of Section 5 concerning the dangers of asbestos dust.*

Removal

1 Remove the brake drum as described in Section 7.

2 Minimise fluid loss by first removing the master cylinder reservoir cap, and then tightening it down onto a piece of polythene, to obtain an airtight seal. Alternatively, use a brake hose clamp, a G-clamp or a similar tool to clamp the flexible hose at the nearest convenient point to the wheel cylinder.

3 Carefully unhook the brake shoe upper return spring, and remove it from both brake shoes. Pull the upper ends of the shoes away from the wheel cylinder to disengage them from the pistons.

4 Wipe away all traces of dirt around the brake pipe union at the rear of the wheel cylinder, and unscrew the union nut. Carefully ease the pipe out of the wheel cylinder, and plug or tape over its end to prevent dirt entry. Wipe off any spilt fluid immediately.

5 Unscrew the two wheel cylinder retaining bolts from the rear of the backplate, and remove the cylinder, taking great care not to allow surplus hydraulic fluid to contaminate the brake shoe linings.

Overhaul

6 Brush the dirt and dust from the wheel cylinder, but take care not to inhale it.

7 Pull the rubber dust seals from the ends of the cylinder body **(see illustration)**.

8 The pistons will normally be ejected by the pressure of the coil spring, but if they are not, tap the end of the cylinder body on a piece of wood, or apply low air pressure - eg, from a foot pump - to the hydraulic fluid union hole to eject the pistons from their bores.

9 Inspect the surfaces of the pistons and their bores in the cylinder body for scoring, or evidence of metal-to-metal contact. If evident, renew the complete wheel cylinder assembly.

10 If the pistons and bores are in good condition, discard the seals and obtain a repair kit, which will contain all the necessary renewable items.

11 Remove the seals from the pistons noting their correct fitted orientation. Lubricate the new piston seals with clean brake fluid, and fit them onto the pistons with their larger diameters innermost.

12 Dip the pistons in clean brake fluid, then fit the spring to the cylinder.

13 Insert the pistons into the cylinder bores using a twisting motion.

14 Fit the dust seals, and check that the pistons can move freely in their bores.

Refitting

15 Ensure that the backplate and wheel cylinder mating surfaces are clean and dry then spread the brake shoes and manoeuvre the wheel cylinder into position. Engage the brake pipe with the cylinder and screw in the union nut two or three turns, to ensure that the thread has started, then refit the retaining bolts and tighten them to the specified torque.

16 Securely tighten the brake pipe union nut then remove the clamp from the flexible brake hose, or the polythene from the master cylinder reservoir (as applicable).

17 Ensure that the brake shoes are correctly located in the cylinder pistons, then carefully refit the brake shoe return spring, ensuring it is correctly located in both shoes.

18 Refit the brake drum as described in Section 7.

19 Bleed the brake hydraulic system as described in Section 2. Providing suitable precautions were taken to minimise loss of fluid, it should only be necessary to bleed the relevant rear brake.

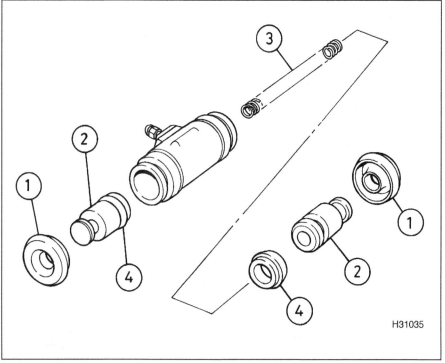

H31035

9.7 Exploded view of a rear wheel cylinder

| 1 Dust seal | 2 Piston | 3 Coil spring | 4 Fluid seal |

10 Master cylinder - removal and refitting

Note: *Before starting work, refer to the warning at the beginning of Section 2 concerning the dangers of hydraulic fluid.*
Note: *New master cylinder retaining nuts and a sealing ring will be needed on refitting.*

Models not fitted with an anti-lock braking system (ABS)

Removal

1 Wipe clean the master cylinder fluid reservoir and remove the reservoir cap. Lift out the filter and syphon the hydraulic fluid from the reservoir. **Note:** *Do not syphon the fluid by mouth, as it is poisonous; use a syringe or an old poultry baster.* Alternatively, open any convenient bleed screw in the system, and gently pump the brake pedal to expel the fluid through a plastic tube connected to the screw (see Section 2).

2 Release the reservoir retaining tang from the cylinder body then ease the reservoir out from its mounting seals and away from the master cylinder.

3 Wipe clean the area around the brake pipe unions on the side of the master cylinder, and place absorbent rags beneath the pipe unions to catch any surplus fluid. Make a note of the correct fitted positions of the unions, then unscrew the union nuts and carefully withdraw the pipes. Plug or tape over the pipe ends and master cylinder orifices, to minimise the loss of brake fluid, and to prevent the entry of dirt into the system. Wash off any spilt fluid immediately with cold water.

4 Slacken and remove the nuts and washers securing the master cylinder to the vacuum servo unit. Discard the nuts, new ones should be used on refitting.

5 Remove the master cylinder from the servo unit along with its sealing ring; discard the sealing ring a new one must be used on refitting.

6 It is not possible to overhaul the cylinder, since no internal components are available separately. If faulty, the complete master cylinder assembly must be renewed. The only components which can be renewed separately are the fluid reservoir mounting seals; both are a push-fit and can simply be pulled out of position.

Refitting

7 Ensure the mating surfaces are clean and dry then fit the new sealing ring to the rear of the master cylinder.

8 Carefully fit the master cylinder to the servo unit making sure the servo unit pushrod enters the master cylinder bore centrally. Fit the washers and new retaining nuts and tighten them to the specified torque.

9 Wipe clean the brake pipe unions and refit them to the master cylinder, tightening their union nuts securely.

10 Ease the fluid reservoir into position in the mounting seals and secure it by clipping its retaining tang onto the cylinder body pin.

11 Refill the master cylinder reservoir with new fluid and bleed the complete hydraulic system as described in Section 2.

Models equipped with an anti-lock braking system (ABS)

Caution: On models equipped with ABS, disconnect the battery before disconnecting any braking system hydraulic union and do not reconnect the battery until after the hydraulic system has been bled. Failure to do this could lead to air entering the hydraulic unit. If air becomes trapped in the hydraulic unit, it may become impossible to remove using the conventional method (see Section 2). If this is the case, the only way to bleed the unit is to take the vehicle to a Skoda dealer who has access to the electronic tester (VAG 1552) required to bleed the hydraulic unit.

Removal

12 Disconnect the battery negative terminal then remove the cap from the master cylinder fluid reservoir. Lift out the filter and syphon the hydraulic fluid from the reservoir. **Note:** *Do not syphon the fluid by mouth, as it is poisonous; use a syringe or an old poultry baster.*

13 Remove the retaining pin securing the reservoir tang to the cylinder body then carefully ease the reservoir out from its mounting seals.

14 Wipe clean the area around the brake pipe unions on the side of the master cylinder, and place absorbent rags beneath the pipe unions to catch any surplus fluid. Unscrew the union nuts then carefully free the pipes from master cylinder. Plug the pipe ends and master cylinder orifices, to minimise the loss of brake fluid, and to prevent the entry of dirt into the system. Wash off any spilt fluid immediately with cold water.

15 Slacken and remove the nuts and washers securing the master cylinder to the vacuum servo unit. Discard the nuts, new ones should be used on refitting.

16 Free the hydraulic unit mounting bracket from the servo unit then remove the master cylinder from the servo unit along with its sealing ring. Once the master cylinder has been removed, seat the hydraulic unit back on the servo unit studs. Remove the sealing ring from the rear of the master cylinder and discard it; a new one must be used on refitting.

17 It is not possible to overhaul the cylinder, since no internal components are available separately. If faulty, the complete master cylinder assembly must be renewed. The only components which can be renewed separately are the fluid reservoir mounting seals; both are a push-fit and can simply be pulled out of position.

Refitting

18 Ensure the mating surfaces are clean and dry then fit the new sealing ring to the rear of the master cylinder.

19 Position the hydraulic unit clear of the servo unit then manoeuvre the master cylinder into position, making sure the servo unit pushrod enters the master cylinder bore centrally. Seat the hydraulic unit bracket back on the servo unit studs then fit the washers and new retaining nuts and tighten them to the specified torque.

20 Ease the fluid reservoir into the master cylinder mounting seals and secure it position with the retaining pin.

21 Before the brake pipes are reconnected to the master cylinder, it is necessary to bleed the master cylinder itself of air. To do this, fill the reservoir with fresh fluid and position a container beneath the master cylinder ports to catch all expelled fluid. Have an assistant depress and release the brake pedal a few times, allowing approximately five seconds between strokes, whilst you keep an eye on the master cylinder. When fluid free of air is being expelled from the ports, remove the plugs from the brake pipes and check that both pipes are full of brake fluid; if necessary fill the pipes with fresh fluid. Have your assistant depress and hold the pedal then reconnect both pipes to the master cylinder, tightening the union nuts securely. Once both pipes are securely reconnected the brake pedal can be released. Remove the container and wash off any spilt fluid immediately with cold water.

22 Top-up the master cylinder reservoir with new fluid and bleed the complete hydraulic system as described in Section 2 before reconnecting the battery.

11 Brake pedal - removal and refitting

Right-hand drive models

1 The brake pedal is part of an assembly with the clutch pedal. Refer to Chapter 6 for removal and refitting details.

2 It is possible to change the brake pedal shaft pivot bushes without removing the pedal assembly (access is poor though). Remove the circlip from either end of the pivot shaft then extract the bushes from mounting brackets. Lubricate the new bushes with multi-purpose grease (Skoda recommend the use of Litol 24 or G000062 grease - available from your dealer) and insert them into the mounting brackets. Refit the circlips to the pedal shaft making sure both are correctly located in the shaft grooves

Left-hand drive models

Removal

3 Remove the clutch pedal as described in Chapter 6.

4 Slide off the retaining clip and withdraw the clevis pin which secures the servo unit pushrod to the brake pedal.

5 Unhook the return spring from the brake pedal to release the spring tension.

12.6a Prise out the centre pin then remove the fastener . . .

6 Slide out the pivot bush then manoeuvre the pedal out from its mounting bracket, along with the return spring.

7 Inspect the pedal for signs of wear or damage, paying particular attention to the pivot bush, and renew worn components as necessary.

Refitting

8 Lubricate the pedal bore, pivot bush and clevis pin with multi-purpose grease (Skoda recommend the use of Litol 24 or G000062 grease - available from your dealer).

9 Fit the return spring correctly to the pedal then manoeuvre the pedal assembly into position. Ensure the pedal is correctly engaged with the servo unit pushrod then slide the pivot bush into position.

10 Align the pedal with the pushrod and insert the clevis pin. Secure the pin in position

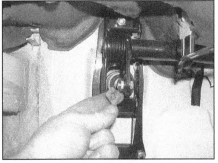

12.7 Slide off the retaining clip and withdraw the clevis pin from the servo unit pushrod

12.8 Ease the pedal mounting bracket away from the bulkhead to gain access to the servo unit mounting nuts (arrowed)

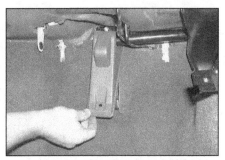

12.6b . . . and lift off the trim cover from the pedal linkage left-hand mounting bracket

with the retaining clip making sure it is securely located in the pin groove.

11 Hook the return spring back over the brake pedal and check the pedal operation before refitting the clutch pedal as described in Chapter 6.

12 Vacuum servo unit - testing, removal and refitting

Testing

1 To test the operation of the servo unit, depress the footbrake several times to exhaust the vacuum, then start the engine whilst keeping the pedal firmly depressed. As the engine starts, there should be a noticeable give in the brake pedal as the vacuum builds up. Allow the engine to run for at least two minutes, then switch it off. If the brake pedal is now depressed it should feel normal, but further applications should result in the pedal feeling firmer, with the pedal stroke decreasing with each application.

2 If the servo does not operate as described, first inspect the servo unit check valve as described in Section 13.

3 If the servo unit still fails to operate satisfactorily, the fault lies within the unit itself. Repairs to the unit are not possible - if faulty, the servo unit must be renewed.

Removal

Note: *New servo unit retaining nuts will be required on refitting.*

4 Remove the master cylinder as described in Section 10. On models with ABS position the hydraulic unit clear of the servo unit, supporting it in some way as to not put any excess strain on the brake pipes.

5 Carefully ease the vacuum hose out from the servo unit sealing grommet. If the sealing grommet shows signs of damage or deterioration it must be renewed.

6 On right-hand drive models, working in the passenger footwell, remove the retaining clip then remove the trim cover from the pedal assembly left-hand mounting bracket. The fastener is released by pressing out its centre pin then prising it out of position. Release the retaining clips and peel back the carpet from

12.6c Slacken and remove the bracket upper and lower mounting nuts (arrowed)

the bulkhead to gain access to the pedal bracket lower mounting nuts. Slacken and remove the nuts securing the pedal assembly left-hand mounting bracket in position and recover the lower mounting plate from the engine compartment **(see illustrations)**.

7 On all models, slide off the retaining clip and remove the clevis pin securing the vacuum servo unit pushrod to the pedal/pedal shaft (as applicable) **(see illustration)**.

8 Slacken and remove the servo unit retaining nuts and washers then free the rubber gaiter and foam sealing cap (where fitted) from the back of the servo **(see illustration)**. Discard the retaining nuts, new ones should be used on refitting.

9 Return to the engine compartment and manoeuvre the servo unit out of position, along with its gasket. The gasket must be renewed if it shows signs of wear or damage. If the servo unit is faulty it must be renewed; overhaul of the unit is not possible.

Refitting

10 Prior to refitting, ensure that the servo unit pushrod is correctly adjusted; the distance from the centre of the clevis pin bore to the servo unit rear surface should be 50 mm **(see illustration)**. To adjust the pushrod, slacken the clevis locknut and rotate the clevis as necessary; once the clevis is correctly

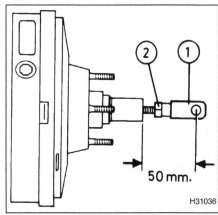

12.10 Ensure the distance from the centre of the pushrod clevis to the rear of the servo is 50 mm. If necessary slacken the locknut (2) and adjust by rotating the clevis (1)

positioned hold it stationary and securely tighten the locknut.

11 Ensure all mating surfaces are clean and dry and fit the gasket to the rear of the servo unit. Manoeuvre the servo unit into position and locate it in the bulkhead.

12 From inside the vehicle, refit the foam sealing cap and/or rubber gaiter to the rear of the servo unit then engage the servo unit pushrod correctly with the brake pedal/pedal shaft (as applicable).

13 Fit the washers and new retaining nuts to the servo and tighten them to the specified torque.

14 Align the pushrod clevis and slide in the clevis pin. Secure the pin in position with the retaining clip, ensuring it is correctly located in the pin groove.

15 On right-hand drive models, have an assistant offer up the lower mounting plate then refit the pedal bracket retaining nuts and tighten securely. Seat the carpet back in position then refit the trim cover to the bracket and secure it in position with its retaining clip.

16 From within the engine compartment, ensure the sealing grommet is correctly located then reconnect the vacuum hose to the servo unit.

17 Refit the master cylinder as described in Section 10.

18 On completion, check the operation of the braking system before using the vehicle on the road.

13 Vacuum servo unit check valve - removal, testing and refitting

Removal

1 The check valve is an integral part of the servo unit vacuum hose and can be removed as follows.

2 Carefully ease the vacuum hose out from the servo unit and remove the sealing grommet **(see illustration)**.

3 Work back along the hose, releasing it from all its retaining clips then slacken the retaining clip and disconnect it from the manifold/vacuum pump (as applicable) **(see illustration)**. Remove the hose assembly from the engine compartment; do not attempt to separate the valve from the hose it is not available separately.

Testing

4 Examine the check valve for signs of damage, and renew if necessary. The valve may be tested by blowing through it in both directions. Air should flow through the valve in one direction only - when blown through from the servo unit end of the valve. Renew the complete hose assembly if this is not the case.

5 Examine the rubber sealing grommet for signs of damage or deterioration, and renew as necessary.

13.2 Ease the check valve hose end fitting (arrowed) out from the servo unit . . .

Refitting

6 Ensure the hose is correctly routed then reconnect it to the manifold/vacuum pump (as applicable), tightening its retaining clip securely.

7 Fit the sealing grommet into position in the servo unit then ease the vacuum hose end fitting into position, taking care not to displace or damage the grommet.

8 On completion, start the engine and check that there are no air leaks.

14 Handbrake - adjustment

Note: *A spring balance will be required to accurately adjust the handbrake.*

1 The handbrake will normally be kept in adjustment by the action of the rear drum brake automatic adjusters. Occasionally, the handbrake mechanism may require adjustment to compensate for cable stretch but adjustment should only be needed if the brake shoes, drums, cables or handbrake lever are disturbed.

2 Prior to checking the handbrake adjustment, firmly apply the footbrake to ensure that the rear brake shoe self-adjusting mechanism is correctly set.

3 Handbrake adjustment is checked by counting the number of clicks emitted from the lever ratchet mechanism whilst apply the handbrake with a force of 100 to 140 N (10 to 14 kg). To accurately measure this force, a

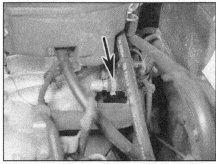

13.3 . . . and disconnect the other end of the hose from the inlet manifold (1.3 litre multi-point injection petrol engine shown)

spring balance will be required; fully release the handbrake lever then hook the balance around the centre of the lever grip and apply the brake using the specified force. When the specified force is applied, the lever should just click onto the second notch of the ratchet mechanism. It is also important that the equaliser plate on the handbrake lever, which links the two cables, is at a right-angle to the lever as this shows that both brakes are being applied equally.

4 If adjustment is necessary, remove the rear section of the centre console to gain access to the handbrake lever (see Chapter 11). On models without a centre console, unclip and remove the handbrake lever cover.

5 Release the handbrake lever then slacken the cable locknuts and rotate both adjuster nuts by the same amount; if the equaliser plate was not at a right-angle to the lever to start with, compensate for this during adjustment. Firmly apply the handbrake several times then recheck the adjustment as described in the previous paragraph, readjusting as necessary.

6 Once both cables are correctly adjusted, hold the adjuster nuts stationary and securely tighten both locknuts. Fully release the handbrake lever and check that both rear wheels rotate freely before refitting the centre console (see Chapter 11) or handbrake lever cover.

15 Handbrake lever - removal and refitting

Removal

1 Remove the rear section of the centre console as described in Chapter 11 to gain access to the handbrake lever. On models without a centre console unclip and remove the handbrake lever cover.

2 Fully slacken the cable locknuts then unscrew the adjuster nuts to obtain maximum freeplay in both cables. Extract the split pin and free the cable equalizer plate from the handbrake lever.

3 Remove the circlip from the handbrake lever pivot pin then slide the pin out of position and remove the lever assembly from the vehicle. Note that the lever ratchet mechanism components are available separately and can be renewed if worn.

Refitting

4 Prior to refitting, ensure that the lever ratchet mechanism components are correctly positioned and apply a smear of multi-purpose grease to the ratchet mechanism and lever pivot bore.

5 Manoeuvre the lever into position and insert the pivot pin. Secure the pin in position with the circlip, making sure it is correctly located in the pin groove.

6 Reconnect the cable equalizer plate to the lever and secure it in position with a new split pin.

7 Adjust the handbrake as described in Section 14.

16 Handbrake cables - removal and refitting

Removal

1 The handbrake cable consists of two sections, a right- and left-hand section which connect the rear brakes to the handbrake lever. Each section can be removed individually as follows.

2 Remove the rear section of the centre console as described in Chapter 11 to gain access to the handbrake lever. On models without a centre console unclip and remove the handbrake lever cover.

3 Unscrew the locknut and adjuster nut and free the front end of the cable from the handbrake lever equalizer plate.

4 Firmly chock the front wheels, then jack up the rear of the vehicle and support it on axle stands.

5 Remove the relevant brake drum (Section 7).

6 Using a flat-bladed screwdriver, lever the handbrake lever out from behind the brake shoe then detach the cable from the lever and free the cable end fitting from the brake backplate.

7 Work back along the cable, noting its correct routing whilst freeing it from any clips or ties. Detach the front end of the cable from the vehicle body and remove the cable from the vehicle. Renew any clips which are damaged on removal.

Refitting

8 Refitting is a reversal of the removal procedure ensuring that the cable is correctly routed and retained by all the relevant clips and ties. Prior to refitting the centre console/cover, adjust the handbrake as described in Section 14.

17 Rear brake pressure-regulating valve - testing, removal and refitting

Note: This procedure only applies to models that do not have ABS fitted.

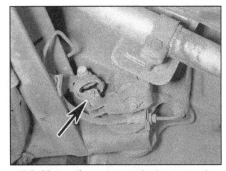

17.9 Make alignment marks between the valve spring bolt (arrowed) and valve lever before slackening it

Testing

1 On models not equipped with ABS, the hydraulic circuit to each rear brake is equipped with a pressure regulating valve to help prevent the rear wheels locking up under hard braking. The valve arrangement can either be of the pressure-sensitive type or the load-sensitive type, depending on vehicle specification.

2 On models with a pressure-sensitive arrangement there are two separate valves which are screwed directly into the rear brake outlet ports of the master cylinder. The master cylinder has a primary and a secondary hydraulic circuit with each circuit operating one front brake and one rear. The regulating valves act as restrictor valves and limit the hydraulic pressure being applied to the rear brakes, ensuring that the front brakes are always applied with a greater force.

3 On models with a load-sensitive arrangement, the valve is mounted onto the underside of the rear of the vehicle and is attached to the rear axle by a spring. The valve uses axle movement to judge load on the rear axle and regulates the hydraulic pressure accordingly.

4 Specialist equipment is required to check the performance of the valve(s). Therefore if there is thought to be a fault the car should be taken to a suitably equipped Skoda dealer for testing. Repairs are not possible and, if faulty, the valve(s) must be renewed.

Removal

Note: Before starting work, refer to the warning at the beginning of Section 2 concerning the dangers of hydraulic fluid.

Pressure-sensitive valve

5 Minimise fluid loss by first removing the master cylinder reservoir cap, and then tightening it down onto a piece of polythene, to obtain an airtight seal.

6 Wipe clean the area around the valve and master cylinder.

7 Slacken the union nut and disconnect the brake pipe then unscrew the valve from the master cylinder. Recover the sealing washer from the valve and discard it; a new one must be used on refitting. Plug or tape over the pipe end and master cylinder port, to minimise the loss of brake fluid, and to prevent the entry of dirt into the system. Wash off any spilt fluid immediately with cold water.

Load-sensitive valve

8 Chock the front wheels then jack up the rear of the vehicle and support it on axle stands.

9 Make alignment marks between the valve spring bolt head and valve lever; these marks can then be used to ensure the bolt is correctly positioned on refitting **(see illustration)**. Slacken and remove the nut and bolt securing the spring to the valve and recover the washers.

10 Wipe clean the area around the brake pipe unions on the valve, and place absorbent rags beneath the pipe unions to catch any surplus fluid. To avoid confusion on refitting, make alignment marks between the pipes and valve assembly.

11 Slacken the union nuts and disconnect the brake pipes from the valve. Plug or tape over the pipe ends and valve orifices, to minimise the loss of brake fluid, and to prevent the entry of dirt into the system. Wash off any spilt fluid immediately with cold water.

12 Undo the retaining screws and remove the valve assembly from its mounting bracket.

Refitting

Pressure-sensitive valve

13 Ensure the master cylinder and valve threads are clean and dry then fit a new sealing washer to the valve. Screw the valve into position and tighten securely.

14 Refit the brake pipe to the valve and securely tighten its union nut.

15 Remove the polythene from the master cylinder reservoir and bleed the complete hydraulic system as described in Section 2.

Load-sensitive valve

16 Manoeuvre the valve assembly into position and tighten its retaining screws securely.

17 Refit the brake pipes to their specific unions on the valve and securely tighten their union nuts.

18 Refit the valve spring bolt, ensuring the washers are correctly positioned and screw on the nut. Align the marks made prior to removal then tighten the nut to the specified torque.

19 Remove the polythene from the master cylinder reservoir and bleed the complete hydraulic system as described in Section 2. Although not strictly necessary, it is recommended that the valve operation is tested by a Skoda dealer.

18 Stop-light switch - removal, refitting and adjustment

Removal

1 The stop-light switch is screwed into the top of the brake pedal mounting bracket.

2 Reach up behind the facia and disconnect the wiring connector from the top of the switch **(see illustration)**.

3 Slacken the switch locknut then unscrew the switch and remove it from the mounting bracket along with its washer.

Refitting and adjustment

4 Ensure the locknut and washer are fitted to the switch then screw the switch back into the pedal mounting bracket.

5 Connect a continuity tester (ohmmeter or self-powered test light) across the switch terminals. Screw the switch in until an open-circuit is present between the switch terminals (infinite resistance, or light goes out). Gently depress the pedal and check that continuity exists between the switch terminals (zero resistance, or light comes on) after the pedal has travelled approximately 10 to 15 mm. If necessary, reposition the switch until it operates as specified.

6 In the absence of a continuity tester, the same adjustment can be made by reconnecting the switch and having an assistant observe the stop-lights (ignition on).

7 Once the stop-light switch is correctly adjusted, securely tighten the locknut and reconnect the wiring connector. Recheck the operation of the stop-lights before using the vehicle on the road.

19 Anti-lock braking system (ABS) - general information

1 ABS was fitted as standard to some models and available as an option on some others. The system comprises of the hydraulic unit, the electronic control unit (ECU) (which is joined to the hydraulic unit) and the four roadwheel sensors. The hydraulic unit contains the hydraulic solenoid valves (two for each brake - one inlet and one outlet) and the electrically driven pump. The purpose of the system is to prevent the wheel(s) locking during heavy braking. This is achieved by automatic release of the brake on the relevant wheel, followed by re-application of the brake. In the case of the rear wheels both brakes are applied at the same time.

2 The solenoid valves are controlled by the ECU, which itself receives signals from the four wheel sensors (which are fitted to the wheel hubs), which monitor the speed of rotation of each wheel. By comparing these signals, the ECU can determine the speed at which the vehicle is travelling. It can then use this speed to determine when a wheel is decelerating at an abnormal rate, compared to the speed of the vehicle, and therefore predicts when a wheel is about to lock. During normal operation, the system functions in the same way as a non-ABS braking system.

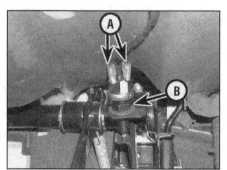

18.2 Disconnect the wiring connectors (A) then slacken the locknut (B) and unscrew the stop-light switch from its bracket

3 If the ECU senses that a wheel is about to lock, it closes the relevant outlet solenoid valves in the hydraulic unit, which then isolates the relevant brake(s) on the wheel(s) which is/are about to lock from the master cylinder, effectively sealing-in the hydraulic pressure.

4 If the speed of rotation of the wheel continues to decrease at an abnormal rate, the ECU opens the inlet solenoid valves on the relevant brake(s) and operates the electrically-driven return pump which pumps the hydraulic fluid back into the master cylinder, releasing the brake. Once the speed of rotation of the wheel returns to an acceptable rate, the pump stops; the solenoid valves switch again, allowing the hydraulic master cylinder pressure to return to the caliper/wheel cylinder (as applicable), which then re-applies the brake. This cycle can be carried out many times a second.

5 The action of the solenoid valves and return pump creates pulses in the hydraulic circuit. When the ABS system is functioning, these pulses can be felt through the brake pedal.

6 The operation of the ABS system is entirely dependent on electrical signals. To prevent the system responding to any inaccurate signals, a built-in safety circuit monitors all signals received by the ECU. If an inaccurate signal or low battery voltage is detected, the ABS system is automatically shut down, and the warning light on the instrument panel is illuminated, to inform the driver that the ABS system is not operational. Normal braking should still be available, however.

7 If a fault does develop in the ABS system, the vehicle must be taken to a Skoda dealer for fault diagnosis and repair. A complete test of the ABS system can then be carried out, using a special electronic diagnostic test unit which is simply plugged into the system's diagnostic connector.

20 Anti-lock braking system (ABS) components - removal and refitting

Hydraulic unit

Caution: On models equipped with ABS, disconnect the battery before disconnecting any braking system hydraulic union and do not reconnect the battery until after the hydraulic system has been bled. Failure to do this could lead to air entering the hydraulic unit. If air becomes trapped in the hydraulic unit, it may become impossible to remove using the conventional method (see Section 2). If this is the case, the only way to bleed the unit is to take the vehicle to a Skoda dealer who has access to the electronic tester (VAG 1552) required to bleed the hydraulic unit.

Note: Before starting work, refer to the warning at the beginning of Section 2

concerning the dangers of hydraulic fluid. Blanking plugs will be needed to seal the hydraulic unit unions once the pipes have been disconnected.

Removal

Note: New mounting nuts should be used on refitting.

1 Disconnect the battery negative lead. Minimise fluid loss by first removing the master cylinder reservoir cap, and then tightening it down onto a piece of polythene, to obtain an airtight seal.

2 Release the retaining clip and disconnect the wiring connector from the hydraulic unit.

3 Wipe clean the area around the brake pipe unions on the master cylinder and hydraulic unit. Mark the locations of the hydraulic fluid pipes to ensure correct refitting.

4 Unscrew the union nuts of the pipes linking the master cylinder to the hydraulic unit and remove both pipes from the vehicle. Working quickly, seal all hydraulic unit ports with the blanking plugs and plug the pipes to prevent dirt ingress and minimise fluid loss. **Note:** *If hydraulic unit unions are not securely plugged there is a risk of air entering the hydraulic unit pump (see Caution at the start of this Section).*

5 Unscrew the union nuts and disconnect the remaining four brake pipes from the hydraulic unit. Working quickly, seal all hydraulic unit ports with the blanking plugs (see previous paragraph).

6 Slacken and remove the nuts securing the hydraulic unit bracket to the servo unit then support the master cylinder and manoeuvre the hydraulic unit assembly out of position.

Refitting

7 Refitting is the reverse of removal, noting the following points.

a) Fit the new mounting nuts and tighten to the specified torque.

b) Prior to reconnection, ensure the pipes and the hydraulic unit unions are full of fluid (see Section 2). Reconnect the pipes to their original unions and securely tighten the union nuts.

c) Ensure the wiring connector is securely held in position with its retaining clip.

d) Bleed the hydraulic system as described in Section 2 then reconnect the battery.

e) On completion, it is recommended that the operation of the ABS system is checked at the earliest opportunity by a Skoda dealer using special electronic test equipment.

Electronic control unit (ECU)

Note: Blanking plugs will be needed to seal the hydraulic unit unions once the electronic control unit (ECU) is to separated from the hydraulic unit.

Removal

8 Remove the hydraulic unit as described in paragraphs 1 to 6.

9 Slacken and remove the bolts securing the ECU to the base of the hydraulic unit then

carefully unclip the ECU and ease it **squarely** away. As soon as the ECU is removed, seal all the hydraulic unit ports with the blanking plugs.
Caution: Do not tilt or rotate the ECU as it is removed from the hydraulic unit as could lead to the valve pins being damaged.

Refitting

10 Refitting is the reverse of removal, taking great care to ensure the ECU engages correctly with the hydraulic unit. Tighten the retaining bolts to the specified torque in a diagonal sequence then refit the hydraulic unit to the vehicle (see paragraph 7).

Front wheel sensor

Removal

11 Disconnect the battery negative lead.
12 Apply the handbrake, then jack up the front of the vehicle and support securely on axle stands. To improve access, remove the roadwheel.
13 Trace the wiring back from the sensor, releasing it from all the relevant clips and ties whilst noting its correct routing, and disconnect the wiring connector.
14 Slacken and remove the retaining bolt and withdraw the sensor from the swivel hub.

Refitting

15 Ensure that the mating faces of the sensor and the swivel hub are clean, and apply a little multi-purpose grease (Skoda recommend the use of Gleitmo 165 or Wolfracote) to the swivel hub bore before refitting.
16 Make sure the sensor tip is clean and ease it into position in the swivel hub. Refit the retaining bolt and tighten it to the specified torque.
17 Work along the sensor wiring, making sure it is correctly routed, securing it in position with all the relevant clips and ties.

Reconnect the wiring connector then lower the vehicle and (where necessary) tighten the wheel bolts to the specified torque.

Rear wheel sensor

Removal

18 Chock the front wheels, then jack up the rear of the vehicle and support it on axle stands. To improve access, remove the appropriate roadwheel.
19 Trace the wiring back from the sensor, releasing it from all the relevant clips and ties whilst noting its correct routing, and disconnect the wiring connector.
20 Slacken and remove the retaining bolt and withdraw the sensor.

Refitting

21 Ensure that the mating faces of the sensor and the hub are clean, and apply a little multi-purpose grease (Skoda recommend the use of Gleitmo 165 or Wolfracote) to the hub bore before refitting.
22 Make sure the sensor tip is clean and ease it into position. Refit the retaining bolt and tighten it to the specified torque.
23 Work along the sensor wiring, making sure it is correctly routed, securing it in position with all the relevant clips and ties. Reconnect the wiring connector then lower the vehicle and (where necessary) tighten the wheel bolts to the specified torque.

21 Vacuum pump (diesel engine models) - removal and refitting

Removal

1 The vacuum pump is situated on the left-hand end of the front of the cylinder block.
2 Release the retaining clip, and disconnect

the vacuum hose from the top of pump.
3 Slacken and remove the retaining bolt and remove the pump retaining clamp from the cylinder block.
4 Withdraw the vacuum pump from the cylinder block, and recover the sealing ring. Discard the sealing ring, a new one should be used on refitting.

Refitting

5 Fit the new sealing to the vacuum pump and apply a smear of oil to it to aid installation.
6 Manoeuvre the vacuum pump into position, making sure that the slot in the drive gear aligns with the dog on the drive shaft.
7 Refit the retaining clamp and tighten its retaining bolt to the specified torque.
8 Reconnect the vacuum hose to the pump, and secure it in position with the retaining clip.

22 Vacuum pump (diesel engine models) - testing and overhaul

1 The operation of the braking system vacuum pump can be checked using a vacuum gauge.
2 Disconnect the vacuum pipe from the pump, and connect the gauge to the pump union using a suitable length of hose.
3 Start the engine and allow it to idle, then measure the vacuum created by the pump. As a guide, after one minute, a minimum of approximately 500 mm Hg should be recorded. If the vacuum registered is significantly less than this, it is likely that the pump is faulty. However, seek the advice of a Skoda dealer before condemning the pump.
4 Overhaul of the vacuum pump is not possible, since no components are available separately for it. If faulty, the complete pump assembly must be renewed.

Chapter 10
Suspension and steering

Contents

Degrees of difficulty

| **Easy,** suitable for novice with little experience | | **Fairly easy,** suitable for beginner with some experience | | **Fairly difficult,** suitable for competent DIY mechanic | | **Difficult,** suitable for experienced DIY mechanic | | **Very difficult,** suitable for expert DIY or professional | |

Specifications

Wheel alignment and steering angles

Front wheel

Models manufactured before November 1994:

Toe setting	1 ± 1 mm toe-in
Toe-out on turns:	
Inner wheel	20°
Outer wheel	18° 45' ± 45'
Camber	0° 20' ± 30'
Castor	1° 30' ± 45'
King pin inclination	12° 20' ± 45'

Models manufactured from November 1994 onwards:

Toe setting	1 ± 1 mm toe-in
Toe-out on turns:	
Inner wheel	20°
Outer wheel	18° 50' ± 45'
Camber	-0° 30' ± 30'
Castor	1° 20' ± 45'
King pin inclination	11° 45' ± 45'

Rear wheel

Toe setting	1.2 ± 1.4 mm toe-in
Camber:	
Pre November 1994 models	-1° 24' ± 30'
November 1994 onwards models	1° 24' ± 30'

Roadwheels

Type	Pressed-steel or aluminium alloy (depending on model)
Size	4.5J x 13, 5.5J x 13 or 5.5J x 14 (depending on model)
Tyre pressures	See Weekly checks on page 0•17

Torque wrench settings

	Nm	lbf ft
Front suspension		
Anti-roll bar:		
Connecting link nuts	33	24
Mounting clamp bolts	25	18
Hub nut	300	221
Lower arm:		
Balljoint retaining bolts (needed for renewal)	25	18
Front pivot bolt nut	90	66
Rear mounting bracket bolts	70	52
Rear mounting bracket nut	7	5
Lower arm balljoint clamp bolt nut	65	48
Subframe mounting bolts	72	53
Suspension strut:		
Upper mounting nuts	20	15
Upper mounting plate nut	50	37
Swivel hub clamp bolt nut	65	48
Rear suspension		
Anti-roll bar retaining bolt nuts	55	41
Axle mounting bracket bolts	70	52
Axle pivot bolt nuts	80	59
Backplate/stub axle bolts	60	44
Suspension strut:		
Lower mounting bolt nut	55	41
Shock absorber piston nut	15	10
Upper mounting nut	30	22
Steering		
Column-to-intermediate shaft clamp bolt	35	26
Intermediate shaft-to-steering gear clamp bolt	35	26
Power steering pipe union bolts	30	22
Power steering pump:		
Mounting bolts	23	17
Pulley retaining bolts	25	18
Steering column mounting bolts	25	18
Steering gear mounting bolts:		
Manual steering	20	15
Power-assisted steering	65	48
Steering wheel nut	35	26
Track rod inner balljoint-to-steering rack	80	59
Roadwheels		
Wheel bolts	110	81

1 General information

1 The independent front suspension is of the MacPherson strut type, incorporating coil springs and integral telescopic shock absorbers. The MacPherson struts are located by transverse lower suspension arms, which utilise rubber inner mounting bushes, and incorporate a balljoint at the outer ends. The front swivel hubs, which carry the wheel bearings, brake calipers and the hub/disc assemblies, are bolted to the MacPherson struts, and connected to the lower arms via the balljoints. A front anti-roll bar is fitted to most models. The anti-roll bar is rubber-mounted onto the subframe, and is connected to the lower arms via connecting links.

2 The rear suspension is of the beam axle type. The axle assembly is mounted onto the vehicle at the front via rubber bushes and the suspension struts are mounted onto the rear of each axle trailing arm and secured to the vehicle body. The axle assembly incorporates an anti-roll bar which links both of the trailing arms.

3 The steering column is connected to an intermediate shaft which incorporates universal joints at its upper and lower ends. The lower universal joint is clamped to the steering gear pinion by means of a clamp bolt.

4 The steering gear is mounted onto the front subframe, and is connected by two track rods, with balljoints at their outer ends, to the steering arms projecting rearwards from the swivel hubs. The track rod ends are threaded, to facilitate adjustment. On models with power-assisted steering the hydraulic steering system is powered by a belt-driven pump, which is driven off the crankshaft pulley.

2 Front swivel hub assembly - removal and refitting

Note: *A new hub nut, lower arm balljoint clamp bolt nut, and swivel hub clamp bolt nut will be required on refitting.*

Removal

1 Remove the wheel trim/hub cap (as applicable) then slacken the driveshaft nut with the vehicle resting on its wheels. Also slacken the wheel bolts.

2 Chock the rear wheels of the car, firmly apply the handbrake, then jack up the front of the car and support it on axle stands. Remove the appropriate front roadwheel.

3 On models equipped with ABS, unbolt the wheel sensor and position it clear of the hub assembly (see Chapter 9). Note that there is no need to disconnect the wiring.

2.4 Unscrew the hub nut and remove the washer

2.5 Using a balljoint separator to free the track rod from the swivel hub

2.6 Unbolt the brake caliper assembly and slide it off the brake disc

4 Slacken and remove the hub nut and washer **(see illustration)**. If the nut was not slackened with the wheels on the ground (see paragraph 1), refit at least two roadwheel bolts to the front hub, tightening them securely, then have an assistant firmly depress the brake pedal to prevent the front hub from rotating, whilst you slacken and remove the driveshaft retaining nut. Discard the hub nut, a new one must be used on refitting.

5 Extract the split pin then unscrew the retaining nut from the track rod balljoint and free the balljoint from the hub. If the balljoint is tight, use a universal balljoint separator to free it **(see illustration)**.

6 If the hub bearings are to be disturbed, remove the brake disc as described in Chapter 9. If not, unscrew the two bolts securing the brake caliper/mounting bracket assembly to the swivel hub, and slide the caliper assembly off the disc **(see illustration)**. Using a piece of wire or string, tie the caliper to the front suspension coil spring, to avoid placing any strain on the hydraulic brake hose.

7 On models with an anti-roll bar, slacken and remove the nut securing the anti-roll bar connecting link to the lower arm and remove the washer and lower mounting rubber.

8 On all models, slacken and remove the lower arm balljoint clamp bolt and nut from the base of the swivel hub **(see illustration)**. Carefully lever down on the lower arm to free the balljoint from the swivel hub clamp; on models with an anti-roll bar take care not to lose the upper mounting rubber and washer from the connecting link. Discard the clamp

bolt nut, a new one should be used on refitting.

9 Undo the nut and withdraw the swivel hub-to-suspension strut clamp bolt **(see illustration)**. Discard the nut, a new one should be used on refitting.

10 Free the swivel hub assembly from the end of the strut, then release it from the outer constant velocity joint splines, and remove it from the vehicle **(see illustration)**. If the swivel hub is a tight fit on the strut, use a large flat-bladed screwdriver to carefully open up the clamp a little and if the driveshaft is a tight fit it can be tapped out of hub using a soft-faced mallet.

Refitting

11 Ensure that the driveshaft outer constant velocity joint and hub splines are clean, then slide the hub fully onto the driveshaft splines. Refit the washer to the outer joint and screw on the new hub nut, tightening it lightly only at this stage.

12 Slide the hub assembly fully onto the suspension strut, aligning the split in the hub clamp with the lug on the back of the strut. Align the hub and strut lug holes then refit the clamp bolt and fit the new nut, tightening it to the specified torque.

13 Align the lower arm balljoint shank with the swivel hub clamp then insert the clamp bolt and fit the new nut, tightening it to the specified torque. On models with an anti-roll bar, align the connecting link with the lower arm as the balljoint is located, making sure the upper mounting rubber and washer are correctly fitted.

14 Where necessary, refit the lower mounting rubber and washer to the anti-roll bar connecting link then refit the retaining nut and tighten to the specified torque.

15 Locate the track rod balljoint shank correctly in the swivel hub bore and securely tighten its retaining nut. Secure the nut in position with a new split pin.

16 Where necessary, refit the brake disc to the hub, referring to Chapter 9 for further information. Slide the caliper into position, making sure the pads pass either side of the disc, and tighten the caliper bracket bolts to the specified torque setting (see Chapter 9).

17 On models with ABS, refit the wheel sensor as described in Chapter 9.

18 Refit the roadwheel then lower the vehicle to the ground and tighten the wheel bolts to the specified torque.

19 With the vehicle resting on its wheels, tighten the hub nut to the specified torque then refit the wheel trim/hub cap (as applicable).

3 Front hub bearings - renewal

Note: *The bearing is a sealed, pre-adjusted and pre-lubricated, double-row roller type, and is intended to last the car's entire service life without maintenance or attention. Never overtighten the driveshaft nut beyond the specified torque wrench setting in an attempt to adjust the bearing.*

2.8 Slacken and remove the lower arm balljoint clamp bolt

2.9 Unscrew the nut and remove the clamp bolt securing the swivel hub to the strut

2.10 Free the swivel hub from the lower arm and strut then slide it off the driveshaft end

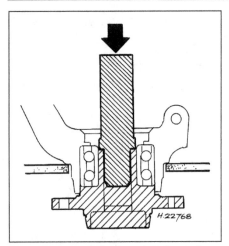

3.2 Pressing out the front hub flange from the bearing

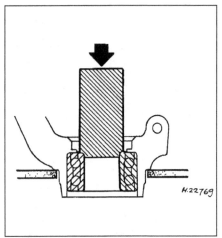

3.4 Pressing the bearing out from the swivel hub

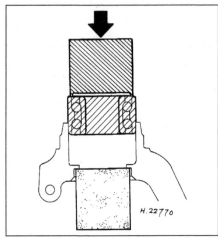

3.7 Pressing new bearing into swivel hub

Note: *A press will be required to dismantle and rebuild the assembly; if such a tool is not available, a large bench vice and spacers (such as large sockets) will serve as an adequate substitute. The bearing's inner races are an interference fit on the hub; if the inner race remains on the hub when it is pressed out of the hub carrier, a knife-edged bearing puller will be required to remove it.*

1 Remove the swivel hub assembly as described in Section 2.

2 Support the swivel hub securely on blocks or in a vice. Using a tubular spacer which bears only on the inner end of the hub flange, press the hub flange out of the bearing **(see illustration)**. If the bearing's outboard inner race remains on the hub, remove it using a bearing puller (see note above).

3 Extract the bearing retaining circlip from the outer end of the swivel hub assembly.

4 Securely support the outer face of the swivel hub. Using a tubular spacer which bears only on the inner race, press the complete bearing assembly out of the swivel hub **(see illustration)**.

5 Thoroughly clean the hub and swivel hub, removing all traces of dirt and grease, and polish away any burrs or raised edges which might hinder reassembly. Check both for

cracks or any other signs of wear or damage, and renew them if necessary.

6 On reassembly, apply a light film of oil (Skoda recommend the use of Optimol VP317 assembly paste) to the bearing outer race and hub flange shaft, to aid installation of the bearing.

7 Securely support the swivel hub, and locate the bearing in the hub. Press the bearing fully into position, ensuring that it enters the hub squarely, using a tubular spacer which bears only on the bearing outer race **(see illustration)**.

8 Once the bearing is correctly seated, secure the bearing in position with the circlip, ensuring that it is correctly located in the groove in the swivel hub.

9 Securely support the outer face of the hub flange, and locate the swivel hub bearing inner race over the end of the hub flange. Press the bearing onto the hub, using a tubular spacer which bears only on the inner race of the hub bearing, until it seats against the hub shoulder. Check that the hub flange rotates freely, and wipe off any excess oil or grease.

10 Refit the swivel hub assembly as described in Section 2.

4 Front suspension strut - removal and refitting

Note: *A new swivel hub clamp bolt nut and strut upper mounting nuts will be required on refitting.*

Removal

1 Open up the bonnet and check wether a strut brace is fitted between the strut upper mountings. If a brace is fitted, slacken and remove the strut upper mounting nuts and lift off the strut brace **(see illustrations)**. Refit the mounting nuts to the struts tightening them lightly only.

2 Chock the rear wheels, apply the handbrake, then jack up the front of the vehicle and support on axle stands. Remove the appropriate roadwheel.

3 On models with an anti-roll bar, slacken and remove the nut securing the anti-roll bar connecting link to the lower arm and remove the washer and lower mounting rubber.

4 On all models, undo the nut and withdraw the swivel hub-to-suspension strut clamp bolt **(see illustration)**. Discard the nut, a new one should be used on refitting.

4.1a On models with a strut brace, with the vehicle on its wheels undo the strut mounting nuts . . .

4.1b . . . then remove the brace and refit the nuts

4.4 Unscrew the nut and withdraw the clamp bolt . . .

4.5 . . . then free the swivel hub from the base of the strut

4.6a Remove the plastic cover from the top of the strut then undo the upper mounting nuts . . .

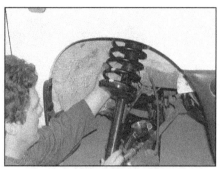

4.6b . . . and withdraw the strut from underneath the wheelarch

5 Lever down on the lower arm to free the swivel hub from the base of the strut, taking care not to strain the brake hose **(see illustration)**. If the swivel hub is a tight fit on the strut, carefully open up the clamp a little using a large flat-bladed screwdriver or similar tool. On models with an anti-roll bar take care not to lose the upper mounting rubber and washer from the connecting link.

6 Working in the engine compartment, remove the plastic cover then slacken and remove the suspension strut upper mounting nuts and washers. Withdraw the strut from under the wheel arch and discard the mounting nuts, new ones should be used on refitting **(see illustrations)**.

Refitting

7 Manoeuvre the strut assembly into position and fit the washers and new upper mounting nuts, tightening them to the specified torque, and refit the plastic cover. If the vehicle is fitted with a strut brace, temporarily fit the original nuts to the mounting and tighten them lightly only at this stage.

8 Engage the lower end of the strut with the hub assembly, aligning the split in the hub clamp with the lug on the back of the strut. On models with an anti-roll bar, align the connecting link with the lower arm as the hub assembly is located, making sure the upper mounting rubber and washer are correctly fitted.

9 Align the hub and strut lug holes then refit the clamp bolt. Fit the new nut to the clamp bolt and tighten it to the specified torque.

10 Where necessary, refit the lower mounting rubber and washer to the anti-roll bar connecting link then refit the retaining nut and tighten to the specified torque.

11 Refit the roadwheel, then lower the vehicle to the ground and tighten the roadwheel bolts to the specified torque.

12 On models with a strut brace unscrew the original nuts from the strut mountings and discard them. Refit the strut brace then fit the washers and new retaining nuts, tightening them to the specified torque **(see illustration)**.

5 Front suspension strut - overhaul

Warning: Before attempting to dismantle the front suspension strut, a suitable tool to hold the coil spring in compression must be obtained. Adjustable coil spring compressors are readily-available, and are recommended for this operation. Any attempt to dismantle the strut without such a tool is likely to result in damage or personal injury.

Note: *A new mounting plate nut will be required.*

1 With the strut removed from the car, clean away all external dirt, then mount it upright in a vice. Fit the spring compressor and compress the coil spring until tension is relieved from the spring seats **(see illustration)**.

4.12 On models with a strut brace, refit the brace then fit the new mounting nuts, tightening them to the specified torque

2 Slacken and remove the upper mounting plate nut whilst retaining the shock absorber piston with a spanner **(see illustration)**.

3 Noting each components correct fitted location, remove the nut and dished washer then lift off the mounting plate. Discard the nut; a new one should be used on reassembly **(see illustrations)**.

4 Remove the bush, bearing locator, bearing and spacer from the strut then lift off the upper spring seat and coil spring **(see illustrations)**.

5 Slide the dust gaiter and rubber bump stop from the shock absorber piston **(see illustration)**.

6 Examine the shock absorber for signs of fluid leakage. Check the piston for signs of pitting along its entire length, and check the shock body for signs of damage. While

5.1 Using spring compressors, compress the coil spring to relieve tension from the spring seats

5.2 Retaining the piston then slacken the upper mounting plate nut

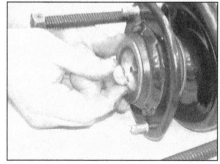

5.3a Remove the nut . . .

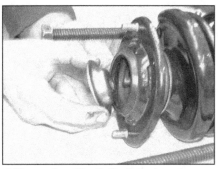

5.3b . . . then lift off the dished washer . . .

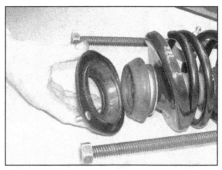

5.3c . . . and remove the upper mounting plate

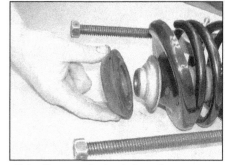

5.4a Remove the bush from the strut . . .

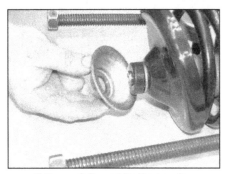

5.4b . . . followed by the bearing locator . . .

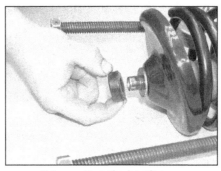

5.4c . . . then the bearing . . .

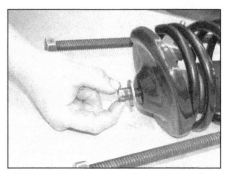

5.4d . . . the spacer and the upper spring seat

holding it in an upright position, test the operation of the shock absorber by moving the piston through a full stroke, and then through short strokes of 50 to 100 mm. In both cases, the resistance felt should be smooth and continuous. If the resistance is jerky, or uneven, or if there is any visible sign of wear or damage to the shock absorber, renewal is necessary.

7 Inspect all other components for signs of damage or deterioration, paying particular attention to the bearing and spacer, and renew any that are suspect.

8 Slide the rubber bump stop and dust gaiter onto the piston, making sure the lower end of gaiter is correctly positioned over the shock absorber end.

9 Refit the coil spring, making sure its lower end is correctly seated against the spring seat stop.

10 Fully extend the shock absorber piston

then fit the upper spring seat, aligning its stop with the spring end **(see illustration)**.

11 Fit the spacer, bearing, bearing locator and bush to the piston then fit the upper mounting plate.

12 Refit the dished washer to the piston and screw on the new nut. Retain the shock absorber piston and tighten the mounting plate nut to the specified torque.

13 Make sure the ends of the coil spring are still correctly located against their stops then carefully release the compressor and remove it from the strut.

6 Front suspension lower arm - removal, overhaul and refitting

Note: *A new lower balljoint clamp bolt nut and a front pivot bolt nut will be required on*

refitting. New spring washers will also be required for the lower arm rear mounting bolts.

Removal

1 Chock the rear wheels, firmly apply the handbrake, then jack up the front of the vehicle and support on axle stands. Remove the appropriate front roadwheel.

2 On models with an anti-roll bar, slacken and remove the nut securing the anti-roll bar connecting link to the lower arm and remove the washer and lower mounting rubber.

3 On all models, slacken and remove the lower arm balljoint clamp bolt and nut from the base of the swivel hub. Carefully lever down on the lower arm to free the balljoint from the swivel hub clamp; on models with an anti-roll bar take care not to lose the upper mounting rubber and washer from the connecting link **(see illustrations)**.

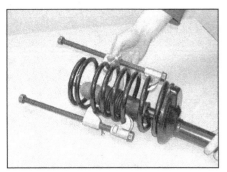

5.4e Remove the coil spring from the strut . . .

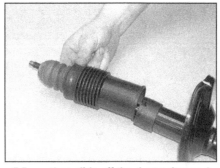

5.5 . . . then slide off the dust gaiter and bump stop

5.10 On refitting ensure the spring ends are correctly located against the spring seat stops

6.3a Remove the lower arm clamp bolt . . .

6.3b . . . then free the balljoint from the swivel hub

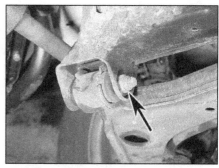

6.4 Slacken and remove the nut from the lower arm front pivot bolt

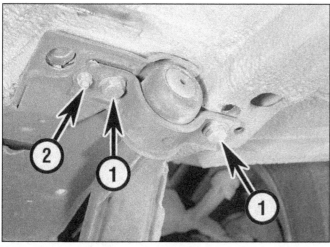

6.5a Slacken and remove the bolts (1) and nut (2) securing the lower arm rear bush to the body . . .

6.5b . . . noting that on some models the nut is replaced with a large pop rivet (arrowed)

Discard the clamp bolt nut, a new one should be used on refitting.

4 Slacken and remove the nut and washer from the lower arm front pivot bush bolt **(see illustration)**. Discard the nut, a new one should be used on refitting.

5 Slacken and remove the nut and bolts securing the lower arm rear pivot bush to the body. Remove the spring washers from the bolts and discard them; new ones should be used on refitting. On some models the nut is replaced by a large pop rivet which will to be drilled out of position **(see illustrations)**.

6 Withdraw the pivot bolt from the front mounting bush and manoeuvre the lower arm assembly out from underneath the vehicle

Overhaul

7 Thoroughly clean the lower arm and the area around the arm mountings, removing all traces of dirt and underseal if necessary, then check carefully for cracks, distortion or any other signs of wear or damage, paying particular attention to the pivot bushes, and renew components as necessary.

8 Renewal of the pivot bushes (the rear bush is particularly tricky) will required the use of a hydraulic press, a bearing puller and several spacers and should therefore be entrusted to a Skoda dealer with access to the necessary

equipment. If the equipment is available, they can be renewed as follows.

9 To renew the front bush first note the correct fitted position of the original then press/draw the bush out whilst securely supporting the arm. Thoroughly clean the arm bore and lubricate the new bush with soapy water before pressing/drawing it into position.

10 To renew the rear bush, first note the correct fitted position of the bush bracket in relation to the lower arm; it is important that the bracket is installed in exactly the same position otherwise excess stress will be placed on the bush. Press the arm assembly out from the bracket then press/draw the bush off from end of the arm. Thoroughly clean the bracket bore and arm and lubricate the new bush with soapy water before reassembling. On reassembly ensure the bush is correctly positioned so that its slot is positioned as shown in relation to the arm **(see illustration)**.

Refitting

11 Manoeuvre the lower arm assembly into position and engage the balljoint shank with the swivel hub. On models with an anti-roll bar, align the connecting link with the lower arm as the arm is fitted, making sure the upper mounting rubber and washer are correctly fitted.

12 Insert the front pivot bolt then refit the washer and screw on the new nut, tightening it finger-tight only.

13 Fit the retaining nut (where fitted) to the rear pivot bush bracket and fit the new spring washers to the retaining bolts. Refit the rear bracket retaining bolts, tighten them to their specified torque setting, then tighten the bracket nut to its specified torque setting. On models where the nut has been replaced with a pop rivet, fit a new rivet.

14 Ensure the lower arm balljoint is correctly seated in the swivel hub and insert the clamp bolt. Fit the new nut to the clamp bolt and tighten it to the specified torque setting.

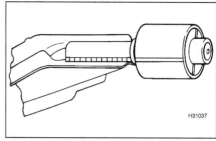

6.10 If the rear bush is being renewed, ensure the bush slot is positioned as shown in relation to the arm

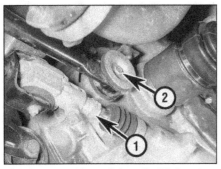

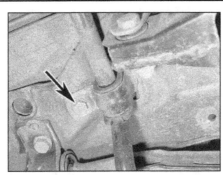

8.2 Remove the retaining clip (1) then tap out the roll pin securing the selector rod to the transmission (2 is the steady rod bolt)

8.6 Unscrew the retaining bolt (arrowed) and unhook each anti-roll bar mounting bracket from the subframe

15 Where necessary, refit the lower mounting rubber and washer to the anti-roll bar connecting link then refit the retaining nut and tighten to the specified torque.

16 Refit the roadwheel, then lower the vehicle to the ground and tighten the roadwheel bolts to the specified torque.

17 Rock the vehicle to settle the lower arm in position then tighten the lower arm front pivot bolt nut to the specified torque.

7 Front suspension lower arm balljoint - removal and refitting

Removal

Note: *Three retaining bolts and nuts will be required on refitting to replace the rivets.*

1 Remove the lower arm as described in Section 6.

2 Carefully grind/drill the heads off from the balljoint retaining rivets then tap out the rivets and remove the balljoint from the lower arm.

Refitting

3 Fit the new balljoint into the arm and insert the retaining bolts from the top of the arm. Fit the new nuts to the bolts and tighten them all to the specified torque setting.

4 Refit the lower arm as described in Section 6.

8 Front suspension anti-roll bar - removal and refitting

Note: *A new selector rod roll pin will be required on refitting.*

Removal

1 Chock the rear wheels, firmly apply the handbrake, then jack up the front of the vehicle and support on axle stands. Remove both front roadwheels.

2 Working at the transmission end of the gearchange selector rod, remove the retaining clip to gain access to the roll pin **(see illustration)**. If the original clip is still fitted, discard it and replace it with a jubilee-type hose clip on refitting. Tap the roll pin out of

position and discard it; a new one must be used on refitting.

3 Slacken and remove the nut and pivot bolt securing the selector rod to the base of the gearchange lever/mounting plate then free the front end of the rod from the transmission shaft and remove the rod from the vehicle. Recover the pivot bush(es) from the gearchange lever.

4 Slacken and remove the bolt securing the gearchange steady rod to the transmission unit and recover the washers and mounting rubber.

5 Remove both anti-roll bar connecting links as described in Section 9.

6 Slacken and remove the bolt securing each mounting bracket in position then unhook both brackets and remove them from the subframe **(see illustration)**.

7 Manoeuvre the anti-roll bar out from underneath the vehicle, and remove the mounting bushes from the bar.

8 Carefully examine the anti-roll bar components for signs of wear, damage or deterioration, paying particular attention to the mounting bushes. Renew worn components as necessary.

Refitting

9 Fit the rubber mounting bushes to the anti-roll bar positioning each bush so that its flat surface is at the top.

10 Offer up the anti-roll bar, and manoeuvre it into position on the subframe. Refit the

9.2 Unscrew the nut (arrowed) and remove the washer and lower mounting rubber from each anti-roll bar connecting link

mounting clamps, ensuring that their ends are correctly hooked behind the subframe, and refit the retaining bolts.

11 Refit the connecting links as described in Section 9 then tighten the mounting clamp bolts to the specified torque setting.

12 Remove all traces of locking compound from the gearchange linkage bolt threads.

13 Ensure the mounting rubbers and washer are correctly positioned then reconnect the rod to the transmission housing. Apply a few drops of locking compound (Skoda recommend the use of Loctite 270 or Three Bond 1305) to the retaining bolt threads then refit the bolt and tighten it to the specified torque setting (see Chapter 7).

14 Ensure the pivot bush(es) are correctly fitted to the gearchange lever and lubricate them with a smear of multi-purpose grease. Refit the selector rod and insert its retaining bolt. Apply a drop of locking compound (see paragraph 13) to the nut then fit the nut to the bolt and tighten to the specified torque (see Chapter 7). Secure the selector rod to the transmission with a new roll pin and secure the roll pin in position using a jubilee-type hose clip.

15 Refit the roadwheels then lower the vehicle to the ground and tighten the wheel bolts to the specified torque.

9 Front suspension anti-roll bar connecting link - removal and refitting

Removal

1 Chock the rear wheels, firmly apply the handbrake, then jack up the front of the vehicle and support on axle stands. Remove the relevant roadwheel.

2 Slacken and remove the nut securing each connecting link to the lower arm and remove the washer and lower mounting rubber from each link **(see illustration)**.

3 Free the connecting links from the lower arms and recover the upper mounting rubber and washer from each link. The links can then be slid off from the ends of the anti-roll bar.

4 Inspect the links for signs of wear or damage, paying particular attention to the mounting rubbers and bushes, renewing worn components as necessary.

Refitting

5 Slide the connecting links onto the anti-roll bar and refit the upper washers and mounting rubbers.

6 Locate the links in the lower arms then refit the lower mounting rubbers and washers and screw on the mounting nuts. Ensure both links are correctly positioned then tighten the mounting nuts to the specified torque.

7 Refit the roadwheel then lower the vehicle to the ground and tighten the wheelbolts to the specified torque.

11.2 Lever out the oil seal from the rear of the brake drum

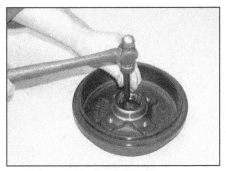
11.4 Tap out the outer bearing outer race from the drum . . .

11.5 . . . then turn the drum over and remove the inner bearing race

10 Front suspension subframe - removal and refitting

Note: *New connecting link nuts and lower balljoint nuts will be required on refitting.*

Removal

1 Chock the rear wheels, firmly apply the handbrake, then jack up the front of the vehicle and support it on axle stands. Remove both front roadwheels.
2 Remove the exhaust system front pipe and catalytic converter as described in Chapter 4D.
3 Remove the anti-roll bar as described in Section 8.
4 Remove both lower arms as described in Section 6.
5 Slacken and remove the steering gear mounting clamp bolts and remove the clamps from the subframe.
6 Slacken and remove the nut and through-bolt from the rear engine/transmission mounting.
7 Make a final check that all control cables/hoses that are attached to the subframe have been released and positioned clear so that they will not hinder the removal procedure.
8 Place a jack and a suitable block of wood under the subframe to support the subframe as it is lowered.
9 Slacken and remove the subframe mounting bolts then carefully lower the subframe assembly out of position and remove it from underneath the vehicle, taking great care to ensure that the subframe assembly does not

catch the power steering pipes as it is lowered out of position.

Refitting

10 Refitting is a reversal of the removal procedure, noting the following points:
   a) Tighten the subframe mounting bolts to the specified torque.
   b) Ensure the steering gear mounting rubbers are correctly positioned with their flat surfaces against the subframe then refit the mounting clamps. Clean the threads of the mounting bolts then apply a few drops of locking compound (Skoda recommend the use of Loctite 270) before refitting them and tightening to the specified torque.
   c) Refit the lower arms and anti-roll bar as described in Sections 6 and 8.
   d) Refit the exhaust system as described in Chapter 4D.
   e) On completion it is recommended that the front wheel alignment is checked (see Section 27).

11 Rear hub bearings - renewal

1 Remove the brake drum as described in Chapter 9.
2 Using a flat-bladed screwdriver, lever the oil seal out of the rear of the drum, noting which way around it is fitted **(see illustration)**.
3 Remove the inner bearing from the drum.
4 Support the hub, and tap the outer bearing outer race out of position **(see illustration)**.

5 Turn the drum over, and tap the inner bearing outer race out of position **(see illustration)**.
6 Thoroughly clean the drum bore, removing all traces of dirt and grease, and polish away any burrs or raised edges which might hinder reassembly. Check the surface for cracks or any other signs of wear or damage, and renew it if necessary. The bearings and oil seal must be renewed whenever they are disturbed, as removal will almost certainly damage the outer races. Obtain new bearings, an oil seal and a multi-purpose grease suitable for wheel bearings.
7 On reassembly, apply a light film of clean engine oil to each bearing outer race, to aid installation.
8 Securely support the drum, and locate the outer bearing outer race in position. Tap the outer race fully into position, ensuring that it enters the drum squarely, using a suitable tubular spacer which bears only on the race outer edge.
9 Turn the drum over, and install the inner bearing outer race in the same way.
10 Ensure both outer races are correctly seated and wipe them clean.
11 Work grease well into both the taper roller bearings, and apply a smear of grease to the outer races **(see illustration)**.
12 Fit the taper roller bearing to the inner bearing outer race **(see illustration)**.
13 Press the oil seal into the rear of the drum, ensuring that its sealing lip is facing inwards. Position the seal so that it is flush with the drum face, or until its lip abuts the rear of the drum. If necessary, the seal can be tapped into position

11.11 Work the grease well into the new bearings . . .

11.12 . . . then fit the inner bearing to the drum

11.13a Fit the new seal to the rear of the drum . . .

11.13b . . . and tap it squarely into position with a tubular drift

using a suitable tubular drift with bears only on the hard outer edge of the seal **(see illustrations)**.

14 Turn the drum over, fit the taper roller bearing to the outer race, and install the toothed washer.

15 Pack the hub bearings with grease then refit the drum as described in Chapter 9.

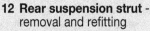

12 Rear suspension strut -
removal and refitting

Note: *A new lower mounting bolt nut will be required on refitting.*

Removal

1 On Hatchback models, unclip the luggage compartment side trim panel to gain access to the strut upper mounting.

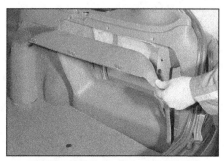

12.2 On Estate models remove the luggage compartment side trim panel and peel back the carpet to gain access to the rear strut upper mounting

2 On Estate models, remove the storage compartment cover from the relevant luggage compartment side trim panel then slacken and remove the panel upper and lower retaining screws. Unclip and remove the trim panel then peel back the carpet to reveal the strut upper mounting **(see illustration)**.

3 On all models, chock the front wheels, then jack up the rear of the vehicle and support it on axle stands. Remove the relevant rear roadwheel.

4 From inside the luggage compartment, remove the cap from the strut upper mounting then slacken and remove the mounting nut and washer. Noting each components correct fitted location, lift off the dished washer and mounting rubber from the top of the strut followed by the collar and spacer **(see illustrations)**.

5 From underneath the vehicle, slacken and

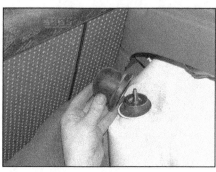

12.4a Remove the cap from the strut upper mounting . . .

remove the lower mounting bolt and nut then manoeuvre the strut assembly out of position. Discard the nut, a new one should be used on refitting. Inspect the upper mounting rubber for signs of damage or deterioration and renew if necessary **(see illustrations)**.

Refitting

6 Manoeuvre the strut into position, making sure it is correctly seated in the body, and insert the lower mounting bolt. Fit the new nut to the mounting bolt, tightening it by hand only at this stage.

7 From inside the luggage compartment, refit the spacer and collar to the top of the strut followed by the mounting rubber and dished washer.

8 Refit the washer and mounting nut to the top of the strut and tighten it to the specified torque. Refit the cap to the top mounting then refit the side trim panel.

12.4b . . . then slacken the mounting nut whilst holding the strut piston with a spanner

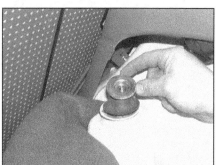

12.4c Lift off the dished washer and mounting rubber . . .

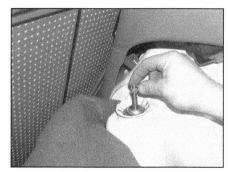

12.4d . . . then remove the collar . . .

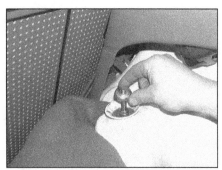

12.4e . . . and spacer from the top of the strut

12.5a Manoeuvre the strut out of position . . .

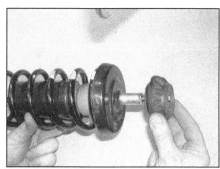

12.5b . . . and inspect the upper mounting rubber for signs of damage

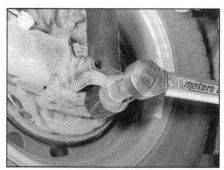

12.9 With the vehicle resting on its wheels, tighten the strut lower mounting bolt to the specified torque

9 Refit the rear roadwheel then lower the vehicle to the ground and tighten the wheel bolts to the specified torque. Rock the vehicle to settle the strut in position then tighten the lower mounting bolt nut to the specified torque setting **(see illustration)**.

13 Rear suspension strut - overhaul

⚠ *Warning: Before attempting to dismantle the front suspension strut, a suitable tool to hold the coil spring in compression must be obtained. Adjustable coil spring compressors are readily-available, and are recommended for this operation. Any attempt to dismantle the strut without such a tool is likely to result in damage or personal injury.*

1 With the strut removed from the car, clean away all external dirt, then mount it upright in a vice. Fit the spring compressor and compress the coil spring until tension is relieved from the spring seats.
2 Slacken and remove the strut piston nut whilst retaining the piston with a spanner.
3 Noting each components correct fitted location, lift off mounting rubber, spacer, spring retainer and spring upper seat.
4 Lift off the coil spring then collar, rubber bump stop and protective sleeve off from the shock absorber piston. If necessary, remove the cap from the top of the shock absorber main body and remove the spring lower seat
5 Examine the shock absorber for signs of fluid leakage. Check the piston for signs of pitting along its entire length, and check the shock body for signs of damage. While holding it in an upright position, test the operation of the shock absorber by moving the piston through a full stroke, and then through short strokes of 50 to 100 mm. In both cases, the resistance felt should be smooth and continuous. If the resistance is jerky, or uneven, or if there is any visible sign of wear or damage to the shock absorber, renewal is necessary.
6 Inspect all other components for signs of damage or deterioration, paying particular

attention to the mounting rubber and spring seat, and renew any that are suspect.
7 Where necessary, fit the lower seat to the shock absorber and clip the cap onto the top of the body.
8 Slide the rubber bump stop and protective sleeve onto the piston then refit the coil spring, making sure its lower end is correctly seated against the spring seat stop.
9 Fully extend the shock absorber piston then fit the upper spring seat, aligning its stop with the spring end.
10 Fit the collar, spring retainer, spacer and mounting rubber and screw on the nut. Retain the shock absorber piston and tighten the piston nut to the specified torque.
11 Make sure the ends of the coil spring are still correctly located against their stops then carefully release the compressor and remove it from the strut.

14 Rear suspension stub axle - removal, overhaul and refitting

Removal

1 Chock the front wheels, then jack up the rear of the car and support it on axle stands. Remove the relevant rear roadwheel.
2 Remove the brake drum as described in Chapter 9. On models equipped with ABS, unbolt the wheel sensor and position it clear of the hub (there is no need to disconnect its wiring connector).
3 Minimise fluid loss by first removing the master cylinder reservoir cap, and then tightening it down onto a piece of polythene, to obtain an airtight seal. Alternatively, use a brake hose clamp, a G-clamp or a similar tool to clamp the flexible hose at the nearest point to the relevant wheel cylinder.
4 Wipe away all traces of dirt around the brake pipe union at the rear of the wheel cylinder, and unscrew the union nut. Carefully ease the pipe out of the wheel cylinder, and plug or tape over its end to prevent dirt entry. Wipe off any spilt fluid immediately.
5 Slacken and remove the bolts securing the brake backplate assembly in position then free the backplate from the axle and remove the stub axle from the vehicle. Whilst the stub axle is removed secure the backplate to the axle with a couple of bolts to prevent the handbrake cable being strained.
6 Inspect the stub axle surface for damage such as scoring, and renew if necessary. Do not attempt to straighten it.

Refitting

7 Ensure the mating surfaces of the axle, stub axle and backplate are clean and dry. Check the backplate for signs of damage, and remove any burrs with a fine file or emery cloth.
8 Manoeuvre the stub axle and backplate assembly into position and refit the retaining

bolts. Tighten the retaining bolts to the specified torque setting in a diagonal sequence.
9 Wipe clean the brake pipe then reconnect it to the rear of the wheel cylinder, tightening the union nut securely.
10 Referring to Chapter 9, remove the hose clamp or polythene, then refit the brake drum and bleed the hydraulic system. Providing precautions were taken to minimise brake fluid loss, it should only be necessary to bleed the relevant rear brake. On models with ABS, it will also be necessary to refit the wheel sensor to the hub.

15 Rear suspension anti-roll bar - removal and refitting

Note: *New retaining bolt nuts will be required on refitting.*

Removal

1 Chock the front wheels then jack up the rear of the vehicle and support it on axle stands.
2 Slacken and remove the retaining nuts and bolts securing the anti-roll bar retaining plates to the underside of the axle then remove both plates and bar from underneath the vehicle **(see illustration)**. Discard the nuts, new ones should be used on refitting.

Refitting

3 Offer up the anti-roll bar and retaining plates then insert the bolts from underneath and fit the washer and new retaining nut.
4 Tighten both nuts to the specified torque then lower the vehicle to the ground.

16 Rear axle assembly - removal and refitting

Note: *New axle pivot bolt nuts and strut lower mounting bolt nuts will be required on refitting.*

Removal

1 Firmly chock the front wheels, then jack up the rear of the car and support it on axle stands. Disconnect the battery negative terminal then remove both rear roadwheels.

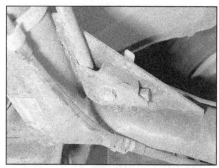

15.2 Rear anti-roll bar is secured to the rear axle by bolts and retaining plates

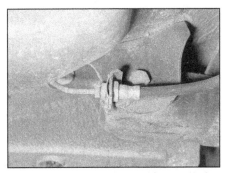

16.2 Disconnect the brake lines at their unions located directly in front of the rear axle

2 Referring to Chapter 9, carry out the following operations.
a) *Slacken and remove the handbrake cable locknuts and adjuster nuts and free both cables from the lever equalizer plate. From underneath the vehicle, free the front of both cables from the vehicle body so they are free to be removed with the axle assembly.*
b) *Trace the brake pipes back from the backplates to their unions on the front of the rear axle assembly* **(see illustration)**. *Remove all traces of dirt then slacken the union nuts and disconnect the pipes. Remove the retaining clips and free the hoses from their mounting brackets then plug the hose/pipe ends, to minimise fluid loss and prevent the entry of dirt into the hydraulic system.*
c) *On models with ABS, trace the wiring back from the rear wheel sensors and disconnect both wiring connectors. Free the wiring from the vehicle body so the sensors are free to be removed with the axle.*
d) *On models not fitted with ABS which are equipped with a load-sensitive pressure regulating valve, make alignment marks between the valve spring bolt and axle. Slacken and remove the nut and bolt and detach the spring.*

3 Make a final check that all necessary components have been disconnected then position a trolley jack beneath the centre of the rear axle assembly. Raise the jack until it is supporting the weight of the axle.
4 Slacken and remove the nuts and bolts securing the suspension strut lower mountings to the rear axle. Discard the nuts, new ones should be used on refitting.
5 With the aid of an assistant, slacken and remove the axle pivot bolts and nuts then carefully lower the jack and axle assembly out of position, and remove it from underneath the car. Discard the pivot bolt nuts, new ones must be used on refitting.
6 Inspect the axle pivot bushes for signs or damage or deterioration and renew, if necessary. Renewal of the pivot bushes will require the use of a hydraulic press and several spacers and is therefore best entrusted to a Skoda dealer or garage with access to the

necessary equipment. If the equipment is available, press out the old bushes and install the new ones using a spacer which bears only on the bush outer edge.
7 If the axle mounting brackets are to be renewed, mark the position of the bracket on the body then slacken and remove the retaining bolts and remove the bracket. Fit the new bracket to the vehicle and refit the retaining bolts. Align the bracket with the marks made prior to removal then tighten the mounting bolts to the specified torque. **Note:** *If the brackets are disturbed, then the rear axle should be checked for parallelism (see Section 27).*

Refitting

8 Raise the rear axle into position and insert the pivot bolts. Fit the new nuts to the pivot bolts, tightening them lightly only at this stage.
9 Refit the suspension strut lower mounting bolts and screw on the new nuts, tighten them lightly only at this stage.
10 Referring to Chapter 9, carry out the following operations.
a) *Where necessary, refit the rear brake pressure regulating valve spring bolt, ensuring the washers are correctly positioned and screw on the nut. Align the marks made prior to removal then tighten the nut to the specified torque.*
b) *On models with ABS, ensure the rear wheel sensor wiring is correctly routed and retained in position with the necessary clips then securely reconnect both connectors.*
c) *Refit the brake hoses to their brackets and secure them in position with the retaining clips. Reconnect the pipes to the hoses and securely tighten the union nuts.*
d) *Ensure both handbrake cables are correctly routed and secured in position with all the relevant clips. Pass the cables up through the body and reconnect them to the lever. Refit the adjuster nuts and locknuts but do not refit the centre console/lever cover yet.*

11 Refit the rear roadwheels then lower the vehicle to the ground and tighten the wheel bolts to the specified torque.
12 With the vehicle standing on its wheels, rock the car to settle the rear axle in position

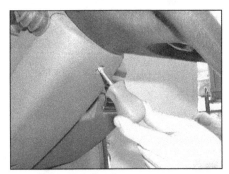

17.8a On models with an airbag, slacken and remove the retaining screw . . .

then tighten both axle pivot bolt nuts and the suspension strut lower mounting bolt nuts to their specified torque settings.
13 Working as described in Chapter 9, bleed the complete braking system then adjust the handbrake cable. On models where the pressure regulating valve is linked to the rear axle, it is recommended that the valve operation is tested by a Skoda dealer at the earliest possible opportunity.

17 Steering wheel - removal and refitting

Note: *Models equipped with a driver's side airbag have the word AIRBAG stamped on the steering wheel pad.*

Models without airbag

Removal

1 Set the front wheels in the straight-ahead position, and engage the steering lock.
2 Using a small flat-bladed screwdriver, carefully prise the horn button from the centre of the steering wheel. Disconnect the wiring connector and remove the horn button from the vehicle.
3 Slacken and remove the steering wheel retaining nut.
4 Mark the steering wheel and steering column shaft in relation to each other. Lift the steering wheel off the column splines.

> **HAYNES HiNT** *If the wheel is tight, tap it up near the centre, using the palm of your hand, or twist it from side to side, whilst pulling upwards to release it from the shaft splines.*

Refitting

5 Refitting is a reversal of removal, noting the following points:
a) *Prior to refitting, ensure that the indicator switch stem is in its central position. Failure to do this could lead to the steering wheel lug breaking the switch tab as the steering wheel is refitted.*
b) *On refitting, align the marks made on removal, and tighten the retaining nut to the specified torque.*

Models with an airbag

⚠ *Warning: Refer to the precautions given in Chapter 12 before proceeding.*

Removal

6 Remove the airbag unit as described in Chapter 12.
7 Position the front wheels in the straight-ahead position and engage the steering lock.
8 Undo the retaining screw from the top of the steering column lower shroud then slide the shroud downwards and remove it from the vehicle **(see illustrations)**.

17.8b ... then unclip the lower shroud and remove it from the steering column

9 Trace the airbag contact unit wiring back to its connector, freeing it from the steering column, then disconnect the connector so the wiring is free to be removed with the steering wheel **(see illustration)**.
10 Slacken and remove the steering wheel retaining nut and washer then mark the steering wheel and steering column shaft in relation to each other **(see illustration)**.
11 Lift the steering wheel off the column splines, taking care not to damage the wiring **(see illustration)**.

 HAYNES HiNT *If the wheel is tight, tap it up near the centre, using the palm of your hand, or twist it from side to side, whilst pulling upwards to release it from the shaft splines.*

18.4 Disconnect the wiring connectors from the horn contacts on the switch holder

18.5 Unclip the surround from around the steering lock/ignition switch

17.9 Disconnect the contact unit wiring connector so the wiring is free to be removed with the wheel

Refitting

12 Refitting is a reversal of removal, noting the following points:
a) Prior to refitting, ensure that the indicator switch stem is in its central position. Failure to do this could lead to the steering wheel lug breaking the switch tab as the steering wheel is refitted.
b) Ensure the front wheels are in the straight-ahead position then refit the wheel, aligning the marks made on removal, and tighten the retaining nut to the specified torque.
c) Ensure the airbag contact unit wiring is correctly routed and securely reconnected before refitting the steering column shroud.
d) On completion, refit the airbag unit as described in Chapter 12

18 Steering column - removal and refitting

Note: *On models equipped with a driver's side airbag, refer to the precautions given in Chapter 12 before proceeding.*

Removal

1 Disconnect the battery negative terminal.
2 Remove the steering wheel as described in Section 17.
3 Remove the combination switches from the top of the steering column as described in Chapter 12.

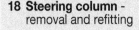

18.6a Undo the retaining screw and nut (arrowed) ...

17.10 Slacken and remove the retaining nut and washer ...

17.11 ... then remove the steering wheel from the column

4 Disconnect the wiring connectors from the horn contacts on the combination switch holder **(see illustration)**.
5 Carefully prise out the surround from around the steering lock/ignition switch housing and remove it from the facia **(see illustration)**.
6 Peel back the carpet then undo the retaining screw and nut and remove the trim cover (where fitted) from the base of the steering column to gain access to the intermediate shaft lower universal joint **(see illustrations)**.
7 Using paint or a suitable marker pen, make alignment marks between the intermediate shaft universal joint and the steering gear pinion then slacken and remove the clamp bolt **(see illustration)**.
8 Slacken and remove the column upper mounting bolts, noting the correct fitted location of the spacers and mounting rubbers,

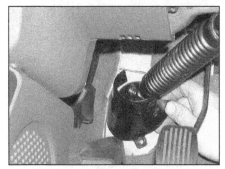

18.6b ... then remove the trim cover from the base of the intermediate shaft

18.7 Slacken and remove the clamp bolt (arrowed) from the intermediate shaft joint

18.8a Slacken and remove the column upper mounting bolts . . .

18.8b . . . and remove the spacers, mounting rubbers and mounting clamp

and remove the mounting clamp **(see illustrations)**.

9 Slacken and remove the column lower mounting bolts, mounting rubbers and spacers then lower the column slightly to gain access to the ignition switch. Note the correct fitted location of each connector then disconnect them from the switch. On models with an immobiliser, carefully unclip the sensor ring from the lock housing and position it clear of the column **(see illustrations)**.

10 Free the intermediate shaft from the steering gear pinion and remove the column assembly from the vehicle **(see illustration)**.

11 Examine the column and mountings for signs of damage and deformation, and renew as necessary. Check the steering shaft for signs of free play in the column bushes, and check the universal joints for signs of damage

18.9a Disconnect the wiring connectors from the rear of the ignition switch . . .

or roughness in the joint bearings. If any damage or wear is found on the universal joints or shaft bushes, the column assembly can be overhauled as described in Section 19.

Refitting

12 Align the marks made prior to removal and engage the intermediate shaft universal joint with the steering gear pinion.

13 Reconnect the wiring connectors to the ignition switch, using the notes made on removal to ensure they are correctly positioned. Where necessary, clip the immobiliser ring securely onto the lock housing.

14 Ensure the mounting rubbers and spacers are correctly fitted to the column lower mounting then seat the column on its mountings **(see illustration)**. Refit the lower mounting bolts then refit the upper mounting clamp and retaining bolts, making sure the spacers and mounting rubbers are correctly positioned. Ensure the column is correctly positioned then tighten all the mounting bolts to the specified torque.

15 Refit the universal joint clamp bolt and tighten it to the specified torque setting. Where necessary, refit the trim cover and securely tighten its retaining screw and nut.

16 The remainder of refitting is a direct reversal of the removal procedure, noting the following:

a) Ensure all wiring is correctly routed and retained by all the necessary clips and ties.

b) Refit the steering wheel as described in Section 17.

c) Prior to refitting the lower shroud, check that a small gap exsists between the steering wheel and the column upper shroud. If necessary, adjust the gap by slackening the combination switch holder clamp and moving the clamp.

19 Steering column - overhaul

Note: On models where an steering wheel adaptor ring is fitted, a puller will be needed to draw the adpator off from the column.

1 Remove the steering column as described in Section 18. Fit the key to the steering lock and position the switch in position0.

2 Using paint or a suitable marker pen, make alignment marks between the column shaft and the intermediate shaft upper universal joint.

3 Slacken and remove the clamp bolt then remove the intermediate shaft from the column **(see illustration)**.

4 Noting each components correct fitted location, remove the spring from the base of the column followed by the spacer, collar. Withdraw the column shaft from the top of the mounting tube and remove the lower bush.

5 Where necessary, using a legged puller, draw the steering wheel adaptor off from the upper end of the steering column shaft.

18.9b . . . and unclip the immobiliser sensor ring (where fitted) from around the lock housing

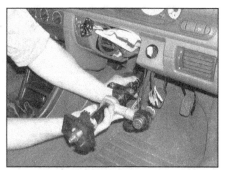

18.10 Free the intermediate shaft from the steering gear and remove the column from the vehicle

18.14 Ensure the mounting rubbers and spacers are correctly fitted to the lower mounting before seating the column in position

19.3 Remove the clamp bolt (arrowed) then separate the intermediate shaft and column

6 Remove the circlip from the upper end of the column shaft and slide off the collar and upper bush.

7 Inspect all components for signs of wear or damage and renew as necessary.

8 On reassembly, fit the upper bush and collar to the top of the column shaft and secure them in position with the circlip. Ensure that the circlip is correctly seated in the shaft groove. Where necessary, fit the steering wheel adaptor to the top of the shaft.

9 Fit the lower bush to the mounting tube then carefully insert the shaft assembly into the top of the tube. Fit the collar, spacer and spring over the lower end of the shaft.

10 Align the marks made prior to removal and refit the intermediate shaft. Ensure the shaft is correctly positioned on the column splines then refit the clamp bolt and tighten it to the specified torque setting.

11 Check the operation of the steering column assembly then refit it as described in Section 18.

20 Ignition switch/steering column lock - removal and refitting

Lock assembly

Note: *New shear bolts will be required on refitting.*

Removal

1 Disconnect the battery negative terminal.

2 Carry out the operations described in paragraphs 1 to 5 of Section 18.

3 Slacken and remove the column upper mounting bolts, noting the correct fitted location of the spacers and mounting rubbers, and remove the mounting clamp.

4 Slacken and remove the column lower mounting bolts, mounting rubbers and spacers then lower the column slightly to improve access to the lock assembly

5 Note the correct fitted location of each connector then disconnect them from the switch. On models with an immobiliser, carefully unclip the sensor ring from the lock housing and position it clear of the column.

6 Using a hammer and suitable punch, tap

the lock housing retaining clamp bolts around until they can be unscrewed by hand. Remove the bolts and mounting clamp and lift the lock assembly away from the steering column.

7 If necessary the complete lock cylinder housing can be separated from its mounting clamp once the shear bolt has been removed.

Refitting

8 Where necessary, fit the lock cylinder housing assembly to its mounting clamp and screw in the new shear bolt. Tighten the bolt lightly only at this stage.

9 Manoeuvre the lock assembly into position and engage it with the column. Refit the mounting clamp and screw in the new shear bolts.

10 Evenly and progressively tighten the shear bolts until both are lightly tightened. Check the operation of the lock assembly then tighten each bolt until its head shears off.

11 Reconnect the wiring connectors to the ignition switch, using the notes made on removal to ensure they are correctly positioned. Where necessary, clip the immobiliser ring securely onto the lock housing.

12 Ensure the mounting rubbers and spacers are correctly fitted to the column lower mounting then seat the column on its mountings. Refit the lower mounting bolts then refit the upper mounting clamp and retaining bolts, making sure the spacers and mounting rubbers are correctly positioned. Ensure the column is correctly positioned then tighten all the mounting bolts to the specified torque.

13 The remainder of refitting is a direct reversal of the removal procedure, noting the following:

a) *Ensure all wiring is correctly routed and retained by all the necessary clips and ties.*

b) *Refit the steering wheel as described in Section 17.*

c) *Prior to refitting the lower shroud, check that a small gap exsists between the steering wheel and the column upper shroud. If necessary, adjust the gap by slackening the combination switch holder clamp and moving the clamp.*

Ignition switch block

Removal

14 Remove the lock assembly as described in paragraphs 1 to 7.

15 Slacken and remove the grub screws and remove the switch assembly from the rear of the lock housing.

Refitting

16 Ensure the switch is correctly positioned then refit it to the rear of the lock housing. Ensure the switch is correctly engaged with the lock and slide it fully into position.

17 Clean the threads of the retaining screws then apply a drop of locking compound to each screw. Refit the screws to the lock assembly and tighten them securely.

18 Refit the lock assembly as described in paragraphs 8 to 13.

21 Steering gear assembly - removal, overhaul and refitting

Removal

1 From inside the vehicle, undo the retaining nuts and remove the footrest from the side of the clutch pedal **(see illustration)**.

2 Peel back the carpet then undo the retaining screw and nut and remove the trim cover (where fitted) from the base of the steering column to gain access to the lower universal joint.

3 Using paint or a suitable marker pen, make alignment marks between the column intermediate shaft lower universal joint and the steering gear pinion then slacken and remove the clamp bolt.

4 Undo the retaining nuts and washers then free the sealing plate and gasket from around the steering gear pinion. If the gasket is damaged it should be renewed.

5 Firmly apply the handbrake then jack up the front of the vehicle and support it on axle stands. Remove both front roadwheels.

6 Extract the split pins then unscrew the retaining nut from each track rod balljoint and free both balljoints from the hubs. If the balljoints are tight, use a universal balljoint separator to free them.

Manual steering gear

7 Slacken and remove the retaining bolts then remove the steering gear mounting clamps from the subframe.

8 Free the steering gear assembly from the intermediate shaft and manoeuvre it out from underneath the vehicle. Remove the mounting rubbers from the steering gear, noting that they are not interchangeable, and recover the sealing plate and gasket from inside the vehicle.

Power-assisted steering gear

9 Using brake hose clamps, clamp both the feed and return hoses near the power steering fluid reservoir. This will minimise fluid loss during subsequent operations.

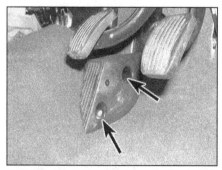

21.1 Unscrew the retaining nuts (arrowed) and remove the footrest from beside the clutch pedal

10 Mark the unions to ensure that they are correctly positioned on reassembly, then unscrew the feed and return hose union bolts from the steering gear assembly; be prepared for fluid spillage, and position a suitable container beneath the pipes whilst unscrewing the union bolts. Disconnect both hoses and recover the sealing washers; discard the washers new ones must be used on refitting. Plug the hose ends and steering gear orifices, to prevent fluid leakage and to keep dirt out of the hydraulic system.

11 Free the power steering hoses from any retaining clips, and position them clear of the steering gear.

12 Slacken and remove the retaining bolts then remove the steering gear mounting clamps from the subframe.

13 Free the steering gear assembly from the intermediate shaft and manoeuvre it out from underneath the vehicle. Remove the mounting rubbers from the steering gear, noting that they are not interchangeable, and recover the sealing plate and gasket from inside the vehicle.

Overhaul

14 Examine the steering gear assembly for signs of wear or damage, and check that the rack moves freely throughout the full length of its travel, with no signs of roughness or excessive free play between the steering gear pinion and rack. On power-assisted steering gear, inspect all the fluid unions for signs of leakage, and check that all union nuts are securely tightened. Renew the mounting rubbers if they show signs of damage or deterioration.

15 It is possible to overhaul the manual steering gear assembly housing components, but this task should be entrusted to a Skoda dealer; the power-assisted steering gear housing is only available as a complete unit.

16 On both types of steering gear the only components which can be renewed easily by the home mechanic are the steering gear gaiters, the track rod balljoints and the track rods. Track rod balljoint/balljoint gaiters, steering gear gaiter and track rod renewal procedures are covered elsewhere in this Chapter.

Refitting

Manual steering gear

17 Fit the mounting rubbers to the steering gear, positioning them with their flat surfaces at the bottom.

18 Ensure the mating surfaces are clean and dry and fit the sealing plate and gasket to the inside of the bulkhead.

19 Manoeuvre the steering gear into position, taking care not to damage the bulkhead sealing plate. With the aid of an assistant, align the marks made prior to removal and engage the intermediate shaft joint with the steering gear pinion splines.

20 Ensure both steering gear mounting rubbers are positioned with their flat surfaces against the subframe then refit the mounting clamps.

21 Remove all traces of locking compound from the steering gear mounting bolts and apply a few drops of fresh locking compound (Skoda recommend the use of Loctite 270) to each bolt. Refit the bolts and tighten them evenly and progressively to the specified torque.

22 From inside the vehicle, ensure the sealing plate is correctly engaged with the steering gear housing then securely tighten its retaining nuts.

23 Ensure the intermediate shaft joint is correctly positioned then refit the clamp bolt, tightening it to the specified torque. Where necessary, refit the trim cover.

24 Locate the track rod balljoints in the swivel hubs and refit the retaining nuts. Securely tighten both nuts and secure them in position with new split pins.

25 Refit the roadwheels then lower the vehicle to the ground and tighten the roadwheel bolts to the specified torque.

26 On completion check and, if necessary, adjust the front wheel alignment as described in Section 27.

Power-assisted steering gear

27 Carry out the operations described in paragraphs 17 to 24.

28 Position a new sealing washer on each side of the steering gear hose unions and screw in the union bolts. Ensure the hose unions are correctly positioned then tighten the union bolts to their specified torque settings before removing the clamps from the hoses.

29 Refit the roadwheels then lower the vehicle to the ground and tighten the roadwheel bolts to the specified torque.

30 Top-up the fluid reservoir and bleed the hydraulic system as described in Section 23.

31 On completion check and, if necessary, adjust the front wheel alignment as described in Section 27.

22 Steering gear rubber gaiters - renewal

1 Remove the track rod balljoint as described in Section 25.

2 Mark the correct fitted position of the gaiter on the housing and track rod, then release the retaining clips and slide the gaiter off the steering gear housing and track rod end.

3 Thoroughly clean the track rod and the steering gear housing, using fine abrasive paper to polish off any corrosion, burrs or sharp edges, which might damage the new gaiter's sealing lips on installation. Scrape off all the grease from the old gaiter, and apply it to the track rod inner balljoint. (This assumes that grease has not been lost or contaminated as a result of damage to the old gaiter. Use fresh grease if in doubt - Skoda recommend the use of Molykote Longterm 2/78).

4 Carefully slide the new gaiter onto the track rod end and locate it on the steering gear housing. Ensure the gaiter is not twisted then align its outer edges with the marks made prior to removal and secure it in position with the retaining clips.

5 Refit the track rod balljoint as described in Section 25.

23 Power steering system - bleeding

1 This procedure will only be necessary when any part of the hydraulic system has been disconnected.

2 Referring to *Weekly checks*, remove the fluid reservoir filler cap, and top-up with the specified fluid.

3 With the engine stopped, slowly move the steering from lock-to-lock several times to purge out the trapped air, then top-up the level in the fluid reservoir. Repeat this procedure until the fluid level in the reservoir does not drop any further.

4 Return the wheels to the straight-ahead position then start the engine and allow it to idle for approximately 5 seconds before switching it off again.

5 Recheck the fluid level, topping-up again if necessary then restart the engine. Slowly move the steering from lock-to-lock several times to purge out any remaining air in the system. Repeat this procedure until bubbles cease to appear in the fluid reservoir.

Caution: Do not hold the steering on full lock for any length of time as this could damage the steering gear.

6 If, when turning the steering, an abnormal noise is heard from the fluid lines, it indicates that there is still air in the system. Check this by turning the wheels to the straight-ahead position and switching off the engine. If the fluid level in the reservoir rises, then air is present in the system, and further bleeding is necessary.

7 Once all traces of air have been removed from the power steering hydraulic system, turn the engine off and allow the system to cool. Once cool, check that fluid level in the reservoir is correct (see *Weekly checks*).

24 Power steering pump - removal and refitting

Removal

1 Firmly apply the handbrake then jack up the front of the vehicle and support it on axle stands.

2 Slacken the bolts securing the drivebelt pulley to the power steering pump then release the drivebelt tension as described in the relevant part of Chapter 2, and unhook the

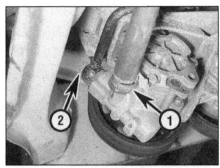

24.5 Slacken the retaining clip (1) and disconnect the supply hose then unscrew the union bolt (2) and disconnect the feed pipe from the pump

drivebelt from the pump pulley. Once the belt is removed, unscrew the retaining bolts and remove the pulley from the pump, noting which way around it is fitted.

3 Using brake hose clamps, clamp both the supply and return hoses near the power steering fluid reservoir. This will minimise fluid loss during subsequent operations.

4 Undo the retaining screw, and free the fluid feed pipe retaining clip from its mounting bracket (where fitted).

5 Slacken the retaining clip, and disconnect the fluid supply hose from the pump then slacken the union bolt, and disconnect the feed pipe **(see illustration)**. Be prepared for some fluid spillage as the pipe and hose are disconnected, and plug the hose/pipe end and pump unions, to minimise fluid loss and prevent the entry of dirt into the system. Recover the sealing washers which are fitted on each side of the feed pipe union and discard them; new ones must be used on refitting.

6 Slacken and remove the pump mounting bolts and withdraw the pump from its bracket.

7 If the power steering pump is faulty it must be renewed. The pump is a sealed unit and cannot be overhauled.

Refitting

8 Manoeuvre the pump into position, then refit its mounting bolts and tighten them to the specified torque.

9 Position a new sealing washer on each side of the feed pipe end fitting then screw in the union bolt. Ensure the end fitting is correctly positioned then tighten the union bolt to the specified torque. Where necessary, refit the pipe retaining clip and securely tighten its screw.

10 Reconnect the supply pipe to the pump, and securely tighten its retaining clip. Remove the brake hose clamps used to minimise fluid loss.

11 Refit the pulley to the pump, tightening its retaining bolts lightly, then and tension the drivebelt as described in the relevant part of Chapter 2. Once the drivebelt is correctly fitted, tighten the pulley retaining bolts to the specified torque.

12 On completion, bleed the hydraulic system as described in Section 23.

25 Track rod balljoint - removal and refitting

Removal

1 Apply the handbrake, then jack up the front of the vehicle and support it on axle stands. Remove the appropriate front roadwheel.

2 If the balljoint is to be re-used, use a straight-edge and a scriber, or similar, to mark its relationship to the track rod.

3 Hold the track rod, and unscrew the balljoint locknut by a quarter of a turn. Do not move the locknut from this position, as it will serve as a handy reference mark on refitting.

4 Extract the split pin then unscrew the retaining nut from the track rod balljoint and free the balljoint from the hub. If the balljoint is tight, use a universal balljoint separator to free it **(see illustration)**.

5 Counting the **exact** number of turns necessary to do so, unscrew the balljoint from the track rod end.

6 If necessary, count the number of exposed threads between the end of the track rod and the locknut, and record this figure. Unscrew the locknut and remove it from the track rod.

7 Carefully clean the balljoint and the threads. Renew the balljoint if its movement is sloppy or too stiff, if excessively worn, or if damaged in any way; carefully check the stud taper and threads. If the balljoint gaiter is damaged but the balljoint assembly seems to be in good condition, the gaiter can be renewed separately. Ensure the balljoint is adequately lubricated (Skoda recommend the use of Molykote Longterm 2/78) then fit the new gaiter and secure it in position with the retaining clips.

Refitting

8 Where necessary, screw the locknut onto the track rod and position it so that the same number of exposed threads are visible, as was noted prior to removal.

9 Screw the balljoint into the track rod by the number of turns noted on removal. This should bring the balljoint to within a quarter of a turn from the locknut. with the alignment marks that were made on removal (if applicable) lined up.

25.4 Using a balljoint separator to free the track rod from the hub

10 Locate the track rod balljoint in the swivel hubs and refit the retaining nut. Securely tighten the nut and secure it in position with a new split pin.

11 Refit the roadwheel, then lower the vehicle to the ground and tighten the roadwheel bolts to the specified torque.

12 Check and, if necessary, adjust the front wheel alignment as described in Section 27, then tighten the balljoint locknut to the specified torque.

26 Track rod - removal and refitting

Note: *A special wrench (Skoda number MP7-601) will be required to remove/refit the track rod inner balljoint from the end of the steering rack. The special wrench engages with the balljoint housing allowing the track rod to be easily slackened/tightened without the risk of damage. Note that without access to the special tool, track rod removal will be difficult, especially without causing damage.*

Removal

1 Remove the track rod balljoint as described in Section 25.

2 Remove all traces of dirt from around the steering gear and gaiter then mark the correct fitted position of the gaiter on the housing and track rod. Release the retaining clips and slide the gaiter off the steering gear housing and track rod end.

3 Using the special wrench (see note at the start of the Section), unscrew the track rod inner balljoint from the steering rack end whilst retaining the rack with an open-ended spanner engaged with the flats on the rack end. Take great care not to allow excess strain to be placed on the steering gear as the joint is unscrewed.

4 Remove the track rod assembly. Examine the track rod inner balljoint for signs of slackness or tight spots, and check that the track rod itself is straight and free from damage. If necessary, renew the track rod; it is also recommended that the steering gear gaiter is renewed.

Refitting

5 Screw the balljoint into the steering rack, and tighten it to the specified torque. Once again, retain the steering rack with an open-ended spanner to prevent any excess strain being placed on the steering gear assembly.

6 Ensure the track rod balljoint is adequately lubricated (Skoda recommend the use of Molykote Longterm 2/78) then carefully slide the gaiter onto the track rod end and locate it on the steering gear housing.

7 Ensure the gaiter is not twisted then align its outer edges with the marks made prior to removal and secure it in position with the retaining clips.

8 Refit the track rod balljoint as described in Section 25.

27 Wheel alignment and steering angles - general information

1 A car's steering and suspension geometry is defined in four basic settings - all angles are expressed in degrees (toe settings are also expressed as a measurement); the steering axis is defined as an imaginary line drawn through the axis of the suspension strut, extended where necessary to contact the ground.

2 **Camber** is the angle between each roadwheel and a vertical line drawn through its centre and tyre contact patch, when viewed from the front or rear of the car. Positive camber is when the roadwheels are tilted outwards from the vertical at the top; negative camber is when they are tilted inwards. The camber angle is not adjustable

3 **Castor** is the angle between the steering axis and a vertical line drawn through each roadwheel's centre and tyre contact patch, when viewed from the side of the car. Positive castor is when the steering axis is tilted so that it contacts the ground ahead of the vertical; negative castor is when it contacts the ground behind the vertical. The castor angle is not adjustable.

4 **Toe** is the difference, viewed from above, between lines drawn through the roadwheel centres and the car's centre-line. Toe-in is when the roadwheels point inwards, towards each other at the front, while toe-out is when they splay outwards from each other at the front. The front wheel toe setting is adjusted by screwing the track rods in or out of their outer balljoints, to alter the effective length of the track rod assembly. The rear wheel toe setting is not adjustable.

5 **Kingpin inclination (sometimes referred to as steering axis inclination)** – is the angle between the steering axis and a vertical line drawn through each roadwheel's centre and tyre contact patch, when viewed from the front or rear of the vehicle. The kingpin inclination angle is not adjustable.

Checking and adjustment

6 Due to the special measuring equipment necessary to check the wheel alignment and steering angles, and the skill required to use it properly, the checking and adjustment of these settings is best left to a Skoda dealer or similar expert. Note that most tyre-fitting shops now possess sophisticated checking equipment. The following are provided as a guide, should the owner decide to carry out a DIY check.

Front wheel toe setting

7 The front wheel toe setting is checked by measuring the distance between the front and rear inside edges of the roadwheel rims. Proprietary toe measurement gauges are available from motor accessory shops. Adjustment is made by screwing the balljoints in or out of their track rods, to alter the effective length of the track rod assemblies.

8 For **accurate** checking, the vehicle **must** be at the kerb weight, ie unladen and with a full tank of fuel.

9 Before starting work, check first that the tyre sizes and types are as specified, then check the tyre pressures and tread wear, the roadwheel run-out, the condition of the hub bearings, the steering wheel free play, and the condition of the front suspension components (see *Weekly checks* and the relevant part of Chapter 1). Correct any faults found.

10 Park the vehicle on level ground, check that the front roadwheels are in the straight-ahead position, then rock the rear and front ends to settle the suspension. Release the handbrake, and roll the vehicle backwards 1 metre, then forwards again, to relieve any stresses in the steering and suspension components.

11 Measure the distance between the front edges of the wheel rims and the rear edges of the rims. Subtract the rear measurement from the front measurement, and check that the result is within the specified range.

12 If adjustment is necessary, apply the handbrake, then jack up the front of the vehicle and support it securely on axle stands. Turn the steering wheel onto full-left lock, and record the number of exposed threads on the right-hand track rod end. Now turn the steering onto full-right lock, and record the number of threads on the left-hand side. If there are the same number of threads visible on both sides, then subsequent adjustment should be made equally on both sides. If there are more threads visible on one side than the other, it will be necessary to compensate for this during adjustment. **Note:** *It is most important that after adjustment, the same number of threads are visible on each track rod end.*

13 First clean the track rod threads; if they are corroded, apply penetrating fluid before starting adjustment. Release the steering gear rubber gaiter outboard clips and peel back the gaiters; apply a smear of grease to the inside of the gaiters, so that both are free, and will not be twisted or strained as their respective track rods are rotated.

14 Use a straight-edge and a scriber or similar to mark the relationship of each track rod to its balljoint then, holding each track rod in turn, unscrew its locknut fully.

15 Alter the length of the track rods, bearing in mind the note made in paragraph 13. Screw them onto or off of the balljoints, rotating the track rod using an open-ended spanner fitted to the flats provided on the track rod. Shortening the track rods (screwing them into their balljoints) will reduce toe-in/increase toe-out.

16 When the setting is correct, hold the track rods and tighten the balljoint locknuts to the specified torque setting. Check that the balljoints are seated correctly in their sockets, and count the exposed threads to check the length of both track rods. If they are not the same, then the adjustment has not been made equally, and problems will be encountered with tyre scrubbing in turns; also, the steering wheel spokes will no longer be horizontal when the wheels are in the straight-ahead position.

17 If the track rod lengths are the same, lower the vehicle to the ground and re-check the toe setting; re-adjust if necessary. When the setting is correct, tighten the track rod balljoint locknuts to the specified torque. Ensure that the rubber gaiters are seated correctly, and are not twisted or strained, and secure them in position with the retaining clips.

Rear axle parallelism check

18 Although no adjustment of the rear suspension settings is possible it is important to ensure that the axle is parallel to the front suspension subframe; this will be difficult to check accurately without the special Skoda jig (see illustration).

19 Chock the front wheels then jack up the rear of the vehicle and support it on axle stands.

20 Measure the distance from the rear of the front suspension subframe to the centre of each rear axle mounting bracket; this distance is equal on both sides. If this is not the case then the axle assembly is not parallel to the subframe.

21 If adjustment is necessary, slacken the axle mounting bracket retaining bolts and reposition the brackets as necessary. Once the distance is the same on both sides, retighten all the mounting bracket bolts to the specified torque whilst ensuring the axle assembly remains stationary.

22 Recheck the mounting bracket positions then lower the vehicle to the ground.

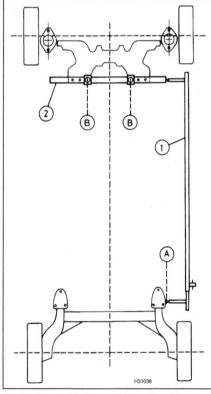

27.18 Skoda jig (1 and 2) for checking rear axle parallelism

a *Centre of rear axle mounting bracket*
b *Locating holes in front subframe*

Chapter 11
Bodywork and fittings

Contents

Degrees of difficulty

Easy, suitable for novice with little experience	Fairly easy, suitable for beginner with some experience	Fairly difficult, suitable for competent DIY mechanic	Difficult, suitable for experienced DIY mechanic	Very difficult, suitable for expert DIY or professional

Specifications

Torque wrench settings	Nm	lbf ft
Bonnet lock:		
Lock striker pin locknut	15	11
Lock striker plate retaining bolts	8	6
Retaining bolts	8	6
Bonnet retaining bolts	15	11
Door hinge bolts	70	52
Door lock:		
Exterior handle retaining nuts	7	5
Lock retaining bolts:		
Inner section to door bolt	5	4
Outer section-to-inner section bolts	20	15
Striker plate retaining screws	20	15
Front seat belt:		
Inertia reel bolt	40	30
Lower mounting bolt	40	30
Tensioner mechanism mounting nut	23	17
Front seat mounting bolts	18	13
Rear seat belt mounting and inertia reel bolts	40	30
Tailgate hinge bolts	15	11
Tailgate lock striker bolts	20	15
Window glass-to-regulator bolts	7	5
Window regulator retaining nuts	7	5

1 General information

1 The bodyshell is made of pressed-steel sections. Most components are welded together, but some use is made of structural adhesives.

2 The bonnet, door, and some other vulnerable panels are made of zinc-coated metal, and are further protected by being coated with an anti-chip primer before being sprayed.

3 Extensive use is made of plastic materials, mainly in the interior, but also in exterior components. The front and rear bumpers and front grille are injection-moulded from a synthetic material that is very strong and yet light. Plastic components such as wheel arch liners are fitted to the underside of the vehicle, to improve the body's resistance to corrosion.

2 Maintenance - bodywork and underframe

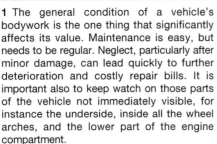

1 The general condition of a vehicle's bodywork is the one thing that significantly affects its value. Maintenance is easy, but needs to be regular. Neglect, particularly after minor damage, can lead quickly to further deterioration and costly repair bills. It is important also to keep watch on those parts of the vehicle not immediately visible, for instance the underside, inside all the wheel arches, and the lower part of the engine compartment.

2 The basic maintenance routine for the bodywork is washing - preferably with a lot of water, from a hose. This will remove all the loose solids which may have stuck to the vehicle. It is important to flush these off in such a way as to prevent grit from scratching the finish. The wheel arches and underframe need washing in the same way, to remove any accumulated mud which will retain moisture and tend to encourage rust. Paradoxically enough, the best time to clean the underframe and wheel arches is in wet weather, when the mud is thoroughly wet and soft. In very wet weather, the underframe is usually cleaned of large accumulations automatically, and this is a good time for inspection.

3 Periodically, except on vehicles with a wax-based underbody protective coating, it is a good idea to have the whole of the underframe of the vehicle steam-cleaned, engine compartment included, so that a thorough inspection can be carried out to see what minor repairs and renovations are necessary. Steam cleaning is available at many garages, and is necessary for the removal of the accumulation of oily grime, which sometimes is allowed to become thick in certain areas. If steam-cleaning facilities are not available, there are some excellent grease solvents available which can be brush-applied; the dirt can then be simply hosed off. Note that these methods should not be used on vehicles with wax-based underbody protective coating, or the coating will be removed. Such vehicles should be inspected annually, preferably just before Winter, when the underbody should be washed down, and repair any damage to the wax coating. Ideally, a completely fresh coat should be applied. It would also be worth considering the use of such wax-based protection for injection into door panels, sills, box sections, etc, as an additional safeguard against rust damage, where such protection is not provided by the vehicle manufacturer.

4 After washing paintwork, wipe off with a chamois leather to give an unspotted clear finish. A coat of clear protective wax polish will give added protection against chemical pollutants in the air. If the paintwork sheen has dulled or oxidised, use a cleaner/polisher combination to restore the brilliance of the shine. This requires a little effort, but such dulling is usually caused because regular washing has been neglected. Care needs to be taken with metallic paintwork, as special non-abrasive cleaner/polisher is required to avoid damage to the finish. Always check that the door and ventilator opening drain holes and pipes are completely clear, so that water can be drained out. Brightwork should be treated in the same way as paintwork. Windscreens and windows can be kept clear of the smeary film which often appears, by proprietary glass cleaner. Never use any form of wax or other body or chromium polish on glass.

3 Maintenance - upholstery and carpets

1 Mats and carpets should be brushed or vacuum-cleaned regularly, to keep them free of grit. If they are badly stained, remove them from the vehicle for scrubbing or sponging, and make quite sure they are dry before refitting. Seats and interior trim panels can be kept clean by wiping with a damp cloth. If they do become stained (which can be more apparent on light-coloured upholstery), use a little liquid detergent and a soft nail brush to scour the grime out of the grain of the material. Do not forget to keep the headlining clean in the same way as the upholstery. When using liquid cleaners inside the vehicle, do not over-wet the surfaces being cleaned. Excessive damp could get into the seams and padded interior, causing stains, offensive odours or even rot. If the inside of the vehicle gets wet accidentally, it is worthwhile taking some trouble to dry it out properly, particularly where carpets are involved. *Do not leave oil or electric heaters inside the vehicle for this purpose.*

4 Minor body damage - repair

Repairs of minor scratches in bodywork

1 If the scratch is very superficial, and does not penetrate to the metal of the bodywork, repair is very simple. Lightly rub the area of the scratch with a paintwork renovator or a very fine cutting paste to remove loose paint from the scratch, and to clear the surrounding bodywork of wax polish. Rinse the area with clean water.

2 Apply touch-up paint to the scratch using a fine paint brush; continue to apply fine layers of paint until the surface of the paint in the scratch is level with the surrounding paintwork. Allow the new paint at least two weeks to harden, then blend it into the surrounding paintwork by rubbing the scratch area with a paintwork renovator or a very fine cutting paste. Finally, apply wax polish.

3 Where the scratch has penetrated right through to the metal of the bodywork, causing the metal to rust, a different repair technique is required. Remove any loose rust from the bottom of the scratch with a penknife, then apply rust-inhibiting paint to prevent the formation of rust in the future. Using a rubber or nylon applicator, fill the scratch with bodystopper paste. If required, this paste can be mixed with cellulose thinners to provide a very thin paste which is ideal for filling narrow scratches. Before the stopper-paste in the scratch hardens, wrap a piece of smooth cotton rag around the top of a finger. Dip the finger in cellulose thinners, and quickly sweep it across the surface of the stopper-paste in the scratch; this will ensure that the surface of the stopper-paste is slightly hollowed. The scratch can now be painted over as described earlier in this Section.

Repairs of dents in bodywork

4 When deep denting of the vehicle's bodywork has taken place, the first task is to pull the dent out, until the affected bodywork almost attains its original shape. There is little point in trying to restore the original shape completely, as the metal in the damaged area will have stretched on impact, and cannot be reshaped fully to its original contour. It is better to bring the level of the dent up to a point which is about 3 mm below the level of the surrounding bodywork. In cases where the dent is very shallow anyway, it is not worth trying to pull it out at all. If the underside of the dent is accessible, it can be hammered out gently from behind, using a mallet with a wooden or plastic head. Whilst doing this, hold a suitable block of wood firmly against the outside of the panel, to absorb the impact from the hammer blows and thus prevent a large area of the bodywork from being 'belled-out'.

5 Should the dent be in a section of the bodywork which has a double skin, or some other factor making it inaccessible from behind, a different technique is called for. Drill several small holes through the metal inside the area - particularly in the deeper section. Then screw long self-tapping screws into the holes, just sufficiently for them to gain a good purchase in the metal. Now the dent can be pulled out by pulling on the protruding heads of the screws with a pair of pliers.

6 The next stage of the repair is the removal of the paint from the damaged area, and from an inch or so of the surrounding 'sound' bodywork. This is accomplished most easily by using a wire brush or abrasive pad on a power drill, although it can be done just as effectively by hand, using sheets of abrasive paper. To complete the preparation for filling, score the surface of the bare metal with a screwdriver or the tang of a file, or alternatively, drill small holes in the affected area. This will provide a good 'key' for the filler paste.

7 To complete the repair, see the Section on filling and respraying.

Repairs of rust holes or gashes in bodywork

8 Remove all paint from the affected area, and from an inch or so of the surrounding 'sound' bodywork, using an abrasive pad or a wire brush on a power drill. If these are not available, a few sheets of abrasive paper will do the job most effectively. With the paint removed, you will be able to judge the severity of the corrosion, and therefore decide whether to renew the whole panel (if this is possible) or to repair the affected area. New body panels are not as expensive as most people think, and it is often quicker and more satisfactory to fit a new panel than to attempt to repair large areas of corrosion.

9 Remove all fittings from the affected area, except those which will act as a guide to the original shape of the damaged bodywork (eg headlamp shells etc). Then, using tin snips or a hacksaw blade, remove all loose metal and any other metal badly affected by corrosion. Hammer the edges of the hole inwards, to create a slight depression for the filler paste.

10 Wire-brush the affected area to remove the powdery rust from the surface of the remaining metal. Paint the affected area with rust-inhibiting paint; if the back of the rusted area is accessible, treat this also.

11 Before filling can take place, it will be necessary to block the hole in some way. This can be achieved with aluminium or plastic mesh, or aluminium tape.

12 Aluminium or plastic mesh, or glass-fibre matting, is probably the best material to use for a large hole. Cut a piece to the approximate size and shape of the hole to be filled, then position it in the hole so that its edges are below the level of the surrounding bodywork. It can be retained in position by several blobs of filler paste around its periphery.

13 Aluminium tape should be used for small or very narrow holes. Pull a piece off the roll, trim it to the approximate size and shape required, then pull off the backing paper (if used) and stick the tape over the hole; it can be overlapped if the thickness of one piece is insufficient. Burnish down the edges of the tape with the handle of a screwdriver or similar, to ensure that the tape is securely attached to the metal underneath.

Bodywork repairs - filling and respraying

14 Before using this Section, see the Sections on dent, deep scratch, rust holes and gash repairs.

15 Many types of bodyfiller are available, but generally speaking, those proprietary kits which contain a tin of filler paste and a tube of resin hardener are best for this type of repair which can be used directly from the tube. A wide, flexible plastic or nylon applicator will be found invaluable for imparting a smooth and well-contoured finish to the surface of the filler.

16 Mix up a little filler on a clean piece of card or board - measure the hardener carefully (follow the maker's instructions on the pack), otherwise the filler will set too rapidly or too slowly. Using the applicator, apply the filler paste to the prepared area; draw the applicator across the surface of the filler to achieve the correct contour and to level the surface. When a contour that approximates to the correct one is achieved, stop working the paste - if you carry on too long, the paste will become sticky and begin to 'pick-up' on the applicator. Continue to add thin layers of filler paste at 20-minute intervals, until the level of the filler is just proud of the surrounding bodywork.

17 Once the filler has hardened, the excess can be removed using a metal plane or file. From then on, progressively-finer grades of abrasive paper should be used, starting with a 40-grade production paper, and finishing with a 400-grade wet-and-dry paper. Always wrap the abrasive paper around a flat rubber, cork, or wooden block - otherwise the surface of the filler will not be completely flat. During the smoothing of the filler surface, the wet-and-dry paper should be periodically rinsed in water. This will ensure that a very smooth finish is imparted to the filler at the final stage.

18 At this stage, the 'dent' should be surrounded by a ring of bare metal, which in turn should be encircled by the finely 'feathered' edge of the good paintwork. Rinse the repair area with clean water, until all the dust produced by the rubbing-down operation has gone.

19 Spray the whole area with a light coat of primer - this will show up any imperfections in the surface of the filler. Repair these imperfections with fresh filler paste or bodystopper, and again smooth the surface with abrasive paper. If bodystopper is used, it can be mixed with cellulose thinners, to form a thin paste which is ideal for filling small holes. Repeat this spray-and-repair procedure until you are satisfied that the surface of the filler, and the feathered edge of the paintwork, are perfect. Clean the repair area with clean water, and allow to dry fully.

20 The repair area is now ready for final spraying. Paint spraying must be carried out in a warm, dry, windless and dust-free atmosphere. This condition can be created artificially if you have access to a large indoor working area, but if you are forced to work in the open, you will have to pick your day very carefully. If you are working indoors, dousing the floor in the work area with water will help to settle the dust which would otherwise be in the atmosphere. If the repair area is confined to one body panel, mask off the surrounding panels; this will help to minimise the effects of a slight mis-match in paint colours. Bodywork fittings (eg chrome strips, door handles etc) will also need to be masked off. Use genuine masking tape, and several thickness of newspaper, for the masking operations.

21 Before starting to spray, agitate the aerosol can thoroughly, then spray a test area (an old tin, or similar) until the technique is mastered. Cover the repair area with a thick coat of primer; the thickness should be built up using several thin layers of paint, rather than one thick one. Using 400 grade wet-and-dry paper, rub down the surface of the primer until it is smooth. While doing this, the work area should be thoroughly doused with water, and the wet-and-dry paper periodically rinsed in water. Allow to dry before spraying on more paint.

22 Spray on the top coat, again building up the thickness by using several thin layers of paint. Start spraying in the centre of the repair area, and then, using a circular motion, work outwards until the whole repair area and about 2 inches of the surrounding original paintwork is covered. Remove all masking material 10 to 15 minutes after spraying on the final coat of paint.

23 Allow the new paint at least two weeks to harden, then, using a paintwork renovator or a very fine cutting paste, blend the edges of the paint into the existing paintwork. Finally, apply wax polish.

Plastic components

24 With the use of more and more plastic body components by the vehicle manufacturers (eg bumpers. spoilers, and in some cases major body panels), rectification of more serious damage to such items has become a matter of either entrusting repair work to a specialist in this field, or renewing complete components. Repair of such damage by the DIY owner is not feasible, owing to the cost of the equipment and materials required for effecting such repairs. The basic technique involves making a groove along the line of the crack in the plastic, using

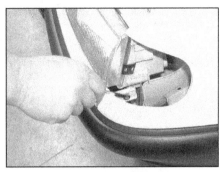

6.1a On early (pre 1998) model slacken and remove the end bolts which are located in the indicator apertures . . .

a rotary burr in a power drill. The damaged part is then welded back together, using a hot air gun to heat up and fuse a plastic filler rod into the groove. Any excess plastic is then removed, and the area rubbed down to a smooth finish. It is important that a filler rod of the correct plastic is used, as body components can be made of a variety of different types (eg polycarbonate, ABS, polypropylene).

25 Damage of a less serious nature (abrasions, minor cracks etc) can be repaired by the DIY owner using a two-part epoxy filler repair material which can be used directly from the tube. Once mixed in equal proportions, this is used in similar fashion to the bodywork filler used on metal panels. The filler is usually cured in twenty to thirty minutes, ready for sanding and painting.

26 If the owner is renewing a complete

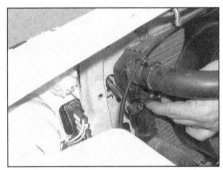

6.1c . . . then slacken and remove the retaining nuts . . .

6.1d . . . and remove the front panel from the vehicle

6.1b . . . and the screws (arrowed) securing the front panel to the crossmember . . .

component himself, or if he has repaired it with epoxy filler, he will be left with the problem of finding a suitable paint for finishing which is compatible with the type of plastic used. At one time, the use of a universal paint was not possible, owing to the complex range of plastics met with in body component applications. Standard paints, generally speaking, will not bond to plastic or rubber satisfactorily, but professional matched paints, to match any plastic or rubber finish, can be obtained from some dealers. However, it is now possible to obtain a plastic body parts finishing kit which consists of a pre-primer treatment, a primer and coloured top coat. Full instructions are normally supplied with a kit, but basically the method of use is to first apply the pre-primer to the component concerned, and allow it to dry for up to 30 minutes. Then the primer is applied, and left to dry for about an hour before finally applying the special-coloured top coat. The result is a correctly coloured component, where the paint will flex with the plastic or rubber, a property that standard paint does not normally posses.

5 Major body damage - repair

1 Where serious damage has occurred, or large areas need renewal due to neglect, it means that complete new panels will need welding-in, and this is best left to

6.6 Slacken and remove the bumper upper nuts and washers (arrowed)

professionals. If the damage is due to impact, it will also be necessary to check completely the alignment of the bodyshell, and this can only be carried out accurately by a Skoda dealer using special jigs. If the body is left misaligned, it is primarily dangerous, as the car will not handle properly, and secondly, uneven stresses will be imposed on the steering, suspension and possibly transmission, causing abnormal wear, or complete failure, particularly to such items as the tyres.

6 Front bumper - removal and refitting

Removal

1 On early (pre 1998) models, remove both front direction indicator lights as described in Chapter 12. Slacken and remove the left- and right-hand front panel retaining bolts, which are accessible through the direction indicator light apertures, and the two screws securing the top of the panel to the bonnet lock crossmember. Unscrew the retaining nuts from the rear of the panel then manoeuvre the front panel away from the vehicle **(see illustrations)**.

2 On later (1998 on) models undo the retaining screws then unclip and remove the trim panels which are fitted inbetween the headlights and bumper.

3 To improve access, firmly apply the handbrake then jack up the front of the vehicle and support it on axle stands.

4 On models with front foglights, disconnect the wiring connector from each light unit and free the wiring from the bumpers.

5 On models equipped with headlight washers, remove both headlight units as described in Chapter 12. Release the retaining clip (where fitted) and disconnect the hose from the rear of each washer jet so the jets are free to be removed with the bumper.

6 On all models, slacken and remove the two nuts and washers securing the top of the bumper to the front of the vehicle **(see illustration)**.

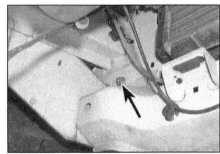

6.7 From underneath, slacken and remove the nuts and washers (arrowed) securing the bumper centre mountings to the body

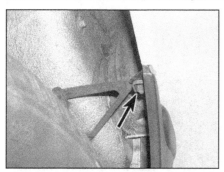

6.8a Loosen the left- and right-hand end nuts (arrowed) . . .

6.8b . . . then free the bumper ends from its mountings . . .

6.8c . . . and remove it from the vehicle

7 From underneath the vehicle, slacken and remove the nuts and washers securing the bumper centre mountings to the front of the vehicle **(see illustration)**.

8 Loosen the nuts securing the left- and right-hand ends of the bumper to its mountings (there is no need to remove these nuts - the bumper holes are slotted) then, with the aid of an assistant, manoeuvre the bumper assembly forwards and away from the vehicle **(see illustrations)**.

9 Inspect the bumper mounting brackets and the reinforcement panel for signs of damage and renew if necessary.

Refitting

10 Refitting is a reverse of the removal procedure, ensuring that the bumper mounting nuts are securely tightened.

7 Rear bumper - removal and refitting

Removal

1 Open up the tailgate. Prise off the trim caps from the bumper upper retaining nuts then slacken and remove all the nuts and washers **(see illustrations)**.

2 If necessary, to improve access to the underside of the bumper, firmly chock the front wheels then jack up the rear of the vehicle and support it on axle stands.

3 From underneath the vehicle, loosen the nuts and washers securing the left- and right-hand ends and the base of the bumper to the body (there is no need to remove these nuts - the bumper holes are all slotted) **(see illustration)**.

4 With the aid of an assistant, free the bumper ends from their mountings and remove the bumper from the vehicle **(see illustrations)**.

Refitting

5 Refitting is a reverse of the removal procedure, tightening the retaining nuts securely.

8 Bonnet - removal, refitting and adjustment

Removal

1 Open the bonnet and place a wad of rag underneath each corner of the bonnet to protect against possible damage should the bonnet slip.

2 Using a pencil or felt tip pen, mark the outline of each hinge relative to the bonnet, to use as a guide on refitting.

3 With the aid of an assistant, support the bonnet then slacken and remove the left- and right-hand hinge to bonnet bolts and washers and carefully remove the bonnet from the vehicle **(see illustration)**.

4 Inspect the bonnet hinges for signs of wear and free play at the pivots, and if necessary renew; each hinge is secured to the body by three nuts.

Refitting and adjustment

5 With the aid of an assistant, align the bonnet with the hinges. Refit the retaining

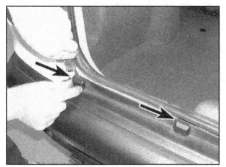

7.1a Open up the tailgate then prise off the trim caps (arrowed) . . .

7.1b . . . then slacken and remove the rear bumper upper retaining nuts and washers (arrowed)

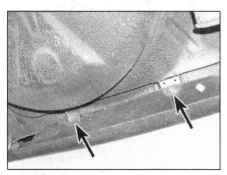

7.3 Loosen all the nuts securing the base of the bumper to the body . . .

7.4a . . . then free the bumper ends from its mountings . . .

7.4b . . . and remove it from the vehicle

bolts and washers and tighten them by hand only. Align the hinges with the marks made on removal, then tighten securely tighten the retaining bolts.

6 Close the bonnet, and check for alignment with the adjacent panels. If necessary, slacken the hinge bolts and re-align the bonnet to suit. If necessary, further adjustment can be gained by slackening the hinge retaining nuts and repositioning the hinge slightly. Once the bonnet is correctly aligned, securely tighten the hinge nuts and/or tighten the bonnet bolts to the specified torque (as applicable). Once the bonnet is correctly aligned, check that the bonnet fastens and releases satisfactorily.

7 If necessary, the height of the bonnet can be adjusted by altering the length of the lock striker pin. As a guide, Skoda state the distance from the striker pin to the bonnet should be 38 ± 1 mm. To adjust the pin, slacken the locknut then screw the pin into/out off (as applicable) the mounting plate **(see illustration)**. Once the pin is correctly positioned, hold it stationary and tighten its locknut to the specified torque.

9 Bonnet release cable - removal and refitting

Removal

1 Remove the bonnet lock as described in Section 10.

2 Work back along the cable, releasing it from its retaining clips and ties whilst noting its correct routing. Free the cable grommet from the bulkhead and tie a piece of string to the end of the cable.

3 From inside the vehicle, reaching up behind the facia, unclip the release cable end fitting from its bracket then extract the lever pivot pin.

4 Manoeuvre the release lever and cable out of position, taking care not to lose its sealing grommet, and remove it from the vehicle. When the end of the string appears from the

8.3 Unscrew the hinge bolts and remove the bonnet from the vehicle

bulkhead, untie it and leave it in position; the string can then be used on refitting to draw the cable back into position. If the sealing grommet shows signs of damage or deterioration it should be renewed.

Refitting

5 Ensure the grommet is in position on the cable then use the string to draw the cable through the into the engine compartment.

6 Seat the outer cable end fitting in the mounting bracket and secure the release lever in position with the pivot pin. Ensure the cable grommet is correctly seated in the bulkhead then untie and remove the string.

7 Ensure the cable is correctly routed and secured in position then refit the bonnet lock as described in Section 10.

10 Bonnet lock - removal, refitting and adjustment

Removal

1 Open up the bonnet then slacken and remove the three bolts securing the lock assembly to the crossmember **(see illustration)**.

2 Free the lock assembly from the underside of the crossmember then unclip the release cable end fitting and unhook the inner cable

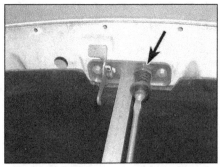

8.7 Slacken the locknut (arrowed) then adjust the lock striker pin as described in text

from the lock lever. The lock can then be removed from the vehicle.

Refitting and adjustment

3 Hook the inner cable onto the lock lever and seat the outer cable in the lock bracket. Check the cable adjustment as follows.

4 With the cable correctly refitted to the lock, there should be no freeplay in the cable and the lock lever should be resting against its stop with a gap of 3 mm between the lever and the edge of the lock striker pin aperture. Adjustment is carried out by opening up and adjusting the release cable clamp **(see illustrations)**. Once the cable is correctly adjusted, secure it firmly in position with the clamp.

5 Once the cable is correctly adjusted, seat the lock on the underside of the crossmember and refit its retaining bolts. Ensure the lock is correctly positioned then tighten the retaining bolts to the specified torque.

6 Lubricate the lock with multi-purpose grease then check the lock operation. If necessary, the lock striker pin position can be adjusted by slackening the mounting plate retaining bolts and repositioning the plate assembly on the bonnet. Once the pin is correctly positioned securely tighten the retaining bolts. Note that the length of the striker pin, which affects the bonnet height, can also be adjusted as described in Section 8.

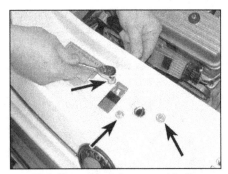

10.1 Bonnet lock is secured to the crossmember by three bolts (arrowed)

10.4a Prior to refitting ensure the release cable is correctly adjusted so there is a gap of 3 mm between the lock lever and striker pin aperture (arrowed)

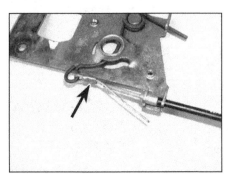

10.4b To adjust the lock, open up the clamp (arrowed) and adjust the cable as necessary before securely reclamping it in position

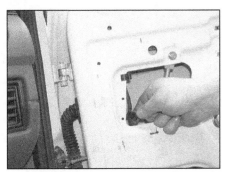
11.2a Unclip the wiring harness . . .

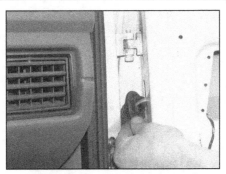
11.2b . . . then free the gaiter and withdraw the wiring from the door

11.3 Slacken and remove the check link pivot bolt

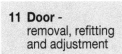
11 Door -
removal, refitting and adjustment

Removal

1 Disconnect the battery negative terminal.
2 If the door contains any electrical components, remove the door inner trim panel as described in Section 12. Peel the insulation panel carefully away from the door then disconnect the wiring connectors and free the wiring from any relevant retaining clips. Ease the rubber gaiter out from the front edge of the door and withdraw the wiring from the door **(see illustrations)**.
3 Slacken and remove the pivot bolt securing the check link to the door then proceed as described under the relevant sub-heading **(see illustration)**.

Front door

4 Have an assistant support the door then, using a hammer and suitable punch, carefully tap out the pivot pins from the upper and lower hinges **(see illustration)**. Take great care not to bend the pins as they are removed; if they are damaged, new ones must be used on refitting.
5 Once both hinge pins have been removed, remove the door from the vehicle **(see illustration)**.
6 Examine the hinges for signs of wear or damage. If renewal is necessary, mark the position of the hinge on the body then undo the retaining bolt and remove the hinge and (where fitted) shim(s) from the vehicle **(see illustration)**. Fit the new hinge, complete with any relevant shims (where fitted), then align the marks made prior to removal and tighten the retaining bolt to its specified torque.

Rear door

7 Draw around the outline of each hinge on the body. Have an assistant support the door then slacken and remove the hinge retaining bolts **(see illustration)**.
8 Remove the door from the vehicle and recover any shims (where fitted) which are positioned between the hinges and body.
9 Examine the hinges for signs of wear or damage. If renewal is necessary, carefully tap out the pivot pin and remove the hinge from the door. Lubricate the new pivot pin with multi-purpose grease then fit the hinge to the door and insert the pin. Tap the pin fully into position and check that the hinge pivots freely before refitting.

Refitting

Front door

10 Lubricate the hinge pivot pins with multi-purpose grease and manoeuvre the door into position. Refit the pivot pins, making sure each one is tapped fully into the hinge **(see illustration)**.
11 Align the check link with its bracket then lubricate the pivot bolt with multi-purpose grease. Insert the pivot bolt and securely tighten its retaining nut.
12 Where necessary, feed the wiring back into the door and seat the rubber gaiter in position. Ensure the wiring is correctly routed and securely reconnected then secure it in position with the necessary clips and ties. Seat the insulation panel back in position and refit the trim panel as described in Section 12.

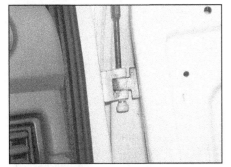
11.4 Support the front door then tap out the hinge pins with a hammer and punch . . .

11.5 . . . and remove the door from the vehicle

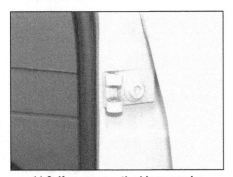
11.6 If necessary the hinge can be unbolted and removed from the body

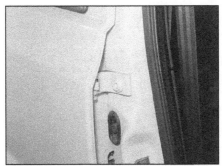
11.7 To remove the rear door undo the bolts securing the hinges to the body

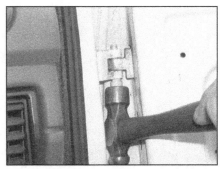
11.10 On refitting ensure the hinge pins are tapped securely into position

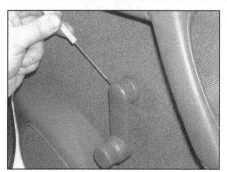

12.2a Prise off the trim cover . . .

12.2b . . . then undo the retaining screw . . .

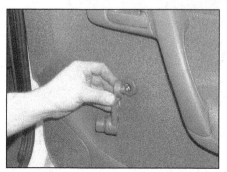

12.2c . . . and remove the window regulator handle and spacer from the door

13 Check the door alignment and, if necessary, adjust then reconnect the battery negative terminal.

Rear door

14 With the aid of an assistant, offer up the door to the vehicle and refit the hinge bolts. Insert any necessary shims (where fitted) between the hinges and body then align the hinges with the marks made before removal and tighten the retaining bolts to the specified torque.

15 Carry out the operations described in paragraphs 11 to 13.

Adjustment

16 Close the door and check the door alignment with surrounding body panels. Slight adjustment of the door position can be made by inserting/removing shims between the hinges and body. If adjustment is necessary, slacken both hinge bolts and add/remove shims as necessary before securely tighten the hinge bolts and rechecking the door alignment. Repeat this procedure as necessary until the door is correctly positioned then tighten both hinge bolts to the specified torque. Note that on the front door access to the hinge bolts is greatly improved if the check link pivot bolt is removed.

17 Once the door is correctly aligned, check that the lock striker enters the door lock centrally and holds the door firmly shut when locked. If necessary, slacken the retaining screws and adjust the lock striker position as necessary. Once the striker plate is correctly positioned tighten its retaining screws to the specified torque.

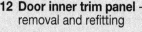

12 Door inner trim panel - removal and refitting

Removal

Note: *Door trim panel design varies according to the equipment level of the vehicle therefore some trim panel fastener locations on your vehicle might be different to those shown in the accompanying illustrations.*

1 Disconnect the battery negative terminal and proceed as described under the relevant sub-heading.

Front door

2 On models with manually-operated windows, unclip the trim cover from the end of the window regulator handle. Undo the retaining screw then remove the handle from the spindle and recover the spacer **(see illustrations)**.

3 Unscrew the locking button and remove it from the top of the operating rod **(see illustration)**.

4 Lift the door lock inner handle then carefully unclip the trim cover from the door handle **(see illustration)**.

5 Slacken and remove the retaining screws and remove the door handle from the trim panel **(see illustration)**. Where necessary, disconnect the wiring connector from the mirror switch as it becomes accessible.

6 Where necessary, prise out the trim cap from panel then slacken and remove the panel retaining screw **(see illustrations)**.

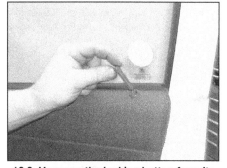

12.3 Unscrew the locking button from its operating rod

12.4 Unclip the trim cover . . .

12.5 . . . then undo the retaining screws (arrowed) and remove the door handle

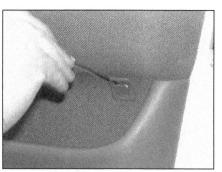

12.6a Prise out the trim cap . . .

12.6b . . . then slacken and remove the panel retaining screw

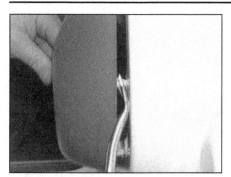

12.7a Release the retaining clips . . .

12.7b . . . then remove the inner trim panel from the door . . .

12.7c . . . disconnecting the wiring as it becomes accessible

7 Carefully unclip the trim panel from the door and remove it from the door. Where necessary, free the wiring harness from the panel and disconnect any relevant wiring connectors as soon as they become accessible (see illustrations).

Rear door

8 Carry out the operations described in paragraphs 2 to 5.
9 Carefully unclip the trim panel from the door and remove it from the door.

Refitting

10 Refitting of the trim panel is the reverse of removal. Prior to clipping the panel in position, ensuring all the wiring (where necessary) is correctly routed and passed through the relevant apertures.

13 Door handle and lock components - removal and refitting

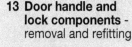

Removal

1 Remove the inner trim panel as described in Section 12 then proceed as described under the relevant sub-heading.

Door lock inner handle

2 Slacken and remove the retaining screw and washer then detach the handle from its operating rod and remove it from the door (see illustrations).

Front door lock cylinder

3 Remove the inner handle as described in

paragraph 2 then carefully peel the insulation panel away from the door sufficiently to give access to the lock components.
4 Position the window so that the bolts securing the window glass to the regulator are accessible. Slacken and remove the retaining bolts and washers then lift the glass fully up and tape it to the door frame to hold it in position (see illustrations).
5 Slacken and remove the nuts and washers securing the window regulator mechanism rear strut to the door and position the strut clear of the lock assembly (see illustrations).
6 Unscrew the retaining nut then remove the retaining clips and manoeuvre the anti-theft cover out from the door to gain access to the lock assembly (see illustrations).

13.2a Undo the retaining screw . . .

13.2b . . . then detach the inner handle from its operating rod and remove it from the door

13.4a Slacken and remove the front . . .

13.4b . . . and rear bolts securing the window glass to the regulator then lift the glass up and tape it to the door frame

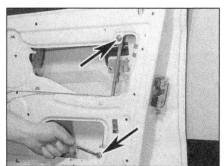

13.5a Undo the regulator rear strut retaining nuts (arrowed) . . .

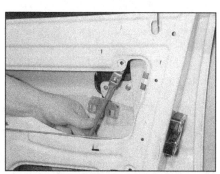

13.5b . . . then free the strut from the door and position it clear of the lock assembly

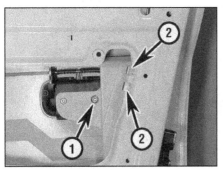

13.6a Slacken and remove the nut (1) and clips (2) . . .

7 Unclip the link rod from the lock cylinder lever balljoint **(see illustration)**

8 Slide the retaining clip to one side then manoeuvre the lock cylinder out of position and remove the clip **(see illustrations)**

13.8a . . . then slide out the retaining clip . . .

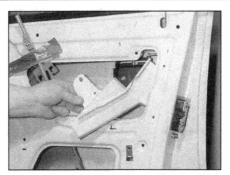

13.6b . . . and remove the anti-theft cover to gain access to the lock assembly

Front door lock

Note: *The lock consists of two pieces, the outer section (which contains the latch) and the inner section (which contains the operating linkage). The outer section can be removed without disturbing the trim panel; the following procedure describes removal of the complete assembly.*

9 Carry out the operations described in paragraphs 3 to 6.

10 Unclip the exterior handle and lock cylinder balljoints from the lock **(see illustration)**.

11 On models equipped with central locking, trace the wiring back from the lock actuator and disconnect it at the connector. Also slacken and remove the additional bolt securing the lock inner section bracket (which houses the actuator) to the door.

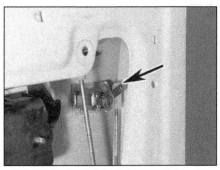

13.7 Unclip the link rod (arrowed) from the lock cylinder balljoint . . .

12 On all models, slacken and remove the two retaining bolts then remove the lock assembly outer section away from the door. The inner section of the lock assembly can then be manoeuvred out from the door, noting the correct locations of the inner button and handle link rods **(see illustrations)**. Note that on models with central locking, the actuator comes out with the lock assembly inner section.

Front door exterior handle

13 Carry out the operations described in paragraphs 3 to 6.

14 Unclip the link rod from the exterior handle balljoint **(see illustration)**.

15 Slacken and remove the handle retaining nut and bracket then manoeuvre the handle out from the door **(see illustrations)**.

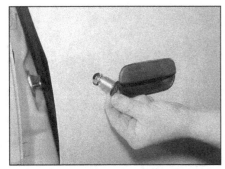

13.8b . . . and remove the lock cylinder from the door

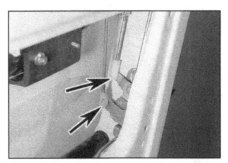

13.10 Unclip the exterior handle and lock cylinder link rods (arrowed) from the front door lock assembly

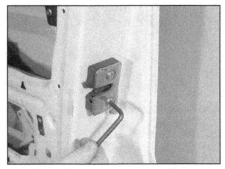

13.12a Undo the retaining bolts . . .

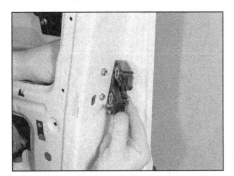

13.12b . . . then remove the outer section of the lock assembly from the door . . .

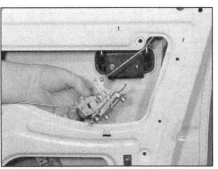

13.12c . . . and manoeuvre out the inner lock section

13.14 Unclip the link rod from the exterior handle balljoint

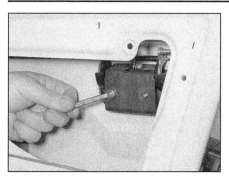

13.15a Undo the retaining nut . . .

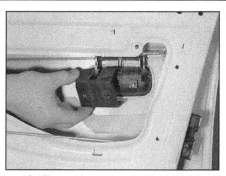

13.15b . . . then remove the retaining bracket . . .

13.15c . . . and manoeuvre the exterior handle out from the door

Rear door exterior handle

16 Carefully peel the insulation panel away from the door sufficiently to give access to the lock components (see illustration).

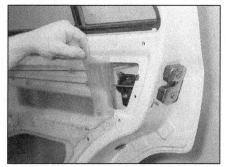

13.16 Peel back the insulation panel to gain access to the rear door lock components

17 Unclip the link rod from the exterior handle balljoint (see illustration).
18 Slacken and remove the handle retaining nuts and bracket from inside the door then manoeuvre the handle assembly out of position (see illustrations).

Rear door lock assembly

Note: *The lock consists of two pieces, the outer section (which contains the latch) and the inner section (which contains the operating linkage). The outer section can be removed without disturbing the trim panel; the following procedure describes removal of the complete assembly.*
19 Remove the exterior handle as described in paragraphs 16 to 18.
20 Slacken and remove the retaining screws and washers then detach the door lock inner

handle from its operating rod and remove it from the door.
21 On models equipped with central locking, trace the wiring back from the lock actuator and disconnect it at the connector. Also slacken and remove the additional bolt securing the lock inner section bracket (which houses the actuator) to the door.
22 On all models, slacken and remove the two retaining bolts then remove the lock assembly outer section away from the door (see illustration).
23 Unclip the link rod from inner button pivot crank then unclip both lock link rods from the door and remove the inner section of the lock assembly (see illustrations). Note that on models with central locking, the actuator comes out with the lock assembly inner section.

13.17 Unclip the link rod (arrowed) from the rear door exterior handle

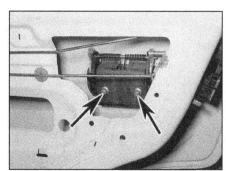

13.18a Undo the nuts (arrowed) . . .

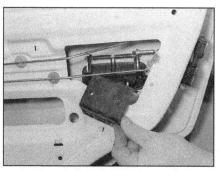

13.18b . . . then remove the retaining bracket . . .

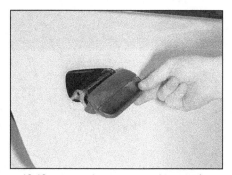

13.18c . . . and manoeuvre the exterior handle out from the rear door

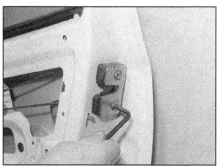

13.22 Undo the retaining bolts and remove the lock outer section from the door

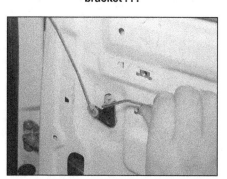

13.23a Unclip the link rod from the inner button crank . . .

13.23b ... then from both rods from their guides ...

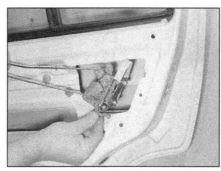

13.23c ... and remove the lock inner section from the rear door

Refitting

24 Refitting is the reverse of removal, noting the following points.
a) Tighten all fasteners to the specified torque settings (where given).
b) Ensure that all link rods are securely clipped onto their balljoints and are correctly adjusted (where possible). Adjustments are made by screwing the end fitting on/off the link rod. Once the end fitting is correctly positioned, clip it securely onto its balljoint.
c) Check the operation of the lock/handles before sticking the insulation panel back onto the door and refitting the trim panel as described in Section 12.
d) On completion check the operation of the lock and check that the rear of the door is flush to the body once shut. If necessary, adjustments can be made by slacken the

retaining screws and repositioning the lock striker slightly. Once the striker is correctly positioned, tighten the retaining screws to the specified torque.

14 Door window glass and regulator - removal and refitting

Removal

1 Remove the inner trim panel as described in Section 12 then proceed as described under the relevant sub-heading.

Front door window glass

2 Slacken and remove the retaining screws and washers then detach the lock inner handle from its operating rod and remove it from the door.

14.5 Unclip the inner sealing strip and remove it from the top of the door

14.6b ... then manoeuvre the glass out of the top of the door

3 Carefully peel the insulation panel away from the top of the door to gain access to the regulator mechanism.
4 Position the window so that the bolts securing the window glass to the regulator are accessible through the door aperture.
5 Carefully ease the window glass inner sealing strip out of position and remove it from the door (see illustration).
6 Slacken and remove the four retaining bolts and washers securing the glass to the regulator mechanism then manoeuvre the glass upwards and out of position (see illustrations).

Front door window regulator mechanism

7 Carry out the operations described in paragraphs 2 to 4.
8 Slacken and remove the four retaining bolts and washers securing the glass to the regulator mechanism then lift the glass fully up and tape it to the door frame to hold it in position.
9 On models with an electrically-operated window, release the retaining clip and disconnect the wiring connector from the motor.
10 On all models, slacken and remove the retaining nuts and washers securing the regulator assembly to the door then carefully manoeuvre the assembly out through the door aperture (see illustrations).

Rear door window

11 Slacken and remove the retaining screws and washers then detach the lock inner handle from its operating rod and remove it from the door.
12 Carefully peel the insulation panel away from the top of the door to gain access to the regulator mechanism.
13 Fully lower the window glass then ease the inner sealing strip out from the top of the door (see illustration).
14 Undo the retaining screws securing the window guide rail to the door then manoeuvre the guide rail and fixed window glass out of position (see illustrations). If necessary, remove the upper sealing strip from the door frame.
15 Using a marker pen, draw around the outline of the window glass to regulator bolt

14.6a Slacken and remove the bolts securing the glass to the regulator ...

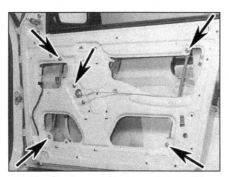

14.10a Slacken and remove the retaining nuts (arrowed) ...

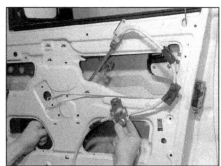

14.10b ... and manoeuvre the regulator mechanism out from the front door

14.13 Lower the window and remove the inner sealing strip from the top of the rear door

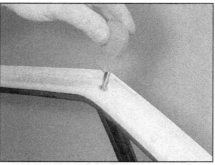

14.14a Slacken and remove the upper retaining screw . . .

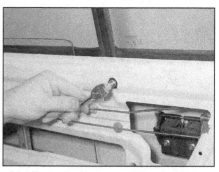

14.14b . . . and lower retaining screw . . .

washers. The marks can then be used on refitting to help position the glass correctly.

16 Slacken and remove the retaining bolts and washers securing the glass to the regulator mechanism then manoeuvre the glass upwards and out of position **(see illustrations)**.

Rear door window regulator

17 Carry out the operations described in paragraphs 2 to 4.

18 Using a marker pen, draw around the outline of the window glass to regulator bolt washers; the marks can then be used on refitting to help position the glass correctly.

19 Slacken and remove the retaining bolts and washers securing the glass to the regulator mechanism then lift the glass fully up and tape it to the door frame to hold it in position.

20 Slacken and remove the retaining nuts

and washers securing the regulator assembly to the door then carefully manoeuvre the assembly out through the door aperture **(see illustrations)**.

Refitting

21 Refitting is the reverse of the relevant removal procedure noting the following.

a) *Ensure all sealing strips are correctly located.*

b) *On refitting the window glass take care to ensure it engages correctly with its guides and securely tighten its regulator bolts.*

c) *Check the operation of the window mechanism prior to sticking the insulation panel in position and refitting the inner trim panel (see Section 12). If necessary, slight adjustments can be made by slackening the retaining bolts and moving the glass slightly on the regulator.*

15 Tailgate - removal and refitting

Removal

Tailgate

1 Open up the tailgate then disconnect the battery negative terminal.

2 On models with a high-level stoplight, remove the light unit as described in Chapter 12 then carefully unclip the caged nuts from the tailgate **(see illustration)**.

3 On all models, remove the rubber plugs from the top of the tailgate to gain access to the spoiler retaining screws. Slacken and remove all the retaining screws then remove the spoiler assembly from the tailgate, disconnecting the washer hose as it becomes

14.14c . . . then manoeuvre the window guide rail and fixed window glass assembly out from the door

14.16a Unscrew the bolts securing the glass to the regulator . . .

14.16b . . . then manoeuvre the glass out of the top of the door

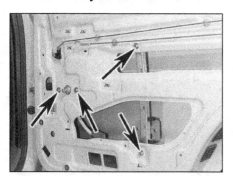

14.20a Slacken and remove the retaining nuts (arrowed) . . .

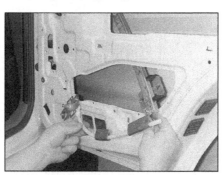

14.20b . . . then manoeuvre the regulator assembly out from the rear door

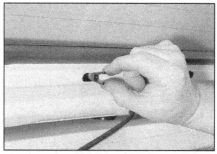

15.2 On models with a high-level stoplight unclip and remove the caged nuts from the tailgate apertures

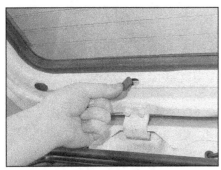

15.3a Remove the rubber plugs from the top of the tailgate . . .

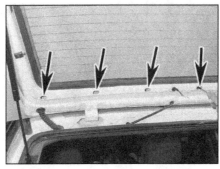

15.3b . . . then slacken and remove the spoiler retaining screws (arrowed)

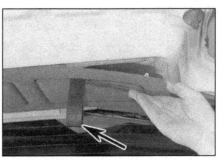

15.4 Unclip the inner trim panel from the tailgate then undo the retaining screw and remove the handle strap (arrowed)

accessible **(see illustrations)**. If necessary, remove the washer jet and grommet from the spoiler then free the hose from the tailgate.

4 Carefully unclip the inner trim panel from the tailgate then slacken and remove the retaining screw and remove the handle strap **(see illustration)**. Peel off the insulation panel to gain access to the wiper motor.

5 Disconnect the wiring connectors from the tailgate electrical components and tie a piece of string to the end of the wiring. Free the wiring from its retaining clips and withdraw it from the tailgate **(see illustrations)**. When the end of the wiring appears, untie the string and leave it in position; it can then be used to draw the wiring back into position on refitting. **Note:** *It may be necessary to free the wiring terminals from the wiper motor connector in order to enable the wiring to be withdrawn from the tailgate. If this is the case, make a note of each wires correct fitted location*

before removing it from the connector.

6 Draw around the outline of each hinge on the tailgate using a suitable marker pen.

7 Have an assistant support the tailgate, then carefully lift the retaining clips and detach both support struts from their balljoints.

8 Slacken and remove the bolts securing the hinges to the tailgate and remove the tailgate from the vehicle **(see illustration)**.

9 Examine the hinges for signs of wear or damage. If renewal is necessary, unclip the trim panel from the roof and carefully peel back the rear of the headlining; each hinge assembly can then unbolted and removed. Fit the new hinge and securely tighten the retaining bolts before refitting the trim panel.

Support strut

10 Have an assistant support the tailgate then, using a small flat-bladed screwdriver, carefully lift the retaining clips and unhook the strut from its balljoints **(see illustration)**.

Refitting

Tailgate

11 Refitting is the reverse of removal, noting the following.

a) *Align the hinges with the marks made before removal and tightening the hinge bolts to the specified torque.*

b) *Prior to refitting the insulation and trim panels, connect the battery and check the operation of all the tailgate electrical components.*

c) *Ensure the tailgate is correctly aligned with all its surrounding body components; adjustments can be made by slacken the hinge bolts and repositioning the tailgate.*

d) *On completion, check the operation of the lock and, if necessary, adjust the lock striker as described in Section 16.*

Support strut

12 Refitting is the reverse of removal making sure the strut is clipped securely in position.

16 Tailgate lock components -
removal, refitting
and adjustment

Removal

Lock assembly

1 Open up the tailgate. Unclip the inner trim panel from the tailgate then carefully peel back the insulation panel to gain access to the lock.

2 Unclip the lock link rod from the lock button and disconnect the wiring connector from the lock switch **(see illustration)**.

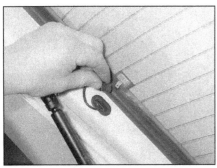

15.5a Disconnect the wiring connectors from the tailgate electrical components . . .

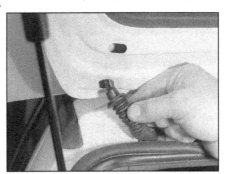

15.5b . . . then withdraw the harness from the tailgate

15.8 Undo the hinge retaining bolts (arrowed) and remove the tailgate from the vehicle

15.10 Carefully lift the retaining clips and detach the support struts from the balljoints

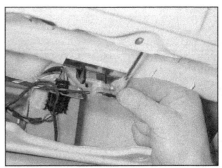

16.2 Unclip the lock link rod from the button balljoint . . .

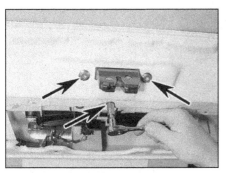

16.3a ... then slacken and remove the retaining bolts (arrowed) ...

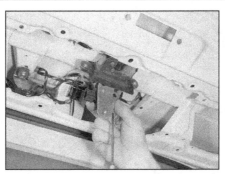

16.3b ... and remove the lock assembly from the tailgate

16.5 Undo the retaining bolts and remove the bracket from above the tailgate lock button

3 Slacken and remove the retaining bolts and remove the lock assembly from the tailgate **(see illustrations)**.

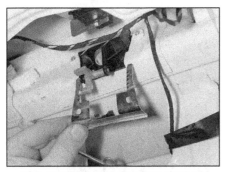

16.6 Unclip the link rod from the lock button then slide out the retaining clip

Lock button assembly

4 Open up the tailgate. Unclip the inner trim panel from the tailgate then carefully peel back the insulation panel to gain access to the lock button.
5 Slacken and remove the retaining bolts and remove the metal bracket which is fitted above the lock button **(see illustration)**.
6 Unclip the lock link rod from the lock button then slide out the button retaining clip **(see illustration)**.
7 Slacken and remove the retaining screws and remove the button assembly from the tailgate **(see illustrations)**.
8 If necessary, remove the circlip, washer and sealing ring from the rear of the lock cylinder then slide the cylinder out from the surround, taking care not to lose the button springs **(see illustrations)**.

Lock striker

9 Open up the tailgate. Remove the retaining screw/fasteners (as applicable) then unclip the tailgate aperture sill trim panel from the body and remove it from the vehicle **(see illustrations)**.
10 Slacken and remove the retaining bolts and remove the striker plate from the vehicle. On models equipped with a remote release lever, it will be necessary to disconnect the release cable from the striker assembly **(see illustration)**.

Refitting

11 Refitting is the reverse of removal. Check the operation of the lock assembly components prior to refitting the trim panel to the tailgate. If necessary, adjust the lock striker as follows.

16.7a Slacken and remove the retaining screws (arrowed) ...

16.7b ... and remove lock button assembly

16.8a Remove the circlip from the rear of the lock cylinder and lift off the washer and sealing ring

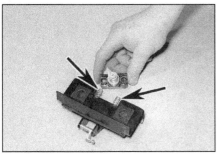

16.8b Separate the lock cylinder from its surround noting the correct fitted locations of the button springs (arrowed)

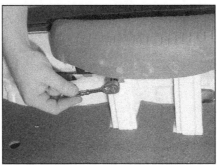

16.9a Undo the retaining screw ...

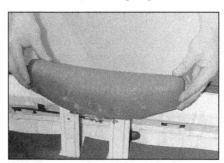

16.9b ... and remove the sill trim panel from the tailgate aperture (trim panel design varies depending on specification)

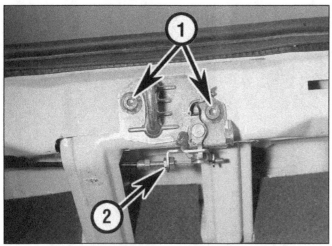

16.10 Undo the retaining bolts (1) and remove the tailgate lock striker. Where necessary, detach the release cable (2)

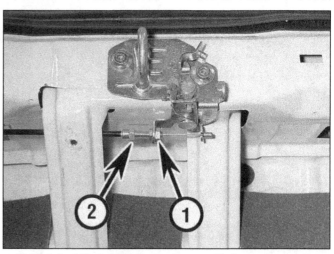

16.12 Adjust the tailgate lock release cable by slackening the locknut (1) and rotating the adjuster (2)

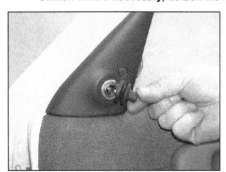

19.1a Remove the rubber gaiter . . .

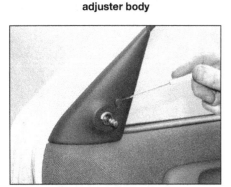

19.1b . . . then unscrew the nut from the adjuster body

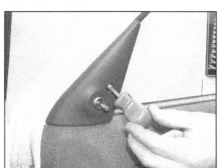

19.2a Prise out the trim cap . . .

19.2b . . . then undo the retaining screw . . .

Adjustment

12 The lock striker should be positioned so that it enters the lock centrally and holds the tailgate firmly shut when locked. If necessary, remove the tailgate aperture sill trim panel (see paragraph 9) then slacken the retaining screws and adjust the lock striker position as necessary. Once the striker plate is correctly positioned tighten its retaining screws to the specified torque. On models with a remote release lever for the tailgate, also make sure that the striker plate lever is against its stop and that a small amount of freeplay is present in the cable; if necessary adjust by slackening the locknut and repositioning the adjuster **(see illustration)**. Once the cable sleeve is correctly positioned hold the adjuster nut stationary and securely tighten the locknut. Check the operation of the lock and (where fitted) remote release lever then refit the trim panel.

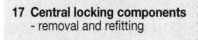
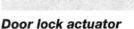
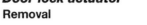

17 Central locking components - removal and refitting

Door lock actuator
Removal

1 Remove the relevant door lock assembly as described in Section 13.

2 Undo the retaining screws then free the actuator from the link rod and remove it from the lock assembly.

Refitting

3 Refitting is the reverse of removal. Prior to refitting any trim panels removed for access thoroughly check the operation of the central locking system.

18 Electric window components - removal and refitting

Window switch

1 Refer to Chapter 12.

Window winder motors

2 At the time of writing, it was unclear wether the window winder motors were available separately or wether the complete regulator assembly would have to be renewed. Refer to your Skoda dealer for the latest information. Regulator removal and refitting is given in Section 14.

19 Exterior mirrors and associated components - removal and refitting

Manually-adjusted mirror assembly

1 Remove the rubber gaiter from the mirror adjustment handle then unscrew the nut from the adjuster body **(see illustrations)**.

2 Prise out the trim cap then undo the retaining screw and remove the mirror inner trim panel from the door **(see illustrations)**.

3 Undo the retaining screws and remove the mirror from the door **(see illustration)**. Recover the insulation which is fitted between the door and mirror; if it is damaged it must be renewed.

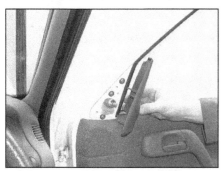

19.2c . . . and unclip the mirror inner trim panel

4 Refitting is the reverse of removal.

Electrically-operated mirror

5 Prise out the trim cap then undo the retaining screw and remove the mirror inner trim panel from the door.
6 Slacken and remove the retaining screws and remove the mirror from the door, disconnect the wiring connector as it becomes accessible. Recover the insulation which is fitted between the door and mirror; if it is damaged it must be renewed.
7 Refitting is the reverse of removal.

Mirror glass

Note: *The mirror glass is clipped into position. Removal of the glass is likely to result in breakage is carried out carelessly.*

8 Tilt the mirror glass fully upwards and insert a wide plastic or wooden wedge inbetween the base of the mirror glass and mirror housing and carefully prise the glass from the motor/adjuster. Take great care when removing the glass; do not use excessive force as the glass is easily broken.
9 Remove the glass from the mirror, where necessary, disconnect the wiring connectors from the mirror heating element.
10 On refitting, reconnect the wiring (where fitted) to the glass and clip the glass onto the motor/adjuster, taking great care not to break it. Apply force only to the centre of the glass to minimise the risk of breakage. Ensure the glass is clipped securely into position and adjust as necessary.

Mirror switch

11 Refer to Chapter 12.

20 Windscreen and tailgate glass - general information

1 These areas of glass are secured by the tight fit of the weatherstrip in the body aperture, and are bonded in position with a special adhesive. Renewal of such fixed glass is a difficult, messy and time-consuming task, which is beyond the scope of the home mechanic. It is difficult, unless one has plenty of practice, to obtain a secure, waterproof fit. Furthermore, the task carries a high risk of

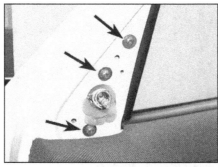

19.3 Undo the retaining screws (arrowed) and remove the mirror from the door

breakage; this applies especially to the laminated glass windscreen. In view of this, owners are strongly advised to have this sort of work carried out by one of the many specialist windscreen fitters.

21 Sunroof - general information

1 Due to the complexity of the sunroof mechanism, considerable expertise is needed to repair, replace or adjust the sunroof components successfully. Removal of the roof first requires the headlining to be removed, which is a complex and tedious operation, and not a task to be undertaken lightly. Therefore, any problems with the sunroof should be referred to a Skoda dealer.

22 Body exterior fittings - removal and refitting

Wheel arch liners and body under-panels

1 The various plastic covers fitted to the underside of the vehicle are secured in position by a mixture of screws, nuts and retaining clips and removal will be fairly obvious on inspection. Work methodically around the removing its retaining screws and releasing its retaining clips until the panel is free and can be removed from the underside

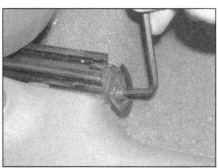

23.2 Slacken and remove the front seat front . . .

of the vehicle. Most clips used on the vehicle are simply prised out of position. Other clips can be released by unscrewing/prising out the centre pins and then removing the clip.
2 On refitting, renew any retaining clips that may have been broken on removal, and ensure that the panel is securely retained by all the relevant clips and screws.

Body trim strips and badges

3 The various body trim strips and badges are held in position with a special adhesive tape. Removal requires the trim/badge to be heated, to soften the adhesive, and then cut away from the surface. Due to the high risk of damage to the vehicle's paintwork during this operation, it is recommended that this task should be entrusted to a Skoda dealer.

23 Seats - removal and refitting

Front seat

Note: *On some later models, side airbags are fitted to the front seats. On these models, refer to the warnings given in the airbag section of Chapter 12 before proceeding.*

Removal

1 On models with side airbag units in the seats, disconnect the battery negative terminal and wait at least one minute before proceeding.
2 On all models, slide the seat fully backwards then slacken and remove the seat rail front mounting bolts **(see illustration)**.
3 Slide the seat fully forwards then slacken and remove the bolts and washers securing the rear of the seat rails in position **(see illustration)**.
4 Carefully manoeuvre the seat out of position. On models with heated seats/side airbags, it will be necessary to disconnect the wiring connector(s) from the seat as they become accessible.

Refitting

5 Refitting is the reverse of removal tightening the mounting bolts to the specified torque. On models with side airbags, refer to the warnings given in Chapter 12 before reconnecting the battery.

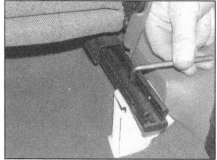

23.3 . . . and rear retaining bolts then lift the seat out of position

Rear seat

Removal

6 Some models are fitted with a one-piece rear seat assembly where as others have a split rear seat assembly. Each section is removed by folding down the seat back down then folding the seat cushion forwards until one of its pivot pins can be lifted and freed from its mounting **(see illustration)**. The seat assembly can then be removed from the vehicle.

Refitting

7 Refitting is the reverse of removal ensuring the seat assembly is correctly engaged with its mountings.

24 Front seat belt tensioning mechanism - general information

1 Models which are fitted with an airbag are also fitted with front seat belt tensioners. The tensioners are designed to instantaneously take up any slack in the seat belt in the case of a sudden frontal impact, therefore reducing the possibility of injury to the front seat occupants. Each front seat is fitted with the system, the tensioner being attached directly to the seat belt inertia reel.

2 Each seat belt tensioner contains an inertia mechanism which is triggered by a frontal impact above a pre-determined force. Lesser impacts, including impacts from behind, will not trigger the system.

23.6 Pivot the rear seat cushion forwards until it is possible to slide its pivot pin out from its mounting

3 When the mechanism is triggered, the fuel inside the tensioner cylinder ignites. This forces the tensioner piston forwards which then removes all slack from the seat belt by retracting and locking the inertia reel. The strength of the explosion in the tensioner cylinder is calibrated to retract the seat belt sufficiently to securely retain the occupant of the seat without forcing them into the seat. Once the tensioner has been triggered, the seat belt will be permanently locked and the assembly must be renewed.

4 Note the following warnings before contemplating any work on the front seat belts.

 Warning: *If the tensioner mechanism is dropped, it must be renewed, even it has suffered no apparent damage.*

⚠ **Warning:** *Do not allow any solvents to come into contact with the tensioner mechanism.*

⚠ **Warning:** *Do not subject the bodywork around the tensioner to any form of shock as this could accidentally trigger the seat belt tensioner.*

⚠ **Warning:** *Do not subject the tensioner assembly to temperatures in excess of 100° C.*

25 Seat belt components - removal and refitting

Removal

Front seat belt - models not fitted with seat belt tensioners

1 Disconnect the battery negative terminal.
2 Remove the relevant front seat as described in Section 23.
3 Unclip the trim cap from the seat belt upper mounting then slacken and remove the mounting bolt and free the seat belt from the height adjuster **(see illustrations)**.
4 Undo the retaining screw securing the upper trim panel to the pillar. Unclip the top of the panel and remove the panel from the vehicle **(see illustrations)**.
5 If necessary, slacken and remove the retaining bolts, noting the correct fitted locations of the washers and remove the height adjustment mechanism from the pillar **(see illustration)**.
6 Unclip the top of the lower trim panel from the door pillar then free the panel from the sill trim panel and remove it from the vehicle **(see illustration)**.

25.3a Remove the trim cap from the seat belt upper mounting . . .

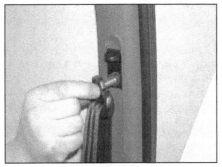

25.3b . . . then unscrew the mounting bolt and detach the belt

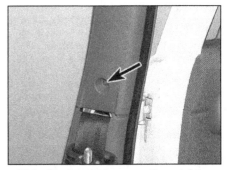

25.4a Slacken and remove the retaining screw (arrowed) . . .

25.4b . . . then unclip the upper trim panel from the pillar

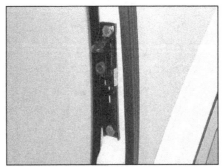

25.5 The height adjuster mechanism is secured to the pillar by two bolts

25.6 Unclip the lower trim panel and remove it from the pillar

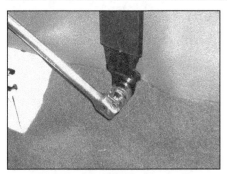

25.7a Unscrew the lower mounting bolt . . .

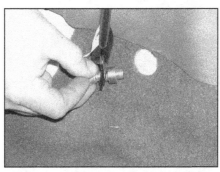

25.7b . . . and free the belt from the floor noting the correct fitted locations of the spacer

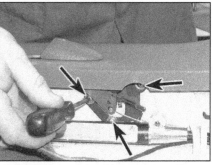

25.10a On models with a remote tailgate release lever, slacken and remove the lever retaining screws (arrowed) . . .

7 Slacken and remove the seat belt lower mounting bolt, noting the correct fitted locations of the washers, then free the belt from sill and recover the spacer from the mounting **(see illustrations)**.

8 Slacken and remove the inertia reel mounting bolt and remove the seat belt assembly from the vehicle.

Front seat belt - models equipped with seat belt tensioners

 Warning: Refer to the warnings given in Section 24 before proceeding.

9 Carry out the operations described in paragraphs 1 to 7.

10 Tilt the rear seat assembly forwards then work along the sill trim panel, releasing its retaining clips by pulling it gently upwards. Once all the retaining clips have been

released, remove the panel from the vehicle. If the driver's side seat belt is being removed and the vehicle is equipped with a tailgate remote release lever, it will be necessary to slacken and remove the lever mounting screws and remove the lever with the trim panel, detaching its cable as it becomes accessible **(see illustrations)**.

11 Unscrew the nut securing the tensioner to its mounting stud (this disables the tensioner mechanism) and the front mounting bracket retaining screw. Slide off the bracket from the front of the tensioner and free it from its mounting **(see illustrations)**.

12 Remove the retaining clip(s) securing the tensioner cable to the body then undo the inertia reel mounting bolt and remove the seat belt assembly from the vehicle **(see illustrations)**.

Rear seat side belt

13 Remove the rear seat assembly as described in Section 23.

14 Slacken and remove the lower mounting bolt securing the seat belt to the floor and recover the spacers and washer fitted between the belt and body **(see illustrations)**.

15 Pull up on the rear of the sill trim panel to release it from the body **(see illustration)**.

16 Unclip the base of the rear seat side trim panel from the body then free it from its upper mounting and remove it from the vehicle **(see illustration)**.

17 Free the luggage compartment cover from the its mountings and remove it from the vehicle. On Estate models also unclip remove the front section of the cover.

18 On models where the tailgate aperture side trim panel overlaps the rear pillar upper

25.10b . . . then unclip the sill trim panel . . .

25.10c . . . and detach the release cable as it becomes accessible

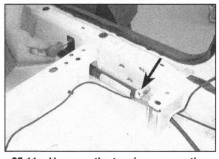

25.11a Unscrew the tensioner mounting nut (arrowed) then undo the retaining screw . . .

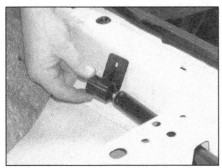

25.11b . . . and slide off the mounting bracket

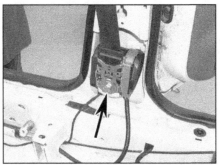

25.12a Slacken and remove the inertia reel mounting bolt (arrowed) . . .

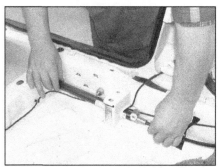

25.12b . . . then remove the seat belt and tensioner assembly from the vehicle

25.14a Unscrew the rear seat belt lower mounting bolt . . .

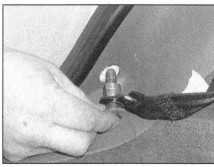

25.14b . . . and recover the spacers which are positioned between the belt and body

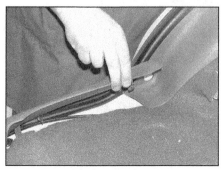

25.15 Free the rear of sill trim panel from the body . . .

trim panel, remove the sill trim panel and the relevant side trim panel. The sill panel is secured in position either by a retaining screw or fasteners; the fasteners can be released by

pressing out their centre pins before remove their outer section. The side trim panel is retained by a single clip **(see illustrations)**.
19 Peel the tailgate sealing strip away from

the body in the area around the edge of the rear pillar upper trim panel then unclip the rear trim panel from the top of the tailgate aperture **(see illustration)**.
20 Undo the retaining screw and washer from the front of the upper trim panel **(see illustration)**.
21 Carefully unclip the handle and remove it from the rear seat back release lever **(see illustration)**.
22 On Estate models, unclip the storage compartment cover from the luggage compartment side trim panel then undo the retaining screws and remove the panel from the vehicle. Slacken and remove the retaining screw securing the rear pillar panel in position **(see illustrations)**.
23 On all models, support the tailgate then carefully lift the retaining clip slightly and free the relevant support strut from its body balljoint **(see illustration)**.

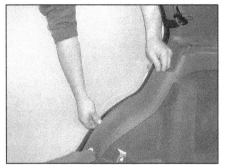

25.16 . . . then unclip and remove the rear seat side trim panel

25.18a Where the tailgate sill trim panel is retained by fasteners, press out the centre pins then remove all fasteners

25.18b Unclip the sill trim panel and remove it from the vehicle . . .

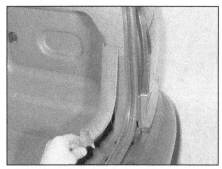

25.18c . . . then unclip the side trim panel (Estate model shown)

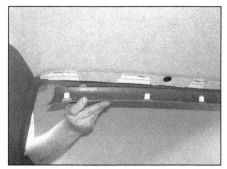

25.19 Unclip the upper trim panel from the top of the tailgate aperture

25.20 Slacken and remove the retaining screw and washer from the front of the upper trim panel . . .

25.21 . . . then unclip the handle from the seat back release lever

25.22a On Estate models unclip the storage compartment cover . . .

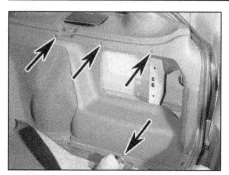

25.22b . . . then undo the retaining screws (arrowed) . . .

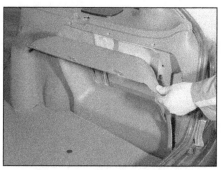

25.22c . . . and remove the luggage compartment side trim panel

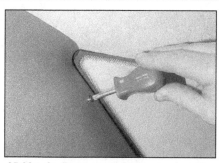

25.22d On Estate models also remove the retaining screw securing the upper trim panel in position

24 Unclip the rear pillar panel from the body and manoeuvre it out of position. Unclip the seat belt guide from the panel then free the panel from the belt and remove it from the

25.23 Support the tailgate then release the retaining clip and detach the support strut from the body

vehicle **(see illustrations)**. Where necessary, disconnect the wiring connector from the luggage compartment light/rear speaker (as applicable) as the panel is removed.
25 Slacken and remove the bolt and free the belt upper mounting from the body **(see illustration)**.
26 Slacken and remove the inertia reel retaining bolt and remove the seat belt assembly from the vehicle **(see illustration)**.

Front seat belt buckle

27 Remove the seat (see Section 23).
28 Pull off the control knob from seat back adjuster then unscrew the retaining bolt and washer and remove the adjuster wheel.
29 Unclip the front edge of the side trim panel then free the rear of the panel and remove it from the seat.

30 Unscrew the retaining bolt, washer and spacer and remove the belt buckle.

Rear seat centre belt and belt buckles

31 Tilt the rear seat assembly forwards then slacken and remove the relevant retaining bolt, noting the correct fitted location of the washer and (where fitted) spacer, and remove the belt/buckle from the vehicle **(see illustration)**.

Refitting

32 Refitting is the reverse of removal, noting the following points.
a) *Make sure the inertia reel is correctly engaged with the body and the washers and/or spacers (as applicable) are correctly positioned on all the belt mounting points.*

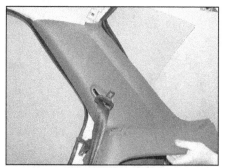

25.24a Unclip the upper trim panel from the body . . .

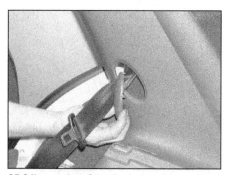

25.24b . . . then free the belt guide and belt from the panel

25.24c Removing the rear pillar panel - Estate models

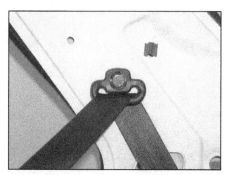

25.25 Slacken and remove the belt upper mounting bolt . . .

25.26 . . . and the inertia reel bolt and remove the rear seat belt from the vehicle

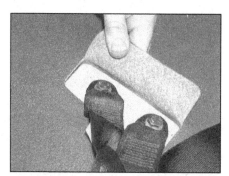

25.31 Rear seat centre belt and buckles are bolted to the floor

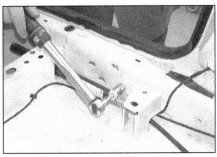

25.32 On refitting tighten the tensioner mounting nut to the specified torque to ensure correct operation

b) Tighten all fasteners to the specified torque (where given) **(see illustration)**.
c) Check the condition of all trim panel retaining clips and renew any that are damaged. Ensure all panels are securely retained by their clips and are correctly joined with all adjoining panels/sealing strips.

26 Interior trim - removal and refitting

Interior trim panels

1 The interior trim panels are secured using either screws or various types of trim fasteners, usually studs or clips.
2 Check that there are no other panels overlapping the one to be removed; usually there is a sequence that has to be followed that will become obvious on close inspection.
3 Remove all obvious fasteners, such as screws. If the panel will not come free, it is held by hidden clips or fasteners. These are usually situated around the edge of the panel and can be prised up to release them; note, however that they can break quite easily so replacements should be available. The best way of releasing such clips without the correct type of tool, is to use a large flat-bladed screwdriver. Note in many cases that the adjacent sealing strip must be prised back to release a panel.
4 When removing a panel, **never** use excessive force or the panel may be damaged; always check carefully that all fasteners have been removed or released before attempting to withdraw a panel.
5 Refitting is the reverse of the removal procedure; renew any clips/fasteners damaged on removal and ensure that all disturbed components are correctly secured to prevent rattles.

Carpets

6 The passenger compartment floor carpet is in one piece and is secured at its edges by screws or clips, usually the same fasteners used to secure the various adjoining trim panels.
7 Carpet removal and refitting is reasonably straightforward but very time-consuming because all adjoining trim panels must be removed first, as must components such as the seats, the centre console and seat belt lower anchorages.

Headlining

8 The headlining is clipped to the roof and can be withdrawn only once all fittings such as the grab handles, sun visors, sunroof (if fitted), windscreen and rear quarterwindows and related trim panels have been removed and the door, tailgate and sunroof aperture sealing strips have been prised clear.
9 Note that headlining removal requires considerable skill and experience if it is to be carried out without damage and is therefore best entrusted to an expert.

27 Centre console - removal and refitting

Removal

Early (pre 1998) models

1 Carefully prise out the blanking plate, which is located directly behind the gearchange lever gaiter, then slacken and remove the storage compartment panel retaining screw which is located behind it **(see illustrations)**.
2 Unscrew the knob from the gearchange lever **(see illustration)**.
3 Lift the rear of the storage compartment panel then free its front retaining clips and manoeuvre the panel and gaiter assembly out of position **(see illustration)**.
4 Prise out the trim cap from the recess at the rear of the centre console rear section then slacken and remove the retaining screw **(see illustrations)**.

27.1a Prise out the blanking plate . . .

27.1b . . . then slacken and remove the storage compartment retaining screw

27.2 Unscrew the knob from the gearchange lever . . .

27.3 . . . then lift off the storage compartment panel

27.4a Remove the trim cap from the rear section of the centre console . . .

27.4b . . . then slacken and remove the retaining screw

27.5a Slacken and remove the retaining nuts and screws (front ones shown) . . .

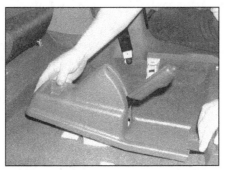

27.5b . . . and remove the console rear section . . .

27.5c . . . and front section from the vehicle

5 Slacken and remove the front and rear retaining nuts and screws then manoeuvre the centre console front and rear sections out of position and remove them from the vehicle (see illustrations).

Later (1998 on) models

6 Remove the storage compartment from inbetween the centre console and facia.
7 Prise out the trim cover from the recess at the front of the console to gain access to the front retaining nuts.
8 On models with electric front windows and/or heated seats, carefully prise the switch assembly out from the top of the console and disconnect its wiring connectors
9 On models not fitted with electric windows or heated seats, prise out the storage compartment from behind the gearchange lever.
10 On all models, unscrew the gearchange lever knob.
11 Prise out the trim cap from the recess at the rear of the centre console rear section then slacken and remove the retaining screw.
12 Slacken and remove the front and rear retaining nuts and washers then lift the front and rear sections out of position and remove it from the vehicle.

Refitting

13 Refitting is the reverse of removal making sure all fasteners are securely tightened.

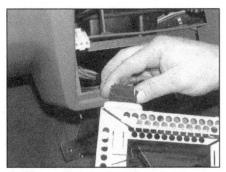

28.6b . . . and unclip the wiring connector

28 Facia panel assembly - removal and refitting

Removal

HAYNES HiNT *Attach an identification label to each wiring connector as it is disconnected. The labels can then be used on refitting to help ensure that all wiring is correctly routed through the relevant facia apertures.*

1 Remove the battery as described in Chapter 5A.
2 Remove the centre console (where fitted) as described in Section 27.
3 Remove the steering column as described in Chapter 10.

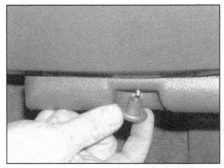

28.5 Unscrew the retainer and lower the fuse/relay box away from the facia

28.7a Unclip the headlight beam adjuster control knob assembly . . .

4 Working as described in Chapter 12, remove the following components.
a) Instrument panel.
b) Radio/cassette unit.
c) Cigarette lighter.
d) Passenger side airbag unit (where fitted).
5 Unscrew the retainer and free the fuse/relay box from the base of the passenger side of the facia (see illustration).
6 Bend back the retaining tangs then slide the radio/cassette mounting frame out of position. Disconnect the aerial lead then unclip the wiring connector and remove the frame from the vehicle (see illustrations).
7 Carefully lever off the complete control knob assembly from the headlight beam alignment adjuster. Loosen the retaining screws by a couple of turns then rotate the adjuster anti-clockwise slightly and free it from the rear of the facia panel (see illustrations).

28.6a Remove the radio/cassette mounting frame from the facia and disconnect the aerial lead . . .

28.7b . . . then slacken the retaining screws and free the adjuster from the facia

28.8 On models with a glovebox, unclip and remove the glovebox insert

28.9a Slacken and remove the facia retaining screws located in the instrument panel aperture . . .

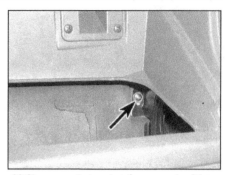

28.9b . . . and glovebox/passenger airbag aperture

8 On models not fitted with a passenger side airbag, open up the glovebox then unclip and lift out the glovebox insert **(see illustration)**.

9 Slacken and remove the two facia retaining screws located in the instrument panel aperture and the single screw accessible through the glovebox/airbag aperture **(see illustrations)**.

10 Work along the bottom edge of the facia and slacken and remove all its lower retaining screws **(see illustration)**.

11 Working in the engine compartment, slacken and remove the six facia retaining nuts and washers; the four upper nuts are located directly beneath the windscreen and the two lower nuts can be found, one on either side. Note the correct fitted locations of the insulation retaining plates fitted to the four upper nuts **(see illustrations)**.

12 From inside the vehicle, with the aid of an assistant, free the base of the facia assembly from the bulkhead then lift it upwards to free its upper studs. Manoeuvre the facia away from the bulkhead and remove it from the vehicle, freeing its wiring from any relevant retaining clips **(see illustration)**.

Refitting

13 Refitting is a reversal of the removal procedure. Prior to refitting the facia mounting nuts and screws, ensure all the necessary wiring connectors are fed through the relevant facia apertures. Refit the retaining nuts and screws, tighten them all by hand at first before going around and tightening them securely. On completion, reconnect the battery and check that all the electrical components and switches function correctly.

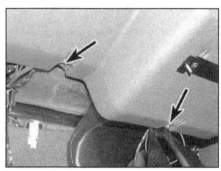

28.10 Slacken and remove all the facia lower retaining screws (two arrowed)

28.11a Working in the engine compartment, unscrew the two lower facia retaining nuts (one arrowed) . . .

28.11b . . . then unscrew the four upper nuts and recover the insulation retaining plates

28.12 Removing the facia from the vehicle

Chapter 12
Body electrical system

Contents

Degrees of difficulty

Easy, suitable for novice with little experience		Fairly easy, suitable for beginner with some experience		Fairly difficult, suitable for competent DIY mechanic	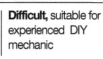	Difficult, suitable for experienced DIY mechanic		Very difficult, suitable for expert DIY or professional	

Specifications

System type . . . . 12 volt negative earth

Bulbs	**Wattage**
Exterior lights	
Headlight	60/55 (H4 type)
Front foglight	55
Front sidelight	5
Direction indicator	21
Direction indicator side repeater	5
Stop/tail	21/5
Reversing light	21
Rear foglight	21
Number plate light	5
Interior lights	
Courtesy light	10
Luggage compartment light	10
Instrument panel bulbs:	
Bulbs with blue holders	1.2
Bulbs with green holders	2

Torque wrench settings	**Nm**	**lbf ft**
Airbag system fixings:		
Control unit nuts	9	7
Driver's airbag unit screws	6	4
Passenger airbag:		
Mounting bracket nuts	15	11
Retaining nut	6	4
Windscreen wiper motor and linkage:		
Linkage spindle nuts	5	4
Wiper motor spindle nut	12	9
Wiper arm nut:		
Tailgate wiper arm	7	5
Windscreen wiper arm	9	7

1 General information and precautions

⚠️ *Warning: Before carrying out any work on the electrical system, read through the precautions given in Safety First! at the beginning of this manual and Chapter 5A.*

1 The electrical system is of the 12 volt negative earth type. Power for the lights and all electrical accessories is supplied by a lead/acid type battery which is charged by the alternator.

2 This Chapter covers repair and service procedures for the various electrical components not associated with engine. Information on the battery, alternator and starter motor can be found in Chapter 5.

3 It should be noted that prior to working on any component in the electrical system, the battery negative terminal should first be disconnected to prevent the possibility of electrical short circuits and/or fires.

Note: *On models with an anti-theft alarm system, disable the alarm system before disconnecting the battery and turn it back on again once the battery has been reconnected (see Section 20).*

2 Electrical fault finding - general information

Note: *Refer to the precautions given in Safety first! and in Section 1 of this Chapter before starting work. The following tests relate to testing of the main electrical circuits, and should not be used to test delicate electronic circuits (such as anti-lock braking systems), particularly where an electronic control module (ECU) is used.*

General

1 A typical electrical circuit consists of an electrical component, any switches, relays, motors, fuses, fusible links or circuit breakers related to that component, and the wiring and connectors which link the component to both the battery and the chassis. To help to pinpoint a problem in an electrical circuit, wiring diagrams are included at the end of this Chapter.

2 Before attempting to diagnose an electrical fault, first study the appropriate wiring diagram to obtain a complete understanding of the components included in the particular circuit concerned. The possible sources of a fault can be narrowed down by noting if other components related to the circuit are operating properly. If several components or circuits fail at one time, the problem is likely to be related to a shared fuse or earth connection.

3 Electrical problems usually stem from simple causes, such as loose or corroded connections, a faulty earth connection, a blown fuse, a melted fusible link, or a faulty relay (refer to Section 3 for details of testing relays). Visually inspect the condition of all fuses, wires and connections in a problem circuit before testing the components. Use the wiring diagrams to determine which terminal connections will need to be checked in order to pinpoint the trouble spot.

4 The basic tools required for electrical fault-finding include a circuit tester or voltmeter (a 12-volt bulb with a set of test leads can also be used for certain tests); a self-powered test light (sometimes known as a continuity tester); an ohmmeter (to measure resistance); a battery and set of test leads; and a jumper wire, preferably with a circuit breaker or fuse incorporated, which can be used to bypass suspect wires or electrical components. Before attempting to locate a problem with test instruments, use the wiring diagram to determine where to make the connections.

5 To find the source of an intermittent wiring fault (usually due to a poor or dirty connection, or damaged wiring insulation), a wiggle test can be performed on the wiring. This involves wiggling the wiring by hand to see if the fault occurs as the wiring is moved. It should be possible to narrow down the source of the fault to a particular section of wiring. This method of testing can be used in conjunction with any of the tests described in the following sub-Sections.

6 Apart from problems due to poor connections, two basic types of fault can occur in an electrical circuit - open circuit, or short circuit.

7 Open circuit faults are caused by a break somewhere in the circuit, which prevents current from flowing. An open circuit fault will prevent a component from working, but will not cause the relevant circuit fuse to blow.

8 Short circuit faults are caused by a short somewhere in the circuit, which allows the current flowing in the circuit to escape along an alternative route, usually to earth. Short circuit faults are normally caused by a breakdown in wiring insulation, which allows a feed wire to touch either another wire, or an earthed component such as the bodyshell. A short circuit fault will normally cause the relevant circuit fuse to blow.

Finding an open circuit

9 To check for an open circuit, connect one lead of a circuit tester or voltmeter to either the negative battery terminal or a known good earth.

10 Connect the other lead to a connector in the circuit being tested, preferably nearest to the battery or fuse.

11 Switch on the circuit, bearing in mind that some circuits are live only when the ignition switch is moved to a particular position.

12 If voltage is present (indicated either by the tester bulb lighting or a voltmeter reading, as applicable), this means that the section of the circuit between the relevant connector and the battery is problem-free.

13 Continue to check the remainder of the circuit in the same fashion.

14 When a point is reached at which no voltage is present, the problem must lie between that point and the previous test point with voltage. Most problems can be traced to a broken, corroded or loose connection.

Finding a short circuit

15 To check for a short circuit, first disconnect the load(s) from the circuit (loads are the components which draw current from a circuit, such as bulbs, motors, heating elements, etc).

16 Remove the relevant fuse from the circuit, and connect a circuit tester or voltmeter to the fuse connections.

17 Switch on the circuit, bearing in mind that some circuits are live only when the ignition switch is moved to a particular position.

18 If voltage is present (indicated either by the tester bulb lighting or a voltmeter reading, as applicable), this means that there is a short circuit.

19 If no voltage is present, but the fuse still blows with the load(s) connected, this indicates an internal fault in the load(s).

Finding an earth fault

20 The battery negative terminal is connected to earth- the metal of the engine/transmission unit and the car body - and most systems are wired so that they only receive a positive feed, the current returning through the metal of the car body. This means that the component mounting and the body form part of that circuit. Loose or corroded mountings can therefore cause a range of electrical faults, ranging from total failure of a circuit, to a puzzling partial fault. In particular, lights may shine dimly (especially when another circuit sharing the same earth point is in operation), motors (eg. wiper motors or the radiator cooling fan motor) may run slowly, and the operation of one circuit may have an apparently unrelated effect on another. Note that on many vehicles, earth straps are used between certain components, such as the engine/transmission and the body, usually where there is no metal-to-metal contact between components due to flexible rubber mountings, etc.

21 To check whether a component is properly earthed, disconnect the battery and connect one lead of an ohmmeter to a known good earth point. Connect the other lead to the wire or earth connection being tested. The resistance reading should be zero; if not, check the connection as follows.

22 If an earth connection is thought to be faulty, dismantle the connection and clean back to bare metal both the bodyshell and the wire terminal or the component earth connection mating surface. Be careful to remove all traces of dirt and corrosion, then use a knife to trim away any paint, so that a clean metal-to-metal joint is made. On reassembly, tighten the joint fasteners

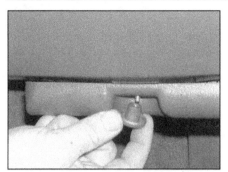

3.2a Unscrew the retainer . . .

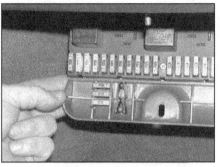

3.2b . . . then pivot the fuse/relay box down from the underside of the facia

3.3 Pull the relevant fuse out of position using the tweezers which are supplied

securely; if a wire terminal is being refitted, use serrated washers between the terminal and the bodyshell to ensure a clean and secure connection. When the connection is remade, prevent the onset of corrosion in the future by applying a coat of petroleum jelly or silicone-based grease or by spraying on (at regular intervals) a proprietary ignition sealer such or a water dispersant lubricant.

3 Fuses and relays - general information

Fuses

1 Most fuses are located in the fuse/relay box, which is fitted to the underside of the facia in the passenger footwell. Some additional fuses (those for the ABS and air conditioning system) are located in holders on the left-hand side of the engine compartment. On Diesel engine models the fuses for the preheating system and cooling fan can also be found on the left-hand side of the engine compartment.

2 To gain access to the main fuse/relay box, unscrew the fastener and pivot the box down from underside the facia **(see illustrations)**. A list of the circuits each fuse protects is given in the wiring diagrams at the end of this Chapter. To gain access to the fuses in the engine compartment, simply unclip and remove the cover (where fitted) from the fuse holder.

3 To remove a fuse, first switch off the circuit concerned (or the ignition), then pull the fuse out of its terminals **(see illustration)**. The wire within the fuse should be visible; if the fuse is blown it will be broken or melted.

4 Always renew a fuse with one of an identical rating; never use a fuse with a different rating from the original or substitute anything else. Never renew a fuse more than once without tracing the source of the trouble. The fuse rating is stamped on top of the fuse; note that the fuses are also colour-coded for easy recognition.

5 If a new fuse blows immediately, find the cause before renewing it again; a short to earth as a result of faulty insulation is most

likely. Where a fuse protects more than one circuit, try to isolate the defect by switching on each circuit in turn (if possible) until the fuse blows again. Always carry a supply of spare fuses of each relevant rating on the vehicle, a spare of each rating should be clipped into the main fuse/relay box.

Relays

6 The majority of relays are also located in the fuse/relay box on the base of the passenger side of the facia. Additional relays (such as the Diesel engine preheating system relay) can be found in the engine compartment.

7 To gain access to the main fuse/relay box, unscrew the fastener and pivot the box down from underside the facia.

8 If a circuit or system controlled by a relay develops a fault and the relay is suspect, operate the system; if the relay is functioning it should be possible to hear it click as it is energised. If this is the case the fault lies with the components or wiring of the system. If the relay is not being energised then either the relay is not receiving a main supply or a switching voltage or the relay itself is faulty. Testing is by the substitution of a known good unit but be careful; while some relays are identical in appearance and in operation, others look similar but perform different functions.

9 To renew a relay first ensure that the ignition switch is off. The relay and then simply be pulled out from the socket and the new relay pressed in.

4 Switches - removal and refitting

Note: *Disconnect the battery negative lead before removing any switch, and reconnect the lead after refitting the switch (see note in Section 1).*

Ignition switch/steering column lock

1 Refer to Chapter 10.

Steering column combination switches

2 Remove the steering wheel as described in Chapter 10.

3 On models not fitted with an airbag, undo the retaining screw then slide the steering column lower shroud downwards, to release its retaining clip, and away from the steering column.

4 On all models, slacken and remove the retaining screw then unclip the upper shroud assembly from the facia/switch holder and remove it from the steering column **(see illustrations)**.

5 Each individual switch assembly can then be removed by depressing its retaining clips and sliding it out of the switch holder before disconnecting the wiring connector(s) **(see illustrations)**.

6 Refitting is the reverse of removal ensuring all wiring connectors are securely reconnected.

4.4a Slacken and remove the retaining screw . . .

4.4b . . . then unclip the steering column upper shroud

4.5a Depress the retaining clips then slide the switch out from its holder . . .

4.5b . . . and disconnect its wiring connector

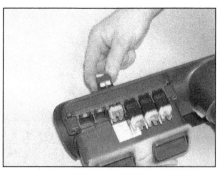

4.8 Depress the retaining clips and slide the relevant facia switch out from the instrument panel shroud

Also make sure that the switch holder horn contact is correctly located before refitting the shrouds.

Facia switch panel switches

7 Remove the instrument panel as described in Section 9.

8 Each switch assembly can then be slid out from the panel shroud once its retaining clips have been depressed **(see illustration)**.

9 On refitting ensure the switch is clipped securely in position then refit the instrument panel as described in Section 9.

Exterior mirror switch

10 Lift the door lock inner handle then carefully unclip the trim cover and remove it from the door handle.

11 Unclip the switch from the door handle and disconnect its wiring connector.

12 Refitting is the reverse of removal.

Electric window/heated front seat switch

13 Taking care not to damage the switch or console, carefully ease the switch assembly out of position using a small, flat-bladed screwdriver.

14 Disconnect the wiring connector(s) and remove the switch from the vehicle.

15 Refitting is the reverse of removal.

Courtesy light switch

16 Open up the door and remove the rubber gaiter from the light switch **(see illustration)**.

17 Release the retaining clips and carefully prise the switch out from the pillar, disconnecting the wiring connector as it becomes accessible **(see illustration)**. Tape the wiring connector to the body to prevent it

disappearing into the pillar. **Note:** *If there is insufficient slack in the wiring to allow the switch to be removed, remove the inner trim panels from the pillar to gain access (see Chapter 11, Section 25).*

18 Refitting is the reverse of removal, ensuring the rubber gaiter is correctly seated on the switch.

Luggage compartment light switch

19 Remove the tailgate lock assembly as described in Chapter 11.

20 Unclip the wiring connector and switch and remove them from the lock assembly **(see illustrations)**.

21 Refitting is the reverse of removal. Check the operation of the switch before refitting the insulation and trim panel.

Stop-light switch

22 Refer to Chapter 9.

Handbrake lever switch

23 On models with a centre console, remove the console as described in Chapter 11.

24 On models with no centre console, unclip the handbrake lever cover and manoeuvre it off of the lever.

25 Undo the retaining screw and lift off the switch cover then remove the switch from the handbrake lever, disconnecting the wiring connector as it becomes accessible **(see illustrations)**.

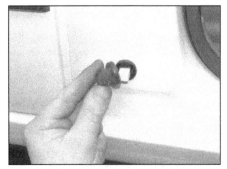

4.16 Remove the rubber gaiter from the courtesy light switch . . .

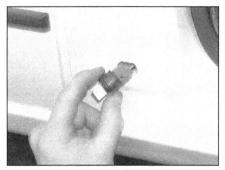

4.17 . . . then release the retaining clips and withdraw the switch from the pillar

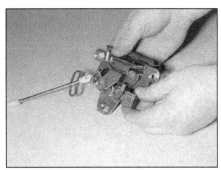

4.20a Unclip the wiring connector and switch . . .

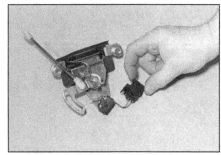

4.20b . . . and remove the luggage compartment light switch from the tailgate lock

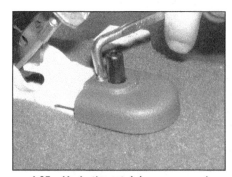

4.25a Undo the retaining screw and remove the cover . . .

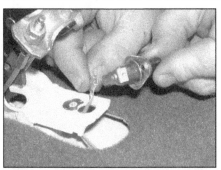

4.25b ... then remove the handbrake lever switch, disconnect its wiring connector as it becomes accessible

26 Refitting is the reverse of removal. Check the operation of the switch before refitting the centre console/cover.

Blower motor switch

27 Remove the heater/ventilation housing assembly as described in Chapter 3.
28 Disconnect the wiring connector from the switch assembly (see illustration).
29 Note the correct fitted location of each cable (the cable end fittings are colour-coded) then, using pliers, release the retaining clips and detach the cables from base of the blower motor and the control panel (see illustration).
30 Unclip the bulb reflector from the front of the control panel.
31 Release the retaining clips and remove the blower motor switch assembly from the control panel (see illustrations).
32 Refitting is the reverse of removal, refitting the housing assembly as described in Chapter 3.

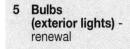

5 Bulbs (exterior lights) - renewal

General

1 Whenever a bulb is renewed, note the following points.
  a) Disconnect the battery negative lead before starting work (see note in Section 1).
  b) Remember that if the light has just been in use the bulb may be extremely hot.

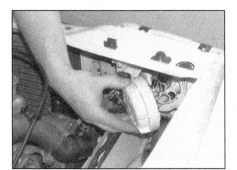

5.2 Remove the access cover from the rear of the headlight unit ...

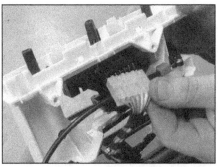

4.28 Disconnect the wiring connector from the blower motor switch

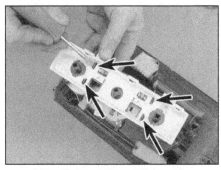

4.31a Release the retaining clips (arrowed) ...

  c) Always check the bulb contacts and holder, ensuring that there is clean metal-to-metal contact between the bulb and its live(s) and earth. Clean off any corrosion or dirt before fitting a new bulb.
  d) Wherever bayonet-type bulbs are fitted (see Specifications) ensure that the live contact(s) bear firmly against the bulb contact.
  e) Always ensure that the new bulb is of the correct rating and that it is completely clean before fitting it; this applies particularly to headlight/foglight bulbs (see below).

Headlight

2 Rotate the access cover anti-clockwise and remove it from the rear of the headlight unit (see illustration).

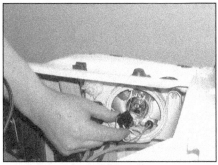

5.3 ... and disconnect the wiring connector from the bulb

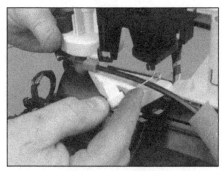

4.29 Unclip the outer cables and detach both inner cables from the base of the heater control panel

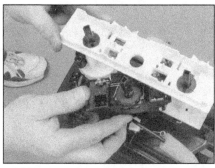

4.31b ... and remove the blower motor switch from the rear of the heater control panel

3 Disconnect the wiring connector from the bulb (see illustration).
4 Unhook and release the ends of the bulb retaining clip and release it from the rear of the light unit. Withdraw the bulb (see illustration).
5 When handling the new bulb, use a tissue or clean cloth to avoid touching the glass with the fingers; moisture and grease from the skin can cause blackening and rapid failure of this type of bulb. If the glass is accidentally touched, wipe it clean using methylated spirit.
6 Install the new bulb, ensuring that its locating tabs are correctly located in the light cutouts, and secure it in position with the retaining clip
7 Reconnect the wiring connector and refit the access cover, making sure it is securely refitted with its TOP marking uppermost.

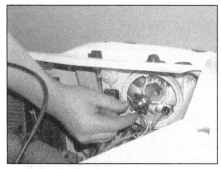

5.4 Unhook the retaining clip and withdraw the bulb

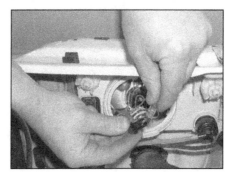

5.9b . . . and pull the bulb out from its holder

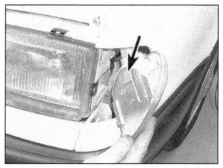

5.17 Depress the retaining clip (arrowed) and slide the indicator light unit out of position

Front sidelight

8 Rotate the access cover anti-clockwise and remove it from the rear of the headlight unit.

9 Remove the sidelight bulbholder from the headlight unit then pull the bulb out from its holder (see illustrations).

10 Refitting is the reverse of the removal procedure making sure the access cover is securely refitted with its TOP marking uppermost.

Front foglight

Note: *The following information is only applicable to pre 1998 models. At the time of writing no information was available for the later models.*

11 Using a small, flat-bladed screwdriver, carefully prise out the foglight trim from the front of the bumper.

12 Undo the retaining screws and free the foglight unit from the bumper. Disconnect the wiring connectors and remove the unit from the vehicle.

13 Release the retaining clip and remove the bulb from the foglight.

14 When handling the new bulb, use a tissue or clean cloth to avoid touching the glass with the fingers; moisture and grease from the skin can cause blackening and rapid failure of this type of bulb. If the glass is accidentally touched, wipe it clean using methylated spirit.

15 Install the new bulb, ensuring that its locating tabs are correctly located in the reflector cutouts, and secure it in position with the retaining clip.

16 Reconnect the wiring connectors then refit the foglight unit to the bumper. Securely tighten the retaining screws then refit the trim panel to the bumper.

Front direction indicator

17 Locate the direction indicator light retaining clip in the front corner of the engine compartment. Depress the clip and slide the light unit out of position (see illustration). If necessary, to improve access to the right-hand indicator, free the air cleaner housing from its mountings (see the relevant part of Chapter 4).

18 Rotate the bulbholder anti-clockwise and remove it from the rear of the light unit. The bulb is a bayonet fit in the holder and can be removed by pressing it and twisting in an anti-clockwise direction (see illustrations).

19 Refitting is a reverse of the removal procedure, ensuring the light unit is securely clipped in position.

Front direction indicator side repeater

20 Reach up behind the wing and ease the light unit out of position.

21 Free the bulbholder from the rear of the lens and remove the bulb. The bulb is of the capless (push-fit) type and can be simply pulled out of its holder (see illustrations).

22 Refitting is the reverse of removal ensuring the lens unit is clipped securely in position.

Rear light cluster

23 Release the retaining clips and remove the bulbholder assembly from the rear of the light unit (see illustration).

5.18a Free the bulbholder from the rear of the light unit . . .

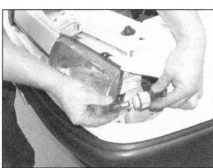

5.18b . . . and remove the bulb by pressing it in and turning anti-clockwise

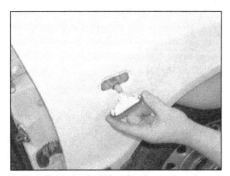

5.21a Free the bulbholder from the rear of the side repeater light unit . . .

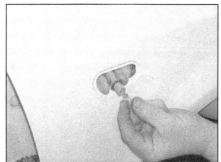

5.21b . . . then pull the bulb out from its holder

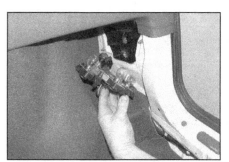

5.23 Release the retaining clips and free the bulbholder assembly from the rear of the light unit

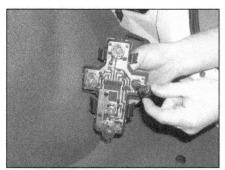

5.24 All bulbs are removed by pressing them in and turning anti-clockwise

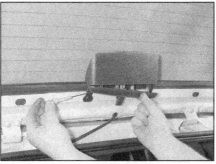

5.26 Release the retaining clip and free the bulbholder assembly from the high-level stoplight . . .

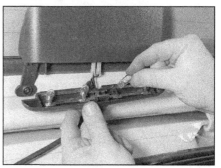

5.27 . . . each bulb is a push-fit in the holder

5.29 Carefully prise the number plate light out from the tailgate . . .

5.30a . . . then free the bulbholder from the light unit . . .

5.30b . . . and pull out the bulb

24 All bulbs have bayonet fittings. The relevant bulb can be removed by pressing in and rotating anti-clockwise (see illustration). Note that the stop/taillight bulb has offset pins to ensure it is fitted the correct way around.

25 Refitting is the reverse of the removal sequence ensuring the bulbholder is securely clipped in position.

High-level stop-light

26 Release the retaining clips and unclip the bulbholder assembly from the rear of the light unit (see illustration).

27 Pull the relevant bulb out from the holder (see illustration). All the bulbs are of the capless (push-fit) type.

28 Refitting is the reverse of removal ensuring the bulb holder is clipped securely in position.

Number plate light

29 Using a small, flat-bladed screwdriver, carefully ease the light unit out from the tailgate (see illustration).

30 Free the bulbholder from the rear of the lens and remove the bulb. The bulb is of the capless (push-fit) type and can be simply pulled out of its holder (see illustrations).

31 Refitting is the reverse of removal ensuring the lens unit is clipped securely in position.

6 Bulbs (interior lights) - renewal

General

1 Refer to Section 5, paragraph 1.

Front courtesy light

2 Using a small, flat-bladed screwdriver, carefully prise light unit assembly out of position to gain access to the bulb (see illustration).

3 Unclip the cover then free the bulb from its contacts and remove it from the light unit (see illustrations).

4 Refitting is the reverse of removal ensuring the bulb is securely held by the contacts.

Rear courtesy light

5 Using a small, flat-bladed screwdriver, carefully prise out the lens from the light unit assembly.

6 Free the bulb from its contacts and remove it from the light unit.

7 Refitting is the reverse of removal ensuring the bulb is securely held by the contacts.

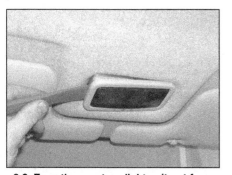

6.2 Ease the courtesy light unit out from the headlining . . .

6.3a . . . then unclip the cover . . .

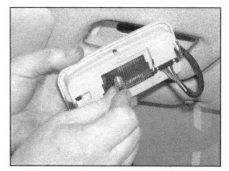

6.3b . . . and remove the bulb from its contacts

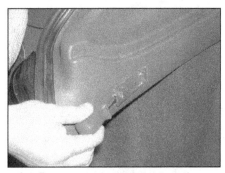

6.8 Remove the luggage compartment light from the trim panel . . .

6.9 . . . and unclip the bulb from its contacts

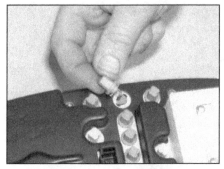

6.12 All instrument panel bulbs are integral with their holders

6.14 Remove the ashtray . . .

6.15 . . . then carefully unclip the faceplate from the heater control panel

6.16a Pull off the control knobs . . .

Luggage compartment light

8 Using a small, flat-bladed screwdriver, carefully prise light unit assembly out of position to gain access to the bulb (see illustration).
9 Free the bulb from its contacts and remove it from the light unit (see illustration).
10 Refitting is the reverse of removal ensuring the bulb is securely held by the contacts.

Instrument panel illumination/warning lights

11 Remove the instrument panel as described in Section 9.
12 Twist the relevant bulbholder anti-clockwise and withdraw it from the rear of the panel; the bulbs are integral with their holders (see illustration). Be very careful to ensure that the new bulbs are of the correct rating,

the same as those removed; bulbs with a blue holder are rated at 1.2W and those with a green holder are 2W.
13 Refit the bulbholder to the rear of the instrument panel then refit the instrument panel as described in Section 9.

Heater control panel illumination bulb

14 Remove the ashtray (see illustration).
15 Taking great care not to damage the facia, carefully prise the faceplate off from the heater control panel (see illustration).
16 Pull off the control knobs then remove the bulb surround from the control panel (see illustrations).
17 Each illumination bulb is of the capless type and is a push-fit in the control panel (see illustration).
18 Refitting is the reverse of removal ensuring the bulb is securely in position.

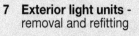

7 Exterior light units - removal and refitting

Note: Disconnect the battery negative lead before removing any light unit, and reconnect the lead after refitting the light (see note in Section 1).

Headlight

1 Remove both front direction indicator lights as described in paragraph 9.
2 On early (pre 1998) models, slacken and remove the left- and right-hand front panel retaining bolts, which are accessible through the direction indicator light apertures, and the two screws securing the top of the panel to the bonnet lock crossmember. Unscrew the retaining nuts from the rear of the panel then manoeuvre the front panel away from the vehicle (see illustrations).

6.16b . . . then remove the bulb surround . . .

6.17 . . . and pull the relevant bulb out from the control panel

7.2a On early (pre 1998) models, slacken and remove the retaining bolt located in each indicator light aperture . . .

7.2b ... and the two screws securing the front panel to the crossmember

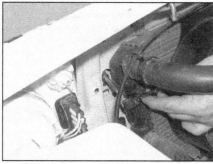

7.2c Undo the retaining nuts securing the rear of the panel in position ...

7.2d ... then manoeuvre the front panel away from the vehicle

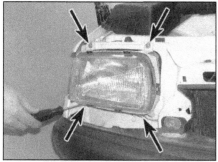

7.4 Slacken and remove the headlight unit retaining screws (arrowed)

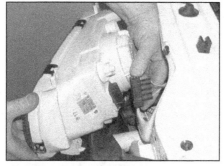

7.5 Disconnect the wiring connector ...

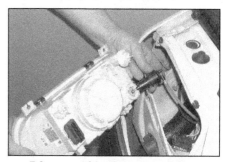

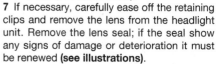

7.6 ... and free the beam adjuster assembly then remove the headlight unit from the vehicle

3 On later (1998 on) models undo the retaining screw then unclip and remove the trim cover which is fitted inbetween the headlight and front bumper.
4 On all models, slacken and remove the retaining screws from the top and bottom of

the headlight unit (see illustration).
5 Slide the unit out of position and disconnect its wiring connector (see illustration).
6 Rotate the headlight beam adjuster assembly to free it from the rear of the

headlight unit then remove the headlight from the vehicle (see illustration).
7 If necessary, carefully ease off the retaining clips and remove the lens from the headlight unit. Remove the lens seal; if the seal show any signs of damage or deterioration it must be renewed (see illustrations).
8 Refitting is a direct reversal of the removal procedure, tightening the retaining screws securely and making sure the adjuster unit is securely clipped in position. On completion the headlight beam alignment should be checked using the information given in Section 8.

Front direction indicator light

9 Locate the direction indicator light retaining clip in the front corner of the engine compartment. Depress the clip then slide the light unit out of position and twist it to free it from the bulbholder (see illustrations).

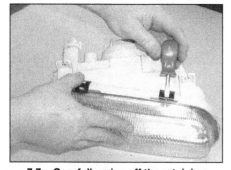

7.7a Carefully prise off the retaining clips ...

7.7b ... then remove the lens unit from the headlight ...

7.7c ... and recover its seal

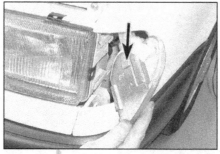

7.9a Depress the retaining clip (arrowed) then slide the indicator light unit out of position ...

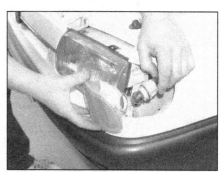

7.9b ... and free it from the bulbholder

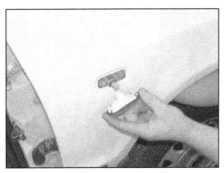

7.15 Push the side repeater light out of position and free it from the bulbholder

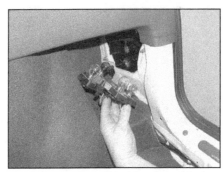

7.17 Unclip the bulbholder assembly . . .

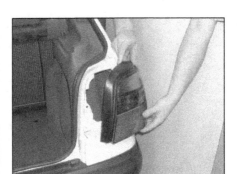

7.18a . . . then undo the retaining nuts (arrowed) . . .

7.18b . . . and remove the rear light from the vehicle

16 Refitting is the reverse of removal ensuring the lens unit is clipped securely in position.

Rear light cluster

17 Release the retaining clips and release the bulbholder assembly from the rear of the light unit (see illustration).
18 Unscrew the retaining nuts and remove the light unit from the vehicle along with its seal (see illustrations). Inspect the seal for signs of damage or deterioration and renew if necessary.
19 Refitting is the reverse of the removal sequence ensuring the seal is correctly fitted.

High-level stoplight

20 Slacken and remove the retaining screws then remove the light unit from the inside of the tailgate, disconnecting the wiring connectors as they become accessible (see illustrations).
21 Refitting is the reverse of removal.

Number plate light

22 Using a small, flat-bladed screwdriver, carefully ease the light unit out from the tailgate.
23 Free the bulbholder and remove the lens unit.
24 Refitting is the reverse of removal ensuring the lens unit is clipped securely in position.

If necessary, to improve access to the right-hand indicator, free the air cleaner housing from its mountings (see the relevant part of Chapter 4).
10 Refitting is a reverse of the removal procedure, ensuring the light unit is securely clipped in position.

Front foglight

Note: The following information is only applicable to pre 1998 models. At the time of writing no information was available for the later models.
11 Using a small, flat-bladed screwdriver, carefully prise out the foglight trim from the

front of the bumper.
12 Undo the retaining screws and free the foglight unit from the bumper. Disconnect the wiring connectors and remove the unit from the vehicle.
13 Refitting is the reverse of removal. If necessary, adjust the foglight aim using the adjuster screw on the light unit.

Front direction indicator side repeater

14 Reach up behind the wing and ease the light unit out of position.
15 Free the bulbholder and remove the lens unit from the vehicle (see illustration).

8 Headlight beam alignment - information and adjustment mechanism renewal

Information

1 Accurate adjustment of the headlight beam is only possible using optical beam setting equipment and this work should therefore be carried out by a Skoda dealer or suitably equipped workshop.

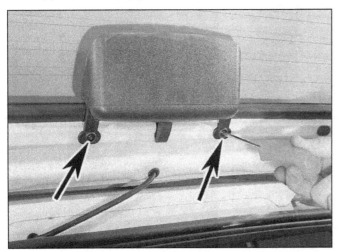

7.20a Undo the retaining screws (arrowed) . . .

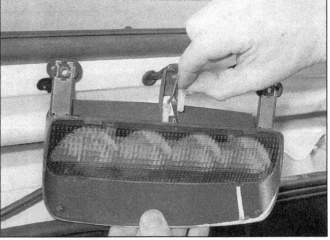

7.20b . . . and remove the high-level stoplight, disconnecting its wiring connectors as they become accessible

2 For reference the headlights are adjusted using the thumbwheels which are fitted to the top of each headlight unit. The outer one alters the headlight beam vertical aim and the inner one the horizontal aim. **Note:** *Ensure that the headlight beam adjuster is set to position 0 before the headlight aim is set.*

Adjustment mechanism renewal

3 The headlight beam adjustment mechanism is hydraulically-operated and consists of two adjusters (one for each headlight) that are linked to the adjustment mechanism by hoses. Note that the adjusters, adjustment mechanism and the hoses linking them must be treated as a sealed unit. If a fault develops, the complete hydraulic mechanism must be replaced as follows.

4 Remove the instrument panel as described in Section 9.

5 Carefully lever off the complete control knob assembly off from the headlight beam adjuster mechanism. Loosen the retaining screws by a couple of turns then rotate the mechanism anti-clockwise slightly and free it from the rear of the facia panel **(see illustrations)**.

6 Working in the engine compartment, locate the adjuster on the rear of the each headlight unit. Rotate each adjuster anti-clockwise to free it from the light unit body then carefully unclip the balljoints from the rear of the reflectors.

7 Work back along the adjuster hoses, noting each ones correct routing, and free them from all the relevant retaining clips and ties.

8 Free the adjuster sealing grommet from the

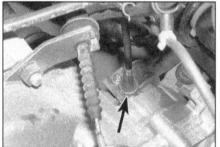

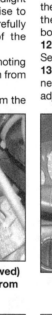

9.2 Unscrew the retaining ring (arrowed) and detach the speedometer cable from the transmission unit

9.5b . . . then unclip the upper shroud from the steering column and switch holder

8.5a Unclip the control knob assembly . . .

bulkhead and remove the complete adjustment system assembly from the vehicle.

9 On refitting, feed the adjustment mechanism in through the bulkhead aperture and seat it correctly in the facia. Securely tighten the retaining screws then clip on the control knob assembly.

10 Seat the sealing grommet in the bulkhead aperture then route the adjuster hoses correctly around the engine compartment, securing them in position with the relevant retaining clips and ties.

11 Clip each adjuster balljoint securely into the rear of the headlight reflector then locate the adjuster body securely in the light unit body.

12 Refit the instrument panel as described in Section 9.

13 Check the operation of the system and, if necessary, have the headlight beam aim adjusted (see paragraphs 1 and 2).

9.5a Undo the retaining screw . . .

9.6a Carefully prise out the blanking plate from the instrument panel shroud . . .

8.5b . . . then slacken the retaining screws and free the adjuster from the facia

9 Instrument panel - removal and refitting

Removal

1 Disconnect the battery negative terminal (see note in Section 1).

2 Locate the transmission end of the speedometer cable then unscrew the retaining ring and detach the cable from the speedometer drive **(see illustration)**.

3 Remove the steering wheel as described in Chapter 10.

4 On models not fitted with an airbag, undo the retaining screw then slide the steering column lower shroud downwards, to release its retaining clip, and away from the steering column.

5 On all models, slacken and remove the retaining screw then unclip the upper shroud assembly from the facia/switch holder and remove it from the steering column **(see illustrations)**.

6 To gain access to the panel shroud upper retaining screws, using a small, flat-bladed screwdriver, carefully prise out the blanking plate (on some models the plate is replaced with the outside temperature display) from the right-hand side (left-hand side on left-hand drive models) of the shroud and remove the trim cover from the centre of the instrument panel shroud vent assembly **(see illustrations)**.

9.6b . . . and remove the trim cover from the centre of the vent assembly

9.7a Remove the inner end cover from the outer switch(es) . . .

9.7b . . . and both end covers (arrowed) from the centre switches

9.8a Slacken and remove the retaining screws (arrowed) . . .

9.8b . . . and remove the instrument panel assembly from the facia . . .

7 To gain access to the panel shroud lower retaining screws, remove the end covers from each end of the centrally-located facia switches and the inner end of the outer switch(es) **(see illustrations)**.

8 Slacken and remove the upper and lower retaining screws then ease the instrument panel and shroud assembly out of position. As they become accessible, disconnect the wiring connectors from the rear of panel then depress the retaining clips and detach the speedometer cable **(see illustrations)**.

9 If necessary, release the retaining clips and separate the panel from its shroud.

Refitting

10 Manoeuvre the assembly into position then securely reconnect the speedometer cable and wiring connectors. Ensure all connections are securely made then seat the instrument panel in the facia.

11 Refit the shroud retaining screws, tightening them securely. Refit the switch end covers, blanking plate and vent trim cover to the shroud.

12 Clip the steering column upper shroud into position and securely tighten its retaining screw. On models not fitted with an airbag also fit the lower shroud.

13 Refit the steering wheel as described in Chapter 10.

14 Reconnect the battery and check the operation of the panel warning lights to ensure they are functioning correctly. If all is well

15 Reconnect the speedometer cable to the drive and securely tighten its retaining ring.

10 Speedometer cable - removal and refitting

Removal

1 Remove the instrument panel as described in Section 9.

2 Working in the engine compartment, unscrew the retaining ring and detach the speedometer cable from the drive on the top of the transmission unit.

3 Work back along the cable, noting its correct routing, and free it from all its retaining clips.

4 Free the cable sealing grommet from the bulkhead and remove the cable from the vehicle.

Refitting

5 Refitting is the reverse of removal ensuring the cable is correctly routed and retained by all the necessary clips.

11 Cigarette lighter - removal and refitting

Removal

1 Remove the instrument panel as described in Section 9.

2 Remove the ashtray then carefully unclip the faceplate and remove it from the heater control panel.

9.8c . . . disconnect the wiring connectors . . .

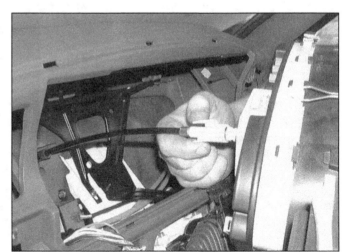

9.8d . . . and speedometer cable as they become accessible

11.3 Undo the retaining screws and free the heater control panel from the facia

11.4a Working in the heater panel aperture, slacken and remove the retaining screws . . .

11.4b . . . then remove the ashtray surround panel/cigarette lighter and disconnect its wiring connector

3 Slacken and remove the heater control panel retaining screws then free the panel from the rear of the facia to gain access to the ashtray surround/cigarette lighter retaining screws **(see illustration)**.
4 Using a right-angled screwdriver, slacken and remove the retaining screws located in the heater control panel aperture then slide the ashtray surround panel/cigarette lighter assembly out from the facia, disconnecting the wiring connector as it becomes accessible **(see illustrations)**. If necessary, the cigarette lighter can be unclipped and removed from the ashtray surround.

Refitting

5 Refitting is a reversal of the removal procedure, ensuring all the wiring connectors are securely reconnected.

12 Horn - removal and refitting

Removal

1 On early (pre 1998) models to gain access to the horn, remove the front panel as described in paragraph 2 of Section 7.
2 On all models, reach in behind the bumper and disconnect the wiring connector from the horn. Slacken and remove the mounting nut and remove the horn from behind the bumper **(see illustration)**.

Refitting

3 Refitting is the reverse of removal.

13 Wiper arm - removal and refitting

Removal

1 Operate the wiper motor then switch it off so that the wiper arm returns to the at rest position.
2 Lift up the wiper arm retaining nut cover then remove the trim cap (where fitted) and slacken and remove the nut **(see illustration)**.
3 Lift the blade off of the glass and pull the wiper arm off the motor. If necessary, carefully lever the arm off of the spindle using a large, flat-bladed screwdriver.

Refitting

4 Ensure the wiper and spindle are clean and dry then refit the arm. Ensure the arm is correctly positioned then refit the retaining nut, tightening it to the specified torque. Refit the trim cap and/or cover.

14 Windscreen wiper motor and linkage - removal and refitting

Removal

1 Operate the wiper motor then switch it off so that the wiper arms return to the at rest position. Disconnect the battery negative terminal (see note in Section 1) and proceed as described under the relevant sub-heading.

Wiper motor

2 Disconnect the wiring connector from the wiper motor **(see illustration)**.
3 Slacken and remove the retaining nut and washer then free the linkage crank from the motor splines **(see illustrations)**.
4 Undo the three retaining bolts and remove the motor assembly from the vehicle **(see illustrations)**.

Wiper motor and linkage assembly

5 Remove the wiper arms as described in the previous Section.
6 Disconnect the wiring connector from the wiper motor.

12.2 Disconnect the wiring connector then undo the retaining nut and remove the horn from the vehicle

13.2 Unscrew the retaining nut then free the wiper arm from its spindle

14.2 Disconnect the wiring connector from the wiper motor

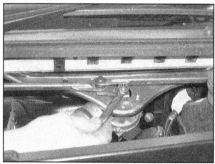

14.3a Unscrew the spindle nut . . .

14.3b ... then release the wiper linkage crank from the motor

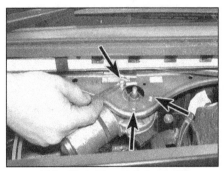

14.4a Undo the retaining bolts (arrowed) ...

14.4b ... and remove the wiper motor from the vehicle

7 Unscrew the plastic retaining nuts and prise out the retaining clips securing the wind deflector panel in position **(see illustrations)**. Free the panel from the base of the windscreen and position it clear of the wiper linkage.

8 Remove the trim cap from each wiper linkage spindle then slacken and remove the linkage retaining nuts, washers and sealing washers **(see illustrations)**.

9 Free the assembly from the body and manoeuvre it out of position noting the correct fitted locations of the spacers and washers which are fitted to the linkage mountings **(see illustrations)**. **Note:** *On left-hand drive models it may prove necessary to remove the retaining clips and lift off the top section of the heater/ventilation housing to gain the clearance required for removal.*

Refitting

Wiper motor

10 If a new motor is being installed, connect the motor to the wiring connector and operate the motor (it will be necessary to reconnect the battery temporarily) before turning it off. This will ensure that the motor is in the at rest position.

11 Manoeuvre the motor into position and securely tighten its retaining bolts.

12 Ensure both wiper arms are correctly positioned in the at rest position then engage the linkage crank with the motor spindle splines. Refit the washer and retaining nut to the spindle and tighten it to the specified torque.

13 Reconnect the wiring connector to the motor then reconnect the battery.

Wiper motor and linkage

14 Refitting is the reverse of removal ensuring the washers and spacers are correctly positioned and the linkage spindle nuts are tightened to the specified torque.

15 Tailgate wiper motor -
removal and refitting

Removal

1 Disconnect the battery negative terminal.

2 Remove the wiper arm as described in Section 13.

3 Remove the cap from the motor spindle then slacken and remove the spindle retaining nut and lift off the washer and outer seal **(see illustrations)**.

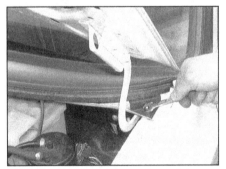

14.7a Unscrew the plastic retaining nuts ...

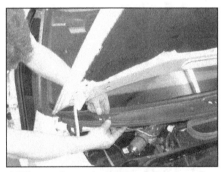

14.7b ... then prise out the retaining clips and position the wind deflector panel clear of the wiper linkage

14.8a Remove the rubber cap from each wiper linkage spindle then unscrew the nut (arrowed) ...

14.8b ... and lift off the washer and sealing washer (arrowed)

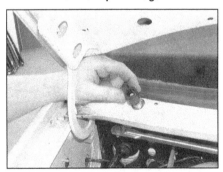

14.9a Recover the spacer and washer from each spindle ...

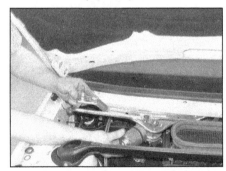

14.9b ... then manoeuvre the wiper linkage assembly out of position

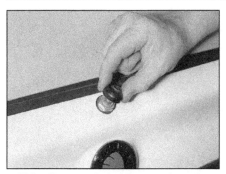

15.3a Remove the rubber cap from the tailgate wiper motor spindle . . .

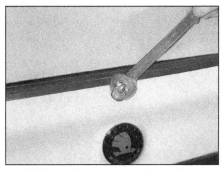

15.3b . . . then unscrew the retaining nut . . .

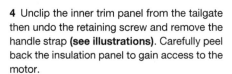

15.3c . . . then lift off the washer and outer seal

4 Unclip the inner trim panel from the tailgate then undo the retaining screw and remove the handle strap **(see illustrations)**. Carefully peel back the insulation panel to gain access to the motor.
5 Undo the retaining bolts and remove the metal bracket which is fitted above the lock button **(see illustration)**.
6 Disconnect the wiring connector then undo the retaining screw and manoeuvre the wiper motor assembly out of position. Recover the inner seal and washer(s) from the wiper spindle and remove the collar from the mounting rubber **(see illustrations)**. Renew the seals and mounting rubber if they show signs of damage or deterioration.

Refitting

7 Slide the washer(s) and inner seal onto the wiper motor spindle.
8 Manoeuvre the motor into position then refit the collar to the mounting rubber and fit the retaining screw.
9 Fit the outer seal and washer to the wiper spindle then refit the spindle nut and tighten it securely.
10 Securely tighten the motor retaining screw then reconnect the wiring connector.
11 Refit the metal bracket to the tailgate, tightening its retaining bolts securely.
12 Seat the insulation panel correctly on the tailgate then refit the trim panel.
13 Refit the wiper arm as described in Section 13 then reconnect the battery.

16 Windscreen/headlight/tailgate washer system components - removal and refitting

1 The windscreen washer reservoir is located in the front left-hand corner of the engine compartment; on models equipped with headlight washers the reservoir also supplies the headlight washer jets via an additional pump.

Windscreen/headlight washer system reservoir

2 Working in the engine compartment, undo the bolts and remove the retaining plate from the top of the reservoir **(see illustration)**.

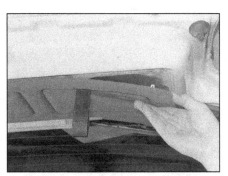

15.4a Unclip the inner trim panel from the tailgate . . .

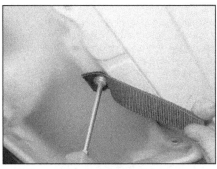

15.4b . . . then undo the retaining screw and remove the handle strap

15.5 Undo the retaining bolts (arrowed) and remove the metal bracket from above the lock button

15.6a Disconnect the wiring connector and undo the retaining screw (arrowed) . . .

15.6b . . . then remove the wiper motor from the tailgate . . .

15.6c . . . and recover the inner seal and washer

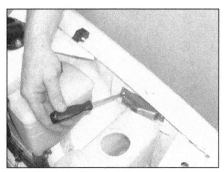

16.2 Undo the retaining screws then remove the retaining plate . . .

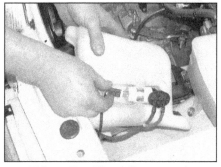

16.3 . . . then lift out the reservoir, disconnecting the washers hoses and wiring connector from the pump(s) as they become accessible

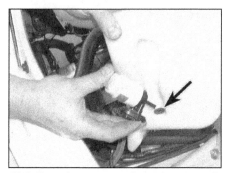

16.6 Ease the pump out from the reservoir and remove its sealing grommet (arrowed)

3 Free the reservoir from its mounting then disconnect the washer hoses, noting each ones correct fitted location. Disconnect the wiring connector(s) from the washer pump(s) and remove the reservoir from the vehicle **(see illustration)**.

4 Refitting is the reverse of removal ensuring that the hose(s) and wiring are securely reconnected; the upper hose is marked for identification. Refill the reservoir and check for leakage.

Washer pump

5 Remove the reservoir as described earlier in this Section.

6 Empty the contents of the reservoir into a suitable container then carefully ease the pump out from the reservoir and recover its sealing grommet **(see illustration)**.

7 Refitting is the reverse of removal, using a new sealing grommet if the original one shows signs of damage or deterioration. Refill the reservoir and check the pump grommet for leaks.

Windscreen washer jets

8 Ease the jet and seal out of position and disconnect the washer hose **(see illustration)**.

9 On refitting, securely reconnect the washer hose then press the jet and seal into position. Check the operation of the jet. If necessary adjust the nozzles using a pin, aiming one nozzle to a point slightly above the centre of

the swept area and the other to slightly below the centre point to ensure complete coverage.

Tailgate washer jet

10 Ease the jet and seal out of position and disconnect the washers hose **(see illustration)**.

11 On refitting, securely reconnect the washer hose then press the jet and seal into position. Check the operation of the jet. If necessary adjust the nozzles using a pin, aiming one nozzle to a point slightly above the centre of the swept area and the other to slightly below the centre point to ensure complete coverage.

Headlight washer jets

12 Remove the front bumper as described in Chapter 11.

13 On early models, slacken and remove the retaining nuts and washers and remove the jet assembly from the bumper. If necessary, the assembly can be dismantled once the retaining clip has been slid out of position.

14 On later models, unclip the jet assembly and remove it from the bumper.

15 Refitting is the reverse of removal, refitting the bumper as described in Chapter 11. Check the operation of the jets. If necessary adjust the nozzles using a pin, aiming one nozzle to a point slightly above the centre of the headlight lens and the other to slightly below the centre point to ensure complete coverage.

17 Radio/cassette unit - removal and refitting

Note: *The following removal and refitting procedure is for the range of equipment fitted by Skoda. Ensure the security code of the radio/cassette unit is known prior to removal.*

Removal

1 Ensure the unit is turned off then depress the button located in the upper, right-hand corner of the unit. The radio/cassette unit can then be pulled out of position with the handle.

Refitting

2 Ensure the unit is still turned off then slide it carefully into position. Push the unit fully into position then switch it on and enter the security code.

18 Loudspeakers - removal and refitting

Removal

Door mounted loudspeaker

1 Carefully prise the speaker grille out of position, noting which way up it is fitted **(see illustration)**.

16.8 Removing a windscreen washer jet

16.10 Removing the tailgate washer jet

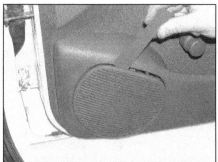

18.1 Carefully prise out the speaker grille from the door trim . . .

2 Slacken and remove the retaining screws then ease the speaker out of position, disconnecting its wiring as it becomes accessible **(see illustrations)**.

Rear speakers - Estate models

3 Working in the luggage compartment, remove the storage compartment cover from the relevant side trim panel. Slacken and remove the upper and lower retaining screws then unclip the trim panel and remove it from the vehicle.

4 Slacken and remove the retaining nuts then lower the speaker out of position and disconnect its wiring connectors. The speaker grille can then be removed from the upper trim panel.

Refitting

5 Refitting is the reverse of removal.

19 Radio aerial - removal and refitting

Removal

1 The aerial mast can be unscrewed from its base. If it is necessary to remove the base (which contains the signal amplifier) proceed as follows.

2 Working in the luggage compartment, unclip the rear trim panel from the roof to gain access to the rear of the headlining.

3 Prise out the retaining clips then carefully peel back the headlining until access is gained to the aerial base **(see illustration)**. Take care not to damage the headlining as it is easily creased.

4 Disconnect the aerial lead and wiring connector from the aerial then slacken and remove the retaining nut. Lift the aerial base away from the roof and recover is seal; the seal must be renewed if it shows signs of wear or damage.

Refitting

5 Refitting is the reverse of removal ensuring good contact is made between the retaining nut washer and the roof.

20 Anti-theft alarm/engine immobiliser system - general information

Note: *This information is applicable only to the system(s) fitted by Skoda as standard equipment.*

1 Some models are fitted with an anti-theft alarm and/or engine immobiliser system as standard. On other models the systems were offered as optional extras.

Anti-theft alarm

2 The alarm is armed and disarmed using the remote transmitter; on models also fitted with central locking the doors will be

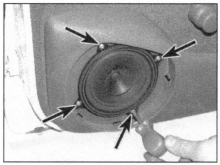

18.2a . . . then undo the retaining screws (arrowed) . . .

locked/unlocked at the same time. When the system is activated, the alarm will sound briefly twice and the indicator light will flash four times. The system remains deactivated for approximately 25 seconds then before being switched on. **Note:** *If the alarm is set when the doors, bonnet and/or tailgate are not probably shut the alarm will sound briefly eight times*

3 The alarm system has switches on the bonnet, tailgate and each of the doors and also monitors movement inside the vehicle via ultrasonic sensors. Should any of the doors, the tailgate or the bonnet be opened whilst the alarm is activated, or movement be detected inside the vehicle, the system will be triggered. When the system is triggered, the alarm will sound and the lights will flash for approximately 30 seconds. After this time the system automatically resets.

4 If required, the ultrasonic sensing facility can be switched off whilst retaining the switched side of the system. To do this, activate the alarm as normal then wait a short while before depressing the on button again. To indicated the sensors have been switched off the indicator lights will flash and the alarm will bleep several times. Now only the switched side of the alarm system is operational. This facility is useful, as it allows you to leave the windows/sunroof open, and still arm the alarm. If the windows/sunroof are left open with the ultrasonic sensing not switched off, the alarm may be falsely triggered by a gust of wind.

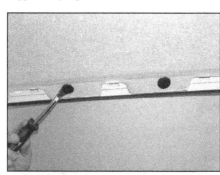

19.3 Prise out the retaining clips and carefully peel back the headlining to gain access to the aerial base

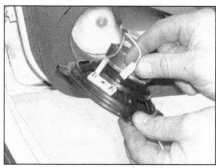

18.2b . . . and remove the speaker, disconnecting its wiring connectors as they become accessible

5 The alarm system has a master switch on the alarm siren which is located at the rear of the engine compartment. To disable the system completely, unclip the protective cap and turn the switch off using the key supplied with the vehicle. Remove the key and refit the protective cap. To enable the system again, simply turn the switch back on again noting the alarm system will be activate as soon as the switch is turned and will need to be turned off immediately using the remote control.

6 Should the alarm system become faulty, disable the system at the master switch and take the vehicle to a Skoda dealer for examination.

Engine immobiliser

7 The engine immobiliser system ensures that the vehicle can only be started using the original Skoda ignition key. The key contains an electronic chip which is programmed with a code. The immobiliser system checks this code, using the sensor fitted to the ignition switch, every time the ignition is switched on. If the key code does not match the immobiliser control unit code, the engine will not start.

8 Bearing this in mind it is essential that you know the ignition key code. The code is printed on a tag originally supplied with the key and should be kept in a safe place. If the key is then lost, a replacement key programmed with the correct code can be ordered from your Skoda dealer. If the key is lost and the code is not known then problems arise and the only solution maybe that a new immobiliser control unit and key set will have to be installed.

21 Heated front seat components - removal and refitting

1 Renewal of the front seat heater pads should be entrusted to a Skoda dealer. Renewal involves dismantling of the complex seat assembly. Heater pad renewal is especially difficult to achieve successfully without ruining the upholstery. The only item which is easily removed/refitted is the operating switch (see Section 4).

22 Airbag system -
general information and precautions

1 Both a driver's and passenger airbag were fitted as standard to some models in the range; on other models they were available as an optional extra. Models fitted with a driver's side airbag have the word AIRBAG stamped on the airbag unit, which is fitted to the centre of the steering wheel. Models also equipped with a passenger side airbag also have the word AIRBAG stamped on the passenger airbag unit which is located in the facia. Some later models are also fitted with side airbags which are fitted to the outside of the front seats.

2 The airbag system comprises of the airbag unit(s) (complete with gas generators), the control unit (with an integral impact sensor) and a warning light in the instrument panel.

3 On models with a driver's airbag or a driver's and passenger airbag, the airbag system is triggered only in the event of a heavy frontal impact above a predetermined force; depending on the point of impact. The airbag is inflated within milliseconds and forms a safety cushion between the driver and steering wheel and (where fitted) the passenger and facia. This prevents contact between the upper body and wheel/facia and therefore greatly reduces the risk of injury.

4 On models also equipped with side impact airbags, the side airbags are triggered in the event of a heavy side impact above a predetermined force. The airbags are inflated within milliseconds and form a safety cushion between the driver/front seat passenger and the doors therefore greatly reducing the risk of injury.

5 Every time the ignition is switched on, the airbag control unit performs a self-test. The self-test takes approximately 4 seconds and during this time the airbag warning light in the instrument panel is illuminated. After the self-test has been completed the warning light should go out. If the warning light fails to come on (check the bulb first before assuming the system is faulty), remains illuminated after the initial period or comes on at any time

when the vehicle is being driven, there is a fault in the airbag system. The vehicle be taken to a Skoda dealer for examination at the earliest possible opportunity. **Note:** *If the warning light flashes for approximately 12 seconds after the initial 4 second test period, the passenger side airbag has been disabled. To have the passenger side airbag switched on again, take the vehicle to a Skoda dealer who will have access to the necessary electronic equipment required.*

⚠ **Warning: Before carrying out any operations on the airbag system, disconnect the battery negative terminal and wait for at least one minute. When operations are complete, make sure no one is inside the vehicle when the battery is reconnected then, with the drivers door open, switch the ignition on from outside the vehicle.**

⚠ **Warning: Note that the airbag(s) must not be subjected to temperatures in excess of 100°C. When the airbag is removed, ensure that it is stored the correct way up to prevent possible inflation.**

⚠ **Warning: Do not allow any solvents or cleaning agents to contact the airbag assemblies. They must be cleaned using only a damp cloth.**

⚠ **Warning: The airbags and control units are both sensitive to impact. If either is dropped onto a hard surface or are damaged they should be renewed.**

⚠ **Warning: Disconnect the airbag control unit wiring plug prior to using arc-welding equipment on the vehicle.**

⚠ **Warning: If a forward-facing child seat is to be used in the front passenger seat, have the passenger side airbag disabled by a Skoda dealer. Once the use of the seat is no longer required, return to your Skoda dealer to have the airbag switched on again.**

23 Airbag system components -
removal and refitting

Note: *Refer to the warnings given in Section 22 before carrying out the following operations.*

1 Disconnect the battery negative terminal, wait at least one minute before proceeding (see note in Section 1).

Driver's side airbag

Removal

2 Slacken and remove the two airbag retaining screws from the rear of the steering wheel, rotating the wheel as necessary to gain access to the screws **(see illustration)**.

3 Return the steering wheel to the straight-ahead position then carefully lift the airbag

assembly away from the steering wheel and disconnect its wiring connector **(see illustration)**. Note that the airbag must not be knocked or dropped and should be stored the correct way up with its padded surface uppermost.

Refitting

4 Ensure the wiring connector is securely reconnected then seat the airbag unit centrally in the steering wheel, making sure the wire does not become trapped.

5 Fit the airbag unit retaining screws and tighten them to the specified torque setting.

6 Ensure no one is inside the vehicle and reconnect the battery. With the driver's door open, turn on the ignition switch and check the operation of the airbag warning light.

Passenger side airbag

Removal

7 Carefully unclip the access cover from the passenger side of the facia to reveal the airbag unit.

8 Slacken and remove the retaining nuts and washers then carefully lift the airbag unit out of position, disconnecting its wiring connector as it becomes accessible.

9 To remove the airbag mounting bracket, slacken and remove the trim panel bracket retaining screws (accessible through the cover panel aperture) then unclip the base of the panel and remove it from the facia. Undo the retaining nuts and washers and remove the mounting bracket from the bulkhead.

Refitting

10 Where necessary, fit the mounting bracket to the bulkhead and tighten its retaining nuts to the specified torque. Clip the trim panel back into position and securely tighten its retaining screws.

11 Securely reconnect the wiring connector then seat the airbag unit on its mounting bracket. Make sure the wiring is not trapped then refit the retaining nuts and tighten to the specified torque. Clip the access cover back into the trim panel.

12 Ensure no one is inside the vehicle and reconnect the battery. With the driver's door open, turn on the ignition switch and check the operation of the airbag warning light.

23.2 Undo the retaining screws securing the driver's side airbag to the steering wheel

23.3 Lift the airbag unit away from the steering wheel and disconnect its wiring connector

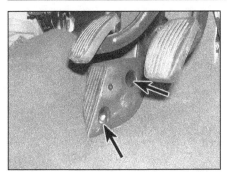

23.16 Undo the retaining nuts (arrowed) and remove the footrest from beside the clutch pedal

23.17a Press out the centre pin then remove the fastener . . .

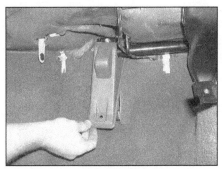

23.17b . . . and lift off the trim cover from the pedal linkage left-hand mounting bracket

Airbag control unit

Removal

13 Remove the centre console as described in Chapter 11.

14 Remove the radio/cassette unit (see Chapter 12) then bend back the retaining tangs and slide the unit mounting frame out from the facia. Disconnect the aerial lead and unclip the wiring connector then remove the mounting frame from the vehicle.

15 Unclip the duct linking the base of the heater/ventilation housing to the rear footwell duct and remove it from the vehicle.

16 Undo the retaining nuts and remove the footrest from the side of the clutch pedal **(see illustration)**.

17 On right-hand drive models, working in the passenger footwell, remove the retaining fastener then lift off the trim cover from the pedal assembly left-hand mounting bracket **(see illustrations)**. The fastener is released by pressing out its centre pin then prising it out of position.

18 On all models, fold back the carpet from the to gain access to the airbag unit which is located underneath the front end of footwell duct.

19 Slacken and remove the retaining nuts and washers and free the control unit from its mountings **(see illustration)**.

20 Release the retaining clip then disconnect the wiring connector and remove the control unit.

Refitting

21 Reconnect the wiring connector and secure it in position with the retaining clip. Refit the control unit to its mountings, making sure the arrow on the top of the unit is pointing towards the front of the vehicle. Refit the mounting nuts and washers and tighten them to the specified torque.

22 Refit the heater/ventilation duct making sure it is correctly engaged with both the housing and rear footwell vent.

23 Fold back the carpet then refit the footrest, tightening its retaining nuts securely.

24 On right-hand drive models, refit the trim cover the pedal assembly left-hand mounting and secure it in position with the retaining clip.

25 On all models, refit the centre console as described in Chapter 11.

26 Clip the wiring connector into the rear of the radio/cassette unit mounting frame and reconnect the aerial lead. Slide the frame into position, securing it in position with the retaining tangs, then refit the radio/cassette unit.

27 Ensure no one is inside the vehicle and reconnect the battery. With the driver's door open, turn on the ignition switch and check the operation of the airbag warning light.

Airbag wiring contact unit

Removal

28 Remove the driver's side airbag unit (see paragraphs 2 and 3) then remove the steering wheel as described in Chapter 10.

29 Make alignment marks between the contact unit and wheel then undo the retaining screws and separate the two components **(see illustration)**. **Do not attempt to rotate the unit when it is removed from the vehicle.**

Refitting

30 Fit the contact unit to the steering wheel, aligning the marks made on removal (where applicable), and securely tighten the retaining screws. Where a new contact unit is being installed, cut and remove the retaining clip.

31 Refit the steering wheel as described in Chapter 10 then refit the driver's side airbag as described in paragraphs 4 to 6.

Front seat side airbag

32 Removal and refitting of the front seat side airbag should be entrusted to a Skoda dealer. Renewal involves dismantling of the complex seat assembly and it is very difficult for the home mechanic to carry out the job without ruining the upholstery.

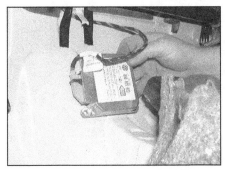

23.19 Slacken and remove the retaining nuts and washers and free the airbag control unit from its mountings

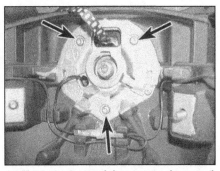

23.29 Undo the retaining screws (arrowed) and remove the contact unit from the rear of the steering wheel

H31123

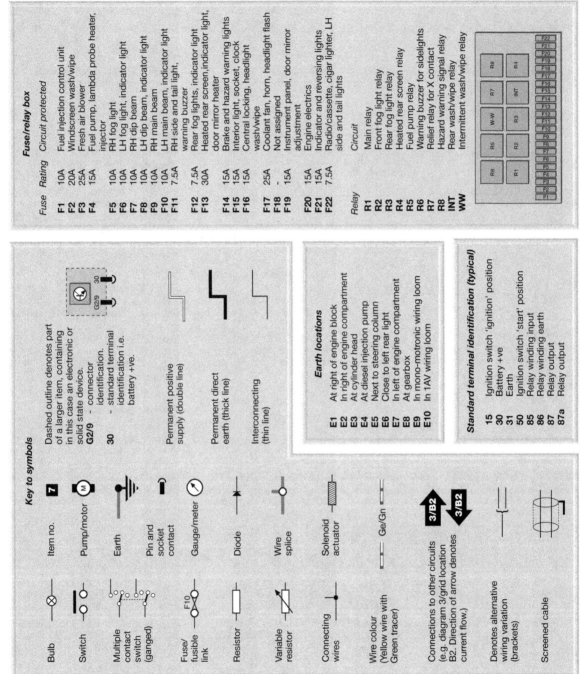

Fuse/relay box

Fuse	Rating	Circuit protected
F1	10A	Fuel injection control unit
F2	20A	Windscreen wash/wipe
F3	25A	Fresh air blower
F4	15A	Fuel pump, lambda probe heater, injector
F5	10A	RH fog light
F6	10A	LH fog light, indicator light
F7	10A	RH dip beam
F8	10A	LH dip beam, indicator light
F9	10A	RH main beam
F10	10A	LH main beam, indicator light
F11	7.5A	RH side and tail light, warning buzzer
F12	7.5A	Rear fog lights, indicator light
F13	30A	Heated rear screen, indicator light, door mirror heater
F14	15A	Brake and hazard warning lights
F15	15A	Interior light, socket, clock
F16	15A	Central locking, headlight wash/wipe
F17	25A	Coolant fan, horn, headlight flash
F18	-	Not assigned
F19	15A	Instrument panel, door mirror adjustment
F20	15A	Engine electrics
F21	15A	Indicator and reversing lights
F22	7.5A	Radio/cassette, cigar lighter, LH side and tail lights

Relay	Circuit
R1	Main relay
R2	Front fog light relay
R3	Rear fog light relay
R4	Heated rear screen relay
R5	Fuel pump relay
R6	Warning buzzer for sidelights
R7	Relief relay for X contact
R8	Hazard warning signal relay
INT	Rear wash/wipe relay
WW	Intermittent wash/wipe relay

Key to symbols

7 Item no.
M Pump/motor
Earth
Pin and socket contact
Gauge/meter
Diode
Wire splice
Solenoid actuator

Bulb
Switch
Multiple contact switch (ganged)
F10 Fuse/fusible link
Resistor
Variable resistor
Connecting wires

Wire colour (Yellow wire with Green tracer) Ge/Gn

Connections to other circuits (e.g. diagram 3/grid location B2. Direction of arrow denotes current flow.) 3/B2

Denotes alternative wiring variation (brackets)

Screened cable

Dashed outline denotes part of a larger item, containing in this case an electronic or solid state device.
G2/9 – connector identification.
30 – standard terminal identification i.e. battery +ve.

Permanent positive supply (double line)

Permanent direct earth (thick line)

Interconnecting (thin line)

Earth locations

E1	At right of engine block
E2	In right of engine compartment
E3	At cylinder head
E4	At diesel injection pump
E5	Next to steering column
E6	Close to left rear light
E7	In left of engine compartment
E8	At gearbox
E9	In mono-motronic wiring loom
E10	In 1AV wiring loom

Standard terminal identification (typical)

15	Ignition switch 'ignition' position
30	Battery +ve
31	Earth
50	Ignition switch 'start' position
85	Relay winding input
86	Relay winding earth
87	Relay output
87a	Relay output

Diagram 1 : Information for wiring diagrams

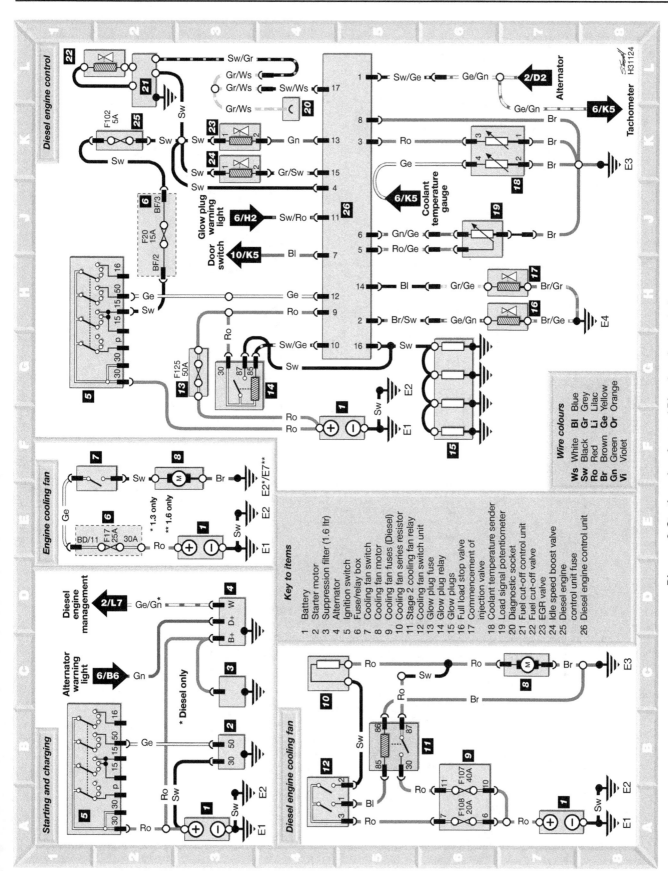

Diagram 2: Starting, charging, and Diesel engine control

Key to items

1 Battery
2 Starter motor
3 Suppression filter (1.6 ltr)
4 Alternator
5 Ignition switch
6 Fuse/relay box
7 Cooling fan switch
8 Cooling fan motor
9 Cooling fan fuses (Diesel)
10 Cooling fan series resistor
11 Stage 2 cooling fan relay
12 Cooling fan switch unit
13 Glow plug fuse
14 Glow plug relay
15 Glow plugs
16 Full load stop valve
17 Commencement of injection valve
18 Coolant temperature sender
19 Load signal potentiometer
20 Diagnostic socket
21 Fuel cut-off control unit
22 Fuel cut-off valve
23 EGR valve
24 Idle speed boost valve
25 Diesel engine control unit fuse
26 Diesel engine control unit

Wire colours

Ws	White	Bl	Blue
Sw	Black	Gr	Grey
Ro	Red	Li	Lilac
Br	Brown	Ge	Yellow
Gn	Green	Or	Orange
Vi	Violet		

Diesel engine control

Engine cooling fan

Starting and charging

Diesel engine cooling fan

* 1.3 only
** 1.6 only
* Diesel only

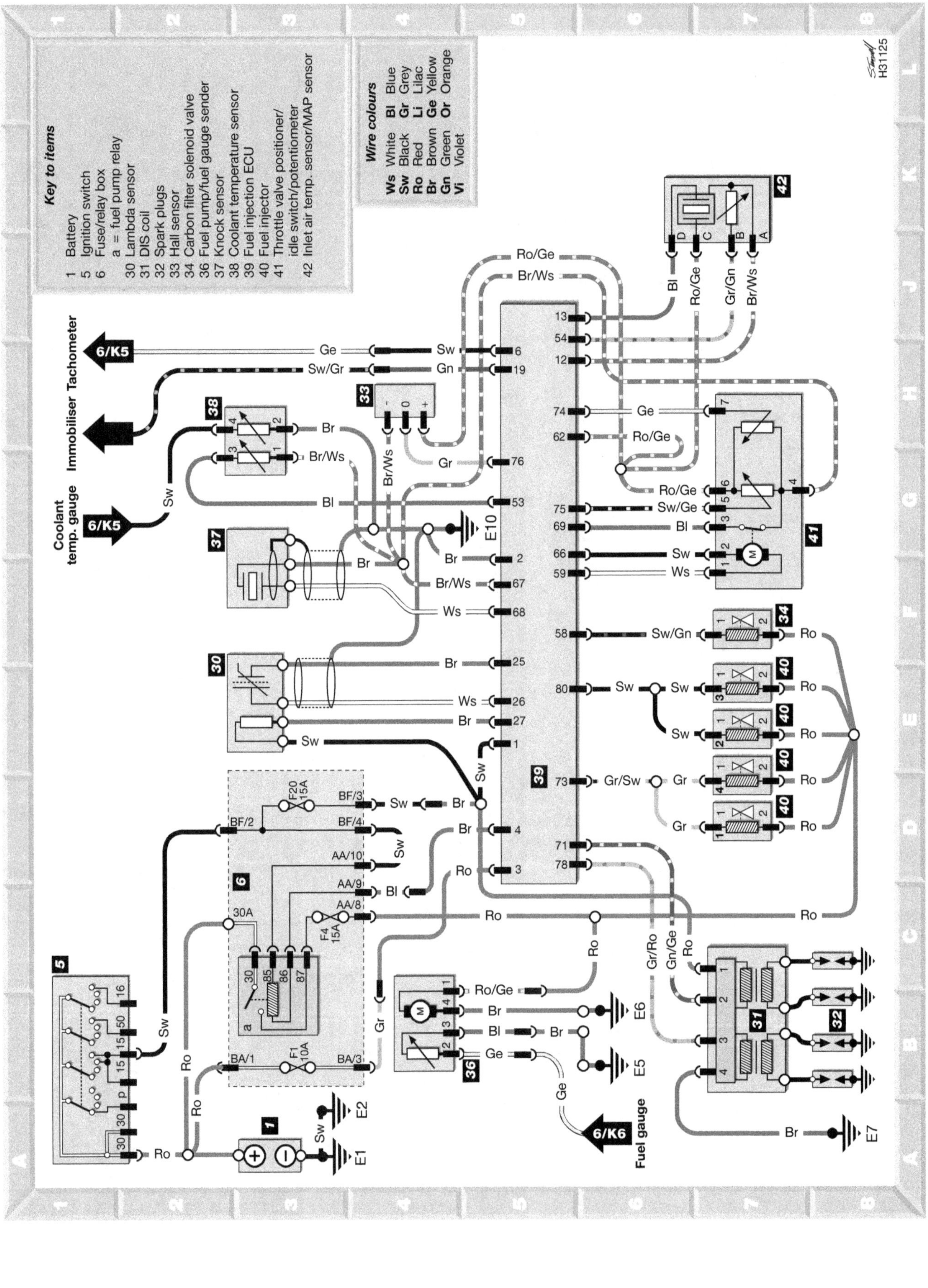
Key to items
1 Battery
5 Ignition switch
6 Fuse/relay box
a = fuel pump relay
30 Lambda sensor
31 DIS coil
32 Spark plugs
33 Hall sensor
34 Carbon filter solenoid valve
36 Fuel pump/fuel gauge sender
37 Knock sensor
38 Coolant temperature sensor
39 Fuel injection ECU
40 Fuel injector
41 Throttle valve positioner/
idle switch/potentiometer
42 Inlet air temp. sensor/MAP sensor
Wire colours
Ws White
Sw Black
Ro Red
Br Brown
Gn Green
Vi Violet
Bl Blue
Gr Grey
Li Lilac
Ge Yellow
Or Orange
Coolant temp. gauge
Immobiliser
Tachometer
Fuel gauge
6/K5
6/K6
E1
E2
E5
E6
E7
E10
H31125
Diagram 3 : Simos 2P engine management

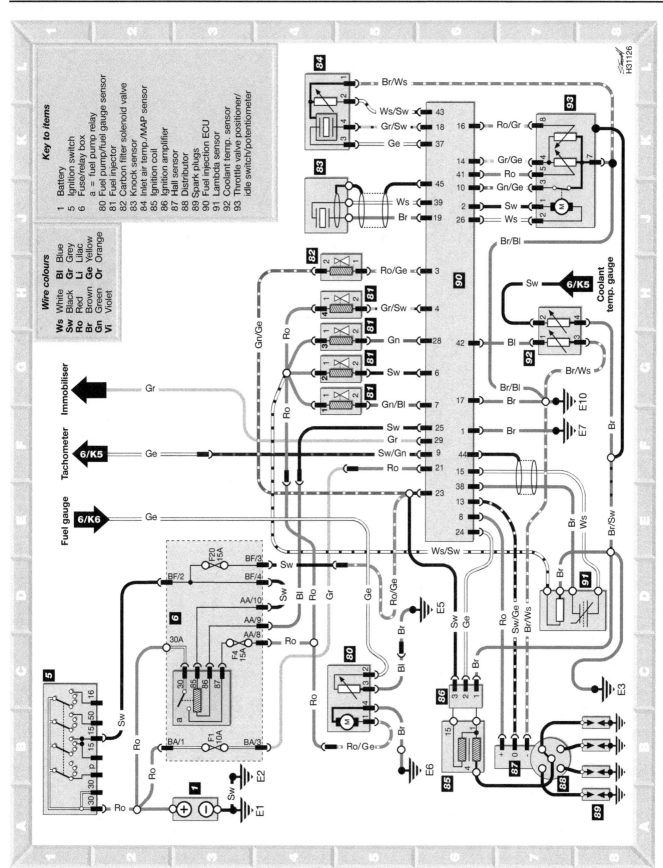

Key to items

1 Battery
5 Ignition switch
6 Fuse/relay box
   a = fuel pump relay
80 Fuel pump/fuel gauge sensor
81 Fuel injector
82 Carbon filter solenoid valve
83 Knock sensor
84 Inlet air temp./MAP sensor
85 Ignition coil
86 Ignition amplifier
87 Hall sensor
88 Distributor
89 Spark plugs
90 Fuel injection ECU
91 Lambda sensor
92 Coolant temp. sensor
93 Throttle valve positioner/
   idle switch/potentiometer

Wire colours

Ws	White	Bl	Blue
Sw	Black	Gr	Grey
Ro	Red	Li	Lilac
Br	Brown	Ge	Yellow
Gn	Green	Or	Orange
Vi	Violet		

Diagram 4 : Magneti-Marelli engine management

H31126

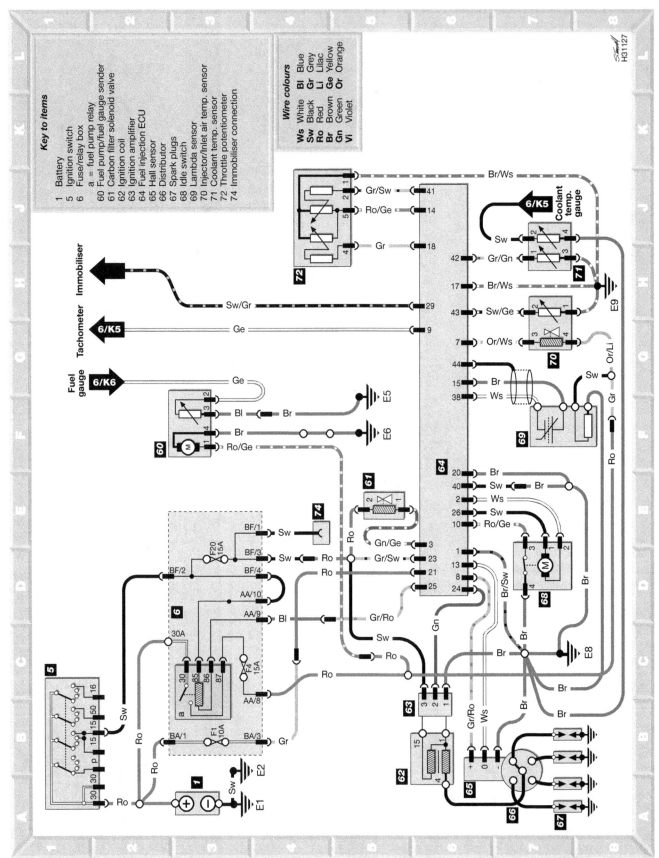

Key to items

1 Battery
5 Ignition switch
6 Fuse/relay box
a = fuel pump relay
60 Fuel pump/fuel gauge sender
61 Carbon filter solenoid valve
62 Ignition coil
63 Ignition amplifier
64 Fuel injection ECU
65 Hall sensor
66 Distributor
67 Spark plugs
68 Idle switch
69 Lambda sensor
70 Injector/Inlet air temp. sensor
71 Coolant temp. sensor
72 Throttle potentiometer
74 Immobiliser connection

Wire colours

Ws	White	Bl	Blue
Sw	Black	Gr	Grey
Ro	Red	Li	Lilac
Br	Brown	Ge	Yellow
Gn	Green	Or	Orange
Vi	Violet		

Diagram 5 : Mono-motronic engine management, from November 1995

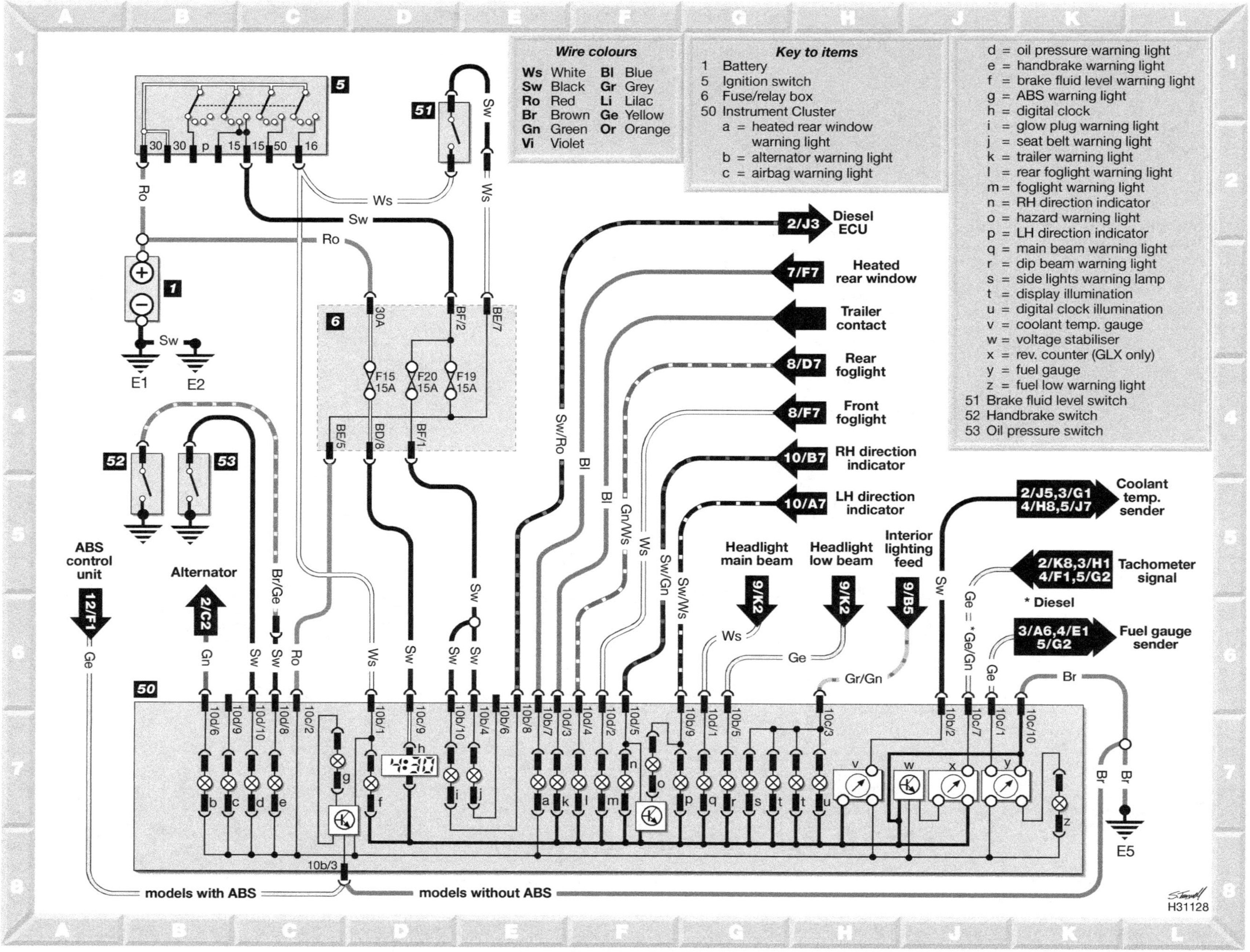

H31128

Key to items

1   Battery
5   Ignition switch
6   Fuse/relay box
50 Instrument Cluster
    a = heated rear window
        warning light
    b = alternator warning light
    c = airbag warning light

d = oil pressure warning light
e = handbrake warning light
f = brake fluid level warning light
g = ABS warning light
h = digital clock
i = glow plug warning light
j = seat belt warning light
k = trailer warning light
l = rear foglight warning light
m = foglight warning light
n = RH direction indicator
o = hazard warning light
p = LH direction indicator
q = main beam warning light
r = dip beam warning light
s = side lights warning lamp
t = display illumination
u = coolant temp. gauge
v = digital clock illumination
w = voltage stabiliser
x = rev. counter (GLX only)
y = fuel gauge
z = fuel low warning light
51 Brake fluid level switch
52 Handbrake switch
53 Oil pressure switch

Wire colours

Ws	White	Bl	Blue
Sw	Black	Gr	Grey
Ro	Red	Li	Lilac
Br	Brown	Ge	Yellow
Gn	Green	Or	Orange
Vi	Violet		

Coolant temp. sender 2/J5,3/G1 4/H8,5/J7

Tachometer signal 2/K8,3/H1 4/F1,5/G2 * Diesel

Fuel gauge sender 3/A6,4/E1 5/G2

Diesel ECU 2/J3
Heated rear window 7/F7
Trailer contact
Rear foglight 8/D7
Front foglight 8/F7
RH direction indicator 10/B7
LH direction indicator 10/A7

Interior lighting feed 9/B5
Headlight low beam 9/K2
Headlight main beam 9/K2

Alternator 2/C2
ABS control unit 12/F1

Diagram 6: Instrument cluster

models without ABS
models with ABS

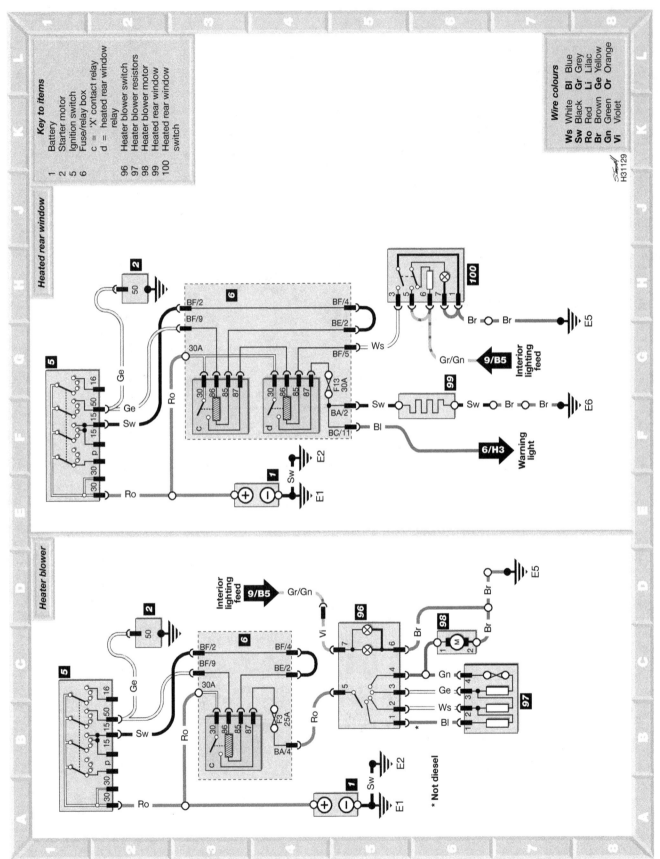

Diagram 7: Heater blower and heated rear window

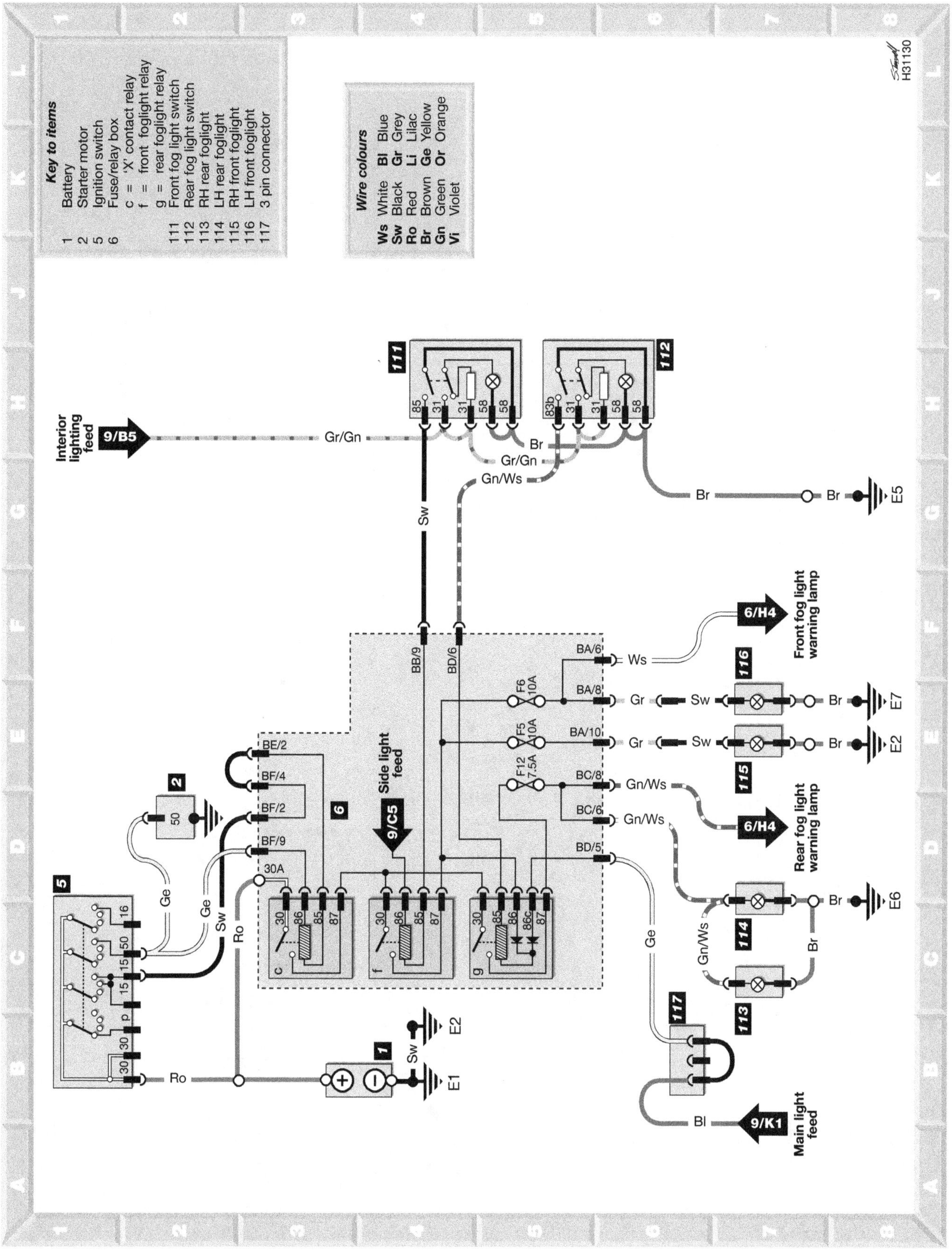

H31130

Key to items

1   Battery
2   Starter motor
5   Ignition switch
6   Fuse/relay box
    c = 'X' contact relay
    f = front foglight relay
    g = rear foglight relay
111 Front fog light switch
112 Rear fog light switch
113 LH rear foglight
114 RH rear foglight
115 RH front foglight
116 LH front foglight
117 3 pin connector

Wire colours

Ws	White	**Bl**	Blue
Sw	Black	**Gr**	Grey
Ro	Red	**Li**	Lilac
Br	Brown	**Ge**	Yellow
Gn	Green	**Or**	Orange
Vi	Violet		

Diagram 8: Foglights

Interior lighting feed 9/B5

Gr/Gn

Br

Gr/Gn

Gn/Ws

Br   Br   E5

Sw

BB/9   BD/6

Side light feed   9/C5

BE/2
BF/4
BF/2
BF/9
30A

2   50

5

Ge   Ge   Sw   Ro

Ro

1   Sw   E2   E1

16   50   15   15   p   30   30

6

c   f   g

30 86 85 87   30 86 85 87   30 85 86 86c 87

F6 10A   BA/6   Ws   6/H4 Front fog light warning lamp

F5 10A   BA/8   Gr   Sw   116   Br   E7

F12 7.5A   BA/10   Gr   Sw   115   Br   E2

BC/8   Gn/Ws   6/H4 Rear fog light warning lamp

BC/6   Gn/Ws

BD/5   Ge   Gn/Ws   114   Br   E6

Gn/Ws   113

117   Bl   9/K1 Main light feed

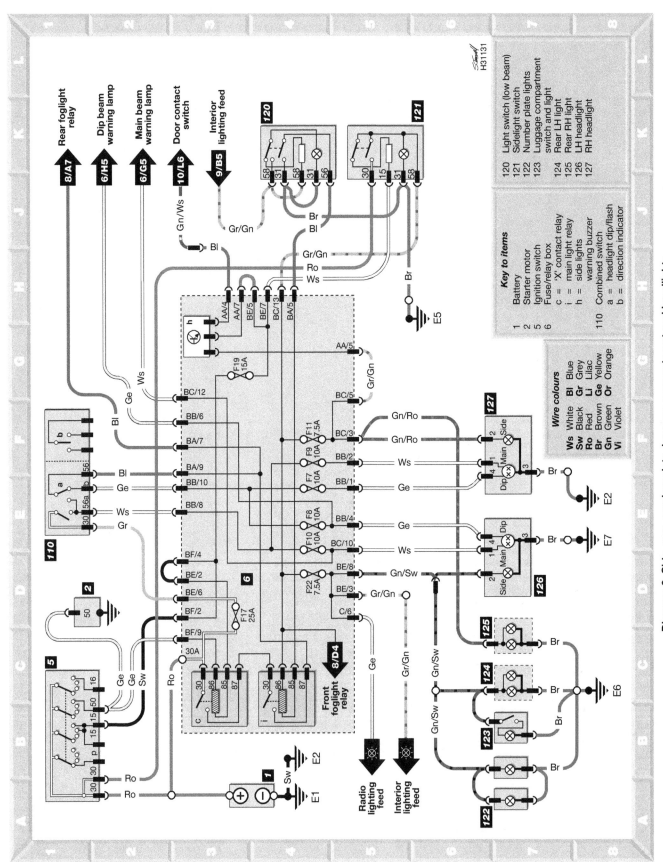

Diagram 9: Side, rear, number plate, luggage compartment and headlights

H31131

Key to items

120 Light switch (low beam)
121 Sidelight switch
122 Number plate lights
123 Luggage compartment switch and light
124 Rear LH light
125 Rear RH light
126 LH headlight
127 RH headlight

1 Battery
2 Starter motor
5 Ignition switch
6 Fuse/relay box
c = 'X' contact relay
i = main light relay
h = side lights warning buzzer
110 Combined switch
a = headlight dip/flash
b = direction indicator

Wire colours
Ws White   Bl Blue
Sw Black   Gr Grey
Ro Red   Li Lilac
Br Brown   Ge Yellow
Gn Green   Or Orange
Vi Violet

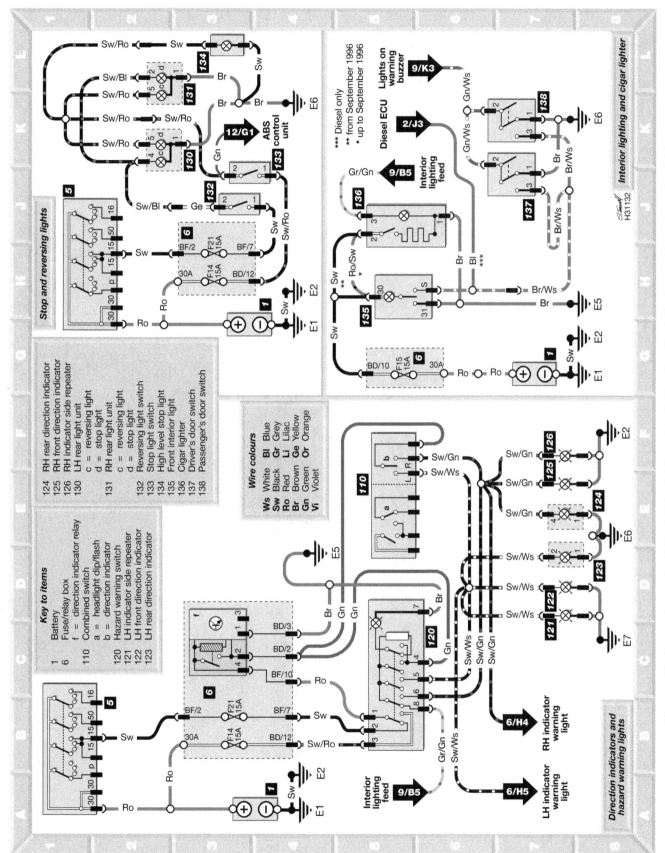

Key to items

1	Battery
6	Fuse/relay box
f	= direction indicator relay
110	Combined switch
	a = headlight dip/flash
	b = direction indicator
120	Hazard warning switch
121	LH indicator side repeater
122	LH front direction indicator
123	LH rear direction indicator
124	RH rear direction indicator
125	RH front direction indicator
126	RH indicator side repeater
130	LH rear light unit
	c = reversing light
	d = stop light
131	RH rear light unit
	c = reversing light
	d = stop light
132	Reversing light switch
133	Stop light switch
134	High level stop light
135	Front interior light
136	Cigar lighter
137	Driver's door switch
138	Passenger's door switch

Wire colours

Ws	White	Bl	Blue
Sw	Black	Gr	Grey
Ro	Red	Li	Lilac
Br	Brown	Ge	Yellow
Gn	Green	Or	Orange
Vi	Violet		

*** Diesel only
** from September 1996
* up to September 1996

Diesel ECU

Stop and reversing lights

Interior lighting and cigar lighter

Direction indicators and hazard warning lights

Diagram 10 : Stop and reversing lights, interior lighting, cigar lighter, direction indicators and hazard warning lights

H31132

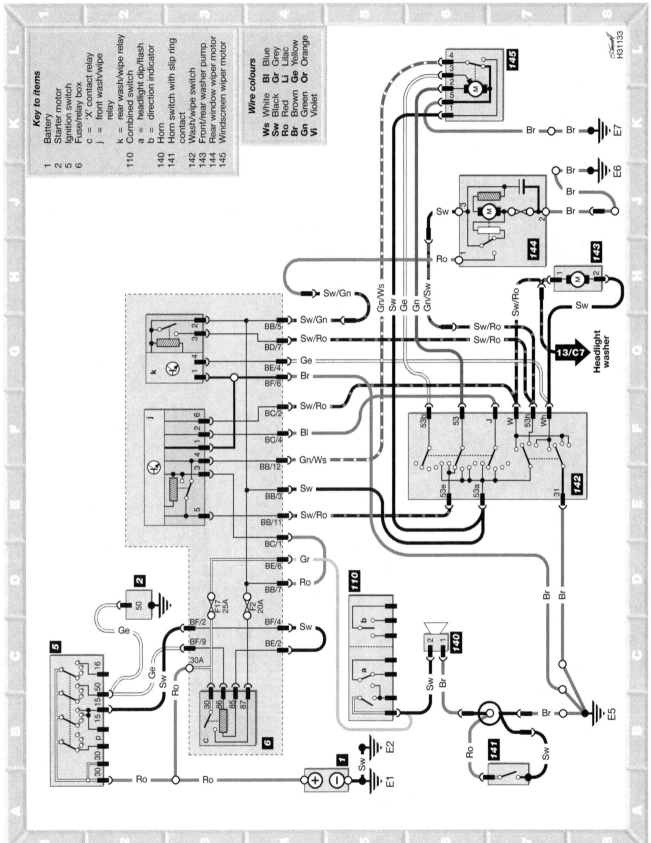

Key to items

1 Battery
2 Starter motor
5 Ignition switch
6 Fuse/relay box
c = 'X' contact relay
j = front wash/wipe relay
k = rear wash/wipe relay
110 Combined switch
a = headlight dip/flash
b = direction indicator
140 Horn
141 Horn switch with slip ring contact
142 Wash/wipe switch
143 Front/rear washer pump
144 Rear window wiper motor
145 Windscreen wiper motor

Wire colours

Ws White Bl Blue
Sw Black Gr Grey
Ro Red   Li Lilac
Br Brown Ge Yellow
Gn Green Or Orange
Vi Violet

Diagram 11 : Horn, front and rear wash/wipe

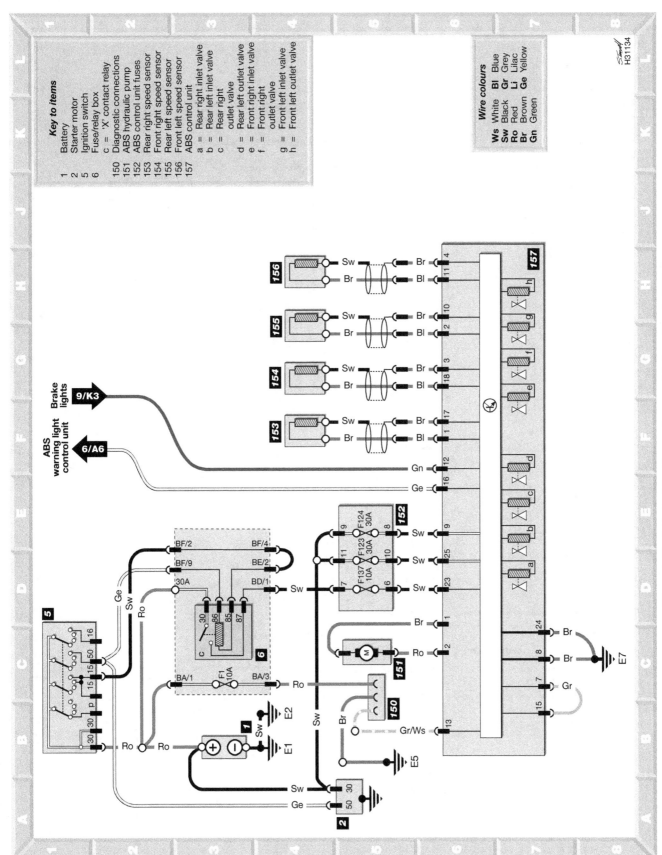

Diagram 12 : Anti - lock braking system, models from March 1995

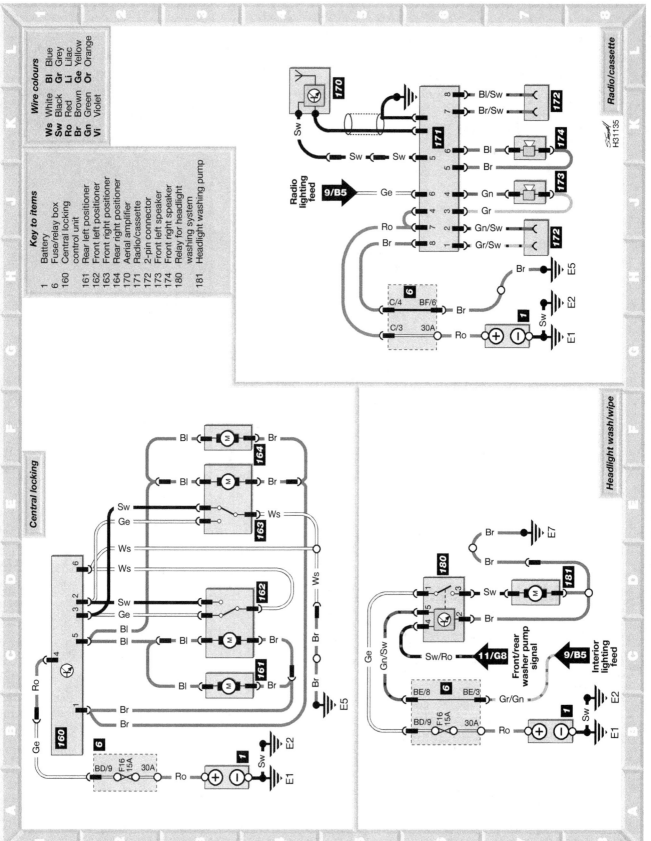

Wire colours

Ws	White	**Bl**	Blue
Sw	Black	**Gr**	Grey
Ro	Red	**Li**	Lilac
Br	Brown	**Ge**	Yellow
Gn	Green	**Or**	Orange
Vi	Violet		

Key to items

1 Battery
6 Fuse/relay box
160 Central locking control unit
161 Rear left positioner
162 Front left positioner
163 Front right positioner
164 Rear right positioner
170 Aerial amplifier
171 Radio/cassette
172 2-pin connector
173 Front left speaker
174 Front right speaker
180 Relay for headlight washing system
181 Headlight washing pump

Radio/cassette

Central locking

Headlight wash/wipe

Diagram 13 : Radio cassette, central locking and headlight wash/wipe

H31135

Dimensions and weights

Note: *All figures are approximate, and may vary according to model. Refer to manufacturer's data for exact figures.*

Dimensions

Overall length:	
Hatchback	3855 mm
Estate and VanPlus	4205 mm
Pick-up	4115 mm
Overall width	1635 mm
Overall height:	
Hatchback	1415 mm
Estate and Pick-up	1420 mm
VanPlus	1830 mm
Wheelbase	2450 mm

Weights

Kerb weight	935 to 1090 kg
Maximum gross vehicle weight	1420 to 1600 kg
Maximum roof rack load	50 kg
Maximum towing weight:	
Braked trailer	900 kg
Unbraked trailer	400 kg
Maximum towing hitch downward load	50 kg

Length (distance)

Inches (in)	x 25.4	= Millimetres (mm)	x 0.0394	= Inches (in)
Feet (ft)	x 0.305	= Metres (m)	x 3.281	= Feet (ft)
Miles	x 1.609	= Kilometres (km)	x 0.621	= Miles

Volume (capacity)

Cubic inches (cu in; in³)	x 16.387	= Cubic centimetres (cc; cm³)	x 0.061	= Cubic inches (cu in; in³)
Imperial pints (Imp pt)	x 0.568	= Litres (l)	x 1.76	= Imperial pints (Imp pt)
Imperial quarts (Imp qt)	x 1.137	= Litres (l)	x 0.88	= Imperial quarts (Imp qt)
Imperial quarts (Imp qt)	x 1.201	= US quarts (US qt)	x 0.833	= Imperial quarts (Imp qt)
US quarts (US qt)	x 0.946	= Litres (l)	x 1.057	= US quarts (US qt)
Imperial gallons (Imp gal)	x 4.546	= Litres (l)	x 0.22	= Imperial gallons (Imp gal)
Imperial gallons (Imp gal)	x 1.201	= US gallons (US gal)	x 0.833	= Imperial gallons (Imp gal)
US gallons (US gal)	x 3.785	= Litres (l)	x 0.264	= US gallons (US gal)

Mass (weight)

Ounces (oz)	x 28.35	= Grams (g)	x 0.035	= Ounces (oz)
Pounds (lb)	x 0.454	= Kilograms (kg)	x 2.205	= Pounds (lb)

Force

Ounces-force (ozf; oz)	x 0.278	= Newtons (N)	x 3.6	= Ounces-force (ozf; oz)
Pounds-force (lbf; lb)	x 4.448	= Newtons (N)	x 0.225	= Pounds-force (lbf; lb)
Newtons (N)	x 0.1	= Kilograms-force (kgf; kg)	x 9.81	= Newtons (N)

Pressure

Pounds-force per square inch (psi; lbf/in²; lb/in²)	x 0.070	= Kilograms-force per square centimetre (kgf/cm²; kg/cm²)	x 14.223	= Pounds-force per square inch (psi; lbf/in²; lb/in²)
Pounds-force per square inch (psi; lbf/in²; lb/in²)	x 0.068	= Atmospheres (atm)	x 14.696	= Pounds-force per square inch (psi; lbf/in²; lb/in²)
Pounds-force per square inch (psi; lbf/in²; lb/in²)	x 0.069	= Bars	x 14.5	= Pounds-force per square inch (psi; lbf/in²; lb/in²)
Pounds-force per square inch (psi; lbf/in²; lb/in²)	x 6.895	= Kilopascals (kPa)	x 0.145	= Pounds-force per square inch (psi; lbf/in²; lb/in²)
Kilopascals (kPa)	x 0.01	= Kilograms-force per square centimetre (kgf/cm²; kg/cm²)	x 98.1	= Kilopascals (kPa)
Millibar (mbar)	x 100	= Pascals (Pa)	x 0.01	= Millibar (mbar)
Millibar (mbar)	x 0.0145	= Pounds-force per square inch (psi; lbf/in²; lb/in²)	x 68.947	= Millibar (mbar)
Millibar (mbar)	x 0.75	= Millimetres of mercury (mmHg)	x 1.333	= Millibar (mbar)
Millibar (mbar)	x 0.401	= Inches of water (inH₂O)	x 2.491	= Millibar (mbar)
Millimetres of mercury (mmHg)	x 0.535	= Inches of water (inH₂O)	x 1.868	= Millimetres of mercury (mmHg)
Inches of water (inH₂O)	x 0.036	= Pounds-force per square inch (psi; lbf/in²; lb/in²)	x 27.68	= Inches of water (inH₂O)

Torque (moment of force)

Pounds-force inches (lbf in; lb in)	x 1.152	= Kilograms-force centimetre (kgf cm; kg cm)	x 0.868	= Pounds-force inches (lbf in; lb in)
Pounds-force inches (lbf in; lb in)	x 0.113	= Newton metres (Nm)	x 8.85	= Pounds-force inches (lbf in; lb in)
Pounds-force inches (lbf in; lb in)	x 0.083	= Pounds-force feet (lbf ft; lb ft)	x 12	= Pounds-force inches (lbf in; lb in)
Pounds-force feet (lbf ft; lb ft)	x 0.138	= Kilograms-force metres (kgf m; kg m)	x 7.233	= Pounds-force feet (lbf ft; lb ft)
Pounds-force feet (lbf ft; lb ft)	x 1.356	= Newton metres (Nm)	x 0.738	= Pounds-force feet (lbf ft; lb ft)
Newton metres (Nm)	x 0.102	= Kilograms-force metres (kgf m; kg m)	x 9.804	= Newton metres (Nm)

Power

Horsepower (hp)	x 745.7	= Watts (W)	x 0.0013	= Horsepower (hp)

Velocity (speed)

Miles per hour (miles/hr; mph)	x 1.609	= Kilometres per hour (km/hr; kph)	x 0.621	= Miles per hour (miles/hr; mph)

Fuel consumption*

Miles per gallon, Imperial (mpg)	x 0.354	= Kilometres per litre (km/l)	x 2.825	= Miles per gallon, Imperial (mpg)
Miles per gallon, US (mpg)	x 0.425	= Kilometres per litre (km/l)	x 2.352	= Miles per gallon, US (mpg)

Temperature

Degrees Fahrenheit = (°C x 1.8) + 32   Degrees Celsius (Degrees Centigrade; °C) = (°F - 32) x 0.56

It is common practice to convert from miles per gallon (mpg) to litres/100 kilometres (l/100km), where mpg x l/100 km = 282

Spare parts are available from many sources, including maker's appointed garages, accessory shops, and motor factors. To be sure of obtaining the correct parts, it may sometimes be necessary to quote the vehicle identification number. If possible, it can also be useful to take the old parts along for positive identification. Items such as starter motors and alternators may be available under a service exchange scheme - any parts returned should always be clean.

Our advice regarding spare part sources is as follows.

Officially-appointed garages

This is the best source of parts which are peculiar to your car, and are not otherwise generally available (eg badges, interior trim, certain body panels, etc). It is also the only place at which you should buy parts if the vehicle is still under warranty.

Accessory shops

These are very good places to buy materials and components needed for the maintenance of your car (oil, air and fuel filters, spark plugs, light bulbs, drivebelts, oils and greases, brake pads, touch-up paint, etc). Parts like this sold by a reputable shop are of the same standard as those used by the car manufacturer.

Motor factors

Good factors will stock all the more important components which wear out comparatively quickly and can sometimes supply individual components needed for the overhaul of a larger assembly. They may also handle work such as cylinder block reboring, crankshaft regrinding and balancing, etc.

Tyre and exhaust specialists

These outlets may be independent or members of a local or national chain. They frequently offer competitive prices when compared with a main dealer or local garage, but it will pay to obtain several quotes before making a decision. Also ask what 'extras' may be added to the quote - for instance, fitting a new valve and balancing the wheel are both often charged on top of the price of a new tyre.

Other sources

Beware of parts or materials obtained from market stalls, car boot sales or similar outlets. Such items are not invariably sub-standard, but there is little chance of compensation if they do prove unsatisfactory. In the case of safety-critical components such as brake pads, there is the risk not only of financial loss, but also of an accident causing injury or death.

Second-hand components or assemblies obtained from a car breaker can be a good buy in some circumstances, but this sort of purchase is best made by the experienced DIY mechanic.

Vehicle identification

Modifications are a continuing and unpublicised process in vehicle manufacture, quite apart from major model changes. Spare parts manuals and lists are compiled upon a numerical basis, the individual vehicle identification numbers being essential to correct identification of the component concerned.

When ordering spare parts, always give as much information as possible. Quote the car model, year of manufacture, body and engine numbers as appropriate.

The *vehicle identification plate* is located on the bonnet lock platform **(see illustration)**. It gives the VIN (vehicle identification number) and vehicle weight information.

The *chassis number* is located on the right-hand front suspension turret **(see illustration)**, and is sometimes repeated on the bonnet lock platform.

The *engine number* is stamped on the cylinder block, in the following location:
a) *On 1.3 litre engines, just above the timing chain cover (see illustration).*
b) *On 1.6 litre engines, just below the distributor.*
c) *On diesel engines, on the front of the block, next to the injection pump.*

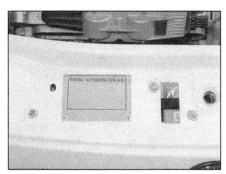

Vehicle identification plate on bonnet lock platform

Chassis number location on right-hand front suspension turret

1.3 litre engine number location on cylinder head

Whenever servicing, repair or overhaul work is carried out on the car or its components, observe the following procedures and instructions. This will assist in carrying out the operation efficiently and to a professional standard of workmanship.

Joint mating faces and gaskets

When separating components at their mating faces, never insert screwdrivers or similar implements into the joint between the faces in order to prise them apart. This can cause severe damage which results in oil leaks, coolant leaks, etc upon reassembly. Separation is usually achieved by tapping along the joint with a soft-faced hammer in order to break the seal. However, note that this method may not be suitable where dowels are used for component location.

Where a gasket is used between the mating faces of two components, a new one must be fitted on reassembly; fit it dry unless otherwise stated in the repair procedure. Make sure that the mating faces are clean and dry, with all traces of old gasket removed. When cleaning a joint face, use a tool which is unlikely to score or damage the face, and remove any burrs or nicks with an oilstone or fine file.

Make sure that tapped holes are cleaned with a pipe cleaner, and keep them free of jointing compound, if this is being used, unless specifically instructed otherwise.

Ensure that all orifices, channels or pipes are clear, and blow through them, preferably using compressed air.

Oil seals

Oil seals can be removed by levering them out with a wide flat-bladed screwdriver or similar implement. Alternatively, a number of self-tapping screws may be screwed into the seal, and these used as a purchase for pliers or some similar device in order to pull the seal free.

Whenever an oil seal is removed from its working location, either individually or as part of an assembly, it should be renewed.

The very fine sealing lip of the seal is easily damaged, and will not seal if the surface it contacts is not completely clean and free from scratches, nicks or grooves. If the original sealing surface of the component cannot be restored, and the manufacturer has not made provision for slight relocation of the seal relative to the sealing surface, the component should be renewed.

Protect the lips of the seal from any surface which may damage them in the course of fitting. Use tape or a conical sleeve where possible. Lubricate the seal lips with oil before fitting and, on dual-lipped seals, fill the space between the lips with grease.

Unless otherwise stated, oil seals must be fitted with their sealing lips toward the lubricant to be sealed.

Use a tubular drift or block of wood of the appropriate size to install the seal and, if the seal housing is shouldered, drive the seal down to the shoulder. If the seal housing is unshouldered, the seal should be fitted with its face flush with the housing top face (unless otherwise instructed).

Screw threads and fastenings

Seized nuts, bolts and screws are quite a common occurrence where corrosion has set in, and the use of penetrating oil or releasing fluid will often overcome this problem if the offending item is soaked for a while before attempting to release it. The use of an impact driver may also provide a means of releasing such stubborn fastening devices, when used in conjunction with the appropriate screwdriver bit or socket. If none of these methods works, it may be necessary to resort to the careful application of heat, or the use of a hacksaw or nut splitter device.

Studs are usually removed by locking two nuts together on the threaded part, and then using a spanner on the lower nut to unscrew the stud. Studs or bolts which have broken off below the surface of the component in which they are mounted can sometimes be removed using a stud extractor. Always ensure that a blind tapped hole is completely free from oil, grease, water or other fluid before installing the bolt or stud. Failure to do this could cause the housing to crack due to the hydraulic action of the bolt or stud as it is screwed in.

When tightening a castellated nut to accept a split pin, tighten the nut to the specified torque, where applicable, and then tighten further to the next split pin hole. Never slacken the nut to align the split pin hole, unless stated in the repair procedure.

When checking or retightening a nut or bolt to a specified torque setting, slacken the nut or bolt by a quarter of a turn, and then retighten to the specified setting. However, this should not be attempted where angular tightening has been used.

For some screw fastenings, notably cylinder head bolts or nuts, torque wrench settings are no longer specified for the latter stages of tightening, "angle-tightening" being called up instead. Typically, a fairly low torque wrench setting will be applied to the bolts/nuts in the correct sequence, followed by one or more stages of tightening through specified angles.

Locknuts, locktabs and washers

Any fastening which will rotate against a component or housing during tightening should always have a washer between it and the relevant component or housing.

Spring or split washers should always be renewed when they are used to lock a critical component such as a big-end bearing retaining bolt or nut. Locktabs which are folded over to retain a nut or bolt should always be renewed.

Self-locking nuts can be re-used in non-critical areas, providing resistance can be felt when the locking portion passes over the bolt or stud thread. However, it should be noted that self-locking stiffnuts tend to lose their effectiveness after long periods of use, and should then be renewed as a matter of course.

Split pins must always be replaced with new ones of the correct size for the hole.

When thread-locking compound is found on the threads of a fastener which is to be re-used, it should be cleaned off with a wire brush and solvent, and fresh compound applied on reassembly.

Special tools

Some repair procedures in this manual entail the use of special tools such as a press, two or three-legged pullers, spring compressors, etc. Wherever possible, suitable readily-available alternatives to the manufacturer's special tools are described, and are shown in use. In some instances, where no alternative is possible, it has been necessary to resort to the use of a manufacturer's tool, and this has been done for reasons of safety as well as the efficient completion of the repair operation. Unless you are highly-skilled and have a thorough understanding of the procedures described, never attempt to bypass the use of any special tool when the procedure described specifies its use. Not only is there a very great risk of personal injury, but expensive damage could be caused to the components involved.

Environmental considerations

When disposing of used engine oil, brake fluid, antifreeze, etc, give due consideration to any detrimental environmental effects. Do not, for instance, pour any of the above liquids down drains into the general sewage system, or onto the ground to soak away. Many local council refuse tips provide a facility for waste oil disposal, as do some garages. If none of these facilities are available, consult your local Environmental Health Department, or the National Rivers Authority, for further advice.

With the universal tightening-up of legislation regarding the emission of environmentally-harmful substances from motor vehicles, most vehicles have tamperproof devices fitted to the main adjustment points of the fuel system. These devices are primarily designed to prevent unqualified persons from adjusting the fuel/air mixture, with the chance of a consequent increase in toxic emissions. If such devices are found during servicing or overhaul, they should, wherever possible, be renewed or refitted in accordance with the manufacturer's requirements or current legislation.

OIL CARE
FOLLOW THE CODE

OIL BANK LINE
0800 66 33 66
www.oilbankline.org.uk

Note: It is antisocial and illegal to dump oil down the drain. To find the location of your local oil recycling bank, call this number free.

The jack supplied with the vehicle tool kit should only be used for changing the roadwheels - see *Wheel changing* at the front of this book. When carrying out any other kind of work, raise the vehicle using a hydraulic (or trolley) jack, and always supplement the jack with axle stands positioned under the vehicle jacking points. If the roadwheels do not have to be removed, consider using wheel ramps - if wished, these can be placed under the wheels once the vehicle has been raised using a hydraulic jack, and the vehicle lowered onto the ramps so that it is resting on its wheels.

Only ever jack the vehicle up on a solid, level surface. If there is even a slight slope, take great care that the vehicle cannot move as the wheels are lifted off the ground. Jacking up on an uneven or gravelled surface is not recommended, as the weight of the vehicle will not be evenly distributed, and the jack may slip as the vehicle is raised.

As far as possible, do not leave the vehicle unattended once it has been raised, particularly if children are playing nearby.

Before jacking up the front of the car, ensure that the handbrake is firmly applied. When jacking up the rear of the car, place wooden chocks in front of the front wheels, and engage first gear.

To raise the front and/or rear of the vehicle, use the jacking/support points at the front and rear ends of the door sills, which are indicated by indentations in the lower sill. Position a block of wood with a groove cut in it on the jack head to prevent the vehicle weight resting on the sill edge; align the sill edge with the groove in the wood so that the vehicle weight is spread evenly over the surface of the block. Supplement the jack with axle stands (also with slotted blocks of wood) positioned as close as possible to the jacking points **(see illustrations)**.

When using a hydraulic jack or axle stands, always try to position the jack head or axle stand head under one of the relevant jacking points.

Providing care is taken, reinforced areas of the floor pan, particularly those in the region of suspension mountings, may be used as support points. Consult a Skoda dealer for advice before using anything other than the approved jacking points, however.

Do not jack the vehicle under any other part of the sill, sump, floor pan, or directly under any of the steering or suspension components.

Never work under, around, or near a raised vehicle, unless it is adequately supported on stands. Do not rely on a jack alone, as even a hydraulic jack could fail under load.

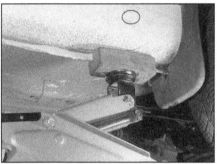
Jack and block of wood positioned under front jacking point

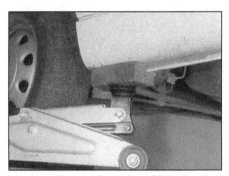
Jack and block of wood positioned under rear jacking point

Hydraulic jack under front jacking point and axle stand under front support point

Radio/cassette unit anti-theft system - precaution

The radio/cassette unit fitted by Skoda may be equipped with a built-in security code, to deter thieves; such units normally have the word CODE on the radio front panel. If the power source to the unit is cut, the anti-theft system will activate. Even if the power source is immediately reconnected, the unit will not function until the correct security code has been entered. Therefore, if you do not know the correct code, DO NOT disconnect the battery negative lead, or remove the radio/cassette unit from the vehicle. On models with a pull-out stereo, the anti-theft system may activate if the unit is removed from the vehicle for more than 24 hours. Refer to your Skoda dealer for further information on whether the unit fitted to your car has a security code. The exact procedure for reprogramming a unit which has been disconnected from its power supply varies from model to model. Consult the radio booklet which should have been supplied with the vehicle for specific details.

Introduction

A selection of good tools is a fundamental requirement for anyone contemplating the maintenance and repair of a motor vehicle. For the owner who does not possess any, their purchase will prove a considerable expense, offsetting some of the savings made by doing-it-yourself. However, provided that the tools purchased meet the relevant national safety standards and are of good quality, they will last for many years and prove an extremely worthwhile investment.

To help the average owner to decide which tools are needed to carry out the various tasks detailed in this manual, we have compiled three lists of tools under the following headings: *Maintenance and minor repair, Repair and overhaul*, and *Special*. Newcomers to practical mechanics should start off with the *Maintenance and minor repair* tool kit, and confine themselves to the simpler jobs around the vehicle. Then, as confidence and experience grow, more difficult tasks can be undertaken, with extra tools being purchased as, and when, they are needed. In this way, a *Maintenance and minor repair* tool kit can be built up into a *Repair and overhaul* tool kit over a considerable period of time, without any major cash outlays. The experienced do-it-yourselfer will have a tool kit good enough for most repair and overhaul procedures, and will add tools from the *Special* category when it is felt that the expense is justified by the amount of use to which these tools will be put.

Maintenance and minor repair tool kit

The tools given in this list should be considered as a minimum requirement if routine maintenance, servicing and minor repair operations are to be undertaken. We recommend the purchase of combination spanners (ring one end, open-ended the other); although more expensive than open-ended ones, they do give the advantages of both types of spanner.

☐ *Combination spanners:*
  Metric - 8 to 19 mm inclusive
☐ *Adjustable spanner - 35 mm jaw (approx.)*
☐ *Spark plug spanner (with rubber insert) - petrol models*
☐ *Spark plug gap adjustment tool - petrol models*
☐ *Set of feeler gauges*
☐ *Brake bleed nipple spanner*
☐ *Screwdrivers:*
  Flat blade - 100 mm long x 6 mm dia
  Cross blade - 100 mm long x 6 mm dia
  Torx - various sizes (not all vehicles)
☐ *Combination pliers*
☐ *Hacksaw (junior)*
☐ *Tyre pump*
☐ *Tyre pressure gauge*
☐ *Oil can*
☐ *Oil filter removal tool*
☐ *Fine emery cloth*
☐ *Wire brush (small)*
☐ *Funnel (medium size)*
☐ *Sump drain plug key (not all vehicles)*

Repair and overhaul tool kit

These tools are virtually essential for anyone undertaking any major repairs to a motor vehicle, and are additional to those given in the *Maintenance and minor repair* list. Included in this list is a comprehensive set of sockets. Although these are expensive, they will be found invaluable as they are so versatile - particularly if various drives are included in the set. We recommend the half-inch square-drive type, as this can be used with most proprietary torque wrenches.

The tools in this list will sometimes need to be supplemented by tools from the *Special* list:

☐ *Sockets (or box spanners) to cover range in previous list (including Torx sockets)*
☐ *Reversible ratchet drive (for use with sockets)*
☐ *Extension piece, 250 mm (for use with sockets)*
☐ *Universal joint (for use with sockets)*
☐ *Flexible handle or sliding T "breaker bar" (for use with sockets)*
☐ *Torque wrench (for use with sockets)*
☐ *Self-locking grips*
☐ *Ball pein hammer*
☐ *Soft-faced mallet (plastic or rubber)*
☐ *Screwdrivers:*
  Flat blade - long & sturdy, short (chubby), and narrow (electrician's) types
  Cross blade – long & sturdy, and short (chubby) types
☐ *Pliers:*
  Long-nosed
  Side cutters (electrician's)
  Circlip (internal and external)
☐ *Cold chisel - 25 mm*
☐ *Scriber*
☐ *Scraper*
☐ *Centre-punch*
☐ *Pin punch*
☐ *Hacksaw*
☐ *Brake hose clamp*
☐ *Brake/clutch bleeding kit*
☐ *Selection of twist drills*
☐ *Steel rule/straight-edge*
☐ *Allen keys (inc. splined/Torx type)*
☐ *Selection of files*
☐ *Wire brush*
☐ *Axle stands*
☐ *Jack (strong trolley or hydraulic type)*
☐ *Light with extension lead*
☐ *Universal electrical multi-meter*

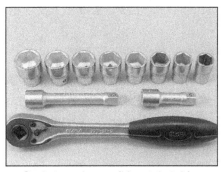

Sockets and reversible ratchet drive

Brake bleeding kit

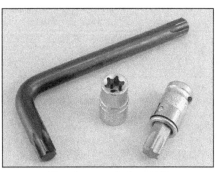

Torx key, socket and bit

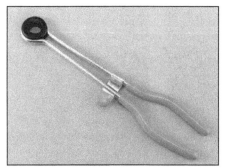

Hose clamp

Angular-tightening gauge

Special tools

The tools in this list are those which are not used regularly, are expensive to buy, or which need to be used in accordance with their manufacturers' instructions. Unless relatively difficult mechanical jobs are undertaken frequently, it will not be economic to buy many of these tools. Where this is the case, you could consider clubbing together with friends (or joining a motorists' club) to make a joint purchase, or borrowing the tools against a deposit from a local garage or tool hire specialist. It is worth noting that many of the larger DIY superstores now carry a large range of special tools for hire at modest rates.

The following list contains only those tools and instruments freely available to the public, and not those special tools produced by the vehicle manufacturer specifically for its dealer network. You will find occasional references to these manufacturers' special tools in the text of this manual. Generally, an alternative method of doing the job without the vehicle manufacturers' special tool is given. However, sometimes there is no alternative to using them. Where this is the case and the relevant tool cannot be bought or borrowed, you will have to entrust the work to a dealer.

- [ ] *Angular-tightening gauge*
- [ ] *Valve spring compressor*
- [ ] *Valve grinding tool*
- [ ] *Piston ring compressor*
- [ ] *Piston ring removal/installation tool*
- [ ] *Cylinder bore hone*
- [ ] *Balljoint separator*
- [ ] *Coil spring compressors (where applicable)*
- [ ] *Two/three-legged hub and bearing puller*
- [ ] *Impact screwdriver*
- [ ] *Micrometer and/or vernier calipers*
- [ ] *Dial gauge*
- [ ] *Stroboscopic timing light*
- [ ] *Dwell angle meter/tachometer*
- [ ] *Fault code reader*
- [ ] *Cylinder compression gauge*
- [ ] *Hand-operated vacuum pump and gauge*
- [ ] *Clutch plate alignment set*
- [ ] *Brake shoe steady spring cup removal tool*
- [ ] *Bush and bearing removal/installation set*
- [ ] *Stud extractors*
- [ ] *Tap and die set*
- [ ] *Lifting tackle*
- [ ] *Trolley jack*

Buying tools

Reputable motor accessory shops and superstores often offer excellent quality tools at discount prices, so it pays to shop around.

Remember, you don't have to buy the most expensive items on the shelf, but it is always advisable to steer clear of the very cheap tools. Beware of 'bargains' offered on market stalls or at car boot sales. There are plenty of good tools around at reasonable prices, but always aim to purchase items which meet the relevant national safety standards. If in doubt, ask the proprietor or manager of the shop for advice before making a purchase.

Care and maintenance of tools

Having purchased a reasonable tool kit, it is necessary to keep the tools in a clean and serviceable condition. After use, always wipe off any dirt, grease and metal particles using a clean, dry cloth, before putting the tools away. Never leave them lying around after they have been used. A simple tool rack on the garage or workshop wall for items such as screwdrivers and pliers is a good idea. Store all normal spanners and sockets in a metal box. Any measuring instruments, gauges, meters, etc, must be carefully stored where they cannot be damaged or become rusty.

Take a little care when tools are used. Hammer heads inevitably become marked, and screwdrivers lose the keen edge on their blades from time to time. A little timely attention with emery cloth or a file will soon restore items like this to a good finish.

Working facilities

Not to be forgotten when discussing tools is the workshop itself. If anything more than routine maintenance is to be carried out, a suitable working area becomes essential.

It is appreciated that many an owner-mechanic is forced by circumstances to remove an engine or similar item without the benefit of a garage or workshop. Having done this, any repairs should always be done under the cover of a roof.

Wherever possible, any dismantling should be done on a clean, flat workbench or table at a suitable working height.

Any workbench needs a vice; one with a jaw opening of 100 mm is suitable for most jobs. As mentioned previously, some clean dry storage space is also required for tools, as well as for any lubricants, cleaning fluids, touch-up paints etc, which become necessary.

Another item which may be required, and which has a much more general usage, is an electric drill with a chuck capacity of at least 8 mm. This, together with a good range of twist drills, is virtually essential for fitting accessories.

Last, but not least, always keep a supply of old newspapers and clean, lint-free rags available, and try to keep any working area as clean as possible.

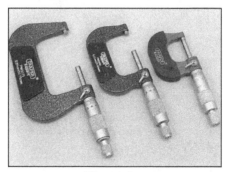

Micrometers

Dial test indicator ("dial gauge")

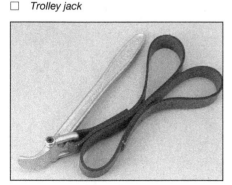

Strap wrench

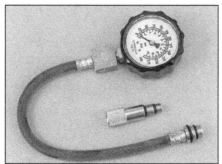

Compression tester

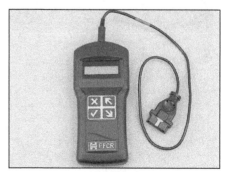

Fault code reader

This is a guide to getting your vehicle through the MOT test. Obviously it will not be possible to examine the vehicle to the same standard as the professional MOT tester. However, working through the following checks will enable you to identify any problem areas before submitting the vehicle for the test.

Where a testable component is in borderline condition, the tester has discretion in deciding whether to pass or fail it. The basis of such discretion is whether the tester would be happy for a close relative or friend to use the vehicle with the component in that condition. If the vehicle presented is clean and evidently well cared for, the tester may be more inclined to pass a borderline component than if the vehicle is scruffy and apparently neglected.

It has only been possible to summarise the test requirements here, based on the regulations in force at the time of printing. Test standards are becoming increasingly stringent, although there are some exemptions for older vehicles.

An assistant will be needed to help carry out some of these checks.

The checks have been sub-divided into four categories, as follows:

1 Checks carried out **FROM THE DRIVER'S SEAT**

2 Checks carried out **WITH THE VEHICLE ON THE GROUND**

3 Checks carried out **WITH THE VEHICLE RAISED AND THE WHEELS FREE TO TURN**

4 Checks carried out on **YOUR VEHICLE'S EXHAUST EMISSION SYSTEM**

---

1 Checks carried out **FROM THE DRIVER'S SEAT**

Handbrake

☐ Test the operation of the handbrake. Excessive travel (too many clicks) indicates incorrect brake or cable adjustment.

☐ Check that the handbrake cannot be released by tapping the lever sideways. Check the security of the lever mountings.

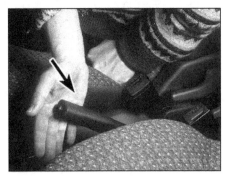

Footbrake

☐ Depress the brake pedal and check that it does not creep down to the floor, indicating a master cylinder fault. Release the pedal, wait a few seconds, then depress it again. If the pedal travels nearly to the floor before firm resistance is felt, brake adjustment or repair is necessary. If the pedal feels spongy, there is air in the hydraulic system which must be removed by bleeding.

☐ Check that the brake pedal is secure and in good condition. Check also for signs of fluid leaks on the pedal, floor or carpets, which would indicate failed seals in the brake master cylinder.

☐ Check the servo unit (when applicable) by operating the brake pedal several times, then keeping the pedal depressed and starting the engine. As the engine starts, the pedal will move down slightly. If not, the vacuum hose or the servo itself may be faulty.

Steering wheel and column

☐ Examine the steering wheel for fractures or looseness of the hub, spokes or rim.

☐ Move the steering wheel from side to side and then up and down. Check that the steering wheel is not loose on the column, indicating wear or a loose retaining nut. Continue moving the steering wheel as before, but also turn it slightly from left to right.

☐ Check that the steering wheel is not loose on the column, and that there is no abnormal

movement of the steering wheel, indicating wear in the column support bearings or couplings.

Windscreen, mirrors and sunvisor

☐ The windscreen must be free of cracks or other significant damage within the driver's field of view. (Small stone chips are acceptable.) Rear view mirrors must be secure, intact, and capable of being adjusted.

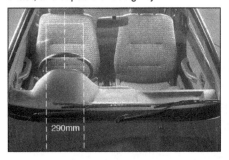

☐ The driver's sunvisor must be capable of being stored in the "up" position.

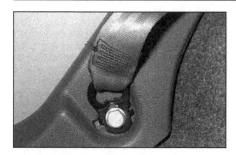

Seat belts and seats

Note: *The following checks are applicable to all seat belts, front and rear.*

☐ Examine the webbing of all the belts (including rear belts if fitted) for cuts, serious fraying or deterioration. Fasten and unfasten each belt to check the buckles. If applicable, check the retracting mechanism. Check the security of all seat belt mountings accessible from inside the vehicle.

☐ Seat belts with pre-tensioners, once activated, have a "flag" or similar showing on the seat belt stalk. This, in itself, is not a reason for test failure.

☐ The front seats themselves must be securely attached and the backrests must lock in the upright position.

Doors

☐ Both front doors must be able to be opened and closed from outside and inside, and must latch securely when closed.

2 Checks carried out **WITH THE VEHICLE ON THE GROUND**

Vehicle identification

☐ Number plates must be in good condition, secure and legible, with letters and numbers correctly spaced – spacing at (A) should be at least twice that at (B).

☐ The VIN plate and/or homologation plate must be legible.

Electrical equipment

☐ Switch on the ignition and check the operation of the horn.

☐ Check the windscreen washers and wipers, examining the wiper blades; renew damaged or perished blades. Also check the operation of the stop-lights.

☐ Check the operation of the sidelights and number plate lights. The lenses and reflectors must be secure, clean and undamaged.

☐ Check the operation and alignment of the headlights. The headlight reflectors must not be tarnished and the lenses must be undamaged.

☐ Switch on the ignition and check the operation of the direction indicators (including the instrument panel tell-tale) and the hazard warning lights. Operation of the sidelights and stop-lights must not affect the indicators - if it does, the cause is usually a bad earth at the rear light cluster.

☐ Check the operation of the rear foglight(s), including the warning light on the instrument panel or in the switch.

☐ The ABS warning light must illuminate in accordance with the manufacturers' design. For most vehicles, the ABS warning light should illuminate when the ignition is switched on, and (if the system is operating properly) extinguish after a few seconds. Refer to the owner's handbook.

Footbrake

☐ Examine the master cylinder, brake pipes and servo unit for leaks, loose mountings, corrosion or other damage.

☐ The fluid reservoir must be secure and the fluid level must be between the upper (**A**) and lower (**B**) markings.

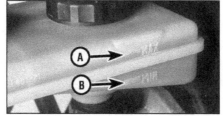

☐ Inspect both front brake flexible hoses for cracks or deterioration of the rubber. Turn the steering from lock to lock, and ensure that the hoses do not contact the wheel, tyre, or any part of the steering or suspension mechanism. With the brake pedal firmly depressed, check the hoses for bulges or leaks under pressure.

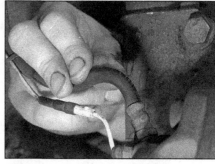

Steering and suspension

☐ Have your assistant turn the steering wheel from side to side slightly, up to the point where the steering gear just begins to transmit this movement to the roadwheels. Check for excessive free play between the steering wheel and the steering gear, indicating wear or insecurity of the steering column joints, the column-to-steering gear coupling, or the steering gear itself.

☐ Have your assistant turn the steering wheel more vigorously in each direction, so that the roadwheels just begin to turn. As this is done, examine all the steering joints, linkages, fittings and attachments. Renew any component that shows signs of wear or damage. On vehicles with power steering, check the security and condition of the steering pump, drivebelt and hoses.

☐ Check that the vehicle is standing level, and at approximately the correct ride height.

Shock absorbers

☐ Depress each corner of the vehicle in turn, then release it. The vehicle should rise and then settle in its normal position. If the vehicle continues to rise and fall, the shock absorber is defective. A shock absorber which has seized will also cause the vehicle to fail.

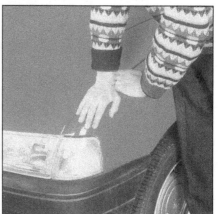

Exhaust system

☐ Start the engine. With your assistant holding a rag over the tailpipe, check the entire system for leaks. Repair or renew leaking sections.

3 Checks carried out **WITH THE VEHICLE RAISED AND THE WHEELS FREE TO TURN**

Jack up the front and rear of the vehicle, and securely support it on axle stands. Position the stands clear of the suspension assemblies. Ensure that the wheels are clear of the ground and that the steering can be turned from lock to lock.

Steering mechanism

☐ Have your assistant turn the steering from lock to lock. Check that the steering turns smoothly, and that no part of the steering mechanism, including a wheel or tyre, fouls any brake hose or pipe or any part of the body structure.
☐ Examine the steering rack rubber gaiters for damage or insecurity of the retaining clips. If power steering is fitted, check for signs of damage or leakage of the fluid hoses, pipes or connections. Also check for excessive stiffness or binding of the steering, a missing split pin or locking device, or severe corrosion of the body structure within 30 cm of any steering component attachment point.

Front and rear suspension and wheel bearings

☐ Starting at the front right-hand side, grasp the roadwheel at the 3 o'clock and 9 o'clock positions and rock gently but firmly. Check for free play or insecurity at the wheel bearings, suspension balljoints, or suspension mountings, pivots and attachments.
☐ Now grasp the wheel at the 12 o'clock and 6 o'clock positions and repeat the previous inspection. Spin the wheel, and check for roughness or tightness of the front wheel bearing.

☐ If excess free play is suspected at a component pivot point, this can be confirmed by using a large screwdriver or similar tool and levering between the mounting and the component attachment. This will confirm whether the wear is in the pivot bush, its retaining bolt, or in the mounting itself (the bolt holes can often become elongated).

☐ Carry out all the above checks at the other front wheel, and then at both rear wheels.

Springs and shock absorbers

☐ Examine the suspension struts (when applicable) for serious fluid leakage, corrosion, or damage to the casing. Also check the security of the mounting points.
☐ If coil springs are fitted, check that the spring ends locate in their seats, and that the spring is not corroded, cracked or broken.
☐ If leaf springs are fitted, check that all leaves are intact, that the axle is securely attached to each spring, and that there is no deterioration of the spring eye mountings, bushes, and shackles.

☐ The same general checks apply to vehicles fitted with other suspension types, such as torsion bars, hydraulic displacer units, etc. Ensure that all mountings and attachments are secure, that there are no signs of excessive wear, corrosion or damage, and (on hydraulic types) that there are no fluid leaks or damaged pipes.
☐ Inspect the shock absorbers for signs of serious fluid leakage. Check for wear of the mounting bushes or attachments, or damage to the body of the unit.

Driveshafts (fwd vehicles only)

☐ Rotate each front wheel in turn and inspect the constant velocity joint gaiters for splits or damage. Also check that each driveshaft is straight and undamaged.

Braking system

☐ If possible without dismantling, check brake pad wear and disc condition. Ensure that the friction lining material has not worn excessively, (A) and that the discs are not fractured, pitted, scored or badly worn (B).

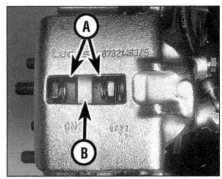

☐ Examine all the rigid brake pipes underneath the vehicle, and the flexible hose(s) at the rear. Look for corrosion, chafing or insecurity of the pipes, and for signs of bulging under pressure, chafing, splits or deterioration of the flexible hoses.
☐ Look for signs of fluid leaks at the brake calipers or on the brake backplates. Repair or renew leaking components.
☐ Slowly spin each wheel, while your assistant depresses and releases the footbrake. Ensure that each brake is operating and does not bind when the pedal is released.

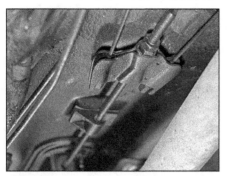

☐ Examine the handbrake mechanism, checking for frayed or broken cables, excessive corrosion, or wear or insecurity of the linkage. Check that the mechanism works on each relevant wheel, and releases fully, without binding.

☐ It is not possible to test brake efficiency without special equipment, but a road test can be carried out later to check that the vehicle pulls up in a straight line.

Fuel and exhaust systems

☐ Inspect the fuel tank (including the filler cap), fuel pipes, hoses and unions. All components must be secure and free from leaks.

☐ Examine the exhaust system over its entire length, checking for any damaged, broken or missing mountings, security of the retaining clamps and rust or corrosion.

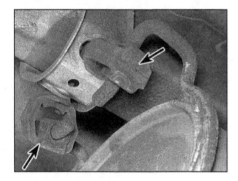

Wheels and tyres

☐ Examine the sidewalls and tread area of each tyre in turn. Check for cuts, tears, lumps, bulges, separation of the tread, and exposure of the ply or cord due to wear or damage. Check that the tyre bead is correctly seated on the wheel rim, that the valve is sound and properly seated, and that the wheel is not distorted or damaged.

☐ Check that the tyres are of the correct size for the vehicle, that they are of the same size and type on each axle, and that the pressures are correct.

☐ Check the tyre tread depth. The legal minimum at the time of writing is 1.6 mm over at least three-quarters of the tread width. Abnormal tread wear may indicate incorrect front wheel alignment.

Body corrosion

☐ Check the condition of the entire vehicle structure for signs of corrosion in load-bearing areas. (These include chassis box sections, side sills, cross-members, pillars, and all suspension, steering, braking system and seat belt mountings and anchorages.) Any corrosion which has seriously reduced the thickness of a load-bearing area is likely to cause the vehicle to fail. In this case professional repairs are likely to be needed.

☐ Damage or corrosion which causes sharp or otherwise dangerous edges to be exposed will also cause the vehicle to fail.

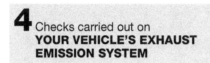

4 Checks carried out on **YOUR VEHICLE'S EXHAUST EMISSION SYSTEM**

Petrol models

☐ Have the engine at normal operating temperature, and make sure that it is in good tune (ignition system in good order, air filter element clean, etc).

☐ Before any measurements are carried out, raise the engine speed to around 2500 rpm, and hold it at this speed for 20 seconds. Allow the engine speed to return to idle, and watch for smoke emissions from the exhaust tailpipe. If the idle speed is obviously much too high, or if dense blue or clearly-visible black smoke comes from the tailpipe for more than 5 seconds, the vehicle will fail. As a rule of thumb, blue smoke signifies oil being burnt (engine wear) while black smoke signifies unburnt fuel (dirty air cleaner element, or other carburettor or fuel system fault).

☐ An exhaust gas analyser capable of measuring carbon monoxide (CO) and hydrocarbons (HC) is now needed. If such an instrument cannot be hired or borrowed, a local garage may agree to perform the check for a small fee.

CO emissions (mixture)

☐ At the time of writing, for vehicles first used between 1st August 1975 and 31st July 1986 (P to C registration), the CO level must not exceed 4.5% by volume. For vehicles first used between 1st August 1986 and 31st July 1992 (D to J registration), the CO level must not exceed 3.5% by volume. Vehicles first

used after 1st August 1992 (K registration) must conform to the manufacturer's specification. The MOT tester has access to a DOT database or emissions handbook, which lists the CO and HC limits for each make and model of vehicle. The CO level is measured with the engine at idle speed, and at "fast idle". The following limits are given as a general guide:

At idle speed -
    CO level no more than 0.5%
At "fast idle" (2500 to 3000 rpm) -
    CO level no more than 0.3%
    (Minimum oil temperature 60ºC)

☐ If the CO level cannot be reduced far enough to pass the test (and the fuel and ignition systems are otherwise in good condition) then the carburettor is badly worn, or there is some problem in the fuel injection system or catalytic converter (as applicable).

HC emissions

☐ With the CO within limits, HC emissions for vehicles first used between 1st August 1975 and 31st July 1992 (P to J registration) must not exceed 1200 ppm. Vehicles first used after 1st August 1992 (K registration) must conform to the manufacturer's specification. The MOT tester has access to a DOT database or emissions handbook, which lists the CO and HC limits for each make and model of vehicle. The HC level is measured with the engine at "fast idle". The following is given as a general guide:

At "fast idle" (2500 to 3000 rpm) -
    HC level no more than 200 ppm
    (Minimum oil temperature 60ºC)

☐ Excessive HC emissions are caused by incomplete combustion, the causes of which can include oil being burnt, mechanical wear and ignition/fuel system malfunction.

Diesel models

☐ The only emission test applicable to Diesel engines is the measuring of exhaust smoke density. The test involves accelerating the engine several times to its maximum unloaded speed.

Note: *It is of the utmost importance that the engine timing belt is in good condition before the test is carried out.*

☐ The limits for Diesel engine exhaust smoke, introduced in September 1995 are:
Vehicles first used before 1st August 1979:
    Exempt from metered smoke testing, but must not emit "dense blue or clearly visible black smoke for a period of more than 5 seconds at idle" or "dense blue or clearly visible black smoke during acceleration which would obscure the view of other road users".
Non-turbocharged vehicles first used after 1st August 1979: 2.5m-1
Turbocharged vehicles first used after 1st August 1979: 3.0m-1

☐ Excessive smoke can be caused by a dirty air cleaner element. Otherwise, professional advice may be needed to find the cause.

Engine

- [ ] Engine fails to rotate when attempting to start
- [ ] Engine rotates, but will not start
- [ ] Engine difficult to start when cold
- [ ] Engine difficult to start when hot
- [ ] Starter motor noisy or excessively-rough in engagement
- [ ] Engine starts, but stops immediately
- [ ] Engine idles erratically
- [ ] Engine misfires at idle speed
- [ ] Engine misfires throughout the driving speed range
- [ ] Engine hesitates on acceleration
- [ ] Engine stalls
- [ ] Engine lacks power
- [ ] Engine backfires
- [ ] Oil pressure warning light illuminated with engine running
- [ ] Engine runs-on after switching off
- [ ] Engine noises

Cooling system

- [ ] Overheating
- [ ] Overcooling
- [ ] External coolant leakage
- [ ] Internal coolant leakage
- [ ] Corrosion

Fuel and exhaust systems

- [ ] Excessive fuel consumption
- [ ] Fuel leakage and/or fuel odour
- [ ] Excessive noise or fumes from exhaust system

Clutch

- [ ] Pedal travels to floor - no pressure or very little resistance
- [ ] Clutch fails to disengage (unable to select gears)
- [ ] Clutch slips (engine speed increases, with no increase in vehicle speed)
- [ ] Judder as clutch is engaged
- [ ] Noise when depressing or releasing clutch pedal

Manual transmission

- [ ] Noisy in neutral with engine running
- [ ] Noisy in one particular gear
- [ ] Difficulty engaging gears
- [ ] Jumps out of gear
- [ ] Vibration
- [ ] Lubricant leaks

Driveshafts

- [ ] Clicking or knocking noise on turns (at slow speed on full-lock)
- [ ] Vibration when accelerating or decelerating

Braking system

- [ ] Vehicle pulls to one side under braking
- [ ] Noise (grinding or high-pitched squeal) when brakes applied
- [ ] Excessive brake pedal travel
- [ ] Brake pedal feels spongy when depressed
- [ ] Excessive brake pedal effort required to stop vehicle
- [ ] Judder felt through brake pedal or steering wheel when braking
- [ ] Brakes binding
- [ ] Rear wheels locking under normal braking

Suspension and steering systems

- [ ] Vehicle pulls to one side
- [ ] Wheel wobble and vibration
- [ ] Excessive pitching and/or rolling around corners, or during braking
- [ ] Wandering or general instability
- [ ] Excessively-stiff steering
- [ ] Excessive play in steering
- [ ] Lack of power assistance
- [ ] Tyre wear excessive

Electrical system

- [ ] Battery will not hold a charge for more than a few days
- [ ] Ignition/no-charge warning light remains illuminated with engine running
- [ ] Ignition/no-charge warning light fails to come on
- [ ] Lights inoperative
- [ ] Instrument readings inaccurate or erratic
- [ ] Horn inoperative, or unsatisfactory in operation
- [ ] Windscreen/tailgate wipers inoperative, or unsatisfactory in operation
- [ ] Windscreen/tailgate washers inoperative, or unsatisfactory in operation
- [ ] Electric windows inoperative, or unsatisfactory in operation
- [ ] Central locking system inoperative, or unsatisfactory in operation

Introduction

The vehicle owner who does his or her own maintenance according to the recommended service schedules should not have to use this section of the manual very often. Modern component reliability is such that, provided those items subject to wear or deterioration are inspected or renewed at the specified intervals, sudden failure is comparatively rare. Faults do not usually just happen as a result of sudden failure, but develop over a period of time. Major mechanical failures in particular are usually preceded by characteristic symptoms over hundreds or even thousands of miles. Those components which do occasionally fail without warning are often small and easily carried in the vehicle.

With any fault-finding, the first step is to decide where to begin investigations.

Sometimes this is obvious, but on other occasions, a little detective work will be necessary. The owner who makes half a dozen haphazard adjustments or replacements may be successful in curing a fault (or its symptoms), but will be none the wiser if the fault recurs, and ultimately may have spent more time and money than was necessary. A calm and logical approach will be found to be more satisfactory in the long run. Always take into account any warning signs or abnormalities that may have been noticed in the period preceding the fault - power loss, high or low gauge readings, unusual smells, etc - and remember that failure of components such as fuses or spark plugs may only be pointers to some underlying fault.

These pages provide an easy-reference guide to the more common problems which may occur during the vehicle's life. These problems and their possible causes are grouped under headings such as Engine, Cooling system, etc. The Chapter and/or Section which deals with the problem is also shown in brackets. Whatever the fault, certain basic principles apply. These are as follows:

Verify the fault. This is simply a matter of being sure you know exactly what the symptoms are before starting work. This is particularly important if you are investigating a fault for someone else, who may not have described it very accurately.

Don't overlook the obvious. For example, if it won't start, is there fuel in the tank? (Don't take anyone else's word on this particular point, and don't trust the fuel gauge either!) If an electrical fault is indicated, look for loose or broken wires before digging out the test gear.

Cure the disease, not the symptom. Substituting a flat battery with a fully-charged one will get you off the hard shoulder, but if the underlying cause is not attended to, the new battery will go the same way. Similarly, changing oil-fouled spark plugs (petrol models) for a new set will get you moving again, but remember that the reason for the fouling (if it wasn't simply an incorrect grade of plug) will have to be established and corrected.

Don't take anything for granted. Particularly, don't forget that a new component may itself be defective (especially if it's been rattling around in the boot for months), and don't leave components out of a fault diagnosis sequence just because they are new or recently-fitted. When you do finally diagnose a difficult fault, you'll probably realise that all the evidence was there from the start.

Engine

Engine fails to rotate when attempting to start

- [ ] Battery terminal connections loose or corroded (*Weekly checks*).
- [ ] Battery discharged or faulty (Chapter 5A).
- [ ] Broken, loose or disconnected wiring in the starting circuit (Chapter 5A).
- [ ] Defective starter solenoid or switch (Chapter 5A).
- [ ] Defective starter motor (Chapter 5A).
- [ ] Starter pinion or flywheel ring gear teeth loose or broken (Chapter 2 or 5A).
- [ ] Engine earth strap broken or disconnected (Chapter 5A).

Engine rotates, but will not start

- [ ] Fuel tank empty.
- [ ] Battery discharged (engine rotates slowly) (Chapter 5A).
- [ ] Battery terminal connections loose or corroded (*Weekly checks*).
- [ ] Immobiliser fault (Chapter 12).
- [ ] Ignition components damp or damaged - petrol models (Chapter 5B).
- [ ] Ignition timing incorrect (Chapter 5B)
- [ ] Broken, loose or disconnected wiring in the ignition circuit - petrol models (Chapter 5B).
- [ ] Worn, faulty or incorrectly-gapped spark plugs - petrol models (Chapter 1A).
- [ ] Preheating system faulty - diesel models (Chapter 5C).
- [ ] Fuel injection system fault - petrol models (Chapter 4A or 4B).
- [ ] Fuel cut-off (stop) solenoid faulty - diesel models (Chapter 4C).
- [ ] Air in fuel system - diesel models (Chapter 4C).
- [ ] Major mechanical failure (eg camshaft drive) (Chapter 2).

Engine difficult to start when cold

- [ ] Battery discharged (Chapter 5A).
- [ ] Ignition timing incorrect (Chapter 5B)
- [ ] Battery terminal connections loose or corroded (*Weekly checks*).
- [ ] Worn, faulty or incorrectly-gapped spark plugs - petrol models (Chapter 1A).
- [ ] Preheating system faulty - diesel models (Chapter 5C).
- [ ] Fuel injection system fault - petrol models (Chapter 4A or 4B).
- [ ] Other ignition system fault - petrol models (Chapter 5B).
- [ ] Low cylinder compressions (Chapter 2).

Engine difficult to start when hot

- [ ] Air filter element dirty or clogged (Chapter 1).
- [ ] Fuel injection system fault - petrol models (Chapter 4A or 4B).
- [ ] Low cylinder compressions (Chapter 2).
- [ ] Ignition timing incorrect (Chapter 5B)

Starter motor noisy or excessively-rough in engagement

- [ ] Starter pinion or flywheel ring gear teeth loose or broken (Chapter 2 or 5A).
- [ ] Starter motor mounting bolts loose or missing (Chapter 5A).
- [ ] Starter motor internal components worn or damaged (Chapter 5A).

Engine starts, but stops immediately

- [ ] Loose or faulty electrical connections in the ignition circuit - petrol models (Chapter 5B).
- [ ] Vacuum leak at the throttle body or inlet manifold - petrol models (Chapter 4A or 4B).
- [ ] Blocked injector/fuel injection system fault - petrol models (Chapter 4A or 4B).

Engine idles erratically

- [ ] Air filter element clogged (Chapter 1).
- [ ] Vacuum leak at the throttle body, inlet manifold or associated hoses - petrol models (Chapter 4A or 4B).
- [ ] Worn, faulty or incorrectly-gapped spark plugs - petrol models (Chapter 1A).
- [ ] Uneven or low cylinder compressions (Chapter 2).
- [ ] Camshaft lobes worn (Chapter 2).
- [ ] Timing belt incorrectly tensioned (Chapter 2B or 2C).
- [ ] Blocked injector/fuel injection system fault - petrol models (Chapter 4A or 4B).
- [ ] Faulty injector(s) - diesel models (Chapter 4C).

Engine misfires at idle speed

- [ ] Worn, faulty or incorrectly-gapped spark plugs - petrol models (Chapter 1A).
- [ ] Faulty spark plug HT leads - petrol models (Chapter 5B).
- [ ] Vacuum leak at the throttle body, inlet manifold or associated hoses - petrol models (Chapter 4A or 4B).
- [ ] Blocked injector/fuel injection system fault - petrol models (Chapter 4A or 4B).
- [ ] Faulty injector(s) - diesel models (Chapter 4C).
- [ ] Distributor cap cracked or tracking internally - petrol models (where applicable) (Chapter 5B).
- [ ] Uneven or low cylinder compressions (Chapter 2).
- [ ] Disconnected, leaking, or perished crankcase ventilation hoses (Chapter 4D).

Engine misfires throughout the driving speed range

- [ ] Fuel filter choked (Chapter 1).
- [ ] Fuel pump faulty, or delivery pressure low - petrol models (Chapter 4A or 4B).
- [ ] Fuel tank vent blocked, or fuel pipes restricted (Chapter 4).
- [ ] Vacuum leak at the throttle body, inlet manifold or associated hoses - petrol models (Chapter 4A or 4B).
- [ ] Valve clearances incorrect - 1.3 litre engine (Chapter 1A).
- [ ] Worn, faulty or incorrectly-gapped spark plugs - petrol models (Chapter 1A).
- [ ] Faulty spark plug HT leads - petrol models (Chapter 5B).
- [ ] Faulty injector(s) - diesel models (Chapter 4C).
- [ ] Distributor cap cracked or tracking internally - petrol models (where applicable) (Chapter 5B).
- [ ] Faulty ignition coil - petrol models (Chapter 5B).
- [ ] Uneven or low cylinder compressions (Chapter 2).
- [ ] Blocked injector/fuel injection system fault - petrol models (Chapter 4A or 4B).

Engine (continued)

Engine hesitates on acceleration

- [ ] Worn, faulty or incorrectly-gapped spark plugs - petrol models (Chapter 1A).
- [ ] Vacuum leak at the throttle body, inlet manifold or associated hoses - petrol models (Chapter 4A or 4B).
- [ ] Blocked injector/fuel injection system fault - petrol models (Chapter 4A or 4B).
- [ ] Faulty injector(s) - diesel models (Chapter 4C).

Engine stalls

- [ ] Vacuum leak at the throttle body, inlet manifold or associated hoses - petrol models (Chapter 4A or 4B).
- [ ] Fuel filter choked (Chapter 1).
- [ ] Fuel pump faulty, or delivery pressure low - petrol models (Chapter 4A or 4B).
- [ ] Fuel tank vent blocked, or fuel pipes restricted (Chapter 4).
- [ ] Blocked injector/fuel injection system fault - petrol models (Chapter 4A or 4B).
- [ ] Faulty injector(s) - diesel models (Chapter 4C).

Engine lacks power

- [ ] Valve clearances incorrect - 1.3 litre engine (Chapter 1A).
- [ ] Timing chain or belt incorrectly fitted or tensioned (Chapter 2).
- [ ] Fuel filter choked (Chapter 1).
- [ ] Ignition timing incorrect (Chapter 5B)
- [ ] Fuel pump faulty, or delivery pressure low - petrol models (Chapter 4A or 4B).
- [ ] Uneven or low cylinder compressions (Chapter 2).
- [ ] Worn, faulty or incorrectly-gapped spark plugs - petrol models (Chapter 1A).
- [ ] Vacuum leak at the throttle body, inlet manifold or associated hoses - petrol models (Chapter 4A or 4B).
- [ ] Blocked injector/fuel injection system fault - petrol models (Chapter 4A or 4B).
- [ ] Faulty injector(s) - diesel models (Chapter 4C).
- [ ] Injection pump timing incorrect - diesel models (Chapter 4C).
- [ ] Brakes binding (Chapters 1 or 9).
- [ ] Clutch slipping (Chapter 6).

Engine backfires

- [ ] Timing chain or belt incorrectly fitted or tensioned (Chapter 2).
- [ ] Vacuum leak at the throttle body, inlet manifold or associated hoses - petrol models (Chapter 4A or 4B).
- [ ] Blocked injector/fuel injection system fault - petrol models (Chapter 4A or 4B).
- [ ] Ignition timing incorrect (Chapter 5B)

Oil pressure warning light illuminated with engine running

- [ ] Low oil level, or incorrect oil grade (*Weekly checks*).
- [ ] Worn engine bearings and/or oil pump (Chapter 2D).
- [ ] High engine operating temperature (Chapter 3).
- [ ] Oil pressure relief valve defective (Chapter 2).
- [ ] Oil pick-up strainer clogged (Chapter 2).

Engine runs-on after switching off

- [ ] Excessive carbon build-up in engine (Chapter 2D).
- [ ] High engine operating temperature (Chapter 3).
- [ ] Fuel injection system fault - petrol models (Chapter 4A or 4B).
- [ ] Faulty fuel cut-off (stop) solenoid - diesel models (Chapter 4C).

Engine noises

Pre-ignition (pinking) or knocking during acceleration or under load

- [ ] Ignition timing incorrect/ignition system fault - petrol models (Chapter 5B).
- [ ] Incorrect grade of spark plug - petrol models (Chapter 1A).
- [ ] Incorrect grade of fuel (Chapter 4).
- [ ] Vacuum leak at the throttle body, inlet manifold or associated hoses - petrol models (Chapter 4A or 4B).
- [ ] Excessive carbon build-up in engine (Chapter 2D).
- [ ] Blocked injector/fuel injection system fault - petrol models (Chapter 4A or 4B).

Whistling or wheezing noises

- [ ] Leaking inlet manifold or throttle body gasket - petrol models (Chapter 4A or 4B).
- [ ] Leaking exhaust manifold gasket or pipe-to-manifold joint (Chapter 4D).
- [ ] Leaking vacuum hose (Chapters 4, 5B and 9).
- [ ] Blowing cylinder head gasket (Chapter 2).

Tapping or rattling noises

- [ ] Valve clearances incorrect - 1.3 litre engine (Chapter 1A).
- [ ] Worn camshaft (Chapter 2).
- [ ] Worn hydraulic tappet (Chapter 2B or 2C).
- [ ] Ancillary component fault (coolant pump, alternator, etc) (Chapters 3, 5A, etc).

Knocking or thumping noises

- [ ] Worn big-end bearings (regular heavy knocking, perhaps less under load) (Chapter 2D).
- [ ] Worn main bearings (rumbling and knocking, perhaps worsening under load) (Chapter 2D).
- [ ] Piston slap - most noticeable when cold - engine worn (Chapter 2D).
- [ ] Ancillary component fault (water pump, alternator, etc) (Chapters 3, 5A, etc).

Cooling system

Overheating

☐ Insufficient coolant in system (*Weekly checks*).
☐ Auxiliary drivebelt broken or drivebelt tensioner faulty (Chapter 1 or 2).
☐ Thermostat faulty (Chapter 3).
☐ Radiator core blocked, or grille restricted (Chapter 3).
☐ Electric cooling fan or thermoswitch faulty (Chapter 3).
☐ Pressure cap faulty (Chapter 3).
☐ Ignition timing incorrect/ignition system fault - petrol models (Chapter 5B).
☐ Inaccurate temperature gauge sender unit (Chapter 3).
☐ Airlock in cooling system (Chapter 1).

Overcooling

☐ Thermostat faulty (Chapter 3).
☐ Inaccurate temperature gauge sender unit (Chapter 3).

External coolant leakage

☐ Deteriorated or damaged hoses or hose clips (Chapter 1).
☐ Radiator core or heater matrix leaking (Chapter 3).
☐ Pressure cap faulty (Chapter 3).
☐ Water pump seal leaking (Chapter 3).
☐ Boiling due to overheating (Chapter 3).
☐ Core plug leaking (Chapter 2D).

Internal coolant leakage

☐ Leaking cylinder head gasket (Chapter 2).
☐ Cracked cylinder head or cylinder bore (Chapter 2D).

Corrosion

☐ Infrequent draining and flushing (Chapter 1).
☐ Incorrect coolant mixture or inappropriate coolant type (Chapter 1).

Fuel and exhaust systems

Excessive fuel consumption

☐ Air filter element dirty or clogged (Chapter 1).
☐ Fuel injection system fault - petrol models (Chapter 4A or 4B).
☐ Faulty injector(s) - diesel models (Chapter 4C).
☐ Ignition timing incorrect/ignition system fault - petrol models (Chapter 5B).
☐ Tyres under-inflated (*Weekly checks*).
☐ Brakes binding (Chapter 1 or 9).

Fuel leakage and/or fuel odour

☐ Damaged or corroded fuel tank, pipes or connections (Chapter 4).

Excessive noise or fumes from exhaust system

☐ Leaking exhaust system or manifold joints (Chapter 1 or 4D).
☐ Leaking, corroded or damaged silencers or pipe (Chapter 1 or 4D).
☐ Broken mountings causing body or suspension contact (Chapter 1).

Clutch

Pedal travels to floor - no pressure or very little resistance

☐ Broken clutch cable (Chapter 6).
☐ Cable out of adjustment (Chapter 6).
☐ Broken clutch release bearing or fork (Chapter 6).
☐ Broken diaphragm spring in clutch pressure plate (Chapter 6).

Clutch fails to disengage (unable to select gears)

☐ Cable out of adjustment (Chapter 6).
☐ Clutch disc sticking on gearbox input shaft splines (Chapter 6).
☐ Clutch disc sticking to flywheel or pressure plate (Chapter 6).
☐ Faulty pressure plate assembly (Chapter 6).
☐ Clutch release mechanism worn or incorrectly assembled (Chapter 6).

Clutch slips (engine speed increases, with no increase in vehicle speed)

☐ Cable out of adjustment (Chapter 6).
☐ Clutch disc linings excessively worn (Chapter 6).
☐ Clutch disc linings contaminated with oil or grease (Chapter 6).
☐ Faulty pressure plate or weak diaphragm spring (Chapter 6).

Judder as clutch is engaged

☐ Clutch disc linings contaminated with oil or grease (Chapter 6).
☐ Clutch disc linings excessively worn (Chapter 6).
☐ Clutch cable sticking or frayed (Chapter 6).
☐ Faulty or distorted pressure plate or diaphragm spring (Chapter 6).
☐ Worn or loose engine or gearbox mountings (Chapter 2).
☐ Clutch disc hub or gearbox input shaft splines worn (Chapter 6).

Noise when depressing or releasing clutch pedal

☐ Worn clutch release bearing (Chapter 6).
☐ Worn or dry clutch pedal bushes (Chapter 6).
☐ Faulty pressure plate assembly (Chapter 6).
☐ Pressure plate diaphragm spring broken (Chapter 6).
☐ Broken clutch disc cushioning springs (Chapter 6).

Manual transmission

Noisy in neutral with engine running
- [ ] Input shaft bearings worn (noise apparent with clutch pedal released, but not when depressed) (Chapter 7).*
- [ ] Clutch release bearing worn (noise apparent with clutch pedal depressed, possibly less when released) (Chapter 6).

Noisy in one particular gear
- [ ] Worn, damaged or chipped gear teeth (Chapter 7).*

Difficulty engaging gears
- [ ] Clutch fault (Chapter 6).
- [ ] Worn or damaged gearchange linkage (Chapter 7).
- [ ] Worn synchroniser units (Chapter 7).*

Jumps out of gear
- [ ] Worn or damaged gearchange linkage (Chapter 7).
- [ ] Worn synchroniser units (Chapter 7).*
- [ ] Worn selector forks (Chapter 7).*

Vibration
- [ ] Lack of oil (Chapter 1).
- [ ] Worn bearings (Chapter 7).*

Lubricant leaks
- [ ] Leaking differential output oil seal (Chapter 7).
- [ ] Leaking housing joint (Chapter 7).*
- [ ] Leaking input shaft oil seal (Chapter 7).*

Although the corrective action necessary to remedy the symptoms described is beyond the scope of the home mechanic, the above information should be helpful in isolating the cause of the condition, so that the owner can communicate clearly with a professional mechanic.

Driveshafts

Clicking or knocking noise on turns (at slow speed on full-lock)
- [ ] Lack of constant velocity joint lubricant, possibly due to damaged gaiter (Chapter 8).
- [ ] Worn outer constant velocity joint (Chapter 8).

Vibration when accelerating or decelerating
- [ ] Worn inner constant velocity joint (Chapter 8).
- [ ] Bent or distorted driveshaft (Chapter 8).

Braking system

Note: *Before assuming that a brake problem exists, make sure that the tyres are in good condition and correctly inflated, that the front wheel alignment is correct, the front wheels are balanced, and that the vehicle is not loaded with weight in an unequal manner. Apart from checking the condition of all pipe and hose connections, any faults occurring on the anti-lock braking system should be referred to a Skoda dealer for diagnosis.*

Vehicle pulls to one side under braking
- [ ] Worn, defective, damaged or contaminated brake pads/shoes on one side (Chapter 1 or 9).
- [ ] Seized or partially-seized front brake caliper/wheel cylinder piston (Chapter 1 or 9).
- [ ] A mixture of brake pad/shoe lining materials fitted between sides (Chapter 1 or 9).
- [ ] Brake caliper or backplate mounting bolts loose (Chapter 9).
- [ ] Worn or damaged steering or suspension components (Chapter 1 or 10).

Noise (grinding or high-pitched squeal) when brakes applied
- [ ] Brake pad or shoe friction lining material worn down to metal backing (Chapter 1 or 9).
- [ ] Excessive corrosion of brake disc or drum - may be apparent after the vehicle has been standing for some time (Chapter 1 or 9).
- [ ] Foreign object (stone chipping, etc) trapped between brake disc and shield (Chapter 1 or 9).

Excessive brake pedal travel
- [ ] Inoperative rear brake self-adjust mechanism - drum brakes (Chapter 1 or 9).
- [ ] Faulty master cylinder (Chapter 9).
- [ ] Air in hydraulic system (Chapter 1 or 9).
- [ ] Faulty vacuum servo unit (Chapter 9).

Brake pedal feels spongy when depressed
- [ ] Air in hydraulic system (Chapter 1 or 9).
- [ ] Deteriorated flexible rubber brake hoses (Chapter 1 or 9).
- [ ] Master cylinder mounting nuts loose (Chapter 9).
- [ ] Faulty master cylinder (Chapter 9).

Excessive brake pedal effort required to stop vehicle
- [ ] Faulty vacuum servo unit (Chapter 9).
- [ ] Faulty vacuum pump - diesel models (Chapter 9).
- [ ] Disconnected, damaged or insecure brake servo vacuum hose (Chapter 9).
- [ ] Primary or secondary hydraulic circuit failure (Chapter 9).
- [ ] Seized brake caliper or wheel cylinder piston(s) (Chapter 9).
- [ ] Brake pads or brake shoes incorrectly fitted (Chapter 1 or 9).
- [ ] Incorrect grade of brake pads or brake shoes fitted (Chapter 1 or 9).
- [ ] Brake pads or brake shoe linings contaminated (Chapter 1 or 9).

Braking system (continued)

Judder felt through brake pedal or steering wheel when braking

☐ Excessive run-out or distortion of discs/drums (Chapter 1 or 9).
☐ Brake pad or brake shoe linings worn (Chapter 1 or 9).
☐ Brake caliper or brake backplate mounting bolts loose (Chapter 9).
☐ Wear in suspension or steering components or mountings (Chapter 1 or 10).
☐ Vibration through pedal - Anti-lock Braking System (ABS) in operation - no fault (models with ABS).

Brakes binding

☐ Seized brake caliper or wheel cylinder piston(s) (Chapter 9).
☐ Incorrectly-adjusted handbrake mechanism (Chapter 9).
☐ Faulty master cylinder (Chapter 9).

Rear wheels locking under normal braking

☐ Rear brake shoe linings contaminated (Chapter 1 or 9).
☐ Faulty brake pressure regulator (Chapter 9).

Suspension and steering

Note: *Before diagnosing suspension or steering faults, be sure that the trouble is not due to incorrect tyre pressures, mixtures of tyre types, worn tyres, or binding brakes.*

Vehicle pulls to one side

☐ Defective or worn tyre (*Weekly checks*).
☐ Tyre pressure low on one side of the car (*Weekly checks*).
☐ Excessive wear in suspension or steering components (Chapter 1 or 10).
☐ Incorrect front wheel alignment (Chapter 10).
☐ Accident damage to steering or suspension components (Chapter 1).

Wheel wobble and vibration

☐ Front roadwheels out of balance (vibration felt mainly through the steering wheel) (*Weekly checks*).
☐ Rear roadwheels out of balance (vibration felt throughout the vehicle) (*Weekly checks*).
☐ Roadwheels damaged or distorted (*Weekly checks*).
☐ Faulty, worn or damaged tyre (*Weekly checks*).
☐ Worn steering or suspension joints, bushes or components (Chapter 1 or 10).
☐ Wheel bolts loose (Chapter 1).

Excessive pitching and/or rolling around corners, or during braking

☐ Defective shock absorbers (Chapter 1 or 10).
☐ Broken or weak spring and/or suspension component (Chapter 1 or 10).
☐ Worn or damaged anti-roll bar or mountings (Chapter 10).

Wandering or general instability

☐ Incorrect front wheel alignment (Chapter 10).
☐ Worn steering or suspension joints, bushes or components (Chapter 1 or 10).
☐ Roadwheels out of balance (*Weekly checks*).
☐ Faulty or damaged tyre (*Weekly checks*).
☐ Wheel bolts loose (Chapter 1).
☐ Defective shock absorbers (Chapter 1 or 10).

Excessively-stiff steering

☐ Incorrect power steering fluid level, where applicable (*Weekly checks*).
☐ Lack of steering gear lubricant (Chapter 10).
☐ Seized track rod end balljoint or suspension balljoint (Chapter 1 or 10).
☐ Broken auxiliary drivebelt or drivebelt tensioner fault - power steering (Chapter 1).
☐ Incorrect front wheel alignment (Chapter 10).
☐ Steering rack or column bent or damaged (Chapter 10).

Excessive play in steering

☐ Worn steering column intermediate shaft universal joint (Chapter 10).
☐ Worn steering track rod end balljoints (Chapter 1 or 10).
☐ Worn rack-and-pinion steering gear (Chapter 10).
☐ Worn steering or suspension joints, bushes or components (Chapter 1 or 10).

Lack of power assistance

☐ Broken or incorrectly-adjusted auxiliary drivebelt (Chapter 1 or 2).
☐ Incorrect power steering fluid level (*Weekly checks*).
☐ Restriction in power steering fluid hoses (Chapter 1).
☐ Faulty power steering pump (Chapter 10).
☐ Faulty rack-and-pinion steering gear (Chapter 10).

Tyre wear excessive

Tyres worn on inside or outside edges

☐ Tyres under-inflated (wear on both edges) (*Weekly checks*).
☐ Incorrect camber or castor angles (wear on one edge only) (Chapter 10).
☐ Worn steering or suspension joints, bushes or components (Chapter 1 or 10).
☐ Excessively-hard cornering.
☐ Accident damage.

Tyre treads exhibit feathered edges

☐ Incorrect toe setting (Chapter 10).

Tyres worn in centre of tread

☐ Tyres over-inflated (*Weekly checks*).

Tyres worn on inside and outside edges

☐ Tyres under-inflated (*Weekly checks*).

Tyres worn unevenly

☐ Tyres/wheels out of balance (*Weekly checks*).
☐ Excessive wheel or tyre run-out (*Weekly checks*).
☐ Worn shock absorbers (Chapter 1 or 10).
☐ Faulty tyre (*Weekly checks*).

Electrical system

Note: *For problems associated with the starting system, refer to the faults listed under Engine earlier in this Section.*

Battery will not hold a charge for more than a few days

- ☐ Battery defective internally (Chapter 5A).
- ☐ Battery terminal connections loose or corroded (*Weekly checks*).
- ☐ Auxiliary drivebelt worn or incorrectly adjusted (Chapter 1 or 2).
- ☐ Alternator not charging at correct output (Chapter 5A).
- ☐ Alternator or voltage regulator faulty (Chapter 5A).
- ☐ Short-circuit causing continual battery drain (Chapter 5A or 12).

Ignition/no-charge warning light remains illuminated with engine running

- ☐ Auxiliary drivebelt broken, worn, or incorrectly adjusted (Chapter 1).
- ☐ Alternator brushes worn, sticking, or dirty (Chapter 5A).
- ☐ Alternator brush springs weak or broken (Chapter 5A).
- ☐ Internal fault in alternator or voltage regulator (Chapter 5A).
- ☐ Broken, disconnected, or loose wiring in charging circuit (Chapter 5A).

Ignition/no-charge warning light fails to come on

- ☐ Warning light bulb blown (Chapter 12).
- ☐ Broken, disconnected, or loose wiring in warning light circuit (Chapter 12).
- ☐ Alternator faulty (Chapter 5A).

Lights inoperative

- ☐ Bulb blown (Chapter 12).
- ☐ Corrosion of bulb or bulbholder contacts (Chapter 12).
- ☐ Blown fuse (Chapter 12).
- ☐ Faulty relay (Chapter 12).
- ☐ Broken, loose, or disconnected wiring (Chapter 12).
- ☐ Faulty switch (Chapter 12).

Instrument readings inaccurate or erratic

Instrument readings increase with engine speed
- ☐ Faulty voltage stabiliser (Chapter 12).

Fuel or temperature gauges give no reading
- ☐ Faulty gauge sender unit/sensor (Chapter 3 or 4).
- ☐ Wiring open-circuit (Chapter 12).
- ☐ Faulty gauge (Chapter 12).

Fuel or temperature gauges give continuous maximum reading
- ☐ Faulty gauge sender unit/sensor (Chapter 3 or 4).
- ☐ Wiring short-circuit (Chapter 12).
- ☐ Faulty gauge (Chapter 12).

Horn inoperative, or unsatisfactory in operation

Horn operates all the time
- ☐ Horn push either earthed or stuck down (Chapter 12).
- ☐ Horn cable-to-horn push earthed (Chapter 12).

Horn fails to operate
- ☐ Blown fuse (Chapter 12).
- ☐ Cable or cable connections loose, broken or disconnected (Chapter 12).
- ☐ Faulty horn (Chapter 12).

Horn emits intermittent or unsatisfactory sound
- ☐ Cable connections loose (Chapter 12).
- ☐ Horn mountings loose (Chapter 12).
- ☐ Faulty horn (Chapter 12).

Windscreen/tailgate wipers inoperative, or unsatisfactory in operation

Wipers fail to operate, or operate very slowly
- ☐ Wiper blades stuck to screen, or linkage seized or binding (*Weekly checks* or Chapter 12).
- ☐ Blown fuse (*Weekly checks* or Chapter 12).
- ☐ Cable or cable connections loose, broken or disconnected (Chapter 12).
- ☐ Faulty relay (Chapter 12).
- ☐ Faulty wiper motor (Chapter 12).

Wiper blades sweep over too large or too small an area of the glass
- ☐ Wiper arms incorrectly positioned on spindles (Chapter 12).
- ☐ Excessive wear of wiper linkage (Chapter 12).
- ☐ Wiper motor or linkage mountings loose or insecure (Chapter 12).

Wiper blades fail to clean the glass effectively
- ☐ Wiper blade rubbers worn or perished (*Weekly checks*).
- ☐ Wiper arm tension springs broken, or arm pivots seized (Chapter 12).
- ☐ Insufficient windscreen washer additive to adequately remove road film (*Weekly checks*).

Windscreen/tailgate washers inoperative, or unsatisfactory in operation

One or more washer jets inoperative
- ☐ Blocked washer jet (Chapter 1).
- ☐ Disconnected, kinked or restricted fluid hose (Chapter 12).
- ☐ Insufficient fluid in washer reservoir (*Weekly checks*).

Washer pump fails to operate
- ☐ Broken or disconnected wiring or connections (Chapter 12).
- ☐ Blown fuse (*Weekly checks* or Chapter 12).
- ☐ Faulty washer switch (Chapter 12).
- ☐ Faulty washer pump (Chapter 12).

Washer pump runs for some time before fluid is emitted from jets
- ☐ Faulty one-way valve in fluid supply hose (Chapter 12).

Electrical system (continued)

Electric windows inoperative, or unsatisfactory in operation

Window glass will only move in one direction

☐ Faulty switch (Chapter 12).

Window glass slow to move

☐ Regulator seized or damaged, or in need of lubrication (Chapter 11).
☐ Door internal components or trim fouling regulator (Chapter 11).
☐ Faulty motor (Chapter 11).

Window glass fails to move

☐ Blown fuse (Chapter 12).
☐ Faulty relay (Chapter 12).
☐ Broken or disconnected wiring or connections (Chapter 12).
☐ Faulty motor (Chapter 11).

Central locking system inoperative, or unsatisfactory in operation

Complete system failure

☐ Blown fuse (*Weekly checks* or Chapter 12).
☐ Faulty relay (Chapter 12).
☐ Broken or disconnected wiring or connections (Chapter 12).
☐ Faulty control unit (Chapter 11).

Latch locks but will not unlock, or unlocks but will not lock

☐ Broken or disconnected latch operating rods or levers (Chapter 11).
☐ Faulty relay (Chapter 12).
☐ Faulty control unit (Chapter 11).
☐ Fault in door lock (Chapter 11).

One solenoid/motor fails to operate

☐ Broken or disconnected wiring or connections (Chapter 12).
☐ Faulty operating assembly (Chapter 11).
☐ Broken, binding or disconnected latch operating rods or levers (Chapter 11).
☐ Fault in door lock (Chapter 11).

A

ABS (Anti-lock brake system) A system, usually electronically controlled, that senses incipient wheel lockup during braking and relieves hydraulic pressure at wheels that are about to skid.

Air bag An inflatable bag hidden in the steering wheel (driver's side) or the dash or glovebox (passenger side). In a head-on collision, the bags inflate, preventing the driver and front passenger from being thrown forward into the steering wheel or windscreen.

Air cleaner A metal or plastic housing, containing a filter element, which removes dust and dirt from the air being drawn into the engine.

Air filter element The actual filter in an air cleaner system, usually manufactured from pleated paper and requiring renewal at regular intervals.

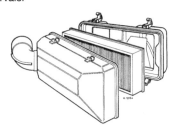

Air filter

Allen key A hexagonal wrench which fits into a recessed hexagonal hole.

Alligator clip A long-nosed spring-loaded metal clip with meshing teeth. Used to make temporary electrical connections.

Alternator A component in the electrical system which converts mechanical energy from a drivebelt into electrical energy to charge the battery and to operate the starting system, ignition system and electrical accessories.

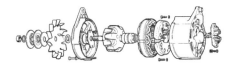

Alternator (exploded view)

Ampere (amp) A unit of measurement for the flow of electric current. One amp is the amount of current produced by one volt acting through a resistance of one ohm.

Anaerobic sealer A substance used to prevent bolts and screws from loosening. Anaerobic means that it does not require oxygen for activation. The Loctite brand is widely used.

Antifreeze A substance (usually ethylene glycol) mixed with water, and added to a vehicle's cooling system, to prevent freezing of the coolant in winter. Antifreeze also contains chemicals to inhibit corrosion and the formation of rust and other deposits that would tend to clog the radiator and coolant passages and reduce cooling efficiency.

Anti-seize compound A coating that reduces the risk of seizing on fasteners that are subjected to high temperatures, such as exhaust manifold bolts and nuts.

Anti-seize compound

Asbestos A natural fibrous mineral with great heat resistance, commonly used in the composition of brake friction materials. Asbestos is a health hazard and the dust created by brake systems should never be inhaled or ingested.

Axle A shaft on which a wheel revolves, or which revolves with a wheel. Also, a solid beam that connects the two wheels at one end of the vehicle. An axle which also transmits power to the wheels is known as a live axle.

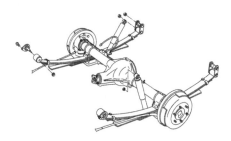

Axle assembly

Axleshaft A single rotating shaft, on either side of the differential, which delivers power from the final drive assembly to the drive wheels. Also called a driveshaft or a halfshaft.

B

Ball bearing An anti-friction bearing consisting of a hardened inner and outer race with hardened steel balls between two races.

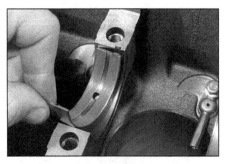

Bearing

Bearing The curved surface on a shaft or in a bore, or the part assembled into either, that permits relative motion between them with minimum wear and friction.

Big-end bearing The bearing in the end of the connecting rod that's attached to the crankshaft.

Bleed nipple A valve on a brake wheel cylinder, caliper or other hydraulic component that is opened to purge the hydraulic system of air. Also called a bleed screw.

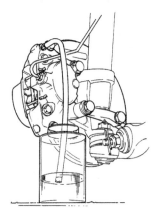

Brake bleeding

Brake bleeding Procedure for removing air from lines of a hydraulic brake system.

Brake disc The component of a disc brake that rotates with the wheels.

Brake drum The component of a drum brake that rotates with the wheels.

Brake linings The friction material which contacts the brake disc or drum to retard the vehicle's speed. The linings are bonded or riveted to the brake pads or shoes.

Brake pads The replaceable friction pads that pinch the brake disc when the brakes are applied. Brake pads consist of a friction material bonded or riveted to a rigid backing plate.

Brake shoe The crescent-shaped carrier to which the brake linings are mounted and which forces the lining against the rotating drum during braking.

Braking systems For more information on braking systems, consult the *Haynes Automotive Brake Manual*.

Breaker bar A long socket wrench handle providing greater leverage.

Bulkhead The insulated partition between the engine and the passenger compartment.

C

Caliper The non-rotating part of a disc-brake assembly that straddles the disc and carries the brake pads. The caliper also contains the hydraulic components that cause the pads to pinch the disc when the brakes are applied. A caliper is also a measuring tool that can be set to measure inside or outside dimensions of an object.

Camshaft A rotating shaft on which a series of cam lobes operate the valve mechanisms. The camshaft may be driven by gears, by sprockets and chain or by sprockets and a belt.

Canister A container in an evaporative emission control system; contains activated charcoal granules to trap vapours from the fuel system.

Canister

Carburettor A device which mixes fuel with air in the proper proportions to provide a desired power output from a spark ignition internal combustion engine.

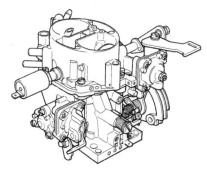

Carburettor

Castellated Resembling the parapets along the top of a castle wall. For example, a castellated balljoint stud nut.

Castellated nut

Castor In wheel alignment, the backward or forward tilt of the steering axis. Castor is positive when the steering axis is inclined rearward at the top.

Catalytic converter A silencer-like device in the exhaust system which converts certain pollutants in the exhaust gases into less harmful substances.

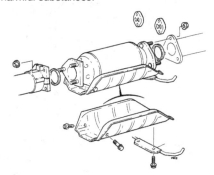

Catalytic converter

Circlip A ring-shaped clip used to prevent endwise movement of cylindrical parts and shafts. An internal circlip is installed in a groove in a housing; an external circlip fits into a groove on the outside of a cylindrical piece such as a shaft.

Clearance The amount of space between two parts. For example, between a piston and a cylinder, between a bearing and a journal, etc.

Coil spring A spiral of elastic steel found in various sizes throughout a vehicle, for example as a springing medium in the suspension and in the valve train.

Compression Reduction in volume, and increase in pressure and temperature, of a gas, caused by squeezing it into a smaller space.

Compression ratio The relationship between cylinder volume when the piston is at top dead centre and cylinder volume when the piston is at bottom dead centre.

Constant velocity (CV) joint A type of universal joint that cancels out vibrations caused by driving power being transmitted through an angle.

Core plug A disc or cup-shaped metal device inserted in a hole in a casting through which core was removed when the casting was formed. Also known as a freeze plug or expansion plug.

Crankcase The lower part of the engine block in which the crankshaft rotates.

Crankshaft The main rotating member, or shaft, running the length of the crankcase, with offset "throws" to which the connecting rods are attached.

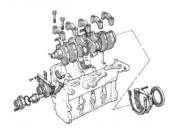

Crankshaft assembly

Crocodile clip See Alligator clip

D

Diagnostic code Code numbers obtained by accessing the diagnostic mode of an engine management computer. This code can be used to determine the area in the system where a malfunction may be located.

Disc brake A brake design incorporating a rotating disc onto which brake pads are squeezed. The resulting friction converts the energy of a moving vehicle into heat.

Double-overhead cam (DOHC) An engine that uses two overhead camshafts, usually one for the intake valves and one for the exhaust valves.

Drivebelt(s) The belt(s) used to drive accessories such as the alternator, water pump, power steering pump, air conditioning compressor, etc. off the crankshaft pulley.

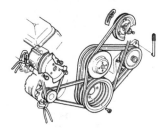

Accessory drivebelts

Driveshaft Any shaft used to transmit motion. Commonly used when referring to the axleshafts on a front wheel drive vehicle.

Driveshaft

Drum brake A type of brake using a drum-shaped metal cylinder attached to the inner surface of the wheel. When the brake pedal is pressed, curved brake shoes with friction linings press against the inside of the drum to slow or stop the vehicle.

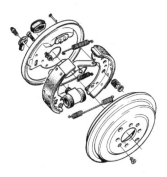

Drum brake assembly

E

EGR valve A valve used to introduce exhaust gases into the intake air stream.

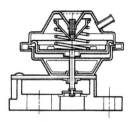

EGR valve

Electronic control unit (ECU) A computer which controls (for instance) ignition and fuel injection systems, or an anti-lock braking system. For more information refer to the *Haynes Automotive Electrical and Electronic Systems Manual.*

Electronic Fuel Injection (EFI) A computer controlled fuel system that distributes fuel through an injector located in each intake port of the engine.

Emergency brake A braking system, independent of the main hydraulic system, that can be used to slow or stop the vehicle if the primary brakes fail, or to hold the vehicle stationary even though the brake pedal isn't depressed. It usually consists of a hand lever that actuates either front or rear brakes mechanically through a series of cables and linkages. Also known as a handbrake or parking brake.

Endfloat The amount of lengthwise movement between two parts. As applied to a crankshaft, the distance that the crankshaft can move forward and back in the cylinder block.

Engine management system (EMS) A computer controlled system which manages the fuel injection and the ignition systems in an integrated fashion.

Exhaust manifold A part with several passages through which exhaust gases leave the engine combustion chambers and enter the exhaust pipe.

Exhaust manifold

F

Fan clutch A viscous (fluid) drive coupling device which permits variable engine fan speeds in relation to engine speeds.

Feeler blade A thin strip or blade of hardened steel, ground to an exact thickness, used to check or measure clearances between parts.

Feeler blade

Firing order The order in which the engine cylinders fire, or deliver their power strokes, beginning with the number one cylinder.

Flywheel A heavy spinning wheel in which energy is absorbed and stored by means of momentum. On cars, the flywheel is attached to the crankshaft to smooth out firing impulses.

Free play The amount of travel before any action takes place. The "looseness" in a linkage, or an assembly of parts, between the initial application of force and actual movement. For example, the distance the brake pedal moves before the pistons in the master cylinder are actuated.

Fuse An electrical device which protects a circuit against accidental overload. The typical fuse contains a soft piece of metal which is calibrated to melt at a predetermined current flow (expressed as amps) and break the circuit.

Fusible link A circuit protection device consisting of a conductor surrounded by heat-resistant insulation. The conductor is smaller than the wire it protects, so it acts as the weakest link in the circuit. Unlike a blown fuse, a failed fusible link must frequently be cut from the wire for replacement.

G

Gap The distance the spark must travel in jumping from the centre electrode to the side

Adjusting spark plug gap

electrode in a spark plug. Also refers to the spacing between the points in a contact breaker assembly in a conventional points-type ignition, or to the distance between the reluctor or rotor and the pickup coil in an electronic ignition.

Gasket Any thin, soft material - usually cork, cardboard, asbestos or soft metal - installed between two metal surfaces to ensure a good seal. For instance, the cylinder head gasket seals the joint between the block and the cylinder head.

Gasket

Gauge An instrument panel display used to monitor engine conditions. A gauge with a movable pointer on a dial or a fixed scale is an analogue gauge. A gauge with a numerical readout is called a digital gauge.

H

Halfshaft A rotating shaft that transmits power from the final drive unit to a drive wheel, usually when referring to a live rear axle.

Harmonic balancer A device designed to reduce torsion or twisting vibration in the crankshaft. May be incorporated in the crankshaft pulley. Also known as a vibration damper.

Hone An abrasive tool for correcting small irregularities or differences in diameter in an engine cylinder, brake cylinder, etc.

Hydraulic tappet A tappet that utilises hydraulic pressure from the engine's lubrication system to maintain zero clearance (constant contact with both camshaft and valve stem). Automatically adjusts to variation in valve stem length. Hydraulic tappets also reduce valve noise.

I

Ignition timing The moment at which the spark plug fires, usually expressed in the number of crankshaft degrees before the piston reaches the top of its stroke.

Inlet manifold A tube or housing with passages through which flows the air-fuel mixture (carburettor vehicles and vehicles with throttle body injection) or air only (port fuel-injected vehicles) to the port openings in the cylinder head.

Glossary of technical terms REF•23

J

Jump start Starting the engine of a vehicle with a discharged or weak battery by attaching jump leads from the weak battery to a charged or helper battery.

L

Load Sensing Proportioning Valve (LSPV) A brake hydraulic system control valve that works like a proportioning valve, but also takes into consideration the amount of weight carried by the rear axle.

Locknut A nut used to lock an adjustment nut, or other threaded component, in place. For example, a locknut is employed to keep the adjusting nut on the rocker arm in position.

Lockwasher A form of washer designed to prevent an attaching nut from working loose.

M

MacPherson strut A type of front suspension system devised by Earle MacPherson at Ford of England. In its original form, a simple lateral link with the anti-roll bar creates the lower control arm. A long strut - an integral coil spring and shock absorber - is mounted between the body and the steering knuckle. Many modern so-called MacPherson strut systems use a conventional lower A-arm and don't rely on the anti-roll bar for location.

Multimeter An electrical test instrument with the capability to measure voltage, current and resistance.

N

NOx Oxides of Nitrogen. A common toxic pollutant emitted by petrol and diesel engines at higher temperatures.

O

Ohm The unit of electrical resistance. One volt applied to a resistance of one ohm will produce a current of one amp.

Ohmmeter An instrument for measuring electrical resistance.

O-ring A type of sealing ring made of a special rubber-like material; in use, the O-ring is compressed into a groove to provide the sealing action.

O-ring

Overhead cam (ohc) engine An engine with the camshaft(s) located on top of the cylinder head(s).

Overhead valve (ohv) engine An engine with the valves located in the cylinder head, but with the camshaft located in the engine block.

Oxygen sensor A device installed in the engine exhaust manifold, which senses the oxygen content in the exhaust and converts this information into an electric current. Also called a Lambda sensor.

P

Phillips screw A type of screw head having a cross instead of a slot for a corresponding type of screwdriver.

Plastigage A thin strip of plastic thread, available in different sizes, used for measuring clearances. For example, a strip of Plastigage is laid across a bearing journal. The parts are assembled and dismantled; the width of the crushed strip indicates the clearance between journal and bearing.

Plastigage

Propeller shaft The long hollow tube with universal joints at both ends that carries power from the transmission to the differential on front-engined rear wheel drive vehicles.

Proportioning valve A hydraulic control valve which limits the amount of pressure to the rear brakes during panic stops to prevent wheel lock-up.

R

Rack-and-pinion steering A steering system with a pinion gear on the end of the steering shaft that mates with a rack (think of a geared wheel opened up and laid flat). When the steering wheel is turned, the pinion turns, moving the rack to the left or right. This movement is transmitted through the track rods to the steering arms at the wheels.

Radiator A liquid-to-air heat transfer device designed to reduce the temperature of the coolant in an internal combustion engine cooling system.

Refrigerant Any substance used as a heat transfer agent in an air-conditioning system. R-12 has been the principle refrigerant for many years; recently, however, manufacturers have begun using R-134a, a non-CFC substance that is considered less harmful to the ozone in the upper atmosphere.

Rocker arm A lever arm that rocks on a shaft or pivots on a stud. In an overhead valve engine, the rocker arm converts the upward movement of the pushrod into a downward movement to open a valve.

Rotor In a distributor, the rotating device inside the cap that connects the centre electrode and the outer terminals as it turns, distributing the high voltage from the coil secondary winding to the proper spark plug. Also, that part of an alternator which rotates inside the stator. Also, the rotating assembly of a turbocharger, including the compressor wheel, shaft and turbine wheel.

Runout The amount of wobble (in-and-out movement) of a gear or wheel as it's rotated. The amount a shaft rotates "out-of-true." The out-of-round condition of a rotating part.

S

Sealant A liquid or paste used to prevent leakage at a joint. Sometimes used in conjunction with a gasket.

Sealed beam lamp An older headlight design which integrates the reflector, lens and filaments into a hermetically-sealed one-piece unit. When a filament burns out or the lens cracks, the entire unit is simply replaced.

Serpentine drivebelt A single, long, wide accessory drivebelt that's used on some newer vehicles to drive all the accessories, instead of a series of smaller, shorter belts. Serpentine drivebelts are usually tensioned by an automatic tensioner.

Serpentine drivebelt

Shim Thin spacer, commonly used to adjust the clearance or relative positions between two parts. For example, shims inserted into or under bucket tappets control valve clearances. Clearance is adjusted by changing the thickness of the shim.

Slide hammer A special puller that screws into or hooks onto a component such as a shaft or bearing; a heavy sliding handle on the shaft bottoms against the end of the shaft to knock the component free.

Sprocket A tooth or projection on the periphery of a wheel, shaped to engage with a chain or drivebelt. Commonly used to refer to the sprocket wheel itself.

Starter inhibitor switch On vehicles with an automatic transmission, a switch that prevents starting if the vehicle is not in Neutral or Park.

Strut See MacPherson strut.

T

Tappet A cylindrical component which transmits motion from the cam to the valve stem, either directly or via a pushrod and rocker arm. Also called a cam follower.

Thermostat A heat-controlled valve that regulates the flow of coolant between the cylinder block and the radiator, so maintaining optimum engine operating temperature. A thermostat is also used in some air cleaners in which the temperature is regulated.

Thrust bearing The bearing in the clutch assembly that is moved in to the release levers by clutch pedal action to disengage the clutch. Also referred to as a release bearing.

Timing belt A toothed belt which drives the camshaft. Serious engine damage may result if it breaks in service.

Timing chain A chain which drives the camshaft.

Toe-in The amount the front wheels are closer together at the front than at the rear. On rear wheel drive vehicles, a slight amount of toe-in is usually specified to keep the front wheels running parallel on the road by offsetting other forces that tend to spread the wheels apart.

Toe-out The amount the front wheels are closer together at the rear than at the front. On front wheel drive vehicles, a slight amount of toe-out is usually specified.

Tools For full information on choosing and using tools, refer to the *Haynes Automotive Tools Manual*.

Tracer A stripe of a second colour applied to a wire insulator to distinguish that wire from another one with the same colour insulator.

Tune-up A process of accurate and careful adjustments and parts replacement to obtain the best possible engine performance.

Turbocharger A centrifugal device, driven by exhaust gases, that pressurises the intake air. Normally used to increase the power output from a given engine displacement, but can also be used primarily to reduce exhaust emissions (as on VW's "Umwelt" Diesel engine).

U

Universal joint or U-joint A double-pivoted connection for transmitting power from a driving to a driven shaft through an angle. A U-joint consists of two Y-shaped yokes and a cross-shaped member called the spider.

V

Valve A device through which the flow of liquid, gas, vacuum, or loose material in bulk may be started, stopped, or regulated by a movable part that opens, shuts, or partially obstructs one or more ports or passageways. A valve is also the movable part of such a device.

Valve clearance The clearance between the valve tip (the end of the valve stem) and the rocker arm or tappet. The valve clearance is measured when the valve is closed.

Vernier caliper A precision measuring instrument that measures inside and outside dimensions. Not quite as accurate as a micrometer, but more convenient.

Viscosity The thickness of a liquid or its resistance to flow.

Volt A unit for expressing electrical "pressure" in a circuit. One volt that will produce a current of one ampere through a resistance of one ohm.

W

Welding Various processes used to join metal items by heating the areas to be joined to a molten state and fusing them together. For more information refer to the *Haynes Automotive Welding Manual*.

Wiring diagram A drawing portraying the components and wires in a vehicle's electrical system, using standardised symbols. For more information refer to the *Haynes Automotive Electrical and Electronic Systems Manual*.

Note: *References throughout this index are in the form - "**Chapter number**" • "**Page number**"*

Preserving Our Motoring Heritage

< The Model J Duesenberg Derham Tourster. Only eight of these magnificent cars were ever built – this is the only example to be found outside the United States of America

Almost every car you've ever loved, loathed or desired is gathered under one roof at the Haynes Motor Museum. Over 300 immaculately presented cars and motorbikes represent every aspect of our motoring heritage, from elegant reminders of bygone days, such as the superb Model J Duesenberg to curiosities like the bug-eyed BMW Isetta. There are also many old friends and flames. Perhaps you remember the 1959 Ford Popular that you did your courting in? The magnificent 'Red Collection' is a spectacle of classic sports cars including AC, Alfa Romeo, Austin Healey, Ferrari, Lamborghini, Maserati, MG, Riley, Porsche and Triumph.

A Perfect Day Out

Each and every vehicle at the Haynes Motor Museum has played its part in the history and culture of Motoring. Today, they make a wonderful spectacle and a great day out for all the family. Bring the kids, bring Mum and Dad, but above all bring your camera to capture those golden memories for ever. You will also find an impressive array of motoring memorabilia, a comfortable 70 seat video cinema and one of the most extensive transport book shops in Britain. The Pit Stop Cafe serves everything from a cup of tea to wholesome, home-made meals or, if you prefer, you can enjoy the large picnic area nestled in the beautiful rural surroundings of Somerset.

> John Haynes O.B.E., Founder and Chairman of the museum at the wheel of a Haynes Light 12.

< Graham Hill's Lola Cosworth Formula 1 car next to a 1934 Riley Sports.

The Museum is situated on the A359 Yeovil to Frome road at Sparkford, just off the A303 in Somerset. It is about 40 miles south of Bristol, and 25 minutes drive from the M5 intersection at Taunton.
Open 9.30am - 5.30pm (10.00am - 4.00pm Winter) 7 days a week, *except Christmas Day, Boxing Day and New Years Day*
Special rates available for schools, coach parties and outings Charitable Trust No. 292048